Yes! Yes! GOD Says Yes!

CREATION HOUSE
A STRANG COMPANY

JUDY SANDERSON PERRIN

YES! YES! GOD SAYS, YES! by Judy Sanderson Perrin
Published by Creation House
A Strang Company
600 Rinehart Road
Lake Mary, Florida 32746
www.creationhouse.com

This book or parts thereof may not be reproduced in any form, stored in a retrieval system, or transmitted in any form by any means—electronic, mechanical, photocopy, recording, or otherwise—without prior written permission of the publisher, except as provided by United States of America copyright law.

Unless otherwise noted, all Scripture quotations are from the King James Version of the Bible.

Scripture quotations marked AMP are from the Amplified Bible. Old Testament copyright © 1965, 1987 by the Zondervan Corporation. The Amplified New Testament copyright © 1954, 1958, 1987 by the Lockman Foundation. Used by permission.

Scripture quotations marked NIV are from the Holy Bible, New International Version. Copyright © 1973, 1978, 1984, International Bible Society. Used by permission.

Scripture quotations marked NKJV are from the New King James Version of the Bible. Copyright © 1979, 1980, 1982 by Thomas Nelson, Inc., publishers. Used by permission.

Scripture quotations marked RSV are from the Revised Standard Version of the Bible. Copyright © 1946, 1952, 1971 by the Division of Christian Education of the National Council of the Churches of Christ in the USA. Used by permission.

Scripture quotations marked TLB are from The Living Bible. Copyright © 1971. Used by permission of Tyndale House Publishers, Inc., Wheaton, IL 60189. All rights reserved.

Scripture quotations marked NJB are from the New Jerusalem Bible, Copyright © 1985, Doubleday, New York.

Scripture quotations marked JPS are from the Jewish Bible Tanakh, The Holy Scriptures, Jewish Publication Society translation, according to the Traditional Hebrew Text, Philadelphia PA/Jerusalem, Israel.

Except where otherwise noted, Hebrew and Greek definitions are derived from *Strong's Exhaustive Concordance of the Bible*, by James Strong, S.T.D., L.L.D. (McLean VA: MacDonald Publishing Company, n.d.).

Cover design by Popcorn Initiative

Copyright © 2006 by Judy Sanderson Perrin
All rights reserved

Library of Congress Control Number: 2005930402
International Standard Book Number: 1-59185-903-4

06 07 08 09 — 987654321
Printed in the United States of America

Acknowledgments

- ∞ Betty Hardin, my faithful friend, for her encouragement and motivation

- ∞ George and Barbara Wagner, my cousins, for their input and support

- ∞ Eric Oppenheimer, my Jewish friend, for his help in researching Jewish history and traditions

- ∞ My son, James, for his constructive criticism

- ∞ My husband, Jim, for his lending ear, proofreading, and patience

- ∞ My late grandmother, Ella Lane of Greenville, Mississippi, who inspired me to write even as a child

Contents

Chapter 1

Our Father

"O GOD, PLEASE LET her live! O God, please let her live! O God, please let her live!"

My infant daughter had drowned! Her limp, gray body lay sprawled on the bathroom vanity. Her dull eyes, wide open, stared expressionless into space.

"O God, please let her live!" My spirit shrieked from within me like a siren, ripping my chest apart as on and on I screamed, "O God, please let her live!"

How well I remember that cool spring morning and the events that led to my carelessness. Busy doing laundry, I had forgotten to watch the clock and had found myself running late for an appointment. *Where has the morning gone?* I had fretted glancing in the mirror, trying to fluff my limp red hair. *Oh dear, I'll have to roll it up. I still have to put on my makeup and dress, and get the kids ready. How can I ever make it on time?*

I always bathed my son—not quite four years old—and my seven-month-old daughter separately. However, hoping to save a few minutes, I decided to put them in the tub together while I got ready in the bathroom. After switching on a wall heater and starting the water, I rounded up their clothes to avoid redressing them in a cooler room. Meanwhile

1

the tub filled fuller than I had intended.

Whatever was I thinking? Instead of draining some water out, I foolishly reasoned, *They'll just have more fun in deeper water.* I never dreamed of leaving them alone.

Although I was barely twenty-three, I prided myself on being thorough in my role of motherhood. Like many wives in the mid-sixties I didn't work outside the home, and I had no desire to do so. I centered almost every waking moment around the needs of my husband and our precious blonde-haired, blue-eyed children. They were my life. And yes, I loved it.

As the children splashed joyfully in their bath that morning it dawned on me that I had forgotten to grab a diaper along with their clothes. With the nursery directly across the hall, I dashed to get one and then realized that all the diapers lay on top of the clothes dryer, where I had folded them.

Laughter came from the bathroom. *They're fine*, I told myself, as I raced to the utility room and back.

But they weren't fine! I opened the door to find my son with face dripping, happily laughing at his tiny sister who had slipped beneath the water. He thought she was playing! In panic I gasped as I saw her eyes, dull and faded, staring blankly through the water where she floated.

Terror whipped through my heart like a tornado. *I had meant to be gone for only an instant! How could I have been so stupid?* Swooping her up, I stretched a lifeless baby on the vanity.

"O God, please let her live!" I screamed while I frantically administered mouth-to-mouth resuscitation. Between each breath I continued crying, "O God, please let her live!"

No vital signs appeared. Again and again I tried. Nothing. I finally stopped. It was no use. I had done all I physically knew to do.

Still, over and over I prayed at the top of my lungs, "O God, please let her live! O God, please let her live!"

Suddenly she whimpered! Pink color flooded into her body. She moved. She cried. My child had come to life! Hugging her against my chest I flew down the hallway to the bedroom and dialed the pediatrician.

"What's she doing now?" he asked.

"Crawling on the bed," I answered, gripping her leg as she circled around me. From the questions that followed, I now realize in retrospect that he was concerned about brain damage.

"Sounds like she's OK," he finally said, "but she has to have water in her lungs. Is she coughing at all?"

"No."

"Well, I won't have you come in now, but at the first sign of anything abnormal—coughing, wheezing, vomiting, a*nything*—bring her in. *Immediately.*"

Praises go to an almighty God who acts in perfection. My daughter never showed a symptom of any kind. Not only did God raise her up, but He also completely healed her.

A CHRISTIAN SINCE childhood, my mind was programmed to call on God in crisis moments. Yet my limited knowledge of all-powerful supernatural Deity left me puzzled. Years slipped by before I became aware of the certainty of His hand in this miracle, years before I gave Him the credit He deserved for answering my cry and freeing my daughter from death's grip.

Though study, prayer, and fellowship with my heavenly Father—I now know Him as a mighty, living God. Many unexplainable things are now explainable, mysteries unveiled. I invite you to meet the glorious One I found, One whose promises never fail. He is a God who, when we call, replies, "Yes, yes, I say, yes!"

> Call unto me, and I will answer thee, and shew thee great and mighty things which thou knowest not.
>
> —JEREMIAH 33:3

Do you ever wonder, *How do I call on God? How should I pray?* Do you long to see great and mighty works of God happen in your life? If your heart cries *yes*, grab your Bible and come along. You're in for a dynamic journey into supernatural wonders of the Almighty. Although this adventure is open for "whosoever will," receiving your utmost requires two important decisions:

1. Leave your traditions behind. You may never wish to pick them up again.

> Making the word of God of none effect through your tradition.
>
> —MARK 7:13

2. Bring your empty cup to be filled to overflowing.

> ...that ye might be filled with the knowledge of his will in all wisdom and spiritual understanding.
>
> —COLOSSIANS 1:9

So get ready! Brace yourself for an explosion of immense excitement, joy, and awareness. Come expecting to be thrilled and amazed as the spectacular power of God unfolds. Prepare for an inner awakening of overwhelming love, compassion, and forgiveness as the majesty of His glory ushers you through doors of new revelation in perception, faith, and understanding.

Using scripture paraphrased for drama and imagining visual concepts, we'll see life emerging from the pages of the Bible. We'll journey through Jewish roots to Christianity, exploring allegories and hidden shadows, discovering metaphoric parallels and previews, unraveling prophetic events and long-lost secrets hidden in His Word.

How will we find our way? We'll use a glorious treasure map to guide us. After a quick look at it we'll be equipped to strike out on our expedition.

> After this manner therefore pray ye: Our Father which art in heaven, Hallowed be thy name. Thy kingdom come. Thy will be done in earth, as it is in heaven. Give us this day our daily bread. And forgive us our debts, as we forgive our debtors. And lead us not into temptation, but deliver us from evil: For thine is the kingdom, and the power, and the glory, for ever. Amen.
>
> —MATTHEW 6:9–13

This is the map—so familiar, so simple to follow—that will steer us on our trip. It is "the Lord's Prayer." Why, it seems that everybody knows it! In the church where I grew up the congregation recited it in unison every Sunday.

What did Jesus intend when He gave us the Lord's Prayer? Did He mean for us to only repeat it repetitiously over and over or maybe just sing it at weddings? Shortly before teaching this prayer Jesus said, "But when ye pray, use not vain repetitions, as the heathens do..." (v. 7).

Let's inspect it closely. Perhaps it's not so simple after all. Like Christ's parables, many underlying jewels glimmer beneath its surface. By following it we'll dig up countless nuggets.

As our travels progress we'll grow to appreciate the never-ending virtues of our heavenly guide. Yet first we come to know Him as "our Father."

OUR FATHER

> "I will be a Father to you, and you shall be My sons and daughters," says the LORD Almighty.
>
> —2 CORINTHIANS 6:18, NKJV

How could One so great, adorned with majesty and possessing all power, desire us as His children? What a supreme privilege to call Him Father!

Yet not everyone always felt this way. Many years ago calling God "Father" triggered shock and anger.

> Therefore the Jews sought the more to kill him [Jesus], because he not only had broken the sabbath, but said also that God was his Father, making himself equal with God.
>
> —JOHN 5:18

This creates a whirlwind of questions. What made these Jews so distraught? As God's chosen people, why didn't they know Him as their Father? If He wasn't a Father to them, how and when did you and I become His children and He our Father?

For complete answers to these questions, we must turn many stones and explore many sites. The first leg of our excursion into the revelation of Father God will whisk us down a long and winding road of Jewish history. We'll emerge shaking our heads, overwhelmed by the Jewish perception of God in ancient times, but we'll gain an understanding of why their view was so alien from the personal Father of grace and mercy Jesus preached. And best of all, at the end we'll understand with thanksgiving how God became our Father.

Are you ready for the journey? Let's begin by changing our first question. Rather than asking why the Jews became so distraught and reacted with such animosity to Jesus' proclamation of God as Father, a more appropriate approach would be to inquire how they—with their background—could even begin to identify with such intimate thinking about God.

Although the Old Testament speaks of God as Israel's Father, this role—to their way of thinking—involved God as founder and overseer of their nation, giver of the Law, and judge. It did not mean He was their personal Father. After all, in Jesus' day, who—except for Jesus and John the Baptist—had ever greeted them with claims of having an inner relationship with the great Jehovah?

No one!

Actually, in comparison to their vast populations, only a handful had been recorded as sharing intimate fellowship with God. Yes, they read of people such as Abraham, Moses, Samson, David, and the prophets hearing directly from Jehovah and sharing personal bonds with Him. Yet it was so long ago!

For four hundred years no God-inspired person had spoken to Israel, until John the Baptist arrived and proclaimed Jesus as the Lamb of God.

What a long stretch to be without any witness from the One who chose them! To compare, consider how distant the issue of the United States Declaration of Independence in 1776 seems today. Not even two hundred fifty years have passed, and yet it seems so long ago.

Realizing all this not only sheds light on reasons the Jews were defiant toward Jesus, but it also shows why multitudes broke with tradition to follow Him. Many were starved for a touch from their Creator, burning in their desire to truly know Him.

Since the ancient Jews lacked personal association with God, what kept them worshiping Him for so many centuries? Answers await as we veer onto a trail often missed by Christians today. It's an extensive walk off the beaten path, and it leads deeper into Hebrew customs, legends, and beliefs to help us understand how God was viewed in Jesus' day.

First, they knew a God of precise plan and purpose. An amazing strategy unfolds as we trace the footsteps of a people set aside in divine destiny. It's an honor no other nation can ever possess, a masterful design unmatched in human history.

God Himself singled them out, promising that from their descendants a Redeemer would be born. From early childhood this knowledge churned inside every Jewish soul. By keeping flawless genealogy records they studied the direct avenue of their bloodline. Knowing its supreme arrangement, their hearts throbbed with awareness that God had established their nation through a man named Abraham, and—down through the ages—had preserved a perfect lineage for the coming Messiah.

Oh, what strategy directed by His unseen hand! And such a wondrous heritage! We travel now into its drama, which begins with Abraham two thousand years before the birth of the Promised Seed in Bethlehem.

BY DIVINE PROMISE Abraham fathered his son Isaac. From this one son an entire Jewish nation developed. Isaac had twin sons, Esau and Jacob. Jacob, renamed Israel, produced twelve sons whose descendants became known as the twelve tribes of Israel. Millions came from them.

The eleventh son of Israel was Joseph, who, sold by ten of his jealous brothers to slave traders at age seventeen, served as an invaluable player in God's perfect plan. In the hands of the Egyptians, Joseph—by miraculous means—overcame the hardships of slavery, false accusation, and imprisonment to win favor with the pharaoh.

By molding a prestigious Joseph in Egypt, God saved His people from great famine in their homeland. Reuniting the household of Israel in Egypt, He uprooted the entire family to live in this region of the Nile. This established them as a unit unto themselves. Now with the necessary separation of His divinely ordained nation from other peoples, God continued to reveal His plan by circumstances only He could direct, thus protecting the line for His Perfect Seed.

As the descendants of Israel increased in this foreign land, a new pharaoh rose to power and made them slaves. Why did this happen to the elect of God? Maybe their faithfulness had dwindled, but we don't know. However, looking at the overall picture we can discern one underlying reason: God's Perfect Seed.

Slavery segregated Israel from the pagan Egyptian culture and protected its people from intermarriage. Throughout centuries in a foreign land their overseeing Lord kept them strong and their lineage pure.

After 430 years in Egypt, when His chosen cried out to Him, God maintained His divine course by raising up Moses as their deliverer. On through the ages of judges and kings, generation after generation, through times of devotion as well as in times of rebellion, God continued to orchestrate a pure bloodline through His appointed Israel.

Yes, the Jews certainly knew the One of precise plan and purpose. Yet they also knew an avenging God of judgment and wrath whose power easily and instantly snuffed out entire wicked populations. Their inspired writings, which we know as the Old Testament, detail His sentence of the great flood on the world in Noah's day and the abrupt doom of Sodom and Gomorrah during Abraham's time. Even so, probably most dramatically stirring in Hebrew minds were the scenes of God's rage when the malicious king of Egypt defied His divine orders—given through Moses—to let the children of Israel go free.

Oh, just look upon the scenes! With hardened heart Pharaoh stood fast in his refusal, causing plagues of terror to wreak havoc on Egyptian life. Their water turned to blood, and there was none left to drink, no way to bathe. Stinging bugs, frogs, and wild beasts descended on them in droves. Boils erupted with unbearable agony. Hailstorms devastated crops, and locusts devoured anything that was left in the field. Total darkness enveloped the land for days. Still, in his rebellious craze, Pharaoh stood firm, prompting the most ghastly plague of all—death. It claimed every firstborn male belonging to an Egyptian—child or beast, young or old. Weeping, sobbing, and screaming exploded from every household. At last their ruler let God's people leave.

Oh, what retribution there was in this final torment! Eighty years earlier under Pharaoh's orders his men brutally murdered male Israelite babies. But no evil act can ever thwart God's plans. Baby Moses was saved.

Have you ever considered the double grief Egyptian women suffered when their heartless leader changed his mind soon after seeing his workforce depart? While mothers still mourned over the loss of their firstborn sons, the Red Sea crashed angrily upon their husbands and other sons, drowning the whole Egyptian army as they pursued the fleeing slaves. Not one survived. It was, no doubt, justice deserved, but anguish surged like hot lava from every soul left in the land of Egypt.

Seeing the precise plan and purpose of their nation transpiring and bearing witness to His wrath, the Jews rightly claimed an awesome God of miracles. They recognized Him as a Mastermind who used mortal men to save them by supernatural means.

> He sent Moses His servant, and Aaron whom He had chosen. They performed His signs among them, and wonders in the land of Ham.
> —PSALM 105:26–27, NKJV

They knew a miraculous Provider who freed them from bondage in wealth and in perfect health.

> He also brought them out with silver and gold, and there was none feeble among His tribes.
> —PSALM 105:37, NKJV

As we peer further into the amazing scene of their escape from Egypt, a vivid picture unfolds. Look at the procession! Somewhere around six hundred thousand men, plus wives and children, departed, herding multitudes of livestock along with them. We can't count them all, but very likely more than two million and possibly as many as six million people make up this caravan. If we listen closely we can hear their shouting and rejoicing. How they praise Moses as their leader who reintroduced their nation to such a wonder-working God after so many years in slavery!

Yet no one preconceived the phenomenon to occur just ahead in their journey. What an indescribable event when the Red Sea split, allowing such massive numbers to pass on dry ground to the other side! Even with the gigantic divide of the waters, several days must have elapsed while so many crossed. But at the instant the last Israelite foot stepped on shore, the sea slammed together, washing their enemies away for good.

Still even greater astonishment unfolded. For forty years God provided extraordinary protection and provision for this immense body in a desolate wilderness. Who can even imagine the amount of manna He showered daily just to feed them all?

Oh, what an undefeatable, insurmountable God the Jew alone could boast! After Israel made it across the Red Sea, Moses sang with his people:

> The LORD is a man of war...
>
> —EXODUS 15:3

Now feel the excitement of Joshua. After enduring forty years in the wilderness, he and the new generation of Israelites marched into the Promised Land with God as their captain. Time after time by the hand of the Lord they conquered powerful enemies in their path.

Centuries later David declared the Lord was a mighty warrior (Ps. 24:8). In a special song of deliverance his lyrics ring:

> The LORD thundered from heaven, and the Most High uttered His voice. He sent out arrows and scattered them; lightning bolts, and He vanquished them.
>
> —2 SAMUEL 22:14–15, NKJV

YES, WHAT A mighty God the Jews knew, worshiping Him for His greatness, sovereignty, and holiness! Yet they knew Him only from a distance. By their own doing they made Him their untouchable, unreachable God. God didn't want it this way. He desired a close relationship.

Come as we venture into the pages of Exodus 19 and 20 to view this for ourselves. We join the people as they set up camp on desert sand at the base of Mount Sinai.

Looming like a monstrous barren rock, the famous mountain protrudes out of stark wasteland, exposing its gray peaks against a hazy sky. With no stirring breeze, the desert air stifles us like an oven. We labor for every breath.

Less than two months have passed since the slaves escaped Egyptian torture, yet we hear grumbling all around. Now concerned only by their weariness of travel and the scorching heat, they seem to have forgotten the miracles God performed to free them.

But not Moses! We catch a blurry glimpse of him high upon a rugged slope as he eagerly scales Mount Sinai to meet with God.

Hurry! Let's scramble after him.

Among the rocks and cliffs Moses waits in silence. We halt nearby. After a while the Lord's voice gently calls: "Moses, remind the people of Israel that they have seen what I did to the Egyptians. Remind them of how I bore them on eagles' wings and brought them unto Myself."

As God continues speaking, it's evident that He desires personal contact with His people. What great reward awaits if they only choose His way! Oh, listen:

"Tell them, Moses, 'Now if you will obey My voice and keep My covenant, then you will be My special people upon the earth. You will be unto Me a kingdom of priests and a holy nation.'"

What music to our ears! With dancing hearts we hurry down with Moses to hear him present these wonderful conditions to the elders.

Excitement blooms. Without hesitation everyone vows in unison, "All God has spoken we will do!"

Caught up in their enthusiasm, we rejoice to follow Moses back up the mountain. We beam when he reports to God the people's instant response and hear with joy their Lord declare, "I will appear in a thick cloud so every person will be able to hear Me when I speak to you. Once they witness My presence, they will always believe you."

With ardent ears we absorb every word as God instructs Moses to set boundaries around Mount Sinai. "Warn the people not to go up the mountain or even touch the boundaries. When the trumpet sounds with one long blast, then they may come to the mountain's edge."

For the next three days zeal fills the campsite. Everyone prepares for God's arrival—bathing themselves, washing their clothes. On the third day each person is bursting with eagerness. Knowing the time of His appearance may happen any moment, their eyes are glued on Mount Sinai.

Oh, look! Here He comes. With lightning the skies erupt. Bolting from the height of heaven, countless streaks set the mountaintop aglow. Ear-shattering thunder rattles the earth. Gigantic clouds swirl with churning force, blanketing the quivering peaks so high above us.

Above it all the trumpet blares, announcing arrival of Jehovah. That's our cue to hurry and gather around the base of Mount Sinai. But we must be extra careful not to cross the designated boundaries. Death marks the penalty for disobedience

In a floodlight of fire the Almighty descends. How His magnificence dazzles our eyes even with the rolling clouds offsetting His radiance. Like an enormous furnace the mountain billows smoke far into the air, rumbling as if it might explode. Beneath our feet the desert reels.

Time and time again the trumpet shrieks. Brighter than a noonday sun, the fire of God lights up the world around us.

Oh, hear Moses! Immersed in praise he calls out with all his mortal strength to his divine Commander.

With stupendous vocal power God responds, "Moses, ascend into My presence!"

Shimmering in the splendor of God's *Shekinah* glory, the human deliverer of Israel walks up into the heights to encounter the Divine. Oh, what a sight!

Like electricity surging through our ears Jehovah vibrates forth the Ten Commandments: "Thou shall have no other gods before Me! Thou shall not make unto yourselves any graven images! Thou shall not use the name of the LORD your God in vain! Remember the Sabbath Day to keep it holy! Honor thy father and thy mother! Thou shall not kill! Thou shall not commit adultery! Thou shall not steal! Thou shall not lie! Thou shall not covet!"

His tremendous exhortation echoes down the slopes and sweeps across the plains. What privilege just to witness such awesomeness. We bask in the glory of His majesty until, to our surprise, the crowd around us turns in panic.

With flapping robes they stampede like cattle, running from the scene that glimmers in holy radiance, screaming as they race toward their tents. A long distance from the boundaries set by God, they stop. Cowering, their eyes ablaze with fear, they turn to stare at the revelation of God's glory.

Come back, our spirits cry. *How can you bear to leave the wonder of His presence?*

But they wail, "Moses, you tell us God's instructions and we'll obey. We don't want Him speaking directly to us because it will kill us!"

With supernatural volume Moses pleads, "Don't be afraid! God has appeared in His awesomeness so you can behold His power. It will instill reverent fear for Him in you, and knowing the greatness of His presence will guard you from sinning."

Despite Moses' appeal everyone backs farther away, still overtaken by terror, muttering in a frenzy.

With heavy hearts we leave Mount Sinai as Moses disappears into its slopes. God's brilliance, now withdrawn because of the people's rejection, is covered in raging smoke. He and His obedient servant meet in solitude. Honoring the people's wishes, the Lord speaks only to Moses as He orders a new concept of Jewish living—the covenant of Law.

HOW SOON THE Israelites forgot their fright of God and their unified pledge of dedication! Only a few weeks after His glorious appearance, as Moses continued conversing with Him high upon the mountain, they molded a pagan calf from the very gold God Himself provided for them from the Egyptians. Turning their backs on their miraculous Redeemer, the children of Israel used their gift of freedom for idol worship and adultery.

From this time forward Jews professed the God of Law—a strict Enforcer of uncompromising regulations. Now unable to approach Him on their own, they had designated priests who interceded with prayers and sacrifices on their behalf.

God never again appeared to the Jewish nation in all His glory. Instead He concealed His splendor in the innermost court of the tabernacle, a large room in the shape of a cube. It was a very secluded holy sanctuary closed to all but the high priest. Never could any other enter into His presence in the most hallowed chamber of all, which they called the holy of holies.

As a tangible concept for His dwelling in the holy of holies God ordered a unique chest built according to the exact specifications He had given to Moses. A beautiful work of art, it was made from special wood and adorned by an overlay of gold. From its golden brilliance rose a throne that was made of gold. It was called the mercy seat, where God Himself manifested His presence. And like heavenly guards two golden statues of cherubim, a special type of magnificent angels, towered in elegance above it all.

God promised, "And I will meet with you there and talk with you from above the place of mercy between the cherubim; and the Ark will contain the laws of my covenant" (Exod. 25:22, TLB).

The ark of the covenant was very precious to the Jews. How they treasured it! Yet under normal circumstances it stayed hidden from the common eye. When it was stationary in the tabernacle, it rested behind an immense veil that blocked entrance into the innermost holy of holies. When the ark was in desert transit this same veil concealed it. The people surely yearned to look upon its glory. But they couldn't.

Did God really dwell there? Being omnipresent He can never be confined to any single place. Without a doubt, however, His majesty abided with the ark because it, being more than a mere item of beauty, proved to be of supernatural function.

In the wilderness the wandering tribes depended on it to go before them, to search out a resting place (Num. 10:33). It radiated with His glory (1 Sam. 4:21–22). It revealed His strength (Ps. 132:8).

Yes, what unimaginable force this superhuman design of God emitted! No human power could control it.

AFTER THE DAYS of the tabernacle of Moses, but before Solomon built a temple, the ark led Israeli troops in battle. Once it wound up in the hands of the enemy, the Philistines.

Oh, what a story!

It was such victory to possess this treasured chest. Or so the Philistines thought until its almighty power showed them wrong.

In their pride they placed it in their temple beside their prized idol Dagon. During the first night Dagon fell flat on his face before the holy ark. Puzzled, the Philistines lifted their pagan god back up to his original position.

Imagine their shock the next morning. Their idol wasn't just sprawled on the floor—his head and both hands were severed. "Only the stump of Dagon was left to him" (1 Sam. 5:4).

This was only the start of a shocking situation. Because of the ark's presence in this unholy land, horrible tumors began killing off the population. Wherever they took the ark these tumors broke out.

Understandably the Philistines soon wanted no part of this powerful structure of the God of Israel. After seven months, unable to bear its presence any longer, they decided they must give the ark back to its rightful owners.

How should they do it?

"Send it back with a guilt offering," the priests and diviners cried, "so the plague will end and we'll be healed!"

God must surely have a sense of humor. From gold the Philistines molded images of their tumors that the Jewish NJPS version of the Bible, *TANAKH, The Holy Scriptures*, calls "hemorrhoids." They also molded golden mice (of all things!) to represent their leaders. These items—mice and hemorrhoids—accompanied the ark on its journey home. Oh, can you picture such a thing!

How did they send it back? They loaded it on a cart drawn by two cows! And from there the unseen hand of God took over and guided it back to its rightful owners.

What a surprise it must have been when out of the blue the ark wobbled into Israeli territory. So elated by its return, the Jewish priests ignored its sacredness and strength and displayed it uncovered upon a large rock. With its beauty exposed for all eyes to see, they offered burnt sacrifices before it.

Perhaps they meant well. But the ark proved too strong for the view of sinful mortal eyes. Thousands died that day because they looked at it. (See 1 Samuel 6.)

The ark was so holy and alive with God's glory that no man could touch its surface. It was to be carried by two poles that were held by rings fastened to the four corners of the ark. When it began to totter from a cart in the course of moving, one single contact of a human hand caused instant death (2 Sam. 6:7).

Following this fatal incident David stored the ark with a righteous man for three months. When the man received great blessings from its presence David retrieved it.

What a glorious homecoming! Such a sight to behold! Leaping and dancing before the Lord with all his being, David—in company with all the house of Israel as it rejoiced and blew trumpets—ushered the ark into Jerusalem (2 Sam. 6:10–15). Eventually this magnificent item found its honorable place once more within the holy of holies inside the fabulous temple built by King Solomon.

WHAT BECAME OF the ark? Where is it today?

Following the destruction of Solomon's temple by the Babylonians, we find no more mention of this object of God's dwelling. *The Zondervan Pictorial Bible Dictionary* says of the second temple rebuilt in Zerubbabel's day, "According to Josephus, the Holy of Holies was empty. Evidently the ark had been destroyed in 587 (B.C.) and was never replaced."[1]

With no pat answers giving positive location or proof of dismantling, legend continues to build around the ark's disappearance. Fictitious accounts like the movie *Indiana Jones: Raiders of the Lost Ark* keep intrigue alive.[2] Research and speculation seems endless.

One often-told story asserts that King Solomon gave the ark as a gift to the queen of Sheba and states that, to this day, it remains in hiding in Ethiopia. We can tell from Scripture that Solomon and this queen acquired a fascination for each other when she visited him in Jerusalem. "And king Solomon gave unto the queen of Sheba all her desire, whatsoever she asked, beside that which Solomon gave her of his royal bounty" (1 Kings 10:13).

A related conjecture, yet with decided differences, also places the lost ark in Ethiopia. It says that the relationship between King Solomon and the queen of Sheba grew to more than simple mutual admiration and produced a son who as a young man brought the ark to his homeland for worship to Jehovah. Solomon is said to have replaced it with a replica. Wow! This could give birth to a whole set of new questions. For starters, what became of the replica?

Another theory, ignoring Josephus' claim of a missing ark, insists that at the completion of Zerubbabel's temple in 538 B.C. the ark remained intact.

It wasn't lost until after 63 B.C. when the Romans took possession of Jerusalem and, as verified by history, confiscated the temple's gold. Is it possible that they took the ark for its gold also?

Even with the Jews suppressed under Roman rule, Herod the Great had enlarged and beautified the temple complex. It stood as the worship center at the time of Jesus. Could it be that neither Zerubbabel's temple nor Herod's remodeled temple ever housed the sacred ark?

With facts uncertain, some prefer to believe the ark did remain in Herod's temple until it was destroyed in A.D. 70. The ark, they say, lies buried in the rubble. Who can prove otherwise? As long as a Muslim mosque sits on the Jewish temple site, excavation seems impossible.

So, with the varied theories about its vanishing and unceasing guesswork about its condition, the mystery of the ark's whereabouts remains unsolved. How heartrending to have the place of God's presence under the Law cease to function! Where did the wondrous glory with its amazing power and redeeming mercy seat go? Oh, how Jewish hearts must still grieve over such a great loss today!

BEFORE IT WAS lost, the ark of the covenant demanded great reverence. When it was set up in the temple, hidden away in the holy of holies, only one person—the high priest—could enter its sanctuary. No other human being could ever step inside. And even the high priest's admittance into the holy of holies was restricted to one day each year—the Day of Atonement.

This day was a very special occasion. Demanding perfect holiness for the Jew, it is still observed by many today, with no ark or temple and without sacrifices. With unwavering commands to be obeyed to the letter while their temple remained, the Day of Atonement entailed an astoundingly strict and solemn performance.

It lasted from sundown to sundown, a full twenty-four-hour period when all of Israel confessed all the sins committed during the past year. Every thought, word, and action centered around repentance, vowing over and over to do better. No food, no bath, and no work or heavy lifting were permitted. Rules for limited walking forbade the wearing of leather shoes. No sleep was allowed, not even a catnap. There was only nonstop acknowledgment of sin.

Anyone who defaulted even slightly faced banishment from his people for the rest of his life. There was no opportunity for repentance, no second chance.

> Indeed, any person who does not practice self-denial throughout that day shall be cut off from his kin; and whoever does any work throughout that day, I will cause that person to perish from among his people.
> —LEVITICUS 23:29–30, NJPS

What were the high priest's duties on the Day of Atonement? In solitude he entered the holy of holies to atone for his own sins, his family's sins, and the sins of the nation. With special incense in one hand and fresh blood from unblemished animal sacrifices in the other, he approached the presence of Almighty Jehovah at the ark of the covenant to sprinkle the blood upon the mercy seat.

What apprehension had to engulf the high priest on this day! If he harbored even one unconfessed sin his mortal body possessed no strength to withstand the immensity of glory abounding from the ark. He would fall dead on the spot.

A popular story asserts that bells dangled from the high priest's robe to signal his movements while he presided in the holy of holies. It says that a rope was tied around the high priest's ankle and stretched into the adjacent inner holy court. If he died and the bells quit jingling, other priests could pull his body from the holy of holies.

Is this really true? No scriptures can be found to support it. The high priest's elaborate ceremonial garment, a blue tunic adorned with alternating bells and pomegranates at its hem, was never worn on the Day of Atonement. For this grave occasion he wore simple white linen, a symbol of holiness and purity.

Why would bells and ropes be needed? If death occurred, the next in line for position of high priest would receive immediate authority to go into the holy of holies, remove the body, and carry on the vital rituals of the day.[3]

THE DAY OF Atonement appears very stern to the Christian. Even though it was just a twenty-four-hour period, upholding its every precept and abiding by all the restrictions without default seem to have been next to impossible.

But pause for a deep breath. We've just begun. As we go on to learn about other uncompromising stipulations and unremitting duties set forth by the covenant of Law, Jewish life becomes staggering to say the least. Yet God saw its necessity. The apostle Paul, a Jew educated to the utmost in every point of the Law, explains:

What purpose then does the law serve? It was added because of transgressions, till the Seed should come to whom the promise was made.
—GALATIANS 3:19, NKJV

God was fed up with defiance and disobedience. As we witnessed at
Mount Sinai, there was continual ungratefulness, murmuring, and rebellion. The Law set the Jew apart until the Messiah would come.

What other good did the Law accomplish? With its relentless demands
it established a sense of devotion to God. Like a grueling schoolmaster it
drilled into the mind a profound awareness and knowledge of sin. By showing the incapability of mortals to keep the Law to perfection, it proved the
necessity for a divine Redeemer.

Yes, easily broken and distracted, vulnerable and inadequate within their
fleshly limits—no matter how hard the people tried, they continuously fell
short in their efforts to obey the Law. Everybody failed!

At this point we ask, couldn't even one person keep the Law? A quick
investigation reveals the answer.

The Law lists 613 basic commands. However, adding all the regulations
required in each made a total of more than 2,700 nonstop and unwavering ordinances that dictated all facets of Hebrew living. Holiness. Worship.
Repentance. Dedication. Wars. Justice. Vows. Social and domestic relations.
Treatment of servants and strangers. Lending to the poor, and more.

Swift punishment (sometimes severe beatings, more often death by
stoning) accompanied moral issues like murder, theft, adultery, lust, idolatry, blasphemy—even lying and jealousy. Constant and rigorous rituals
compelled exactness in food preparation, dietary restrictions, personal
hygiene, purification, and sanitation. Specific unconditional statutes
governed hundreds of religious rites, confessions, various tithes, alms,
daily offerings, and sacrifices. Mandatory guidelines directed feasts and
celebrations.

Unrelenting and unbreakable restrictions ruled the Sabbath and its "no
work" policy. One man received the death penalty for gathering sticks
(Num. 15:32–36).

Although the Day of Atonement issued the most rigid laws for any single
day, other areas of disobedience could also cause a person to be cut off from
his people: eating flesh or fat from certain sacrificial offerings (Lev. 7:21,
25). Failing to bring a sacrifice to the entrance door of the tabernacle (Lev.
17:9). Partaking of blood (Lev. 17:10). Indulging in sex during a woman's
period (Lev. 20:18). And except for certain exemptions, a man refraining
from offering a Passover sacrifice (Num. 9:13).

Every iota of the Law, all of its more than 2,700 instructions, demanded full obedience.

> What thing soever I command you, observe to do it: thou shalt not add thereto, nor diminish from it.
> —DEUTERONOMY 12:32

Nothing, no matter how small, could be broken or overlooked.

> For whosoever shall keep the whole law, and yet offend in one point, he is guilty of all.
> —JAMES 2:10

Have you ever thought that the judgment Moses received for his single recorded transgression in the wilderness seemed awfully harsh? When Israel needed water, he disregarded God's command to speak to the rock and struck it in anger instead. As a result, God barred him from entering the Promised Land.

In studying the Law and the exactness it commanded, we find justification in Moses' penalty. As leader of the Israelites, he stood as their prime example. Since their code of living permitted no person even one tiny violation, how would it have looked if Moses, who disobeyed direct orders from God Himself, had escaped severe punishment?

Oh, how hard the laws of God are!

As we close our investigation our question changes. We no longer ask if even one person could keep the Law. Now we ask, How could any mortal being have possibly obeyed its every aspect to the letter?

The obvious answer—they couldn't!

But not only did mankind fail the Law, but also, just as tragically, the Law failed man. "Law brings wrath," says the apostle Paul (Rom. 4:15, NIV). Hebrews 7:18 calls it "weak and useless" (NIV).

Yes, sadly the Law proved to be unable to produce perfection, the state of being without defect or fault. "For the law made nothing perfect" (Heb. 7:19).

It was unable to justify us, clear us of guilt, and make us as if we had never sinned. "Knowing that a man is not justified by the works of the law…" (Gal. 2:16).

The Law was unable to bestow righteousness, right standing with God. "Now do you see it? No one can ever be made right in God's sight by doing what the law commands. For the more we know of God's laws, the clearer it becomes that we aren't obeying them; his laws serve only to make us see that we are sinners" (Rom. 3:20, TLB).

And it was unable to save souls. "For it is not possible that the blood of bulls and of goats should take away sins" (Heb. 10:4).

Though the Law burdened man with the impossible task of earning his own salvation, the religious Jew never regarded it as a straitjacket. With pride he accepted its obligations and looked on it as a superior way of life, as do many today.

Most certainly the Law yielded many positive aspects. Authored by divine Intellect it discloses a wholesome and healthy lifestyle in diet and sanitation, thereby supplying knowledge far superior to any other culture in ancient times. Later we'll take a closer look at some of these benefits.

And not all was somber. Even the Sabbath in its strictness brought a happy time for family sharing and supplied needed rest, as well as being a day set aside to truly acknowledge God in worship and thankfulness.

Despite all the rules, festivals and feasts produced celebration with joy and gaiety. These events along with other factors of the Law and Old Testament customs hold a treasure chest of knowledge too long neglected and ignored by the Christian church. Prophetic of Jesus, they gleam with enlightenment for us. In our travels we'll discover many of their jewels, and we'll come to realize how the New Testament can never be fully revealed without the Old Testament.

Great promises such as life, well-being, and prolonged days accompanied lawful obedience. The rewards of Deuteronomy 28:1–14 bless the heart of anyone who reads them. But oh, such a list of curses in the remainder of that chapter for anybody who chose to disobey!

Listen to the voice of Moses as he warns of consequences for neglecting God's commandments:

> Beware that thou forget not the LORD thy God, in not keeping his commandments, and his judgments, and his statutes....And it shall be, if thou do at all forget the LORD thy God, and walk after other gods, and serve them, and worship them, I testify against you this day that you shall surely perish. As the nations which the Lord destroyeth before your face, so shall ye perish; because ye would not be obedient unto the voice of the LORD your God.
>
> —DEUTERONOMY 8:11, 19–20

Yes, the Jewish view of God was so different from Jesus' teaching about the personal Father of mercy and grace. Now we may understand why, but we see what a hard road the Jewish people chose to travel.

By their denial of Christ as their Messiah, they rejected the idea of an actual Father God who, as a parent, loved each of them individually. Once more they backed away from the One who longed to bring them into His presence. Instead, they chose to continue living a long distance from Him as they had at Mount Sinai. They chose the Law. Oh, why didn't they choose Jesus and the freedom He offered!

BUT WAIT! WHY pick on them? The Jews didn't cause a distant and broken relationship to develop between man and God. Throughout history men have chosen to tread down a grim and painful road. It started long before the existence of a Hebrew nation, and it still prevails today.

Why? Our quest for answers sweeps us all the way back to the beginning of humanity. Here we'll witness the original separation of man and God. We'll learn His perfect will.

Look! The land of paradise! We're just in time to behold the making of mankind, the most glorious of all creation.

> And God said, Let us make man in our image, after our likeness. . . . So God created man in his own image, in the image of God created he him; male and female created he them.
> —Genesis 1:26–27

Here is the species of man—male and female—fashioned after God's own image. It sounds grand. And it is! Let's leave no stone unturned and gather every tool we can to find out just how grand it is.

For deeper understanding we search the Hebrew language. Since the Old Testament was originally written in Hebrew, we'll uncover revelation by the Hebrew definition of a word. At times we'll trace the verbal root because Hebrew words stem from verbs and, even in another form, carry verbal meanings.

The word for *image* in the above scripture translates as "phantom, illusion, resemblance."[4] Doesn't this show us a glorious spiritual impression? Just think, human beings modeled after the invisible spiritual image of Almighty God!

What a day, that sixth day of creation when God made man! He first gave him a body from the earth, and then from His own breath He gave him life.

> And the Lord God formed man of the dust of the ground, and breathed into his nostrils the breath of life; and man became a living soul.
> —Genesis 2:7

God called him Adam. In Hebrew the name is *Awadawm*, meaning "mankind" or "human being." Traces to the root verb *awdam* define it as "show blood in the face, flush, turn rosy."[5]

Such a picture! As God breathed His very own supreme breath into man, divinely inspired crimson blood gushed throughout his veins.

Yes, God formed Adam's body from dust, but by His own breath He created a soul and spirit in the likeness of Himself. Because of sin the earthy substance of man dies and returns to dust. Yet the invisible parts of man patterned in the image of the Creator never cease to be. Eternal like Him, they exist forever.

What an honor that God, Himself a Spirit Being, uniquely fashioned mankind with His own characteristics—making humans an unequaled race of everlasting spirit, life, and destiny! Empowered with a conscience, reasoning ability, freedom of choice, language, intellect, and emotions, He gave His esteemed human creatures qualities far superior to any other creature of the earth.

Such was the glorious being God had made of Adam. And oh, the Garden of Eden—the breathtaking paradise He placed him in! Let your mind wander over crystal rivers as they wind through vast velvet landscapes glistening with gold and sparkling gems. Breathe in the delightful fragrance of sweeping meadows embroidered with miles of vivid flowers alive with dancing butterflies. Listen to the symphony of birds playing hide and seek among emerald leaves of massive trees rich with every type of fruit imaginable. Pet the enormous lion and delicate lamb snuggled against each other on downy beds of clover. Behold hundreds of other tame creatures, some napping, many frolicking together, all in total harmony.

What an exciting occasion when Adam named all his friendly animals! It bore witness to the superb mind man possessed before sin entered in.

Even with such perfection God saw that Adam needed human companionship. At the close of His six-day extravaganza, as His man slept, God reached down with compassionate hands. In loving care He gently removed a rib, a bone covering the very heart of His most prized creation, and made woman to share man's life.

Adam and Eve. There they stood together, a reflection of the very Creator Himself. How God loved them! He blessed their union and granted them supreme authority to govern not only the glorious garden but also the entire planet.

> And God blessed them, and God said unto them, Be fruitful, and multiply, and replenish the earth, and subdue it: and have dominion over the fish of the sea, and over the fowl of the air, and over every living

thing that moveth upon the earth.... I have given you every herb bearing seed... every tree...

—GENESIS 1:28–29

Yes, God relinquished His control of Earth—every animal, every plant—to His beloved mankind. And He blessed them with the opportunity of replenishing the entire surface of the world with their offspring in an atmosphere of love and purity. There was no death, no sorrow, no pain, no hate, no ugliness. At this time it was, and still is today and forever will be—God's perfect will for humanity.

At the beginning in the excellence of Eden, Adam and Eve knew no sin. They walked in the perfect light of the Lord God, who visited them face-to-face. Some scholars theorize that while they were in sinless perfection they glowed so from the brightness of God's glory that they needed no clothing. This explains why they didn't care that they were naked. However, could they really have such brilliance?

After Moses met with the Almighty on Mount Sinai, his face shone so brightly the children of Israel feared to venture near him (Exod. 34:29–30). And how Jesus gleamed from standing in the presence of the Father when Peter, James, and John beheld His transfiguration with Elijah and Moses. "His face shone like the sun, and His clothes became as white as the light" (Matt. 17:2, NKJV).

Envision His face as bright as the sun. At one time or another haven't we all attempted to gaze at this ball of fire, only to have its blinding rays overtake our naked eye? This gives us but a concept of the awesome brightness caused by the visible manifestation of God's holy presence.

Can you conceive a world without any darkness? In the sinless eternal domain of the New Jerusalem at the end of the ages, only the perfect light of God will shine forth. So great is the brilliance of His *Shekinah* glory that it alone will forever illuminate the Holy City and all its righteous residents (Rev. 21:23).

Psalm 104:2 tells us the Lord covers Himself with light as a garment. Visualize sinless Adam and Eve clothed in the excellence of the glory radiating from God's presence in the Garden of Eden.

Such was the grandeur of man's original state, most likely far beyond anything ever imagined by mortal minds today. With pleasure God scanned the final results of His majestic design:

And God saw every thing that he had made, and, behold, it was very good.

—GENESIS 1:31

NOT JUST PART of His creation was very good. *Everything* was very good. It was not just simply good. It was *very* good. Oh, such splendor! Such happiness! The overwhelming satisfaction of the Creator swept throughout His earthly kingdom, which was now ruled by His mankind!

> Thus the heavens and the earth were finished, and all the host of them.
> —GENESIS 2:1

Although this "host" is commonly taught to mean the stars, planets, sun, and moon, the Hebrew word for *host*—as used in this verse—actually describes a mass of persons or things organized for war, an army awaiting their appointed time.[6] In His infinite wisdom God realized the need for heavenly warriors to be stationed on Earth. After all, He knew that Lucifer (Satan) roamed about.

> How art thou fallen from heaven, O Lucifer, son of the morning! how art thou cut down to the ground, which didst weaken the nations!
> —ISAIAH 14:12

Jesus said in Luke 10:18, "I beheld Satan as lightning fall from heaven." Yet in spite of all this danger to the earth, the Creator, so pleased with His handiwork, entrusted rulership to the ultimate of all His creation—mankind. And He released an army of angelic hosts to watch over it.

All seemed secure at the conclusion of that sixth day as the eyes of the Almighty surveyed His splendor with all its wonders: the tiniest of beasts to the gigantic whale, bountiful fruit, beautiful flowers and herbs, spacious rivers, complete with human beings—made after His supreme image. He had finished His marvelous creation.

> And God blessed the seventh day, and sanctified it: because that in it he had rested from all his work which God created and made.
> —GENESIS 2:3

From the original Hebrew word we discover that God's blessing was "an act of adoration" of the seventh day.[7] Here the word *sanctified* could be read, "He observed it as clean and consecrated it as holy."[8] *Rested* in this verse means "cease" and "celebrate."[9] God not only ceased His work of Earth's creation, but He also celebrated His perfect job. Let's pause for a moment and try to sense this joyous party. But how can we even begin to identify with the jubilee and excitement that must have taken place? Can you recall the happiest moments of your life?

I remember the first time I nestled each of my newborn children in my arms. A bubbling spring of warm bonding and overwhelming love surged through my veins with bliss too great for words. Other glad occasions—baptisms, graduations, weddings, anniversaries, reunions, recognition, achievements, rewards—leap to mind. At the top of my list I put my decision to follow Jesus. Maybe every event combined might compare in a vague way.

No! How could any human event, no matter how precious, reach the ecstasy of our Maker when He surveyed His supreme masterpiece? What a glorious day—that happy seventh day when He ceased from work and celebrated His creation!

Divine love and tranquility reigned throughout the flawless abode God designed and released to Adam and Eve. Except for only one command concerning a single tree, no rigid rules or regulations burdened them.

> But of the tree of the knowledge of good and evil, thou shalt not eat of it: for in the day that thou eatest thereof thou shalt surely die.
> —GENESIS 2:17

From the word *rested* in Genesis 2:3 another Hebrew meaning can apply—"cause (made) to fail."[10] Yes, God knew what lay ahead, but He didn't design living souls in His image to be programmed robots or puppets on a string. The instant He blew His breath into their being, they became agents of their own will.

No matter how it hurts Him to watch humans go astray, He has never forced anyone to worship Him. God desires allegiance only by man's decision. This one tree of commandment gave Adam and Eve the liberty to choose. And God knew their choice ahead of time.

When He handed exclusive control over to them, they held full authority to cast Satan out of their garden and order him to never return, and they could have called on angels to back them up. At the onset, as God blessed them He told them to subdue the earth.

What a different world we would have if they had done just that! God and mankind's fellowship would never have been challenged. No sin or evil of any kind could ever have taken over. Only perfection and goodness would exist. How could they be so foolish?

But wait! Let's not judge Adam and Eve too harshly. How can we be so sure that we could have fared any better against the devil's subtle ways?

When Satan, a master of deception and disguise, approached Eve in the guise of a serpent, "... more cunning than any beast of the field which the

LORD God had made..." (Gen. 3:1, NKJV), she had never experienced anything other than truth, love, and purity.

With gnawing passion to rule the world, this "father of lies" (John 8:44) descended upon Eve with his con-artist smooth talk. No one had ever lied to her before. Eve stood before Satan as easy prey, and he knew it. How he must have gloated as he watched her press the forbidden fruit against her lips and then sink her teeth into its flesh, dispersing deadly poison through her glowing sinless body.

Even after she swallowed it and stood openly in stark nakedness, Adam still maintained the power and right to conquer this epitome of evil. But if he did, his precious helpmate could be no longer his. She had sinned and would surely die as God had said.

There Adam held the fate of the whole world in his hands with the love of his life clinging helplessly to his side. He took the fruit. Although the serpent had deceived Eve, he didn't deceive Adam (1 Tim. 2:14). Defying God, Adam opted to tread the path of sin. The crown of all creation chose to die!

And thus man's broken fellowship with God began. Oh, the hurt, the sorrow endured by man and God from that day forward.

And what terrible agony Adam and Eve suffered. The name *Eve* means "life," for she became the mother of all living. How sad to give birth in a land of sickness, pain, and death when she and Adam had experienced paradise so pure and free.

How God must have grieved. Though He would never leave or forsake His human race, now He must step aside. The decision of His most treasured of all creation, His precious man and woman creatures, separated them from Him and transferred Earth's rulership to Satan. Evil triumphed over good, bringing the bondage of sin and death to all.

> Therefore, as sin came into the world through one man, and death as the result of sin, so death spread to all men, [no one being able to stop it or to escape its power] because all men sinned.
>
> —ROMANS 5:12, AMP

As the God of perfect righteousness He could never participate in or even look upon their sin.

> Thou art of purer eyes than to behold evil, and canst not look on iniquity.
>
> —HABAKKUK 1:13

As the God of absolute truth, He couldn't go against His Word and reclaim His rule of Earth. Once He gave dominion to man, only a man could take it back from Satan. It must be a man who would refuse all sin. But how could anyone accomplish this?

As the God of all wisdom, He had a plan to redeem the world. From the gates of Eden it spun into motion.

God cursed the serpent, sentencing it to a life of crawling on its belly and eating dust. To Satan He proclaimed war!

> And I will put enmity between thee and the woman, and between thy seed and her seed, It shall bruise thy head, and thou shall bruise his heel.
>
> —Genesis 3:15

Someday at the appointed time a battle would rage between Satan and this seed of woman. The seed, a sinless Man, would triumph over evil. As the God of amazing grace and mercy, He would redeem mankind by the blood of this perfect Man. The very Son of God would come to Earth, born of a virgin, made of human flesh and blood.

Then sinful man, enlightened by the history of evil's devastation and no longer ignorant of Satan's devices, would be able to regain the authority that was lost in Eden. It would be accomplished by the wonders of the righteous seed, the sacrifice of His sinless flesh, the power of His spotless blood.

As the God of eternal faithfulness, He would forever abide by His human race. Sin may have placed Him outside of His creation looking in. But longing for man's allegiance, He would walk throughout the ages ever present as their guide, as much as man himself allowed.

IMMEDIATELY FOLLOWING ADAM'S and Eve's disobedience, God began weaving His divine plan of redemption, preparing His special people whose bloodline would usher forth the promised Redeemer in mortal flesh. In defiance Satan would sew constant threads of delusion with a blood-thirsty obsession to stop the lineage of this great Messiah and cut a lethal gash in the relationship between man and God.

But as the God of total knowledge, our all-seeing Creator scanned the centuries with eyes of love. Seeing every generation, even you and me, in the fullness of time He honored His redemption promise. He gave His Son for us.

> For God so loved the world, that he gave his only begotten Son, that whosoever believeth in him should not perish, but have everlasting life.
>
> —JOHN 3:16

Aware of the torture He faced in order to redeem man, this beloved Son still elected to leave His heavenly state to become human and suffer as a man. Entering the world as a baby, born of the virgin Mary in a primitive stable, He grew as all humans do into adulthood, the Man who would recover the creation Satan stole and restore life in full measure to humanity.

> The thief cometh not, but for to steal, and to kill, and to destroy: I am come that they might have life, and that they might have it more abundantly.
>
> —JOHN 10:10

What a restoration! Oh, the wonders of redemption and the treasure of knowing Jesus as our Savior. Sin no longer reigns.

> The sin of this one man, Adam, caused death to be king over all, but all who will take God's gift of forgiveness and acquittal are kings of life because of this one man, Jesus Christ. Yes, Adam's sin brought punishment to all, but Christ's righteousness makes men right with God, so that they can live. Adam caused many to be sinners because he disobeyed God, and Christ caused many to be made acceptable to God because he obeyed.
>
> —ROMANS 5:17–19, TLB

Reach out! Take the gift of His pardon and forgiveness. Become a new creature in Him, transformed into a king of abundant life. It is God's gift to us, free for the asking, made possible only by His sinless perfection as a Man who died for our redemption. What a Savior! Once for all and forever He paid the price for sin with the sacrifice of His spotless human blood.

Oh, the sacrifice of spotless blood! It lifted us from the bondage to sin and into freedom, beyond the rigid covenant of law into a loving covenant of grace.

> For sin shall not have dominion over you: for you are not under the law, but under grace.
>
> —ROMANS 6:14

Oh, the sacrifice of spotless blood! It not only set the New Covenant into motion, but it also inscribed it upon our hearts and minds.

> This is the covenant that I will make with them after those days,
> saith the Lord, I will put my laws into their hearts, and in their
> minds will I write them; and their sins and iniquities will I remem-
> ber no more.
>
> —Hebrews 10:16–17

Oh, the sacrifice of spotless blood! It abolished the distant approach to God that the Jews knew—for at the instant of Christ's death, entry into the holy presence of God became available for all. No longer is He in a place where man can never go, hidden behind a veil in the holy of holies.

COME NOW AS we gather among the crowd at the feet of our Savior while He hangs in disgrace, cruelly nailed upon the cross at Calvary.

Three hours of midday darkness envelop the earth. It seems like an eternity as we stand without hope...waiting...trembling, lost in a despair of utter helplessness.

How can this be happening to the One we love so much? Our hearts blaze with heaving pain like hot lava pumping in our chests. We weep in total anguish...and we wait.

Piercing the silence like a thousand jagged swords His voice shrieks out in agony. It stabs into our burning grief as we grasp His final words. "Father, into Thy hands I commit my spirit!"

"Oh, no!" we scream. "He can't be gone!" With tear-blurred eyes we squint through the uncanny blackness and gape in horror as the last breath of life is sucked from His naked, blood-drenched body.

The earth trembles. Before we have time to absorb the nightmare of His torture and the shock and sorrow of His death, a violent earthquake flings us to the ground. We wail in fright and disbelief. The shaking stops. But we muster no strength, make no effort to lift ourselves out of the dust. Beneath the lifeless, battered form of our Savior on the cross we stay sprawled, wretched in grief, convulsing uncontrollably.

There is sobbing all around! Many have now come to grips with the truth. *Surely this man was the Son of God!*

How quickly news travels. We learn that at the exact instant of the earthquake the temple veil supernaturally ripped from top to bottom.

Yes! This man is the Son of God!

The veil blocking the entrance into the holy of holies has split apart. As we examine this massive curtain, the impact of this miracle leaps to life. So beautifully designed in a radiance of blue, purple, and crimson lavishly embroidered with angelic cherubim on white fine-spun linen—its dimensions are GIGANTIC.

Ancient records reveal it as a curtain reaching as high as sixty feet. That compares to a six-story building! And its width stretched over thirty feet. Now picture this huge work of art tightly woven into a density as wide as a man's palm—four inches thick! No wonder legend says two teams of oxen attached to the veil and pulling against each other couldn't tear it apart.[11]

Yet the powerful sacrifice of His spotless blood tore it into shreds for us! Do you realize what this means? With the veil gone—with God no longer isolated from man—He becomes our ever-available Friend. The entrance into His presence is wide open, unrestricted, accessible for all. With an open invitation His welcome extends to everyone. What a privilege and honor to be able to enter with freedom into the innermost sanctum of a most holy God. We have freedom to stand in His presence at any time for any reason. It is a freedom with boldness—not without reverence—but without fright. It's the kind of boldness that grows from intimate friendship, total trust, and confidence.

Yes, with complete freedom and boldness we can come to Him to share all we are, our every thought, need, and desire. And more than any true and faithful friend, He will always be there for us to provide fellowship, comfort, forgiveness, and love. What a privilege for man!

> Therefore, brethren, having boldness to enter the Holiest by the blood of Jesus, by a new and living way which He consecrated for us, through the veil, that is, His flesh, and having a High Priest over the house of God...
>
> —HEBREWS 10:19–21, NKJV

Oh, the sacrifice of spotless blood! It established a High Priest for us!

> He came as High Priest of this better system which we now have. He went into that greater, perfect tabernacle in heaven, not made by men nor part of this world.
>
> —HEBREWS 9:11, TLB

Jesus Christ is our High Priest. With His perfect and final sacrifice for sins the need no longer exists for an earthly high priest to preside as a mediator between man and God in an earthly tabernacle. Our High Priest in a perfect heavenly tabernacle presides not as a mere man making intercession to God for us, and not as a mere man allowed to enter into God's presence only one day each year. Our High Priest is the victorious Lamb of God who makes intercession for us, remaining constantly in the Father's presence, eternally at His side.

> But this man, after he had offered one sacrifice for sins for ever, sat down on the right hand of God.
>
> —HEBREWS 10:12

Yes! Our High Priest is "made higher than the heavens" (Heb. 7:26). He sits at "the right hand of the throne of the Majesty in the heavens" (Heb. 8:1). Yet in spite of such greatness, our High Priest completely understands our pain, our stress, and our temptations. He loved us enough to suffer them Himself.

> For we do not have a High Priest who cannot sympathize with our weaknesses, but was in all points tempted as we are, yet without sin. Let us therefore come boldly to the throne of grace, that we may obtain mercy and find grace to help in time of need.
>
> —HEBREWS 4:15–16, NKJV

Oh, the sacrifice of spotless blood! Only because of its purity can we find mercy and grace in the presence of a most holy God, for by its cleansing power His blood covers us in His righteousness. And through the righteousness of His perfect blood, God looks upon His less-than-perfect creatures in mercy and grace without seeing their sin.

> God made him who had no sin to be sin for us, so that in him we might become the righteousness of God.
>
> —2 CORINTHIANS 5:21, NIV

What a plan of redemption! A design of such wisdom boggles the human mind. Can we ever completely comprehend the magnitude of His spotless blood?

Such power! It not only opened the door of His throne room for all humanity, but it also reopened the door of His entrance into His beloved creation. Because Christ Jesus took on the nature of man in a perishable body of flesh and blood, He became Our kinsman—one with us.

Yes, Jesus is our blood relative, brother to mankind! Therefore fellowship between the Creator and His human creatures has forever been restored for all who believe on Him. Secured by the spotless blood, this long-awaited reunion remains sealed throughout eternity.

What a privilege, what benefits, what joy! Through the wonders of the blood, our God so holy, sovereign, perfect, and pure adopted us despite our many faults and failures. Joined by the blood of His Son, believers will always be His children. This infinite and almighty God is forever our Father!

> But when the fulness of the time was come, God sent forth his Son, made of a woman, made under the law, to redeem them that were under the law, that we might receive the adoption of sons.
>
> —GALATIANS 4:4–5

Adoption entitles us to inheritance. "...if children, then heirs; heirs of God, and joint-heirs with Christ" (Rom. 8:17). Just think of it, we are joint-heirs!

Adoption entitles us to family bonds. We are "no longer strangers and foreigners, but fellow citizens with the saints and members of the household of God" (Eph. 2:19, NKJV). We're members! We belong to His household!

Does His adoption include everyone? Yes, yes, God says yes! His adoption is available, not for just a chosen sect, but for every single person who accepts Jesus as Lord and Savior. "But as many as received him, to them gave he power to become the sons of God, even to them that believe on his name" (John 1:12).

Yes, by faith in Christ Jesus we become children of God. Now no distinction exists in the eyes of God between Jews or Gentiles, slave or free, male or female. As Christians we are one and the same. (See Galatians 3:26–28; 1 Corinthians 12:13.)

Adoption entitles us to family rights. "And because ye are sons, God hath sent forth the Spirit of his Son into your hearts, crying, Abba, Father. Wherefore thou art no more a servant, but a son; and if a son, then an heir of God through Christ" (Gal. 4:6–7). We are no longer servants, but sons and daughters with the right to call Him "Abba, Father!" Jesus prayed "Abba, Father" on the night of His betrayal (Mark 14:36). In Romans 8:15 we read, "For ye have not received the spirit of bondage again to fear; but ye have received the Spirit of adoption, whereby we cry, Abba, Father."

ABBA FATHER. SUCH a personal title. Most scholars agree that the word *abba*, although it means "father," denotes a closer and more intimate fellowship. It is like the word *daddy*.

As a ten-year-old child I shared this kind of fellowship with God, as a daughter shares relationship with her daddy. My "Abba" Father and I met often under the shade of an elm tree behind my home. As I walked and talked with Him in the nearby meadow, His presence overwhelmed me and I sensed His hand upon my life. Then one day I told someone—a grown-up!

I thank God that today my mind doesn't recall who the person was. It must have been someone I looked up to, someone I trusted, because I remember how crushed I felt when this person said God no longer walks and talks with people the way He did in Bible times.

"It must have been your imagination," this person explained.

Feeling empty and forsaken, I stopped going to my special places to commune with the Father. Yet all was not lost. I knew God heard my prayers.

At age eight I pranced up to my mother with red curls bouncing and excitement in my voice. "Mother, can I have a baby sister?"

Her large brown eyes narrowed. "No," she said, "you have a brother. The two of you with Daddy and me makes our family complete. We don't need more children."

"Well, is it OK if I pray for a baby sister?"

"Yes," she smiled, "you can pray about it."

A year later she gave birth to my baby sister!

As humorous as this sounds, it grounded my faith. After once savoring the delicacy of answered prayer and tasting the sweet nectar of divine fellowship, my spirit never ceased in hungering for more of Him. Following the negative "grown-up" counseling, I hid in my bedroom devouring stories in my Bible. Perhaps in my childlike thinking I feared the joy I'd discovered in God's Word might also be stolen, so I kept it a secret. And I shied away from sharing any deep feelings about my heavenly Father with anyone.

Yet the Holy Bible continued to take root in my heart. In Sunday school we journeyed with Moses and the Israelites from Egypt to Canaan and constructed a replica of the tabernacle. How I yearned to be like the people of that day and witness mighty miracles of God. But the church I attended never taught that anyone in modern times experienced God's power. I didn't know the scriptures that say He never changes:

> For I am the LORD, I change not...
>
> —MALACHI 3:6

> Jesus Christ the same yesterday, and to day, and for ever.
>
> —HEBREWS 13:8

In the sixth grade the teacher asked each student to share what they wanted to be when they grew up. My chest pounded and my face burned like fiery coals as my turn drew near. How I wanted to call out, "Missionary!" But the word choked inside me. I simply couldn't share the union I felt with my heavenly Father. With throbbing heart I dropped my eyes, and as so many of the girls had answered before me I mumbled, "Nurse."

During the next school year a pretty dark-haired girl who was usually quite reserved announced with great enthusiasm to the entire class, "Last night we went to a tent crusade and my daddy got healed!"

I remember how those words just bubbled out of her. My heart froze as I waited for someone to volunteer that God no longer did things the way He did in biblical times. Nothing but dead silence followed. Nobody said a word, not even the teacher. It was as though the girl never said it. But I never forgot it.

Sadly, this tiny episode constituted my first and only hint of any ongoing divine healing until after I reached adulthood. Despite its briefness it deepened my gnawing appetite for intense spiritual knowledge. With this yearning inside me I wandered aimlessly, haunted by the "grown-up" words, blinded by tradition and doctrine, not knowing how or where to soothe my hunger pangs.

WHY, OH WHY, did it take so long to find the truth?

Ignorance is such a flimsy excuse. I owned many Bibles, God's infallible Word that holds the only true answers. Yet soon after my daughter's mysterious drowning event, with eagerness to search out supernatural power I nibbled unknowingly upon forbidden fruit—the occult!

Completely unaware of its abomination to God and its wickedness, I deviated into perilous webs of deceit and tunneled dangerously through darkness. How easily we veer into sin if we don't know God's Word. And dabbling in sin, even in innocence, separates us from God. "We wait for light, but behold obscurity; for brightness, but we walk in darkness" (Isa. 59:9).

Let me warn you now. Before our travels end we'll venture into the slimy crevices of evil—the serpent's den, Satan's world of lies and perverseness—where deceptions hide, poised and waiting like rattlesnakes.

> They hatch vipers' eggs and weave the spider's web; he who eats of their eggs dies, and from that which is crushed a viper breaks out.
> —Isaiah 59:5, NKJV

But don't panic. When the time comes, we'll march with confidence upon demonic turf possessing full awareness of its deadly venom. With knowledge of God's Word we'll attack, dressed in the whole armor of our

Father. As our guide, He will triumphantly lead our way.

Had I not already known Jesus as my Savior when I toyed with evil powers, I wonder where I would be today. Patiently waiting in the midst of all my wayward turns the Lord stood by, ready to untangle me from the web of darkness and usher me into His sunshine and freedom. When I learned to seek His righteousness through His Word, it fed my flaming passion for His truth, which had never stopped burning within my spirit.

In His sermon on the mount Christ promises, "Blessed are they which do hunger and thirst after righteousness: for they shall be filled" (Matt. 5:6). Just as He furnished manna for the Israelites, He sent His living bread to me to nourish my famished heart.

In ways I'd never experienced before, words in the Bible spoke life, health, and miracles. The gifts of His Holy Spirit (1 Cor. 12:1–12) emerged, real and alive and for today. While praying one day with a lady minister on Christian television, I received instant healing from nosebleeds, a condition I apparently inherited from my grandmother. New insight and strong faith awakened inside my being.

Yet for some reason the memory of my daughter's drowning incident stayed tucked away in an unused closet of my brain. Years had passed since the door of that memory opened even a crack.

Then one night after my daughter reached her teen years, she drove off with some friends. Feeling uneasy I paced the floor, praying for her protection. Suddenly I froze in my tracks as a Voice thundered inside my being.

I saved her from drowning, didn't I?

As I recovered from the shock, my heart burst forth with thanksgiving. The mystery of so long ago had come to light. For the first time I knew beyond any doubt the miracle-working hand of almighty God had truly raised her from death. How sad that I hadn't known to give Him full honor for this miracle before! From that moment forward I began testifying to everybody how God heard my cries to Him and supernaturally saved my infant daughter. I vowed to never again allow anyone to steal my boldness to speak out in behalf of my heavenly Father.

THE GOD I know today not only still walks and talks with those who seek Him, but He performs miracles, too!

How wonderful that at our adoption into the family of God we didn't have to forfeit an astounding God of marvels and wonders. How wonderful that when we received open access into His presence we didn't lose a sovereign holy God. So gracious is His mercy that, as His children, we no longer need to fear an avenging God of wrath and judgment. We serve a Father of love.

> Behold, what manner of love the Father hath bestowed upon us, that we should be called the sons of God.
>
> —1 JOHN 3:1

How blessed we are. In the great exchange of law for grace we received adoption by a forgiving Father of love, a merciful Father who cares about our every need.

Jesus instructs us not to worry if we'll have enough food to eat or clothes to wear. God feeds the ravens that don't plant, harvest, or have barns to store food.

> And you are far more valuable to him than any birds!
>
> —LUKE 12:24, TLB

Our Father clothes the lilies whose beauty is here today and gone tomorrow. He cares for the fields and the grass.

> Your heavenly Father knows your needs. He will always give you all you need from day to day if you will make the Kingdom of God your primary concern."
>
> —LUKE 12:30–31, TLB

Can you imagine such a loving God who even cares about every sparrow that falls to the ground, a God who cares so individually for each of us that He numbers every single hair on our head?

> So don't worry! You are more valuable to him than many sparrows.
>
> —MATTHEW 10:31, TLB

> If a child asks his father for a loaf of bread, will he be given a stone instead? If he asks for a fish, will he be given a poisonous snake? Of course not! And if you hardhearted, sinful men know how to give good gifts to your children, won't your Father in heaven even more certainly give good gifts to those who ask him for them?
>
> —MATTHEW 7:9–11, TLB

God our Father is love. He is a forgiving God, a God of compassion, a gracious God. He is more than able to do immeasurably above what we can ask or imagine. He is an ever-present help in time of need, our shelter from the storm, our stronghold in trouble. He is our God of glory, hope, peace, truth, and comfort. He is always with us as our provider, our light, our shield, our guide, our rock, our strength, and our healer.

God is unlimited, awesome, powerful, mighty, majestic, forever faithful, and glorious beyond compare. He is the Great I AM, the Judge of all the earth, the Lord God Almighty, the Lord of hosts, the Lord Most High. He is the Creator of heaven and Earth, the only true and living God, the King above all and owner of all kingdoms.

He is all this and more. His vastness reaches higher than our minds can fathom. Yet, even in all His excellent greatness, God is our Father—our Abba Father—who loves us and cares about our every need. Even though we did nothing to earn it and certainly don't deserve it, He gave us the free gift of redemption through the blood of His dear Son.

Yes, what love!

When we pray *Our Father*, it brings us into a personal intimate fellowship with Him. As we realize that we are truly His children and He is truly our Father, a loving respect floods our souls and humbles our hearts.

> I bow my knees unto the Father of our Lord Jesus Christ, of whom the whole family in heaven and earth is named.
>
> —Ephesians 3:14–15

All who know Jesus as Lord and Savior are part of God's wonderful family. Thank You, God, for adopting us. Thank You for being our Father, our Abba Father.

Chapter 2

Heaven

WHERE COULD I be?
So vivacious and free—in a state of euphoria—I felt suspended in space, gliding through a long black tunnel. Sparkling radiance lined both sides, billions of lights alive with gorgeous colors, more vibrant than I can describe and so close I could almost reach out and touch them. Yet darkness engulfed the center where an unseen force swept me forward. On and on I flowed, throbbing with vitality in wondrous ecstasy and absolute glory.

What are these magnificent lights? I pondered.

Instantly an answer transcended into my being, *Each light represents an aborted baby.*

Although not fully understanding the meaning of these words, calm assurance embraced me. I sensed myself being drawn into a world of tranquility and joy. And I loved it.

Then boom! Like a human firecracker I blasted into the physical world. A blinding flash of boiling red liquid exploded behind my eyes, charging like a grenade against my skull, jolting horrendous pain throughout my body.

"Mrs. Perrin, Mrs. Perrin, wake up!" a human female voice burst into a pulsating channel of my brain.

"No! No! Let me go back!" I screamed—whether aloud or just within myself I don't know.

A second woman's voice shot against my eardrums, "Wow! She was *really* knocked out!"

I ached all over. My right arm weighed a ton. My body felt welded to a stretcher. Forcing my eyelids apart I squinted up at two blurry figures. Women in nurses' smocks? *Leave me alone,* I wanted to yell. *Please stop shaking me!*

"Where am I?" I finally moaned in audible voice.

"Recovery room. Your surgery's over."

Surgery? In slow motion the crisis trickled into my memory... *shattered arm... hospital... bone graft...*

In semi-consciousness I squeezed my eyes shut, trying to revert to oblivion. My heart agonized with every beat, and I longed for the utopia I had almost entered.

Because so many accounts about near-death encounters have surfaced in modern times and also since no one ever admitted that I neared the brink of death, I hesitated to write of this experience. But it wouldn't leave me alone—stirring inside my spirit, pressing me to share this supernatural wonder of my Father.

Perhaps He took me into this dimension so that I would tell it to bring consolation to those who suffer regret and guilt because of choosing abortion. Whatever the reason, I know God showed me that these innocent babies are not forgotten. A light beams for every infant denied a life on Earth.

Mothers (and fathers), be assured that God forgives. Let Him fill the void in your life and soothe the grief that eats into your heart. Somewhere your child resides safely and securely in heavenly arms of love—yes, perfect love. For a moment I basked in its excellence as it overflowed from God's celestial home. I gazed upon brilliance shimmering beyond imagination, and I became immersed in the glories of a better world.

Yet His Word tells me so much more awaits.

> But as it is written: "Eye has not seen, nor ear heard, nor have entered into the heart of man the things which God has prepared for those who love Him." But God has revealed them to us through His Spirit. For the Spirit searches all things, yes, the deep things of God.
>
> —1 CORINTHIANS 2:9–10, NKJV

WITH HIS SPIRIT as our guide we continue our travels to search out "the deep things of God." Let the wonder of "the things God has prepared for those that love Him" fill our spirits as we sense them whisking us into a fabulous land of majesty. Yes, come! Join me for the next stop on our treasure map. A tour of the holy residence of our gracious Host, our Father...

"WHICH ART IN HEAVEN"

Oh, what a glorious place where our Father resides. Perfection to the fullest in holiness, beauty, splendor, peace, love, harmony, light, magnificence, elegance, and everything good. The awesome infinity of His solar system presents a preview of its greatness.

> The heavens declare the glory of God; and the firmament showeth his handiwork.
>
> —PSALM 19:1

Overwhelmed by my mortal frailty, I often stare into outer space, amazed at the vastness of His heavens. Nothing proclaims the magnitude and glory of our Creator like a clear night's starlit sky. Surely David's heart throbbed with this same soul-stirring affection as he wrote:

> When I consider thy heavens, the works of thy fingers, the moon and the stars, which thou hast ordained; what is man, that thou art mindful of him?
>
> —PSALM 8:3–4

How can human intellect possibly comprehend why such a boundless Being loved wanton mankind enough to step from the glories of heaven into such suffering and humiliation to become a docile Lamb, slain for our sins?

> But [you were purchased] with the precious blood of Christ (the Messiah), like that of a [sacrificial] lamb without blemish or spot. It is true that He was chosen and foreordained (destined and foreknown for it) before the foundation of the world...
>
> —I PETER 1:19–20, AMP

What love! Our heavenly Father knew even before the beginning of man the necessity of His Son to be sacrificed as the Lamb of God. A story I heard at church often often burns inside my heart:

One day a man took a job at a meat slaughtering plant. Because he was the youngest worker, the most gruesome task—slitting the throats of the animals—fell to him. When pigs, goats, or cows came to be butchered, they raged savagely while men laced their legs together and hung them on the conveyer belt. In ferocious frenzies they bellowed until the young man's knife severed their jugular veins. As hard as it may seem, each evening when he stripped off his bloodstained coveralls and departed for home, he managed to blot the day's work from his mind.

Then one day men herded some sheep to slaughter. While the lad stared, they brutally grabbed a lamb, slamming it down to bind its legs. The lamb offered no resistance. Dangling upside down the helpless creature moved toward its death. Still it made no struggle.

As the slayer lifted the blade to the lamb's neck wide, frightened, pleading eyes looked at him. A soft "baa" gurgled out as the instrument dug deep into its flesh. Warm blood gushed, spraying on the young man's sleeve, streaming down his glove. In its last fleeting breath the dying lamb reached out with a gentle tongue and licked its own blood from the hand that took its life.

Tears welled from the man's eyes. He cast aside the bloody knife, threw off the gloves, and peeled off his coveralls one last time. That day he quit his job. But the memory could not be blotted out. He never forgot the lamb he had slain... [1]

With deep regret my heart agonizes knowing that, due to our sinful weakness, Christ, as an innocent Lamb, was brutally led to slaughter.

The LORD hath laid on him the iniquity of us all. He was oppressed, and he was afflicted, yet he opened not his mouth: he is brought as a lamb to the slaughter, and as a sheep before her shearers is dumb, so he openeth not his mouth.

—ISAIAH 53:6–7

With faith and adoration I cherish His unconditional love and divine gift of redemption with an ever-grateful heart. But how can humanity ever express enough gratitude for such limitless commitment? Will we ever understand why this One of infinite creation cares so much for us?

I once read that at least fifty billion galaxies exist, with more than four hundred billion stars in our galaxy alone. Yet God not only positions every heavenly body in outer space, but He also personally identifies each one.

He determines the number of the stars and calls them each by name. Great is our Lord and mighty in power; his understanding has no limit.

—PSALM 147:4–5, NIV

When in the black of night I spot the tiny twinkling of the North Star, a sense of excitement rushes through my veins. It puzzles me that it never changes its location, and I wonder if somewhere near this star a world of total peace and joy—our Father's home, heavenly Mount Zion—exists.

Great is the LORD, and greatly to be praised in the city of our God, in His holy mountain. Beautiful in elevation, the joy of the whole earth, is Mount Zion on the sides of the north, the city of the great King.

—PSALM 48:1–2, NKJV

GOD PLACES MANY parallels, types, previews, and metaphorical pictures within His Word and also in Jewish customs. During our adventures together many of His semblances will lead us to His greatness by shedding light on darkened areas, steering us into seldom traveled regions and revealing plans for future events.

Let's begin our tracking series with the above text about Mount Zion. Although it describes earthly Jerusalem, it easily symbolizes the elevated celestial city of the great King. Even the word *north* gives a possible simile of Jerusalem to God's supernal location since other scriptures support the idea of heaven being in the north.

When Lucifer defied God, threatening to ascend to heaven and exalt his throne above the stars of God, he boasted, "I will sit also upon the mount of the congregation, in the sides of the north" (Isa. 14:13).

A whirlwind bringing Ezekiel a vision of heaven swirled out of the north (Ezek. 1:4). In the Book of Job we read, "He comes from the north as golden splendor, with God is awesome majesty" (Job 37:22, NKJV).

It seems that the psalmist Asaph also places God in the north when he says, "For exaltation comes neither from the east nor from the west nor from the south. But God is the Judge" (Ps. 75:6–7, NKJV).

So much fascination with heaven churns inside man, and many questions seem unanswerable. For example, how high is it? Although we cannot fully know, we are certain that it exists far beyond Earth's atmosphere.

The LORD is high above all nations, and his glory above the heavens.

—PSALM 113:4

Job declared, "Is not God in the height of heaven? and behold the height of the stars, how high they are!" (Job 22:12). Upon announcing Christ's birth, angels praised, "Glory to God in the highest" (Luke 2:14). Jesus "ascended up far above all heavens" (Ephesians 4:10). Paul tells of being caught up into the third heaven. (See 2 Corinthians 12:2.)

Our Father dwells somewhere high above our solar system. His throne abides far beyond the Milky Way. And exalted at His right hand the Lamb of God now sits in great authority. With His sacrifice of spotless blood He earned a position "far above all principality, and power, and might, and dominion, and every name that is named, not only in this world, but also in that which is to come" (Eph. 1:21). But oh, the price He paid for this honor.

Always aware of the cost, Jesus bore a burdened soul. He had to accept an undeserved death sentence to redeem the world. Although He was totally innocent, He was savagely beaten, forsaken, belittled, betrayed, and displayed naked before all eyes. Without a struggle our Lamb yielded to the torment. Like the gentle lamb at the slaughterhouse He offered no resistance. Just as the lamb's tongue tenderly licked the one who thrust the blade into its throat, our Savior cried with compassion from the cross, "Father, forgive them, for they know not what they do."

At last relieved from His mortal mission He exclaimed in victory, "It is finished!"

LET'S LOOK IN on our Lord's final evening before His arrest and eventual crucifixion. With an aching heart He dreads His approaching torture, yet He reclines with His beloved disciples during His last supper with them.

Tonight they eat the Passover meal. This occasion established by God from the days of Moses commemorates the delivery of the Jews from slavery in Egypt when they smeared the sacrificial blood of an unblemished male lamb on their doorposts. It presents striking parallels to the spotless blood of our Savior; even Egypt is a prototype of sin.

The Passover celebration adds impact to the words spoken by John the Baptist, some three years before, when Jesus came to be baptised—"Behold the Lamb of God, which taketh away the sin of the world" (John 1:29).

The Jews knew that from the time of Adam's son Abel, the lamb held first place as the preferred sacrifice. They understood how under the covenant of Law the lamb's blood gave a temporary covering for sin, yet only for the Jew.

John the Baptist proclaimed that this Lamb's blood would not simply cover sin. It would take sin away—not only for the Jew, but also for the entire world. How the people must have pondered this!

Many would soon know its meaning. However on this night with Him at His last supper, the disciples haven't even grasped the effect of Jesus' departure, though they do have a sense of uneasiness. Knowing this, Jesus casts aside His own troubling thoughts of the approaching crucifixion and comforts them with this assurance:

> In my Father's house are many mansions: if it were not so, I would have told you. I go to prepare a place for you. And if I go and prepare a place for you, I will come again, and receive you unto myself; that where I am, there ye may be also.
>
> —JOHN 14:2–3

Although these words bring hope and peace to us today, they held much deeper revelation for those who were at His last supper. They prompted questions from His disciples, but they also painted a picture of a glorious reunion. To understand the significance of this as His disciples did, we must open a door into Jewish customs and step into their society two thousand years ago.

Upon entering Jerusalem we spy a Jewish lad picking his way along a dusty trail. His calf-length robe overlaid with a tasseled tunic sways from side to side with his brisk and determined stride. In the crook of one arm jostles a skin of wine as it keeps time with the rhythm of his steps.

As we hurry to catch up with him, he suddenly halts. Closing his eyes he sucks in a long breath before turning and entering the forecourt of a Hebrew home. Under the shelter of rough stones laid in intricate perfection, he fidgets with the wine and waits for entrance into the living quarters. He gulps as the door opens.

With quivering lips and paling face he greets an older gentleman who seems to be expecting him. As he moves inside the man motions for a petite maiden with wide shining eyes. She joins them. Beneath a beige shawl dark, flowing hair frames her delicate features and smooth olive skin. She appears no older than her teens.

From the folds of a burgundy sash belted at his waist the visitor pulls out a document, a legal contract proposing marriage. His black eyes twinkle ever so slightly as he catches a glance from the girl, and we realize he seeks her as his bride. Blushing, she drops her eyes.

In a graceful sweep her soft blue robe swishes across her feet as she draws closer to the elder man's side. She peers up to him in wonderment. With the loving focus of a father's eyes he meets her gaze in a deepness that seems to search into the very pulse of her tender soul. *This girl, my child so innocent, is she ready to take on the duties of a wife?*

He sighs and shifts his eyes to an older lady who looks on with other family members from across the room. We sense that she is the young girl's mother. Then with hands tanned and gnarled from years of work in the vineyards he reaches for the document.

The potential bridegroom's heart pounds like a hammer against his rib cage as with a frozen stare he watches the father read with solemn face. Frantically his young thoughts spin. *Surely her father will except my proposal! I'm offering the most lavish dowry I can possibly afford. Surely, oh surely, he will realize what a sacrificial price I'm paying to have his daughter as my bride!*

He swallows the lump in his throat. *What if the father agrees to the contract, but she doesn't?* His jaw tightens, as he recognizes that the final decision rests with her. As his mind races on, the thudding of his heart now beats a melody of love. How vividly he recalls the day he met her. Even though his father picked this girl for him, he desired her for his life's companion from first sight.

The father nods. He accepts! In jubilation the young man pours the wine. And now comes the most crucial moment of all—will the one he desires so greatly want him for her husband?

With trembling hand he fills a cup with the scarlet liquid—knowing her acceptance or rejection of his wine will reveal the feelings of her heart. If she refuses to drink from the cup, all wedding plans are off. The hammer in his chest pounds even harder. For a second he hesitates to raise his head—then slowly, slowly, ever so slowly he peers up into her glistening eyes. Peace surges through his veins and floods his soul with bliss as she smiles with true affection.

With face aglow she lifts the cup to her lips. She sips the wine! Dancing in his spirit he in turn drinks of the cup to honor her acceptance. Tears of joy spill onto her cheeks, and he reaches out with a gentle hand to wipe them all away.

Hallelujah! The marriage covenant is sealed! From one of the onlookers a waiting trumpet rings in celebration.

Bursting with love the accepted bridegroom readily pays her father the full price stated in the contract. Though it's torture to leave now, he must say good-bye to his betrothed.

"I am going to prepare a place for you at my father's house," he assures her. "When it's ready, I'll come back to take you there." With this promise he departs.

Building the honeymoon chamber begins. It's quite a task for the bride-groom. First it must be lovely. Next it must meet his father's approval. Only when it does can the son return for his bride. And his father alone decides when the time will be.

In the meantime she waits, knowing that it might be a year—or even two—before her beloved comes back. She waits, watching, believing, ever-ready to go with him. As the days fade into weeks and the weeks turn into months, she continues to wait, hoping that his appearance will occur at any moment.

Without warning, probably in the dead of night, the bridegroom will come to steal his bride away with him. He will fulfill his vows to cherish and love her, keeping her first in his heart, always at his side. There will be no more parting. They will be united as one.

What a symbolic illustration Jesus plants in the minds of His disciples at His last meal with them. He tells them that He is going away to prepare a place for them, and He gives them wine from His cup.

They have often heard Him refer to Himself as a bridegroom. All four Gospels record such instances. In the parable of the ten virgins the bride-groom, addressed as "Lord," represents none other than Christ Himself. He cautioned, "Watch therefore, for ye know neither the day nor the hour wherein the Son of Man cometh" (Matt. 25:13).

Similar advice occurs in Matthew 24, Mark 13, and Luke 21, where Jesus taught on the signs of the end of this age—the time when He will appear to whisk His bride away. Most certainly Jesus will keep His word. Someday, with the bridal chamber complete, He will return.

> But of that day and that hour knoweth no man, no, not the angels which are in heaven, neither the Son, but the Father.
>
> —MARK 13:32

Listen to Paul's description of the wonders that will happen when Christ appears to claim His bride.

> For the Lord himself shall descend from heaven with a shout, with the voice of the archangel, and with the trump of God: and the dead in Christ shall rise first: Then we which are alive and remain shall be caught up together with them in the clouds, to meet the Lord in the air: and so shall we ever be with the Lord.
>
> —1 THESSALONIANS 4:16–17

Oh, picture it! In a flash, we will rise into the clouds to be forever united with our Bridegroom who paid the price for us. You may know of this event as the rapture, which simply means a catching away. It will happen so quickly.

> In a moment, in the twinkling of an eye, at the last trump: for the trumpet shall sound, and the dead shall be raised incorruptible, and we shall be changed.
>
> —1 CORINTHIANS 15:52

At that moment all who know Christ will receive new, glorified, and everlasting bodies.

> For our earthly bodies, the ones we have now that can die, must be transformed into heavenly bodies that cannot perish but will live forever.
>
> —1 CORINTHIANS 15:53, TLB

As His bride we must all stay on alert, ready to go, eagerly awaiting this glorious union. At the shout of the archangel and the heavenly trumpet blast all the redeemed must be prepared for immediate departure.

FOR YEARS QUESTIONS stirred in my mind when I heard of the rapture. Where are the righteous dead today since this meeting with Jesus in the sky has not yet taken place? Many traditional Christian teachings indicate man's spirit and soul ascend immediately to walk on golden streets and sing with choirs of angels. However, if the saints already reside where Jesus went to prepare a place in His Father's house, why would it be necessary for them to be caught up to meet Him in the air to "ever be with the Lord"? In our search for answers, let's explore paradise in the New Testament.

Dying on a cross next to Jesus, a thief pleads, "Remember me when you come into Your kingdom!" Jesus assured him, "Today you will be with me in Paradise." (See Luke 23:42–43.)

In relating his visit to heavenly realms, Paul wrote, "And I know that this man—whether in the body or apart from the body I do not know, but God knows—was caught up to paradise. He heard inexpressible things, things that man is not permitted to tell" (2 Cor. 12:3–4, NIV).

The Spirit divulges to John, "To him that overcometh will I give to eat of the tree of life, which is in the midst of the paradise of God" (Rev. 2:7).

What is paradise? Is it different from the heavenly city where golden streets stretch for miles enclosed by walls of precious gems and gates of solid pearl?

Since most of the New Testament was originally written in the Greek language, let's examine the word *paradise* from its Greed roots. In *Strong's Exhaustive Concordance* we find that the Greek word *paradeisos* means "a park as Eden."[2] *Vines Expository Dictionary of New Testament Words* defines it as "the figurative antitype of that in Eden, held out to the overcomer, is spoken of as being in 'the Paradise of God'... 'garden,' as in Gen. 2:8."[3]

For more detailed information, we turn to *The Complete Word Study Dictionary*:

> This is an oriental word which the Greeks borrowed from the Persians, among whom it meant a garden, park, or enclosure full of all vegetable products of the earth. In Xenophon's economics, Socrates said that the King of Persia took particular care, wherever he was, to have gardens or enclosures full of every beautiful and good thing the earth could produce. These were called paradises. The original word *pardes* occurs in Neh. 2:8; Eccl. 2:5; Song 4:13.
>
> In Sanskrit *paradesha* and *paradisha* meant a land elevated and cultivated. In Armenian, *pardes* means a garden around the house planted with grass, herbs, and trees for food and ornament. The Sept. uses it to refer to the Garden of Eden (Gen. 2:8). In later Jewish usage and in the NT *paradeisos* is used for the abode of the blessed after death. Paradise, before Christ's resurrection, has been thought to be the region of the blessed in Hades, although it was not specifically called by that name. Luke 23:43
>
> The expression "the paradise of God" means the celestial paradise where the spirits of the just dwell with God.[4]

Has paradise, the dwelling place of the spirits of the just, always been a celestial kingdom? Come with me, but only if you have the stomach to endure it, for a trip into eerie crevices deep inside the earth to visit the abode of the dead before the victory of the cross.

As our journey begins, we witness the death of two men—a pitiful beggar named Lazarus and a prominent rich man. In mortal life they knew each other and also in their state thereafter. (See Luke 16:19–31.)

Lazarus dies first. He suffered so terribly during his earthly sojourn. In constant hunger he grappled with dogs for scraps from the rich man's table.

But did the rich man care? Not in the least. He gave the poor man nothing, not even a dab of salve to relieve his agony. Dogs licked pus from the beggar's oozing sores, but even so, it didn't phase the rich man.

How death changes things as a glorious band of angels escort a healed and pain-free Lazarus to a land of safekeeping, the holding place for righteous souls.

Look, there's Abraham! As father of the Jews he welcomes all newcomers, ministering in fellowship and comforting in love.

What a blessing for Lazarus! His mortal days are over. No longer suffering, he relishes his new life and its essence of joy and kindness. At first glance his surroundings present a picture of a perfect paradise.

But listen! Do we hear weeping, wailing, and gnashing of teeth? Can it be that pain and torment lurk nearby? Yes! The location of this "paradise" is next to a cesspool of torture for the wicked dead. Only a gaping gulf separates the two. How awful! We stare in horror at a region engulfed in fire. Rising with its flames, a putrid stench worse than boiling sewer scum makes us gag. Below, writhing balls of worms cover the ground with smoldering slime. In a never-ending death people flounder about.

We gasp as we see the rich man. While tossing back and forth he scans the land of the righteous. Oh, he recognizes Lazarus sitting at the feet of Abraham! *Why did I treat that beggar so badly?* he moans to himself.

Now naked and powerless, he so desperately needs help. If only Lazarus can come to his aid! With all his strength he shrieks above the deafening howls of those around him and over the ear-shattering cracking of the blazes, "Father Abraham! Have mercy on me! Send Lazarus over to help me. If only he may just dip the tip of his finger in water to soothe my burning tongue!"

But it can't be done. As we hear Abraham's refusal, we weep for the foolish rich man and his wasted years on Earth. His cries of remose continue, and with aching hearts we close our ears and run away from this horrendous pit of torture.

In one last glance we view the righteous in their abode. They know that hope awaits. The sacrifice of spotless blood will free all saints. Then they will dwell far from the devil's grip, out of the tragic sight and sounds of the wicked.

Yes, by the account in Luke we can surmise that although Satan never tormented the righteous dead, he evidently gained authority through his triumph in Eden to hold them captive adjacent to his quagmire for the unrighteous. How he must have gloated over his domain.

But hallelujah! A victorious Savior put an end to his authority! After His conquest on the cross, the mighty Seed of the woman descended into the bowels of hell, possessing power and boldness never imagined by Satan or his cohorts. How every fallen angel and all the demonic forces must have squawked at the sight of their defeated prince when Jesus Christ, Son of Man, emerged as conqueror!

Holding the keys of hell and death and ringing out His victory, He marched the righteous out of Satan's clutches, away from the horrible sight of the evil dead, forever into freedom! (See Revelation 1:18; Colossians 2:15; Ephesians 4:8–9.)

What a perplexing sight when some of those who had been delivered stopped off in Jerusalem and walked among the people.

> And the graves were opened; and many bodies of the saints which slept arose, and came out of the graves after his resurrection, and went into the holy city, and appeared unto many.
> —MATTHEW 27:52–53

In reading this, I wonder, Where did the rescued dead go after they left Jerusalem? Jesus hadn't yet prepared the place in His Father's house. And what about the promise of the rapture? Is it possible that all the godly dead abide in a new land of bliss far away from the gaze of wicked souls? Is there a re-created paradise positioned in the realm of heaven where souls eagerly anticipate the ultimate catching away to be with their Redeemer?

Above the heavens of Earth's atmosphere and above the starry curtains, there is a definite paradise that displays its beauty in the heavenly kingdom of God. No longer in the depths of Earth, today paradise claims its site in the heights of the "third heaven."

Earlier we read about the tree of life being located in the paradise of God (Rev. 2:7). Describing trees in the Garden of Eden, Genesis 2:9 notes "the tree of life also in the midst of the garden." Could the tree Jesus mentions in Revelation as being in the paradise of God be the same species as the tree of life planted by the Lord in His original paradise for mankind?

John also testifies of living fountains of waters (Rev. 7:17). Just consider—living fountains! And can you picture entire mountains made of gleaming metals? In a vision Zechariah saw horse-drawn chariots descending from heaven between two mountains of brass (Zech. 6:1–3).

Trees of life, living fountains, brass mountains, horses, chariots. Are these all part of the paradise of God? We'll know for sure someday when we set foot in God's celestial land, but for now exact design and locations can only be surmised. Although no one can factually state the paradise of God is a special region for the righteous at death, one thing I do know with all my being—paradise definitely exists and heaven is a reality. Their existence is as literal as Planet Earth.

The sphere of heaven must be limitless. God's chariots "are tens of thousands and thousands of thousands" (Ps. 68:17, NIV). Here the Hebrew word for *chariot*s means "vehicle, team, cavalry, multitude."[5] The King James Version includes angels in this verse. Can you picture millions of chariots, pulled by horses and perhaps driven by angels? What a sight to behold!

Isaiah prophesies that "the LORD will come with fire, and with his chariots like a whirlwind, to render His anger with fury, and his rebuke with flames of fire" (Isa. 66:15). Oh, what a time of confusion and panic for many on that terrible judgment day! How sad for those who denied the Lord in this life when they face Him as Judge in eternity.

A story is told of a young lawyer who often jogged along the beach. One evening he stopped dead in his tracks. *Had he heard screams for help?* Frantically he searched the waves.

"Help!" a desperate wail echoed above the ocean's roar again as a small boy's head surfaced for a moment and then submerged. With no thought for his own life, the lawyer dove into the treacherous incoming tide. By his alert actions and swimming skills he brought the child to safety.

Years passed. As the rescued boy grew into manhood he led a life of crime and was caught in the act of cold-blooded murder. Found guilty at his trial, he stood for sentencing.

"With this verdict and considering your merciless act, I must sentence you to death," came the voice behind the bench.

"Your Honor!" the guilty man cried, knowing the judge to be the same young lawyer who had pulled him from the ocean so many years before, "You rescued me! Remember? I'm the little kid you saved from drowning!"

The judge paused and studied the pleading man's face. "Yes, I remember." With tear-filled eyes he spoke again, "On that day I was your savior. But this day I am your judge."[6]

Today as we tour our Father's heavenly home we'll view Him only as a loving Savior and behold the glorious future awaiting the redeemed. In another chapter at the end of our travels we'll return to witness Him as Judge. But only those guilty of denying Him will need to fear as they stand before His throne for sentencing.

WALK WITH ME now as we seek out the wonders of His throne and His heavenly residence. Proceeding alongside chosen men in the Bible we'll witness His majesty and set our eyes on His eternal splendor through their visions.

Thy throne, O God, is for ever and ever.

—PSALM 45:6

The prophet Micaiah glimpsed God on His throne with vast throngs of angels beside Him (2 Chron. 18:18). Truly millions upon millions, even trillions upon trillions of heavenly host glorify God in heaven. There are too many to count!

> But ye are come unto mount Sion, and unto the city of the living God, the heavenly Jerusalem, and to an innumerable company of angels.
>
> —HEBREWS 12:22

Isaiah beheld God sitting on His throne high and lifted up. The magnificent train of God's robe, a portrayal of His *Shekinah* glory, flooded the entire temple. Above His throne seraphim, an awesome type of angel, praised Him with vigor: "Holy, holy, holy, is the LORD of hosts: the whole earth is full of his glory." Their voices rang with such force that the foundations shook and smoke permeated throughout the temple (Isa. 6:1–4).

Another astounding description of God's throne unfolds in the Book of Ezekiel. Out of the north a whirlwind spins, propelling a cloud of gleaming fire. Constant flames engulfing themselves blaze with amber brilliance (Ezek. 1:4).

In lively detail Ezekiel 1 portrays four living creatures each having four faces, four wings, human hands, and wheels. They flame like burning coals of fire surrounded by lightning bolts. Later Ezekiel identifies them as cherubim (Ezek. 10:15).

What unique angelic beings! Did the figures of golden cherubim guarding God's mercy seat above the ark of the covenant look like this? They must have!

"Expressibly beautiful!" Ezekiel breathes. He gapes in sheer astonishment. Above the mighty cherubim the sky glitters with a most exquisite throne where the Almighty Eternal One reigns in splendor. Oh, what an awesome sight!

> For high in the sky above them was what looked like a throne made of beautiful blue sapphire stones, and upon it sat someone who appeared to be a Man. From his waist up, he seemed to be all glowing bronze, dazzling like fire; and from his waist down he seemed to be entirely flame, and there was a glowing halo like a rainbow all around him. This was the way the glory of the Lord appeared to me.
>
> —EZEKIEL 1:26–28, TLB

Yes, such awesomeness. And the spectacular has only begun! We're in for marvels inexpressible with an excursion into the last book of the Bible. So open your inner being to dynamic panoramic views of God's abode. Prepare to gaze upon majestic beauty, hear angelic voices ring through all the kingdom, bow in gratitude for His mercy and grace, and delight in His rewards as His ecstasies for His redeemed unravel.

WHAT A SHAME that so many forgo blessings by seldom reading the Book of Revelation and saying that the judgments of the Great Tribulation seem beyond understanding. They miss the fact that, sandwiched between the expressions of God's wrath, a beautiful and loving picture of eternal salvation emerges.

First we step into chapter 4 to locate John, who will lead our way. How haggard he appears in rags, a prisoner exiled on the Isle of Patmos. Yet as we approach him, we see that he walks in dignity, undefeated, unafraid, on fire for Jesus.

Why is he so excited as he peers up into the clouds? Oh, see it? There's an open door leading all the way into the highest realm of heaven!

Listen! Someone calls with the voice of a mighty trumpet. "Come up here, and I will show you future events!"

Instantly John rises, caught up in the Spirit of God. Hurry! We can't be left behind.

Our minds hum—*trumpet... loud voice... Come up. Where have we heard this*? In Paul's description of the rapture! Recall his words, "...with a shout... voice of the archangel... trump of God... caught up..." Can this be a metaphor portraying the "moment in the twinkling of an eye" when saints rise to be with Jesus?

Yes. Though I personally do not see this as signifying the actual moment of the rapture in sequence with Tribulation events (as you will see later), anyone can perceive how John's catching away to heaven illustrates how Jesus will call His people up to be with Him. Other places in the Bible show previews of the rapture, the transfiguration of Christ in Matthew 17:1–7 being one example. Yet the rapture did not occur at that moment.

Could the significance of this metaphoric picture of John's ascension into heaven, which happens before the tribulation begins, indicate that the rapture will occur prior to the onset of this grievous time? Although I believe it does, opinions do differ. Some are closed to any catching-away transpiring until after the tribulation, leaving all here to suffer until the end. However, the two most popular views are pretribulation and midtribulation.

Why do most, including myself, lean toward belief in a pretribulation rapture? One reason is the debut of the Antichrist. He must remain obscure until a force against him has departed.

> As for the work this man of rebellion and hell will do when he comes, it is already going on, but he himself will not come until the one who is holding him back steps out of the way. Then this wicked one will appear...
>
> —2 THESSALONIANS 2:7–8, TLB

Who holds him back? The church of Jesus Christ! If Christians are here when the seven-year era begins, they will stand against the Antichrist, shouting his satanic identity and openly revealing his scheming notions to all the world.

Those who insist that the rapture will take place at midtribulation say the Antichrist will be recognized only as his demeanor of peacemaker transforms into a temperament of utter evil halfway into the tribulation. But how can any Christian who knows prophecy fail to spot him on the start?

The Bible alerts us that this tyrant, referred to in 2 Thessalonians 2 as the man of sin, son of perdition, and wicked one, rises to notoriety by signing a seven-year peace pact with Israel. "And he shall confirm the covenant with many" (Dan. 9:27). This appears to be the event that will thrust the seven years into motion. From this the Antichrist's fame spreads with no hint of hindrance as he devises unprecedented global remedies for social problems, economical devastation, and religious conflicts. "Even him, whose coming is after the working of Satan with all power and signs and lying wonders" (2 Thess. 2:9).

The next verse says, "He will completely fool those who are on their way to hell because they have said, 'no' to the Truth" (2 Thess. 2:10, TLB). But those *on their way to heaven* who have said *yes* to the Truth cannot be fooled! Yes, without doubt his works will be restrained if Christians are not raptured beforehand.

Another reason some believe in a midtribulation rapture is that Paul says the saints will rise "at the last trump" (1 Cor. 15:52). They identify this as the last trumpet judgment of Revelation 11:15–19, which appears to take place around the middle of the tribulation. But how can this be? Paul taught this passage around A.D. 52, some forty-three years before John received his Revelation vision. So in Paul's day nobody knew anything about any trumpet judgment.

But they knew about the trumpets of the Jewish wedding!

After the father accepted the bridegroom's contract and the maiden sipped the wine, a *first* trumpet sealed the agreement. After completion of the wedding chamber, when he returned for his bride, an attendant blew the *last* trumpet just outside her door to announce his arrival.

Midtribulation believers reinforce their belief by saying that Paul calls the rapture a mystery (1 Cor. 15:51). They relate this to Revelation 10:7: "But in the days of the voice of the seventh angel, when he shall begin to sound, the mystery of God should be finished, as he hath declared to his servants the prophets." Yet the rapture was never preached by the prophets.

Roman 11:25 tells us not to be ignorant of "this *mystery* ... that blindness in part is happened to Israel, until the fullness of the Gentiles be come in" (emphasis added). *This* mystery *wa*s declared by the prophets of old. They prophesied many times about the blindness of Israel, the rise of a Gentile age, and a final restoration of His chosen to Himself. When will this mystery be "finished?" In the tribulation period!

Still another reason I stand by a pretribulation rapture comes from my extensive search in the Old and New Testaments. No scriptures show believers facing any part of End-Time woe. All my findings indicate otherwise.

First, Jesus Himself says that the tribulation will come as a snare (a trap or noose) upon all who dwell on the earth He adds:

> Watch ye therefore, and pray always, that ye may be accounted worthy to escape all these things that shall come to pass, and to stand before the Son of man.
>
> —LUKE 21:36

Why would He tell us to pray to be "worthy to to escape all these things" and "stand before the Son of of Man" (as in the rapture) if He intends for us to stay to endure even a tiny bit of the turmoil? If we are destined to not "escape all these things," such prayer is futile!

Paul, in his teaching about this, says, "For God hath not appointed us to wrath, but to obtain salvation by our Lord Jesus Christ" (1 Thess. 5:9). In this verse the word *wrat*h translates as punishment in the form of anger, indignation, vengeance.[7] It refers to judgment from God to be inflicted upon the wicked. *Salvatio*n means rescue or safety, deliver, health, save.[8] So God has not appointed us as part of His punishment, but to be rescued and delivered. Does this sound like Christian saints will remain here to endure untold hardship and devastation?

Reading the entire Book of Revelation mounts more support for pretribulation rapture. Its first three chapters deal exclusively with the church, using the word *church* or *churches* nineteen times, yet the word appears no more until verse 16 of the last chapter.

From the immediate onset of the seven years God's attitude toward Earth and its inhabitants switches from mercy and compassion to fury. Divine security is mentioned for only three groups—144,000 Jewish evangelists sealed by God, two supernatural witnesses who arrive from the portals of heaven, and a remnant of Israel who flees into the desert to a safe haven prepared by God. If Christ's beloved church is not raptured, where, oh, where, is it?

First John 4:8 says, "God is love." Would any loving father turn his back on his children, purposely leaving them in harm's way with no instruction to fend against a vengeance that traps every living soul?

> For as a snare shall it come on all them that dwell on the face of the whole earth.
>
> —LUKE 21:35

Why would any father want his children to endure horrors that in Jesus' own words will be such as was not since the beginning of the world to this time, no, nor ever shall be" (Matt. 24:21)?

Jesus promises:

> Because you have kept My command to persevere, I also will keep you from the hour of trial which shall come upon the whole world, to test those who dwell on the earth.
>
> —REVELATION 3:10, NKJV

Notice He says "keep you from," not "keep you in the midst." God has always made a way of escape for His own. He kept Noah and his family from every raindrop and escorted the family of Lot away from harm before the judgments of the wicked struck.

This is not to say that Christians will never suffer. Jesus Himself declared that in this world we will have tribulation (John 16:33). Throughout history Christians have suffered persecutions. A *Reader's Digest* article titled "The Global War on Christians" states, "Never before have so many Christians been persecuted for their beliefs. An estimated 200 million to 250 million Christians are at risk in countries where such incidents occur."[9]

Many Christians have had to stand against opposition to their faith, but they have not had to endure through God's wrath on the wicked. Furthermore, I cannot believe that the Bridegroom will leave His bride to be raped by the Antichrist during the global ravages of the Great Tribulation. Most prophecy students agree.

ASSUMING THEN THAT the rapture occurs before the start of the Tribulation, does this mean the seven-year judgment on Earth immediately follows? Yes, I believe it does. Let's take another peek into the marriage customs of the ancient Jew.

Oh, behold the merriment! The bridegroom is returning for his bride. With lamps ablaze an entire wedding party of friends accompanies him. There is music, singing, laughing, and dancing! Oh, such fun!

An instant before the bridegroom's arrival at the door of his betrothed, a member of the wedding party runs ahead and shouts with jubilee. Another blows the trumpet.

With eagerness the waiting bride leaps to attention. Her wedding garments, so long spread out in splendor, now adorn her youthful body. She veils her face and grabs her well-trimmed lamp. Friends and sisters who are waiting to serve as bridesmaids also have their lanterns filled with oil, ready for departure on the spot.

Oh, what a parallel to the rapture! Arrayed in sparkling jewels and graced in a flowing white robe designed with exquisite embroidery, the bride beams with delight as she is whisked away by her beloved. Soon arriving at the house of the bridegroom's father, nothing is too extravagant. As host the father clothes guests in festive garments and sets crowns on many heads. What a celebration that lasts for seven days.

Seven days? Is this a mere coincidence, or does it symbolize the seven years of tribulation? Yes, I think it does!

With twinkling eyes the honored pair quickly steal away inside the place the groom has prepared. How wonderful to finally be alone together. What a blessing that this day of their union, so long in coming, has finally arrived.

After the consummation of their union, the bridegroom alerts an attendant who waits just outside the door. Hooray! The guests resume their merrymaking.

Who, in allegory, are the guests? Can they be angels? I believe so. After all, angels will accompany Jesus at the rapture of His bride. These are the very souls they watched over while they were fragile mortal beings. In the presence of angels there is joy over every sinner who repents (Luke 15:10).

One of the many duties of angels is to minister to the heirs of salvation (Heb. 1:14). Such a vital part they've played to see this wedding day!

Inside the nuptial chamber, alone in unity, the wedding couple remain until the seventh day. Then with veil removed, all behold the bride's gleaming face as she emerges at the side of her groom to face the wedding party.

Listen to the cheers. Gaze at the elegant table overflowing with sumptuous fruits, meats, and vegetables—arrayed in fine dishes and complemented with the most exquisite wine. The wedding banquet commences! What a spectacular climax to this week of grandeur.

And what is symbolized by the wedding banquet? It's an event scheduled in heaven at the close of the Great Tribulation on Earth. In our tour of heaven we'll soon behold this celebration—the Wedding Supper of the Lamb!

After the seven-day Jewish ceremony, the bridegroom stays at home for an entire year, resuming no work or activities that require him to leave his beloved new wife. Striving to keep her cheerful, he demonstrates true love and devotion as her husband.

Her life is committed to serving and following him. Always she will be a member of his family clan. In every way she works to be an asset to him, knowing that "a virtuous woman is a crown to her husband" (Prov. 12:4).

One year of working together, growing in dedication to the marriage. Could one year signify the one-thousand-year reign of peace on Earth, that time immediately following the Great Tribulation when the saints serve as priests and kings with Jesus? Yes, I believe it must!

Soon the young couple is eager to establish a residence of their own. So hand-in-hand and heart-in-heart they go to dwell together in a permanent home.

The New Jerusalem will be a glorious place of dwelling for the saints and their Bridegroom after their thousand-year reign on Earth with Him. During our visit in heaven we'll also view its wonders.

Oh, when can we get started? Right now! Keep your eyes on John while up, up, up we fly behind him like shooting stars across the sky.

AMAZED BEYOND OUR wildest dreams we zip through the vastness of our universe into the cosmic heavens. All at once a spectacular planet ablaze in lights appears in our path, and we feel ourselves being pulled into its world of splendor. Overcome by a sense of holiness, as soon as our feet touch down we kneel. Like Moses in God's presence at the burning bush, we remove our shoes, for only in total humility and submission do we dare to stand on heaven's holy ground.

Welcome to our Father's home! Jubilant events greet us. In our raptured bliss we frolic after John until a sudden radiance beyond description sweeps us into the majesty of Revelation 4 and 5.

"What a gorgeous throne!" John cries, "Oh, behold the One who sits upon it! How He shines in beauty! Sparkling like diamonds! Shimmering like rubies! Such a lovely glow encircling Him. A gorgeous emerald rainbow!"

We see a rainbow, just as Ezekiel witnessed a rainbow around the throne so many years before. So wonderfully eternal and unchanging is our God!

Beside the King of glory we glimpse twenty-four elders occupying their own personal thrones. Arrayed in snowy white garments and crowns of gold, they gleam as jewels in the brightness streaming from the throne above all thrones.

Oh, the magnificence of the moment! Like colossal torches seven blazing lampstands illuminate the view while electrifying brilliance flashes all around, rumbling like thunder throughout the kingdom. Even so, nothing can drown out the myriads of angelic voices ringing in praise of the One who sits upon the seat of power.

Captivated in the splendor we gaze upon the breathtaking luster of a crystal sea before His scepter. On and on into the vast domain it sparkles like glazed diamonds far beyond our realm of human sight and far beyond our human words for beauty. Its radiance magnifies the scene.

Our hearts stand still at the glory of the awesomeness mirrored by the sea. The Almighty's reflection, dazzled by billions of diamonds and crimson rubies in the midst of flames and lightning, takes our breath away. At His side gleams His court of twenty-four in their robes of radiant white and glimmering crowns. From the rainbow soft hews of green shimmer across the crystal waters to form a halo reaching far above the wondrous image of His countenance.

With so much to drink in, only now do we notice four living creatures flying above the throne. What magnificent beings! How could we have missed them? They appear so similar to the cherubim also in Ezekiel's vision. Full of eyes in front and back, each with six wings, they circle the air and never rest from praising God. Theirs are the wondrous voices we hear: "Holy, holy, holy, Lord God Almighty, which was, and is, and is to come!"

In utter happiness and perfect pitch they sing, never stopping: "Glory and honor and thanks to the Almighty One upon the throne who lives forever and ever."

As we watch, the elders step from their thrones and bow before the Him. Beaming with devotion they lift their priceless crowns and lay them at His feet. Their voices also swell in song: "You are worthy, O Lord, to receive glory, honor and power for You created all things. And for Your pleasure they are and were created!"

All of a sudden we realize something is amiss. Do we detect someone crying nearby? Why, who could possibly be unhappy during this fabulous occasion? Turning our eyes to John we see him weeping. Oh no, what can be wrong?

One of the elders calls, "Don't be sad! Behold, the Lion of Judah, the Root of David! He has conquered!"

We gasp. In the middle of the throne surrounded by the living creatures and the elders stands a Lamb who looks as if He had been slain. He is a precious Lamb bearing the scars of sacrifice, a glorious Lamb of princely elegance and noble virtue, an almighty Lamb endowed with seven horns and seven eyes.

Oh, precious Lamb of God—the One who shed His blood for us, the One who bore the cross to become mankind's Redeemer, the One who triumphed over evil, the One who forever reigns in power, positioned at the right hand of the Father. We stand in awe, overwhelmed by His eternal beauty as the elder announces, "He alone is worthy to break the seals of future judgment coming upon the earth!"

Gladness floods John's face as he hears this. We relax knowing all is well. Even though the greatest tribulation known to man will soon assault the Earth, jubilation permeates heaven. Trusting God's justice for the inhabitants who are left to face His wrath, we rest in the perfection of our Father's home.

Rapturous music saturates the kingdom with excellence as the magnificent living beings and the elders strum harps before the Lamb. Bowing, they present Him with incense burning in bowls of gold. Smoke arises as if to create a veil of admiration all around the throne.

Ah! We inhale in total ecstasy as luxurious aroma escapes. It is so rich and sweet, with such exquisite essence, purer than any scent we've ever dreamed of breathing. This sweet-smelling ceremony appears to be so pleasing to the Lamb that a stirring inside our spirits causes us to question, "Why does this delight our Lord so much?"

These are prayers of the saints. Filled with praise, they release a fragrance so delightful that it rises all the way into the realm of heaven. What are their prayers?

Just as though they heard our thoughts, the living beings and elders break out in concert with a new song, vibrating with words extolling the Lamb for His redemption. Since only the redeemed can claim such honor, they must be repeating the words of their praises: "You are worthy to take the book and open its seals, because You are the One who was slain. With Your blood You redeemed mankind to God, bringing people of every race, language, and of all nations as gifts for God. You have made us to be kings and priests united to serve, to reign upon the earth!"

Our eyes open to trillions of angelic choirs encircling the throne as with extra gusto they unite in worship: "Worthy is the Lamb who was slain to receive power, riches, strength, honor, glory, and blessing!"

As we consider this moment, we ask, "Where are the saints?" John shows us no picture of them. Have they reached the realm of glory? Not quite yet, for as John relates more of their praises, he says in present tense, "And every creature which *is* in heaven, and on the earth, and under the earth, and such as *are* in the sea, and all that *are* in them, heard I saying, 'Blessing, and honor, and glory and power, be unto Him that sits on the throne, and unto the Lamb forever and ever.'"

Whether they are living on Earth or abiding in paradise, the saints offer praise to God. Grateful for redemption by the blood, they know that as the seals are broken, the Bridegroom will appear to catch them up from every location.

Upon hearing John's words to us, the four beasts shout, "Amen!" The twenty-four elders fall down in worship as the seals of the book are about to be opened. Will we see what they are? Not on this visit. We must wait until we view the tribulation judgment in the final stage of our journey. As we stand at the end of the ages, we will hear those who remain on Earth after the rapture plead for the mountains and rocks to fall on them to hide them from the wrath of the Lamb. Knowing that the tribulaton begins at this point, they will mourn, "For the great day of his wrath is come; and who shall be able to stand?" (Rev. 6:17).

John turns to go. Although we're absorbed in wonderment, the time has come for us to depart this scene. As we leave, we hear the four creatures shout, "Amen." We glance back to catch a glimpse of the twenty-four elders falling down before the throne, still worshiping the Lamb.

WHAT GLORY WE'VE encountered. In awe we now gasp at its magnificence. Can we ever know the meaning of it all? Probably not in this life. Yet come, let's probe to understand a portion of the marvels we have beheld.

We have stood trembling before our Savior, the Lion of the tribe of Judah, the Root of David and yes, the precious Lamb slain for our redemption. *The Bible Reader's Companion* explains it all so well:

> The jolt implied in looking for a Lion and seeing a bloody Lamb is intended. Both "Lion of Judah" and "Root of David" are titles of the conquering Messiah. The vision reminds us that Jesus conquered by giving His life for us. The bloodstained Lamb, still bearing the visible marks of His execution, is about to be revealed as the executor of God's final judgment![10]

Through the eyes of John we have witnessed this Conqueror endowed with seven horns and seven eyes. In God's Word, a horn represents power. Eyes portray the all-seeing and all-knowing attributes of God. Displaying omnipotence (infinite power), omniscience (limitless knowledge), and omnipresence (ability to be all places at once), our sacrificial Lamb, though still bearing scars of the cross, now reigns triumphant.

All these invincible characteristics make up "the seven Spirits of God sent forth into all the earth" (Rev. 5:6), which are also portrayed by the seven blazing lampstands at the throne. A preview of heaven, the earthly Jewish tabernacle kept a seven-branched lampstand continuously burning just outside the holy of holies, the sanctuary of God's dwelling.

What are the "seven Spirits" of God? Some declare they refer to angels, yet most speculate that they are the sevenfold virtues of His Spirit like those told by Isaiah:

> The Spirit of the LORD shall rest upon Him, the Spirit of wisdom and understanding, the Spirit of counsel and might, the Spirit of knowledge and of the fear of the LORD.
>
> —ISAIAH 11:2, NKJV

The number *seven*, which represents perfect completion throughout the Bible, emerges time and time again in Revelation. In addition to seven horns, seven eyes, seven Spirits, and seven lamps, we find seven stars in His right hand, seven angels, seven churches, seven seal judgments, seven bowl judgments, seven trumpet judgments, seven archangels with seven trumpets, seven thunders, and seven new things.

What about the crystal sea before the throne? Since the Bible sometimes uses the word *sea* to denote a great assembly of people, some commentators believe this "sea" may indicate multimillions of saints who will gather after the rapture. For several reasons (some I have already expressed and some I will not reveal until our final chapter), I personally believe the rapture has not yet happened at this point in John's vision. Yet this idea of the crystal sea presents a beautiful allegory—as I've heard it said crystal is the only substance that can never hide a flaw, and Christ will come for:

> ...a glorious church, not having spot, or wrinkle, or any such thing; but that it should be holy and without blemish.
>
> —EPHESIANS 5:27

Who are the living creatures? Evidently they are cherubim like those in Ezekiel's vision. What strength they must possess. God assigned them, as special angelic beings, to prevent entrance into Eden after man sinned (Gen. 3:24). A song of David says God Himself "rode upon a cherub [singular for cherubim], and did fly" (2 Sam. 22:11).

Other accounts associate these angels with God's throne. Not only did replicas of cherubim hover over the mercy seat above the ark of the covenant and grace the veil blocking access into the holy of holies, but they also decorated the temple walls. How superbly this typifies their most sacred duty as guardians of our Lord's heavenly temple and His divine presence.

Who are the twenty-four elders? As we ponder the similarities between them and the saints of God, excitement should ripple through our hearts. Might they typify believers?

They wore crowns. Will saints wear crowns? Yes. Scripture reveals five types of crowns that are prepared for those who love Him and prove faithful. They are crowns of joy, righteousness, life, glory, and incorruptibility.

They had their own thrones. Will saints have thrones? At the Last Supper Jesus told His disciples:

> And I appoint unto you a kingdom, as my Father hath appointed unto me; that ye may eat and drink at my table in my kingdom, and sit on thrones...
>
> —LUKE 22:29–30

Yet will all who are redeemed have a throne? Hear the promise of our Savior:

> To him that overcometh will I grant to sit with me in my throne, even as I also overcame, and am set down with my Father in his throne.
>
> —REVELATION 3:21

The elders denote believers in other ways. How intriguing that their number, twenty-four, equals the twelve apostles and twelve tribes of Israel. This is a picture of the fact that salvation is available for all and reveals that Old Testament and New Testament saints make up the church triumphant in its entirety. Acts 7:38 says that Moses "was in the church in the wilderness with the angel which spake to him in the mount Sina..."

Might these elders also be showing us a preview of the royal priesthood that awaits the redeemed? In the Jewish temple twenty-four orders of priests ministered. As a symbol of ascending prayers priests burned incense in a golden vessel. We observed the twenty-four elders performing this priestly duty when they presented to the Lamb their golden bowls of incense, "which are the prayer of saints" (Rev. 5:8).

Can you imagine such honor as presiding as a priest with Jesus? How would you like to receive the reward of being appointed a king to rule and reign by His side?

> Unto him that loved us, and washed us from our sins in His own blood, and hath made us kings and priests unto God and his Father; to him be glory and dominion for ever and ever. Amen.
> —REVELATION 1:5–6

Oh, the marvels of His heavenly plan. What rewards await us. With our human brain too inept to grasp the magnitude of His truly inconceivable wonders, it is only by faith that we can dream of the splendor He has revealed today. But someday all the redeemed will understand completely. Someday we shall see Him face-to-face and share in the fullness of His majesty.

NOW JOHN CALLS us to come along with him. Stepping into Revelation 7:4–17, the feeling of God's love and compassion overwhelms us. Even during the ravages that are upon the earth our Father offers salvation for those who have been left behind to face the wrath that has come.

We learn that 144,000 direct descendants of the twelve tribes of Israel have been marked by God, called out to evangelize Jews. They are the natural seed of Abraham, converted, believing in Jesus as the Messiah. They are an anointed force endowed with power from the Holy Spirit preaching Jesus as the Son of God, turned on at high speed to win souls for heaven.

While we digest this good news our attention shifts to new activity before the throne. Look, there's an enormous congregation of human beings!

"Far too many for anyone to count," John exclaims, "gathered before the Lamb at His throne! All races and creeds. All languages and nations!"

Astounded, we look out as far as possible, straining to take in this huge group assembled in the presence of the Lamb. In unison everyone sways together waving palm branches to glorify Him with honor and thanksgiving. It's such a lovely sight.

Envision it if you can. Row upon row, line upon line, mile after mile, stretching on and on into the distance, joyous people are arrayed in snow-white linen with swirling greenery above their heads. They are shouting to the Lamb, "Salvation to our God who sits upon the throne and to the Lamb!"

Excitement soars throughout the kingdom. All the many millions of angels gather around His throne. Consumed in worship, the twenty-four elders bow before Him.

Turning to John, an elder asks, "Do you understand who this multitude in white are, and where they come from?"

"No, I have no idea. But you must know. Please, sir, explain to me who they are!"

"These are people who have come out of great tribulation, who washed their robes white in the blood of the Lamb. They stand before His throne serving Him day and night in His temple, knowing He will always dwell among them. They will never be hungry or thirsty again. The sun will scorch their skin no more. Nothing will ever burn them. The Lamb in the center of the throne will feed them and lead them to living fountains of water, and God will wipe every tear from their eyes."

Hallelujah! These raptured saints all suffered tribulations while they were mortals. As the scriptures say:

> In the world ye shall have tribulation: but be of good cheer; I have overcome the world.
>
> —JOHN 16:33

> We must through much tribulation enter into the kingdom of God.
>
> —ACTS 14:22

> Blessed be God, even the Father of our Lord Jesus Christ, the Father of mercies, and the God of all comfort; who comforteth us in all our tribulation.... For as the sufferings of Christ abound in us...
>
> —2 CORINTHIANS 1:3–5

> Wherefore I desire that ye faint not at my tribulations for you, which is your glory.
>
> —EPHESIANS 3:13

We see innumerable risen souls with spirits ablaze basking before the throne in the presence of the Lamb. They are celebrating their redemption in perfect glorified bodies, magnificent bodies made without flaw. New and incorruptible, their bodies are everlasting. They will never decay, never age, never die. Heavenly models of supernatural capabilities, they are as swift and mighty as angels. They are no longer composed of perishable flesh and bone and no longer depend on blood to live. Instead, they have an anatomy designed in sinless perfection to last forever.

> So also is the resurrection of the dead. The body is sown in corruption,
> it is raised in incorruption. It is sown in dishonor, it is raised in glory.
> It is sown in weakness, it is raised in power. It is sown a natural body,
> it is raised a spiritual body.
>
> —1 CORINTHIANS 15:42–44, NKJV

The natural vessel of man has been transformed into a spiritual powerhouse. Fragile human traits are now eternally replaced with His wholeness. Gathered into the brightness of His glory, the saints stand before the throne in flawless form. They will remain throughout eternity with the One who paid the price for their salvation. No longer do they wait to be called from an earthly habitat into the heavens. Oh, the wonders of the rapture!

> God has told us His secret reason for sending Christ, a plan He decided
> on in mercy long ago; and this was His purpose: that when the time is
> ripe He will gather us all together from wherever we are—in heaven or
> on earth—to be with him in Christ, forever.
>
> —EPHESIANS 1:9–10, TLB

As we gaze across the multitudes we view only a huge assembly in God's presence, a mass of righteous people gathered at the throne. Yes, we see a crowd. But the Lamb discerns each heart separately, distinguishing every thought and personality, recognizing every face, knowing every name. Sinful flaws have been washed away by His spotless blood, and with eyes of grace He sees righteousness shine forth from the depth of every single soul. He surveys each individual with His eternal love and outstretched arms.

Praises still ring as every tongue in heaven proclaims, "Blessing and honor! Glory and power unto Him who sits on the throne and unto the Lamb forever and ever!"

Can you even imagine yourself being part of such a great assembly? Can you really picture such a multitude standing before the throne?

In reality, my mind finds it difficult to fathom such an immense number assembled in one accord in one place. Yet, my spirit churns in anticipation of such a glorious gathering where there will be no hate or murder, no gossip or lying, no cheating or adultery, no rioting or drunkenness. Such thoughts jog my memory.

Several years ago at a major league baseball game in a crowded stadium of *only* 40,000 I felt swallowed up by the magnitude and chaos. It most certainly was *not* a scene of one accord.

Stuffed among the fans I cringed as many, intoxicated from beer sold by vendors, cursed and screamed out crude insults—instead of disgust I found myself overcome with compassion for their souls. With anguished heart I wondered, *If the rapture occurs at this instant, how many will be left behind?*

Oh, I mourned, *how God must grieve because society gets so wrapped up in useless worldly pleasures with no thought for eternity.* Feeling so tiny, completely insufficient, I agonized for those at the game that day. How blessed we are to have a God who always knows our thoughts. Amid the clamor I sensed His presence as I bowed my head and prayed for the salvation of those around me.

The crowd's vile accusations switched to wild delirium as people scrambled, then fought with each other, for a baseball that had been hit into the stands. What idols athletes have become.

I scanned the field. Like a neon sign the life of every major leaguer flashed the word *success* to the crowd. But with my mind focused on eternity—success glowed with brighter, much more enduring color.

My spirit whispered to my heart, *In all of time nothing matters except our accomplishments for God. The only things that can accompany us to heaven are souls we've won to Him. This measures true success. All worldly gain perishes like the maple leaf when summer ends. Truly life passes like a vapor appearing for such a little while then vanishing away, as James wrote in James 4:14. But eternity never ends. It goes on and on forever.*

Inside I wept. I knew my prayer was not enough. *Show me how to reach the multitudes,* I cried.

And in my heart He breathed, *Yes, I will.*

What a loving, caring One we serve!

Returning to the scene with John, my heart dances with gratitude. How wonderful that such a multitude has been delivered from Earth's tribulation—many of them martyrs for their faith—to rise redeemed in His presence.

With overflowing tenderness let your heart absorb the picture as they rejoice face-to-face with a God of mercy. They worship a loving Lamb with outstretched arms, an abundant God who provides, a caring God who wipes away all tears forever.

Bathed in God's everlasting goodness, how hard it is for us to give up this precious moment and leave with John. But as we see him walk away, we know we can't linger. As we scurry along to catch up, he leads us into Revelation 19:6–9.

WHAT GLORIOUS MUSIC pierces the very depths of our souls! Where does it come from? Is it possible another glorious occasion lies just ahead?

Yes! We have come upon the Marriage Supper of the Lamb!

"Hallelujah! Salvation! Glory! Honor and power to the Lord our God!" the exaltations ring.

Good news! The seven-year reign of terror on Earth is drawing to an end. Sweet words of victory circulate through heaven: "True and righteous are the judgments of He who has judged the corruption of the earth and avenged the blood of His servants!"

Again and again voices rich and strong excel in harmony. Before the throne the elders and living beings remain prostrate in worship.

"Amen! Hallelujah! Praise the Lord!" It's a melody so sweet, unknown to mortal ears.

Like waves of a hundred oceans sweeping upon the seashore, as awesome as the voice of mighty thunder, thousands upon thousands sing out, "Hallelujah! For the Lord God omnipotent reigns!"

What gaiety! What cheer! What fellowship! The celebration of love is far too great for words. We squeeze in close to John, captivated by its festivities, elated in the merriment, absorbed in absolute bliss.

"The bride is ready and prepared, adorned in fine linen, pure and white. Fine linen for the righteousness of the saints."

The glorious bride sweeps before our eyes. Unveiled for all the hosts of heaven to behold, she is adorned in purest white and radiant in righteousness. Just as the virtuous woman is "a crown to her husband," the bride of Christ shall forever be His crown.

> You shall also be a crown of glory in the hand of the Lord, and a royal diadem in the hand of your God. . . . And as the bridegroom rejoices over the bride, so shall your God rejoice over you.
>
> —Isaiah 62:3, 5, NKJV

Behold the gleaming Bridegroom with His bride arrayed in wedding splendor! Aglow in His *Shekinah* glory, the bride draws near to the bosom of His comfort and into His lap of peace, drinking with affection from His everlasting cup of holiness, wisdom, love, and beauty.

Great cheers ring out from the angels—the guests. All heaven rejoices.

With throbbing hearts we gaze upon His treasured bride. Bought with His priceless sacrifice, she is redeemed, forever pledged to the Lamb in perfect love. Reaffirming now to follow Him in His shining path of endless sovereignty and majesty, she partakes of His everlasting greatness and goodness. Promising to bestow all adoration to Him as her devoted Husband, she walks from this day forward in His blessings. She is in unity with Him—hand in hand and heart in heart—throughout eternity. They are one forevermore.

We rejoice to learn of the plans the Bridegroom has in store. Very soon His redeemed, His cherished Bride, will leave the Father's house to serve on Earth with Him, the reigning Lamb, for a thousand years. After a final war yields victory over wickedness, a millennium of peace and happiness awaits to demonstrate the perfect love and dedication of their eternal marriage.

With longing souls we desire to visualize all these upcoming events right now, but this must happen later in the final chapters of our travels. At this point we cannot deviate from this tour and its awaiting splendor.

"Come," John is urging, "there's so much more to see of heaven."

Casting one last peek, we tear ourselves away from the wedding celebration. Over our shoulder we catch an angel's voice beaming to John, "Write these words: 'Blessed are all who are called unto the marriage supper of the Lamb!'"

Oh, that we should be so blessed!

Deep longing swells inside the core of our being. Our spirits cry, "O Lamb of God, keep us ever true so on Your wedding day we'll stand redeemed before You as part of Your righteous bride—so blessed eternally in purity, happiness, excellence, and majesty at Your side—forever cleansed in the blood of the Lamb."

Our prayer continues until we emerge with John into the episodes of Revelation 21 and 22. Look, oh look, at the fabulous sight manifesting before us. With God wonders never cease!

TOWERING INTO UNIMAGINABLE heights, a gleaming mountain materializes before us. In an instant, as though whisked on angel's wings, we ascend with John into its peaks. With stirring wonder we discover a perfect view set aside just for us. We hurriedly settle in our places.

What awaits us now? Why are we here? Anticipation booms like a drum inside our chests as we bide our time.

All of a sudden an angel appears, proclaiming, "Behold the bride, the Lamb's wife!"

Like a flash a lustrous city unfolds before us. Now we know. The thousand-year millennial reign on Earth has ended. Zipping beyond its time we've come to glimpse the eternal residence of the redeemed—the New Jerusalem!

Descending from heaven, it is radiant like a bride in her wedding gown. Overflowing in God's glory her brightness shines like a most exquisite diamond, dazzling, glittering, sparkling with luster beyond words.

"Having the glory of God! Her light is like a jasper stone, clear as crystal!" John utters in amazement.

Even in this moment of breathtaking beauty we exchange puzzled glances over the angel's description of the city. He called it the bride, the Lamb's wife.

What? This is a city, the New Jerusalem! How can it be the Lamb's wife? What can the angel mean?

In our last scene we attended the wedding supper of the Lamb with all of His redeemed. The actual span of time between then and this announcement of the New Jerusalem has been a thousand years.

At the wedding we heard a mighty voice heralding the occasion. Now we need to examine all that was spoken:

> Let us be glad and rejoice, and give honour to him: for the marriage of the Lamb is come, and his wife hath made herself ready. And to her was granted that she should be arrayed in fine linen, clean and white: for the fine linen is the righteousness of saints.
> —REVELATION 19:7–8

This picture of the bride certainly doesn't resemble the Holy City!

We also recall the allegory of the Jewish wedding. And in previous texts we heard Jesus portray Himself as our Bridegroom, not the Bridegroom of a city. Surely His righteous are His bride.

However, can the bride of the Lamb also be a city, the New Jerusalem? If so, how can Jesus, or any bridegroom, wed an inanimate object? Wouldn't this be impossible?

Just who is the actual bride of Christ? To seek out an explanation we must temporarily detach ourselves from the wonders of the city.

Not only the parables of Jesus Himself, but also other scriptures affirm Christ as the Bridegroom of His people. Probably the most direct analogy lies in Ephesians 5. Christ, characterized as the Head of the church, simulates a beautiful illustration of His role as Husband: "The husband is head of the wife, as also Christ is head of the church" (v. 23, NKJV). The husband, as the "head" of the wife, is likened to Christ, the "Head" of the church and therefore the Husband of its members.

As we evaluate other semblances in this text, the wife is portrayed as parallel to the church and the husband as parallel to Christ: "Husbands, love your wives, just as Christ also loved the church and gave Himself for her" (v. 25, NKJV). How perfectly this symbolizes the love a husband gives to his wife as the same love Christ gave to His church (His saints). This further identifies the church as His spiritual wife.

In wedding vows a man pledges his life for his bride: "In sickness and in health, for better or worse, from this day forward until in death we do part." Likewise, Christ pledged His life for His church.

But if the church is His body, how can it also be His wife? Just as the Head and the body are one, in marriage a bridegroom and his bride are also one. Grasping the underlying parable in these words clarifies this answer:

> So husbands ought to love their own wives as their own bodies; he who loves his wife loves himself. For no one ever hated his own flesh, but nourishes and cherishes it, just as the Lord does the church. For we are members of His body, of His flesh and of His bones. "For this reason a man shall leave his father and mother and be joined to his wife, and the two shall become one flesh." This is a great mystery, but I speak concerning Christ and the church.
>
> —EPHESIANS 5:28–32, NKJV

Do you see the pattern? Just as the wife becomes one flesh with her husband, a member of his body—so the church becomes the same with Christ. Although the text gives guidelines for marriage, the "mystery" is that it also portrays the eternal Bridegroom and His bride.

Even with so much scripture verifying Christ as Bridegroom of the church, some still hold a view that says, "Christ is our brother. Siblings don't wed!"

Again we delve into prototypes displayed in God's Word. By matching similarities we see that Abraham parallels Christ in many ways.

Abraham left his homeland to further God's plan of redemption. Jesus left Heaven to finish His redemptive plan. Abraham was accounted righteous by his faith. Jesus was accounted righteous by His perfection. Through the bloodline of Abraham multitudes were born. Through the blood of Jesus multitudes are born again.

Abraham met the ultimate requirement of God, willing to give his son in sacrifice. Jesus met the ultimate requirement of the Father and gave His own life in sacrifice. Abraham is called the faithful friend of God. Jesus is the faithful Son of God.

Without question these parallels create a beautiful composite picture, but the metaphor that presents Abraham as a symbol of the heavenly Bridegroom is often unnoticed. Abraham married his sibling! Although Abraham and Sarah were one in holy matrimony as husband and wife, Sarah was also Abraham's sister. They had different mothers but the same father.

How gloriously this foreshadows the marriage of Christ to the redeemed. Our Brother shares the same heavenly Father but has a different earthly mother. When we recognize this about the bride of Christ, the entire Song of Solomon becomes an beautiful allegory depicting the Bridegroom and His bride.

> Thou hast ravished my heart, my sister, my spouse.... How fair is thy love, my sister, my spouse!... A garden inclosed is my sister, my spouse; a spring shut up, a fountain sealed.
> —Song of Solomon 4:9–10, 12

Think about a garden. It consists of chosen plants, not just one or two, but many gathered in one setting. Not there by happenstance, the garden grows in a selected plot. The gardener cultivates and maintains each and every seedling, enriching it with proper nutrients for growth, pulling the weeds that would choke it, faithfully watering it. He makes it his pride and joy, an enclosed site capturing his devotion as he awaits the day of harvest. What a model of the bride of Christ!

Solomon's description of his sister as his spouse—"a spring shut up," "a fountain sealed," and "a fountain of gardens, a well of living waters" (v. 15)—gives obvious symbolism. Jesus says:

> Whoever drinks of the water that I shall give him will never thirst. But the water that I shall give him will become in him a fountain of water springing up into everlasting life.
> —John 4:14, NKJV

He gave Himself for the church:

> That he might sanctify and cleanse it with the washing of water by the word, that he might present it to himself a glorious church, not having spot, or wrinkle.
> —Ephesians 5:26–27

"Thou art fair, my love, there is no spot in thee," says Song of Solomon 4:7. In his teaching on the coming of the Lord Peter says:

> Wherefore, beloved, seeing that ye look for such things, be diligent that
> ye may be found of him in peace, without spot, and blameless.
>
> —2 Peter 3:14

Paul gives a parallel to "a fountain sealed" when he says that believers are sealed by the Holy Spirit until the day of redemption (Eph. 4:30). When is that day? It is the day we meet Him in the air!

Yes, the bride of Christ is "a spring shut up, a fountain sealed" until the Bridegroom returns to take us "without spot" to the house He has prepared for us.

> He brought me to the banqueting house, and his banner over me
> was love.
>
> —Song of Solomon 2:4

And so we behold the glorious bride of Christ!

Who is included in the "church" that is His bride? I believe Scripture shows that the church represents all believers since the beginning of time. All, both male and female, every race and creed, those who lived by the Old Covenant before the days of Jesus and those living by the new since His first coming. Why are all included? Every single saint who ever walked on Earth had to be redeemed by His sacrifice of spotless blood. There is, nor never has been, any other way.

Earlier we visited the domain of Satan and witnessed how after Jesus' victory of the cross He freed the righteous who had been held captive. These died under the Old Covenant, yet it was Christ who broke their bonds. Recall a verse we mentioned earlier:

> This is he [Moses], that was in the church in the wilderness with the
> angel which spake to him in the mount Sina...
>
> —Acts 7:38

What a glorious bride, the "church" of all saints throughout the ages! Blameless, in peace, redeemed in entirety, with no spot or wrinkle, the church is joined in union with the Lamb for all eternity.

In this verse the Old Testament reveals the chosen of Israel as the wife of the Redeemer:

> For thy Maker is thine husband; the Lord of hosts is his name; and
> thy Redeemer the Holy One of Israel; The God of the whole earth shall
> he be called.
>
> —Isaiah 54:5

Yes! This portrays Christ!

Jesus is the Maker. "All things were made by him; and without him was not anything made" (John 1:3).

Jesus is the LORD of hosts. The Hebrew word for LORD is *Yahwe*h (Jehovah). The name *Jesus* means "Yahweh is salvation." The word *hosts* can include all creation—stars, angels, men. Jesus, in the direct human bloodline of Israel (Jacob), truly fits the profile of the Holy One of Israel.

Jesus is God of the whole earth. He has earned this title. As the Lamb of God He alone is its Redeemer who was promised as Savior to all at the gates of Eden.

Indeed this "great mystery" concerning Christ and His church challenges our finite thinking. But some great day we will stand face-to-face in perfect union with the Lamb of God. Only then can we completely comprehend the devotion of such spiritual depth and glorious bond. The mystery will be completely solved, and we will be one with Him forevermore.

STILL WHAT ABOUT the city of New Jerusalem? Again we ask, if the city isn't the bride, why does the angel declare as he presents the city to John, "I will show thee the bride, the Lamb's wife"? (Rev. 21:9).

Let's think back to the moment when the angel referred to the city as the bride and the Lamb's wife. Remember John's immediate response, "Having the glory of God: and her light was like unto a stone most precious, even like a jasper stone, clear as crystal" (v. 11)?

Here lies the missing piece of the puzzle—found as we unearth the definition of *phoste*r, the Greek word this verse uses for *ligh*t. It is defined as something or someone who gives forth light. In the entire New Testament the only other scripture that uses this identical word for *light* is Philippians 2:15, referring to Christians who shine as lights to the world.

Let's draw from the expertise of William Barclay, who explains the light of the New Jerusalem this way:

> There is a certain difficulty of translation here. The word used for light is *phoster*. The normal Greek word for light is *phos*, and *phoster* is normally the word used for the lights of heaven, the sun, the moon and the stars, for instance in the Creation story (Genesis 1:14).
>
> Does this, then, mean that the body which illumined the city was like a precious stone? Or does it mean that the radiance which played over all the city was like the glitter of jasper? We think the word must describe the radiance over the city; it is later quite distinctly said that

the city needs no heavenly body like the sun or moon to give it light, because God is its light. What, then, is the symbolism? H. B. Swete would find a hint in Philippians 2:15. There Paul says of the Christians at Philippi: "You shine as lights in the world." The holy city is inhabited by thousands and thousands of the saints of God, and it may well be that it is the light of these saintly lives which gives it this glittering glow.[11]

Yes! The "light of saintly lives" reflects the radiance of God in the New Jerusalem—the bride of the Lamb arrayed in God's *Shekinah* glory!

Immediately after describing the judgment of the wicked at the end of the world Jesus declares, "Then shall the righteous shine forth as the sun in the kingdom of their Father" (Matt. 13:43).

Envision millions of saints in the New Jerusalem gleaming with the awesome light of Almighty God. It is the same *Shekinah* glory that shone from Moses after he stood in the Lord's presence and the same *Shekinah* glory that streamed like the sun from Jesus when He was transfigured in the presence of the Father.

WITH EVERY PUZZLE piece now in place we rush with clear minds to rejoin John, filled to overflowing with eagerness to soak up more of the city's grandeur. We gasp at its immensity as it soars higher and stretches farther than mortal eyes can see.

Fifteen hundred miles high! Science tells us that breathable air surrounding Earth extends only about twenty miles. One hundred miles would place a person in outer space.

The New Jerusalem also spreads fifteen hundred miles square. Will this hold all the bride of the Lamb? Yes, yes, God says, yes! With over two million square miles just on the ground floor, there's ample room for everyone.

Although a few speculate that the city may be shaped like a pyramid, I believe it is a cube. The cube is God's symbol for perfection. In the Jewish temple the holy of holies where He manifested His presence was a cube. Now we behold the *Shekinah* glory of His presence enveloping every inch of New Jerusalem.

A heavenly voice proclaims, "Behold the tabernacle of God is now among mankind. He will live with them and they shall be His people. Yes, God Himself will dwell among them. There will be no more death. No sorrow. No crying. No pain. All these horrors are gone forever."

Such peace floods our souls. Such melody swells in our ears. Such beauty stretches before our eyes as we behold the New Jerusalem—a place of unequaled excellence running over with tranquility and love, goodness and gladness, so superior and so supreme. And precisely in the center of its splendor towers a glorious throne, unparalleled in loveliness and majesty. It is a sovereign throne, high and lifted up, visible from all directions as far as the eye can see, aglow with holiness and righteousness, shining brighter than the sun with unblinding, perfect light. Yes, it is the throne of our Lord and our precious Lamb.

With joyous hearts we tremble in awe and reverence while the redeemed radiate with thanksgiving and praise and worship. They belong forever to the Bridegroom, and nothing can ever harm them.

Look! Every forehead bears a new name, the name of the Lamb of God! What does it mean?

At the moment of salvation we, as believers, received the name of Jesus. All the authority and power of this name became ours the day of our adoption into the royal family of God. Yes, it is our family name.

But now in heaven the redeemed have received their Husband's name. As any bride acquires the husband's name in marriage, the bride of the Lamb now bears the name of her eternal Bridegroom. It is a new and glorious name to be worn with devotion and dignity by His wife throughout eternity.

> He who overcomes, I will make him a pillar in the temple of My God, and he shall go out no more. And I will write on him the name of My God and the name of the city of My God, the New Jerusalem, which comes down out of heaven from My God. And I will write upon him My new name.
>
> —REVELATION 3:12, NKJV

The city glows throughout with faultless Light. There is no more night, not one hint of darkness or shadows of any kind. Never will the slightest flicker of a candle or a lamp be needed, not even a ray of sunshine, for the Lamb Himself is the light. In His unlimited *Shekinah* glory His bride will always live.

Oh, the splendor of New Jerusalem, with its virtuous bliss and ravishing beauty. It is an exquisite cube twinkling like billions of sequins, arrayed in perfect light. Endowed throughout in purest gold, so refined it gleams as clear as glass, even its streets are paved in this golden brilliance.

Like perfectly cut diamonds, magnificent walls tower in gigantic elegance, measuring over two hundred feet across. Their twelve foundations, richly layered in precious gems, dazzle the city's boundaries and glitter with the name of each apostle. Within the walls twelve incredible gates, each fashioned from a single pearl, bear names of the tribes of Israel. An angel graces every entrance with gates swung open wide. They never need to be shut since all evil is abolished and no darkness ever occurs.

Glistening brighter than the finest crystal a majestic river dances from the throne. Its fountains never run dry. With living water they refresh anyone who desires a drink.

Like a rippling mirror the river reflects a forest—a vast and majestic species of trees towering along its banks. The tree of life flourishes in the New Jerusalem. Every branch thrives with savory fruit as each month features a special delicacy, ripened to perfection, begging to be eaten. The soothing leaves, plentiful and available for everyone, bestow perfect health and healing for all nations. No need goes unheeded, no hurt unhealed.

This is absolute utopia, eternal paradise. Here stretch the golden streets and gates of pearl that we hear so much about. But this exclusive city, the ultimate home of all the redeemed, stands reserved until Satan is locked away forever, after every battle has been fought and wickedness exists no more. Then the Father's marvelous and miraculous plan of redemption, conceived before the beginning of time and set in motion at the Garden of Eden, will be complete.

As we depart the realms of heaven with John, we tremble to hear the voice of the Almighty declare in final victory from the throne that all is truly finished:

> And he said unto me, It is done. I am Alpha and Omega, the beginning and the end. I will give unto him that is athirst of the fountain of the water of life freely.
>
> —REVELATION 21:6

So great, so holy, so awesome is our Father, who art in heaven!

Chapter 3

Hallowed Be Thy Name—Yahweh

TWO PEOPLE KILLED! My fairy-tale "happily-ever-after" ideas exploded like gasoline thrown into a raging fire. One awful misjudgment branded a nightmare inside my brain to smolder ever after with the question, Could my mother and I have prevented these deaths?

It was the dawning of the 1960s. I barely knew the word *bad* existed. I had a crisp high school diploma in my possession, and life sang carefree melodies of delight. My small-town upbringing involved church, a close-knit family, crinoline petticoats, drive-in movies, and curb service at a teen burger hangout. Elvis was the rage, television still a novelty.

In my young eyes the world displayed a pleasant arena as all over the globe our country captured the highest of respect. President Eisenhower had recently built esteem by visiting foreign soil in the name of peace and good-will with warm welcomes embracing him at every stop. "The Star Spangled Banner" rang from hearts with zest as patriotism soared across our land. With enthusiasm and expectation we energetically entered outer space as our astronauts raced the Soviets for first place in its exploration.

Despite my summer job in a nearby factory I saw no crucial upsets or disorder. The horror of assassinations and civil unrest that erupted later in the decade would have seemed beyond belief, and the demon of drug culture had yet to raise his ugly head. I'd never even heard of marijuana. How could I have realized that my idealism tottered on the edge of a crumbling cliff and was about to plummet headlong into the flames of death and guilt? If only I'd had the slightest inkling.

When I rounded the corner of our white country house, I'd probably been home from work about an hour. Against a thin waist I hugged a heaping basket of fresh laundry I'd taken off the clothesline as I made my way toward the back door.

A swanky automobile whipped into our driveway. *Who can that be?* Shaking a strand of reddish-blonde hair out of my eyes, I squinted against the sunset's blinding rays to watch a hefty man in a black suit unfold his six-foot stature from the car.

He looks familiar. Where have I seen him? Then it hit me. *That's Mr. Bower.* A prominent banker, his picture had appeared in local newspapers. Though I had never met him personally I knew him also as Mike Bower's father.

He shuffled over to me, thrusting a business card in my face and saying, "We're opening a new branch bank."

I shifted my basket to one side to reach for his card. *Yuk, he smells putrid!* I backed up to keep from gagging.

Because of his important standing in the community, his disheveled appearance surprised me. Wearing a rumpled suit, his hair was tangled and his face was so flushed that beads of perspiration glowed like embers above his loosened tie and stiff unbuttoned collar. As I peered up into his puffy bloodshot eyes, they traveled down every button of my blouse, over the laundry, outlined my Bermuda shorts, bare knees, bobby socks, and saddle oxfords. Then they shifted upward over the same path.

"You're quite a gal," he grinned. "I see why my son likes you."

Inside I cringed. Yet being brought up to respect age and position. I remained polite and asked about his son, now in college, and tolerated his chatter about his new bank. As he talked—with roving eyes—my revulsion grew, prompting a definite urge to end his social call.

"I'll give your card to my mother." Like lightning I shot toward the house and scrambled up steps leading into the kitchen. Balancing my bulging load and squeezing his card, I fumbled with the doorknob.

Oh no! I felt the heat of his repugnant breath on the nape of my neck. *Why is he following me?*

As the door opened he chuckled and slapped me on the rear. I stumbled across the linoleum, sprawling over toppled clothes. My heart raced. *What's wrong with this old man?*

As she spun around from a sink of dishes, my mother's big brown eyes grew huge. Her mouth flew open as she caught sight of me on the floor with Mr. Bower snickering above. I saw question marks spinning in her head.

"Mother, we have company." Rolling my eyes in frustration I retrieved scattered items. "Mr. Bower's here. Mike Bower's father."

"Inviting you to our Grand Opening," he said approaching her and shoving an invitation in her wet hand. In a flash he sneaked a juice glass from the dish rack, slipping it inside his coat.

"Where's your bathroom?" Not waiting for directions he proceeded through the living room and down the hallway until he found it.

"Mother, he hit me on my behind," I whispered.

Her lips tightened, and I sensed her concern. "He's been drinking," she said, drying her hands and removing her apron. She drew a deep sigh and headed for the living room. By a flick of her head she beckoned me to follow.

"Drinking?" I laughed. The only "drunk" people I'd ever seen were hilarious actors on television.

My mother frowned, "It's not funny!" Under her breath she added, "Alcohol can make a person violent. As soon as he comes out we'll insist he leave, but we must try our best not to make him angry."

As he emerged, bumping against the wall, Mother and I exchanged glances. *Did he use the glass for more liquor?*

Before we managed to speak, he plopped down on the sofa. Instantly he regained composure and without batting an eye he started describing—in explicit detail—scanty costumes of waitresses at the "Bunny Club."

"Some say they wear shoes, but who notices their feet?" he cackled while his eyes wandered over every square of my mother's blue-check gingham dress.

I grimaced, waiting for her reaction. To my surprise she seemed to pay no attention, yet I knew better. At that point I realized her seriousness when she said not to upset him.

But why was she worried? He didn't seem dangerous. Obnoxious, yes, but not mean. Because of my lack of knowledge, happy-go-lucky outlook, and the influence of sitcoms, the scene played like a live comedy to me. I saw no reason for concern.

"This is an inconvenient evening for a visit, I'm so pushed for time," my mother said. "Maybe you can come sometime when my husband is here, then you can chat with him."

At those words he dropped his eyes and massaged his forehead. *What is he up to?* Without twitching a muscle I stood waiting in curiosity. My focus shifted to my mother. With her eyes glued on his thinning crown, her head rotated slightly from side to side. And she just waited, too.

Finally he raised a somber face now speckled in patchy red. "I don't need to talk to your husband. This is the real reason I'm here...to ask a favor from her." His comments zeroed in on my mother, but he motioned in my direction. "My son Mike speaks highly of your daughter. Says she's a nice gal. He kinda likes her, you know...looks up to her. Well, to get to the point, Mike's making some birdbrain decisions and I need her to talk to him. Change his mind."

While he continued eyeing my mother, I stepped off to his side and caught her glance. *How silly drunk people think!* With wrinkled nose I shook my head. *Surely she senses my feelings.*

Why would this man want me, of all people, to talk to his son? I chuckled to myself at such a notion. Although Mike and I once ran in the same circles, we were never more than casual friends, living in different towns, attending separate schools. Our paths hadn't crossed in over a year.

Mike Bower? Look up to me? How absurd! Just imagining his reaction if I told him his father had sent me to give him personal advice made me giggle out loud, which brought on a stern once-over from my mother.

On and on Mr. Bower babbled, "Mike refuses to even consider a banking career. He's got this girlfriend. He's thinking of getting married, quitting college, and settling for some penny-ante job. Maybe joining the navy or..."

Turning his roaming eyes toward me he winked. "I'd kinda like it if he'd marry you. Is it true redheads have a lot of temper?"

Though I found this comical, my mother failed to see the humor. She stiffened. "If your son wants to speak with my daughter about his life, I'm sure he'll contact her." As a warning not to convey my feelings on the matter, her glare centered in on me.

What a riot! Attempting to hide my amusement, I sank into a nearby chair.

In the next breath Mother added, "Mr. Bower, I insist that you go. My husband's due home any second, and I need to get supper cooked, because we do have to rush off to a meeting tonight. I don't mean to be rude, Mr. Bower, but you must leave. Now."

Still he made no effort to budge. In a nonstop drawl he switched back and forth from the perils of his son to lewd remarks and sexual insinuations. All the while he kept making eyes at my mother.

Although a delicate five-foot-two, her spunk often amazed me. *She has to be fuming,* I thought. *But she acts so aloof, keeping her cool, insisting that my dad will enter at any moment.* In spite of our dilemma I stifled another chuckle.

For a split second she shot a hard look my way. Her demeanor changed. She'd had enough of my silliness and our drunken intruder. With new firmness in her voice, she spoke words that finally caused Mr. Bower to take notice, "Perhaps you should stay after all. When my husband gets here, I'll relate all the things you've mentioned—not just about your son, but the Bunny Club, your comments about their outfits and shoes, and, of course, your flirtatious advances. He'll find it all quite interesting."

At these remarks Mr. Bower's cocky expression dropped like a veil. Venom shot from his stare. He leaned forward in his seat. With wrinkled forehead and narrowed eyes he studied my mother's face.

Did she forget she shouldn't make him mad? I squirmed against my chair uneasily. *Maybe she was right! He may get violent.*

But my mother stared back at him without a flinch. *Oh, no, doesn't she realize she's provoked him?* In the pit of my stomach my teenage giggles transformed into a flock of nervous butterflies.

"Judy, why don't you call your father at his office in case he's working late. He should know Mr. Bower is here." Her eyes never left his gaze.

Instantly I jumped up and headed for the phone. *Such an act of bluffing!* My heart flip-flopped. She and I both knew Daddy wasn't at the office.

Mr. Bower stood up. I stopped in my tracks as he started toward me. Then to my astonishment he actually seemed gentlemanly. "No, don't bother. I'll be going now so your mom can finish in the kitchen."

In a flash he darted out to his car with no apparent waver in his walk. We locked the door behind him, gasping with relief. As he pulled away, his driving shocked us.

"What should we do?" my mother asked, seeing his lavish sedan weaving in the road. "I didn't realize just how drunk he is. Should we call the police?"

Knowing his position with the bank, we certainly didn't want to mar his character or suffer repercussions for hurting him and smearing his reputation. So because of his prominent name, we agreed that we should not notify the authorities.

How uneducated we both were about the impending danger. Dealing with Mr. Bower's condition thrust us into unfamiliar territory, and with television constantly portraying drunkenness as funny, the hazards of driving while intoxicated weren't stressed to the public as they are now. Even after seeing his instability behind the wheel, it never entered our minds that he might not make it home. How could we have been so ignorant?

At the factory early the next morning, standing in line to punch timecards, my coworkers buzzed with news about the wreck. With horror I soaked it in, feeling as if sizzling sludge had been dumped into my heart.

Mr. Bower was dead!

Just about thirty minutes after he had left us the evening before, he zoomed up a hill in the wrong lane and crashed head-on into an oncoming car. Not only did he end his life, but he also killed a passenger in the other vehicle, a nine-year-old boy who was my little sister's age.

No, it's not true! my brain exploded in disbelief. At first I hoped to awaken from a bad dream. But of course I didn't. I waited for someone to admit that it was all just a horrid joke. But no one did. As I accepted the stark reality, my head throbbed with burning anguish that sent my young idealistic philosophy up in ashes.

Rumors circulated. In the afternoon of the previous day, earlier than the time Mr. Bower showed up at our house, police in a neighboring county had picked him up. After they realized who he was, they released him though he was far from sober. Other drivers had witnessed his zigzagging vehicle, and some had pulled off the road for him to pass. Even as people vowed that these stories were true, nothing soothed my blazing guilt.

How I agonized! *Mr. Bower, in a drunken state, had gone to face his Maker. My mother and I may have been the last people to ever talk with him. Not only his life but also the life of an innocent boy had been snuffed out. How could I have ever considered his condition funny? Why were we so foolish? Why, oh, why didn't we report him?*

Our decision was so dumb, so irrational, a choice we made because of Mr. Bower's well-known name. Now I will always have to wonder if we could have possibly stopped this tragedy.

OH, THE POWER in a name!

> A good name is better than precious ointment.
>
> —ECCLESIASTES 7:1

> Dead flies make the perfumer's ointment give off an evil odor; so a little folly outweighs wisdom and honor.
>
> —ECCLESIASTES 10:1, RSV

How quickly a good name can be defiled. How easily "dead flies" corrupt. How treacherous even a "little folly" can be. Mr. Bower had been killed instantly, his reputation drenched in disgrace as knowledge of his "little folly"—his drunken stupor—pulsated throughout the community like "dead flies" polluting his name in the minds of those who heard.

What weight the "little folly"—the wrong decision my mother and I made—bears upon my soul. In one fleeting moment two people died. Yet the memory of that moment lives on in timeless space. Adhering to the apostle Paul's advice, "forgetting those things which are behind" (Phil. 3:13), I refuse to let this memory overtake me, yet sometimes without warning it bubbles up like simmering poison in my head.

With my youthful heart engulfed in flaming heaviness, the only consolation I found was to seek forgiveness and in making a heartfelt vow. *Heavenly Father*, I prayed, *please forgive me. If ever I face another compromising situation, I promise to the best of my ability to choose what's right. Regardless of the persons involved, no matter how well their names are known or what the consequences, I'll trust You as my Protector and Guide.*

Years later another accident called my hand on this—also a painful event that on occasion boils up in my thoughts, a scene we'll encounter shortly in our trip ahead. But for now we must push forward, leaving despair behind, accepting the fact that nothing in the past can ever be changed, knowing that God forgives our mistakes then forgets them.

Another verse about names says, "A good name is rather to be chosen than great riches" (Prov. 22:1). Great riches, undeniable value, precious ointment, so costly. What makes a name so treasured?

Fellow travelers, throw aside all heaviness and come away with me. At this very moment happier times call for us to blaze our way into the seldom explored territory of names.

NAMES? IT MAY sound like a humdrum adventure, but it's not. To be sure, we'll explore intriguing trails and hidden paths leading us to fresh awareness, appreciation, and esteem of our Father and His Word. Secrets and mysteries await.

With names?

Yes, names can be fascinating. Stop a minute and consider their necessity. How could we even live without them? Life would be chaotic to say the least.

Never has man known a time when names did not exist. From the very beginning of history they marked identity in God's creation. Soon after forming man He named him Adam; then He gave Adam the privilege of naming all the animals since they also needed to be identified.

God created woman. For a while both male and female, being of the species of man, shared the name *Adam*, meaning "man."

> When God created man, He made him in the likeness of God. He created them male and female and blessed them and named them [both] Adam [Man] at the time they were created.
>
> —Genesis 5:1–2, AMP

Following the breach caused by sin, the male retained the name of Adam, but of the female we read, "And Adam called his wife's name Eve; because she was the mother of all living" (Gen. 3:20). The name *Eve* means "living."

In the antiquities the meaning of a name carried much significance. It stood as a building block for a person's life, revealing traits and character. Many times a name decreed the destiny of an individual, and sometimes it even revealed the future to whole populations.

In our present-day society people seldom know or even care about definitions of their names. Some names hold biblical or family significance, but many are simply picked for their popularity. Though a name is important as a unique gift of identity at birth, it develops its own worth wrapped by reputation, tied in ribbons of character, and decorated with titles of achievement. We see this illustrated in the expression, "He made a name for himself."

Perhaps because the definitions of names have lost importance in modern times, we often miss the enlightenment of their meanings buried in Bible stories. Now as we unearth several, we'll find their significance amazing.

First we dig up the name *Methuselah* from Genesis 5:21. In contemporary minds it clicks with the recollection of the oldest man who ever lived and has generated the cliché "as old as Methuselah."

Yet much more inspiration is found in its actual meaning. Can you believe that this name *Methuselah* issued a dire alarm for the entire world? Well, it did. It prophesied that his death would usher in the Flood of Noah!

Matthew Henry's Commentary on the Holy Bible tells us, "Methuselah signifies, 'he dies, there is a dart,' or, 'a sending forth,' namely, of the deluge, which came the very year that Methuselah died. If, indeed his name was so intended, and so explained, it was fair warning to a careless world a long time before the judgment came."[1]

Methuselah lived 969 years (Gen. 5:27), and it wasn't mere coincidence, when precisely as his name proclaimed, he died the exact year of the Flood. To possess the knowledge to give him such a dynamic name, Methuselah's father must have experienced an awesome personal encounter from God. Who was his father? Enoch, the man who walked in such perfect unity with

God that he was caught up from Earth to heaven, never facing death.

Yet when did his devout relationship with the Lord begin? Evidently at age sixty-five at the birth of the son he named Methuselah. Genesis 5:21–22 says Enoch walked with God for three hundred years after he begat Methuselah (until his rapture into heaven). Perhaps the naming of his son, surely a name chosen by the Almighty Himself, electrified Enoch with his devout faith and flawless commitment unparalleled by any mortal soul.

Let's look into the name *Enoch*. It means "teacher, dedicate, initiate, discipline, train up."[2] We've seen that, from the birth of Methuselah, Enoch fulfilled his name by disciplining his entire being in dedication to God. But can we find biblical evidence of his teaching others?

Yes. And more than simple instruction, Enoch gave a startling prophecy that is nestled in the tiny Book of Jude:

> The Lord is coming with millions of his holy ones. He will bring the people of the world before him in judgment, to receive just punishment, and to prove the terrible things they have done in rebellion against God, revealing all they have said against him.
>
> —JUDE 14–15, TLB

These words spoken by Enoch about five thousand years ago still wait to be fulfilled. How chilling to realize that from age to age so many have ignored Enoch's prophecy of judgment in the same way the people of his time ignored the approaching Flood. The Flood was readily revealed to them in the divinely appointed name of Methuselah for nearly a thousand years and confirmed by Noah 120 years while he built the ark. Yet they did not listen to God's warning.

Wake up, world! Not only does the Bible tell of the Flood, but also scientific discoveries verify that it happened. Because the same unchangeable God reigns today, we can be sure that Enoch's teaching of End-Time events will come to pass just as surely as the prophecy in Methuselah's name. Many other scriptures back up Enoch's words with virtually identical predictions. Be ready! Fulfillment could be very soon. Just as in the days of Noah, disaster awaits all who refuse to heed.

Noah's name denotes rest. Moved by holy fear (Heb. 11:7, NIV) in the midst of looming peril, Noah rested his faith and trust in the Lord, following His instructions to the letter. Oh, the rest all the others could have also had in God if they had only listened and repented!

The same holds true today.

TO UNCOVER MORE biblical names our exploration whisks us over many centuries until we spring into the dawning of the Hebrew nation and behold name changes for Abram and Sarai. God Himself gave them new names to reset their course in life, shine new light into their destinies, and affect all future generations.

Abram means "high father,"[3] which in everyday terms expresses that any man is exalted by being a father. God changed *Abra*m to *Abraham*, "the father of a multitude."[4]

This new title announced Abraham as the actual father of many descendants. For two names that sound so much alike that's quite a difference in meaning! At the transformation of his name God vowed:

> I will make you very fruitful; I will make nations of you, and kings will come from you. I will establish my covenant as an everlasting covenant between me and you and your descendants after you for the generations to come, to be your God and the God of your descendants after you.
>
> —Genesis 17:6–7, NIV

Sarai, meaning "my princess (i.e., Abraham's)," was changed to *Sarah*, distinguishing her as a woman of great honor by its definition of "princess" (for all the race).[5] She will always be known as the wife of Abraham whose seed produced Isaac, the son of God's promise from whom the perfect Seed is born.

Yet at this time of their name changes, Abraham had no children by Sarah. And she was far beyond the age of child-bearing. Still God assured Abraham:

> And I will bless her and also give you a son by her; then I will bless her, and she shall be a mother of nations; kings of peoples shall be from her.
>
> —Genesis 17:16, NKJV

Hearing this Abraham fell on his face in worship. What joy it was to have God's affirmation that Sarah would bear this promised child. Yet such faith was required of the father of multitudes. With Sarah? His heart throbbed in happiness knowing God's words as truth. He pictured Sarah conceiving at age ninety and himself becoming a father at one hundred. He burst out laughing.

God Himself gave Abraham and Sarah's son the name *Isaac*, meaning "laughter."[6] Not only laughing because they heard the promise of his conception, surely they also laughed with uncontrollable happiness at his birth. What joy this child must have overflowed into their aging lives!

Do you think others may have not simply laughed—but scoffed at this old man who suddenly called himself "Abraham" and his wife "Sarah" before he had even one child by her? Surely people must have doubted the possibility of his ever fathering any children by his barren and aged wife. Yet because Abraham believed God he accepted his name without shame or embarrassment. Rewarding his faithful obedience, his truthful God fulfilled His promise of "father of a multitude," and more than once as years slipped by He would reassure Abraham of His everlasting covenant:

> And I will establish my covenant between me and thee and thy seed after thee in their generations for an everlasting covenant, to be a God unto thee, and to thy seed after thee.
>
> —GENESIS 17:7

> That in blessing I will bless thee, and in multiplying I will multiply thy seed as the stars of the heaven, and as the sand which is upon the sea shore; and thy seed shall possess the gates of his enemies; and in thy seed shall all the nations of the earth be blessed; because thou hast obeyed my voice.
>
> —GENESIS 22:17–18

Yes! God established an *everlasting* covenant in which *all* nations would be blessed. Do you realize what this means?

This covenant remains forever. It holds as true and strong today it did back then. Never throughout all the passing generations have *any* of its promises ever ended. They will remain through all eternity.

During ancient times this covenant met the needs of Abraham's offspring, the children of Israel. God's blessings were bountiful when they lived faithful to God, but only meager essentials when they turned their backs on Him. However, because God gave His word, He has never forgotten the descendants of Abraham.

Consider the miracle of the present Hebrew population. Although they have suffered indescribable persecutions down through history, they always prevail. In the vilest movement against them in modern history, Hitler zeroed in to annihilate them. As a vicious leader he murdered millions, but defeated and in disgrace he met his death. Jews survived in honor.

How many Amorites do you know today? How many Hittites, Perizzites, Philistines? None. They vanished long ago. The children of Israel have far surpassed any sect of people in migration and wandering, enduring for nearly two thousand years without a country of their own. Not only did they retain their identity, but also in 1948 these descendants of Abraham reestablished their own nation of Israel, an unheard-of possibility by natural means.

Why have they survived when all others failed? They have the covenant of Abraham, an everlasting promise insured by the word of Almighty God. It is still in effect today and forevermore. And as God promised, it is a covenant that extends blessing to all nations of the earth.

SO DOES THE covenant grant blessing to us? Yes, yes, God says, yes! Why? Because of Jesus!

> He redeemed us in order that the blessings given to Abraham might come to the Gentiles through Christ Jesus, so that by faith we might receive the promise of the Spirit.
>
> —GALATIANS 3:14, NIV

Exactly how does this occur? Grab your walking shoes and come along as we wend our way through other parts of Galatians 3.

> Consider Abraham: "He believed God, and it was credited to him as righteousness." Understand, then, that those who believe are children of Abraham. The Scripture foresaw that God would justify the Gentiles by faith, and announced the gospel in advance to Abraham: "All nations will be blessed through you." So those who have faith are blessed along with Abraham, the man of faith.
>
> —GALATIANS 3:6–9, NIV

From the moment the Lord presented the Abrahamic covenant it could never be canceled, not even by the Law. God made this covenant of promise four hundred years before the Law. It was not just for Abraham, but for all of his descendants. (See Galatians 3:16.)

"Now to Abraham and his Seed were the promises made. He does not say, 'And to seeds' as of many, but as of one, 'And to your Seed,' who is Christ" (v. 16, NKJV). Hallelujah! Christ, the *Seed* of Abraham. By our belief in Christ, the anointed Son of God born as a Man of Jewish lineage—we become grafted into Abraham's family tree. "Those who believe are children of Abraham" (v. 7, NIV). Yes, oh yes, we are blessed with Abraham as heirs of the everlasting covenant just as certainly as God's chosen Israel.

> You are all sons of God through faith in Christ Jesus, for all of you who
> were baptized into Christ have clothed yourselves with Christ. There is
> neither Jew nor Greek, slave nor free, male nor female, for you are all
> one in Christ Jesus. If you belong to Christ, then you are Abraham's
> seed, and heirs according to the promise.
>
> —GALATIANS 3:26–29, NIV

Heirs according to the promise! All the blessings of Abraham are ours.
Just what does this mean? We already know he was blessed with long life,
fertility, and countless descendents. But what other ways was he blessed?

He was blessed by spiritual union with God. He had intimate fellowship
with the Almighty who spoke with him as a personal friend.

He was blessed with divine favor. God gave him special honor because of
his undaunted obedience to the course He set before him.

He was blessed with almighty protection. God told him, "Do not be
afraid, Abram, I am your shield, your very great reward" (Gen. 15:2, NIV).

He was blessed materially. God supplied him with abundant earthly wealth:
"And Abram was very rich in cattle, in silver, and in gold" (Gen. 13:2).

He is blessed in eternal bliss. Jesus states that many will sit down with
Abraham, Isaac, and Jacob in the kingdom of heaven. (See Matthew 8:11.)

Even though the blessings of Abraham belong to every believer, many
seem to never receive them in fullness. Why? There may be many reasons:
lack of faith and commitment, disobedience, fear, murmuring, worrying,
unforgiveness, and unrepentance.

Some may not receive the blessing of Abraham because of lack of knowledge or simply not asking. Just as with any inheritance, one must know it
exists and take hold of it. In the natural this sometimes requires claiming
and maybe even fighting for rightful belongings. In the spiritual it demands
active faith and fortitude. This means putting faith into action by doing
works like Abraham, who accompanied his faith with works. Jesus said:

> If ye were Abraham's children, ye would do the works of Abraham.
>
> —JOHN 8:39

ONLY BY EXAMINING Abraham's life can we determine his works. His
first "work" was simply choosing God above all. Although history tells us he
grew up in a land of idol worship, he desired to serve only the one true and
living God. Follow now as we enter into an ancient Hebrew legend to spy
on a scene that happened four thousand years ago.

While he was away on business, Terah left his young son to tend his idol shop. Now at the end of a busy day the child feels alone and apprehensive even though his father's many "gods" surround him. He frowns with distaste while he scans each cold lifeless statue.

Suddenly a fitful urge overtakes him. Grabbing a nearby club he smashes every idol, except the biggest one, into bits. Then in the hands of the one left standing he positions the telltale club. He sits down and waits, slightly smiling, although fidgeting nervously. How his heart churns, knowing that his father will soon return.

Before long shuffling footsteps approach the shop entrance. His father steps inside. With a gulp the boy leaps to his feet and stands erect.

In shock Terah cries, "Oh, son! What happened?"

"The big one did it!" He points to the huge image gripping the club. "See? He broke them all!"

Terah rages. "No! That can't be true! How could it be? None of these gods can do anything. Why, they can't even think!"

"Oh, Father, let the words of your mouth enter into your heart, and truly hear what you are saying!" responds the son.[7]

Yes, this legend speaks of the young boy Abram—destined by a true and living God to become Abraham, the father of the Jews, the father of multitudes. His bloodline would give birth to the promised *Seed*, extending blessings to everyone who chooses Christ by the unending covenant confirmed with him. Even though the account of the idol shop may be just a story handed down through the ages, Scripture confirms that Abraham wholeheartedly chose God above all else—supplying much bona fide evidence with demonstrations of his trust and obedience in Almighty Jehovah.

In His first vow God told Abram:

> And I will make of thee a great nation, and I will bless thee, and make thy name great; and thou shall be a blessing: And I will bless them that bless thee, and curse him that curseth thee; and in thee shall all families of the earth be blessed.
>
> —GENESIS 12:2–3

Yet before he could receive these promises Abram had to obey God by forsaking his homeland for a foreign land. Without question he chose obedience:

> Abraham trusted God, and when God told him to leave home and go far away to another land which he promised to give him, Abraham

obeyed. Away he went, not knowing where he was going.

—HEBREWS 11:8, TLB

Abraham's works include other qualities becoming to God. His unselfish nature allowed his nephew Lot to take the best land for himself (Gen. 13:9). In unconditional love he fought a battle to rescue Lot from enemy forces and later interceded to save him from the fate of Sodom and Gomorrah (Gen. 18:20–33).

His works include giving to God. From the blessings of his material wealth Abraham tithed (Gen. 14:20). It so happened that immediately after Abraham gave his tithe God vowed that his seed would become as countless as the stars (Gen. 15:5). Even with all his riches Abraham's trust relied not in this world. He placed his hope in a heavenly city "whose builder and maker is God" (Heb. 11:10).

Abraham trusted God as his leader, totally following divine direction and yielding his life in submission. He proved his faith to the utmost—even to the point of his willingness to sacrifice his and Sarah's divinely promised son:

> Was not Abraham our father justified by works, when he had offered Isaac his son upon the altar? Seest thou how faith wrought with his works, and by works was faith made perfect?
>
> —JAMES 2:21–22

The Living Bible says:

> You see, he was trusting God so much that he was willing to do whatever God told him to; his faith was made complete by what he did, by his actions, his good deeds.
>
> —JAMES 2:22

By faith Abraham showed himself to be a man of genuine trust—willing to obey, to give, to sacrifice. His work displayed his character, certainly qualifying him for the esteemed title "Friend of God."

> And the scripture was fulfilled which saith, Abraham believed God, and it was imputed unto him for righteousness: and he was called the Friend of God.
>
> —JAMES 2:23

Abraham, what a man of works! Choosing God above all and trusting Him as his Leader, he obeyed God and went wherever He sent him. Demonstrating unselfishness to others, he gave back to God from his material wealth. He was willing to trust and obey God even to the degree of sacrificing his own son. His heart was attuned to eternity, his spiritual eyes on his eternal home.

Abraham's works validated his great faith. In our Christian walk we must also do the same.

> Even so faith, if it hath not works, is dead, being alone. Yea, a man may say, Thou hast faith, and I have works: shew me thy faith without thy works, and I will shew thee my faith by my works. Thou believest that there is one God; thou doest well: the devils also believe, and tremble. But wilt thou know, O vain man, that faith without works is dead?
>
> —James 2:17–20

Do you want the blessings of Abraham to be yours? Then do the works!

Faithful Abraham, the "father of a multitude" was blessed beyond measure with long life. He was fruitful spiritually, materially, eternally. God blessed him with a covenant of promise that carried on through the loins of his son Isaac, his grandson Jacob, and his great-grandson Judah to usher forth the promised *Seed*—extending the promise to every nation. What a glorious fulfillment of the destiny spoken in his name!

Another name—*David*—attracts our attention as we skip on down our path of names. What endearing insight it produces in its rendering of "beloved." Oh, the heart of David! Many psalms give witness to the power of his pen as he bared his innermost emotions to reveal his devotion to God. In spite of his failures and shortcomings his love remained true, and in the middle of his human weaknesses he readily acknowledged his sins and sought forgiveness. With a broken spirit, praise and worship flowed from his entire being.

And God responded with His boundless love. He affirmed His beloved David as "a man after mine own heart" (Acts 13:22), and just as with Abraham, God also honored him with an everlasting covenant:

> And thine house and thy kingdom shall be established for ever before thee: thy throne shall be established for ever.
>
> —2 Samuel 7:16

We have seen what loyalty, faith, and trust radiated from David, Abraham, Noah, and Enoch in their relationships with God and the intimacy they shared with Him. Can we say the same about ourselves?

Examine your heart with honesty. Does it show works like Abraham's? Is it repentant like David's? Does it express belief like Noah's? Is it dedicated like Enoch's? What kind of closeness do you share with your heavenly Father? How well do you actually know Him? Do you know His names?

At an initial introduction one usually learns a person's first and last names and oftentimes his titles. Yet many Christians live in total unawareness of the marvelous names and titles belonging to their heavenly Father.

And now we enter into another adventure on our treasure map. For many miles we will be traveling on sacred ground as we explore the depths of...

"HALLOWED BE THY NAME"

David expressed, "And they that know thy name will put their trust in thee" (Ps. 9:10). He also said, "Bless the LORD, O my soul...bless his holy name" (Ps. 103:1).

WHAT IS GOD'S name?

To discover the answer we must walk, in reverence of a holy, eternal Deity, upon a whole new path of names. It is a majestic trail into astounding knowledge, leading us to many names and titles of our Lord. It is a walkway overflowing with insight into every facet of His being, beaming with splendor indescribable.

Hurry, fellow travelers, for the next adventure on our treasure map awaits as we flow into God's majesty with praise upon our lips for our Father, which art in heaven, hallowed be thy name! Yahweh! How glorious is this name!

> I am the LORD [Hebrew, *Yahweh*]: that is my name.
>
> —ISAIAH 42:8

The definition of *Yahweh* (or as some say, *Jehovah*) is simply "(the) self-Existent or Eternal."[8] But by the acts attributed to God under the name *Yahweh* we discover the complete fullness of His total Being, the magnitude of His Deity, and everything He is. We learn of His absolute supremacy, utmost sovereignty, super-superlative entity. We stand in awe for He is holy, righteous, majestic, total power and might, all-revealing, transcendent, infinite, utterly independent, permanently self-existent.

Although many names and titles of God reveal certain attributes, various functions, and specific qualities of His nature, *Yahweh* stands alone in totally expressing God in His entirety. As Yahweh He demonstrates His unconditional love, unwavering compassion, unlimited resources, and total protection for His people. By this name He deals with mankind as the covenant-fulfilling God and the Judge of Righteousness. This Name incorporates His every other name and title. It identifies Him as Head of all.

> Our help is in the name of the LORD [*Yahweh* in Hebrew], who made heaven and earth.
>
> —PSALM 124:8

Hallowed is the name of Yahweh. It is holy, sanctified, consecrated, and set apart for sacred use, a name to be worshiped, honored, and adored.

Yahweh. Yes, what a glorious name!

Could a name so significant somehow be lost? This notion sounds preposterous, yet because of a decision made around 300 B.C. it actually happened. Because of the emphasis placed on the importance of names and in fear of the consequences for breaking the third commandment, the Jews became afraid to use the name *Yahweh*.

> Thou shalt not take the name of the LORD [Yahweh] thy God in vain: for the LORD [Yahweh] will not hold him guiltless that taketh his name in vain.
>
> —EXODUS 20:7

In the days of Moses a man who blasphemed the name was stoned to death by orders from the Lord. Afterwards, God told Moses to say to the Israelite people:

> If anyone curses his God, he will be held responsible; anyone who blasphemes the name of the LORD must be put to death. The entire assembly must stone him. Whether an alien or native-born, when he blasphemes the Name, he must be put to death.
>
> —LEVITICUS 24:15–16, NIV

The Jews determined that they could only obtain certain and absolute obedience of never using His name without complete reverence and respect if they no longer said "Yahweh." So they resolved to only imply it by expressions like "the Name," "the Great and Terrible Name," "the Peculiar Name," "the Separate Name," "the Unutterable Name," "the Ineffable Name," "the Incommunicative Name," "the Holy Name," "the Distinguished Name."[9]

Only one limited exception allowed the name Yahweh to be spoken. This was a whispered utterance by the high priest on the Day of Atonement, that one day a year when the high priest conversed alone with God in the holy of holies.

The name *Yahweh* could not even be written. As a result, *Adonai*, meaning "Lord, Master, Owner,"[10] found its way into Scripture as the written substitution for *Yahweh*. In *TANAKH: The Holy Scriptures*, the King James Version, and several other versions of the Old Testament, the replacement for Yahweh appears in small capital letters as "LORD" or "the LORD." The few times *Lord* is written in lowercase indicates that in the initial scripture the name Adonai was used to mean "Lord, Master and Owner," and not the sacred name. For instance:

> O LORD our Lord, how excellent is thy name in all the earth!
> —PSALM 8:1

Notice one *LORD* in small capital letters and the other *Lord* in lowercase. This should actually read, "O Yahweh our Adonai, how excellent is Your name in all the earth!"

Here, the word *excellent* in Hebrew expresses "wide, large, powerful, famous, gallant, glorious, goodly, lordly, mighty, noble, principal, worthy."[11] This describes Yahweh! How unfortunate to have generations pass never hearing the name spoken or seeing it in print. It's no wonder uncertainties arose concerning the exact pronunciation and correct spelling. Following so many decades of silence, the only absolute surety existed in four Hebrew consonants, *YHWH* (sometimes shown as *JHWH, YHVH,* or *JHVH*), known as the Tetragrammaton. Centuries after deletion of the true name, scribes inserted vowels from their Hebrew rendering of Adonai within the Tetragrammaton to form Yahweh.

Amazingly, modern-day archeology supports this rendition, yet even so, its exactness is still debated and spellings vary. The English rendering of Yahweh, which has been in usage only since around 1521 and which many scholars deem inappropriate, is Jehovah.

I prefer using the Hebrew name Yahweh above Jehovah. Before we move onward, I must share a few reasons from underlying insights in the Hebrew language.

First, in speaking the sounds of *yah* and *weh* one can feel the very breath that the Holy Spirit of Almighty God breathed into the soul of man and that we exhale back unto His glory. Speak it now, and you will see.

Another reason I favor the name Yahweh is that Yah, a shorter version for Yahweh sometimes used in Scripture, comes alive in syllables throughout God's Word. When the Lord changed the name Abram to Abraham He chose letters that inserted His own name into Abram's name, Abr—*ah* (for Yah)—am. This can be more readily observed in the Hebrew alphabet. For another example, hear the name *Yah* leap forth in the word *alleluia* (or as we often say say, *hallelujah*), which is a universal word meaning "praise the Lord."

As we travel we will interchange these two, Yahweh and Jehovah, because of the more popular use of Jehovah and also to familiarize them as being one and the same in identifying God in His fullness. Yahweh is the Hebrew name, and Jehovah is the modern version.

Regardless of history, in spite of disagreement—how wonderful is the excellence of this name. Yahweh! Jehovah! Solomon proclaims:

> The name of the LORD [Yahweh] is a strong tower; the righteous run to it and are safe.
>
> —PROVERBS 18:10, NKJV

Yes, beaming like a floodlight over our pathway a most magnificent tower of strength extends from this name. It manifests for us a mighty fortress where we can run for safety and security, a wonderful refuge where at any time we may enter welcomed and unafraid.

In life's travels this tower can always go with us as a lovely steeple with golden lights declaring the splendor of His holy name. With our every step we may gaze upon its glory to steer us in the right course. At anytime along life's way, should we feel the slightest need, we can climb into its shelter.

OH, SO BRIGHTLY now the name Yahweh glows as we begin a stroll down a winding trail under His tower of protection. As we amble soft music fills the air. Someone sings. Where can this be coming from?

Enchanted we round the corner to discover a robust man from early Bible days. Clothed in a flowing purple robe of finest linen with the gleam of satin, his auburn hair falls in waves upon his broad and burly shoulders.

King David! Such prestige he radiates, arrayed in all his royal wealth. Without one sign of arrogance he praises Yahweh with all his being. Psalm 145, a song composed from David's heart, is a daily prayer of orthodox Jews today.

We gather now around King David as with this psalm, accompanied by sweet notes of his harp, his deep melodious voice tells of Yahweh's virtues.

"Great is the LORD (Yahweh) and greatly to be praised!...His greatness is unsearchable...mighty acts...glorious splendor of Your majesty...wondrous works...awesome acts...greatness...goodness...righteousness...gracious and full of compassion...slow to anger...great in mercy...good to all...tender mercies...glory of Your kingdom, majestic, everlasting...Your power...dominion...upholds all who fall...raises up all who are bowed down...You give them food...satisfy the desire of every living thing...The LORD is righteous...gracious...near to all who call...preserves all who love Him...all the wicked He will destroy. My mouth shall speak the praise of the LORD, and all flesh shall bless His holy name" (NKJV).

David's tribute to Yahweh closes. He falls to his knees and lifts his face toward heaven, unashamed and beloved by the Eternal One he praises.

Such a psalm. How well it shows the many attributes of Yahweh and the reverence David held for Him. No wonder God called David a man after His own heart and honored this earthly king with an everlasting throne.

Numerous chapters in the Book Psalms also display Yahweh's never-ending wonders. David wrote many of them. Before we leave this scene, let's linger a moment longer to hear a few more of his writings expressing the enormity of God's most holy name. These come from *The New Jerusalem Bible*, which instead of using *LORD*, rightly prints the actual name in its translation.

> I will bless Yahweh at all times, his praise continually on my lips, I will praise Yahweh from my heart; let the humble hear and rejoice. Proclaim with me the greatness of Yahweh, let us acclaim his name together.
>
> —PSALM 34:1–3, NJB

> The Law of Yahweh is perfect, refreshment to the soul; the decree of Yahweh is trustworthy, wisdom for the simple. The precepts of Yahweh are honest, joy for the heart; the commandment of Yahweh is pure, light for the eyes. The fear of Yahweh is pure, lasting for ever; the judgements of Yahweh are true, upright, every one.
>
> —PSALM 19:7–9, NJB

Unending qualities are revealed in this name—His majesty, holiness, goodness, mercies, power, sovereignty, and judgments. The above psalm deals exclusively with Yahweh's nature as the Righteous Judge—declaring His Law, decrees, precepts, and commandments as perfect, trustworthy, honest, pure, upright, and true. By His judgments the earth stands firm.

> For ever, Yahweh, your word is planted firm in heaven. Your constancy
> endures from age to age; you established the earth and it stands firm.
> Through your judgements all stands firm to this day, for all creation is
> your servant.
> —PSALM 119:89–91, NJB

From the beginning of mankind God set up an order of obedience, insti-
tuting rules with consequences for those who break them. His standards for
good and evil abide today and always will remain the same. As a Being of
perfect holiness, Yahweh has no choice. By His purity he must judge sin. In
His sovereignty He must require obedience and enforce justice.

> I know, Yahweh, that your judgements are upright, and in punishing
> me you show your constancy.
> —PSALM 119:75, NJB

How He surely grieved when Adam and Eve, His mankind made in His
image, in righteousness and perfection, fell short of His requirements. Nevertheless, He didn't hesitate to punish them for going against His command
and eating of the tree of the knowledge of good and evil.

With no reservation He dictated the Flood in Noah's day, destroyed
Sodom and Gomorrah, and pronounced plagues on the Egyptians. By enact-
ing the Law He demanded the submission of a rebellious Hebrew nation.
He allowed them, His chosen offspring of Abraham, to be captured by the
Babylonians in Daniel's day, live under Roman rule in Jesus' time, and pos-
sess no country of their own for another two thousand years.

Judgment also came to individuals. Because of his weakness to enforce
righteousness in his family, Eli, the priest and judge, met his death. Samson suffered terribly for his wrongdoings. King Saul died by his own hand.
Even King David, God's beloved, could not escape the consequences of his
sins—as we'll witness firsthand farther along our road together.

Not only under the Old Covenant did God's hand of correction govern.
In the Book of Acts, Ananias and Sapphira dropped dead on the spot for
lying to the Holy Spirit (Acts 5:1–10). As eyewitnesses we'll soon see why
divine reproof constantly accompanied the apostle Paul, even though he
willingly gave his life to preach the gospel and, inspired by God Himself,
wrote much of the New Testament.

What about divine discipline in our day? Does it still exist?

Yes! Of all of Yahweh's qualities, why is His nature as Judge so frowned
upon in our society? Many Christians seem to believe that since the cross of
Calvary brought mercy and grace, God no longer serves as a disciplinarian.

But as wonderful as the benefits of the New Covenant are, they do not remove consequences for sin or cause the heavenly Father to withdraw from His role as Judge.

God never varies. True, by His virtue of perfect love, He pardoned us by giving His Son whose spotless blood redeems us, covers us with His righteousness, and grafts us by adoption into His family. Yet the necessity for Yahweh's justice and penalties has never ceased. How could a never-changing God punish for disobedience in bygone eras and wink at sin today?

He couldn't!

To do so would annul His authority over evil, place a stamp of approval on defiance, and enable wickedness to run rampant with nothing to keep it in check. There would be no right or wrong, no way of righteousness, no holy God.

But, oh, my friends, there is a holy God. Throughout His Word we find examples of instructions with penalties for transgression. These proceed directly from the mouth of Jesus:

> Take heed that you do not do your charitable deeds before men, to be seen by them. *Otherwise you have no reward from your Father in heaven.*
> —MATTHEW 6:1, NKJV, EMPHASIS ADDED

> Judge not, that you be not judged. *For with what judgment you judge, you will be judged;* and with the same measure you use, it will be measured back to you.
> —MATTHEW 7:1–2, NKJV, EMPHASIS ADDED

> And whenever you stand praying, if you have anything against anyone, forgive him, that your Father in heaven may also forgive you your trespasses. *But if you do not forgive, neither will your Father in heaven forgive your trespasses.*
> —MARK 11:25–26, NKJV, EMPHASIS ADDED

Consequences for noncompliance sound severe. Yet the Righteous Judge gives them not with wrath but in love to reveal the need for right living and to control wrong desires within His children. He is working to squelch sin and restore, reconcile, and refine hearts. He is producing patience, toughening character, building faith, teaching us to depend on His grace, and uniting our spirits to His in righteousness.

I like what Andrew Jukes, dedicated lecturer and author of the nineteenth century, says, "The highest righteousness, while it judges sin, can never rest until it makes the sinner righteous."[12] This so defines the intentions of our Righteous Judge.

IN OUR ENCOUNTER with this facet of Yahweh we are about to come face-to-face with a just Deity of highest excellence. Get ready for travel in rugged terrain, tearing through underbrush and scrambling over cutting rocks as we tackle a trail of suffering and hardship. Painful, yes, but what strength develops by endurance. And such blessings wait for all who grasp the joy of understanding, knowing and accepting God as Yahweh, Judge of Righteousness.

> Beloved, do not be surprised at the fiery ordeal which comes upon you to prove you, as though something strange were happening to you. But rejoice in so far as you share Christ's sufferings, that you may also rejoice and be glad when his glory is revealed. If you are reproached for the name of Christ, you are blessed, because the spirit of glory and of God rests upon you. But let none of you suffer as a murderer, or a thief, or a wrongdoer, or a mischief-maker; yet if one suffers as a Christian, let him not be ashamed, but under that name let him glorify God. For the time has come for judgment to begin with the household of God.
>
> —I PETER 4:12–17, RSV

Our human nature desires that all things will miraculously, instantly, drop into place. We vehemently detest struggle and waiting.

If parents could give their children immediate rewards, without facing hardships in achievements or consequences for wrong actions, would this be a good and perfect gift? In the long run what sort of self-esteem, perseverance, personality, and character would develop in these children? Would they realize purpose or set any goals in life? With these thoughts we can begin to perceive the value of Yahweh's disciplinary wisdom.

Why did Abraham need to withstand wanderings in foreign lands, waiting over twenty years from the time God first promised him the birth of Isaac? What purpose did it serve for Moses to forfeit royal standing and endure as a shepherd for forty years before he delivered the Israelites?

Is it not true that God, in His power, could instantly remove every adverse circumstance man has ever faced? Did He actually have to depend on the rod of Moses to part the Red Sea? Was it necessary for that there be a human march to collapse the wall of Jericho? Did God need the slingshot of David to defeat Goliath?

No!

And certainly with one sweep of His might He could have brushed away every obstacle awaiting the Israelites in the Promised Land. He could have given Samson strength even with his head shaved and kept Daniel from the lions' den and the three young Hebrew men from the fiery furnace.

But oh, what courageous character and unshakable maturity grew in the lives of those who experienced these ordeals. And how God revealed through them the glory of His sovereignty, His ever-abiding faithfulness and power.

Within our weak human selves we find deficiency to survive on our own. In Him we can discover supernatural fortitude. What strength blooms in us when we resolve to live by faith and rest in His supremacy. Despite any situation we stand in victory, boasting of His ability, glorying in His strength and greatness, exalting Him and not ourselves.

Like the apostle Paul.

Oh, to have his fortitude! Prepare for pain as we enter the trail of hardships to accompany him. Listen intently to his testimony. Feel his anguish. Absorb his agony. How it will break your heart. Still, what joy to see his bravery and hear his declaration of victory even in the midst of torture.

> From the Jews five times I received forty stripes minus one. Three times I was beaten with rods; once I was stoned; three times I was shipwrecked; a night and a day I have been in the deep; in journeys often, in perils of waters, in perils of robbers, in perils of my own countrymen, in perils of the Gentiles, in perils in the city, in perils in the wilderness, in perils in the sea, in perils among false brethren; in weariness and toil, in sleeplessness often, in hunger and thirst, in fastings often, in cold and nakedness—besides the other things, what comes upon me daily: my deep concern for all the churches.
>
> —2 CORINTHIANS 11:24–28, NKJV

Can you even conceive of such vicious attacks, intense sufferings, and distress? Not even counting his three beatings with rods, Paul endured a total of 195 lashes from a leather whip, possibly studded with metal that dug into his flesh. Have you ever been struck by even one small rock? Imagine being pelted with stone after stone and finally left for dead. Picture being shipwrecked and drifting on the water, mugged and abused over and over again, going without food and water, having no clothes. How could Paul have ever survived?

Only by the strength of God. Paul knows this, and so next he adds, "If I must boast, I will boast of the things that show my weakness" (v. 30, NIV). But he could have bragged of so much more.

Following this He tells of a wonderful trip into the highest realm of heaven where he beheld paradise and heard unspeakable words. He says, "That experience is something worth bragging about, but I am not going to do it. I am going to boast only about how weak I am and how great God is to use such weakness for his glory" (2 Cor. 12:5, TLB).

Oh, how Paul wants to flatter himself. But he knows he'd be a fool to do so (v. 6). Still he fought with temptation to put himself on a pedestal, and for this reason he received a hardship—his notorious "thorn in the flesh"—to discipline him.

> And lest I should be exalted above measure through the abundance of the revelations, there was given to me a thorn in the flesh, the messenger of Satan to buffet me, lest I should be exalted above measure.
>
> —2 CORINTHIANS 12:7

Much speculation about this "thorn in the flesh," almost to the point of fantasizing, circulates from pastors and Bible teachers. Some insist that it was a sickness or perhaps dim eyesight. But was it?

No. Read his words again. His thorn was a worker for Satan, a messenger to buffet him. It was a disciplinary measure, allowed by God, to keep Paul from boasting and exalting himself. This "messenger" caused the very infirmities and hardships Paul just related. He never mentioned one physical illness.

However, let's not stop short in this exploration. We must not leave until we are positive of the meaning of Paul's thorn in the flesh, so come with me to dig deeper beneath the surface.

Although we've searched translations of both Greek and Hebrew on many subjects in our travels, this excursion requires a bit more excavation. But never fear. Grab your shovel. Together we can do it.

QUITE OFTEN READING different versions of scripture can shed insight. The Amplified Bible is especially beneficial because it defines many words according to their Greek or Hebrew meanings. Let's check it out as we begin our probe:

> And to keep me from being puffed up and too much elated by the exceeding greatness (preeminence) of these revelations, there was given me a thorn (a splinter) in the flesh, a messenger of Satan, to rack and buffet and harass me, to keep me from being excessively exalted.
>
> —2 CORINTHIANS 12:7, AMP

This reads simple enough. Why did God allow this messenger of Satan? To keep Paul from being puffed up about his revelations from God and over-exalting himself. What did the messenger do? Make him sick or give him a physical handicap? No! He came to "rack and buffet and harass." In other words, he beat him up.

Paul himself identifies his "thorn" as "the messenger of Satan sent to buffet me." *Messenger* translates as "angel."[13] The word *buffet* means to rap with fist and comes from a Greek word defined as "to curtail, to chastise or reserve for infliction."[14] Digging deeper we find that in this particular passage *buffet* expresses "to mistreat."[15]

This should clear up any misunderstanding of Paul's afflicting thorn, giving us an undeniable picture of his types of mistreatments and agreeing with his own account of his adversities—beaten, stoned, shipwrecked, robbed, weary, hungry, thirsty, cold, and naked. From day to day Paul lived in relentless perils that often led him to the point of death. After stoning him, the people dragged Paul's unconscious body outside the city, leaving him for dead (Acts 14:19). Do you suppose it may have been during this ordeal that God lifted him into paradise?

Paul's list of perils, his revelation of paradise, and his "thorn in the flesh" are all a prelude to his declaration to boast only in his weakness and thereby magnify God's strength. Nothing indicates sickness. Think about it—do any of the afflictions he relates sound like some disease God refused to heal, as some sermons have led many to believe?

I think not. In this discourse Paul does not describe sickness but only types of dangers and hardships that he faced from the unremitting harassment of Satan's messenger. This "thorn," though sent by Satan, was allowed by God for two good reasons. It disciplined Paul and kept him turning to God for help instead of being "exalted above measure" and bragging of his grand experiences and achievements.

Did Paul want afflictions? Of course not. Paul was as human as we are. And just as we would do in the same situation, Paul cried out to God for relief from such dreadful abuse. He begs to have this buffeting angel, his painful "thorn in the flesh" removed: "Concerning this thing I pleaded with the Lord three times that it might depart from me" (2 Cor. 12:8, NKJV).

Yes, God could have removed all hardships. But a much greater Paul developed from the discipline caused by his hounding angel and in the wisdom of God's answer, which kept him ever dependent on God's awesome power: "My grace is sufficient for you, for My strength is made perfect in weakness" (v. 9, NKJV).

What promises this statement holds. The Amplified Bible reads, "My grace (My favor and loving-kindness and mercy) is enough for you [suffi-cient against any danger and enables you to bear the trouble manfully]; for My strength and power are made perfect (fulfilled and completed) and show themselves most effective in [your] weakness."

When Paul says, "My strength is made perfect in weakness," the word *weakness* is a precise reference to the Adamic sin.[16] This further verifies that the weakness Paul endured had nothing to do with sickness. Consider this—was Adam's sin because of sickness? Of course not. It was because of human weakness to give into temptation.

The exact Greek word for *weakness* in this text also appears in 2 Corinthi-ans 13:4, which says of Christ, "For though He was crucified in weakness, yet He goes on living by the power of God. And though we too are weak in Him [as He was humanly weak], yet in dealing with you [we shall show ourselves] alive and strong in [fellowship with] Him by the power of God" (AMP). According to *Vine's Complete Expository Dictionary*, weakness in this passage "is said in respect of the physical suffering to which Christ volun-tarily submitted in giving Himself up to the death of the cross."[17]

Was Christ crucified because He was sick? No, of course not. As far as we know, in His sinless state He never suffered illness during His life on Earth. Yet His human body consisted of the same weak, mortal flesh as all humans. Otherwise He wouldn't have been able to die at all. Because of bodily human weakness, He suffered physical pain and death from injuries sustained at His crucifixion like any earthly creature.

Paul's weakness was not sickness and disease, but mortal weakness. He was unable to conquer Satan's messenger by his own mere human strength, and this kept him humble, realizing he must depend on the sufficient grace of God. What triumphant growth Paul showed from this discipline. What glory his life gave to God.

This is such comforting news for us. What a relief when we understand that God isn't telling Paul He won't heal him from sickness and disease. Instead He is saying that because of the gift of His grace—He, Almighty Jehovah, can come upon any scene whenever Paul needs Him with divine delivering power. This same grace abides for you and me today!

No wonder Paul immediately proclaims, "Therefore most gladly I will rather boast in my infirmities, that the power of Christ may rest upon me. Therefore I take pleasure in infirmities, in reproaches, in needs, in persecu-tions, in distresses, for Christ's sake. For when I am weak, then I am strong" (2 Cor. 12:9–10, NKJV).

Oh, the power of God's grace! Oh, the need of His discipline!

It is no wonder that Paul—educated in the best of schools, taught by the highest esteemed scholars, called to repentance in such a dramatic way on the road to Damascus, anointed to carry the gospel to the Gentiles, and shown the glories of Paradise—harbored overwhelming urges to boast of his own credibility. Only because of the bitter judgment of the "thorn," a disciplinary measure permitted by the One knowing all hearts, did Paul stay in right standing with Him. Without question the greatest of all his revelations were his acknowledgment of his own meager status as a human being and his reliance on the wonder-working strength of divine grace.

The pain Paul endured produced a humble, consecrated man who conceded hopelessness on his own and received the divine Authority as his lifeline. By his perseverance he demonstrated his undying determination and commitment to spread the gospel. He trusted God despite all obstacles, knowing that He remained constantly by his side with His sufficient grace so strong, available, and able to assist whenever havoc arose.

And Paul's constant confession of triumph by God's strength in spite of the buffeting reveals the supernatural power of Yahweh's sufficient grace, the amazing grace he had to depend upon. "I have learned, in whatever state I'm in, therewith to be content" Paul declared in Philippians 4:11. Of God he boasted, "I can do all things through Christ who strengthens me" (v. 13, NKJV).

How wonderful to experience the amazing grace of God to such an extent. Although it was so hard for Paul to bear the thorn, it was also so rewarding.

FOLLOW NOW AS we converge upon an era many centuries before our time, around the year A.D. 67 or 68.

Oh dear, where are we headed?

An eerie feeling overtakes us as we grope down a narrow stone corridor that is dimly lit by blackened lamps of oil. As we fumble downward into the earth, a gagging stench of human waste and rancid body odors invades our nostrils. Dampness chills us to the bone.

Is this some kind of wretched cave?

As the passageway levels into a flat and wider murky area we realize we're standing in the sludge of a cold, dark Roman dungeon, a jail of horror where offenders await Nero's execution.

The rustling of parchment draws our attention to a tiny cubicle. When our eyes adjust to the darkness, we make out the shadow of a prisoner seated in the corner and leaning forward under the faint flickering light. Bound by heavy chains to a filthy wall, this famished and tiny figure of a man comes into view.

Who can this poor person be? We surmise his age as somewhere around sixty, though in such gaunt condition he could pass for much, much older.

In wonder we peer at him. Seemingly oblivious to his vile surroundings, he appears excited as his bony hand glides over a scroll spread across his lap. With great vigor and intensity he writes.

Suddenly we sense an overwhelming power from the Holy Spirit vibrating from his pen. We fall upon our knees. Uncaring that the damp mire with its stench closes in around us, our bodies tremble at the presence of Almighty God. Amazed we stare and listen as this frail being starts quoting mightily from his manuscript.

How inspired are his writings! How elegant his dialect. How can one so debilitated in body be so strong in voice?

"To Timothy, my dearly beloved son. Grace, mercy, and peace from God the Father and Christ Jesus our Lord..."[18]

Oh, do you recognize the words? Can it be? Oh, yes, it is! The apostle Paul!

In overwhelming compassion our faces burn with tears. Captivated by his divine inspiration as he continues with great force from his anointed script, we absorb with tender ears a heartrending letter of instruction and encouragement to his young friend Timothy.

How wholeheartedly Paul loves him. Again he addresses him as "my son" while he pours out his heart in edifying words of guidance. "Stir up the gift of God which is in you...be a partaker of the afflictions of the gospel according to the power of God...hold fast the strong words you have heard of me in faith and love of Christ Jesus...be strong in the grace that is in Christ Jesus...endure hardness as a good soldier of Jesus Christ...study to show yourself approved unto God...follow righteousness, faith, charity, peace...be watchful in all things, endure afflictions and fulfill your ministry of an evangelist."

Paul realizes his earthly days are drawing near an end. "The time of my departure is at hand," he says, "I have fought a good fight. I have finished the race. I have kept my faith. Finally there is laid up for me the crown of righteousness—which the Lord, the righteous Judge, will give me on that Day. And not to me only, but also to all who love His appearing."

Through blurred vision we watch the stamina of this emancipated human being so filled with the Holy Ghost. We know his strength can only be possible by God's sustaining grace. In awe we feed upon his every word.

With courage his voice rings on, "The Lord stood with me and strengthened me so His message could be preached fully through me, and so all Gentiles might hear. I was delivered out of the lion's mouth. And the Lord will deliver me from every evil work and preserve me for His heavenly kingdom. To Him be the glory forever and ever!"

In closing, Paul expresses to Timothy his care and concern for other friends and "all the brethren." Our souls ache in hearing his voice fade away with this final note, "The Lord Jesus Christ be with your spirit. Grace be with you. Amen."

So ends this precious letter to Timothy—the last recorded words penned by the hand of the apostle Paul before his martyrdom. Very soon now Paul will be beheaded for his faith.

How well Paul knew the ever-sustaining power of God's sufficient grace. All the hardship, affliction, perils, and human weakness he encountered could not smother his burning passion to preach Jesus Christ. No amount of buffeting by Satan's messenger could even begin to quench the flaming burden he carried for the gospel, the church, and "all the brethren."

Although Paul's last letter was written to Timothy many centuries ago, it applies for us today. As Christians we too share the honor of being his brethren. And just as it did for the apostle Paul, the same abiding grace of God abounds for us today.

What faith blossomed in Paul. What strength the discipline of infirmities carved into his life as through each whittle of the Carver's knife he recognized God's greatness and learned to depend upon His sufficient grace. With every chip that fell Paul developed divine temperament and awe-inspiring faith. His afflictions and persecutions only produced greater loyalty and determination to live for Christ and boast of God's delivering power. By accepting the discipline of the Judge of Righteousness, beauty is chiseled out of adversity.

James, quite possibly the brother of Jesus, challenges us to count it all joy when we face various trials. In doing so we build genuine faith. We mature in patience and endurance. We develop knowledge of our need to depend on God, learning to seek His wisdom, efficiency, and strength. Listen now to these words of James:

> Dear brothers, is your life full of difficulties and temptations? Then be happy, for when the way is rough, your patience has a chance to grow. So let it grow, and don't try to squirm out of your problems. For when your patience is finally in full bloom, then you will be ready for anything, strong in character, full and complete.
>
> —JAMES 1:2–4, TLB

Do you see Yahweh's purpose to produce through divine discipline His power and qualities in our lives? He's carving warriors from hardwood, not wimps of soft mush. He's developing warriors to stand for Him regardless of the situation or the cost, warriors destined by Him to conquer corruption—to stand at the end of the Great Tribulation as an undefeatable army led by the triumphant King of kings and Lord of lords.

> I saw heaven standing open and there before me was a white horse, whose rider is called Faithful and True. With justice he judges and makes war.... He is dressed in a robe dipped in blood, and his name is the Word of God. The armies of heaven were following him, riding on white horses and dressed in fine linen, white and clean.... Then I saw the beast and the kings of the earth and their armies gathered together to make war against the rider on the horse and his army. But the beast was captured, and with him the false prophet...
>
> —REVELATION 19:11, 13–14, 19–20, NIV

Yes, Yahweh must exercise His role as Judge of Righteousness with divine discipline in order to produce in mankind a glorious work of art, polished and perfected by His sufficient grace. Day by day and chip by chip, He whittles until that final time, when with unconquerable faith and character we accompany Him as mighty soldiers unafraid, washed by His blood, carved into the very likeness of His image.

How wonderful that His discipline builds champion character and develops staunch faith. But wait. There's more. His discipline reveals His love as our Father.

> My son, do not make light of the Lord's discipline, and do not lose heart when he rebukes you, because the Lord disciplines those he loves, and he punishes everyone he accepts as a son. Endure hardship as discipline; God is treating you as sons. For what son is not disciplined by his father?
>
> —HEBREWS 12:5–7, NIV

How could a parent truly love his children without proper penalties to teach, direct, and inspire them? By the same token, how could God be a Father of love without doing the same?

> If you are not disciplined (and everyone undergoes discipline), then you are illegitimate children and not true sons.... Our fathers disciplined us for a little while as they thought best; but God disciplines us for our good, that we may share in his holiness. No discipline seems

pleasant at the time, but painful. Later on, however, it produces a harvest of righteousness and peace for those who have been trained by it.
—HEBREWS 12:8, 10–11, NIV

Reward comes as we grow in His discipline. When we accept the training
of the Judge of Righteousness, we realize the wonders of His grace just as
Paul did.

Teach me, Yahweh, your ways, that I may not stray from your loyalty;
let my heart's aim be to fear your name.
—PSALM 86:11, NJB

Chapter 4

El Shaddai, El Elyon, Elohim, and Adonai

O H, THE VASTNESS of the name Yahweh. Such value, such insight, such dimension it brings to light. How unfortunate that so few have knowledge of the endless height, depth, length, and breadth of God displayed in the magnitude of this name.

> Let them praise the name of Yahweh, for his name alone is sublime, his splendour transcends earth and heaven.
>
> —PSALM 148:13, NJB

Had it not been substituted in Scripture by Adonai and written as "LORD," the name Yahweh would appear in the Bible nearly seven thousand times, far more than any other name or title used of God. This fact stabs my heart. The word *lord* can indicate the rank of any man, but Yahweh is the sacred name specifying the one eternal, true, and living Deity in His totality.

As we've explored His nature as the Judge of Righteousness we've seen that Yahweh—even in all His majesty and splendor, total power and might, supremacy and sovereignty, purity and righteousness—is a God of individual care. He is a parent who wants to build character in His children, a Father of unconditional, faithful, and enduring love.

As tenderly as a father treats his children, so Yahweh treats those who fear him.

—Psalm 103:13, njb

Even at the height of our rebellion, despite our shortcomings and failures, God walks beside us. Forgiveness for even the most horrific sin is only a heart's cry away. Yahweh's loving arms are always open.

Although He is deeply grieved by man's rejection, He loves regardless. In its perfection His love bonds so much stronger and reaches far beyond the most profound feelings of any earthly parent. The anguish we suffer for a wayward child can rip our insides into shreds. Yet in comparison to His love, our ability to love falls by the wayside. Still our human love must be patterned after His—unconditional, faithful, and enduring—or it really isn't love at all.

As we resume our journey, I take you now into another private place tucked deep inside my heart.

"Your son has had a wreck!" A young hysterical voice shrieked over the phone.

With no knowledge of our teenager's condition, my husband, Jim, and I bolted out of the house and raced to the scene in our pickup truck. As we neared a horseshoe curve, blue lights cut circles in the black sky and whipped across silhouettes of a gathered crowd.

I strained my eyes to take it in. *Oh, no!* In the middle of the road I spotted our station wagon upside down. A large patrolman stooped beside it.

"Look! There's our car!" I exclaimed. "But where is our son?"

"There he is!" my husband shouted with relief, "See? Standing beside the state trooper."

"Yes, yes! Oh, thank You, God!" A river of gratitude surged through me. Leaping from the truck we both dashed to his side.

"Are you hurt?" I reached out to his quivering body. To my dismay he reeked of beer. "You've been drinking!"

The officer straightened up. In his hand he gripped an empty beer can he had salvaged from the wreckage. With disgust he crumpled it just inches from our boy's terrified eyes. Trying to hold back tears, I clamped my lower lip between my teeth as he spoke.

"I know where you got this. I know who's selling it to you kids." He named the place and the man who sold it. Our son nodded.

"Why don't you stop the guy?" I asked.

"Getting someone to have the guts to turn him in ... finding one person who's not afraid to testify against him ..." The officer just shook his head. "I know that beer he's sold to minors is responsible for at least one death. But this man's a big name. Nobody will take a stand against him."

Like a bomb inside my head I remembered my vow to God. I dropped my eyes. *What should we do?* I peered up into my husband's face. He knew the story of Mr. Bower, and he saw into my heart.

I swallowed hard. "I have no choice," I said to him.

"We'll do it. We'll take a stand," my husband said. We turned to our son, who nodded in agreement.

And we did. To ban that man from selling beer to minors we acted on everything the patrolman advised. As parents we signed papers that very night. Later our son testified in court. The judge fined the guilty man and pulled his license. Although for years to follow he still snarled about the litigation, God took care of every repercussion that might have come our way.

This couldn't bring back Mr. Bower. It couldn't bring back the nine-year-old boy he killed. But perhaps it saved other lives. I want to think it did.

Yet oh, such woe lurked ahead. If anyone had said to me, "This is only the beginning of heartbreak with your son," I would have exclaimed, "That's not so!"

I would have thought their words insane, utterly crazy. But years of pain were yet to surface. My firstborn, the baby I claimed for God while I sang lullabies and dreamed of his future, my Boy Scout who made straight As in school—went from alcohol to drug addiction, even crack cocaine.

Oh, the venom of the serpent. Not only do his fangs sink poison into the victim of his deception, but they also puncture without mercy into hearts of those who love...and pray...and wait.

As hard as it may be, we are also obligated, in the likeness of our Father, to discipline our children and point them to the road of righteousness. We do this by issuing penalties in spite of their arguing or rebellion. It is imperative that we never ignore their evil or compromise with their sin. We must never make excuses for their wrongdoings, but we must let them learn that they must accept responsibility, paying the consequences for their own actions. Our challenge is to always seek God's direction in reprimanding and balance it with unwavering love that is patterned after His.

> Alleluia! Give thanks to Yahweh for he is good, for his faithful love endures for ever.
>
> —Psalm 136:1, njb

Yahweh promised this faithful love to Israel when He said:

Yea, I have loved thee with an everlasting love: therefore with loving-kindness have I drawn thee.

—JEREMIAH 31:3

Jesus spoke of this enduring love with a burdened soul when He cried out to the holy city that mistreated Him so terribly:

O Jerusalem, Jerusalem, the one who kills the prophets and stones those who are sent to her! How often I wanted to gather your children together, as a hen gathers her chicks under her wings, but you were not willing!

—MATTHEW 23:37, NKJV

In the phrase "as a hen gathers her chicks under her wings" we see the quality of *El Shaddai*, another name used for God.

Why does Yahweh use different names?

Sometimes God chooses names other than Yahweh (Himself in fullness) to emphasize special distinctions of His personality. As creatures patterned in His image, let's look at ourselves for help in understanding this.

In spite of being given legal identification (usually a first, middle, and last name) at birth, people fill many roles that require extra titles. For instance, the same man can be called a "teacher" by his students or a "deacon" at his church. His wife refers to him as her "husband" and calls him "honey." He's known as "father" to his children, and they call him "daddy." His parents know him as their "son." Some friends use his first name, others a nickname. Those less acquainted acknowledge him by his last name preceded by "Mr." And the list goes on—"brother," "uncle," "granddaddy," "neighbor."

While this one man fulfills the roles of all these names and titles, everyone does not know him in each capacity. Nor is it necessary, even though a person may know him well, to recognize him in all his facets. And depending on the title used, he deals with people in various ways.

How much more unlimited are the attributes of an infinite God! His many names and titles greatly broaden our perspective of His indescribable depth. From our knowledge of Him as Yahweh we may think we know Him well, but we'll soon find that to truly know Him is unending. Now as we wander farther on our path of names to discover God's various titles, we start with *El Shaddai*.

WHO IS EL Shaddai? As the One who is so all-sufficient, He is more than enough. *El* reveals almightiness. *Shaddai* shows unlimited bountifulness, but more than this it exposes the tenderness of God's nurturing care in its root word *shad*, which by its meaning "breast" presents God as "the Breasted One," "the Pourer or Shedder-forth."[1] It reveals a most secure and satisfying way to experience Him in His powerful abundance.

In the Old Testament this name is written as "Almighty." Why? Perhaps Andrew Jukes explains it best:

> Mothers at least will understand it. A babe is crying,—restless. Nothing can quiet it. Yes: the breast can. A babe is pining,—starving. Its life is going out. It cannot take man's proper food: it will die. No: the breast can give it fresh life, and nourish it. By her breast the mother has almost infinite power over the child...[2]

Abraham, Isaac, and Jacob lived in the loving provisions of El Shaddai:

> God spoke to Moses and said to him, "I am Yahweh. To Abraham, Isaac and Jacob I appeared as El Shaddai, but I did not make my name Yahweh known to them."
>
> —Exodus 6:2–3, NJB

The word *known* in this context does not mean that Abraham, Isaac, and Jacob had no awareness of God's name Yahweh. In scriptures concerning them the name is used often. In Genesis 15:7 (NJB) God Himself tells Abraham, "I am Yahweh." However, as He began fulfilling His covenant of promise with his faithful servant at age ninety-nine:

> Yahweh appeared to him and said, "I am El Shaddai."
>
> —Genesis 17:1, NJB

The word *known* conveys a close, intimate observation and deep experience with Yahweh as God in total personality. Though God never ceases in His complete integrity as Yahweh, He deemed it unnecessary to exercise His every aspect with Abraham, Isaac, or Jacob. Instead He dealt with them in the nurturing care and all-sufficiency of the Almighty, El Shaddai.

On the other hand, in raising up Moses to deliver Abraham's seed from slavery, Yahweh revealed His total Being. Yahweh's eternal nature surfaced as He began fulfilling the covenant He made with Abraham so many years before by their deliverance. In His punishment of the Egyptians and later using strict discipline with His chosen, they experienced Yahweh as the Righteous Judge. At Mount Sinai they witnessed the fullness of Yahweh's *Shekinah* glory. Yahweh's independent self-existence was demonstrated by

His provisions in the desert. The tabernacle displayed Yahweh's absolute holiness.

What a blessing to abide in the care of El Shaddai as Abraham, Isaac, and Jacob did. Again, the words of Andrew Jukes:

> "Jehovah" bears a sword. But "El Shaddai," the "Almighty," here revealed to Abram, is not the "sworded" God. His Almightiness is of the breast, that is, of bountiful, self-sacrificing love, giving and pouring itself out for others. Therefore He can quiet the restless, as the breast quiets the child: therefore He can nourish and strengthen, as the breast nourishes.[3]

What picture is more heartwarming than that of a mother as she cuddles her baby against her breast? Words cannot describe the cherished affection, growing adoration, and richness of sharing life-sustaining nourishment. At every feeding, mother and child bond in deeper unity with a new wave of immeasurable attachment.

This picture reveals the deep, loving nature of our God. In human weakness a mother's care may fail, her heart forget, the bonds of love be severed. However, we have a God who never leaves His children or forsakes them.

> Can a mother forget the baby at her breast and have no compassion on the child she has bore? Though she may forget, I will not forget you!
> —ISAIAH 49:15, NIV

Almighty El Shaddai longs to cuddle His own, to cradle us in His arms. In affectionate greatness His nature yearns not just to walk by our side, but to lift us up and nestle us into His abundant stability and safety. He is more than enough to meet our needs—fostering, delivering, doting, and protecting us.

ABIDING A LITTLE longer in the virtues of El Shaddai we find this name intertwined with other names of God in an inspiring psalm composed by one who certainly knew the virtues of God. Many believe it to be words from the heart of Moses. I like to think so, too.

> He who dwells in the secret place of the Most High shall abide under the shadow of the Almighty. I will say of the LORD, "He is my refuge and my fortress; my God, in Him I will trust." Surely He shall deliver you from the snare of the fowler and from the perilous pestilence.

He shall cover you with His feathers, and under His wings you shall take refuge.

—Psalm 91:1–4, NKJV

Oh, the richness of this message!

In the original script it conveys even greater inspiration. We miss so much by not having the actual names printed in today's versions, for buried within these few verses hide four names of God. *El Elyon* is translated as "Most High," *El Shaddai* as "Almighty," *Yahweh* as "the Lord," and *Elohim* as "God."

Like a garden of fragrant flowers, the combination of these names glows in beauty, giving us heart-stirring awareness of the endless wonder of our Maker. The letters *El* found in many of names of God define a Deity of power and might, able to meet any need. He is capable of overturning natural impossibilities with supernatural miracles.

First, the psalm introduces El Elyon, "the Most High"—"He who dwells in the secret place of the Most High." This name discloses a most-powerful, supreme, and sovereign ruler. He is the towering commander, controller above all, the divine watchman over every puff of air, every particle of dust, all the earth, the surrounding universe, countless stars, and infinite galaxies. He is the Most High Overseer of all creatures and all existence.

This reveals the splendor and majesty of El Elyon. He, the Most High, finds pleasure in abiding with us, His human creatures, in *His* secret place, His special hideaway inside each being. That intimate spot belongs to Him alone, and it is a private room that we reserve for only Him. This "holy of holies," His innermost sanctuary in the temple of our hearts, is where our spirits live in precious solitude with the watchful Most High El Elyon. It is a sacred meeting place in the glory of His presence, in the marvel of His peerless position.

When we dwell with the Most High El Elyon, our spirits rise into the heavenlies to be with Jesus, our Most High Priest, "who is set on the right hand of the throne of the Majesty in the heavens" (Heb. 8:1). We find ourselves exalted by One "rich in mercy" and of "great love," who has made us alive together with Christ, who "hath raised us up together, and made us sit together in heavenly places with Christ Jesus" (Eph. 2:4–6).

Oh, what joy to fellowship with our Redeemer at the Father's throne in the chambers of the holiest of all. And no matter where we go or what we encounter, the welcome mat extends all the way from His throne into our heart, inviting us to join Him every minute of every day—to worship, to petition, to intercede, or just to visit. Oh, the wonders of our Most High.

Oh, what serenity to abide in the secret place of El Elyon.

In a shopping mall you can dwell with Him in His secret place. You can abide there in the middle of a parade, in a crowded stadium, in the beauty of the woods, in the privacy of your home, or in a dark and dismal alley. Everywhere at any time you can dwell with Him in His secret place. No other person knows the closeness that you share together in its solitude.

Oh, the blessings of His secret place! How deeply this supreme and sovereign God of all loves His human beings!

We receive blessings without measure by acknowledging God as El Elyon, our Most High God, and dwell (constantly abide) in the intimacy of His secret place. It stations us under the boundless care of the all-sufficient, ever-abundant, powerful, and nurturing El Shaddai. There we "remain stable and fixed under the shadow of the Almighty" [Whose power no foe can withstand]" (Ps. 91:1, AMP).

What a picture! El Shaddai compassionately and completely overshadows us with almighty ability and tender abundance. And as long as we continue dwelling in the secret place of El Elyon, we remain under the provisions of El Shaddai's marvelous shadow. Oh, the hovering comfort of El Shaddai. Like a devoted mother who pampers her child, He covers and protects.

This psalm bestows more blessings as we move farther in our study of this Most High and Almighty One in His complete essence of Yahweh. Honoring Him by His holy, sacred name—"I will say of the LORD" (v. 2)—gives recognition to the always existing One in His entirety. Declaring Yahweh as our "refuge" (our point of safety) and our "fortress" (our wall of protection), the palmist calls Him "my God," which translates as "Elohim."

This name, *Elohim*, distinguishes God as the divine Creator, powerful Triune Being, and eternal covenant-maker. Soon we'll visit Him in depth.

The unconquerable strength of the Almighty surfaces again in the promise, "For [then] He will deliver you from the snare of the fowler and from the deadly pestilence" (Ps. 91:3, AMP).

Although the name *El Shaddai* doesn't appear again in this text, how well it portrays the Almighty who reacts with the same protectiveness as a mother if someone attacks her children. The Almighty, whom no foe can withstand, stands ever ready to deliver His children "from the snare of the fowler" (Satan's traps of deception) and "from the noisome pestilence" (deadly, life-threatening disease and epidemics).

Then in verse 4 we identify El Shaddai's unlimited tenderness and nurturing as He covers those who trust in Him with His feathers, snuggling them safely beneath His wings. He shelters them like a mother hen with her chicks.

Travel with me now to the farming community where I grew up, where as a child I became familiar with the doting hen. Whenever I see farmers burning harvested wheat fields in preparation to sow another crop this story always pops into my memory.

Smoke rises to the sky in a blinding screen while stubbles of wheat crackle in the flames. As the farmer stands by to watch the direction of the fire, he hears his wife calling. "Have you seen our mama hen anywhere? She and all her babies are missing!"

Oh, no! they realize *the chickens must be trapped in the blazing field!*

In the evening when the fire dies down, the farmer and his wife go out to the smoldering land. Step by step, row by row they scan each inch together.

"Peep, peep, peep," comes the faintest cry. *Little chicks? If so, where can they be?*

The farmer spies a blackened heap. *Oh no, his hen!* With a sigh he lifts her lifeless body. Six chicks, all of them unharmed, scurry from underneath her wings. These baby chicks, trusting her sustaining power, received life in the midst of death.[4]

Trust in God. Dwell in the secret place of El Elyon, where life awaits under the shadow of El Shaddai. He longs to shelter you beneath His wings of safety, to snuggle you in the softness of His feathers. Yes, El Shaddai, more than capable to meet any need, always cares for us with a tender heart that is as enduring as a mother's love in the midst of any trouble.

How well I know. More than a protective mother hen, He's been there for me through divorce, rejection, bad decisions, burning memories, the heartbreak of a wayward son, gnawing guilt, the death of a loved one, financial disaster, and overwhelming debt. As I have trusted His ever-ample nurturing and overcoming power, the almighty and loving El Shaddai has overshadowed me with His care, lifted me by His love, and carried me beyond it all.

He will do the same for you. If you are hungry, He's standing by to sustain you with the bread of life. If you are thirsty, He'll quench your thirst with living water. He will give you light that you may see even in the darkest hour. I know. He did it for me. Trust Him; He will do it for you.

Thank You, El Shaddai.

ABRAHAM LIVED IN the blessings of El Shaddai, never having to experience the judgments and bare necessities his descendants did centuries later in the wilderness. Why? The reason is that he not only trusted God completely, but he also made Him his Adonai. This is the name that acknowledges God as Master, owner, and Lord. Often Abraham addressed Him by this name.

Adonai speaks of total submission to God, the surrender of ourselves, releasing our will to Him. Every other name of God denotes His obligation of covenant relationship with man, His commitment to us. The name Adonai stands alone in our vow of commitment to Him.

In the original Hebrew text of the Old Testament the name Adonai appears more than three hundred times. With the Jewish emphasis on the meanings of names, each time they spoke or read "Adonai," they were surely reminded of the dedication due to their God. Therefore, in their compulsion to substitute Adonai for the sacred name Yahweh, it would seem a wise choice. However commitment must come, not from vainly spoken words, but from the heart:

> And they remembered that God was their rock, and the high God their redeemer. Nevertheless they did flatter him with their mouth, and they lied unto him with their tongues. For their heart was not right with him, neither were they steadfast in his covenant.
>
> —PSALM 78:35–37

Even today with the Holy Spirit to freely guide our human spirits, we see this same complacency and shallow commitment among many professing Christians. Prayers are repeated, scriptures quoted, hymns sung, and sermons heard without any stirring of the heart. Many churches have become little more than social clubs. What a lukewarm spirit!

We sing, "I surrender all." But do we? God longs for our wills in obedience and our hearts in worship. With sincere dedication, total submission, and true reverence, Yahweh in His entirety should be our Adonai. Not only does He yearn to be the flaming desire of our hearts as Master, owner and Lord—but He also requires it.

> So then because thou art lukewarm, and neither cold nor hot, I will spue thee out of my mouth.
>
> —REVELATION 3:16

With burning faith, obedience, and a desire to please Yahweh, Abraham claimed Him as Adonai, and Yahweh dealt with him in His virtues as the powerful, bountiful, and nurturing El Shaddai. Centuries passed until Moses' day when God deemed it necessary to again reckon with man in His full spectrum of Yahweh—the time had arrived to proceed with His plan of redemption and begin fulfilling His covenant of promise. However, because the people of Israel failed to yield their hearts to Him as Adonai, they never knew the all-sufficient and abundant sweetness of El Shaddai that Abraham enjoyed.

In the character of Elohim God spoke to Moses when He said, "I am Yahweh. To Abraham, Isaac and Jacob I appeared as El Shaddai, but I did not make my name Yahweh known to them." As Elohim He added, "I also made my covenant with them to give them the land of Canaan" (Exod. 6:2–4, NJB).

ELOHIM—THE COVENANT MAKER, the Creator, the Triune God-head. Investigating this name requires us to whiz many years back into time, ages before Moses and the Jewish nation, even thousands of years before Abraham and the covenant of promise, preceding the days of Noah.

For an instant we spot his ark upon the waves. Oh, can we stop? No, but we'll return for a visit later to witness how Noah, trusting Yahweh in fullness, also experienced the glory of Elohim to the utmost.

We pause briefly over Eden. Before Adam and Eve encountered the judgment of Yahweh, they knew only the glory of Elohim as the Creator who designed paradise and fashioned them in such splendor and the covenant maker who presented them with the contract of dominion over all the earth.

Oh, why can't we tarry here awhile?

Very soon we'll come back, but we can't stay now. We must keep going deeper into the past, until at last ...

Elohim! From spaceless infinity and timeless eons long before the age of man, in the very first sentence of His Holy Word the name appears. "In the beginning God (Elohim) ..." (Gen. 1:1).

Elohim! A glorious masterwork of proficiency, expertise, and versatility unfolds with this name. It's the name that holds the amazement of creation, that knits our spirits to His by His priceless promises and treasures of commitment. It leads us into the wonders of His being, giving us a view of His absolute oneness, yet three in personality.

What grandeur unveils when we explore the richness of this name. As we continue His Trinity sparkles all along our path like mystifying diamonds.

Just as plural words end with "s" in the English language, plural words in Hebrew end with "im." For instance, *cherubim* is the plural for *cherub.* The word *Elohim,* a plural noun, paints a most intriguing portrait of God in plural personality.

But stop. We must understand that Eloh in plurality as Elohim doesn't indicate more than one God. Remember *El* means a deity of power. The name Eloh plus "im" signifies a multiplication in the power of the living God as our Creator. And the "im" also multiplies—or to use a better word, *intensifies*—the oneness of our Creator as by the name Elohim He displays the plurality of His being and the trinity of His nature.

Behold now the workings of Elohim as He speaks in Triune Deity using plural pronouns, "Let us make man in our image, after our likeness" (Gen. 1:26).

Draw near as we ponder this intricate picture of Elohim. Together with probing minds and searching hearts let's inspect the multi-personality, power, promises, and plans of Elohim as we enter the glory of Creation. In the pages of the Hebrew Bible, just as in most instances *LORD* translates to "Yahweh," and *God* translates to "Elohim."

> In the beginning God [Elohim] created the heaven and the earth. And the earth was without form, and void; and darkness was upon the face of the deep. And the Spirit of God [Elohim] moved upon the face of the waters.
>
> —GENESIS 1:1–2

Immediately the Holy Spirit (often spoken of as Third Person of the Trinity) displays the power of Elohim. What a grand illustration of His magnificence as He sweeps His might over the dark formless void of Earth.

Next the Word takes center pose. To the darkness the Word of Elohim commands, "Let there be light." Light appears! With the overpowering authority of His Word Elohim has only to speak and the solar system forms in obedience.

> Through faith we understand that the worlds were framed by the word of God.
>
> —HEBREWS 11:3

The Word of God is a portrayal of Jesus—"In the beginning was the Word, and the Word was with God, and the Word was God....And the Word was made flesh, and dwelt among us" (John 1:1, 14).

Searching deeper into the design of Creation we bring to light the remaining personality of Elohim, nestled in the sacred name of Yahweh:

> And the LORD God [translates Yahweh-Elohim] formed man...
>
> —GENESIS 2:7

With this reference to Yahweh we see the completed masterpiece of the Trinity. With glowing insight the psalmist saw it, too.

> By the word of the LORD were the heavens made; and all the host of them by the breath of his mouth.
>
> —PSALM 33:6

In both Hebrew and Greek the word for *spirit* is the same word used for *breath, air,* and *wind.* Thus, this verse, like an artist's stroke, profiles the image of the divine Trinity at Creation: The "word" is Jesus; the "LORD" is Yahweh; the "breath of God" is the Holy Spirit.

Why would the personality of the Godhead whom we identify as Father be represented by the fullness of the name Yahweh? Because the Father encompasses all.

Once more we turn to an analogy of ourselves for clarity. Ideally household operation stems from the father. He produces life in his son. As an extension, an express image, of the father the son carries on this life. In proper relationship the son abides according to will of his father and their spirits knit together. The oneness of spirit working in them results in lifelikeness, achieving a special unity of love and devotion unlike any other.

In God we see the will of the Father, carried out by His Son. Jesus says:

> For I have come down from heaven, not to do My own will, but the will of Him who sent Me.
>
> —JOHN 6:38, NKJV

The Son, whose "name is called The Word of God" (Rev. 19:13), is the brightness of the Father's glory, the express image of His person (Heb. 1:3). And all is made evident in our hearts by His Spirit.

> No man can say that Jesus is the Lord, but by the Holy Ghost.
>
> —1 CORINTHIANS 12:3

Within every person the working of the God's Spirit is mandatory in order to fulfill the purpose of His Word and to accomplish His will. Although man first must hear the Word and yield to the will of God, success comes by the function of the Spirit. Throughout the Bible it was through this "third Person" of the Trinity that men attained supernatural feats:

> But the Spirit of the LORD came upon Gideon...
>
> —JUDGES 6:34, NKJV

And the Spirit of the LORD came mightily upon him [Samson]...

—JUDGES 14:6, NKJV

Samuel took the horn of oil and anointed him [David]...and the Spirit of the LORD came upon David from that day forward.

—1 SAMUEL 16:13, NKJV

Then Peter, filled with the Holy Spirit...

—ACTS 4:8, NKJV

But he [Stephen], being full of the Holy Spirit...

—ACTS 7:55, NKJV

...Paul, filled with the Holy Spirit...

—ACTS 13:9, NKJV

Before beginning His ministry Jesus received the anointing of the Spirit (Matt. 3:16). On the night of His betrayal Jesus said, "But the Helper, the Holy Spirit, whom the Father will send in My name, He will teach you all things, and bring to your remembrance all things that I said to you" (John 14:26, NKJV). All believers are told to be filled with the Spirit. (See Ephesians 5:18.)

So now we see Elohim as three-in-one: *Will* (Yahweh, Father), which encompasses all, *Word* (Christ, Son), and *Work* (Helper, Holy Spirit). Each with many responsibilities and specific duties but together as *one* God. Perfect unity stemming from His will, which is one with His Word and work.

For there are three that bear record in heaven, the Father, the Word, and the Holy Ghost: and these three are one.

—1 JOHN 5:7

Arise now to envision the baptism of Jesus. Before our eyes the Trinity unfolds: the Spirit of God, the voice from heaven, the beloved Son:

And Jesus, when he was baptized, went up straightway out of the water: and, lo, the heavens were opened unto him, and he saw the Spirit of God descending like a dove, and lighting upon him: And lo a voice from heaven, saying, This is my beloved Son, in whom I am well pleased.

—MATTHEW 3:16–17

The revelation of the Trinity surfaces often in Scripture. At the Last Supper Jesus reveals the Triune Godhead as He promises, "But the Comforter, which is the *Holy Ghost*, whom the *Father* will send in *my* name, he shall teach you all things and bring all things to your remembrance, whatsoever I have said unto you" (John 14:26 emphasis added).

We see the Trinity again as moments before His ascension Jesus leaves us with these final words, "It is not for you to know times or seasons which the *Father* has put in His own authority. But you shall receive power when the *Holy Spirit* has come upon you; and you shall be witnesses to *Me* in Jerusalem, and in all Judea and Samaria, and to the end of the earth" (Acts 1:7–8, NKJV, emphasis added).

Revealing the Trinity the apostle Paul ends his letter with, "The grace of the Lord *Jesus Christ*, and the love of *God*, and the communion of the *Holy Ghost*, be with you all. Amen" (2 Cor. 13:14, emphasis added).

Except through the name Elohim we seldom see clear distinction of the Trinity in the Old Testament. However in Isaiah 63 we find reference to each characteristic: " . . . the lovingkindness of the LORD . . . He became their Savior . . . the Angel of His Presence saved them . . . they rebelled and grieved His Holy Spirit" (vv. 7–10, NKJV).

Of the Angel mentioned here the Lord declares in Exodus 23:21 (NKJV), "My name is in Him." Later in our journey we'll see why Bible scholars view this Angel as Jesus pre-incarnate.

"Holy, holy, holy! merciful and mighty," voices ring in song today, "God in three persons, blessed Trinity!"[5]

Like the word *rapture*, the actual term *Trinity* is not found in the Bible. It appears to have been coined about A.D. 200 by Tertullian.[6] Many expressions have been used to describe the threefold nature of God—magistrates, personalities, characteristics, functions, facets, conscious centers—but can we actually comprehend our one God in three Persons? Perhaps these words from *The Complete Who's Who in the Bible* best convey our thoughts:

> There are three persons but one God. Such teaching, when taken together, implies a mode of existence far removed from anything we can understand. It is for this reason that human analogies will invariably break down when talking of the Trinity.[7]

Scriptural interpretations vary. Arguments arise. Doctrines build around differing opinions. Truly the magnitude of our Creator boggles our finite minds, and His Holy Trinity may never be explained or understood to complete satisfaction. Nevertheless, perhaps by peering again into our likeness of His image, a tiny ray of light may chase away some shadows from our limited perceptions. Consider these words about our makeup from the apostle Paul:

> Now may the God of peace Himself sanctify you completely; and may your whole spirit, soul, and body be preserved blameless at the coming of our Lord Jesus Christ.
> —1 THESSALONIANS 5:23, NKJV

The Trinity of Elohim patterned mortals from Himself. Behold the trinity of mankind—spirit, soul, and body!

Our spirit, the deepest inner part of us, is like a candle that only the Spirit of God can light—"The spirit of man is the candle of the LORD, searching all the inward parts of the belly" (Prov. 20:27). It instills a spiritual nature in us, is enlightened to God, and allows us to commune with Him. It spawns our desire to praise and worship and gives us a quality that is unique to God's creation, setting us apart from any other creature of Earth.

Our soul, consisting of our mind, will, and emotions, supplies us with the ability to make decisions and sets us far above all animals in levels of intelligence and understanding. It equips us with superior faculties to converse, reason, learn, design, invent, plan, express feeling, and assert our will.

Our body is a temporary temple for the Holy Spirit, our earthen vessel, "a living sacrifice, holy, acceptable unto God" (Rom. 12:1).

HOW COULD WE ever separate the three of us? It takes all of us to function. And yet at death, the body, "our living sacrifice," separates from us—just as the perfect Living Sacrifice had to do to fulfill the plan of redemption. Imagine how hard it was for the ultimate Three-in-One to face the separation of Himself when He gave His Word in human form.

Risen from the dead, the Living Sacrifice again resides, incorruptible, at the Father's side in majesty and honor. And our body, our living sacrifice, awaits the fullness of time to also rise to incorruptibility reunited with our spirit and soul—to reside in majesty and honor at our Savior's side.

Before the foundation of the earth, Elohim, the almighty Creator, knowing that His man creatures would sin and his once glorious Lucifer would stake his claim on the world, still created us. In a purely hypothetical way, with childlike imagination, let us take a moment to explore eternity past before the time of man began.

In creative reflection Elohim, our covenant-making Creator and wondrous Three-in-One, scans a blob of cold, dead matter. It is the earth in utter darkness.

Artistic plans stir inside His being. *Let Us shine Our light upon this planet and design a wondrous garden filled with life. Plants. Animals. And human beings in Our image. By being in Our image they must have the right to choose. Living totally in Our righteousness they will have the strength needed to withstand the wicked adversary. Such perfection it will be!*

But as His all-seeing eyes sweep the ages of the future, Elohim sees perfection turn to chaos. His humankind won't stand! From the beginning they will fail, every single one. Death will reign over His precious beings. He weeps.

We must design a redemptive plan to restore them, a way of grace and mercy for their salvation. We must provide a means of cleansing them from sin to restore them into Our holy presence. Oh, how hard it will be. Once We give dominion away, We can't demand Earth back. Only the death of a sinless man can redeem it. Only spotless blood from the veins of a mortal body can ever triumph over evil. A perfect human sacrifice. How can it be done?

For a moment all is silent. Elohim as the Will, the Word, and the Work, seems to be in deep thought. Then the plan is born: God must become a man! *Can We do it? What suffering it will involve! Who of Us would commit to carry out such a painful plan?*

Without hesitation the Word comes forth. *I'll do it! In order to redeem the world, yes, I'll do it!*

Elohim grieves. *Though We'll still be one, We will have to walk in separation. As hard as it may be, the Word must be made flesh, or Our humans will be eternally doomed. As three in one We will work together.*

By My Will We'll devise the way of redemption. My Work will reveal the Spirit of truth. My Word will restore abundant life. As the Son of God He will present all three—the way, the truth, and the life. As Son of man He will become the perfect sacrifice, redeeming mankind in the threefold love of Elohim. In oneness we can do it!

Yet at the instant the Son becomes sin for man upon the cross, Our holiness will have to pull away entirely. The Son must be forsaken. Our oneness will be totally severed! Can We bear it? Yes, yes, oh yes, We must!

In an everlasting book, the Covenant of Redemption, We must transcribe this plan. This shall be a never-ending pledge to our human creatures.

By the work of His Spirit Elohim moves upon the face of the book with might and inspiration. In deep compassion and total commitment by His Word He quotes a vow of promise, grace, and mercy for its eternal pages. By

His will He orchestrates the pathway, refines each detail, and sets a perfect timetable. And so the eternal covenant for mankind, spun into motion even before the age of man, began.

Oh, the inexplicable nature of Elohim! What a covenant maker! What a Creator! What a planner! What a privilege to be created in His image!

NOW THE HOUR is here when we return to Eden. Oh, but how it's changed! Where is all the joy?

On the road ahead a warning sign glares: "Disappointment Ahead!" Hand in hand, with chests pounding, we tiptoe into the garden to face the initial judgment of mankind. For the first time the intertwining of the names *Elohim* and *Yahweh* as "Lord God" will be revealed to His human creation. We approach the sorrowful moment when Adam and Eve are tottering on the brink of confrontation with the combined natures of the covenant-making Creator Elohim and the covenant-fulfilling Yahweh, Judge of Righteousness.

Oh, no! What has happened to mankind's glory? Having eaten the forbidden fruit, Adam and Eve gape at one another in horror. No longer are they covered in the luster of Elohim. Now they look so drab and ugly. They feel so helpless—a sensation they've never known before.

What can they do? Soon Elohim will come to fellowship with them. How can they bear for Him to see them in such disgrace!

In panic they grab fig leaves, the largest they can snatch from the lush vegetation. But with every heaving breath their lungs shriek, "These can't suffice to conceal our wretched flesh!"

Yet their hands work frantically to bind them together. It's so futile, they know. But what else can they do? *Oh no, rustling in the thicket. Has Elohim arrived?* Together Adam and Eve cower behind the density of the plants. Their hearts shudder as they hear His footsteps coming nearer.

How fearful His presence seems! Can this be Elohim, their glorious Creator, who walks with them in the cool of each evening? As the words of the "Lord God" (Yahweh Elohim) fall upon their ears their bodies tremble and their spirits recoil apart with regret. They realize they can never hide from God.

"Where are you?" calls Yahweh Elohim.

In submission Adam rises, peeking out between green branches. He sobs in embarrassment and shame, "I hid in fright. I couldn't bear for You to find me naked!"

"Who revealed your nakedness?" Yahweh Elohim booms. "Did you go against My word and eat the only fruit I prohibited?"

"Yes, the woman You gave me handed it to me, and I ate it."

By Adam's side Eve slumps. How she agonizes.

Yahweh Elohim thunders to her, "How could you do such a thing?"

"The serpent. He tricked me into eating it."

Yahweh Elohim curses the serpent. Then at His announcement that someday the Seed of woman will demolish the evil one, His covenant of redemption begins its long and gruesome journey.

Our hearts erupt in anguish as Yahweh Elohim mourns the devastation His humans have released on the world by straying from His righteousness. Now stained with sin, they must leave the ecstasy of Eden.

Pain and death applaud in victory as the grieving Yahweh Elohim pronounces judgment and evicts His man and woman, supremely modeled in His image, now so frail from sin, to face a plight of toil and sweat. How heart-wrenching to give them up to Satan's bondage. Despair laughs as they blunder in the darkness on the sinful road they chose for humankind to tread. Like heavy fog, sorrow saturates the earth.

Though we turn away in tears our minds radiate in awe, realizing we have beheld the immeasurable magnitude of Yahweh Elohim. With deep reverence we stagger at the concept of this dramatic combination of His nature.

Still drenched in His magnificence we spin over sixteen hundred years from Eden to the Flood. In spending time with Noah we'll discover that the names *Yahweh* and *Elohim* not only intertwine, but they also interchange.

Calling to Noah in His creative name of Elohim, God reveals the design for the ark (Gen. 6:13–16). After the Flood, Elohim repeats to Noah and his sons the identical instructions He once spoke to Adam and Eve: "Be fruitful, and multiply, and replenish the earth" (Gen. 9:1).

But sadly, this time Elohim can't add the words "subdue it." Even the cleansing of the mighty waters can't rid the world of sin. Even the dedication and obedience of Noah can't regain power and authority over Earth. No sin-weakened human can reclaim dominion. The Seed of woman still must come to free mankind—at the proper time set aside on Yahweh's calendar.

What a day of rejoicing has finally arrived for Noah. We observe such great relief, such a sense of freedom churning in this man and his family the instant their toes dig into soil after the Flood. For 120 years Noah built the ark, and for the past year they have all lived with the animals in the confines of the ship, weathering the storm, tossing to and fro day after day, waiting for a sign from God to be released.

Now down the mountain, into valleys, and over the plains beasts scurry, frolicking, leaping, and rolling in new tender sprouts of grass. Absorbing the sunshine's warmth and being caressed by gentle winds they seek out new domain. Oh, what joy to behold the earth alive again, budding in the splendor of Elohim.

Praise bubbles like a spring from the depths of Noah's spirit. He builds an altar of sacrifice. Yahweh in His holy and loving qualities inhales its sweet-smelling savor. Ahh, such delight!

In His nature as Judge, Yahweh decrees to never again curse the ground even though man will continually turn to evil. He declares to never again smite every living thing as He did with the Flood. As long as Earth remains, Yahweh gives His word that seedtime and harvest, cold and heat, winter and summer, day and night will not cease. (See Genesis 8:21–22.)

In the name of Elohim, the Covenant-Maker, He vows:

> And I will establish my covenant with you; neither shall all flesh be cut off any more by waters of a flood; neither shall there any more be a flood to destroy the earth.
>
> —GENESIS 9:11

Also in the name of Elohim, the covenant maker, He makes His promise of the rainbow:

> And the bow shall be in the cloud; and I will look upon it, that I may remember the everlasting covenant between God [Elohim] and every living creature of all flesh that is upon the earth.
>
> —GENESIS 9:16

With every rainbow man witnesses the loveliness of Elohim, our glorious triune Creator and covenant maker. Every rainbow also sparks remembrance of the Flood, the worldwide judgment of Yahweh.

Holy, eternal Yahweh. Faithful, unchangeable Jehovah. Our covenant fulfiller. Oh, the glory of His names!

Yahweh. Jehovah. Elohim. Adonai. El Elyon. El Shaddai. Such blessings to absorb into our hearts.

And more is yet to come. Ahead glows an entire vein of shimmering gold and precious stones—shining titles that complement and accompany the name of Yahweh, our Lord, Jehovah. The more we travel the more we realize what a mighty One we serve.

Of Him there is no end.

Chapter 5

Shalom, Sabaoth, and Shammah

S LEEPY PUFFS OF clouds meander across a soft blue sky, and rambling honeysuckle decorates a split-rail fence as our road winds through spacious countryside. We stroll into a forest of emerald trees. Safely tucked inside we find a secret park aglow with streams of warm sunbeams and crimson roses.

From a gurgling brook water tumbles leisurely over stones to feed a crystal pond. Swans glide across its surface. Under water lilies goldfish and tadpoles play a game of tag while a croaking bullfrog referees. How fast they all scatter when a doe and her young fawn amble up to get a drink.

Nearby a ballet of yellow butterflies perform to the symphony of songbirds gathered on flowing arms of a massive oak. Under its shade sways a whitewashed swing, gently wooing us to stay and rest awhile. *Come,* it coaxes. *Let the breeze caress you with perfume of roses and wrap you in the soothing scent of honeysuckle drifting from the meadow.*

We pause. *Can we spare a moment to do nothing more than relax, basking in the lovely peacefulness of our Creator?*

Ahh, yes, our hearts agree. *And let's slip off our shoes to let the velvet moss stroke our weary feet while our thoughts roam free with tranquility and bliss, absorbed in the beauty of His holiness and bathed in the sweet serenity of Jehovah Shalom, our God of perfect peace.*

> Peace I leave with you, my peace I give unto you: not as the world giveth, give I unto you. Let not your heart be troubled, neither let it be afraid.
>
> —JOHN 14:27

Whenever I hear this verse memories burst forth inside my being. And I am reminded of a supernatural, caring heavenly Father.

What calmness flowed into my life through these words long years ago! And although time has flown by like fleeting wind, the comfort of this verse remains. His peace still cascades within my spirit. Without doubt I know that His promises are real. Always I'll remember the wonderful way Jehovah Shalom, the God of peace, brought His Comforter to me.

"Lord, please send me Your Comforter," I prayed. My heart wept with every beat as I paced the floor like a zombie. For three days I did little more than cry, "O God, I need Your Comforter!"

My oldest child, a year past his accident and now eighteen, had stupefied himself with the partying scene of the seventies—marijuana, uppers, downers—who knows what else. Inside I felt such guilt. *Had I failed him as a mother?*

Eleven years earlier I had fled with him and his sister from my marriage to their father. After almost nine years of a bad marriage, my self-esteem registered zero. Rejection had gnawed my heart to pieces.

In time, by the strength of God, I managed to pick up the fragments of my life and rebuild. Nevertheless, with a mother's empathy, I knew that even a devoted stepfather couldn't erase the scars divorce had left upon my son and daughter—especially my son.

Following a summer's stay with his father he had returned bombed-out on drugs. Although his adverse tendencies had previously surfaced in our home, we had always been able to discipline him and reason with him. In rebellious rages, now my son refused any kind of guidance.

Fervently I prayed for him. Pointing blame inward, I searched myself for guilt while my heart cried out for the Comforter.

Majestically the Comforter came to me. As I slept He applied warm peace like soothing ointment to my aching soul, bandaged me in His calm assurance, and relieved my hurts and fears. How can I explain it? It defies all human logic.

I remember how with burdened thoughts I drifted into sleep that night.

Somehow in the deepness of my slumber His words spilled into my mind and gushed to every throbbing section of my body. Time and time again they streamed in constant flow, "Peace I leave with you. My peace I give unto you. Not as the world giveth, give I unto you. Let not your heart be troubled. Neither let it be afraid."

When I rose the following morning these words vibrated like honey through my veins, spreading indescribable comfort and peace. Convinced that they came from the Comforter, I questioned myself, *Are they Scripture?*

In those days I knew very little about how to pinpoint specific subjects in the Bible, but I did have a book of biblical quotations where I discovered the exact words. At first I couldn't believe it. I scanned them again. *Yes, there they are, word for word in one verse.*

My spirit overflowed in a fountain of praise as again and again I quoted the verse aloud. Knowing that I could always turn to it in the quotation book, I didn't bother noting its location in the Bible. Later I wondered, *Did God Himself shield this knowledge from me to further confirm His miracle of peace?*

Surely He directed my hand when I sat down that afternoon and opened my Bible to the fourteenth chapter of John. As I read, "And I will pray the Father, and he shall give you another Comforter, that he may abide with you for ever," my heart cheered. *This talks about His Comforter, the very One I've been praying for!*

Like a child eating an ice cream cone in summer heat, I couldn't devour the words fast enough. Then my racing eyes fell on this, "But the Comforter, which is the Holy Ghost, whom the Father will send in my name, He shall teach you all things, and bring all things to your remembrance, whatsoever I have said unto you."

O Lord, my heart exploded, *this tells precisely what You did for me last night. Just as I asked, You sent Your Comforter to bring Jesus' teaching of His peace to my remembrance.* Through tears of joy I scanned the next verse. It leaped out to me with "Peace I leave with you..." These were the very words He had instilled within me while I slept!

Many years of drug abuse would follow, but staunch assurance rests within my heart even today. By these words of Jesus, Jehovah Shalom enveloped me in a peace beyond all understanding, a glorious peace that never leaves.

And just as surely as He did this for me, He can do it for you. Seek His Comforter. He will come. In Him you'll discover, as I have, Jehovah Shalom, God of perfect peace. The giver of peace throughout all ages, He washes away all worry.

WE TRAVEL NOW to Judges chapter 6, which begins our story of Gideon. He came to know this peace over three thousand years before our time, but what dismal days he had until he found it. Existing in a state of hopelessness, his life burdened with defeat, he had lost all confidence and every ounce of self-esteem.

Israel was under constant siege, in a time of unremitting anguish. Its people were hungry and impoverished with no relief in sight. The entire nation was doomed to devastation, until Jehovah Shalom moved on Gideon with the miracle of His peace.

Plodding into these dark times we spot Gideon hard at work. In a steady tempo, without pausing, he toils like a machine. He's all alone, and he never glances up. Beneath his unfeeling motion we detect the weight of agony in his soul.

How demeaning it is to hide inside a winepress while I thresh wheat, his heart moans. *This stone trough is designed for crushing grapes, not wheat!*

But what's a man to do? With a heavy rod, in total drudgery he beats the stalks over and over and over.

During normal times kernels of grain would be removed on flat open ground by oxen tramping over cut wheat as they drag a weighted sled. In the evening men would thrust the golden grain into the air with pitchforks and rejoice in their harvest while breezes blew the chaff away.

But these aren't normal times. For seven years ruthless Midianites and Amalekites have invaded the land, coming in droves on camelback.

Oh, those dreadful camels! The downright ugly beast is strong enough to carry a four-hundred-pound load. Able to go an entire week without drinking a single drop, it could easily trek a hundred miles in one day. How defenseless Israel is with only its meager donkeys.

In relentless succession the enemy has demolished their crops, seized their goods, and stolen their livestock. With delight they butcher any person who happens to be in their path. What horrid brutality.

But what can Israel do? Without supernatural intervention from Jehovah, how can they ever come against the mighty troops of Midian?

They can't.

Gideon pounds the wheat with a constant rhythm. With every stroke the word *defeated...defeated...defeated...* booms against his eardrums.

Well, at least I've mustered enough courage to not run away, he reasons. *Plus I'm doing a little something to ward off starvation for my people. Most Israelis simply hide in mountain caves.*

The despairing word continues, *defeated...defeated...defeated...*

Payment for evil. Why did his nation turn their backs on Jehovah, the one true and living God, to worship useless idols? Did they think they could continue in existence on their own? Gideon shakes his head. Without Jehovah's leading and protection he knows their days are numbered.

Defeated... defeated... defeated... beats his rod.

His chest heaves. What can his people do? Not long ago they cried out to the Lord, but did He help? No. He just sent a prophet who rebuked them.

"Thus says the LORD God of Israel," His prophet said, "I delivered you from bondage in Egypt and out of the hands of all who oppressed you. I drove the heathen Amorites out. I gave you their land, ordering you not to turn to their idols but you refused to listen."

Defeated... defeated... defeated... on and on it drones inside his skull, keeping perfect time as he whips the wheat. On and on and on...

Listen! What's that? Gideon freezes in motion. *Did someone speak?* With a ghastly face he lifts his eyes. He gapes in utter shock. Before him looms the mighty Angel of the Lord!

"Jehovah is with you," the Angel announces, "for you are a man of fearless courage."

"Sir," Gideon responds, "if Jehovah is with us, why have we suffered such disaster and defeat? Where are all His wonders we've heard so much about? Didn't Jehovah bring our people out of Egypt? Why has He forsaken us?"

At the familiarity of his outcry our hearts shudder. How closely this resembles the response of people today. They go their own way, live worldly lives, do their "own thing"—until trouble strikes. Then they moan, *O God, why have You left us?*

How can Israel expect God to work miracles while their hearts remain in sin? Idols of Baal pollute the hills and defile their countryside. Will God move toward a solution to their problems just because they've cried to Him—before they accept responsibility for their wicked ways—before they turn to Him in remorse? Yes! Oh, His gracious mercy! He will do it through the sincere heart of one insignificant mortal—Gideon! With the leadership of Gideon the people shall once again acknowledge Jehovah as their only God, repent, and find acceptance in His sight.

The Angel orders Gideon, "Go in your might and save Israel out of the hands of Midian. I am sending you!"

Oh, how despair has sown seeds of low-esteem in Gideon's mind! Echoes of his threshing rod must still rumble in his head. *Defeated... defeated...*

Gideon wails, "But, sir, how can I save Israel? My family is poor in the tribe of Manasseh. I am least in my father's house..."

"I, Jehovah, shall be with you! You shall win over the army of Midian as if only one man stands against you."

"If this is true," Gideon replies, "if I've really found such favor with Jehovah, then give me a sign proving He truly speaks."

As Gideon sucks in a deep breath we sense a frightening thought flash through his mind. *What if this is really Jehovah? I dare not take any chances. I must show honor to this visitor.*

"Please stay here until I return with a present for you."

Honoring his request, the angel of the Lord settles by a big rock. Gideon dashes home to roast a young goat and bake a large cake of unleavened bread. Somewhat later, with the meal cooked, we spy Gideon rushing back, bread swinging in a basket on one arm and broth sloshing in a pot against his chest.

"Place the meat and bread upon that rock," says the angel, "then pour the broth over it."

What a strange request! In curiosity we stare while, without hesitation, Gideon obeys.

The angel thrusts out his staff and touches the food. An instant blaze erupts from the rock, consuming every morsel. We stand aghast.

So does Gideon. With terrified eyes he searches for the angel.

"Oh, no! Where is He?" he gasps in panic. "The angel of the Lord has vanished!"

We gape in amazement at the scene. Yes, the holy Being has departed. The only evidence of His presence remains in ashes glowing on the rock.

"Without a doubt I stood face-to-face with the Angel of the Lord. With my own eyes I beheld Him! No, oh, no," he sobs, "now will I be struck dead?"

But Jehovah calls with assurance, "Peace be unto you. You need not be afraid. You shall not die!"

Like a mighty surf trust rises in Gideon. With one billowing wave hope breaks up his puny thinking and dissolves his inferiority complex. His newfound confidence whisks away worries of defeat and replaces fear with peace. Praise swells inside his heart as the new Gideon of fearless courage assembles an altar, naming it Jehovah Shalom, proclaiming, "My Lord is peace!"

OH, WHAT A proclamation. Yes, Jehovah Shalom, our Lord is peace. Constant serenity directs those whose thoughts remain on Him. Isaiah declares it with these words:

> You will keep him in perfect peace, whose mind is stayed on You, because he trusts in You.
>
> —Isaiah 26:3, NKJV

Jehovah Shalom. Paul experienced His continual presence. By following Paul's example so can we.

> The things which you learned and received and heard and saw in me, these do, and the God of peace will be with you.
> —Philippians 4:9, nkjv

Jehovah Shalom, Jesus personified:

> But now in Christ Jesus you who once were far off have been brought near by the blood of Christ. For He Himself is our peace.
> —Ephesians 2:13–14, nkjv

Jehovah Shalom, the Holy Spirit manifested:

> But the fruit of the Spirit is love, joy, *peace*, longsuffering, kindness, goodness, faithfulness, gentleness, self-control. Against such there is no law.
> —Galatians 5:22–23, nkjv, emphasis added

Jehovah Shalom, also manifested in the Holy Spirit by His indwelling Comforter. By your wholly trusting God's Word and truly believing its promises, His Comforter will abide in your heart, filling it with total faith to bring peace regardless of circumstances. This peace doesn't have to come supernaturally as it did with me that one time. Through other painful trials He has showed me this is true. Later I'll muster the courage to take you to these places.

Yes, in many personal experiences I have found that Jehovah Shalom always stands by, offering His sweet serenity to rise above all problems and all stress. We only have to look to Him, relax, and receive.

By accepting the message from the angel of the Lord, the peace of Jehovah Shalom conquered Gideon's fright and dispelled his hopelessness. From then on, even in the midst of his country's havoc he never feared, but charged ahead with undaunted bravery into what looked like impossible feats.

Oblivious to danger, he destroyed Israel's prized altars of Baal. This alone could well have cost him his life, but the terror of death no longer plagued him. By following God's miraculous strategy a courageous Gideon led his remnant army of only three hundred and completely annihilated the immense forces of Midian just by shouting and uncovering torches in the dark. For more than forty years the peace of Jehovah Shalom reigned in Israel with Gideon as their leader.

Such a transformation from his cowardly personality occurred because of his encounter with the angel of the Lord. Who is this mighty Angel? Had Gideon actually seen the Lord Himself? Is that why he expressed such a fear of sudden death after standing in the angel's presence?

No doubt he recalled the recorded words God had given to Moses on Mount Sinai some generations before:

> You cannot see My face; for no man may see Me, and live.
> —EXODUS 33:20, NKJV

In human frailty no one can withstand the magnitude of Jehovah's divine splendor. Moses experienced this *Shekinah* glory, but he could only look at His backside (Exod. 33:22). After this encounter Moses glowed with light.

In no way did the angel who came to Gideon possess the overwhelming power and brilliance of Yahweh at Mount Sinai. He appears to be much more than one chosen from heaven's multitude of heavenly hosts.

For another glimpse of the angel of the Lord, let's peer briefly into the story of Sarai's servant-girl Hagar in Genesis chapter 16. Hagar, like Gideon, perceives this angel as Deity.

Even though childless Sarai decides to have Hagar bear a son with Abram, Sarai rages with jealousy when Hagar conceives. Her harshness causes the pregnant girl to flee into the desert alone.

At least she thinks she's alone. But not so! We have a God who sees us in all our dilemmas wherever we are.

The angel of the Lord finds Hagar beside a fountain in the wilderness. "Return to thy mistress and submit to her authority. I will multiply this seed within you so greatly that his descendants cannot be numbered. Name the child Ishmael."

Such a promise! Within her womb stirs an Arabian nation. The descendants of Ishmael, still so prevalent today, have always battled with Israel—the descendants of Sarah through Isaac, Ishmael's half-brother—in a long and grueling jealousy that has never ended. What a legacy for a little servant girl. And what an event she experienced that day in the desert.

She acknowledges this angel not as an mere angel but as the Lord (Yahweh). She also addresses Him by the name *El Roi*, which means "the God Who Sees."

So here surfaces a name worthy for only God Himself. The name *El Roi* defines His all-seeing character with complete knowledge of every happening in the life of every individual—a quality not endowed to actual angels. He alone not only sees but also oversees every situation, presented in the name *El Roi* and here manifested in the image of the angel of the Lord.

How can this be? Is it possible that God made Himself visible through angelic form? To better understand the identity of the angel of the Lord, who appears quite often in the Old Testament, let's wander over the enlightening road of Bible resources:

Nelson's Illustrated Bible Dictionary informs us, "A mysterious messenger of God sometimes described as the Lord Himself but at other times as one sent by God. The Lord used this messenger to appear to human beings who otherwise would not be able to see Him and live."[1]

Dake's Annotated Reference Bible relates, "The phrases the angel of the Lord and the angel of God are used many times in Scripture of the appearance of one of the persons of the Divine Trinity, who is the angel (messenger) of or from God, the head of the Godhead. The second person of the Trinity is no doubt the manifestation of God in such appearances."[2]

The Zondervan Pictorial Bible Dictionary says, "In the OT we find the oft-recurring phrase 'the angel of the Lord', in which in almost every case, the messenger is regarded as deity, and yet is distinguished from Jehovah. There is good reason for thinking that He is the pre-incarnate Logos, his appearance in angelic or human form foreshadowing His coming in the flesh."[3]

Logos in the Greek language means "word." In both Greek and Hebrew *angel* translates "messenger." By this thinking, the Angel of the Lord then could be called the Messenger of Yahweh's Word. Jesus, the Word who "was made flesh and dwelt among us" (John 1:14).

By definition all angels are God's messengers. Whether using the Word of His Trinity, the angel of the Lord in the Old Testament, or choosing angelic messengers from His innumerable heavenly beings, Jehovah has used angels to minister to His fallen humans throughout the ages. We have a fabulous Lord who directs countless throngs of spiritual hosts, willing ambassadors, and faithful representatives who stand ready to deliver His tidings and do His bidding.

THIS SUBJECT BRINGS us to another marvelous title of God. *Yahweh Tsebaoth,* transliterated as "Jehovah Sabaoth," means "Lord of hosts."

Oh, the complexity of God's many facets. Jehovah Sabaoth, Master of all hosts—stellar bodies, beast and fowl, humans and angels. As Jehovah Sabaoth He owns and supervises all.

Have you ever considered what supreme management this requires? Pause a moment and ponder the extent of His wisdom, authority, and endless responsibility.

He orders the systematic rotation of the planets and they never get off course, yet once at His desire they obediently moved backward (2 Kings 20:11). Another time He stopped the sun in motion (Josh. 10:12–13). By His might the fountains of the deep erupted and the windows of heaven gushed forth in torrents for forty days (Gen. 7:11). He caused the Red Sea to flow backwards, drying out the land so the children of Israel could cross it (Exod. 14:21).

> I am Yahweh your God who stirs up the sea, making its waves roar—
> Yahweh Sabaoth is my name.
> —Isaiah 51:15, njb

He directs the animals at will. When Noah released a dove from the ark, it returned to him with an olive leaf (Gen. 8:8–11). After swallowing Jonah, a great fish escorted him to the seashore and spewed him out on dry land (Jon. 2:10). A donkey once spoke in human words (Num. 22:28). Ravens sent by God fed Elijah (1 Kings 17:6). At the Master's call even beast and fowl obey.

Insuring His plan of redemption, our Lord God of hosts guides human nations, tribes, governments, and armies—raising up individuals and orchestrating their course to accomplish His eternal will. He watches over believers with the eyes of a merciful Father, encamping the Angel of the Lord around those who fear Him (Ps. 34:7) and sending heavenly ministers to aid all who inherit salvation (Heb. 1:14).

Oh, the wonder of His angels!

Come as we continue our journey and explore the marvels of Jehovah Sabaoth's righteous spirit world. Prepare for entrance into a realm of fascination, a domain invisible and invincible. We'll stand face-to-face with the magnificence of His divine rule, emerging with a valuable awareness of the magnitude of His indestructible unseen armies, realizing our utter helplessness as human beings without Him.

Step now into His glorious angel kingdom. Visualize our Father on His throne surrounded by trillions upon trillions of mighty attendants to carry out His orders. These are the majestic creatures who at creation sang together and shouted for joy (Job 38:7). They are the eternal creatures who carry out the judgments of the Great Tribulation, casting Satan into the bottomless pit for a thousand years (Rev. 20:1–3). In the past, the future, and today they stand ever poised with power and desire, obeying His slightest nod to dispatch messages, win wars, and provide protection and provisions for His children. Their functions can be wondrous and dynamic, yet also very personal.

> Are they not all ministering spirits, sent forth to minister for them who shall be the heirs of salvation?
>
> —Hebrews 1:14

The angels are ministers for the heirs of salvation—for us! Does this mean that angels are available for believers now?

Yes! I believe they surround every believer at this very moment. Though I've never knowingly seen one, my faith affirms that angels cushioned my son's fall...thirty feet onto concrete!

It was Christmas Eve. Now age twenty-one, my son lived over seven hundred miles away.

When we returned home after a festive evening with my parents we noted that we hadn't heard from him. He said he would call to wish everyone a merry Christmas at their house. *He's probably just out celebrating with friends,* we reasoned.

But he wasn't.

At daybreak on Christmas morning the telephone jarred me awake. As a voice on the other end began to speak, before I was aware that a horrible accident had occurred, an inner voice broke into my heart—*Your son is going to be all right!*

Calmly I absorbed the gruesome details. After mentioning to friends that he was stepping outside to make a call from a pay phone, he left a wild Christmas party. In a drugged and drunken stupor he plunged from the roof of a three-story building to the paved parking lot below.

His chin was crushed, both jaws were shattered, and he had a broken nose. His extremities were smashed—one knee crushed, the other leg splintered, a fractured pelvis, and a broken elbow and wrist.

Someone discovered him lying in a pool of his own blood. In such a fall experts told us he should have splattered like a watermelon, yet no internal organ received even the slightest injury.

Did angels cushion his fall? What other explanation can there be? Especially, when one considers that for days on end I'd prayed, "Lord, please keep Your angels watching over my children." In concern for this son's life amid his world of darkness, I often added, "Wherever he is at this second and wherever he goes, keep Your angels always surrounding him."

God answers prayer. In the virtue of Jehovah Sabaoth He sent His angels to my son. At the issue of His order they sped in power, just as His Word says:

> Bless the Lord, ye his angels, that excel in strength, that do his

commandments, hearkening unto the voice of his word. Bless ye the LORD, all ye his hosts; ye ministers of his, that do his pleasure.

—PSALM 103:20–21

Our Lord of host speaks, and angels comply. Jesus knew this. At His arrest in the Garden of Gethsemane He turned down help from His disciples, saying, "Do you think I cannot call on my Father, and he will at once put at my disposal more than twelve legions of angels?" (Matt. 26:53, NIV). With Israel under Roman rule, they knew a Roman legion consisted of approximately six thousand soldiers. Multiply that by twelve. Over seventy-two thousand angels! What an army awaiting divine direction.

But that was for the Son of God. What about us?

Rejoice! As Christians we become joint-heirs with Christ Jesus. Today, tomorrow, every day at "the voice of His word" angels speed forth to do His bidding—for His Son then, for His sons down through the ages, for us now and always.

OUR ROAD BECKONS us to travel deeper into the vastness of His angelic world. But how can we continue? A towering wall of fantasies with three cutting ledges blocks our way. From each ledge slippery misconceptions glare down, daring us to climb up and confront them.

Listen! Can that be demons laughing? Oh, what should we do? Turn and run?

No, charge ahead; let truth win out! Regardless of any hostility facing us, God's Word is stronger. It's time to come to grips with all distortions and rise above them. So swallow a cup of gumption, exchange your flimsy costumes of traditional myths for durable fatigues of truth, grab your sword of the Spirit to fight off clinging fables and to pop balloons filled with secular notions, lace up your climbing boots, and march with me toward the wall.

But take warning. Our outfits aren't stylish, and they can dig into flesh like cactus needles. Also, the climb may be steep, requiring great effort. But no matter how hard it is to reach the top, please don't give up. Success depends on courage to overpower every deception and to cast down all preconceived ideas.

Watch out! On the first ledge we wrestle with notion number one.

What do angels look like? Are they delicate, beautiful ladies in flowing white gowns? Are they naked baby "cherubs" with little wings, fluttering around and shooting tiny bows and arrows?

No, no, no! How does man come up with so many misconstrued ideas?

In God's Word angels appear as powerful masculine beings. This might be a tough balloon to burst, but in truth, not one female angel ever appeared to anyone in Scripture. The closest biblical presentation of any feminine figure that could possibly be regarded as an angel is in Zechariah's vision of two winged women (Zech. 5:9), but they only denote prophetic symbols, not angels. No feminine form of the word *angel* exists.

And certainly angels aren't babies. As created beings they never experience infancy or grow from children into adults. The images of cherubs (or correctly cherubim) hovering above the mercy seat of the ark of the covenant and glorifying the luxurious temple walls and veils displayed powerful creatures truly colossal in strength and superb in beauty.

Yes, strong, chosen to guard the gates of Eden with flaming swords (Gen. 3:24). God not only dwells between cherubim (Isa. 37:16), but He even rides upon them (Ps. 18:10).

Yes, beautiful! In Ezekiel's vision spectacular cherubim escort the Lord in fire and with wheels as He departs the temple. With such a vivid description, it's impossible for our minds to conceive it all:

> Every one had four faces apiece, and every one four wings: and the likeness of the hands of a man was under their wings.
>
> —EZEKIEL 10:21

They possess tremendous wingspread—"And the sound of the cherubims' wings was heard even to the outer court.... And the cherubim lifted up their wings, and mounted up from the earth in my sight: when they went out, the wheels also were beside them" (Ezek. 10:5, 19).

And to think Satan himself once held the honor of the most glorious of all cherubim. Oh, what magnificence he forfeited as Lucifer, son of the morning (Isa. 14:12), when he rebelled against his Maker:

> You were the seal of perfection, full of wisdom and perfect in beauty. You were in Eden, the garden of God; every precious stone was your covering.... You were the anointed cherub who covers; I established you.... You were perfect in your ways from the day you were created, till iniquity was found in you.
>
> —EZEKIEL 28:12–15, NKJV

Hold on tight! Directly above a still sharper ledge looms with notion number two.

What size are angels? Do they range from gigantic to microscopic?

Once as I taught on angels a man spoke up. "No one knows how many angels can fit on the head of one pin," he said as a matter of fact.

For a long time I assumed this statement to be some type of fairy tale dancing in his head, but even though years and miles stretched between them, another person made this same comment not long ago. I didn't know whether to laugh or cry. Where is there any basis for angels being no larger than germs?

Although the Bible transcribes no exact proportions, it never gives the slightest indication of tiny spiritual hosts. In most accounts people stood in fear and awe at their super powerful appearance. Nowhere in Scripture did angels arrive in miniature, although at times they manifested themselves in the physical image of man such as the occasions with Abraham, Sarah, and Lot (Gen. 18:1–8; 19:1–3). God's Word cautions us, "Do not forget to entertain strangers, for by so doing some people have entertained angels without knowing it" (Heb. 13:2, NIV).

Not only does God's Word fail to mention even one small-scale angel, but it also does not record any astronomical figure able to hover around the entire globe or tower above cities as we sometimes see in pictures. As supernatural beings they accomplish incomprehensible feats. In Revelation 7:1 John saw "four angels standing on the four corners of the earth, holding the four winds of the earth, that the wind should not blow on the earth, nor on the sea, nor on any tree." Powerful, yes, yet there is no mention that stupendous stature is needed to succeed in this or any of their many incredible duties during the Great Tribulation.

Are heavenly hosts colossal in strength and impressive in size? *Yes.* Can they appear as man? *Yes.* Are they bigger than skyscrapers or small as wee little beings? *Bah, humbug!*

Are you still hanging on? Please dig in and don't let go. One last ledge, and we're over the wall. Notion number three:

Do people become angels? Never! Nowhere in the Holy Word do we read a single account or find the slightest hint that any human being ever became or ever will become an angel. Angels are always created beings, not born like humans or the beasts of Earth who all multiply by birth of their own kind. And in our eternal state we won't suddenly find ourselves reconstructed into angels. This common idea bears no scriptural backing. The only "created" (not born) of mankind are Adam and Eve. Just as surely as our Creator Elohim designed the heavens in all its fullness from nothing, He also created every angel.

> Praise ye him, all his angels: praise ye him, all his hosts. Praise ye him, sun and and moon: praise him, all ye stars of light. Praise him, ye heavens of heavens, and ye waters that be above the heavens. Let

them praise the name of the LORD: for he commanded, and they were created.

—PSALM 148:2–5

Men and angels differ in other ways. God gave humans the right to choose, and He also gave them a way of repentance. Angels have ability to choose but not the right. They cannot repent of their wrongdoing, and no plan of redemption exists for them.

Like man, however, angels do possess curiosity. They look with wonder upon God's amazing plan of salvation for humans: "... so strange and wonderful that even the angels in heaven would give a great deal to know more about it" (1 Pet. 1:12, TLB).

And like men, angels feel emotion. "There is joy in the presence of the angels of God over one sinner that repenteth" (Luke 15:10). When God is happy, so are His angels. When God becomes displeased, His angels share His displeasure, as we'll soon find out.

In their timeless state angels outrank humans today in strength, vitality, intelligence, and performance. Their bodies never grow old, and they never die. Although humans never transform into angels, in eternity the redeemed will become like them in these respects.

Being of one gender, angels never marry. As the bride of the Lamb people in immortal state will no longer marry one another. A perfect bond, a spotless union, a flawless love will exist between everyone.

The roles of resurrected saints as priests and kings with Christ differ from the duties of angels. As children of God and children of the resurrection, saved from sin by the spotless blood, mankind will always stand apart from angels.

> The children of this world marry, and are given in marriage: But they which shall be accounted worthy to obtain that world, and the resurrection from the dead, neither marry, nor are given in marriage: Neither can they die any more: for they are equal unto the angels; and are the children of God, being the children of the resurrection.
>
> —LUKE 20:34–36

It seems that angels—though not all-knowing, all-seeing, or omnipresent as only God is—have always had the benefit of viewing both the natural and spiritual worlds. Not so for humans. At least 110 angelic appearances occur in the Bible, yet for the most part, Jehovah Sabaoth's spiritual domain evades man's limited sight. Perhaps this explains why today's society finds it so easy to fantasize about angel's physical features and Hollywood delights in making movies of people changing into angels after death. Maybe this also accounts for modern ideas that scoff at the reality of principalities and powers in force today.

But never be fooled. Angels certainly do exist.

At last we're over the wall! That wasn't so bad after all, now was it?

WITH THESE FALSE notions far behind us we're prepared to scale without barriers into utmost heights, able to view angels in a truest sense. Rise in expectation. Let your spirit excel in the never-ending glory of the Lord God of hosts. So much more remains to learn about His wondrous spirit creatures. *O God, illuminate our hearts to receive. And open our eyes to see the way Elisha saw in 2 Kings 6:8–23.*

"Who is the traitor in our midst?" asks baffled King Ben-hadad. "I demand to know who is giving Israel inside information!"

"Sir," volunteers one officer, "not a single soldier has ever leaked our battle plans. Your informer is none other than Israel's prophet Elisha. He even knows words spoken in your bedroom!"

What a reputation has traveled with this man of God since he witnessed Elijah's spectacular exit from Earth. Because of his persistence to stay by Elijah's side, Elisha obtained his desire to be endowed with a double portion of Elijah's miracle-working spirit. Oh, such anointing!

Now Elisha possesses unshakeable faith. He speaks; miracles happen. With his spiritual awareness stretching like a super pipeline straight up to the mind of almighty God, he is sensitive to terrorist acts against Israel. His ear taps in to even the most private conversations of this opposing Syrian king, Ben-hadad. More than once he has spoiled their planned attacks by revealing their strategies against Israel.

When Ben-hadad learns the informant's identity he rages. Elisha, Israel's prophet! Syria must capture this man at once. After releasing spies who pinpoint Elisha's whereabouts, the king forms a massive raiding party to cut him down with vengeance.

Oh, such vanity. And oh, so foolish. Does the king actually believe he can be victorious in this pursuit? How does he fail to reason that even with his multitudes of men he'll never be a match against Elisha's divine inside information?

During the night the Syrian army creeps in to encircle the city where Israel's famous prophet sleeps. By dawn countless troops flanked by horses and chariots poise like coiled serpents at every strategic site.

"Alas, my master!" Elisha's servant boy convulses with fear in the early morning light. "What can we do!"

Do you think Elisha even bats an eye? No, of course not. Most likely he expected them. And besides, this man knows the Lord God of Hosts, Jehovah Sabaoth.

"Don't be afraid. Our army far outnumbers theirs." He lifts his face toward heaven. "Jehovah, I pray thee, open my servant's eyes. Let him see..."

Oh, what the boy beholds! The mountains come alive with majestic horses and chariots. Looming above the troops of Syria an immense angelic force waits for God's command.

"Lord, let blindness befall our enemy," Elisha prays.

What a laugh. The deluded Syrians become putty in Elisha's hands. With blinded eyes and unbeknownst to them, led into Israel's city of Samaria by Elisha himself, they are captured without any bloodshed, given a meal, and sent home.

So humiliating! Needless to say, from then on King Ben-hadad and his soldiers dared not tamper with God's people.

How superbly Jehovah Sabaoth rules. Always on the scene with His awesome hosts, He is ready to direct His created beings who excel in supernatural strength.

Next we come upon Israel's King Hezekiah praising God. We find him calling specifically on the name of Jehovah Sabaoth, the Lord of hosts.

> O LORD of hosts, God of Israel, the One who dwells between the cherubim. You are God, You alone, of all the kingdoms of the earth.
> —ISAIAH 37:16, NKJV

With continuing prayer he asks God to save his kingdom from the aggression of powerful enemy forces. Jehovah Sabaoth honors his request.

> Then the angel of the LORD went out, and killed in the camp of the Assyrians one hundred and eighty-five thousand.
> —ISAIAH 37:36, NKJV

Can you imagine that? One hundred eighty-five thousand conquered at the hands of one single angel! As we realize that this protection remains available for all who reverence the Lord's holiness, our hearts overflow with gratitude!

> The angel of the LORD encampeth round about them that fear him, and delivereth them.
> —PSALM 34:7

How tragic that so many know so little about the true grandeur of the heavenly hosts and are completely unaware of their abilities. It is so sad that such spiritual blindness prevails in our "world-educated" society. *O Lord of hosts, open our spirits beyond worldly sight to perceive the greatness of angelic beauty and might.*

> God speaks of his angels as messengers swift as the wind and as servants made of flaming fire.
>
> —HEBREWS 1:7, TLB

O God, increase our awareness of the constant presence of Your angels in our midst. Give us faith to believe the marvelous benefits that await us as we abide with You.

> Because you have made the LORD, who is my refuge, even the Most High, your dwelling place, no evil shall befall you, nor shall any plague come near your dwelling; for He shall give His angels charge over you, to keep you in all your ways. In their hands they shall bear you up, lest you dash your foot against a stone.
>
> —PSALM 91:9–12, NKJV

Oh, what power God's Word holds. Meditate on it and memorize it in preparation to call out to God for angelic help in times of trouble. It could save your life.

Charles H. Lightoller, one of the officers of the *Titanic*, related the miracle of his survival. As the ship sank he found himself struggling in vain against the suction of an air shaft when water gushed in, sucking him down to his death. With his body underneath the icy ocean, the promise of Psalm 91 surfaced in his being: "His angels shall have charge over thee!"

At that instant a boiler blew up, throwing him free. He felt another suction overtaking him. Though not able to recall the details, again the grips of death released him. Surfacing near an overturned lifeboat holding several other passengers, he managed to grab the rope and pull himself to safety. Then as the mighty *Titanic* plummeted deeper, a terrific wave swept the lifeboat clear of danger. Instead of a tragic, untimely death, Lightoller lived out his life, passing away in 1952.[4]

Even Satan realizes the power that is available in God's Word. Tempting Christ in the desert, he used this same passage from Psalm 91 to dare Jesus to leap from the holy temple in Jerusalem:

> If thou be the Son of God, cast thyself down: for it is written, He shall
> give his angels charge concerning thee: and in their hands they shall
> bear thee up, lest at any time thou dash thy foot against a stone.
>
> —MATTHEW 4:6

How foolish could Satan be? What was he thinking? He should know
that the true Son of God couldn't be tricked into putting angels to this
foolish test. To deliberately jump to prove a point to Satan would no doubt
displease the Father and thus provoke His angels.

Can angels be provoked?

Yes.

Once again we enter into the wilderness with Moses and the Israelites.
Our arrival takes place a short time after Israel's awesome experience with
Jehovah on Mount Sinai. What a faithful Lord we have. Even after His people backed away at His appearing, He loves and watches over them. Listen
while He presents an amazing guarantee of His security:

> Behold, I send an Angel before thee, to keep thee in the way, and to bring
> thee into the place which I have prepared. Beware of him, and obey his
> voice, provoke him not; for he will not pardon your transgressions: for
> my name is in him. But if thou shalt indeed obey his voice, and do all
> that I speak; then I will be an enemy unto thine enemies, and an adver-
> sary unto thine adversaries. For mine Angel shall go before thee, and
> bring thee in unto the Amorites, and the Hittites and the Perizzites, and
> the Canaanites, the Hivites and the Jebusites: and I will cut them off.
>
> —EXODUS 23:20–23

God's promises continue. Not only will their special angel guide them,
but also if they will just obey him and consecrate themselves to God, great
blessings lie in store. They will have plenty of food and water. There will be
no more sickness, miscarriages, or barrenness. God assures them that His
terror will cause the enemies of the land to flee, and He will bring confusion,
even sending hornets to attack opposing forces.

Their two requirements—worship the Lord, and follow and heed their
anointed angel, being careful not to offend him. That's all. Then this land
that flows with milk and honey will belong to them and their descendants.
What a deal!

NOT LONG AFTER this day of promise they stand at the edge of the
Jordan River staring across into the beautiful, far-reaching terrain that can

soon be theirs. As we enter now into Numbers 13 and 14 we wonder, *Will they rush in to stake their claim?*

No. We hear Moses appointing twelve spies, one from each tribe, to slip in and check it out. Well, that sounds like the proper thing to do in preparation for their invasion. For forty days they'll be gone from camp. Shall we accompany them? Yes, let's trail along behind.

How lush the country is, with scenery so overwhelming that it surpasses description. In total awe we soak up its richness. Beyond a winding brook stretches enormous vineyards more spectacular than any we could have ever imagined. One single cluster of grapes requires two men to share the weight, balancing it on a staff between them. And look—oodles of other luscious fruit. Pomegranates and figs abound in all directions.

Oh, but what about the wicked people here? They're so many and so mighty, huge populations with monstrous giants. It's quite a challenge, but with the angel endowed to lead them, God's people can endure and conquer. There's no need for worry.

What's that? Do we catch a wind of murmuring among the spies? Did we overhear someone mutter "too many obstacles"? Can there be a sense of apprehension spreading through the group? Surely not.

However, when they return to camp and report to Moses and the people, our hearts faint from disappointment. "There's no denying the land flows with milk and honey," ten of the spies announce in agreement, "but the people living there are giants! And their cities, fortified and enormous! Why, they'll crush us like measly grasshoppers!"

Only two spies, Joshua and Caleb, disagree. "With God's help we can do it!" they shout. Yet outnumbered by the others, their words fall on unbelieving ears.

Oh, please, our hearts cry, *watch your attitudes, or you'll offend your angel. Didn't you hear God say that if you provoke the angel he won't pardon your transgressions?*

But they can't read our hearts, and they refuse to heed Joshua and Caleb and their pleadings to march forth in faith. We ache inside. Why won't they listen?

People scream, "We wish we had died in Egypt! We'd be better off to return to slavery there!" They even talk of stoning Joshua and Caleb.

Foolishly they reject God's wondrous promises, but there's nothing we can do. We must leave them to the consequences of their actions. Not only have they provoked their angel, but they've also kindled God's fury.

"How long will these people provoke me?" He thunders to Moses. "How can they refuse to believe Me after all My miracles they've seen?"

He threatens to destroy His entire nation and start anew. Moses begs Him not to do it. And He won't. But no adults other than Joshua and Caleb will live to enter the land God promised for His chosen. From age twenty years and upward, all who have murmured against Him have doomed themselves to die in the desert.

> Surely they shall not see the land which I sware unto their fathers, neither shall any of them that provoked me see it.
>
> —NUMBERS 14:23

In an effort to understand their actions we pause to reflect. Why are they foolish?

They have hearts that are still bound by slave mentality!

During their years in bondage they worked hard, but the Egyptians made decisions for them. Although they escaped in a blaze of Jehovah's mighty miracles, the only thing that was required of them was that they sacrifice a lamb, eat it, and paint its blood on their doorposts.

When God worked by His might they had no trouble following, but what a foreign concept it is to act in faith now. Looking at the problem with natural eyes as they have always done, instead of relying on the Problem-solver with trusting hearts, they rebel.

They murmur, whine, and complain about everything. "What shall we drink? Give us meat to eat!" Hardening their hearts against divine direction, they refuse to believe the power of His word.

No wonder they fail the big test—the call to conquer the Promised Land. How sad that they turn away in unbelief at the very entrance to their blessing of rest and plenty. Instead of entering an abundant life in the land of milk and honey, they settle for forty years of bare necessities and never leave the wilderness.

> For some, when they had heard, did provoke.... But with whom was he grieved forty years? was it not with them that had sinned, whose carcasses fell in the wilderness?... So we see that they could not enter in because of unbelief.
>
> —HEBREWS 3:16–19

Unbelief is the number one weapon of the adversary. Though it starts in small ways, it soon forms the taproot from which all rebellion springs. How it grieves God. And when He becomes upset, so do His angels.

Check yourself. Do you murmur when things don't go just right? Be ever mindful of your words and their importance!

He that keepeth his mouth keepeth his life: but he that openeth wide
his lips shall have destruction.

—PROVERBS 13:3

What have you been saying? Are you a slave to worry, to the traditions of
the world, to powerless doctrine? Have murmuring and unbelief provoked
the angel who ministers to you and also barred you from entering into
abundant blessings from God? Be careful! Angels despise wavering faith,
and penalties result from it.

BY HIS UNBELIEF a priest named Zacharias provoked his angel. Come
along now as the story unfolds in Luke 1:5–25 shortly before the birth
of Jesus.

How busy it is as many bring sacrifices to the temple. Some buy them at
the gate. Throngs mingle in the outer temple courtyard praying while priests
burn offerings on the brazen altar.

Entering alone into the inner holy court, Zacharias prepares for the daily
duty of burning incense for their prayers. Even in his blue ceremonial robe
with its hem of bells and pomegranates, and his breastplate of twelve precious stones—his grandeur seems overpowered by the vastness of the room.
Passing between a table graced with twelve loaves of bread and a flaming
seven-branched lamp stand, he approaches a golden altar of incense located
in front of the veiled entrance of the most sacred holy of holies. He sighs;
only on the Day of Atonement can he venture beyond the holy court into
the holiest of all. Today is not that day.

Soon a soft glow enhances the beauty of the tremendous curtain that for-
bids access into the innermost sanctuary. A trail of incense begins rising to
the ceiling as sweet fragrance penetrates the air around Zacharias. Serenity
envelops the inner holy quarters.

Then like a lightning bolt, an angel of the Lord appears. The stunned
priest backs away and gapes in terror, face-to-face with his mighty messenger.
"Fear not, Zacharias! God has heard your prayer! Elisabeth shall bear a son!"

Wonderful news! If anyone deserves such a blessing, Zacharias and Elisabeth do. With their enduring love for God, they always try their best to
stand blameless in His sight, to meet every commandment of the Law in
spirit as well as in letter.

Nevertheless, despite their righteous living and years of praying, Elisabeth has never conceived. This presents such a heartbreaking situation. To
be childless brings disgrace and dishonor upon any Jewish woman, and now

they've grown old with no one to carry on the family line. Yes, what grand news the angel brings!

With zeal the angel continues, "You must name your baby John. Not only will you and your wife rejoice at his birth, but many others will also share your joy, because your son shall be great in the sight of the Lord. Before he is even born he will be filled with the Holy Ghost. He will never taste wine or any strong drink. As he goes forth in the spirit and power of Elijah, many Jews will return to the Lord. By his teaching, father's hearts will be restored to their children, and the disobedient will come to know the wisdom of the just. Your son will prepare the people for the coming of the Messiah!"

After so many long years of praying for a son, why isn't Zacharias leaping with delight and praising God? Our hearts fall as we hear his reaction.

"How do you expect me to believe such a thing? I am an old man, and my wife is advanced in years!"

Were all his days of prayer just words in unbelief? Didn't he have faith that God would answer?

Oh, no! Has his unbelief provoked the angel? Yes, it has!

Immediately the angel in his anger states his high position. "*I*," he exclaims, "am Gabriel! I stand in the very presence of God! I am sent to you with this glad news. Because you have not believed me, you are stricken dumb, unable to speak anymore until after the birth of your son. At the proper time my words *shall* come to pass!"

Just as Gabriel declared, Elisabeth soon conceives and bares a son. And sure enough, following his birth Zacharias's voice returns—after he obeys the angel's instructions to name his son John, a name meaning "given by Jehovah."

We know his son as John the Baptist. A blessing to his parents and a blessing to the world, he baptized our Savior, who said:

> Among them that are born of women there hath not risen a greater than John the Baptist.
>
> —MATTHEW 11:11

Because of Zacharias and Elisabeth's dedication the Lord chose them to be parents despite Zacharias's questioning faith. But why did the angel become so angered at his skepticism? Gideon also doubted. Why wasn't his angel provoked with him? By comparing the lives of the two men, we find that the difference lies in three factors—upbringing, circumstance, and attitude.

Zacharias, born into the priestly lineage of Levi, had been taught the letter of the Law from childhood and had been trained to perform sacred duties of the temple. At his first glimpse of Gabriel's anointed presence, the angel had every right to expect great faith, not stark disbelief of the divine message and doubt about God's capability to bring it to pass. Without question Zacharias should have recognized this proclamation as the long-awaited answer to his prayer and readily received it.

Gideon, on the other hand, lacked the advantages of Zacharias. God understood Gideon's plight and met him on his level. As a lowly descendent from the half-tribe of Manasseh coping alone in a national dilemma, he hesitated at the thought of his worthiness to actually receive such an esteemed visitor. He rated himself poor and unimportant, doubting his own ability. But he never questioned the ability of Jehovah. Once Gideon established in his mind that God Himself actually acknowledged him as a worthy vessel, he totally trusted the heavenly message in such dimension that supernatural faith erupted from him as he gratefully obeyed his divine appointment to the letter.

Today, God still meets you where you are, at your level, according to your knowledge. If you feel that unbelief has hindered your walk with God and kept angels from working on your behalf, never fear. Repent of all your murmurings. Begin speaking words of faith and act on them. You'll find a God of abundant blessings awaits with open arms.

> Come now, and let us reason together, saith the LORD: though your sins be as scarlet, they shall be as white as snow; though they be red like crimson, they shall be as wool.
>
> —ISAIAH 1:18

Cast doubt aside. Even if you feel all alone, the Lord of hosts watches over you. Though you may feel that your prayers go unheeded, He always listens. As the story of Zacharias and Elisabeth shows, He never overlooks our needs. But just as it was with Zacharias, too often while Christians wait for answers from the Lord, doubt creeps in and hinders Him from doing what they ask. Oh, how hard it is to wait without doubt and murmuring!

I once heard someone say that time steals more answers to prayer than anything else. As time lapses Satan delights in feeding a person's mind with unbelief. Before long the person's mouth expresses doubt. Sometimes at the brink of a breakthrough the heart gives up. Jesus tells us:

> Therefore I say unto you, What things soever ye desire, when ye pray, believe that ye receive them, and ye shall have them.
>
> —MARK 11:24

When you pray, believe from that moment on, not when the answer materializes. Pray expecting.

Things might get worse or look impossible, but keep on believing and expecting, regardless of the circumstances. In spite of what others say, no matter how bad the situation looks, refuse to succumb to unbelief.

Train your spirit to wait in faith. Human nature refuses to wait, but as you discipline your spiritual nature to become the stronger of the two, waiting plants strong seeds of faith that are unattainable any other way. They are seeds that sprout and blossom into blessings if only you continue to believe, never losing hope.

Be a Joshua and Caleb. It took forty years for them to enter into the Promised Land, but they made it. The ten spies who brought the evil report "died by the plague before the LORD" (Num. 14:37).

Speak words of good report. Rely on God, never forgetting the power of His angels to go before you and keep you in the way. Never provoke them by words that displease God. Keep believing!

> I would have lost heart, unless I had believed that I would see the goodness of the LORD in the land of the living. Wait on the LORD; be of good courage, and He shall strengthen your heart; wait, I say, on the LORD!
>
> —Psalm 27:13–14, NKJV

I HAD PRAYED for my son and his drug problem so long. Three years had passed since his fall. Although the peace of Jehovah Shalom had never subsided and worry had never returned, on this particular day my soul ached with waiting.

Heavenly Father, how long? I cried.

He led me to the above passage of Psalm 27. So much like the fourteenth chapter of John and its teaching about His Comforter, these words flooded me with comfort. They seemed to leap from the written page into the pining of my heart, coming alive inside my spirit.

Just a few minutes later I flipped on the television to watch a Christian program. The camera zoomed in on a woman's face. I heard her reciting these exact two verses. It was an affirmation from God, a total reassurance of hope for my wayward son.

Still many years of addiction have followed and trials have arisen, but this Word has strengthened my heart with the capability to wait in "good courage." It has helped me to continue believing and never lose hope.

Resting in faith, I know that someday the portals of glory will burst forth with rejoicing in the presence of angels at my son's salvation.

> Likewise, I say unto you, there is joy in the presence of the angels of God over one sinner that repenteth.
>
> —LUKE 15:10

Every day I expect it to happen. In the name of Jesus I stand against the devil, quoting Scripture and pleading the blood of Jesus. My faith is renewed by studying, by memorizing and meditating on God's Word, by praying and fasting. Listening to Christian music, watching Christian programs, and reading Christian books, I find encouragement in the testimonies of people who have been delivered from dependence on drugs and alcohol. I find strength in the fellowship of church.

In the natural things have often looked worse. There have been arrests, jail, recovery programs, treatment center after treatment center. Bloody fights have happened, and when he has disappeared, I have sometimes not known where or how to find him.

Through all this I've come to depend on the virtue of another name of God—Jehovah Shammah, the One who is always there. No matter where my son may venture, my heart savors the knowledge that Jehovah Shammah is already there. I might not know the whereabouts of my loved one, but I rest in the fact that my Father knows. I don't know his every situation, but I always know my Father knows. And every day I place my prodigal child in my Father's hands.

Jehovah Shammah. This bountiful name surfaces in the very last verse of Ezekiel's writings (Ezek. 48:35). After foretelling of the destruction of the Jewish temple and the ages of its desolation, Ezekiel describes a new and prefect temple that will someday dwell on earth. "The name of the city [Jerusalem] from that day shall be: THE LORD IS THERE" he prophecies (NKJV).

In the Hebrew language this reads "Yahweh Shammah." As we contemplate the presence of Yahweh/Jehovah, we realize that He abides everywhere. The writer of the book of Hebrews tells us of God's promise: "I will never leave thee, nor forsake thee" (Heb. 13:5). Even if you try, you can never escape His presence:

> Whither shall I go from thy Spirit? or whither shall I flee from thy presence? If I ascend up into heaven, thou art there: if I make my bed in hell, behold, thou art there. If I take the wings of the morning and dwell in the uttermost parts of the sea; even there shall thy hand lead

me, and thy right hand shall hold me. If I say, Surely the darkness shall cover me; even the night shall be light about me. Yea, the darkness hideth not from thee; but the night shineth as the day: the darkness and the light are both alike to thee.

—PSALM 139:7–12

In His magnitude Jehovah Shammah overflows throughout Earth and fills up all the heavens. His boundless presence stretches far beyond human comprehension—yet He is a personal, loving, ever-present God. Before we reach our destination He's already there, and He travels with us every step along the way. He stays after we have gone, but He also goes with us when we leave. Even when we stray from Him we're not alone. He remains with us to gently lead us back to His fold.

The day arrived when my son turned his heart toward God. The answer to my prayers had manifested—or so I thought.

With a sincere heart he renewed his childhood commitment to Jesus and learned anew of Him. Absorbing God's Holy Word, he walked with Him.

Three years passed. Then Satan jerked him back. The battle began all over. Back and forth, in and out.

Demonic situations arose. His business went belly-up, and he suffered personal bankruptcy. He pawned his possessions—his television, VCR, microwave, washing machine, clothes dryer, and even toys, bicycles, and collections that belonged to his children—all to purchase drugs. His family and possessions, everything he owned, took second place to crack cocaine.

Then he vanished. No one knew his whereabouts. But my husband Jim and I rested with the knowledge that wherever he might be, Jehovah Shammah was there, too. And instead of doubt and worry, we confessed God's Word.

Within his AA group a report circulated that he'd been murdered. Though in truth he had been put out on the street to die, a friend from another town showed up out of the blue, rescued him, and checked him into a treatment center more than one hundred miles away.

My son notified us of his residence, but we had no inkling of the rumor or his frightful circumstances. Weeks later when he returned and walked into an AA meeting, shock spread across the room. When he told us this, we knew without a doubt that once again God had saved his life.

Sometimes people ask me, "Why don't you worry? It's abnormal not to worry!"

When one truly meets the peace of Jehovah Shalom, the protection of Jehovah Sabaoth, and the presence of Jehovah Shammah, the need to worry disappears.

After my son escaped the grips of death and pulled himself together, he and his wife felt called to help others who were on drugs and in jail. They attempted to head an outreach called "Addiction to Christ Ministry" through their church. With understanding hearts they reached out to anyone who suffered the effects of chemical dependency—those addicted to drugs or alcohol, their families, and their friends.

But even after this, darkness overtook my son once more. His home broke up, and for a while he chose to live on the streets and in his car. We didn't know where to find him, but our heavenly Father knew. As we prayed, He reached down and brought him back to us. Today he's doing well and growing strong again.

Over twenty-six years have elapsed since the night the Comforter flowed peace into my heart. Others may give up hope, even belittle my son's past futile efforts. Nevertheless, in steadfast faith his stepfather and I stand together. And we wait, trusting God, without murmuring, looking ahead for his complete deliverance.

Yes, someday this man will walk in total freedom. Day by day he grows in strength. Through his desire to help others, he'll lead them to know the same way, truth, and life that come only from the power of God, by accepting Jesus Christ and walking in His ways. Then he will proclaim a new addiction:

> They have addicted themselves to the ministry of the saints.
> —1 CORINTHIANS 16:15

Thank You, faithful Father, Jehovah Shalom, Jehovah Sabaoth, Jehovah Shammah. Day by day we abide in Your peace, the protection of Your angels and Your ever-abiding presence.

Chapter 6

Tsidkenu and M'Kaddesh

ARRIAGE IS SUCH a beautiful commitment. The wedding, with songs of love, blessings, joy, happiness, bonds two as one. Glowing with hope and expectation, a man and a woman proclaim their love and devotion for better or worse till they are parted by death. They commit to uphold a most sacred pledge, a heartfelt vow spoken before a holy God, that opens the way into a lifetime of devotion, shared dreams, and cherished family unity. How God honors marriage—the highest esteemed of all covenants existing between man and woman.

> Wherefore they are no more twain, but one flesh. What therefore God hath joined together, let not man put asunder.
> —MATTHEW 19:6

Enter divorce, such an ugly force. Divorce screams defeat, rejection, lies, and heartbreak. It spews despair, confusion, hardship, loneliness, fear, and depression. The bond of oneness is ripped apart, and cutting wounds seep with vengeance, bitterness, hate, and distrust. It leaves scars of failure, weakness, guilt, and shame. A breech of promise punctures dreams and shatters the family unit. Not only does it destroy relationships between the two people involved, but it also inflicts pain on many hearts. How God hates divorce, this pain that can continue for generations.

> For I hate divorce, says the LORD the God of Israel, and covering one's garment with violence, says the LORD of hosts. So take heed to yourselves and do not be faithless.
>
> —MALACHI 2:16, RSV

Consider Yahweh. A perfect God, Yahweh shines in holiness, purity, righteousness, and with no darkness. He abides in faithfulness, truth, and excellence. With an eternal bond to mankind by His Holy Spirit, He speaks through His Word. He gives guidelines for moral, honorable, and upright living and requires obedience, devotion, and dedication. The designer of the union of holy matrimony never intended that the glorious togetherness between husband and wife should fail. Holy Yahweh desires relationships to be unending. He—the God who fulfills His Word and never breaks His covenants—never fails. How I failed Him!

> For the woman which hath a husband is bound by the law to her husband so long as he liveth.
>
> —ROMANS 7:2

Can the One so faithful to His promises tolerate broken marriage vows? He must surely turn His back on those divorced.

At least that's the way I decided He felt toward me. It hurts to let you peer into this dark closet of my past, but I know the time has come for me to take you there.

How naïve I was at seventeen! Having dated only high school boys, I fell so easily for the suave young sailor I met when he came home on leave that autumn. After his return to the military base he delighted me with letters, gifts, and phone calls.

We dated constantly when he came back for Christmas. In the spring he popped in for my eighteenth birthday to surprise me with an engagement ring. Engulfed in clouds of romance, I accepted it despite frantic protests from my parents. "Please wait until you're older to even think of marriage. You're just eighteen, so inexperienced. You've spent so little time with him. At least put off wedding plans until you know each other better. What about your college plans?"

Like distant thunder their words rumbled in my brain to alert me that they were right. But the love song in my heart drowned them out.

He managed to make it home once more in May for my high school graduation. In September we married. Less than three months following our blissful wedding day, while living a thousand miles from my hometown and already having morning sickness, I realized there was a serious problem in our marriage.

Life wasn't altogether bad. After his discharge from the Navy in less than a year, we settled in the area where we both grew up, at home again among friends and family. He met the requirements to become a medical therapist. During our first four years together we had two beautiful children and built our first home. Yet problems mounted. At times we separated, then we would unite again to try to work things out. Finally our differences overtook our marriage vows. After more than eight years our marriage ended in divorce.

My heart mourned for my vanished "happily-ever-after" dreams and for the loss of the home life I had desired for my children. But I felt the deepest pain because of my broken wedding vows—vows I had made before a pure and holy God, the Abba Father I loved since childhood.

Chaste when I married, I now felt so used, so dirty and forsaken. Sinking in a sea of spiritual hopelessness and overcome with guilt, I concluded, *God surely must turn His back on those divorced!*

My marital situation had robbed me of self-worth. After jumping from high school and a brief summer job into years of being a housewife, how could I muster courage to strike out on my own? Could I even get a job? Who would ever want me? Yet how could I give up on life? Looking beyond my pain into the innocent faces of my son and daughter, I knew I couldn't wallow in self-pity and whine about past mistakes. At least for them I had to begin anew.

In effort to stay above my circumstances I began to seek the positive things of God. Norman Vincent Peale's book *The Power of Positive Thinking*[1] found its way into my hands, and I devoured it. Slowly I began moving forward, yet my heart still ached. How could I ever regain favor with a holy, righteous God? Years passed before I found the answer.

Today I understand that He looks not for a flawless heart, but rather a willing heart. Today I realize that as long as I seek Him, He will never turn His back on me. Today I've come to know His priceless name that brings me into His everlasting safekeeping regardless of my shortcomings. He is Yahweh Tsidkenu, Jehovah our Righteousness, so full of grace and mercy.

Are you hurting from some big mistake? Do guilt and condemnation throb within your heart? Then come with me to fellowship with Yahweh Tsidkenu. Together we'll abide in the hope He delivers in this name.

> Behold, the days come, saith the LORD, that I will raise unto David a
> righteous Branch, and a King shall reign and prosper, and shall execute
> judgment and justice in the earth. In his days Judah shall be saved, and
> Israel shall dwell safely: and this is his name whereby he shall be called,
> THE LORD OUR RIGHTEOUSNESS.
>
> —JEREMIAH 23:5–6

YAHWEH TSIDKENU, THE LORD OUR RIGHTEOUSNESS. The
title Yahweh/Jehovah speaks directly of Jesus, the righteous Branch of David
who came to Earth as Man, the King who will return to judge and govern
Earth in righteousness forever. Christ in His glorified authority exempli-
fies every name of Yahweh, especially Tsidkenu, for Christ Himself is our
Righteousness.

We can never be perfect. We all fail time after time. But His righteousness—no other—suffices for man. From the writings of Isaiah we read:

> But we are all as an unclean thing, and all our righteousnesses are as
> filthy rags.
>
> —ISAIAH 64:6

The apostle Paul agrees: "There is none righteous, no, not one" (Rom.
3:10).

Even if we always make correct and noble decisions...no matter how
hard we try within ourselves—the only way anyone can ever stand righteous
before our pure and holy Father is through our Redeemer's perfect sacrifice.
The only way we can claim any means of righteousness is to respond to Him
with a repentant heart and accept His payment for the penalty of sin. We
must believe that He is the Son of God and make Him Lord of our lives.
Paul goes on to say:

> But now the righteousness of God without the law is manifested...even
> the righteousness of God which is by faith of Jesus Christ unto all and
> upon all them that believe.
>
> —ROMANS 3:21–22

The righteousness of God is not just for some who believe. It is not for
any selected few, but it is unto all and upon all who believe. It is for every
believer.

Another time Paul states:

> For He made Him who knew no sin to be sin for us, that we might become the righteousness of God in Him.
>
> —2 Corinthians 5:21, NKJV

What a Savior! Yes, in Him we become the righteousness of God! Our own righteousness covers our imperfect flesh like mangy rotten rags. What a putrid stench it is to holy nostrils.

Yet complete in Christ we wear the clean and shining robes of His perfect righteousness. Adorned in the sweet savor of His purity we can stand before our Father. In the fullness of His authority our prayers rise as fragrant incense in His presence.

> For in him [Christ] dwelleth all the fullness of the Godhead bodily. And ye are complete in him, which is the head of all principalities and powers.
>
> —Colossians 2:9–10

Yes, in all aspects of Christ we are complete in Him. He is the One who sits in authority over all principalities and powers, the Redeemer who became sin for us on the cross. The Man Jesus, who lived as a mortal man and experienced Earth's temptations, sufferings, and grief, is the Messiah who understands our shortcomings. As the heavenly High Priest, He sits at the Father's right hand and makes intercession on our behalf. He is the precious Lamb who freely sacrificed His life so that the Father can look upon us through His spotless blood and see us as though we have no sin. This is our Lord who bestows His righteousness upon us.

Our own efforts can never be enough. Without the righteousness of Jesus we'd be lost in utter hopelessness forever, but because of it we can rest assured that when we sin and fail…

> If we confess our sins, he is faithful and just to forgive us our sins, and to cleanse us from all unrighteousness.
>
> —1 John 1:9

Regardless of past blunders, a true repentant heart finds reconciliation in Him. Sins are washed away, purity restored. No longer stained, we become complete in Him and His righteousness.

In His *Shekinah* glory His righteousness shines like the sun. Malachi 4:2 proclaims, "But unto you that fear my name shall the Sun of righteousness arise with healing in his wings."

Yahweh Tsidkenu, the brilliant Sun of righteousness, Christ Himself. He desires to heal your every hurt. With the gleaming radiance of His righteousness He longs to free you from your despair, confusion, hardship, bitterness, grief, anger, loneliness, illness, and depression—whatever has ripped your life apart.

Open your heart. Seek His righteousness and receive the healing in His wings. No matter what you've done or where you've been, no matter how many times you've made the wrong decision and missed the mark—His righteousness avails. He gives us His assurance that all who hunger and thirst after righteousness will be blessed (supremely happy) and filled (most abundantly satisfied) (Matt. 5:6). So if your heart is sorrowful for any wrongdoings and mistakes and passionate after His ways, He will nourish your yearning spirit back to health.

He did for me. After a long battle within myself—feeling unworthy, not good enough, totally rejected—I learned to depend on His righteousness, not on my own. Now restored and cleansed, in right standing before Him and set apart as His, I walk with Him every day. Yes, I strive for a holy life, but it is by His victory, not mine.

In addition to this expression of His nature God reveals another title that speaks of His work to bring us into perfection with Him. He is Yahweh M'Kaddesh, the Lord Who Sanctifies.

> Sanctify yourselves therefore, and be ye holy: for I am the LORD your God. And ye shall keep my statutes, and do them: I am the LORD which sanctify you.
>
> —LEVITICUS 20:7–8

To sanctify means to cleanse, purify, refine, and set aside as holy. In the name of Yahweh M'Kaddish He purges the sin of His people and separates them unto Himself as holy. He requires all to sanctify themselves by wholeheartedly pursuing Him, living according to His Word, and acting in faith. Therefore, sanctification for any believer becomes an ongoing process of embracing His righteousness and growing in holiness—not by a sinless life, but by a life of continual progression toward righteousness.

Sanctification should govern the Christian's spirit and establish a right way of conduct. It is God's work of guiding our thoughts and emotions and conforming us into His likeness.

> And be renewed in the spirit of your mind; and that ye put on the new man, which after God is created in righteousness and true holiness.
>
> —EPHESIANS 4:23–24

> And be not conformed to this world: but be ye transformed by the
> renewing of your mind, that ye may prove what is that good, and
> acceptable, and perfect, will of God.
>
> —ROMANS 12:2

Sanctification calls for daily renewal and pressing on to perfection. It is
not only that we become complete in Him but also truly one with Him,
members of His body, part of His glorious church.

> That he might sanctify and cleanse it with the washing of water by the
> word, that he might present it to himself a glorious church, not hav-
> ing spot, or wrinkle, or any such thing; but that it should be holy and
> without blemish.
>
> —EPHESIANS 5:26–27

Yes, cleansed, purified, refined, set apart, and consecrated for His purpose, we are one with Him.

> For we are members of his body, of his flesh, and of his bones.
>
> —EPHESIANS 5:30

Andrew Murray, a nineteenth-century minister, spoke of the process of
sanctification as "Holy-making." I like this definition he gives: "Sanctified is
cleansed from sin, taken out of the sphere and power of the world and sin,
and brought to live in the sphere and power of God's holiness in the Holiest
of All."[2]

Can mere man ever reach the ultimate of sanctification to dwell at a
level above the grips of temptation? Has anyone ever truly accomplished
this?

Well, it seems that four men did. Daniel lived in this sphere of God's
holiness and triumphed in the lions' den. His three colleagues—Shadrach,
Meshach, and Abednego—lived accordingly, and they emerged in victory
from the fiery furnace. What examples for us to follow!

How did they do it? With fortitude and determination they chose a sanctified life. Not half-hearted in their decision, they remained totally sold out
to God regardless of their situation, always keeping His statutes and performing them. Perhaps we need a hands-on look.

OH, THE WONDERLAND of Babylon! With Jerusalem captured by the
Babylonian King Nebuchadnezzar, these four young Hebrews, chosen for

special service by the king himself, awaken to an exquisite world of partying and luxury.

There is such splendor to behold. The city spreads out in grandeur on both sides of the Euphrates River. Palaces stretch high into the sky. Towers spiral above the multitudes of temples and shrines honoring many gods. Spacious courtyards and houses stretch beyond our sight into the distance.

Home after home and structure after structure are fortified within a massive wall and heavily guarded gates. Each entrance presents a superb work of art, yet none compare to the magnificent Gate of Ishtar with its miles of enameled walls displaying masterpieces of dragons and bulls.

Inside the city statues of ferocious lions line the main avenue, which is paved with smooth stones. Groves of stately palm trees lend their shade to it as well as to numerous other streets and walkways. Nothing lacks in beauty. The entire landscape flourishes from an abundance of water drawn from amazing underground canals.

But the most spectacular site of all—the famous Hanging Gardens—reach like a majestic mountain far above the heights of the city. How they dazzle the horizon with breathtaking greenery. An exotic oasis, it is a bewitching pleasure ground prized for its wonder throughout the entire world. Exquisitely terraced and superbly manicured, it is absolute perfection and loveliness beyond belief.

Oh, the intrigue of Babylon! With its hustle and bustle it is the focal point of trade where merchants congregate from regions far and wide to buy and sell. Countless processions of caravans arrive daily. A few noblemen sport fine chariots while throngs clamor about on camels, horses, and donkeys. Others pour in by boat. All rush after precious gems, perfumes, oils, fabrics, grains, spices, produce, art, and other exotic treasures of the city.

Drawn by excitement, people draped in bright fashions and adorned in jewelry swarm like bees in the courtyards and temples. Life vibrates with constant celebration here. Lively pagan festivals, elaborate parades, banquets, and dancing fill the social calendar. With harps, flutes, cornets, and bagpipes, merrymaking bursts to life. Thrilling sports events, especially the most popular lion fighting, take place inside a gigantic arena. Cheering rings through the streets.

Yes, what glamour Babylonian culture unveils before the eyes of Daniel, Shadrach, Meshach, and Abednego. Temptation lurks in every corner, and they have every opportunity to partake.

King Nebuchadnezzar has appointed them to attend the finest school Babylon has to offer. It is a most prestigious training center for magistrates, wizards, counselors, and all the elite with its grand location inside the king's palace. Arrayed in the best of garments and lavished in finery, these boys no doubt realize the superb privilege and esteem of being selected.

What pride these vibrant Jewish teenagers could feel! They are at such a vulnerable age to be seduced by this rich society of black magic. How typical it would be that they in their youthfulness would succumb to peer pressure and desire to blend in with the other students and gain acceptance as part of the group. Oh, the urge to enter into the full swing of Babylon must be overpowering.

But they don't give in. Even amid such a captivating culture of indulgence their devotion remains fixed upon their God. Although the king changes their Hebrew names that esteem Yahweh to names glorifying false gods of Babylon, he can never change their hearts.

What boldness these boys display. When their first test of faith arises and they ask permission to be excluded from the rich feasts of the king's diet, which defiles their Jewish laws, they don't merely jeopardize their status with other students; they risk their very lives. Yet the king's official honors their request without even becoming angered.

How God blesses their stand for Him. They receive promotion among their peers and are so mightily increased in godly wisdom and insight that they amaze the king and all his court.

They continue to honor Jehovah with sanctified lives, sold out to Him, throughout many years of living among the Babylonians. We find no history of any wavering. Even after nearly twenty years of exposure to pagan ways Shadrach, Meshach, and Abednego choose being thrown into the fire over worshiping Nebuchadnezzar's golden image. And Daniel, as an elderly man around the age of eighty, faces hungry lions rather than defy his God—still choosing to be set apart and consecrated for God's service.

Yes, what an example of sanctification for us to follow! Can we do it? As I did when my marriage ended, you may be saying, "I've failed already."

Look up! You may have faltered in God's plan for you, and your dreams may have burst into shambles, but unless you refuse to pull yourself out of your rubble and rebuild, you haven't failed. We have an understanding God.

> If thou, Lord, shouldest mark iniquities, O Lord, who shall stand? But there is forgiveness with thee, that thou mayest be feared.
>
> —Psalm 130:3–4

In His mercy God gives hope and a new beginning. His grace flows with freedom from guilt. With a repentant heart you can walk anew. Forgiveness is yours. Push aside your faults, and make a sincere effort to move ahead with the One who sanctifies. Yahweh M'Kaddesh has a destiny for you.

CONSIDER ABRAHAM, THE father of our faith, the man whose great faith was accounted unto him as righteousness. Certainly he lived a life sanctified by God. Yet he faltered more than once.

However, Abraham never let his imperfections deflect him from his destiny with God. Neither did God cast Abraham aside because he wasn't always perfect. When called to leave his homeland, Abram didn't hesitate to go. God said:

> Get thee out of thy country, and from thy kindred, and from thy father's house, unto a land that I will shew thee.
>
> —GENESIS 12:1

What about Lot, the son of Abram's deceased brother? His nephew was certainly his "kindred." But Abram allowed Lot to tag along. Did God mean, "Take some of your kinfolks if you want to"?

No. Abram conformed God's instruction to suit his own desire. Taking Lot with him proved to be a troublesome decision. Before long his herdsmen and Lot's herdsmen began to quarrel.

This brought about another alteration in God's plan. With generous virtue Abram let his nephew choose land for himself. Lot wanted the best, and, without balking, Abram let him have it. On the surface this seems quite nice of Abram. It certainly reveals his unselfish nature, which without question shows a quality to be admired.

But let's look further. God had promised that all the land would belong to Abram and his descendants, not to his nephew. Did Abram possess the right to give any of it away?

No. And this decision almost caused total disaster for Lot. Only the pleadings of Abram to Jehovah saved Lot from the doom of Sodom in the nick of time.

Not until Abram and Lot parted did God begin fulfilling His promises to Abram. The name *Lot* means "veiled." It seems that until the "veil" (hindrance) was removed, God delayed His action.

Yet even so, Abram and Sarai decided that He was moving too slowly. So they adjusted God's timetable by devising their own way to produce a son. Hagar the servant girl could complete God's promise. But could she?

No. This decision only brought heartache and complications, which still exist today between the Jews and the Arabs.

Abraham faltered in his walk with God another time when he deceived a king about Sarah's real identity as his spouse. "She's my sister," he declared. This was true to a degree, since she was indeed his half-sister. However,

Abraham risked an adulterous situation by covering up the fact Sarah was his wife. Why did he do this? Because he, this man of great faith, feared for his life. What, we have to wonder, happened to his faith at this point?

Yet in viewing the way he pushed on to accomplish his destiny with God, we see that in spite of his shortcomings, his splendid faith gave him right standing in God's sight. And God called Abraham His friend (James 2:23).

Even though Abraham faltered on the road to spiritual maturity, his true goal never wavered as his heart embraced his purpose in God's plan. Because of this, despite his human faults, he continued on in a lifestyle sanctified unto the Lord—pressing on until his faith matured to withstand any challenge. Hs faith was so strong that even the greatest trial could no longer cause him to blunder.

God never forsakes His people despite their imperfections. Although many suffer condemnation for making wrong decisions, they don't have to continue under such oppression. God accepted Abraham because of his faith, not because of his perfection. God will do the same for us today.

> And because of Abraham's faith God forgave his sins and declared him 'not guilty.' Now this wonderful statement—that he was accepted and approved through his faith—wasn't just for Abraham's benefit. It was for us, too, assuring us that God will accept us in the same way he accepted Abraham—when we believe the promises of God who brought back Jesus our Lord from the dead. He died for our sins and rose again to make us right with God, filling us with God's goodness.
>
> —Romans 4:22–25, TLB

AT CALVARY JESUS justified us (made us just as if we never sinned), filling us with the righteousness of God in Him. By His perfect sacrifice we became His, sanctified forever.

> We are sanctified through the offering of the body of Jesus Christ once for all.... For by one offering he hath perfected for ever them that are sanctified.
>
> —Hebrews 10:10, 14

If only I had realized this sooner. After my divorce I struggled with guilt. Had I just understood the benefits of Yahweh Tsidkenu, the Lord our Righteousness, and Yahweh M'Kaddesh, the One who sanctifies, I could have walked in freedom with Jesus instead of being trapped by condemnation.

When I married again a year and half after my divorce, I floundered in the mire of shame for eight more years. Just about the time I would climb out, Satan's deception would hurl me down into the mud again.

One incident especially pains my heart. I tuned in to a phone-in radio program and heard a preacher answering questions. An anguished caller poured out her heart, crying for help in a story somewhat like this.

"My husband left me for another woman who was expecting his baby. After our divorce he married her, and they moved away. He never contacts our four children anymore. Though he pays some child support, I simply can't make ends meet. My question is, can a woman in this situation marry again and still remain right with God?"

"No," the preacher said emphatically.

"But you see," she said, "I met this man at church. He's a Christian and so good to me. He loves my kids as his own. Last week we got married. We so want God's blessing!"

Without compassion the preacher read Romans 7:2–4: "For the woman which hath a husband is bound by the law to her husband so long as he liveth; but if the husband be dead, she is loosed from the law of her husband. So then if, while her husband liveth, she be married to another man, she shall be called an adulteress: but if her husband be dead, she is free from that law; so that she is no adulteress, though she be married to another man."

In his own words he added, "As long as your husband lives, you are never free to marry again. And you should leave the man you're with now. Or be lost."

Crash! A new mudslide of condemnation slammed down on me. I too had already remarried. Jim came as a beautiful rainbow after a terrible storm. The children and I loved him so, and he loved us. How could I ever cast him aside?

But if I didn't, was I doomed forever as an adulteress? My heart boomed with grief and fear.

Today, after extensive probing into these verses, I realize that Paul writes them to contrast the Old Covenant of law and our New Covenant of grace. He wasn't teaching on remarriage after divorce, but only using the strict order of the Mosiac Law on this subject (something the people of this day understood) in a metaphorical sense.

Notice that Paul says she is "bound by the law." Under the Law a woman could never leave her husband and marry again as long as he lived.

Also under the Law, the man always obtained the divorce, never the woman. This passage says being "loosed from the law of her husband." After a man divorced a woman, he was no longer considered or ever called her "husband" again. Therefore, this passage speaks not of a divorced woman, cast aside by a former husband, but rather a wife, bound by the Law, who left her husband.

Paul spoke these words to illustrate a point. In allegory he speaks of Christians as no longer "married" to the Law, which in a sense "died" when the New Covenant came into effect.

For Paul to say no pardon could ever be given for any divorce—no matter what the reason—would contradict other New Testament teachings, including not just his own statements but also those of Jesus.

But at the time I heard that radio preacher, my understanding in the meat of the Word was so limited. I didn't know how to search out the answer for myself, so I grieved inside, feeling so unworthy, trapped in shame, a prisoner to past mistakes, cast aside, and forever filthy in the eyes of God.

Several told me that Jesus (in His sermon on the mount) gives the act of fornication (sexual sin) as a pardonable reason for divorce. (See Matthew 5:31–32.) Nevertheless, in my state of self-condemnation, my mind would argue, *He directed His words about fornication to the man and not to the woman*—"But I say unto you, That whosoever shall put away his wife, saving for the cause of fornication..." (v. 32).

What about adulterous acts of the husband? my heart would pound. *Do they give the woman a right to divorce?* Today I realize the customs of that time and understand that Jesus spoke to Jews still under the Law, which allowed only for the man to "put away" the wife. To speak of a woman seeking divorce would only bring confusion.

In secret desperation I fought with guilt for so very long while feelings of unworthiness deadlocked my spiritual growth. Yet as my heart yearned for Him, I prayed each day and sought the guidance of His ways. Little by little the seeds of His Word began to grow through the soil of my anguish. Despite all opposition wisdom sprouted.

> If any of you lack wisdom, let him ask of God, that giveth to all men liberally, and upbraideth not; and it shall be given him.
>
> —JAMES 1:5

Guided by His wisdom, I obeyed His advice and shared the inner shame that haunted me with a Christian friend:

> Confess your faults one to another, and pray one for another, that ye may be healed. The effectual fervent prayer of a righteous man availeth much.
>
> —JAMES 5:16

Oh, my traveling companions, if you receive nothing else from our journey together, believe this—God's Word works! It never, never fails!

Although my friend had no inkling of how deeply guilt ate at me, God soon used her to open my eyes to the Sun of Righteousness with His healing wings. I remember the time she said, "I'm reading a book, *Second Fiddle*, and feel overwhelmed to read this part to you." Then from the autobiography of Henry Harrison, a Christian talk show co-host who remarried after a disastrous marriage, she preceded with his own words:

> One day at CBN I went to Pat Robertson and said, "Pat, you have met Susan, and you know her. I feel that the Lord has ordained that she and I should be married. I'd like to ask you if you would see fit to perform the ceremony?"
>
> "Henry," he said, "I see no reason why not." He pointed me again to a Scripture he had used in counseling me at various times through the years, stating that 1 Corinthians 7:15 means that if the unbelieving partner in a marriage would depart, let him depart. A brother or a sister is not under bondage in such a case, for God has called us to peace. Pat pointed out that in the original Greek the words "the believer is no longer under bondage, and no longer bound," the literal meaning is that when the unbeliever has departed that it's the same as if they were dead because spiritually that is true. In such a case the believer no longer being bound is free to marry. It's a beautiful thing when the Word of God and the truth we feel from the Lord are in perfect harmony.

While my friend continued reading my heart stood still. Each word sent cold chills over me as guilt and hopelessness burst like a geyser from my being:

> The thing that probably did more to set me free from the previous entanglement and to give me peace in my heart about my marriage to Susan is the fact that I know in my heart, I serve a God who is capable and lovingly forgives a person of any sin or anything that a person will bring to Him in confession and repentance. A God who can forgive murder (Moses), robbery, adultery (David), and anything else that is not pleasing to Him can also forgive a mistake in marriage. I have received this forgiveness, and I thank the Lord for it. In tracing the genealogy of Jesus in Mark 1:6 [actually Matthew 1:6], we find that He was a direct descendant of Solomon, who was born to David the king, by she who had been the wife of Uriah.[3]

Isn't God good? A few years later He gave me an opportunity to tell Henry Harrison in person how his book delivered me from such a miry grave of guilt.

Oh, the depth with God my newfound freedom brought. It released me from my cesspool of pain and caused my spirit to sparkle like a redeemed sunken treasure. Never could I have freed myself—it took His Word, spotless blood, and righteousness to cover the transgression of my mistake in marriage. In addition to my repentance, it required my acceptance of His forgiveness before I could experience the glory of His sanctification, cleansed and consecrated for His purpose.

No one needs to live with gnawing fear, bogged down in guilt! God isn't lording it over His children with a blackjack ready to strike them down into eternal damnation. Never let past mistakes hinder your spiritual walk, as I did in ignorance of His mercy. God stands by with grace and love eager to free you from all condemnation. He forgives. So forgive yourself! And feel His freedom flow.

> There is therefore now no condemnation to them which are in Christ Jesus, who walk not after the flesh, but after the Spirit.
>
> —Romans 8:1

Free from condemnation, you can walk after the Spirit in a sanctified life. Even if you falter you'll never fail. If you slip, admit your mistake and climb back upon the road of cleansing, never letting a wrong step bind you in guilt and shame. Go as the apostle Paul, never looking back:

> Brethren, I do not count myself to have apprehended; but one thing I do, forgetting those things which are behind and reaching forward to those things which are ahead, I press toward the goal for the prize of the upward call of God in Christ Jesus.
>
> —Philippians 3:13–14, nkjv

Yes, forget and move forward. Press—pushing hard, not giving up—until you receive the reward of your high calling, your destiny in Christ Jesus. Renewed you stand before Him without blemish, justified, just as though you never sinned. You are His. Spirit, soul, and body, with perfect heart, fixed and true.

Yet this presents only the beginning for believers!

After allowing His cleansing and receiving His forgiveness, don't stop. Go on to discover His complete wholeness and healing—not only emotionally and spiritually—but physically as well. We have a God who heals in every single aspect.

In this virtue He bears another title. Yahweh Rophe. Jehovah our Health. The Lord Who Heals.

Are you ready for another excursion? Brace yourself as our path takes a daring turn to investigate this name and move beyond the ordinary. In Yahweh Rophe we will find the strength available to stand against disease, to recover from injury, to alleviate pain, and to daily walk in health.

Oh, the awesomeness of God!

Chapter 7

Rophe

YAHWEH ROPHE—THE TITLE of our God who heals.

Then why did Cynthia have to die?

Bewildered, my heart burned with grief. Cynthia believed whole-heartedly that God would heal her disease. With many others I stood by her in prayer and faith. But Cynthia died.

I miss her so. For thirty years we'd been close friends. Our friendship, which had budded when we were frivolous teenagers, blossomed into a deep-rooted spiritual bond as adults. Then at age forty-four she suffered a most painful death.

Maintaining a strong belief that she lived in divine health Cynthia refused to accept the fact of her illness, telling only her husband about it for a long while. When I detected something amiss she said, "I'm fighting a physical condition, and I'll be OK. By the stripes of Jesus I am healed."

Cynthia loved Jesus. Her heart ballooned with care and compassion for others, overflowing in Christian works. She trusted God's healing power with all her being. *If anyone deserves to be healed*, I thought, *Cynthia does*. I waited in expectation.

But Cynthia died.

Why, oh, why, did it happen?

Some said that because of her goodness God wanted her to be in heaven with Him. I believe this idea is absurd. Why would God desire an untimely death for a mother who is rearing her young children to live in devout admiration of Him? Why, when she took in foster children and also instilled Jesus in their neglected hearts? Why, when time after time she read in the local newspaper about strangers in distress and then looked them up, ministered to their needs, and turned their lives upon the road to heaven? Yes why, when Cynthia practiced such dedication to God's purposes on Earth, would He prefer for her to be in heaven?

Several said God made her sick to teach her something. Others said she suffered for His glory. Ludicrous! What kind of father wants to watch his loving child agonize, wither away to forty pounds, then die in order to teach her something? What good could she or anybody else learn by this? And how can God find glory in such horror?

Some declared God no longer heals today. From experiences in my own family, which I'll share with you very soon, I know this is not true.

Some remarked, "It wasn't His will for her to be healed." Or, "It was just her time to go."

Aching for consolation I searched all aspects of physical healing—spiritual means by faith in God, man's power within himself, and natural means with doctors, exercise and diet. And now as I take you on my exploration, come in childlike wonder and leave biased opinions behind.

In our past excursion we came to know the qualities of Yahweh Tsidkenu (the Lord Our Righteousness) and M'Kaddesh (our Sanctifier). We touched upon His emotional and spiritual healings. However, Yahweh bears the title *Rophe* for all His healing virtues, including wellness for the whole person— spirit, soul, and body. Yes, Yahweh Rophe, Jehovah Our Health, the Lord Who Heals. Glorious are His benefits.

How tragic it is that most people never abide in the fullness of His nature, but wander instead in the wilderness of infirmity. Why? Giants! They lurk throughout the land of promise—a land that flows with vitality and strength. But the land belongs to every child of God who is willing to contend for it.

Is it possible to defeat the giants? Yes. Together we made it over a wall of fantasies concerning angels, and together we can triumph over every obstacle that bars our way to health. In this adventure our roads may be rough and the battlefields fierce, but victory belongs to all who determine to overcome. Prepare for many confrontations as we travel, and brace yourself now to face our first menace head-on.

The Giant of Uncertainty

Uncertainty roars with troubling questions, "Is it always God's will for His people to be well? Isn't affliction often for His glory?" With Bible in hand we search for evidence. We see two times when God was glorified, not from afflictions, but by His healing!

When Mary and Martha sent Jesus word that their brother Lazarus was sick, Jesus said, "This sickness is not unto death, but for the glory of God, that the son of God might be glorified thereby" (John 11:4).

How was He glorified? By raising Lazarus from the dead!

There was another time when Jesus said a physical ailment was for God's glory. And again, glory came through healing. After restoring sight to a blind man, Jesus said the blindness had occurred "that the works of God should be made manifest in him" (John 9:3).

So yes, God can receive glory from affliction, if the one who is sick experiences miraculous recovery and gives God the glory for his healing. Are you undergoing sickness for His glory? Flee from the anti-healing crowd that hovers over you, and turn a deaf ear to uncertainty. Let the works of God be made manifest in you. Be healed. That is what gives Him glory.

Uncertainty erupts again, this time with scripture:

> Beloved, think it not strange concerning the fiery trial which is to try you, as though some strange thing happened unto you: But rejoice, inasmuch as ye are partakers of Christ's sufferings; that, when his glory is revealed, ye may be glad also with exceeding joy.
>
> —1 Peter 4:12–13

Are sickness and disease the fiery trial that makes us partakers of Christ's sufferings and revealing His glory? The very next verse (v. 14) tells us how Christ is glorified—"If ye be reproached for the name of Christ." The word *reproach*ed means railed, chided, taunted, reviled, upbraided, defamed, assailed with abusive words.[1] Not one definition even hints at sickness.

James 1:2–3 tells us to count it as joy when we fall into various temptations for the *trying* of our faith. The Greek word for *trying* means a testing, trying, and by implication—trustworthiness.[2] Here we see trials of resisting temptation as tests of faith, not trials of being sick.

Still the giant of uncertainty bellows, "You're supposed to be sick. As a man Christ suffered, and so should you." To substantiate this notion he brings up another verse:

> For to this you have been called, because Christ also suffered for you,
> leaving you an example, that you should follow in his steps.
> —1 Peter 2:21, rsv

Wait just a minute. How should we follow in Christ's steps? By examples He left us. Exactly what examples of suffering did He leave? The next two verses say:

> He committed no sin; no guile was found on his lips. When he was reviled, he did not revile in return; when he suffered, he did not threaten; but he trusted to him who judges justly.
> —1 Peter 2:22–23, rsv

We notice that this doesn't talk about suffering by being sick. For reinforcement, let's look at a couple more scriptures that shed light on Christ's suffering:

> For in that he himself hath suffered being tempted...
> —Hebrews 2:18

> For Christ also hath once suffered for sins, the just for the unjust, that he might bring us to God, being put to death in the flesh.
> —1 Peter 3:18

During His ministry on Earth Jesus suffered, being tempted and resisting temptation, willing to give His life for the cause of His kingdom. Without struggling against the Father's will He suffered His ordeal of death, carrying out the plan of redemption. None of this suffering included being sick. As we found in studying the sufferings of Paul, never does the Bible record that Christ suffered any illness during His life on earth.

How should we in turn suffer for Him? First Peter 3:14 tells us: "for righteousness' sake," being happy and not afraid or troubled by the terror of evildoers. Three verses down we read, "For it is better, if the will of God be so, that ye suffer for well doing, than for evil doing" (v. 17).

To follow the example of Christ our suffering should be as His—suffering for well doing. How? By battling for the purposes of His kingdom, not in weakness, but strong in spiritual, emotional, and physical being. We are to proclaim the gospel and live for God by faith, overcoming temptation and its trials.

> Ye are in heaviness through manifold temptations: That the trial of your faith, being much more precious than of gold that perisheth, though it

be tried with fire, might be found unto praise and honour and glory at
the appearing of Jesus Christ.

—1 PETER 1:6–7

Yes, these things bring Him glory. Sickness, however, is found in the
category of diabolic cruelties, not as suffering for Jesus!

Still the giant of uncertainty refuses to give up: "At times God makes you
sick to teach you something!"

We turn to the Bible again to see if Yahweh ever transmitted sickness or
disease to man to teach him something. At times He did. He allowed such
things as plagues, leprosy, and even fatal snake bites. But when God chose
such drastic measures, there was a single cause—sin.

It may have been blatant rebellion, whining, pouting, belittling His plan,
responding to Him in fright and unbelief, refusing to submit and obey, or
sometimes just plain old brutality and wickedness among men. But always
due to sin, at God's sanction torment struck. It was only in judgment for
wrongdoing, no other reason.

So, friend, if you feel that your suffering comes from God to teach you
something, then by all means repent and recover. On the other hand, if you
believe your illness is somehow God's will but not a judgment for sin, I must
reinforce what an evangelist once said: "If it's His will for you to be sick and
to suffer, then why do you pray to get well or even go to a doctor? Instead,
shouldn't you be telling Him, 'Heap more sickness on me. Just pour it on,
Lord. Teach me more!'"

Sickness doesn't come from God but from the enemy! The Bible declares
that our heavenly Father is a giver of good and perfect gifts (James 1:17), a
God not only of love but a God who is love (1 John 4:8). He does not will
pain and agony on His obedient children to teach them something.

NOW THE GIANT of uncertainty spits out an avalanche of controversy
with the heated, age-old query: what about Job? God called him a perfect
and upright man who feared Him and avoided evil. Why then did He per-
mit Satan to attack Job with sickness and sorrow?

Abraham was also declared right in God's sight, yet we've seen that he
sometimes fell short. Like Abraham, Job was human. Perfect in his pursuit
for the ways of God perhaps, but only Christ stands as a sinless Man. So
what did Job do wrong? For one thing, he harbored fear. When disaster
struck, he admitted:

For the thing which I greatly feared is come upon me, and that which
I was afraid of is come unto me.

—Job 3:25

Is fear sin?

Yes. Although this fact may hit you like falling rock, all fear except reverent fear for God definitely ranks as sin. For starters, fear is disobedience.
Over and over the Bible admonishes us not to fear. Why? Fear shows doubt
and distrust. You cannot entertain faith and fear at the same time because
they stand in opposition. In fact, fear devours faith. And without faith it is
impossible to please God (Heb. 11:6).

Jesus asked His disciples, "Why are ye so fearful? How is that ye have
no faith?" (Mark 4:40). Jesus told Jairus, "Be not afraid, only believe"
(Mark 5:36).

Fear can be a death sentence. Because they were afraid of giants in the
Promised Land, the Hebrews died in the wilderness.

So did Job's fear cause a break in the hedge of safety God had built around
him (Job 1:10)? Did fear give Satan a loophole to persuade God to let him
worm his way beyond the hedge and into Job's domain?

Possibly. But no one can state absolutely that this once-mentioned fault
gave foothold for the devil to invade Job's life with such havoc.

Nevertheless, one thing is certain. Even though God granted permission
for Satan to persecute Job, it was not His will for Job to *remain* diseased,
defeated, destitute, or in despair.

We find the turning point of Job's predicament in the last chapter of his
story. Here we also detect another fault. Until his devastation Job evidently
considered himself a most remarkable being. However, immediately before
his deliverance his view completely changes. As he recognizes his own insig-
nificance in comparison to his supreme, holy, eternal Creator, Job pulsates
with remorse realizing and admitting his human status in humbled perception. He sees himself not as some ideal specimen but a mere mortal, an
appalling subject in contrast to God Almighty. In humility he cries:

My ears had heard of you but now my eyes have seen you. Therefore I
despise myself and repent in dust and ashes.

—Job 42:5–6, NIV

Only after Job's repentance did God restore him. He blessed Job not only
by renewing his health but also by giving him far more in the end than he
possessed in the beginning.

Ah, ha! As the sovereignty of God honored the trusting and contrite heart of Job, Satan lost in his battle of oppression. The healing virtue of Yahweh was manifested! And Job, never wavering in faith throughout his ordeal, developed a much deeper awareness of the Lord's restoring power:

> I know that you can do all things; no plan of yours can be thwarted.
> —Job 42:2, NIV

Yes, in the end Job emerged healed and whole, a wiser, humbler man. His afflictions definitely "taught him something."

What about present times? Can modern man, like Job, learn through physical devastation? Yes, of course he can.

Can God teach through sickness even now? He surely can. God never changes. Many positive things can take place during illness.

Injury and disease often walk hand in hand with repentance. Suffering can bring one to his knees until like Job, he sees himself as nothing compared to the greatness of God. Bcoming aware of their mortal limitations without help from above, many learn how to truly rely on God.

Faith often takes root in moments of difficulty. As the person with physical afflictions meets alone with God in the place of prayer, his fellowship with God grows.

The right response to sickness can develop compassion for the suffering of others. It can also resolve problems of unforgiveness, make ongoing disagreements with friends or family members seem trivial, and thereby settle long-held bitterness.

We can list other expressions of spiritual growth, but certainly pain and hardship are not prerequisites for teaching such things. If we sincerely seek Christ, spiritual closeness and charitable virtues will flow naturally. It doesn't take pain and misery to make a heart right with God.

It has never been God's plan to force us to serve Him. What an insult to the One who designs perfection! Before we go any further, let's place blame where it is due. On us! In the beginning, mankind himself brought sorrow, sickness, and sin into the world. Because of our shortcomings, all these continue to thrive today.

Still in His mercy God never deserts us. When we begin to sink in our man-made mire, He steps in with a solution for all who seek and accept it. He always has.

OH, THOSE GRUMBLING Israelites! In Numbers 21:1–9 we read about another of Israel's wilderness experiences. The Lord had given them a glorious victory over the aggressive Canaanite King Arad, but as usual they soon became bogged down again in desert hardships. Despite their supernatural triumph they blasphemed God's goodness.

"Moses! Why have you brought us out of Egypt to die in this desert? There's no bread. No water. And we hate this manna!"

Because of their murmuring and rebuke Yahweh in His righteous judgment dispersed fiery serpents among them. Many died from bites. But when they admitted their sins and repented, pleading with Moses to intercede for their deliverance, the Lord sent His solution to save them.

"Moses, make a brass serpent and erect it upon a pole. All who look upon it shall live."

Moses followed God's instructions. Anyone who had been bitten by a live snake only had to peer up at the brazen one that was hanging on a pole, and he would live instead of die. It was such a simple act to by which the people could receive healing. But the tragedy is that their dilemma was so unnecessary. Long ago Yahweh told them:

> If thou wilt diligently hearken to the voice of the LORD thy God, and wilt do that which is right in his sight, and wilt give ear to his commandments, and keep all his statutes, I will put none of these diseases upon thee, which I have brought upon the Egyptians: for I am the LORD that healeth thee.
>
> —EXODUS 15:26

With these words He introduced Himself as Yahweh Rophe. Healing belonged to them. Divine health was theirs if they would just obey.

Yet they mumbled and complained in unbelief, refusing to take God at His word, listening instead to the voice of uncertainty. And they missed out on their promise of a whole and healthy lifestyle. They lost touch with their healing LORD, Yahweh Rophe.

Is dealing with adversity much different today? How do you react to unpleasant situations? Have you been grumbling and complaining? Do you feel as if you've been bitten by a fiery serpent? Are you defeated by your circumstances, trapped in pessimism, too weak to pull yourself out, ready to die?

Don't listen to uncertainty another second. Ask forgiveness for your misdoings, and turn to your heavenly Father in obedience. He's still the same "LORD that healeth thee" today. And He offers the same simple solution to turn your life around. Jesus reveals it in John 3:14–15:

> And as Moses lifted up the serpent in the wilderness, even so must the

Son of man be lifted up: That whosoever believeth in him should not perish, but have eternal life.

Look to Jesus on the cross. Emotional healing and physical healing begin with spiritual healing. The Greek word *salvation* means deliver, health, save, rescue, safety deliverance, preservation from danger or destruction.[3] All this is supplied by the Son of God, our Savior. The psalmist writes:

> He sent his word, and healed them, and delivered them from their destruction.
>
> —Psalm 107:20

God sent His Word in the flesh—Jesus, who always did the will of the Father—to bring healing to all. Not once did He deny any who asked to be healed. Never did He say, "It's not my Father's will for you to be made well. He wants you sick."

John, the disciple of Jesus who wrote the Gospel of John, three New Testament letters, and the Book of Revelation, tells us:

> Beloved, I wish above all things that thou mayest prosper and be in health, even as thy soul prospereth.
>
> —3 John 2

Would Almighty God let John announce in His inspired Word that "above all things" he wishes for his "beloved to prosper and be in health" if being healed was ever against His will?

Of course not. Believe His Word! Make a vow to never again agree with or even entertain an unsure thought. Let faith arise with power like a fountain within, washing away all inclination that it is not God's will for you to be whole spiritually, emotionally, and physically. And watch the giant of uncertainty vanish as quickly as a campfire on the beach when the high tide rolls in.

But don't let your guard down. Even with uncertainty defeated our fight has just begun. Other giants work to block our way to wellness. Watch out! The next one is attacking, and he's violent.

The Giant of Power Denial

This giant probably thwarts a person's recovery more than any other by teaching against God's ability to heal today. Completely opposed to any thought of divine healing, he convulses with ingrained secular thinking as well as powerless religious doctrine.

We hear him yell, "What good does prayer do? If medical science says it's terminal and doctors have done all they can, accept it. Whatever will be, will be."

But God's Word says to act on our adverse circumstances! Attack!

> Be strong in the Lord, and in the power of his might. Put on the whole armour of God, that ye may be able to stand against the wiles of the devil.
>
> —EPHESIANS 6:10–11

Oh dear, have we provoked this giant? In defiance he rises like a demon breathing lethal fumes, closing our minds even tighter, suffocating us with hopeless beliefs, poisoning us with deadly differences among God's people.

Dare we still oppose him? Yes, but to escape such toxins we must bind ourselves together in love with open minds to find out what the Bible truly says.

This giant deals death. Our only chance of overthrowing him exists in relying on God's capability and turning away from any doctrine "having a form of godliness, but denying the power thereof" (2 Tim. 3:5).

How loudly this monster cries, "God's supernatural acts of healing are no longer available for you today. He only performed miracles before man possessed the completed New Testament as his guide. When its writing was finished, man no longer needed to see manifestations of His power. Reading about them is all you need now. You live under the New Covenant. Miracles passed away with the Old."

Honestly, do such notions make any sense? Isn't the New Covenant of grace better than the Old Covenant of law? Jesus said He came to bring us life more abundantly (John 10:10).

How would not having the Lord God to heal us make a more abundant life? After all, even though the Bible reached completion nearly two thousand years ago, His healing power is still needed. People do get sick!

Sadly, God's time of miracles *has* ended for those who choose to believe the lie that it has. In accepting such teaching they trade a supernatural God for one who just sits on a throne and watches His people suffer sickness here on earth. This false perception grieves my heart because I know it is not true.

Why, oh, why, do churches disagree about God's miracle power today? How can anyone believe that He can still hear prayer, forgive sins and save souls, but can no longer heal bodies? Aren't all these miraculous acts?

What gives anyone authority to say that part of the Bible is for today and part is not? How can Scripture be separated? It's beyond my comprehension why some insist on tossing certain verses aside. Yet let's examine an instance where this frequently happens.

Immediately before His ascension Jesus left this mandate:

> And He said to them, "Go into all the world and preach the gospel to every creature. He who believes and is baptized will be saved; but he who does not believe will be condemned. And these signs will follow those who believe: In My name they will cast out demons; they will speak with new tongues; they will take up serpents; and if they drink anything deadly, it will by no means hurt them; they will lay hands on the sick, and they will recover."
>
> —Mark 16:15–18, nkjv

It baffles me why some church denominations reject the words "And these signs will follow those who believe…" by declaring that these evidences of Christ are no longer in effect for modern times, However, I thank the Lord they haven't discarded all of His vital commission. They wholeheartedly believe in the call to tell the world about Jesus. Being baptized also remains a definite requirement in their teachings.

Nevertheless, how can anyone deny the power Jesus gives believers? It is provided to show signs that have been identified by the very Son of God Himself. Why would the Holy Spirit withdraw His power from man today? What would be the purpose?

According to this teaching, the supernatural acts listed by Jesus extended only to those original eleven disciples who were with Him in person that day. It says that He gave this power only for establishing the early New Testament church. But where does the Bible state this? Nowhere!

Why did God bestow these signs on Paul? He wasn't present when Jesus spoke them. At that time Paul not only didn't believe in Jesus as the Messiah, but he also hated Him and would later have believers killed. However, after Paul gave His life to Christ, these marvels most certainly accompanied him in his ministry.

> And God wrought special miracles by the hands of Paul.
>
> —Acts 19:11

He cast out demons (Acts 16:18). He spoke with new tongues (1 Cor. 14:18). When a snake bit him, it didn't hurt him (Acts 28:3–5). He healed a lame man (Acts 14:8–10) and even brought a dead man back to life (Acts 20:9–10). Because of the signs following him, people believed the gospel, "being astonished at the doctrine of the Lord" (Acts 13:12).

The Bible shows us, especially in the Book of Acts, that at the coming of the Holy Spirit after Jesus' ascension into heaven, healing power still prevailed for those who believed. Just coming into the range of Peter's shadow cured people (Acts 5:15). The healing miracles of Paul stirred all of Asia. Through sending out handkerchiefs or aprons that had touched his body, many received healing and restoration (Acts 19:10–12).

How can we truly know that God means for believers to continue doing His divine wonders? Because the apostle Paul, called to the Gentiles by Jesus Himself (Acts 22:21), writing under the inspiration of the Holy Spirit tells us:

> Those things, which ye have both learned, and received, and heard, and seen in me, *do*.
> —PHILIPPIANS 4:9, EMPHASIS ADDED

If God's healing power and miracles were predestined to pass away at the death of Paul and the disciples, then these instructions make no sense. How could anyone pattern their lives after Paul's without the "signs following believers"?

I'm not against denominations. God will sift through denominational differences on Judgment Day. I *am* against putting God in a box and saying that He can only do things in limited fashion, not according to the almighty Lord of the Word, but according to a doctrinal teaching.

Our God is almighty El Shaddai! He can accomplish His purpose however, wherever, and whenever He decrees. He works and moves by His limitless power, His infinite wisdom, and His boundless love. He is not limited by any devised conception of Him or by restrictions man places on Him.

Why not believe all God's Word? Throwing out various texts can be a risky business. Who can know which verse to cast aside and which one to keep? What about John 3:16, "For God so loved the world, that he gave his only begotten Son, that whosoever believeth in him should not perish, but have everlasting life"? What if this lost its effectiveness for today? Where, oh, where, would that leave you and me?

Every word of the Bible is still relevant! The Sun of Righteousness has healing in His wings now as well as long ago. In His healing title of Yahweh Rophe, God proclaimed, "I am the Lord thy God who heals thee." He continues now the same as then, never changing. Yahweh Rophe. Jehovah Our Health is The LORD Who Heals even at this moment.

God has never altered His character or removed His healing benefits. If you're having problems believing this, just read His Word. Doesn't He Himself claim to remain unchanged? Yes, yes, God says, yes!

> For I am the Lord, I change not.
>
> —Malachi 3:6

Throughout all generations He has never changed, and He never will. Never does He vary.

> Every good gift and every perfect gift is from above, and cometh down from the Father of lights, with whom is no variableness, neither shadow of turning.
>
> —James 1:17

Does this sound as if God withdrew His healing power from Earth in this day and time? No! God's promises are everlasting. Just stop murmuring and believe them all. In both the Old and New Testaments His Word never fades or fails.

> Bless the Lord, O my soul, and forget not all His benefits: Who forgives all your iniquities, who heals all your diseases, who redeems your life from destruction, who crowns you with lovingkindness and tender mercies, who satisfies your mouth with good things, so that your youth is renewed like the eagle's.
>
> —Psalm 103:2–5, NKJV

What insight this gives into the complete restoring character of Yahweh Rophe. He gives total healing—spiritual, emotional, physical. Let's inspect each benefit listed in this psalm one by one.

"Who forgives all your iniquities." This is spiritual healing, pardon for our sins. God brings us as a new creation into His family and continually forgives us when we make mistakes.

"Who heals all your diseases." This is physical healing, not just for certain kinds of sickness, but *all* maladies. God eliminates pain, renews strength, and restores health.

"Who redeems your life from destruction." God gives healing for the spirit, soul, and body. He brings us back from harmful paths we've taken—paths that led us away from Him into condemnation, bitterness, sinfulness, and sickness. He frees our lives from Satan's bondage.

"Who crowns you with lovingkindness and tender mercies." The verb *crowns* means to encircle for attack or protection."[4] How can we even think of failing when He encircles us and protects us from attack with His loving-kindness and tender mercies? What power this gives over any opposition from the enemy!

"Who satisfies your mouth with good things." This means that God gives us joyful and favorable words that are beautiful, best, bountiful, cheerful, at ease, fine and glad.[5] What other words can we speak after we experience His benefits? Knowing the reality of His forgiveness, healing, restoration, lovingkindness and tender mercies, encircled in His protection—our mouth overflows with the satisfaction of these good things as we testify of them to others.

Next is the reward! "So that your youth is renewed like the eagle's." What a promise. What a gift. Oh, the lesson God teaches with the picture of an eagle in need of restoration.

It has been said that when this magnificent bird grows old and weak, it hides itself on the side of a cliff, finding refuge in the crevice of a rock. Its once sturdy feathers, now thin and worn, cannot repel rain as they once did. No longer can they elevate this tired body to the great altitudes where it used to soar with ease. Will it just give up and die?

No! While pain must shoot like needles, the eagle uses its beak to yank out each feather one by one. Sometimes they number as many as seven thousand. Ouch, ouch, ouch!

Seeking sunshine by day the disabled eagle may waddle a few feet, yet it never ventures far from the security of the rock. Stripped of all beauty, cold and naked, no longer able to fly, it depends on other eagles to bring it food. Day by day the broken fowl bides its time, looking only to the loving nature of its Maker, believing its ugly skin will be replenished and its withered strength restored. In its helplessness it rests and regains vitality, waiting as long as it takes, protected by the cleft of the rock.

And sure enough, new feathers sprout and grow. One day, covered again with loveliness and renewed in youthful vigor, the aged bird flies to unknown heights again. In majesty it glides with restored wings spread out in elegance across a bright horizon.[6]

Yes, oh, yes. What a picture of God's restoration and renewal!

When we seek refuge in the crevice of our Rock, bowing before our Maker, stripped of vanity with a broken and contrite heart...when we stand in faith while we rest and wait, believing His Word as absolute truth...when we bless Him with all our being, trusting in His benefits and testifying of them...when we, with fixed hearts, can say like David, "Lead me to the rock that is higher than I" (Ps. 61:2)...when we can claim, "He only is my rock and my salvation: he is my defence; I shall not be moved. In God is my salvation and my glory: the rock of my strength, and my refuge, is in God" (Ps. 62:6–7)...when we can solely put such trust in Him that His promise comes alive...it is then that He truly renews the strength of our youth just as surely as He renews the eagle's. Oh, what healing goodness is ours when we believe!

The very essence of God's ministry is renewal, reconciliation, and restoration. Run to the Rock. He's there, not just in the Old Testament, but also in the New—available for you today with rejuvenating power. When your soul has run dry, when you're down and depressed, when you're sick and undone, feeling lost in the wilderness, drink from the Rock.

> And did all drink the same spiritual drink: for they drank of that spiritual Rock that followed them: and that Rock was Christ.
>
> —1 Corinthians 10:4

Jesus Christ, the Rock of our salvation, gives us living water:

> But whosoever drinketh of the water that I shall give him shall never thirst.
>
> —John 4:14

THROUGH JESUS THE promises of God's healing under the Old Covenant remain alive for us today. Twice God's Word states that we receive healing by the stripes (wounds from scourging) Jesus endured as part of His agony for our salvation. Just as He bore our sins (spiritual healing), He also bore our sorrows and griefs (emotional healing) and our sicknesses and diseases (physical healing).

In the Old Testament, Isaiah prophesied:

> Surely he hath borne our griefs, and carried our sorrows: yet we did esteem him stricken, smitten of God, and afflicted. But he was wounded for our transgressions, he was bruised for our iniquities: the chastisement of our peace was upon him; and with his stripes we are healed.
>
> —Isaiah 53:4–5

In the New Testament, Peter affirmed:

> Who his own self bare our sins in his own body on the tree, that we, being dead to sins, should live unto righteousness: by whose stripes ye were healed.
>
> —1 Peter 2:24

When many people are asked what Jesus' death accomplished, they answer, "Atonement for sin."

This is absolutely true. Yet as we see in these words of Isaiah and Peter His death achieved much more. It brought complete redemption and entire restoration: pardon, peace, health, wholeness in every respect. If you have any lingering concern about healing always being the will of God, these scriptures should put an end to your doubts. All the stripes Jesus suffered were in vain unless they bring healing to our bodies.

We must never forget Christ's suffering, its purposes and benefits. In fact, He established the Lord's Supper so that we will remember His death. What blessings this ordinance of Holy Communion holds for the believer.

First, giving the cup of wine to His disciples Jesus says:

> For this is my blood of the new testament, which is shed for many for the remission of sins.
>
> —MATTHEW 26:28

We should never forget the blessings of His blood with its absolute power to redeem the human race. One benefit we often overlook is the provision Holy Communion gives for the well-being of our bodies. As we recall the brokenness of His human body we need to acknowledge what it did for us.

Explaining the bread Jesus says:

> Take, eat: this is my body, which is broken for you: this do in remembrance of me.
>
> —1 CORINTHIANS 11:24

We should realize and never forget what was accomplished by the bodily abuse He endured. His brokenness atoned for our healing.

I believe this is why Paul tells us:

> For he that eateth and drinketh unworthily, eateth and drinketh damnation to himself, not discerning the Lord's body. For this cause many are weak and sickly among you, and many sleep.
>
> —1 CORINTHIANS 11:29–30

The Complete Word Study Dictionary, New Testament expounds on the word *unworthily*: "irreverently, as in an unbecoming manner, treating the Lord's Supper as a common meal without attributing to it and its elements their proper value."[7]

In his book *The Meal That Heals*, international evangelist Perry Stone Jr. says, "Do not underestimate the power of the Communion meal. Confessing your sins and believing upon Jesus Christ will bring you salvation and eternal life, but the Communion meal can actually preserve and keep you during your earthly life. The bread and the cup are so important that Christ said He would eat it again when we enter the kingdom at the marriage supper of the Lamb (Rev. 19:19)."[8]

Hallelujah! The healing virtues of Yahweh Rophe are extended by the victory of the cross, and we keep them in our remembrance by discerning Christ's body in Holy Communion. Forgiveness, mercy, grace, redemption, salvation, health, and healing are all part of His atonement.

What a joy to accept the truth of His whole Word, to truly know that God has never changed and never will. All His benefits, all His promises, in the Old and New Testaments remain in operation. None will ever pass away.

At this moment shed the doctrine of "miracle have-nots" as fast as a snake sheds its skin, and leave the giant of power denial stewing in his lethal lies. Put on the doctrine of "miracle-manifestations." You'll be marching triumphantly with the almighty God of unsurpassed power who gives life abundantly and whose blessings never cease.

Although this battle may be behind us, don't rest just yet. A new conflict rages as another troublemaker leaps out at us. Ouch, he fights with fiery accusations! "If all scripture holds true for you today, why don't you witness supernatural healings everywhere?"

THE GIANT OF UNBELIEF

His question often burns in Christian hearts. To overcome his flames faith must open the floodgate for God's power to work in us and saturate our beings in the river of life. This will quench all burning doubt as we search out an answer.

Why, oh, why don't we see more healing by the hand of God? Because of this very giant—unbelief. While the power of the Bible remains ever available and Yahweh Rophe is ever able to perform, He ministers through His church according to the amount of power at work within each individual.

> Now unto him that is able to do exceeding abundantly above all that we ask or think, according to the power that worketh in us.
>
> —Ephesians 3:20

If we live in unbelief, not trusting that God is able to do "exceeding abundantly above all that we ask or think," no power can ever work in us. Whether skepticism stems from tradition, powerless doctrine, lack of knowledge, or plain old rebellion, it reduces our blessings to ashes.

How did Jesus respond to faith? How did He act toward scoffers? We'll find out as we ask Him to lead us safely out of the searing reach of unbelief.

As the woman who suffered for twelve years from an issue of blood (Matt. 9:20–23) pushed through the crowd, her inner being cried, "If I may but touch His garment, I shall be whole."

According to the Law, her bleeding made her unclean. What a sentence this was, since unclean Jews spent their lives cut off from their loved ones. If anybody so much as brushed against this poor lady, they suffered from contamination and were required to be in isolation for days while they went through tedious cleansing acts. No one dare go near her.

How lonely her life must have been. Besides the weakness and physical pain she undoubtedly endured, she must have also agonized emotionally.

What determination and courage she showed by even venturing into a crowd. Yet the power of faith exploded within her spirit and she did it. She touched the hem of the Savior's tunic.

Jesus turned to her, "Daughter, be of good comfort. Your faith has made you whole!" From that very moment she was well!

Faith. Oh, what power it produces. In Matthew 9:27–29 Jesus healed two blind men. Before restoring their sight He asked, "Do you believe I am able to do this?"

"Yes, Lord!"

He touched their eyes, saying, "According to your faith be it unto you." And their eyes received sight!

These dynamic results happened because of faith. Faith unlocks "the power that worketh in us." Faith releases His healing power. Lack of faith limits His ability.

We go now to Mark 6:2–6, where we find Jesus teaching in the synagogue on the Sabbath in the region where He grew up. Having known Him since childhood people snub their noses.

"Where has this man learned such things? What gives Him wisdom to produce any mighty works? Isn't this the carpenter, son of Mary, brother to James, Joses, Judah, and Simon? Aren't these his sisters among us?"

Their doubt astounds Jesus. Other than laying His hands on a small number of ailing followers to heal them, no mighty miracles can be performed.

Have things changed much today? Is Jesus still astounded at man's unbelief and unwillingness to receive? This next question reveals the answers. How often do people snub their noses and get offended simply at the mention of His healing power working today?

Just as when He physically walked among men, His healing power still lies within us and according to our faith. I have often heard this little rhyme, "Believe and receive. Doubt and do without!" How true it is.

What a sight the pool of Bethesda had to have been in the days of Jesus. Can't you just see sick people sprawled all around, waiting for the angel to come and stir the water? Though many gathered hoping for a miracle, only the first person into the swirling pool got healed.

One poor soul had lain there for thirty-eight long years. I've heard the teaching that this man had grown accustomed to his life the way it was and didn't really care about being well, since he didn't instantly shout yes when asked if he wanted to be healed.

But how differently I perceive him! This man had lain there day after day, not giving up, still hoping for his healing. Why else would he be there? As Jesus walked along the side of the pool He saw something special in this individual; evidently He sensed sincerity in his persistence.

"Do you want to be well?" Jesus asked, seeking an earnest opinion. In actuality He was saying, "Do you have faith within you to be made whole?"

The invalid explained that since no one ever helped him into the moving water another always got ahead of him. On the outside we hear his weariness. But Jesus looked into the untiring diligence of a faithful heart. How wonderful it must have sounded when Jesus said, "Get up, pick up your sleeping pad, and walk!" Instantly the man experienced healing and obeyed (John 5:2–9).

What about the other afflicted people at the pool? Why didn't they cry out to this anointed Man? Did they just turn their heads in unbelief? The Bible doesn't say. But it records no other healings at Bethesda that day.

Years ago I received an instant healing of nosebleeds. A television evangelist described my condition to the letter—a sore that never healed, often gushing forth with blood. "If you will place your hands on your nose and believe with me in prayer, you will be healed," she said.

What if I had sat in unbelief? What if I hadn't obeyed the instructions of the television evangelist? What if I had argued that God's healing power isn't available today? What if I had balked, saying that He couldn't heal over the airwaves? Would I have been healed anyway?

No, without a doubt I would not. I had never been taught by some great theologian or given a divine revelation about God's healing power. But I obeyed. And from that day my nosebleeds stopped. Within three days the abrasion I'd suffered with for years disappeared, never to return.

Although it's hard for me to fathom such reasoning, someone once told me my healing came from Satan not from God. "Miracles have passed away," she insisted with staunch conviction.

What could I say? To try to convince her that the same supernatural God of old still exists would just stir up argument. Yet without forethought I posed two questions:

- ∞ When did the Devourer become a healer of God's children?
- ∞ Where is any scripture to support this belief?

I still wait for her answers.

Are you needing to be healed, longing to go through life whole and well? Flee unbelief with a heart that is fixed on God and determined to trust His power in times of trial. Be fully persuaded to follow Him, never veering. Then watch His blessings flow.

> The LORD is nigh unto them that are of a broken heart; and saveth such as be of a contrite spirit. Many are the afflictions of the righteous: but the LORD delivereth him out of them all.
>
> —PSALM 34:18–19

Yet, as with any promises of God, we must do our part in receiving, building up the power that works in us by staunch faith and devotion. Keep this thought. We'll need it in our upcoming battle with the deterrent rising just ahead. Using subtle methods he seeks to destroy our road to healing.

THE GIANT OF HALFHEARTEDNESS

How friendly this giant seems. He doesn't roar like the others but simply points us to a lovely, winding trail. Its stately evergreens cast playful shadows while its tantalizing breath of cedar lures us into its nooks and crannies.

"Come on in," the giant simply smiles. "Dare to venture off your faith route so straight and narrow. With my lead you'll always have religion but with satisfactory balance—keeping one foot in the Word, the other in the world. It's just a slight deviation, and you won't forsake your faith entirely. You know, moderate Christianity is accepted by any group. Be a Sunday Christian, yes, but stroll the remainder of the week with me, never being labeled as one of those Jesus fanatics."

Marking entrance into the giant's trail a gate stands open wide, giving easy access to amble in its shade. It appears so broad and well-worn, so we know a multitude before us chose its way of secular conformity and casual spiritual commitment. Can so many be wrong?

It looks like easy hiking with a perfect climate—not too hot or cold, just comfortably lukewarm. We can be carefree with no binding decisions, free to be double-minded and go with the flow of the moment. Since we won't be bound by rigid rules we can be self-sufficient. How welcoming this broad way seems. Should we take it?

Opening in the opposite direction the gate to God's promises stands so separate and secluded that few even locate it. Its path appears so unbending—firm and fixed, uncompromising, self-sacrificing, and demanding utter commitment. Unconventional and unpopular with the public, it is seldom traveled. Yet, its way is right.

> Enter ye in at the strait gate: for wide is the gate, and broad is the way, that leadeth to destruction, and many there be which go in thereat: Because strait is the gate and narrow is the way, which leadeth into life, and few there be that find it.
>
> —Matthew 7:13–14

How tempting to forsake the gate of inflexibility and yield to this giant's coaxing. After all, his way is more familiar in today's society and sounds logical by world standards.

No! Beware of such deception!

> There is a way that seemeth right unto a man; but the end thereof are the ways of death.
>
> —Proverbs 16:25

Shun the ways of death and embrace the way that leads to life. There you will find your healing.

> Be not wise in thine eyes: fear the Lord, and depart from evil. It shall be health to thy naval, and marrow to thy bones.
>
> —Proverbs 3:7–8

Yes, by all means, flee the halfhearted giant. At first glance his direction may appear quiet and unassuming, but don't be fooled. Danger lurks at every turn. All who follow Him risk becoming lost, even tottering on a shaky bridge over currents of desperation that rumble so loudly with pain and hardship any voice of hope is stifled. There overcoming power drowns in doubt, and faith can find no way to surface. Prayer goes unanswered.

Are you truly seeking healing and desiring to function daily in good health? Then you have no choice but to walk away from wishy-washiness and convert to single-mindedness toward God. Ask for His benefits in total submission, believing, trusting, and never wavering.

> But let him ask in faith, with no doubting, for he who doubts is like a wave of the sea that is driven and tossed by the wind. For that person must not suppose that a double-minded man, unstable in all his ways, will receive anything from the Lord.
>
> —JAMES 1:6–8, RSV

Nothing equals the strength that comes from giving yourself completely to faith in the Word of God. It creates an inner force of rejuvenation that empowers and sustains you against all attacks of disease, injury, and adversity. It supplies authority for answered prayer:

> If ye abide in me, and my words abide in you, ye shall ask what ye will, and it shall be done unto you.
>
> —JOHN 15:7

Every step won't be easy. Yet if you sincerely wish to know Yahweh Rophe, it takes more than halfhearted submission. It takes wholehearted devotion—abiding in Jesus, staying on the straight and narrow, saturating your heart in God's ways until you find the life and health He offers through His Word.

> My son, attend to my words; incline thine ear unto my sayings. Let them not depart from thine eyes; keep them in the midst of thine heart. For they are life unto those that find them, and health to all their flesh.
>
> —PROVERBS 4:20–22

His Word is life! His Word is health! The Bible flows with healing and well-being. The more it becomes a part of you, the more victories you win. Freedom from oppression surges inside your body, soul, and spirit as the Word you know and believe becomes a living weapon within your inner being.

The Bible calls His Word the sword of the Spirit (Eph. 6:17) and proclaims it to be "quick, and powerful, and sharper than any twoedged sword" (Heb. 4:12). By quoting the Word, Jesus fought Satan in the desert (Matt. 4:1–11), and in the final battle over evil when He returns to Earth, "out of His mouth goes a sharp sword, that with it He should strike the nations" (Rev. 19:15, NKJV).

How powerful it is! Just before Joshua set out to conquer giants in the Promised Land the Lord commanded:

> This Book of the Law shall not depart from your mouth, but you shall meditate in it day and night, that you may observe to do according to all that is written in it. For then you will make your way prosperous, and then you will have good success.
>
> —JOSHUA 1:8, NKJV

When we read, study, meditate, memorize, believe, and act on God's Word, success is bound to follow. We prosper in His power, not our own, as the Word in us slashes like a mighty sword against all the ploys of Satan. What a weapon at our disposal just waiting for us to use it.

How well are you equipped to fight with it? Is your knowledge of God's Word strong enough to keep you from faltering? Are you walking daily in faithfulness to Him, or are you fence-straddling?

Who is guiding you? The divine Comforter or the six-o'clock newscaster?

Who gives you instruction? The Holy Word or Hollywood?

Whom do you trust? The hand of the Almighty and His promises, or government programs and social services?

What are you pursuing? Eternal life or earthly treasure?

Whom do you serve?

> No man can serve two masters: for either he will hate the one, and love the other; or else he will hold to the one, and despise the other, Ye cannot serve God and mammon.
>
> —MATTHEW 6:24

Victorious healing and walking in divine health require that you turn from double-minded behavior to staunch devotion to God's Word. Do it until it becomes a natural response to speak the Scriptures and act on them in every situation. Only then will your success and vitality become certainties. Yes, then what blessings flow!

> Blessed is the man that walketh not in the counsel of the ungodly, nor standeth in the way of sinners, nor sitteth in the seat of the scornful. But his delight is in the law of the LORD; and in his law doth he meditate day and night. And he shall be like a tree planted by the rivers of water, that bringeth forth his fruit in his season; his leaf also shall not wither; and whatsoever he doeth shall prosper.
>
> —PSALM 1:1–3

What a declaration! This says that all the ways of a person who enjoys living by and meditating on the God's Word will be prosperous, strong like a tree beside the streams, always fruitful in season, never withering. Many trees when well watered have been known to live for hundreds of years, strong and free from disease. In this scripture *meditate* not only means to ponder and think about—but to murmur, mutter, roar, speak, study, talk, utter.[9] Prosper here is an action word with its meaning of pushing forward as to break out or come mightily.[10] The word *whatsoever* in verse 3 includes all endeavors—with family, friends, and co-workers, in finances, and in health. The Word says it. Believe it.

Read, reflect, respond—the three "Rs" of genuine success. Truly it requires undying effort, but end results bring jubilation as His power takes root and grows inside your spirit. He bestows life abundantly. Stress releases. Worry flees. Healings occur. And His glory abounds.

Immediately? Not always. Oftentimes we must give God time to act. He alone knows the right moment and season.

A person who has recently left the path of halfheartedness to walk in wholehearted commitment to God should not expect overnight solutions to the struggles in his life. Neither should those who have long abided on the straight and narrow. Every child of God must be willing and determined to endure in faith until blessings materialize. So before we travel one more step, make a true heart's decision to never withdraw no matter how bad things get. Otherwise, the next giant will jerk your healing out from under you, laughing all the while.

THE GIANT OF INSTANT RESULTS

What a line he throws our way: "God isn't going to answer your prayer or He'd have already done it. You'll never be well again. You're dying!"

Lift your sword against him! He may sound powerful, but he's all bluff. As time goes by, yes, it's tough to wait. When things seem to get worse instead of better, it's tough to believe. When you pray and pray with no results, it's tough to keep trusting. But if you give up, this giant wins. Determine to wait on God and trust Him to act no matter how bad the situation becomes, never losing heart and continually expecting to be healed.

Does God always require waiting? No, not always. How sweet it is when our Father reaches down the moment we approach Him and meets our needs.

Several years ago my sister walked through her home reading Psalm 91 aloud, claiming its promises for her husband who lay in bed with the flu. "Because thou hast made the LORD, which is my refuge, even the Most High, thy habitation; there shall no evil befall thee, neither shall any plague come nigh thy dwelling."

Though he was in another room and unaware of her actions, just as she finished reading, her husband's fever broke. His symptoms vanished and he rose in health. Yes, what power lives within God's Word!

But the giant of instant results cries, "Oh, you've tried things like that. They never work for you."

What about the times when healings don't manifest immediately? Does that mean God's promises don't work, at least not for everyone?

No! Hold firmly to your faith. Your answer may be right around the corner. Even if it is not, still believe. Results will come.

I recall when my granddaughter at age ten attended a healing crusade with her parents. Dermatologists had failed to cure the warts on her hands. Although I feel sure that she envisioned herself on the stage facing the internationally acclaimed pastor with her warts dissolving before everyone there, it didn't happen that way. However, in her seat that night she claimed healing and declared her warts as gone. Even though the unsightly protrusions stood out on her tender skin as big and ugly as ever, she never wavered in her claim. "They *are* healed," she insisted. "They're going to disappear!"

In a few days they began peeling away. Within two weeks, just as she claimed, the warts completely vanished.

In the next two years my granddaughter fell on some hard times, and her faith in God began to waver. And, to everyone's surprise, one small wart appeared on her finger. *Why*, I wondered, *would another wart appear after such a miraculous healing?* Then, not long ago, my now adult granddaughter told me, "He gave one back as a reminder to me, so I would never forget to keep my faith in Him."

God's Word always works. The failing lies in us when we let go. Like Job sometimes we must hold on to God in faith. Sometimes we must wait in persistence as the man at the pool of Bethesda did. And sometimes we should turn to other believers for help.

> Is any sick among you? let him call for the elders of the church; and let them pray over him, anointing him with oil in the name of the Lord: And the prayer of faith shall save the sick, and the Lord shall raise him up....Confess your faults one to another, and pray one for another, that ye may be healed. The effectual fervent prayer of a righteous man availeth much.
>
> —JAMES 5:14–16

This instructs the sick person to call for the elders of the church. Why, then, do those who are ill so often wait for church leaders to call on them to pray and anoint them with oil? And why do others secretly ail and do nothing?

Just as many who were distressed sought Jesus for healing when He was here on earth, so those who are afflicted today should seek Him through Christian believers. This doesn't mean that Jesus can't or won't heal in other ways. At times He came to the sick as He did with the man beside the pool, but most would have never been healed had they not called on Him.

Don't just sit around waiting. Act, step out in faith, and earnestly seek God for healing. Call for the elders of the church. Ask for prayer and to be anointed with oil. Admit and confess your shortcomings. Pray for and with others. Keep believing.

The giant of instant results yells, "Why make yourself look silly? Give up!" But he's a liar. Never take him seriously.

For more than twenty-six years now I've waited, continuing in prayer and firm in belief for God to deliver my son from his addictions. Someday God will intervene. Until then my duties consist of continuing to hold on in faith knowing that my prayers are answered. The rest is up to my Abba Father.

When you can't understand the reason for your circumstances, stop trying to figure it out. Wait for His timing, trust His wisdom, and leave it with Him.

> For my thoughts are not your thoughts, neither are your ways my ways, saith the LORD. For as the heavens are higher than the earth, so are my ways higher than your ways, and my thoughts than your thoughts.
> —ISAIAH 55:8–9

Put worry behind you and place your dilemma in the hands of the One who has all the answers. Give Him praise even when nothing seems to be happening. Develop a Joshua mentality. As you shift your mind away from what you're going through and center in on what you're going to, you'll find that waiting just makes you stronger. Keep your thoughts tuned into God for deliverance, being faithful in the wilderness even if you can't understand, and you'll soar on His wings above all fear.

> Ye have seen what I did unto the Egyptians, and how I bare you on eagle's wings, and brought you unto myself.
> —EXODUS 19:4

Again God uses the picture of an eagle. What a glorious revelation of Himself is presented in His design of this feathered creation.

In some countries an eagle has a wingspread as wide as fourteen feet, enabling its elegant form to speed across the horizon at one hundred miles an hour and glide into towering heights with no fear. On the wind of a storm it finds power to ascend safely until it is safely beyond the reach of all turmoil.

How wise the mother eagle is when she builds the nest for her eggs. Locating it far above the danger of wild beasts, she lines the bottom with prickly twigs and then pads it with her own downy feathers so her babies can snuggle warm and secure. She dotes over them, bringing food to their wide-open mouths and often cuddling them beneath her.

Then the day arrives when they must learn to fly. What squawking and fluttering takes place inside the nest when the mother tosses the soft layer of down into the air. How loudly her little ones screech, watching their cozy home torn apart as the sharp briars begin jabbing them. Ouch! They have to get out right away. But where, oh, where can they go?

Upon the open wings of their mother! With sweet cooing she reaches down to them, and to escape the pain they readily climb aboard. *Can this be the same one who has cared for us?* they seem to wail, as they rise into the sky clinging to her in awful fright. Over and over the mother returns to deposit her children harshly into their piercing bed as if to say, *Today you must give up your baby crib, trust me, and fly!* Each time as fast as possible they scurry back to the protection of her strong wings, only to lift off once more while hanging on. Oh, no! Without warning their former loving care-giver dumps them in midair. What must she be thinking!

Plummeting they shriek. In their panic they spread and flap their wings. The mother quickly swoops underneath them to catch them on her wings, but again she shakes them off. Time after time she repeats this action until finally all of her young have overcome their fear. With outstretched wings they can soar on their own and climb to heights unknown with all the other eagles.

But where do you think they go? Straight back to their nest of thorns. Yipes! No longer can they live here! Soon, one by one they zoom beyond the clouds to realize the wisdom of a mother's love and the wonders of their heritage.[11]

> As an eagle stirreth up her nest, fluttereth over her young, spreadeth abroad her wings, taketh them, beareth them on her wings: so the LORD alone did lead him, and there was no strange god with him. He made him ride on the high places of the earth.
>
> —DEUTERONOMY 32:11–13

When you wait for answered prayer, what do you need to fear? Climb aboard Yahweh's wings—He's always near to cuddle you, ready to "cover thee with his feathers" and comfort you if "under his wings shalt thou trust" (Ps. 91:4). Reverence Him, knowing that in the fullness of His time He'll arrive for you "with healing in His wings" (Mal. 4:2).

In your waiting, be encouraged also by the aging eagle. Recall the pain it endures physically and emotionally as it yanks out all its precious feathers. Observe that in waiting, its beauty is replenished and its robust nature returns. But know that the hardest agony of the old eagle's ordeal must surely be in waiting for its restoration. In soreness, yet sitting patiently, it rests peacefully and waits, waits, waits. Shivering in nakedness, it refuses to give up.

Be like the eagle! Learn to soar above the turmoil when you find your coziness in shambles. Learn to wait when any situation requires it. No matter how ugly your condition may look—meditate on the promise, not the problem. Have faith that all will be restored. Rely on God—His wisdom, knowledge, and goodness. Never, never give up.

> And let us not be weary in well doing: for in due season we shall reap, if we faint not.
>
> —GALATIANS 6:9

And rejoice as you wait, for great joy lies ahead. All wonders of the eagle belong to those who wait.

> They that wait upon the LORD shall renew their strength; they shall mount up with wings as eagles; they shall run, and not be weary; and they shall walk, and not faint.
>
> —ISAIAH 40:31

AS WE ROAM through the pages of Scripture we learn that healing power didn't always materialize instantly. Let's first explore the story of Hannah in 1 Samuel 1–2:1–21.

Hannah desperately wanted a child, and in faith she turned to God. She prayed fervently that she would conceive and vowed to give the baby to God and His purposes. And her infertility was healed.

Was it instantaneous? The King James Version says, "When the time was come, she conceived." The Living Bible puts it, "In due process."

The Lord made her womb whole, but she first had to abide in faith, believing in the goodness of God, knowing in her heart that a miracle took place the day she prayed. And in due time it came to pass. Following the wondrous birth of Samuel, her firstborn son, she honored her vow and presented her baby to the Lord.

Put yourself in her place. Oh, to let go of the child she had waited so long to hold and love. How it must have torn her nurturing heart. Yet she kept her word, turning her precious baby over to Eli the priest, releasing her special child to grow up in the temple. Never forgetting God's goodness when she returned to Shiloh every year, she brought a sacrifice to the Lord in gratitude for her healing miracle. And such blessings followed:

> And the LORD visited Hannah, so that she conceived, and bare three sons and two daughters. And the child Samuel grew before the LORD.
> —1 SAMUEL 2:21

Yes, the Lord rewarded Hannah with other children. And He blessed Israel with the life and ministry of Samuel. After a dark and dismal season in Israel, a new time of enlightenment opened through this miracle son of Hannah's prayer, the product of her healing, the blessing of her waiting and evidence of her faith. Samuel became a shining instrument—an anointed prophet, priest, and judge—in God's hands.

Sometimes, in addition to waiting, seekers must follow special orders. Ten lepers cried out to Jesus, "Have mercy on us!" "Go show yourselves to the priest," Jesus instructed. As they went, obeying Jesus, their leprosy vanished. (See Luke 17:13–14.)

As you believe in faith, look to Him for answers and listen for His voice. Even today He can give specific instructions that will bring about your healing. Oh, how well I know.

A few years ago a tiny spot on my husband's ear grew into a black crusty sore. After days of treating it with commercial ointments, Jim visited the doctor.

At one glance the doctor declared, "I can run tests and you could wait for results, but if this thing was growing on my ear, I'd get it removed immediately."

Jim agreed for the doctor to set up the next available appointment with a plastic surgeon. It would be about two weeks before a consultation, but in the meantime we did not sit idle.

That very night Jim requested prayer during Bible study at a friend's house. Upon returning home I anointed his ugly lesion with oil, and we praised God for hearing our request and for His promises to heal. "Father, we thank You that You are restoring health to this ear."

The next morning I knew exactly what we needed to put on the growth. In a natural-based substance I mixed a gooey concoction of natural anti-oxidants. With Jim's agreement I plastered it over the abrasion and stuck a bandage over it. Within three days it started shrinking.

"How did you know what to use?" Jim asked.

Without thinking, the words burst from my lips, "The Holy Spirit told me." From that point we knew without one doubt that He had supplied us with divine knowledge.

By the time Jim met with the plastic surgeon, the incrustation had shrunk from the shape and size of a large kidney bean to that of a round pencil eraser. Jim told the surgeon how, with the treatment of our home remedy, its size had been reduced.

He scoffed, "Well, it is cancer, no doubt about it. I'll have to remove a large portion of your ear, and then remake it with skin from your thigh. The sooner, the better."

Because of his busy schedule he set the surgery twelve days later. In the meantime we kept applying a new coat of our "medicine" each day. The scab continued to shrink rapidly. Every day we could see a difference as it grew smaller and smaller.

Three days before the scheduled operation I thought, *Should we postpone the surgery?* I stopped in my tracks as words pounded in my chest, *God's timing is perfect!*

The following evening Jim took the bandage off for treatment. My heart leaped with joy. Although it was still black, the "cancer" was no longer an unsightly protrusion. It appeared flat and no larger than the dot of a pencil lead embedded in a circle of white flaky skin.

"Jim," I said, "why not try removing the skin around it?"

Looking in a mirror he gently blotted it with a tissue. It simply fell off. No evidence of any sore remained, not even a red spot. It was completely gone!

Explaining this miracle to the surgeon's skeptical receptionist, Jim canceled his appointment. He then returned to our family physician to have the healing confirmed.

Astonished, the doctor shook his head. "I remember the place. It was so bad I wasn't about to touch it. What God has healed I can't charge you for."

Our second miracle! The doctor's visit that day was free!

Oh, how God was glorified! Amazement filled Jim's work place as people paraded by him just to stare. Relatives and friends stood in awe. What a mighty Healer we have!

Trust His healing power even though it may not arrive the instant you ask or in the way you expect it. Throw out any inclination of instant results that seeks to rob your faith. Pray believing. Stand trusting. Listen for His voice. Rely upon His wisdom. Heed His instructions even if they seem crazy and even if they don't suit your fancy.

Remember the story of Naaman? God required him to dip in the Jordan River seven times to receive freedom from leprosy. How Naaman balked!

Not only did he expect immediate recovery, but he also anticipated special recognition when he and his men pulled up in fine chariots to meet Elisha. What a prick to his ego when the man of God made no effort to come out and greet him. Naaman was livid.

Didn't Elisha realize that he, a leader of great wealth, famous throughout the entire nation of Syria as army captain and the most prized confidant of the king himself, stood in his midst? How dare this man ignore him!

To make matters even more demeaning, this so-called prophet sent a common messenger in his place with utterly ridiculous orders. What? Wash seven times in the muddy waters of Jordan? How could that make anybody well?

Naaman fumed, "I expected Elisha to come out to see me. I thought he would just wave his hand over my leprosy, call upon the Lord his God, and heal me!"

Only as he relented, obeyed, and acted on the words of Elisha's messenger did Naaman receive his recovery. He overcame yet another giant who opposes our healing.

THE GIANT OF PRIDE

This giant boasts of himself by an array of deadly names—smug, egotistical, arrogant, haughty, dogmatic. He sets in our path the deadly traps of social clout, political standing, proper upbringing, money, education, beauty, and dyed-in-the-wool theories and attitudes. It is his purpose to make us snarl, "Me. Mine. Myself. My way. I will. I, I, I . . ."

Are you caught in his snares, bound by pride's evil powers? Do God's blessings fail to materialize simply because you hang on to unmerited self-esteem—unable to admit that you might be wrong, afraid that you may appear foolish if you obey directions from the Most High?

Don't let pride block your way to healing!

So what if you fall under the power of the Holy Spirit in front of a congregation? What difference does it make if you look silly or feel foolish, as long as you walk away healed? How sad it is that people still fit into the category of Naaman because of pride.

Why question the ways of God? Instead of resisting Him, lean on His wisdom, and you will find the way of true salvation. The very meaning of the word *salvation* teaches that God saves, delivers and rescues us, and gives us health and safety. To receive His salvation in fullness, we must overcome pride.

So humble yourself to accept God's design for you boldly and without shame. Conquer the giant of pride. How free you'll feel to truly be yourself with friends and family—and best of all, with your Father.

Uh oh, we're about to encounter another monstrosity. Phew! This one reeks like rotten garbage, and, look out, he's shooting fiery darts at us!

THE GIANT OF ABUSIVE HABITS

Get ready for blisters. Dodging his aim may be impossible. Plan for nausea. His putrid odor may cause you to gag. Nevertheless, the way to wellness requires us to dig in our heels and overcome him, regardless of our discomfort.

So far we've mainly fought with spiritual warfare. Now our road takes a different turn. Are you willing to make physical changes for your well-being? Endure some pain? As we fight this giant we'll not only be attacking in the spiritual but also warring in the flesh. And, oh dear, how it can smart!

Abusive habits—what strongholds this giant presents. And what courage we must muster, for each of us must stand alone in our own defense. Yes, though we support one another, we must separately subdue our individual unhealthy practices.

Why? We have no power to change each other's free will, not even through our strongest prayers. By our authority in the name of Jesus we can come against the working of darkness in another's life, but even then that person must choose the right path himself.

So the battle must take place within each of us as we determine to discipline ourselves for better health, to face the truth about our lifestyles, and to conquer personal hindrances. Are you ready to move forward in this?

Diet. How do you eat? Do you find yourself declaring, "Tomorrow I'll do better," but tomorrow never comes?

The old saying "garbage in, garbage out" proves true in the body, mind, and spirit. Our whole being is made up by what we take in, whether it be spiritual, emotional, or physical food.

As the temple of the Holy Spirit we are expected to present our bodies as "a living sacrifice, holy, acceptable unto God" (Rom. 12:1). Sacrifices in the Old Testament had to be offered without blemish. How do we expect a God of purity and holiness to meet us in His "temple" and miraculously heal our bodies from the consequences of our actions if we habitually defile His "temple" with junk foods processed in poisons and chemicals—if we overload with sugar, starches, bad fats, and caffeine...if we pump nicotine, drugs, and alcohol into our bloodstream...if we constantly overeat?

> Do you not know that you are the temple of God and that the Spirit of God dwells in you? If anyone defiles the temple of God, God will destroy him. For the temple of God is holy, which temple you are.
> —1 Corinthians 3:16, nkjv

Exercise. How well do you fair with it? Do you overdo it, or as most—get far too little?

First Timothy 4:8 tells us that bodily exercise profits us only slightly compared to spiritual training, which has the promise of "the life that now is, and of that which is to come."

The Bible hardly speaks on the subject of physical exercise. Observation, experience, and common sense let us know that regular activity makes a strong and able body. We all realize an unused muscle soon grows weak and that the more a person exercises the stronger his muscles become. Be determined to get up and get moving. But also beware. Health complications do arise from overindulgence. A sound anatomy depends on action, not addiction. Scripture warns against excess in anything except our wholehearted pursuit of Him.

Rest. This antidote to stress is so vital for well-being. Do you find yourself going nonstop until you are exhausted, burdened with anxiety, and preoccupied with problems? Are you too busy, too tired, and too overwhelmed by daily pressure to spend time with God?

I heard a minister say, "If Satan can't get you into sin, he just gets you too busy." Stop and consider your lifestyle. If you're racing on the road to early death, slow down and get off. Place your worries with Jesus, who calls:

> Come unto me, all ye that labor and are heavy laden, and I will give you rest.
> —Matthew 11:28

Make time to rest physically, emotionally, and spiritually and watch your overall state improve.

I learned to take care of myself the hard way. Years ago when I owned a store I lifted merchandise and heavy racks of clothes until my back screamed, "Enough!"

After one stay in the hospital and another time when I spent twelve days in bed on muscle relaxants and pain pills, I declared all-out spiritual war. How nice it would have been if God had reached down and restored my back instantly, but no, He chose another route for me—warring not only in the spiritual realm but also in the natural realm.

At the persuasion of a friend I visited a chiropractor. Observing his adjustment positions I would go home and stretch my back in the same way. A friend taught me an exercise to relieve muscle tension, and I later learned others. And I used caution in lifting!

Now I thank the Lord for this experience. It taught me that our bodies are breakable. And I realized that God heals in many ways—sometimes by supernatural means and sometimes by teaching us to use common sense and proper care.

I still do these same exercises every day. I take a readily absorbable calcium tablet and occasionally other joint-sustaining supplements. To the best of my capability I eat right—avoiding processed foods, unnatural additives, white flour, hydrogenated oils, and desserts.

How is my back? Jim and I grow vegetable gardens without using pesticides and herbicides, which means that we spread mulch and manure and pull weeds. I maintain beds of various herbs and all kinds of flowers. People rave about our yard, but I rave about the restoration of my back.

What an enabling God we have, even in the natural arena of life. He designed the body with a supernatural function to heal itself and an immune system to resist disease. However, it is essential that we do our part by not mistreating our bodies and thus shutting down the marvelous health mechanisms within us. Good nutrition, wholesome eating patterns, avoiding addictions, sensible exercise, and proper rest all work together to build and maintain strong physical health.

For the sake of health as well as pleasing God, we must break bad habits by exercising fortitude, discipline, and perseverance to overcome them. Don't look for an easy way out. None exists. Habits don't develop overnight, and except for a supernatural deliverance they won't disappear overnight. Where does a person start?

Begin with true desire to be all that you can be for God, and then strive for it. Recognize the fact that as much as humanly possible we must keep our bodies as living sacrifices to Him, without spot or blemish. Never forget that your body is the temple of His Holy Spirit, and view it this way each day. Be aware of everything you put into your system and everything to which you subject it, asking if Jesus would be pleased. And fight debilitating urges and thoughts by keeping your mind renewed. Paul says:

> And be not conformed to this world: but be ye transformed by the
> renewing of your mind, that ye may prove what is that good, and
> acceptable, and perfect, will of God.
>
> —Romans 12:2

Why? The mind is the breeding place for all we do. As well as directing
physical actions, thoughts build attitudes and determine speech. This brings
us to another abusive habit we must conquer—speaking negative words!

> Thou art snared with the words of thy mouth, thou art taken with the
> words of thy mouth.
>
> —Proverbs 6:2

> The tongue of the wise is health.
>
> —Proverbs 12:18

> He that keepeth his mouth keepeth his life.
>
> —Proverbs 13:3

> A wholesome tongue is a tree of life.
>
> —Proverbs 15:4

> Death and life are in the power of the tongue.
>
> —Proverbs 18:21

Jesus Himself said:

> For by your words thou shalt be justified, and by thy words thou shalt
> be condemned.
>
> —Matthew 12:37

The things we say, as well as what we listen to, change and rearrange
situations—either as helpful tools to victory or destructive weapons of
gloom and doom. Avoid and abstain from expressions that are without
hope, faith, or motivation. Focus on life-building words to see sickness run
and health return.

Even in statements that may at first seem trivial, consider the frame of mind
they create. Which points to victory—saying "I'm taking a cold" or "I'm fighting cold symptoms"? Which sows seeds of faith, "There is no hope" or "I have a
miracle-working God"? Which do you see releasing angels to your defense?

Are you facing sickness now? Certainly sickness cannot be denied.
Without a doubt it does exists. Ignoring it accomplishes nothing. So

what do you do? Just give in?

No! You may get knocked down occasionally, but determine that you will not be knocked out. When illness tries to overtake you, go to God in prayer, abide in faith, and speak against the symptoms. Even before you see healing taking place, let your vocabulary claim it. It may seem foolish at first, but God says to do it: "Let the weak say, I am strong" (Joel 3:10).

Friends, we serve a God "who quickeneth the dead, and calleth those things which be not as though they were" (Rom. 4:17). He called Abraham the father of multitudes before any sign of Sarah's conception. At the instant God promised, it was considered done.

His Word declares that we are healed by the stripes of Jesus. Don't moan and groan because you haven't seen evidence of your healing. Take God at His Word and confess the outcome now. He promises it. It is done!

> For I am the LORD that healeth thee.
>
> —EXODUS 15:26

> There shall no evil befall thee, neither shall any plague come nigh thy dwelling.
>
> —PSALM 91:10

> Who healeth all thy diseases, who redeemeth thy life from destruction.
>
> —PSALM 103:3–4

> By whose stripes ye were healed.
>
> —1 PETER 2:24

Learn to demand the submission of your body. It may desire junk food, crave substances of addiction, rebel at exercise because of laziness, or refuse rest because it sees so much to do. Don't give in to it. Command to it from the depths of your conscience, "You are a living sacrifice unto a holy God and the temple of His Spirit. Now act like it!"

Your body may scream, "I'm sick!" because it hurts.

Train your spirit to cry the truth, "His Word says I am healed!"

It is true because God says it. Know His Word. Declare its certainty every day in every way.

Seems foolish? So what!

> But God hath chosen the foolish things of the world to confound the wise.
>
> —1 CORINTHIANS 1:27

Know this. Proclaiming His promises as truth in spite of circumstances keeps you strong even when affliction tries to dig its claws into your flesh. Denying its right to dwell in you amplifies the character of the Creator who Himself formed the worlds by the power of His words. Yes, speak His promises even though it sounds silly to the world and the fulfillment of His Word seems impossible. Store life-giving verses in your mind. Absorb them in your heart. Keep them on your lips.

By doing these things you set your lifestyle on a joyous mode. Modern science recognizes that optimism promotes healing. Many doctors now admit that the positive outlook of a heart of faith is the best prescription for fast recovery. The Bible revealed this long ago!

> A merry heart doeth good like a medicine: but a broken spirit drieth the bones.
>
> —PROVERBS 17: 22

The spiritual and natural realms of healing are harmonized by a passion for the power of His living Word and a lifestyle of weighing words, maintaining a healthy attitude, and developing wholesome physical habits. This happens as we do not give in to warning signals but search out the reason for them and work to correct their cause. It is effective as we pray and wholeheartedly stand against symptoms in faith, paving the road to divine health and walking daily under His protection.

Oh, dear! Another enemy rises before us with a familiar question: "If you believe in divine health and supernatural healing, shouldn't you do away with medicine and never seek a doctor's help?"

THE GIANT OF OUTLANDISH NOTIONS

Consider again God's word in Proverbs 17:22. "A merry heart doeth good *like a medicine.*" According to this, medicine does good.

So does God approve the use of medicine? Does He ever use earthly means as a healing source or to prevent disease? Yes.

Throughout the Israelites' desert journey God not only worked in the supernatural but also in the natural through the Law. With its cleansing rituals, dietary regimens, and hygienic and quarantine requirements, God gave them health measures far better than the practices of ancient days, which would have been disastrous to their health. Even though he had been reared in Egyptian royalty, Moses never exercised their barbaric medicinal practices, such as using concoctions of animal parts, dung, and dead insects. What would have happened without the sensible, practical demands of the Law?

This should boggle the mind of the atheist—God's instructions were so far advanced that science has only lately begun catching up with them. Before the invention of the modern microscope germs had never been identified, and until just before the end of the nineteenth century, the spread of disease remained a mystery. Yet, more than thirty centuries before the discovery of germs, obeying the sanitary rules of God kept them in check for the children of Israel.[12]

For further amazement, consider cholesterol. How many laymen even heard this word before the 1970s? In studying the Hebrew Law we find that the very animals God forbade the Jews from eating are the evil culprits of this fatty substance that builds up in man's bloodstream and brain. On the other hand, every food He allowed turns out to be very healthy and nutritious. And ponder this—olive oil, their staple, has proven to be a most beneficial and effective oil in regulating and even counteracting bad cholesterol.

Through godly wisdom Moses proclaimed:

> For the life of the flesh is in the blood.
>
> —LEVITICUS 17:11

How could it have taken so many thousands of years for man to grasp this simple knowledge? Today we realize the value of blood in giving life, combating illness, and maintaining strength, but as late as the nineteenth century people extracted great amounts of blood from the sick to supposedly drain away their disease. History reveals that George Washington met his death due to this bizarre practice called "bleeding."

Did Jesus ever use natural means when He healed? We know of two instances when He used His own saliva. Once He put it upon a blind man's eyes. "Do you see anything?" He asked.

"I see men that look like trees walking," answered the man.

Again Jesus touched his eyes. As the man looked up he received complete restoration and saw everything clearly. (See Mark 8:22–25.)

Another time Jesus made a poultice from His spittle and clay and put in on the eyes of a blind man. "Go wash in the pool of Siloam," He said.

As the blind man obeyed and cleansed his eyes, he was healed. He walked away seeing for the first time in his life. (See John 9:6–7.)

How did Jesus feel about doctors? In Matthew 9:12 Jesus makes the statement "They that be whole need not a physician, but they that are sick." Later, the apostle Paul certainly placed no condemnation on Luke who was a physician (Col. 4:14).

I believe that God has revealed knowledge to those who practice modern medicine. No one can overlook the fact that properly administered treatments can restore, maintain, and save lives. To refuse the services of medicine in the name of faith reminds me of this often repeated illustration.

As flood waters ravage an area a man stands trapped on the roof of his house. A boat floats near. "Jump in with me!" yells the man inside.

"No," the stranded man calls back. "God will save me!"

The water continues to rise, leaving hardly a place for the man to stand. Still he refuses rescue from another boat. "God will save me!" he exclaims again.

Later, perching upon his chimney, the man hears a helicopter overhead. "Grab the rope and climb up!" comes a voice over the loudspeaker.

"No!" he cries. "The Lord will save me!"

A few hours later standing before the throne in heaven, this same man asks, "Why, Lord, did You let me drown?"

God answers, "I didn't. I sent you two boats and a helicopter."[13]

Is it a good witness for God when people refuse a doctor's help in the guise of faith and die (or even let their own children die)? That's not faith. That's foolishness. How quickly and loudly the media jump on such cases and make Christianity look crazy. Does that glorify God?

It is solid advice to use medicinal remedies under God's instruction, not in excess or overdose, but with godly wisdom. In receiving medical help, stay abreast of reality, be on constant alert, and know that all healing, whether directly or indirectly, comes through God. Realize that except for antibiotics, medicines do not cure illness; they only control or camouflage symptoms.

Beware of complications from medicine. Dangers are obvious. Overdosing, intermixing, and side effects can cause serious problems, even death.

The best advice is that you consult your physician while you pray to the Great Physician. Sin comes not from seeking aid through the medical field, but in neglecting to first seek God in all things, in placing more trust in the power of doctors than in the healing hand of Yahweh Rophe.

> And in the thirty-ninth year of his reign, Asa became diseased in his feet, and his malady was severe; yet in his disease he did not seek the LORD, but the physicians. So Asa rested with his fathers; he died in the forty-first year of his reign.
>
> —2 Chronicles 16:12–13, NKJV

Seek the knowledge of doctors when you need it, but first pursue health and healing from above. Never magnify the earthly physician as a god by believing a bad report over trusting in the Word of God. I despise the word *terminal.* For the most part, leprosy in ancient times fell into the no-hope, incurable-disease category, but God had a solution for those who sought it. In this century as well as long ago, He still holds the solution. Be thankful for doctors, but never stop battling with the mighty sword of the Spirit. Always remember:

> The things which are impossible with men are possible with God.
>
> —LUKE 18:27

NOW AS WE near the end of our highway to health, the question still arises. What about my friend Cynthia? Why wasn't she healed? Did she have unconquered giants? Perhaps she did.

AS WE HAVE seen, God deals with mankind in both the supernatural and the natural. God requires trust and obedience in every part of our lives. Satan hit his mark in the natural side of Cynthia. He couldn't win over her spirit, which stayed attuned to God. In the beginning he couldn't penetrate her will and emotions because of her unwavering faith. So he began by aiming at her body, the one part of her being that she neglected.

Her lifestyle was one of working beyond physical limits and eating foods that were not always nutritious. When she was approached about her diet, Cynthia responded, "What does it matter what we eat, as long as we ask God to bless it?" Another time I heard her comment that our bodies produce their own vitamins and minerals in spite of the food we consume. I believe Satan saw an opening in this foolishness and wormed his way into her life.

During her sickness Cynthia's friend prepared natural foods for her. She made fresh fruit and vegetable juices, but Cynthia shrugged her shoulders and continued eating whatever struck her fancy.

I believe Cynthia was a victim of outlandish notions. When her disease first surfaced, she sought a doctor for diagnosis, but relying only on faith she refused any treatment until the very last stages of her illness.

With her determination to live and her rock-solid faith she seemed to be overcoming—until the devourer attacked her through another avenue. Her marriage began to fail. Even though she still claimed her healing by speaking God's Word, her physical condition declined as she agonized for her marriage. One day she went to bed and just never got up. I believe she simply lost her will to live.

I may never completely understand every reason for her death. You may also know someone who believed they would be healed and yet died. But don't let it ruin your trust. Who can question the wisdom of the One who made us? Who can know the inner heart of any person but God Himself?

Have you lost faith because of disappointment, from trying to reason with God, from listening to worldly opinions? Perhaps you carry guilt from past mistakes as I did. Do you live with insecurity because you feel you have failed at something? Do resentment, bitterness, and unforgiveness eat away at body and soul? Any one of these can be a monstrous hindrance to your ability to be healed. If any of these problems or any giant we've encountered haunts you, receive from Christ the courage you need to triumph over them. Only then will you be able to overcome this last hindrance.

THE GIANT OF NATURAL REASONING

Quit trying to figure out solutions on your own, and stop thinking that you must understand every move of God before you can trust His ways. Throw away your heavy baggage of "grown-up" logic. Pick up a lightweight backpack of absolute trust and wear it wherever you go. This giant will quickly turn and run when you walk with untainted childlike faith in Christ.

> Verily I say unto you, Except ye be converted, and become as little children, ye shall not enter into the kingdom of heaven.
> —MATTHEW 18:3

After five years of marriage God blessed Jim and me with a new baby—a son. My son and daughter, who would soon be ages fourteen and eleven, were elated and showered him with love as if they were his second parents, not merely his siblings. We named him James. In his infancy Jim and I dedicated James to the Lord.

At that time I still treaded on the road of bondage due to guilt from my divorce. A true heartfelt relationship with a living Jesus was new to Jim because he had been reared in a church of legalistic beliefs. However, new light began to shine inside our home. By the time James turned three, I walked in freedom from the ravages of my first marriage and Jim fulfilled his rightful role as spiritual head of our family.

One by one hindrances to spiritual growth were plucked away, and deep knowledge of God sprouted like new, strong eagle feathers. Soaring into heights beyond our dreams we realized the meaning of His grace and the magnitude of His spotless blood. We experienced dynamic wonders of the Holy Spirit and encountered a healing heavenly Father.

How easily He works through childlike faith. Little James readily, without question, absorbed all that God had to offer. At three years of age he lay in bed with an upset stomach, a frequent occurrence because he had contracted an awful stomach virus that seemed to weaken his digestive system.

"James, how are you feeling?" I ran my palm across his feverish brow.

"Not too good."

"Let's pray you'll be healed. You know the Bible tells us we are healed by the stripes of Jesus. I believe Jesus wants you well, don't you?"

He nodded. "Pray, Mommy."

I had just come into the knowledge of divine healing a short time before, yet I put my hands on His stomach and prayed. "You're healed!" I said. "Now I'm going out to pick grapes to make jelly. If you need someone, your sister is in her room, and I'll be just outside the door."

No sooner had I begun to fill my pail than James skipped down the steps. Dressed and vibrant, he beamed, "I'm healed!"

Moments later I saw him popping grapes into his mouth. "Oh, James! You shouldn't be eating those."

He looked at me and sighed, "Mom, I'm healed."

How could I argue? I nodded, "Yes, my son, you're healed."

We both laughed as he continued to stuff his cheeks. Not only did he have no adverse effects, to this day James, now a grown man, has never had another bout with the stomach virus.

Oh, the blessings of childlike faith!

Another time we visited a large church to hear a nationally known singing group. James fell against me in the pew.

"I feel awful," he moaned looking up with listless eyes. He burned with fever.

"Feel his head, Jim," I whispered.

About that time one of the singers said, "Everyone stand and join us in a song. We believe there are people here who need healing. As we sing, reach out to Jesus and receive it."

James stood with us. After the song he felt cool and clammy against my hand and his eyes sparkled.

"Do you want to go home?" I asked.

"No, I feel fine now," he said. "Jesus healed me."

Whatever had attacked him never returned. How graciously Yahweh Rophe appears when we are open to receive. These are simple healings, not something magnificent like opening blinded eyes or making deaf ears hear. But they show how our heavenly Father cares even about our little needs and how He honors complete trust and faith that knows no doubt.

Hurl natural reasoning behind you and rest with childlike love in His lap. A glorious, miracle-working God awaits!

Do you need spiritual healing? God is waiting for you to come. With outstretched arms He longs to cleanse your heart with the spotless blood of Christ and reconcile you unto Himself with the healing balm of love and forgiveness. He wants you to become His child. Ask Him to take you in. He's there for you right now.

Do you need emotional healing? Let God erase your hurts. Give Him your depression, your grief, your guilt, and all the wounds of the past. He'll heal your soul with soothing peace and turn your sadness into joy. He'll wrap you in His righteousness and sanctify your heart. Just ask Him and believe. He's standing by with healing just for you.

Do you need physical healing? Throw away doubt and unbelief. Reach out and touch the hem of Christ's garment. Envision yourself arising, taking up your bed, and walking. Seek Him, trust Him, and follow Him. Act on His Word. Hold on and never give up. Believe, believe, believe. He's always available for you.

He is a healing God. He is Yahweh Rophe, who made provisions for our health through our Redeemer at Calvary. Does any giant still hinder your walk on the road to well- being? Renew your mind with the Word and take authority over the enemy. Call on the Healer with faith. His power lies within you through your obedience and trust. No matter how high and mighty any obstacle may seem, you can overcome with faith.

> And Jesus answering saith unto them, Have faith in God. For verily I say unto you, That whosoever shall say unto this mountain, Be thou removed, and be thou cast into the sea; and shall not doubt in his heart, but shall believe that those things which he saith shall come to pass; he shall have whatsoever he saith. Therefore I say unto you, What things soever ye desire, when ye pray, believe that ye receive them, and ye shall have them.
>
> —Mark 11:22–24

> As thou has believed, so be it done unto thee.
>
> —Matthew 8:13

Chapter 8

Jireh, Rohi, Nissi, I AM, and Jesus

SUCH A BUMPER crop of dill we grew the summer of 1978. In our farming area many households canned pickles, so fresh dill—usually quite scarce—was always in demand. In a local newspaper we ran a classified ad that read simply, "Need dill for pickling?" and listed our phone number.

How amazed we were at the number of people who called, then flocked to our backyard garden to fill brown grocery bags with the herb's fragrant yellow blooms. "How much do we owe you?" they invariably asked.

My husband or I answered quoting Jesus' words in Luke 6:38, "The Bible says, 'Give, and it shall be given unto you; good measure, pressed down, and shaken together, and running over, shall men give into your bosom.'" Next we added, "You don't owe us anything."

Like a type of drama practice, Jim and I delighted to play this scene over and over. One day after I recited the verse to a gentleman he asked me to write it down for him to put in his bag. "I picked this dill for a co-worker who's not a Christian. He plans to pay me tomorrow, but I'll just tell him Jesus took care of it."

The man left, and the incident escaped my mind. But oh, what a surprise God had in store by it!

A few nights later as our family sat around the dinner table my fourteen-year-old daughter asked, "When are we getting corn to put in our freezer?"

Because corn was her favorite vegetable, she always willingly helped me shuck three hundred ears, shave it off the cob, blanch and bag it. Though it involved hours of messy work, canned or frozen varieties in supermarkets could in no way compare in freshness and flavor. But that year corn failed to produce not only in our garden but also for most farmers. The price was sky high.

"We can almost buy a side of beef for what enough corn for us would cost. And we need the meat instead, so we won't be buying corn."

As I read disappointment in her face I heard an inner assurance within my spirit, *You'll have corn.*

Without understanding I secretly pondered these words. But not for long. A few days later as Jim and I dressed for Wednesday night church, we heard a knock at our front door. While I continued getting ready he went to answer it.

Then that same inner voice spoke to me again, *Your corn is here.*

In a few minutes Jim rushed back for his shoes smiling from ear to ear. "Just wait until you hear what's going on," he said tying his laces. "I'm so stunned by the things God does."

"Oh, Mama, we have corn!" our daughter ran into the bedroom waving an ear in each hand.

A warm feeling ran through me as Jim beamed with the rest of the story. "A man we don't even know is standing at our door with three hundred ears of corn for us. A gift!

"Since we're going to church he offered to take them around back to the patio where I'll spread them out and spray them with the hose to keep them moist and cool overnight."

"Why is he doing this?" our daughter asked.

Jim laughed and looked at me. "When we gave away our dill while back, did you write down that verse about giving for anybody?"

"For a young man."

"Well, when that man took the dill to work to give to someone, he placed it under an office air conditioner so it would stay fresh. And guess what—his boss saw the card with the Bible verse on top of the dill and was so moved he decided to give us corn from his own field when it was picked. So here he is!"

So true are God's promises. What a loving, giving One He is!

And now His title for this virtue gleams from our pathway. Behold, Yahweh Yireh! Jehovah Jireh. The LORD our Provider. We discover now His name of great provision, first introduced by Abraham at the sacrificial site of his son Isaac.

> Abraham called this place "Yahweh provides," and hence the saying today: On the mountain Yahweh provides.
>
> —GENESIS 22:14, NJB

> And Abraham called the name of that place, Jehovah-jireh: as it is said to this day, In the mount of the LORD it shall be seen.
>
> —GENESIS 22:14

On a mountain of Moriah Abraham's faith passed its supreme test. Could anything show greater faith than his total willingness at the Lord's command to give up his and Sarah's most prized possession, their long-awaited son of promise, by binding him on an altar, killing him with a knife by his own hands, then watching the body of their beloved Isaac burn as a sacrifice to God?

Let's venture back to the beginning of this scene in Genesis 22 to understand why Abraham gave the name of "Jehovah Jireh" to his mountain of victory. We're just in time to witness the voice of God.

"Abraham!"

"Yes? Here I am," he responds.

"Take your only son, yes, Isaac, the son you treasure so dearly, into the land of Moriah. As a burnt offering to Me sacrifice him upon a mountain I will point out to you."

How shocking! How can God order such a thing, especially since He vowed to carry out His covenant of promise through Isaac's offspring? Isaac has no children, has never even married. According to God Himself, only by Isaac can the promised Seed come. How can he possibly die?

At this point what races through Abraham's mind? We can only speculate, but one thing is evident. He trusts God's wisdom. He knows a capable El Shaddai who has protected him through famine and battle. He knows a nurturing El Shaddai who brought about the birth of Isaac despite overwhelming impossibilities. Abraham knows a God who keeps His word. A God who never lies.

Surely God has not forgotten the promise. Certainly He cannot betray His faithful servant. So whatever Yahweh has in store for him, unwavering Abraham never questions. He blindly trusts and obeys.

And he doesn't hesitate. Rising early the very next morning Abraham saddles his donkey and entreats two of his servants to accompany him and his precious son. As soon as he splits wood for the offering fire, the pilgrimage begins. They travel three days before the designated mountain of Moriah finally looms into view.

Abraham says to his men, "Stay with the donkey while the lad and I go away and worship. Then we'll be back."

To worship? Such reverence and devotion this tells us that Abraham holds for God. Did we actually hear him declare that *both* he and Isaac will be back?

Yes. Such words of total trust.

On his young shoulders Isaac balances the wood while his father carries the fire and knife. Together they climb the slope.

"Father, we have fire and wood, but where is a lamb for the offering?"

Without falter in his voice Abraham responds, "God Himself will provide the lamb."

Provide the lamb? Isaac is to be the lamb! Is his father simply lying, or is he calling things that be not as though they were in an act of faith?

Finally they reach the specified place where now the most crucial test begins. Is Abraham really going through with this? Evidently so.

Abraham begins his work constructing the altar. Methodically he places the wood in order. Oh no, now he binds Isaac, stretching his beloved son upon the rugged structure. The son, obedient to his father, never even struggles.

Without stalling Abraham grips the knife. He lifts the blade to slay his son for God. Oh, how can we bear to watch?

"Abraham! Abraham!" a Voice calls from heaven.

Oh, how wonderful! It is the Angel of the Lord!

"Put the knife down!" He orders. "For you have shown God is truly first in your life by not withholding your only son."

Oh, the faith of Abraham! Yes, oh yes, he passed the test!

> By faith Abraham, when he was tried, offered up Isaac: and he that had received the promise offered up his only begotten son, Of whom it was said, That in Isaac shall thy seed be called: Accounting that God was able to raise him up, even from the dead.
>
> —HEBREWS 11:17–19

Unshakeable trust. Unbreakable faith. Abraham had no doubt that God would keep His word. The seed of Isaac must go on, so he knew that even if the blade plunged into his son's heart...even if his lifeless body burned to ashes...God could and would resurrect him to carry out His promise.

Now Abraham lifts his eyes. Look! Something struggles in bushes nearby. Why, it's an animal caught by its horns among the branches. A ram just right for the sacrifice!

Yes, exactly as Abraham had claimed earlier to Isaac, Jehovah has provided!

So this explains why Abraham calls this site "Jehovah Jireh." What rejoicing! To the top of his lungs we hear him shout, "On the mountain of Jehovah it is provided!"

As his voice echoes over the mountains, carries into the valleys and across the plains, we know that all generations are blessed through this man's faith. What a reason this gives for us, too, to erupt with glee. Yet even more joy awaits as we open our hearts to receive the prophetic revelation of our heavenly Father and His promised Son in this story of Abraham and Isaac. How amazingly it metaphorically previews our Savior—Isaac, the seed of promise, was the only legitimate son of Abraham. Christ, the Seed of Promise, is the only direct Son of God. Isaac, through whose bloodline Abraham became father of nations. Christ, through whose bloodline God became personal Father of mankind. Isaac bore the wood for his sacrifice. Jesus bore the wooden cross. Isaac, obedient to his father, showed no resistance. Christ, obedient to His Father, also did not resist.

So prophetic are the words of Abraham when he announced, "On the mountain of the LORD it will be provided" (Gen. 22:14, NIV), for Moriah is the same mountain range as Calvary where two thousand years later the Lamb of God was sacrificed. Today some declare this very spot became the location of Solomon's temple.

Prophecy also rings from Abraham's words in his answer to Isaac, "My son, God will provide himself a lamb" (Gen. 22:8). For us God Himself provided the Lamb!

Could it be that Abraham understood this composite picture, knowing that through faith he had fulfilled his part in the covenant God confirmed with him? Without a doubt Abraham received great insight into these things, for Jesus tells us, "Your father Abraham rejoiced to see my day: and he saw it, and was glad" (John 8:56).

In the virtues of El Shaddai, Abraham already knew Yahweh as his provider. He provided protection. He provided wealth. He provided Isaac. But dearest of all provisions came when God gave the ram to take the place of Isaac on the altar. And the dearest of all provisions for us transpired when Yahweh Yireh, Jehovah Jireh, our Provider gave the Lamb who took our place upon the cross.

Yes, Jehovah Jireh provides. To give abundantly is His nature. He longs to supply our every need.

So why doesn't He always do so? Because of our failure to fulfill our part in His promises. Yes, man himself limits the Provider.

It was more than four hundred years after this ultimate testing of faith with Abraham that Jehovah freed Abraham's descendants by the hands of Moses from slavery in Egypt.

Such a grand Provider. Not only did He provide His awesome power in deliverance; in overflowing abundance He supplied their every need.

> He also brought them out with silver and gold, and there was none feeble among His tribes.
>
> —PSALM 105:37, NKJV

What a downhill plunge they took after leaving Egypt so blessed. If they had only gone forth in the example of faith their father Abraham had set before them, they could have continued in God's bountiful blessings. Yes, if only they had passed their tests of faith—accepting His wisdom, acting in trust and following His direction without question. Yet in spite of their rebellion Yahweh continued to provide in the desert. He supplied miraculous food and water. By a supernatural cloud each day and fire at night He guided them. But they could have known so much more.

No longer in Egyptian bondage, they became in bondage to themselves, bound by their unbelief. Instead of forty years of struggling in a barren land of bare essentials, they could have crossed over into to a superabundant land flowing with milk and honey. But because they failed their trials of faith, refusing in murmuring and fear to fulfill God's plan, they missed out on a lifestyle of limitless provisions. How sad to partake in God's splendor, to behold His mighty miracles that gained them freedom and to bask in His benefits while departing Egypt—then afterwards to behave as spoiled children who wanted no responsibility, choosing not to trust, believe, and stand in faith when adversity arose.

Oh, how it pains me to recall the time when I also failed the test of faith, even after God had demonstrated His supernatural provisions to me. Yes, so easily in exchange for our dill, corn miraculously found its way to our doorstep. At that time I heard His voice so clearly and witnessed the wonders of His reciprocity.

Why then, after seeing His goodness, would Jim and I waver a few years later when our business failed and debt engulfed us like a flood? Why, oh, why did we slam the door on His bountiful blessings when an ultimate test arose?

So foolish man becomes by refusing to trust God's way in difficulty. Yes, we steal our own blessings. Jim and I know. In financial devastation we found out firsthand.

To experience the utmost of Jehovah Jireh as abundant provider we must abide in faith. Trusting Him, we should have kept on giving regardless of hardship. We knew this, yet we failed. To look back on this time of darkness stabs like an ice pick into my innermost being.

While I know that later I'll lead you into this shadow of my pain, I feel compelled to keep its entrance under padlock just now. As hard as it will be for me, when the time proves right I'll locate the key, open the door, and take you inside. I promise. Somehow I'll muster fortitude to relive the sadness Jim and I endured in order to share with you the lessons we learned and show you how our faith matured in turmoil.

Once we decided to give despite our need, God's waiting hand lifted us over our self-made mire into a new freshness of His blessings. By it all we experienced His faithfulness, and without reservation we can proclaim He never forsakes us. Now Jim and I also know, without a doubt, that to receive His promises to the utmost, we must fulfill our part. To live in His abundant goodness and fully know Him as Jehovah Jireh, every element of us must surrender to trust, delight, and commitment in Him.

> Trust in the LORD, and do good; so shalt thou dwell in the land, and verily thou shalt be fed. Delight thyself also in the LORD; and he shall give thee the desires of thine heart. Commit thy way unto the LORD; trust also in him; and he shall bring it to pass.
>
> —PSALM 37:3–5

So often people seek answers to prayer and claim God's promises without even realizing *their* requirements in order to receive. A good example arises with this verse in Philippians 4:19: "But my God shall supply all your need according to his riches in glory by Christ Jesus."

In expectancy people frequently quote this marvelous passage. Without a doubt it asserts that God will meet all your need. And He will, but there are stipulations. Are you doing your part to release the fullness of the provisions in this promise?

Let's examine it in context. Why does Paul assure the Philippians that God will meet all their need?

Because first they gave!

By backing up to verse 10 of this chapter we find Paul saying, "But I rejoiced in the Lord greatly, that now at the last your care of me hath flourished again." Then in verse 15 he tells them, "No church communicated with me concerning giving and receiving, but ye only."

The church of Philippi gave to Paul's ministry to further the gospel of Christ. In doing so they gave to God. Notice how Paul speaks of giving and receiving together. Throughout the pages of the Bible these two—giving and receiving—work as partners hand in hand. We give. We receive. Our needs are met by giving.

Jehovah Jireh desires to meet our every need. So give! Like the force of a bulldozer, giving pushes our pile of unmet needs out of the way.

Yes, give. It unloads fertile soil of receiving upon barren pastures. Seeds from giving spring up and crops flourish. Giving, both in monetary means and of ourselves in service to Him, reveals that we place Him first in all aspects. Giving brings abundant harvests of His blessings as we demonstrate our trust, our delight, and our commitment in Him.

When we pray, "Give us this day our daily bread," we ask for our material needs to be met. And concerning these things—our food, drink, and clothing—Jesus says, "But seek ye first the kingdom of God, and his righteousness; and all these things shall be added unto you" (Matt. 6:33).

As Jehovah Jireh He provides for us. His abundant blessings await those of faith, doing whatever He asks, giving of themselves unafraid, trusting His wisdom and guidance. Once established upon His road of giving and receiving, you'll wonder how you ever survived before.

Never desiring to return to the road of holding back in faith, you place your hand in His and follow Him wherever He leads. You become His sheep, and He becomes your ever-present Shepherd.

> He will feed His flock like a shepherd; He will gather the lambs with His arm, and carry them in His bosom, and gently lead those who are with young.
>
> —ISAIAH 40:11, NKJV

With this in mind we come upon another of His names. Yahweh Raah. Jehovah Rohi. Our Shepherd.

> Know ye that the LORD he is God: it is he that hath made us, and not we ourselves; we are his people, and the sheep of his pasture.
>
> —PSALM 100:3

Why, you may be saying, are we referred to as sheep instead of a more eloquent animal? If you really want to know the truth, then swallow your pride and read on.

Has it ever crossed your mind that goats or cows don't have anyone to direct them in open fields? Have you considered that before fences, herdsmen weren't stationed to watch camels, cows, or donkeys? Herds of buffalo, horses, deer, and goats can thrive on their own in the wild. Why do only sheep need a constant guide?

Because of such profound stupidity! It seems about all they can do right without being told is bleat, and most of the time they baa the loudest over situations brought on by themselves. And they are so helpless on their own. One may roll over on its back, then bleat and bleat, unable to get on its feet without a shepherd's help. So oblivious to its surroundings, if a sheep wanders away from the flock it may topple off a ledge or blindly graze its way into a ditch. Left unattended, sheep have no inkling how to search out fresh pasture, locate suitable drinking water, or even find their way home. So docile and defenseless, without an overseer they have no means of protection, yet they can be so determined to go the wrong way.[1] At times a lamb may wander off time and time again until finally the shepherd finds it necessary to take drastic measures. He fractures one of the lamb's legs. If it still hobbles away, he breaks another leg. Then, with tenderness he swoops his injured animal up into his arms and hoists it across his shoulders, where he carries it until its legs heal. By that time the lamb has grown so fond and dependent on the shepherd's care it never desires to stray again.

> All we like sheep have gone astray, we have turned every one to his own way.
>
> —Isaiah 53:6

Without acknowledging Jesus, man is lost. Without His guidance, we do compare to sheep with no shepherd. And so much like sheep, oh, how loud we all can bleat when we find ourselves in a pickle!

So now you know why we are called His sheep. We need an ever-present Shepherd. Every one of us. We all do foolish things, so thoughtless and irresponsible, sometimes even to the point of death, but God shows up and bales us out. He does things like that. Yes, He really does.

Cool springtime has always been Jim's favorite season to go fishing. Knowing he couldn't swim very well and panicked in deep water always concerned me when he fished from a boat without wearing a life jacket.

"But I have floating seat cushions. I can always grab one of them if I need to," he assured me.

However, things don't usually happen as we plan. So well I remember the morning my fisherman burst through the kitchen door dripping wet and shaking like a lost puppy.

"Jim, what happened?" I exclaimed.

In his own words I relate his story.

"Alone on the lake in my small jon-boat, I turned off my trolling motor and drifted with the breeze. While I was casting for bass, somehow the screws under my pedestal seat pulled loose, throwing me flat on my back in the boat. This should have been warning enough, but not so. After all, how could I bare to stop fishing so soon? Why, I just got started!

"So struggling to get myself back up, I set the disconnected seat into its position and very carefully I sat down on it, ready to fish again. Dumb, dumb, dumb!

"Returning to my casting shifted my weight and caused the seat to plunge me headfirst, along with my best rod and reel, into the part of the lake known to be around fourteen feet deep. No life preserver. Bone-chilling temperature. Heavy coat. All alone. My first thought groaned, *What a fine pickle this turned out to be!*

"My next thought shrieked, *Is it going to end like this?* Then my brain clicked; I'll yell for help.

"An inner voice told me, 'No one will hear you.'

"For the second time I went under. When I resurfaced the boat had floated about eight feet beyond me. What could I do?

"Another voice said, 'Calm down.' With that I gained presence of mind to reach out with both hands in big strokes, which to my surprise kept me afloat and moved me closer to the boat.

"What a sigh of relief I breathed when I reached the stern. 'What now?' I asked.

"Clinging to the side I inched my way to the bow. As I held on with one hand I reached up with the other, turned on the trolling motor and headed toward the shore holding to the boat. Near the bank I climbed upon a big rock covered by about six inches of water. Overflowing with thanksgiving for just being alive, my mind wildly surveyed the picture. There was so much to be grateful for.

"Usually I fished with the motor running, but because of the nice breeze, it wasn't needed. Had it been on, for sure the boat would have left me.

"God took care of every detail. He must have a great sense of humor. When I raised my foot to step into the boat I saw a fishhook caught in the sole of my shoe. A line was attached to it. I pulled and up came my rod and reel!

"Isn't that just like the Lord?" Jim laughed. "Nothing lost except my dignity."

I laughed with him. And perhaps the Lord laughed, too.

What a Shepherd! So desperately we need Him.

Within the name of Yahweh Raah many virtues of our Lord magnify through His constant shepherding. How enlightening Psalm 23 (NKJV) becomes when we see His names come alive in it:

The LORD [Yahweh] is my shepherd [Raah or Rohi];
I shall not want [Yireh or Jireh, our Provider].
He makes me to lie down in green pastures:
He leads me beside the still waters.
He restoreth my soul [Rophe, our Healer];
He leads me in the paths of righteousness [Tsidkenu, our righteous-
    ness] for His name sake.
Yea, though I walk through the valley of the shadow of death, I will
    fear no evil [Shalom, our peace];
For You are with me [Shammah, ever-present];
Your rod and your staff [Nissi, our banner], they comfort me;
You prepare a table before me in the presence of my enemies;
You anoint my head with oil;
My cup runs over [El Shaddai, more than enough].
Surely goodness and mercy shall follow me
All the days of my life [Elohim, our Covenant-maker];
And I will dwell in the house of the LORD [Yahweh] forever.

With loving-kindness the true herdsman supplies all the needs of his flock, including medical assistance, security, peace, and constant guidance. With his rod (or staff) he comforts them. With it the shepherd leads his creatures through danger. If a fall occurs, his rod takes over as a rescue tool when with its crook the shepherd pulls the animal back to safety. While in route his staff keeps the flock in line and guides their way. As a weapon the rod defends against wild beasts.

The sheep respect discipline from the shepherd's rod and look to it to steer them safely as they follow their master. With ears attuned to his voice and watching his staff, the trusting creatures live in confidence.

A most important item of identity for the shepherd, his rod represents his profession, his way of life, a safeguard in peril, and his authority over his sheep. No herdsman dares to walk the hills or plains without the prized shepherd's staff in his hand. As we understand more about this tool of love and protection, we discover another name revealing Yahweh as our banner. Come as we learn of Yahweh Nissi.

Let's take a look at the staff of Moses. For forty years Moses served as a shepherd. What a reverse lifestyle from that of Egyptian royalty.

Can you imagine his sorrow? In compassion he desired to help the slaves of Egypt, but acting in haste he failed. When they misconstrued his efforts, which put his life in jeopardy, he fled his homeland alone, hiding out in the land of Midian for forty years. No longer a noble prince, but a mere shepherd. A foreigner in desert country.

ALONG THE ROAD

I walked a mile with Pleasure;
She chattered all the way,
But left me none the wiser
For all she had to say.
I walked a mile with Sorrow,
And ne'er a word said she;
But oh, the things I learned from her
When Sorrow walked with me!

—ROBERT BROWNING HAMILTON[2]

Oh, what sorrow Moses endured because of the rejection his rashness caused. Still what things he learned during desolate shepherd years. Fortitude. Endurance. Patience. Meekness. Discipline. Dedication. Responsibility. And maturity.

In time God knew Moses had gained these qualities and had at last reached maturity to become savior to the Israelites. Come, as we join him, beginning in Exodus 3.

Leading his flock through wilderness, Moses starts up a slope on Mount Horeb. In silence he stirs dry sand under his feet while directing the docile animals with his staff along a narrow trail winding between hot, barren boulders. The sheep push against each other and bleat for want of food and water until at last they reach a shady plateau with green pasture and a bubbling stream.

As they begin their feast, a weary Moses squats to get a drink. One weathered hand pushes his long gray beard aside while the other one cups the water. How it soothes his parched throat. He pats its coolness over his brown leathery cheeks and furrowed brow, then moves to the shade.

Keeping his eyes on his feeding flock he relaxes in the grass, and with a sigh of exhaustion he fans his drab shepherd's robe to stir the air. His self-esteem ebbs mighty low.

For half of his eighty years now, he has tended these smelly balls of wool in this forlorn countryside. Once he indulged in riches. Ah, those were the days. Residing in the luxury of the palace, wearing exquisite garments, dining at the finest tables. Esteemed as a prince, Pharaoh's grandson. But he threw it all away.

Why, oh, why did he murder that Egyptian taskmaster?

In all honesty he knows the reason. He felt so chosen by God. And he really thought the Hebrew slaves—after all, his true people—would understand his act of mercy and look up to him. Yes, he envisioned himself as their hero from the Lord. But no. They, his own flesh and blood, didn't even try to understand. They looked on him as a common murderer.

Why had he felt so called to their defense? Look where it got him. In this backside of nowhere, sprawled here on the ground, just a stinking shepherd.

What good does it do to reminisce? He can't change former things. And after all these years Egypt has probably forgotten his very existence. Sometimes he wonders if even God remembers him.

If only he could forget. Erase his painful memories, put the failure of his past behind him and truly enjoy his lot in life, for he loves his wife and sons immensely and holds such great respect for his father-in-law.

Deep within he knows that even if he still resided in wealth among the royalty, he could never know true happiness.

Not as long as the Hebrews remained slaves. Why after all this time does he still harbor this nagging burden for those people? Why? Why can't he forget them?

A tear spills down his cheek. It seems so odd to us a man who appears so calloused and rugged possesses a heart so soft. Surely God has not forgotten.

Baa! Baa! The sheep stir wildly. In a split second Moses leaps to his feet with rod in hand. Why such commotion? Is danger lurking?

Fire! A bush aflame!

But how?

No time to try to figure it out. He must protect his herd. Like a flash Moses races with his staff to whip out the blaze. In the next instant he halts dead-still in his tracks. What is going on? His brain screams, *Have I gone crazy? This can't be!*

"The bush burns," he wails, "but it's not consumed!"

Look! Is someone inside the flames? Yes, it is the angel of the Lord!

"Moses, Moses, here I am," thunders His voice. "Don't come any closer! Stop. Take off your shoes. You stand on holy ground."

With trembling fingers Moses stoops to untie his dusty sandals. His sheep now graze quietly, but they no longer have the attention of their master. At this moment nothing matters anymore to him except the Lord Almighty.

The tender heart of this misplaced shepherd pounds as he rises to face the mysterious burning bush. In bare feet he stands in awe before the presence of a pure and holy God.

"I am the God of your ancestors. The God of Abraham, Isaac, and Jacob."

Moses hides his face, afraid to look.

The Lord goes on, "I have seen the terrible misery of My people in Egypt. I have heard their pleas to be freed from their harsh taskmasters, and I know their deep despair. I shall deliver them from their bondage and bring them into a bountiful land that flows with milk and honey. I am sending you to Pharaoh to demand that he let you lead My people out."

Forty years of sorrow, failure, and rejection slam like an avalanche inside Moses' skull. From his throbbing brain escapes these anguished words, "Who am I that I could even begin to accomplish a thing so great? How can the likes of me ever go before Pharaoh and deliver the children of Israel from his grip?"

"Certainly *I* will be with you! As proof that I am the One sending you, after their deliverance you shall worship Me upon this very mountain."

"But what about before that?"

The memories of so long ago swirl with the force of a torrid sandstorm throughout his every vein. These very slaves shunned his help when he held position in the royal family, so why would they accept him now as a lowly shepherd?

"If I go to the people and announce the God of your fathers has sent me, they will surely mock me saying, 'Which God are you talking about?' What name must I tell them?"

God replies, "I AM that I AM! Announce that I AM has sent you! I AM, the Lord God of your fathers, the God of Abraham, Isaac, and Jacob. My name I AM will be remembered throughout all generations!"

I AM! Ever-existent Yahweh, always having been and eternally forever! For a moment let us step aside from this scene with Moses and consider the magnitude of I AM.

Yes! I AM forever. Yesterday, today, always. For all generations the Lord, our almighty God, reigns as the great I AM. The unchangeable, ever-existent, eternal I AM. The One who sent His Son to Earth to free man enslaved to sin, to portray the great I AM in human flesh for all the world. Jesus tells us:

> Jesus said, "Most assuredly I say to you, before Abraham was, I AM.
> "I *am* in the Father and the Father in me,
> "I *am* in my Father, and you in Me, and I in you.
> "I *am* the bread which came down from heaven.
> "I *am* the living bread.
> "I *am* the light of the world.
> "I *am* the door of the sheep.
> "I *am* the good shepherd.
> "I *am* the resurrection and the life.

"I *am* the way, the truth, and the life.

"I *am* the true vine.

"I *am* the Alpha and the Omega, the Beginning and the End who is and who was and is to come, the Almighty.

"I *am* the First and the Last.

"I *am* the Root and Offspring of David, the Bright and Morning Star."

The high priest asked Him, "Are you the Christ, the Son of the Blessed?"

And He said, "I *am*."

They all said, "Are you then the Son of God?"

And He said to them, 'You rightly say that I *am*."

—FROM JOHN 8:58; 14:11, 20; 6:41, 51; 8:12; 9:5; 10:7, 11; 11:25; 14:6; 15:1, 5; REVELATION 1:8, 11; 22:13, 16; MARK 14:61–62; LUKE 22:69–70, NKJV, EMPHASIS ADDED

Yes, just as Moses fulfilled his duties, announcing the Great I AM, freeing His people from bondage and being their shepherd, so has Jesus done the same for us. Those who believed Moses were saved. Those who didn't died in sin. And so it is for us with Jesus.

Now we return to the site of the burning bush on Mount Horeb.

Even after hearing God's plan of deliverance, Moses remains skeptical of himself. Past failure still shoots like a blazing arrow, piercing the core of his heart. "They won't believe me, or even pay attention to anything I tell them. They'll scoff and say, 'Yahweh never appeared to you!'"

God says, "What do you hold in your hand?"

He peers at his shepherd's staff and frowns, "A rod."

"Cast it to the ground."

Moses' obedience symbolizes total submission. By surrendering his rod, representative of his way of life, arm of protection, means of authority between him and his sheep, Moses allegorically transfers all control to the great I AM. With his compliance a common rod arises as an honorable ensign, a glorious banner, to unfurl inconceivable wonders before both Egyptians and Hebrews.

Transformation takes place this very day on Mount Horeb. Lo and behold, in the grass before the eyes of Moses his rod wriggles into a snake—certainly a prototype of evil. But the submissive hand of Moses gains power over the evil one, when at the instruction of I AM he retrieves it.

The hissing serpent changes back into a rod in the grip of a man yielded to God.

Although chosen by One so great, Moses still moans his inefficiency.

Maybe to give him self-esteem and boldness God anoints his shepherd's staff as a point of faith. At first identified to God by Moses as simply "*a* rod" (Exod. 4:2), God now refers to it as "*this* rod" as He reveals, "And you shall take this rod in your hand, with which you shall do the signs" (Exod. 4:17, NKJV).

Next, we find *this* rod converts into the *rod of God*!

> And Moses took his wife and his sons, and set them upon an ass, and he returned to the land of Egypt: and Moses took the rod of God in his hand.
>
> —EXODUS 4:20

Yes, his shepherd's staff bore him honor and security as the mighty miracle-working rod of God!

Just imagine. As Moses leaves Midian to return after forty long years to the place of his birth, the home of his adolescence, the land of his young adulthood, how both anticipation and anxiety no doubt churn inside his chest like a windmill in a thunderstorm. But as he clutches the rod of God, his courage swells and faith abounds.

With the rod of God escorting him like the touchable presence of the living God Himself, Moses announces I AM with super confidence. He displays before the wickedness of Egypt his shepherd's staff, now a powerful flagstaff of victory. With the rod of God in his hand Moses evolves from a failure and a runaway into a valiant leader, an unbeatable savior, a fearless shepherd over a multitude of people.

His anointed shepherd's staff brought forth hail, lightning, and locusts upon the Egyptians. It parted the Red Sea and delivered water from the desert rock. An emblem of faith, it stood as an ensign in battle, a glorious banner of victory.

As we leap ahead to Exodus 17:8–16 we witness a renewed Moses. No longer is he the defeated shepherd of Midian, but now a courageous leader on the eve of war with the armies of Amalek.

"Joshua," Moses' voice rings with fearless authority, "assemble an army to march into battle. For we must fight! Tomorrow I'll stand at the top of the hill with the rod of God in my hand!"

Oh no, our hearts sink. What can Moses be thinking? The men of Israel are not trained to fight. Only a few weeks ago they served as slaves to Pharaoh. Does Moses expect them to be instant soldiers?

Yet after examining the situation we agree with him. They have no choice. With the Hebrew's trip across the plains barely begun, the wicked

Amalekites have already sneaked up in their rear and cut down all who lagged behind. These bloodthirsty men claim no respect for Yahweh or His chosen people.

Yes, something must be done to stop them. However, we wonder if Moses sounds a bit over zealous and too confident in his battle strategy. Standing on a hilltop and holding up his rod? Do his men realize its significance as the mighty rod of God? And even if they do, can this alone spurn untrained fighters to victory? We can only wait and see.

With excitement Joshua beams; troops are assembled, swords in place, eager to charge. No apprehension seems to spread within the camp. Most certainly they trust the wonders of the rod.

With Aaron and Hur at Moses' side, they dash up the hill with him. They stop at the highest point, making sure their leader stands in plain view of his soldiers. Moses strikes a pose with his hands stretched toward the heavens to showcase his shepherd's staff, the magnificent rod of God, high above the battlefield. How it glows against the sun.

Our hearts cheer as we observe such an unbelievable confidence this rod generates for those approaching danger of death. What assurance it instills. What courage it evokes. We realize now, as Moses and Joshua knew all along, success lies not in man's ability but in faith produced by God in His unconquerable rod.

Hooray! Israel prevails.

But soon, before the eyes of his army, Moses' arms grow weary. They quiver from utter exhaustion and every muscle screams with pain. In agony Moses grits his teeth. Veins pop out in big blue whelps across his sweaty forehead. His robe, dripping with perspiration, sticks to his pumping chest as with all his might he staggers to not lose his stance. Finally, he can hoist the rod no longer.

Heaving one last enormous sigh, he drops his aching limbs to his sides. In alarm his blurry eyes widen and his face reddens. His jaw falls open with gasping breaths, but no sound emerges. Helpless now, this man so fearless just moments before, now stares at panicking troops below.

Without the rod of God displayed against the sky, Israel's pathetic soldiers take a drastic downhill turn.

Look out! Our spirits yell with vigor as the enemy advances. Oh, no! Joshua and his army are losing the battle! Oh, Moses, somehow you must find strength to lift your hands. Unless the soldiers can focus on the rod as their mighty banner of Jehovah soon, they'll all be dead!

In the nick of time Aaron and Hur rush to the rescue. They quickly roll a stone to make a seat for Moses. Then with one at each side, they stand to support his weakened arms. Once again the rod of God broadcasts victory across the horizon for all to view.

By dusk Israel overtakes the Amalekites. Oh, the wonders of the Lord! In one day the war is won. Glowing in the sunset, brave Joshua and his men march into camp with shouts of praise ringing across the land. Aaron and Hur run down to join them.

A most grateful Moses lingers. Overlooking the site of victory, he erects an altar of remembrance and fellowships with the Great I AM. In His honor Moses names the hill of conquest "Yahweh Nissi," "Jehovah, our Banner."

How marvelous to realize that with the God's rod for a banner, despite man's own incapability, only these possible outcomes exist. Success! Triumph! Victory!

Can we expect the same results today?

Yes, yes, God says yes!

Because we possess an even greater banner—the mighty cross of Jesus. Never let the hill of Calvary escape your view, for that is where our Savior held up His hands for all to see. In agony He stretched out His arms until victory was won.

Oh, the allegory of our Bridegroom in the Song of Solomon! In eternity as we sit as Christ's bride at the heavenly wedding feast, we'll realize the total magnitude and conquest of His banner.

> He brought me to the banqueting house, and his banner over me was love.
>
> —SONG OF SOLOMON 2:4

First and foremost God is love. Before the foundation of the world Yahweh loved us enough to establish His plan of redemption. His love spans through the sands of time, guiding the linage of the perfect Seed. He loved us enough to release a part of Himself, as His Son, into the pains of Earth to shed His spotless blood to free mankind from sin, grief, sorrow, and sickness. With everlasting arms of love Father, Son, and Spirit hold the banner of the cross up before us for all eternity.

Yes, the cross purchased freedom forever. There is no way into the splendor of Yahweh, except through its victory.

> Whosoever denieth the Son, the same hath not the Father: [but] he that acknowledgeth the Son hath the Father also. Let that therefore abide in you, which ye have heard from the beginning. If that which ye have heard from the beginning shall remain in you, ye also shall

continue in the Son, and in the Father. And this is the promise that he
has promised us, even eternal life.

—1 John 2:23–25

Through Jesus we know the Father. Above all the many names and titles
we've experienced in our travels, the most special and endearing name we
can ever know Him by is Abba Father. Even with His endless magnitude, in
all His glory and majesty, in His almighty power and strength, His boundless knowledge and wisdom, He remains to all believers Abba Father, fulfilling the role of Daddy to His children.

In gratitude let us review the wonder of our adoption, trying once
again to fathom how it came about. How marvelous the mercy, how
amazing the grace, and how deep the love of God to give His Son to save
the human race.

Yes, when Deity became human, born into this sinful world with mortal flesh and mortal blood through an earthly mother, He carried through
His Father the linage of God Himself. On His mother's side He became
mankind's brother.

On His Father's side He became mankind's Redeemer.

By acknowledging Him for who He truly is—our precious Lord and
Savior, the only begotten Son of God—a supernatural adoption takes place.
In the natural we were born to earthly parents. In the spiritual we are reborn
into the family of Almighty God. Joint heirs with His Son. Temples of His
Holy Spirit. Members of His royal household with the legal right to use our
family name.

One more name we must probe. And this name belongs to us. Jesus, a
transliteration of the name Joshua (Yhowsuwa in Hebrew), means "Jehovah
(Yahweh) is salvation."

Jesus! A superior name, exalted higher than the name of any angel!

Being made so much better than the angels, as he hath by inheritance
obtained a more excellent name than they.

—Hebrews 1:4

A name above all names!

And being found in human form he humbled himself and became
obedient unto death, even death on a cross. Therefore God has
highly exalted him and bestowed on him the name which is above
every name, that at the name of Jesus every knee should bow, in
heaven and on earth and under the earth, and every tongue confess

that Jesus Christ is Lord, to the glory of God the Father.

—PHILIPPIANS 2:8–11, RSV

The name that saves!

> Neither is there salvation in any other: for there is none other name
> under heaven given among men, whereby we must be saved.

—ACTS 4:12

Saved in this text is defined as to save, deliver or protect, heal, preserve,
do well, be (made) whole.

The name that gives life!

> But these are written, that ye might believe that Jesus is the Christ, the
> Son of God; and that believing ye might have life through his name.

—JOHN 20:31

The name that brings His presence!

> For where two or three are gathered together in my name, there I am
> in the midst of them.

—MATTHEW 18:20

Such power in this name!

> And the seventy returned again with joy, saying, Lord, even the devils
> are subject unto us through thy name.

—LUKE 10:17

> And these signs shall follow them that believe; In my name shall they
> cast out devils; they shall speak with new tongues; They shall take up
> serpents; and if they drink any deadly thing, it shall not hurt them;
> they shall lay hands on the sick, and they shall recover.

—MARK 16:17–18

> …that signs and wonders may be done by the name of the holy child
> Jesus.

—ACTS 4:30

This name gives authority over sickness!

> Is any sick among you? let him call for the elders of the church; and let
> them pray over him, anointing him with oil in the name of the Lord:

And the prayer of faith shall save the sick, and the Lord shall raise him up; and if he have committed sins, they shall be forgiven him.

—JAMES 5:14–15

Sins are pardoned through this name!

...that through his name whosoever believeth in him shall receive remission of sins.

—ACTS 10:43

Oh, the workings of this name with the Holy Spirit!

But ye are washed, but ye are sanctified, but ye are justified in the name of the Lord Jesus, and by the Spirit of our God.

—1 CORINTHIANS 6:11

And the Holy Spirit Himself is given by this name!

But the Comforter, which is the Holy Ghost, whom the Father will send in my name...

—JOHN 14:26

What glorious rewards in using this name!

And in that day ye shall ask me nothing. Verily, verily, I say unto you, Whatsoever ye shall ask the Father in my name, he will give it you.

—JOHN 16:23

And rights to this name belong to all who believe!

For there is no difference between the Jew and the Greek: for the same Lord over all is rich unto all that call upon him. For whosoever shall call upon the name of the Lord shall be saved.

—ROMANS 10:12–13

JESUS! Name above all names. Name of everlasting victory. Alive and powerful with deliverance, protection, healing, and wholeness. The family name of all believers to freely rely upon. To use in all we do, in all we say.

And whatsoever ye do in word or deed, do all in the name of the Lord Jesus, giving thanks to God and the Father by him.

—COLOSSIANS 3:17

Do you want His everlasting victory? If you've never truly said yes to His plan of redemption, will you say yes now? With all submission, will you agree to be His child? To trust His Word and follow in His way? Will you be washed, sanctified, and justified by the power of His name and Holy Spirit? Will you bow in true repentance, confessing Jesus as your Savior?

> That if thou shalt confess with thy mouth the Lord Jesus, and shalt believe in thine heart that God hath raised him from the dead, thou shalt be saved.
>
> —ROMANS 10:9

Saved—delivered, protected, healed, preserved, made whole.[3] Have you called upon His name for this salvation? Do you believe He is the Son of God so that you can walk hand in hand with Him "saved" throughout eternity?

Can you honestly proclaim, "Yes, yes, my heart says yes"? If not, then ask Him in the name of Jesus to receive you now: "Father, will You forgive my sins and accept me me as righteous in Your sight because of the spotless blood Your Son Jesus shed for me?"

Loud and clear we hear His voice. "Yes, yes," God says. "Yes!"

Chapter 9

Thy Kingdom Come

A S TRAVELERS TOGETHER our feet have touched God's paths of glory. We have walked hand in hand in the magnitude of His creation, the marvel of His redemptive plan, the brilliance of His *Shekinah* glory, the power of His might.

We now know Him by His names and many virtues. We have stood in awe of his holiness and excellence, majesty and splendor, unconditional love and nurturing, discipline and judgment, mercy and grace, peace and healing, sanctification and righteousness, provisions and promises, ever-abiding presence and faithfulness. We have caught a glimpse of His innumerable angelic hosts, His glorious Throne, and beautiful heavenly city. We have seen Him as our Savior on the cross.

Through the revelation of Himself as Father, Son, and Holy Ghost—three, yet one—we know Him. How blessed we have been to meet Him as Creator, Abba Father, the Living Word, the Holy Spirit, Conqueror, Banner, Guide, Shepherd, Brother, Redeemer, the Lamb, High Priest, Bridegroom, the Almighty, the Most High, the Son of Righteousness, the Alpha and Omega, eternal Deity. He is all these things to us because of His everlasting testament, His blood-sealed covenant to mankind.

Yes, oh yes, we know Him!

Awareness of His infinite nature calls us to greater responsibility. Now with our treasure map in hand we will travel in new places that will refine us by His kingdom policies. They will give us wisdom for mortal living today and prepare us to be future partakers in life beyond imagination, molding us to become glorified beings and reign with Him for all eternity. From this point until our journey's end we'll be striving for this goal—"Thy kingdom come. Thy will be done in earth, as it is in heaven."

Will God's total will ever be done on Earth as it is in heaven? Absolutely! Jesus never tells us to pray a hopeless prayer. Someday a perfect kingdom will exist on this planet just as in heaven, but until then His kingdom lives in us. When Jesus came, He brought God's kingdom into the world. It was not manifested externally, but by the Holy Spirit it dwells within the innermost being of all believers.

Jesus stresses this in Luke 17:20–21 where the Pharisees ask when the kingdom will come. "The kingdom of God does not come with signs to be observed or with visible display, nor will people say, Look! Here [it is]! or, See, [it is] there! For behold, the kingdom of God is within you [in your hearts] and among you [surrounding you]" (AMP).

How can His "inner" kingdom be defined? It is His way of doing things, His governmental system of heaven's operation on Earth. God's kingdom is the work of His principles enabling good to triumph over evil. It is proficiency from above, establishing His excellence within all who are covered by the blood.

> Now may the God of peace who brought up our Lord Jesus from the dead, that great Shepherd of the sheep, through the blood of the everlasting covenant, make you complete in every good work to do His will, working in you what is well pleasing in His sight, through Jesus Christ, to whom be glory forever and ever. Amen.
>
> —Hebrews 13:20–21, NKJV

His kingdom working in us makes us "complete in every good work to do His will." Living by kingdom rules, doing "what is well pleasing in His sight," our spirits rise beyond the natural realm into heavenly heights with Him.

> If ye then be risen with Christ, seek those things which are above, where Christ sitteth on the right hand of God. Set your affection on things above, not on things on the earth.
>
> —Colossians 3:1–2

As we participate in the richness of His kingdom and discover its precepts, prepare yourself for a daring ride into vibrant perceptions in the natural law of His creation and spiritual law in His living Word. In a more intense probe than ever before, we'll search out amazing mysteries and uncover hidden patterns, previews, and parables meant only for His followers and not for the world to know.

> Because it is given unto you to know the mysteries of the kingdom of heaven, but to them it is not given.
>
> —MATTHEW 13:11

Oh, what intrigue unfolds in the remainder of our trip. With increased understanding of His kingdom abiding within us we can learn how to operate solely within its structure and fine-tune ourselves for success now and forever.

Although we've touched on many kingdom rules in our preceding travels, we have now entered the place of absolute reliance upon our Lord and total observance of His ways. After all, how can we be content to stand still (or stop growing) in the knowledge we've gained so far?

We can't! We can never rest in the deception that we have achieved all. Instead, we must always continue striving to be our best in Him.

> Not that I have already attained, or am already perfected; but I press on that I may lay hold of that for which Christ Jesus has also laid hold of me.
>
> —PHILIPPIANS 3:12, NKJV

BEFORE STARTING OUR expedition let's pause to acknowledge Christ as our Leader. From now on we'll recognize Him as the Conductor of our destiny on a train leading us all the way to glory. Arise with glee, friends, as a whole new venture jolts into motion!

Like a flash of lightning the Jubilee Express streaks into the station to pick us up. It screeches to a halt, and its door flies open. The joyous song of a thousand voices overflows from its chambers, filling the air with lyrics: "This train is bound for glory, this train!"[1]

Eagerness overwhelms us. Anticipation mounts. Above the wild pounding of our hearts and the volume of the choir's singing, the train whistle summons all to come.

The Conductor calls, "All aboard!"

Hurray! We're bound for glory, on our way to discover the inner workings of the mighty kingdom of God. Our tickets have been purchased by the blood of Christ. Our passage has been made possible by His righteousness, mercy, and grace. A most glorious light shines from the Jubilee Express, brightening the darkest tunnel and beaming with radiance through the blackest night.

In flowing harmony the melody of the choir switches to a softer note, "Just as I am, without one plea, but that Thy blood was shed for me...O Lamb of God, I come."[2]

In humility we pause—"giving thanks to the Father who has qualified us to be partakers of the inheritance of the saints in the light. He has delivered us from the power of darkness and conveyed us into the kingdom of the Son of His love, in whom we have redemption through His blood, the forgiveness of sins" (Col. 1:12–15, NKJV).

With great desire we gaze toward the light of His kingdom. Our hearts burn with appreciation in contemplation of being partakers of our inheritance. How could we ever deserve such blessings?

"...but that Thy blood was shed for me..."

We qualify by His blood, not by our own merits. Come just as you are, accepting His provisions and ride the train to glory. Climb aboard. The wheels will soon start rolling.

Whoops, we can't go yet. How could I overlook the one requirement for departure? Each of us must have a ticket. Even though every single ticket was purchased for us two thousand years ago, we must personally claim our very own. Let me tell you about the time I got mine.

Oh, how amazing our Father is! Undoubtedly He cares about our every thought.

I was so blessed to hear my sister speak at our church some years ago. She lived in a nearby town and was part of a lay-witness group that came and gave testimonies for Christ. As the speakers shared how Jesus turned their wayward lives around, the congregation absorbed their stories of salvation. The Holy Spirit filled the room like a pleasant aroma. I especially experienced His sweet bliss because of the endearing spot my sister holds in my heart.

Toward the end of the service one man said, "If you can't recall a specific time you gave your heart to Jesus, you never have, and you need to do it now." His words penetrated the crowd.

One young lady dashed to the platform. Many knew her as the dedicated wife of a minister, a loving mother, a person devoted to God and the church. In no way would anyone have questioned her salvation or love of Jesus.

However, in a broken voice she spoke, "Although I've always believed I was saved, I can't pinpoint a specific day when I invited Jesus to be my Savior, so I'm doing it right now. From this night on, I'll claim this date as my day of salvation, pledging my life to Him anew." Joyful tears spilled down her cheeks.

My heart gave her a standing ovation. How I admired her boldness in affirming her commitment to God before the church—because I also couldn't declare an exact moment I asked Jesus into my life.

Racking my brain, I thought back to days gone by. I knew without a doubt that from early childhood I had believed and trusted God. At age eleven I had made a public confession and joined the church. At nineteen I had rededicated my life to Him at a crusade. *But when,* my heart boomed, *did I first ask Jesus to become my Lord and Savior?*

After the service, caught up in an hour of refreshment and fellowship, I dismissed this probe. But overwhelmed by a compelling urge, I told people how my sister was conceived after I as a little girl prayed her into being. "Our mother gave my prayer the credit for her conception," I assured them. "She wrote it in her baby album."

Each time I repeated the story I asked myself, *Why do I keep doing this?* Nevertheless, over and over in the course of conversation I would suddenly relate the account to yet another person.

At home the following day, still baffled and somewhat embarrassed by my compulsion, I asked, "Why, Lord, did I tell so many about my prayer for a sister when I was at church yesterday?"

Like comforting warmth the answer radiated through my soul, *On the day of her birth you asked Me into your heart.*

In praise I lifted my hands. Yes, through the years I had often recalled that special day. Even now I grope for words to describe the sheer joy that raced through every tender cell of my body when the phone rang at the relative's house where my brother and I were staying. "It's your daddy calling from the hospital. It's a girl!" came the message. Knowing the story of my prayer, my older cousin added, "Your baby sister is here!"

Later she laughed as she related to others how I skipped down the hallway, "then without a single word Judy bolted out the front door!"

Although she delighted in my happiness, how could she even begin to suspect the way my young heart exploded in thanksgiving? Inside I cried, *God gave me a baby sister! A baby sister! A baby sister!* But I couldn't make my lips utter one word out loud. I felt God calling me to come to Him. I had to be alone.

In the backyard behind the garage I located a secluded area. I remember worshiping God, thanking Him over and over. Now I know at that very place in time I gave my fragile heart away and placed the rest of life into the outstretched hands of Jesus.

Yes, on that special day at age nine I became a citizen in His kingdom and took possession of my ticket to glory. Paid for by the spotless blood that flowed so long ago at Calvary, it cost me nothing but to come to Him.

That's the only requirement to enter into His kingdom, to be a passenger on board the train bound for glory. Come with a sincere heart just as you are to the One who paid the price. With unconditional love He issues a ticket to every single person who comes. No plea is needed except that His blood was shed for you. So come in faith. The ticket's free.

But don't put it off. The train could leave without you as quickly as the twinkling of an eye.

Once more the Conductor calls all who haven't already come. He has a seat reserved for all, so claim your ticket now, climb aboard, and settle in your seat. It's time to be on our way.

AS THE JUBILEE Express begins to stir, its wheels awaken with a gentle hiss. After a quick spring forward they chug with a pleasant rhythm on straight and narrow rails that gleam in the kingdom light like brilliant scarlet threads as they stretch far into the distance. The train will take us through miles of desert, over mountains high, into valleys deep until we reach the realms of glory. We will travel many miles and make many stops before we come to our final destination, but at last we're on our way.

Clang, clang the bell peals with happiness. The whistle joins in with notes of joy. The mighty engine puffs with steam that billows like a swirling cloud of cotton candy. With gaiety great voices arise in another song, "Where He leads me I will follow...I'll go with Him, with Him all the way."[3]

With eyes of love our Conductor threads His way down the aisle greeting each passenger. Authority and power stream from His countenance, and kindness radiates from His face. Any trace of anxiety vanishes because we have no need to worry under His leadership. He's already won every battle we can possibly encounter. On His hands we see scars of victory as, while confirming each ticket, He passes out free tokens labeled "Reassurance."

Tokens of reassurance? Bewildered we look to Him. Exactly what are these for?

They are given as reminders of His everlasting testament, recollections of His plan of redemption, precious mementos of His spotless blood that makes His kingdom a possibility for all. These reassuring tokens are found in hidden pictures scattered among the pages of God's Word.

> And the blood shall be to you for a *token*.
> —EXODUS 12:13, EMPHASIS ADDED

Like lightning our train whisks us far back to the ages of eternity past before the world began. There is no need to linger because we visited here before and witnessed the making of the covenant by the trinity of Elohim.

We sweep into the Garden of Eden, remembering the day when God first declared to Adam and Eve that a redeemer—the Seed of the woman—would arise to defeat the devil and free the human race. We've already been here, too, so why are we stopping?

Oh, we see why. This is the first token of blood, revealed in the making of clothes for Adam and Eve. By His own hand the Lord God slaughters an undefiled beast made of His perfection. Innocent blood spills upon the new creation to provide covering for the sinful flesh of fallen man. His promise of the Seed of the woman is sealed for all mankind in guiltless blood, confirmed by an unblemished sacrifice, and established for all eternity.

At a slower pace our ride resumes because just over the hill we'll make another stop. This time we will be on new ground that we haven't explored before, Genesis 4:8–15, the site of Abel's blood.

Is it just a coincidence that the first shedding of man's blood on Earth's soil is righteous blood, as Jesus Himself called it in Matthew 23:35? This is such a parallel to our Savior's spotless blood.

Is it incidental that Abel chose to be a shepherd and is murdered by his own brother? Jesus is our shepherd, "...our Lord Jesus, that great shepherd of the sheep, through the blood of the everlasting covenant" (Heb. 13:20). Abel is like our Savior, our Brother, who was murdered by His own. Such likenesses are hidden tokens to remind us of the covenant.

After Cain kills his brother Abel, God approaches him. "What have you done?" He thunders. "The voice of your brother's blood cries out to me from the ground!"

If Abel's blood, the blood of an imperfect mortal, has power to cry out—greater beyond measure is the ability of the blood of the infallible Son of God. It cries on our behalf, pleading our case before the Father.

> And to Jesus the mediator of the new covenant, and to the blood of sprinkling, that speaketh better things than that of Abel.
> —HEBREWS 12:24

Abel's blood cries for vengeance on his brother, and Cain received a lifelong sentence. God says to Cain, "Now you are cursed from the earth, whose mouth has opened to receive the blood of your brother, shed by your hand."

Jesus' blood cries, not for vengeance, but for mercy and forgiveness for His brothers. All of us are guilty of His death, for He died for all our sins. But instead of a curse, His blood cries for our atonement. Instead of a lifelong sentence, His blood gives everlasting life.

As the Jubilee Express glides through the centuries a beautiful rainbow appears across a royal blue horizon. Its loveliness radiates with a reminder of the grace of God.

> And God said, This is the *token* of the covenant which I make between me and you and every living creature that is with you, for perpetual generations: I do set my bow in the cloud, and it shall be for a *token* of a covenant between me and the earth....And the bow shall be in the cloud; and I will look upon it, that I may remember the everlasting covenant between God and every living creature of all flesh that is upon the earth. And God said unto Noah, This is the *token* of the covenant.
>
> —GENESIS 9:12–13, 16–17, EMPHASIS ADDED

We remember from our earlier visit with Noah, how upon descending from the ark he "built an altar to the LORD, and took of every clean animal and every clean bird, and offered burnt offerings on the altar" (Gen. 8:20, NKJV).

The blood of clean animals is a reminder of the promise from the gates of Eden. In the delight of the sweet aroma of Noah's devotion, God vows:

> I will never again curse the ground for man's sake...nor will I again destroy every living thing as I have done.
>
> —GENESIS 8:21, NKJV

And so we have the token of the rainbow to verify His Word, to put us in remembrance.

OUR TRAIN SPEEDS into another chapter in time. Peering from our windows into Genesis 15 we recognize a familiar face. Abram! Joy radiates in his movements. We hear him praising God as he works. How happy and busy he is.

What in the world is he doing? Cutting slaughtered animals apart.

For sacrifice? No, for the validation of God's promise.

In a vision God has just reaffirmed the surety of Abram's everlasting seed, from which the perfect Seed will come. And God has just presented His faithful friend with a title deed to the Promised Land—the land of Canaan, given to Abram for the nation that will spring from his loins.

We know this nation by the name of Abram's grandson Israel, the only nation ever born by the sovereignty of God. All the generations of Israel have been aware that God Himself gave their land to Abram, whose name He changed to Abraham and thereby qualified to be the father of many nations. Knowing this we comprehend the magnitude of the guarantee God presents this day as we look on.

Abram asks, "Oh, my Master Yahweh, how can I be sure You will give this land to me?"

He will know beyond any doubt by a blood covenant. God says to kill a heifer, a female goat, and a ram, each three years old, a turtledove and a young pigeon. Abram slays them and separates the larger animals into halves. He arranges the animal pieces side by side in two lines on the ground. We can tell by his actions that he knows exactly what's going on, yet we are baffled. Exactly what does all this mean?

Jeremiah 34:18 gives us a clue when Jeremiah speaks of the ancient blood covenant, "when they cut the calf in twain, and passed between the parts thereof."

Abram knows these rules. And with his instructions coming from the Lord Himself, he expects Him to show up and pass between the butchered parts.

While we wait to see what happens, let's draw more from a history of the times. Generally the persons making a covenant joined hands, recited the provisions agreed upon, and solemnized its terms by each proceeding down an aisle between the slain pieces. It was as if to say, "If I break this testament, may the same fate as these beasts come to me." How binding and unconditional, how unbreakable and serious the enactment of the blood covenant was.

Now just think; Almighty God is willing to carry out such a custom to substantiate His word on the human level. A supernatural God plans to confirm His word to Abram by arriving on the scene and passing between bloody, cut-up animals. What an amazing demonstration of His love.

But when will He show up? Although Abram must be wondering, he waits in faith. Hungry buzzards swoop down to devour the carcasses. Abram fights them off.

As the sun begins setting on his long and strenuous day, Abram yawns and closes his eyes in sleep. Beside the dead creatures he collapses on the ground. Oh no, will he miss the Lord?

What profound stillness! Has he drifted into a coma?

In the next instant the voice of the Supreme Ruler of all heaven and Earth recites the terms of the covenant to His sleeping servant. As He finishes, darkness descends like a heavy blanket over the area and envelops Abram. Seconds later God in His *Shekinah* glory blasts into the atmosphere. Like a mighty sweeping fire, a tremendous smoking furnace, a torch blazing brighter than words can describe, He touches the earth and passes between the fleshly parts.

Now we realize why Abram had to sleep in total darkness. The light of God is so bright, with such magnificence and splendor. No human being can look upon its magnitude and live. How can a God so great love mere man so much!

Abram awakes, aware of the miracle that has just taken place. We wait for him to rise and also pass between the parts, but nothing happens. Even though ancient rules obligate each person involved in the covenant to bind their word by walking the blood-drenched path, Abram doesn't have to do it. God alone binds Himself without conditions.

No man could adequately fulfill the terms, for it required the perfect Seed. He took man's place when by His own blood He met all the obligations and extended the covenant that began with Abram to all humanity. God's willingness to bind His word in human fashion gives us another reassuring token.

OUR TRAIN MOVES on until we reach the wicked city of Jericho. Within its walls a harlot, Rahab, gives us another symbol of remembrance. By her courageous faith the saving power of the blood of Christ is previewed in a single scarlet thread.

Though she is not a Jew, she risks her very life for the purposes of God. Because of Rahab's kindness and heroic efforts to save the lives of the two Hebrew spies sent into the city, she along with her family survives its doom. With a sincere heart she bravely acknowledges the sovereignty of Yahweh as Creator:

> For the LORD your God, he is God in heaven above, and in earth beneath. Now therefore, I pray you, swear unto me by the LORD, since I have shewed you kindness, that ye will also shew kindness unto my father's house, and give me a true *token*: And that ye will save alive my father, and my mother, and my brethren, and my sisters, and all that

they have, and deliver our lives from death.
—JOSHUA 2:11–13, EMPHASIS ADDED

Heeding instruction from the men of Israel, she places a scarlet thread in her window until their return. It is a token of their promise to return and deliver her from doom. A sign for her safety, it is a reminder of their redemptive promise, a similitude of God's redemptive promise.

And so our train zooms forward on rails of scarlet thread. So many token reminders leap from His Word. Every Old Testament circumcision, every marriage to a virgin, every animal sacrifice takes on new significance as they reveal the redemptive covenant of our Creator. They portray not what tarnished man pledges to God, but what a pure and holy God has pledged to man.

Offering unblemished beasts covers man's guilt, but only for a season. With repeated offerings their blood suffices as a token until the blood of God's Son will drip on Earth's soil to free souls forever.

> For if the blood of bulls and of goats, and the ashes of a heifer sprinkling the unclean, sanctifieth to the purifying of the flesh: How much more shall the blood of Christ, who through the eternal Spirit offered himself without spot to God, purge your conscience from dead works to serve the living God?
>
> —HEBREWS 9:13–14

Before the rules for sacrifices were issued from Mount Sinai the Jew understood the power of the blood. By smearing the blood of an unblemished lamb above their doorposts at its center and also on both sides, the avenging angel passed over their houses.

> And the blood shall be to you for a *token* upon the house where ye are: and when I see the blood, I will pass over you, and the plague shall not be upon you to destroy you, when I smite the land of Egypt.
>
> —EXODUS 12:13, EMPHASIS ADDED

They also experience supernatural healing from the lamb's flesh. After eating all of it at God's command, they escape Egypt the next day with "not one feeble person among their tribes" (Ps. 105:37).

Why does our Lord of limitless power use a simple lamb for their salvation? The answer is obvious, but many fail to see it. This foreshadows the Messiah and reveals God's redemptive plan. Why put blood on the door in such a pattern that it would drip from the center and from each side to the ground? Blood would drip from Jesus, our Door—from His body at the center of the cross and from His outstretched hands at the sides.

Because of the night when they were saved by the lamb and death passed over them, Jews still celebrate an annual Feast of Passover. It is a token of remembrance set forth by God Himself.

THE JUBILEE EXPRESS now whips us into a depot to let us off. As we step down, the Conductor hands out invitations to a Seder, the Jewish Passover meal. We're going to a party! Hidden in this event lie tokens that show the essence of Christianity. And we're about to uncover them!

Patterns emerge even before we arrive at the Feast. Four days before the death angel came upon Egypt, the Israelites selected their lambs, and four days before His death, Jesus rode into Jerusalem. On the night of the Seder He was arrested. He was dead at the close of the Passover, with the Feast of Unleavened Bread beginning immediately. *Unleavened*, symbolizing sinlessness, presents a type of Christ's body. Next followed the Feast of First Fruits. During its celebration Christ was raised from the dead, becoming "the firstfruits" of the resurrection (1 Cor. 15:23).

We'll soon see how Passover Feasts remain unchanged from age to age as Jews perform the same basic rituals and repeat the same prayers word for word. What an honor it is to attend!

On the way a lingering touch of winter teases us, its lively breeze ruffling our hair like a playful child. In mischievous twirls it zips among the almond trees to bring attention to their dancing veils of ivory blossoms. A neon sun forms a glowing halo around a distant mountain and bids good day. As it sinks behind the horizon, the first full moon of spring debuts like a golden marble and lights our way to a bustling Hebrew household.

Just moments before the Seder begins we step inside the home of a large family. Vivacious children, giggling teenagers, and smiling adults are waiting in anticipation. We spot the distinguished father of the home dressed in white garments.

Glancing around we realize that several days of devoted preparation have taken place. From ceiling to floor everything sparkles in cleanliness. White decorations adorn the dining room. The table gleams with a white tablecloth, special dishes, a goblet at each setting, and tall ivory candles waiting to be lit. Every nook and cranny expresses purity on this night of honoring Israel's exodus from Egypt and the freedom made possible by the blood of a lamb. Even all leaven, a symbol of sin, has been purged from the house. As we watch the gaiety we can see the rituals unveil the true Lamb of God.

> Purge out therefore the old leaven, that ye may be a new lump, as ye are unleavened. For even Christ our passover is sacrificed for us.
>
> —I CORINTHIANS 5:7

Excited about getting started, the children gather around. Their faces beam as the father boasts of their helpfulness in getting things so clean and perfect. How they love being a part of the merriment of the Passover.

The mother of the house lights the candlesticks, and the festivities begin. How unusual that a woman puts the night in motion, since by Jewish custom the female rarely holds even a slight role in religious ceremonies. Yet it is so appropriate, for a Jewish maiden gave us Jesus, the light of the world (John 8:12).

In line with the theme of purity, the father wears his simple white robe with matching headdress, so like the costume of the high priest on the Day of Atonement when he entered into the holy of holies to sprinkle sacrificial blood in the presence of God. Two thoughts ignite, reminding us that Christ's garments glowed "as white as the light" (Matt. 17:2) at His transfiguration and also that He by His own blood "offered himself without spot to God" (Heb. 9:14) to serve as our heavenly High Priest:

> But Christ being come an high priest of good things to come, by a greater and more perfect tabernacle, not made with hands, that is to say, not of this building; Neither by the blood of goats and calves, but by his own blood he entered in once into the holy place, having obtained eternal redemption for us.
>
> —HEBREWS 9:11–12

The family reclines around the table, expressing relaxation that signifies their freedom from slavery. We notice an empty chair, reserved perhaps for a late arrival. Did someone call it Elijah's seat? What can that mean? *Shh!* We'll find out later as the celebration continues.

With explicit precision the father surveys the table setting. Every item has to be in exact accordance with the Law, unchanged from the previous year and every year before. No one dares to breathe. With all eyes glued on him, the father checks each detail by a special book. When he reaches out to pour the first of four goblets of wine, tension disappears and cheer breaks out. Called the Cup of Sanctification, it serves to sanctify the table and all the preparation of the feast.

That he [Jesus] might sanctify and cleanse it [the church] with the washing of water by the word.

—EPHESIANS 5:26

Next the father holds up three flat loaves of matzo, bread baked without leaven. They resemble large crackers, but what a picture they show of our Savior. A special unleavened bread, matzo is a symbol of sinlessness. The process by which it is grilled makes stripes across it.

By whose stripes ye were healed.

—1 PETER 2:24

Matzo has holes from piercing.

They shall look on him whom they pierced.

—JOHN 19:37

The father selects a special napkin on the table. A beautiful white fringed cloth, it is embroidered with gold thread and contains three pockets. In each pocket he places one flat loaf of matzo.

This signals the beginning of a game, and the children squirm with excitement. In its rules we see a pattern of the Father, Son, and Holy Spirit unfold. Holding the center section (the pocket typifying the Son), the father breaks the matzo down the middle.

He leaves one broken piece in the center pocket between the two whole loaves. Removing the other he wraps it in a white linen cloth and hurriedly hides it. Did he put it behind a pillow in his chair or in a compartment under the table? All eyes strain to see where the middle loaf is buried, but they must wait in suspense until the time of its resurrection. How this signifies Jesus.

And when Joseph had taken the body [of Jesus], he wrapped it in a clean linen cloth, and laid it in his own new tomb.

—MATTHEW 27:59–60

In the beauty of this first night of Passover we decipher many more prototypes of the Messiah. A plate in front of the father holds the roasted shank bone of a lamb, a variety of bitter herbs, a sweet delight of apples and nuts and cinnamon mixed with a little wine, and a hard-boiled egg. Let's examine each item.

The unbroken shank bone reminds us of the lamb that gave his life for them. By God's command no trace could remain the next day and no bone could be broken.

> They shall leave none of it unto the morning, nor break any bone of it: according to all the ordinances of the passover they shall keep it.
> —NUMBERS 9:12

How obviously this reveals the Lamb of God who gave His life for us. His body was not left upon the cross until the morning "because it was the preparation, that bodies should not remain upon the cross on the sabbath day" (John 19:31).

Joseph of Arimathea moved the body of Jesus to the tomb on the evening of the crucifixion.

Although it was customary to break the legs of all who had been crucified, Jesus was already dead when the soldiers came to Him, and they decided it unnecessary. "For these things were done, that the scripture should be fulfilled, A bone of him shall not be broken" (John 19:36).

Bitter herbs remind us of the bitterness of slavery in Egypt. This is a shadow of sin and the world, so bitter for anyone without the saving grace of Jesus.

Everyone at the table dips the bitter herbs into a bowl of salt water and thereby illustrate their way to freedom from Egypt by the Red Sea. It is a symbol of baptism—a demonstration of our freedom from sin through the blood.

Apples, nuts, and cinnamon in wine represent the brick mortar of Egypt. In this we find that the sweetness of life under the blood (symbolized in the wine) holds us together in His kingdom amid a world of sin.

The hard-boiled egg was possibly added in later years, and controversy arises over its definite meaning. Overcooked like a stone, it is sometimes thought to represent Pharaoh's heart. Does the Easter egg originate from the Seder plate as some Christians would like to believe? My research found no tangible evidence of this, but rather that the Easter egg comes from pagan Babylonian culture.

When the plate is removed from the table, the smallest child—a tiny boy with dark curls and bubbling smile—leaps to his feet. His eyes twinkle as he quotes from memory four long questions about the reason for Passover. It is a feat to memorize, yet such an honor to be chosen to recite them.

The father answers all four inquiries, reading an entire narration on the exodus of Israel from his Seder book, "That thou mayest remember the day of thy going forth from Egypt, all the days of thy life... 'The days of thy life' refer to this world only, but' all the days of thy life', include the time of the Messiah."[4]

Next we examine the second goblet of wine, the Cup of Judgment. Each person dribbles its scarlet liquid one drop at a time into an empty white plate before them. Ten droplets fall, signifying the ten plagues the Egyptians suffered. As each drop spills the father utters the plagues by name, "Blood, frogs, vermin, wild beast, pestilence, boils, hail, locusts, darkness, slaying of the firstborn."[5] With sadness all express compassion for the victims of the horrible plight required for their deliverance.

Ten is God's number for redemption. With sorrow we remember the ten sufferings Jesus endured for our deliverance—the great drops of blood He perspired under terrible duress, His betrayal and desertion by His friends, the merciless flogging of the Roman whip, the torturous crown of thorns placed upon his brow in mockery, the beatings of a reed upon His head, the plucking out of His beard, the vile spitting in His face, the weight of the cross on His bleeding back, the nails, the thirst.

Before His ordeal Jesus prayed three times:

> O my Father, if it be possible, let this cup pass from me: nevertheless not as I will, but as thou wilt.
>
> —Matthew 26:39

But the cup had to be endured. Jesus drank our cup of judgment.

After agonizing over this somber cup, joy returns to the family as a festive meal, a literal feast, emerges from the kitchen. Delicious aromas fill the room. Amid laughter and conversation they enjoy a luscious dinner. As Christians we relate this to the joy that returned to Jesus' disciples at His glorious resurrection after His somber cup of Calvary.

In olden days an entire lamb graced the table, but since the destruction of the temple in Jerusalem another meat is substituted. Without a place of sacrifice, a sacrificial lamb for the Passover has been deemed inappropriate. We rejoice knowing that no sacrificial lamb has been needed since the day Christ triumphed over His somber cup.

> But this Man, after He had offered one sacrifice for sins forever, sat down at the right hand of God.
>
> —Hebrews 10:12, NKJV

Soon all eyes turn to watch the pouring of the third goblet of wine, the Cup of Redemption. The father prays, "Blessed art thou, O Lord, our God, who creates the fruit of the vine."[6]

This prayer, some thirty-five hundred-years old, still speaks through Jesus today:

> I am the vine, ye are the branches: He that abideth in me, and I in him,
> the same bringeth forth much fruit.
>
> —JOHN 15:5

It's time to find the hidden matzo! Like a game of hide and seek, children scurry to locate the buried bread. With glee a little girl brings it forth for all to see. Oh, what a precious profile of our Savior as He is brought forth from death.

> He is not here; for He is risen, as He said. Come, see the place where
> the Lord lay.
>
> —MATTHEW 28:6, NKJV

The father reaches for the matzo. But no, the boys and girls laugh and shake their heads. He can't have it until he buys it back. Within our head the words swirl, "For ye are bought with a price" (1 Cor. 6:20).

According to rules of the game, the father redeems the bread with silver. This brings another scripture to our minds:

> Forasmuch as you know that ye were not redeemed with corruptible
> things, as silver and gold ... but with the precious blood of Christ, as of
> a lamb without blemish and without spot.
>
> —1 PETER 1:18–19

After carefully removing this "middle" loaf from its white linen wrapping, the father breaks it into many pieces. This is the last solid nourishment of the evening. We listen carefully to the blessing recited over the matzo, "Blessed art Thou, O Eternal, our God, King of the Universe, Who bringest forth bread from the earth."[7]

Our minds shift to Jesus and His Passover meal the night before the cross:

> Jesus took bread, and blessed it, and brake it, and gave it to the dis-
> ciples, and said, Take, eat; this is my body.
>
> —MATTHEW 26:26

Adhering to the Seder observance, Jesus passed matzo to His disciples. How did He bless it? Undoubtedly He said that same prayer still repeated each year by Jews today.

The words of Jesus echo in our spirits:

> I am the living bread which came down from heaven.
>
> —JOHN 6:51

Each person partakes of the broken bread and drinks from the Cup of Redemption as if this bread and wine contain a mysterious sustaining quality. We know the mystery!

> And when he had given thanks, he brake it and said, Take, eat: this is my body, which is broken for you: this do in remembrance of me. After the same manner also he took the cup, when he had supped, saying, This cup is the new testament in my blood: this do ye, as oft as ye drink it, in remembrance of me.
>
> —1 CORINTHIANS 11:24–25

The father now fills the wine goblet at the empty chair. But who will drink it? No one.

Yes, this seat is reserved for Elijah. This cup waits for Elijah to come and drink it, for Scripture says:

> Behold, I will send you Elijah the prophet before the coming of the great and dreadful day of the LORD.
>
> —MALACHI 4:5

Hope fills the room. Maybe Elijah will walk in this year, take his seat, and announce that the centuries of waiting are over at last. How they yearn to hear the prophet cry, "The Messiah has come!"

But Elijah doesn't arrive. A designated child dashes outside to look for him, but he's nowhere in sight. So they must wait another year for yet another Passover, the day of their salvation. For another year they will build their hopes, confident that then the prophet will at last show up.

Before Christ's ministry began, John the Baptist, in the spirit and power of Elijah, announced the coming of God's kingdom and proclaimed Jesus as the Lamb of God who takes away the sin of the world.

> And Jesus answered and said unto them, Elias truly shall first come, and restore all things.... Then the disciples understood that he spake unto them of John the Baptist.
>
> —MATTHEW 17:11, 13

However, the "great and terrible day of the LORD" spoken of by Malachi will occur in the future, shortly before the mighty Word of God as King of kings and Lord of lords descends with His armies of saints to bind Satan for a thousand years. During the tribulation period the true Elijah will return to preach on Earth again as one of the two witnesses mentioned in Revelation 11:1–13.

And I will give power unto my two witnesses, and they shall prophesy a thousand two hundred and threescore days, clothed in sackcloth.

—REVELATION 11:3

How sad it is that some still wait for the Messiah's first arrival. Our hearts long to exclaim to everyone, "He has already come!"

We scan each face. Surely the mood of the Passover now reflects disappointment. But no, the last glass of wine is a joyous one, the Cup of Praise. Filling it the father reads prayers of praise, asking God to reestablish the temple, praying, "Rebuild Jerusalem, Thy holy city, speedily, in our days."[8]

As the service ends, vibrant voices lift in song. Courage rings in every note and even soars within our spirits as we scurry back to our train with midnight fast approaching.

WHAT A WONDERFUL evening! Yet we have not explored one significant aspect of the Passover. We have just witnessed a prelude to our celebration of Holy Communion, the Lord's Supper. A sacrament that Jesus Himself gave us to commemorate His death, this New Testament token of remembrance is His supreme reminder of the victory He attained for us by His spotless blood and broken body.

As we scamper along in the moonlight Christ's words surge within us:

Take, eat; this is my body which is broken for you; do this in remembrance of Me.

—1 CORINTHIANS 11:24, NKJV

We recall the accomplishments of His broken body. He bore the excruciating pain of the whip that tore His flesh into shreds for our healing—spirit, mind, and body. The tearing of His flesh also opened the way into the heavenly holy of holies. As Hebrews 10:20 tells us, His flesh symbolized the temple veil which ripped from top to bottom at His death.

Picture our blessed Savior holding the cup of wine the evening of the Seder and saying:

This do, as often as you drink it, in remembrance of Me.

—1 CORINTHIANS 11:25, NKJV

In obedience, we recall the purpose of His blood. It paid the price for our redemption. Its perfection cleanses our sins so we can enter boldly through the shredded veil into His presence. It gives us blood relationship to Him and membership in His kingdom. It assures us of eternal life and previews His second coming.

After Jesus drank from the cup with His disciples, He said:

> I will not drink of this fruit of the vine from now on until that day when I drink it new with you in My Father's kingdom.
> —Matthew 26:29, nkjv

The heavenly wedding feast! Each time we drink the Bridegroom's wine it reminds us of His return for His bride. It brings us into a renewal of betrothal to Him—a rededication of our lives to Him until He comes.

The Christian experience encompasses three aspects of knowing Christ. As we've just seen, Holy Communion typifies all three.

First, we know Him through the cross as Savior, Redeemer, Christ our Brother. We draw near to Him in repentance, accepting His forgiveness, healing, and peace.

Second, the destruction of the veil opens the way for us to enter into the heavenly sanctuary, to know Him as the ascended Christ. He is the King on the throne on high, seated at the right hand of Majesty as our High Priest, mediator, intercessor, head of the church. We draw near to Him in our commitment of total surrender to and dependence on His authority, seeing Him in His divine fullness as Conqueror.

Third, by drinking the wine Christ signified His vow to return and take us to the place He is preparing for us. Through this we know Him as our Bridegroom. We draw near to Him by betrothal, united as one with Him, serving, loving, and living in His presence forevermore.

Oh, what depth of meaning is found in Holy Communion, the Lord's Supper. It is a natural act that brings us into spiritual union with Him. A time for gladness and thanksgiving, it is far-reaching in significance yet so lightly realized. It is such a special requirement that Jesus gave it as the first instruction for His church, even before the act of water baptism.

How often should we partake of Holy Communion? The early church shared it at least once a week—"And upon the first day of the week, when the disciples came together to break bread..." (Acts 20:7) and possibly daily—"And they, continuing daily with one accord in the temple, and breaking bread from house to house..." (Acts 2:46).

At close scrutiny the phrase *breaking bread* points only to joining together in Holy Communion—and not just in a church-building, but from house to house.

I've heard it said that Smith Wigglesworth, a renowned Pentecostal evangelist in the early twentieth century, took Communion every day. A biography, *Smith_Wigglesworth: Apostle of Faith*, credits his ministry as empowered with miracles, supernatural faith, and unshakable boldness—even telling how he brought a corpse back to life.[9] Could Jesus' sacred ordinance "in remembrance of Him" have contributed to his success? It certainly did not hinder him!

How often do most Christians take Communion? Probably not often enough. It seems that its importance as well as any heartfelt desire to participate in it has diminished in many congregations. With flimsy reasoning they excuse themselves by saying that constant practice would make it mundane.

Really? Does asking a blessing each time we eat make it humdrum? Is daily Bible reading a useless routine? What about Paul's order, "Pray without ceasing" (1 Thess. 5:17)?

Certainly all these practices keep the door open to heartfelt fellowship with God. They build faith and increase devotion. And so does Holy Communion.

So why do so many Christians believe that partaking of this sacrament too often would minimize its effect? They simply don't understand its importance.

But why not? Because of the deceiver! He hates the enlightenment into the healing of the body and the destruction of the veil between man and God. The enemy despises the revelation of forgiveness by the power of the blood. He wants no reminder of the Lord's return, so he fights to the hilt to weaken our awareness of its benefits. Satan wishes that we would never remember our Redeemer's death. After all, it defeated him. And this is yet another reason for us to celebrate when we observe the Lord's Supper.

> Insomuch than as the children have partaken of flesh and blood, He Himself likewise shared in the same, that through death He might destroy him who had the power of death, that is, the devil, and release those who through fear of death were all their lifetime subject to bondage.
> —HEBREWS 2:14–15, NKJV

Our frequent practice of Holy Communion is so vital in the eyes of Jesus! In His evaluation of the church in Ephesus He praises their works of labor, patience, shunning evil, detecting false apostles, and perseverance. Yet He adds:

> Nevertheless I have this against you, that you have left your first love.
> —REVELATION 2:4, NKJV

First love? Had they left Jesus? I had always heard it taught that the church in Ephesus had grown cold toward Jesus, as a wife may lose the fervent desire of a newlywed for her husband. But two factors puzzled me. Jesus would not have praised their acts if they had not been done with heartfelt devotion. Also, all their actions showed their dedicated love for Him.

My perplexity lifted when I heard a Messianic Jewish evangelist teach that this "first love" pointed to neglect in observing the Lord's Supper. He said that *agape*, the Greek word used for *love* in this scripture, is the deepest God-kind of love and can mean "love feast."[10]

In my research I found this to be true. I also discovered that *philandros,* the Greek word meaning affection as a wife for her husband, is an entirely different word than *agape*, which Jesus used when He scolded the Ephesus church.

He identifies this "first love" as works:

> Remember therefore from where you have fallen; repent and do the first works, or else I will come to you quickly and remove your lampstand from its place—unless you repent.
>
> —Revelation 2:5, nkjv

History reveals that the early church had charity banquets not just to share with the less fortunate, but also for the purpose of observing the Lord's Supper. Since, as we mentioned earlier, this observance was the first order Jesus gave the church—might He have been addressing the church in Ephesus about their neglect of the "love feast" and their need to be reminded of His death? Had the almost impeccable church of Ephesus lost its fervor in participating in the Eucharist, the "first work" Jesus instituted as He passed the bread and wine to His disciples on the last night before His death? This seems quite plausible.

Oh, how churches need this lampstand to guide them beyond the darkness of the world and walk in the conquering light of the kingdom. With each Communion service we, as believers, participate in a worshipful memorial. In His token of remembrance for all that He achieved by His victorious death, we honor Him as our Savior, High Priest, and Bridegroom.

In this context Holy Communion expands into a gala celebration of our everlasting guarantee from Almighty God. It is not a somber occasion but a glorious commemoration. A powerful token reminding us of His never-ending testament sealed by His death, it establishes us in His kingdom now and forever. His is a spiritual kingdom that brings heavenly life into our hearts and a literal kingdom that is coming in His power and glory.

We have seen so much in the Seder—the Jewish Passover meal—in its portrayal of our Messiah and as a prelude to the Lord's Supper. Overflowing with reverence, gratitude, joy, love, and wonder, we approach the station where the Jubilee Express waits for us. What a marvelous welcome we receive. Praise erupts from every car. Later from our sleeping berth we hear voices softly harmonizing.

Like a lullaby the hymn soothes away all lingering stimulation from our busy evening. How blessed we are to know that we can rest in calm assurance with the tokens of His precious blood in our possession, reminding us of our salvation by the victory His death. By it we are made members of His kingdom. By it our destiny is sure.

As we drift into slumber and the singing fades, a soft hum of metal wheels secure upon their scarlet rails will comfort us through the night. At dawn we'll arise to new adventure. But sleep well till then, my companions, renewing your strength to face strenuous challenges of faith as we awaken to explore God's principles of kingdom economy.

Chapter 10

Give Us This Day Our Daily Bread

DOWN, DOWN, DOWN our business spiraled like a ship that was being sucked to destruction in a whirlpool. Eight years of sacrificial investment and diligent work gurgled into a sewer of no return, leaving us with a sinking sense of failure and despair. Heartbroken, I felt as if my chest held the weight of a lead bomb that was ready to explode.

The store had been my baby. I had nurtured it, and it had grown and prospered. Then in a heartbeat it sank before my eyes. Jim and I tried so hard to save it, but all effort proved in vain. Every prayer went unanswered. Now our store was gone.

On December 31, 1991, Jim and I finished sweeping the last debris from an empty building, and only one factor remained—debt. Our debt was thousands upon thousands of dollars, and we had no idea how we would ever pay it. What a bleak New Year's Eve!

Like venomous fangs the severity of our financial crisis bit deep into our souls. As Jim locked the door to our business for the final time, I looked into the soft blue of his eyes and read their anguish. His tight lips and grim expression reflected the emotions we both felt. How desperately we had worked, but to no avail. I burst into tears as we limped away with tired, defeated hearts.

As if to taunt us even further, a nasty wind cut to the bone and a frigid drizzle spit into our faces as we crossed the parking lot in silence. Jim clutched my hand. Together we had yearned for some type of consolation—a kind expression of concern, a brief note of support, a mere flicker of compassion—from anyone.

But none had come.

It looked as if we suffered alone except for each other against a vicious world. With trembling lips I crawled into the passenger side of our van and brushed my icy tears aside. Throughout our twenty-one years of marriage Jim, so steadfast in optimism, always served as my fountain of encouragement. Somehow even now it overflowed. Before starting the motor his big hand reached out and squeezed my shoulder.

"It'll be all right. God will bring us through."

"I know. It's just so hard to say good-bye."

As we pulled away, vibrant colors danced in reflection on the dashboard. Except for the desolation of our one dark building, the entire shopping center gleamed in holiday luster. I slumped against the seat, and though I shut my eyes to protest the sight, my brain blazed with the picture of our window display two years earlier.

People came just to stand and gaze at it. Twinkling with thousands of lights, a huge star had flowed with glittering streams into a manger scene. Life-size mannequins portrayed Mary, Joseph, and baby Jesus while other ivory figures robed in white and with enormous wings hovered over them. Our shop captured first place in the citywide decoration contest.

Yes, it was so hard to say good-bye!

But I knew Jim was right. Rising above my despondency my heart did believe God would bring us through. Only by His miracle-working hand could we ever overcome our mountain of financial obligations. From deep within I decreed, *Through Him we will overcome!*

Shivering, I withdrew inside my down-filled coat and sighed, *If only Daddy were here!* Although the heater in our van warmed my body, the chilling nightmare of our business loss along with my father's untimely death played like a Stephen King novel in my head.

I had phoned him on a Sunday evening in June. "Daddy, I desperately need you to look over the store finances and give me advice."

How blessed we were to have my father. Because of his unique ability in financial matters, the local bank had put him on their board and often called for his opinion. Jim and I, as well as others in our family, depended on his expertise. As I talked to him that Sunday I felt relieved that we were planning to join him and my mother for a vacation on Thursday.

At my father's recommendation we had opened an outlet clothing business in 1983. He put us in touch with an international catalog company that sold us top-notch fashions at fantastic savings and helped us set up shop.

Following my father's suggestion, Jim stayed in his profession while I managed the store. With overflowing enthusiasm for our new venture we poured all our energy and spare money into making it succeed. Since we owed only five hundred dollars on our home, we refinanced it for inventory.

For the first six years our store flourished. Then, without warning, our supplier of discount merchandise dissolved overnight. Our store, as well as others like it, plunged into devastation. Most closed right away, but in optimism we sought new avenues. Although we searched high and low, we located no large-scale source that offered high-quality merchandise at low prices, which our large clientele had grown to expect.

Our profit margin dwindled. Sales plummeted, bills soared, and new debt accumulated. Our last two years in business produced only constant struggle and heartache.

Now on the way home passing lawns and houses that flashed with holiday lights, my thoughts flashed for a brief moment to a happy period. When our store first opened, my father lived only minutes away and visited every day. In my mind I saw his snow-white hair, ruddy face, and twinkling eyes. Wearing his usual khaki slacks and crisp white shirt, he was smiling—greeting customers, ringing up sales, and pricing and stocking merchandise.

How I missed him when after three years of selling in our hometown, Jim's job transfer relocated us and our store over 250 miles away. Though my father could no longer be physically present every day, Jim and I still treasured his input on fiscal matters.

Then unexpectedly, time ran out. Our phone conversation in June was the last we would ever share in this lifetime.

"I was shocked last week as I posted May's sales," I had told him. "I thought liquidation of our old stock in January, then remodeling the entire store and restocking with all new inventory would stimulate sales, entice new customers. I was wrong. We just sank deeper into dept. Every idea we tried backfired in our faces. Our new grand opening in February, the promotions and contests with elaborate prizes and gifts, all our extensive advertising just gobbled up our profit. Month by month we've hung on by a thread, but now sales have hit rock bottom. We owe so, so much. And I don't know anything else to do!"

"It can't be all that bad," my father had said. "Just bring your records when you come Thursday. We'll look over them together."

That night a violent illness struck my father. Within moments my brother and mother rushed him to the hospital. By morning he was dead.

At the funeral home a relative commented, "After the initial shock of his death, it hit me—what will we do if we face another financial crisis?"

My heart leaped into my throat. I knew that my father's guidance had once spared this man from bankruptcy in his business and from losing his home. His words mixed with my mourning and smoldered within me. Day by day the burning intensified while our store sank deeper to the point of no return.

As we traveled in our van amid the roadside's flickering bliss that New Year's Eve, I claimed a new beginning and vowed that the torment of my heart would soon be quenched. *Next year we'll celebrate the holidays with joy,* I assured myself.

Forcing a smile I said, "Yes, Jim, it *will* be all right. In God's eyes our debt is puny. His resources never run out. He will bring us through."

With my one last ounce of strength I cried privately inside my being, *Lord, please help us overcome!*

And He did. But oh, what struggle lay ahead. How far we had to navigate in our cold and heartless sea of debt. How much we had to learn before our heavenly Father could begin His work in our financial restoration. It was a gruesome course that I do not wish to take again, and yet I now treasure its savage waves and blows for the place to which they brought us.

We thought our faith was strong, but how immature it proved to be. For years we had claimed God as the One who met our needs; nevertheless, in a pinch we had cherished the comfort of knowing that my father stood nearby with a solution.

And what happened? Without him our lives nose-dived into a monetary mess. Swept away by panic we sought the world's opinion, but the input rang cold and uncaring: "Declare bankruptcy and forget it."

My father had co-signed one initial note to launch our business. Due to the expense of our move we still had not fully paid it. Our complete renovation meant still another loan, this time a personal note from my father. His death left my mother responsible for them both if we failed to pay.

We also owed other creditors. While our consciences cried out that we should not let anyone down, how could we ever pay our debts? Without God we couldn't. For the first time in my life I had no choice but to rely wholly on Him without leaning on my father. Continuing to assert that God would bring us through, Jim and I spoke all the right words. However, for a long while our actions showed little trust as we attempted to work things out by our own efforts.

How foolish we are when we try to fit God's master design into our meager plan. In our failure to abide in His kingdom mode of operation, we floundered like goldfish in an ocean. Immersed in our human reasoning, engulfed by carnal endeavors, we paddled frantically yet never made any progress.

Only the Lord's merciful love kept us from drowning. Through all our blundering not once did He deny us as His children or abandon us like orphans who were lost in ignorance, unable to reach the shore. Instead, with patience He kept us afloat until we grew to completely trust His spiritual system above our natural effort. He faithfully cared for us until at last we realized that our heavenly Father, not our earthly father, holds first position as our source and supplier.

With grace and truth, He taught us until we came to know the necessity of conquering problems by doing things according to His rules and learned the magnitude in His principles of giving. Giving activates receiving. God's kingdom law of reciprocity is the key to overcoming.

Stay with me as we travel through and rise above the years of turbulence Jim and I endured. Witness how God's divine discipline instills His wisdom to the searching soul. See how day by day, stroke by stroke, precept upon precept Jim and I emerged from our abyss of errors into His river of living water. Discover how finally in true and tested faith we came to know our Savior as our daily living bread.

Oh, what a relief it was when we yielded totally to His way. We were no longer tossed blindly about in murky waves, but we were guided by His lighthouse. No longer did we simply hope for a miracle out of the blue, but we followed His methods for living abundantly in His daily provisions. As we move into this next venture on our treasure map, you'll discover as we did solutions to unlock the mysteries to your problems and revelation to release your reservoirs of blessings.

OUR GLORY TRAIN waits. It's time to be on our way—once again relinquishing leadership to our Conductor and placing full confidence in the scarlet rails. Sit tight as we ride into an area of responsibility, obedience, and service to grow in deeper appreciation of the promises and provisions of His kingdom as we pray.

GIVE US THIS DAY OUR DAILY BREAD

Yes, sit tight, fellow travelers! Come and gain new wisdom in God's kingdom light. We'll zoom on shaky bridges above raging waters, so clutch your blood-bought tickets and blood-dipped tokens and cling to the assurance they provide as you rely on Him daily for your bread.

In this petition, "Give us this day our daily bread," bread typifies practical need. In John 6:51 Jesus calls Himself the living bread. What a precious promise of God's provision.

In ancient cultures grain provided a most important food, to such a degree that people quite often referred to all food and daily necessities as bread. This expression carries over into today's world, and still today bread remains a staple in our natural diet. How important it is that we consider the living bread a daily necessity and the staple of our spiritual diet.

Bread is often referred to as the staff of life. Just as surely as Moses' staff became the rod of God, Christ serves as our Staff, the anointed *Rod of God*—to see us through the storm, to guide us in the night, to feed our hungry souls, to be the staple of our lives.

Give us *this* day our *daily* bread shows that we should ask our Father every day to meet our needs, one day at a time. Yet asking consists of much more than merely repeating words.

Abiding in Jesus is the criteria for asking. "If ye abide in me, and my words abide in you, ye shall ask what ye will, and it shall be done unto you" (John 15:7). *Abiding* means dwelling, remaining, and thereby knowing the power of His Word.

Asking requires His name. How do we acquire authority to use someone's name? By being a family member. Accept Jesus as Brother and God as Father and become part of His heavenly family.

> Both the one who makes men holy and those who are made holy are of the same family. So Jesus is not ashamed to call them brothers.
> —HEBREWS 2:11, NIV

What a mighty Brother! He entrusts believers with the full authority of His name (Mark 16:17–18), a name above all names (Phil. 2:9). What a privilege we receive:

> And I will do whatever you ask in my name, so that the Son may bring glory to the Father. You may ask me for anything in my name, and I will do it.
> —JOHN 14:13–14, NIV

Our rights as a family member give us access to a name. If you walk into a bank and demand money from an account in a name you have no right to use, the banker will scoff and likely see that you are escorted out the door. Likewise demons scoff and exercise their authority over anyone who attempts to use the name of Jesus without ever having made a commitment to Him (as in Acts 19:13–16). But just read the entire Book of Acts. Oh, what power exists for those who have genuine access to His name!

Asking includes seeking and knocking. Jesus tells us to ask and it will be given, to seek and we will find, to knock and the door will be opened (Matt. 7:7). Seeking and knocking reflect faith that does not give up.

Asking demands faith. Jesus says that whatever we ask in prayer, if we believe we have received it, we shall have it (Mark 11:24). In James we read:

> But when he asks, he must believe and not doubt, because he who doubts is like a wave of the sea, blown and tossed by the wind. That man should not think he will receive anything from the Lord; he is a double-minded man, unstable in all he does.
>
> —JAMES 1:6–8, NIV

Asking depends on His will.

> This is the confidence we have in approaching God: that if we ask anything according to his will, he hears us. And if we know that he hears us—whatever we ask—we know that we have what we asked of him.
>
> —1 JOHN 5:14–15, NIV

Asking requires that we live for Him.

> And whatsoever we ask, we receive of him, because we keep his commandments, and do those things that are pleasing in his sight.
>
> —1 JOHN 3:22

Asking insists that we turn from greediness.

> When you ask, you do not receive, because you ask with wrong motives, that you may spend what you get on your pleasures.
>
> —JAMES 4:3, NIV

Asking compels us to abstain from sin. Yahweh, the Judge of Righteousness, still rules. His sovereignty did not diminish with the New Covenant or in modern times. Even with members of His kingdom He refuses to hear petitions from a wayward heart. However, He is always open to a repentant heart. We see this as He speaks to His chosen:

> When you spread out your hands in prayer, I will hide my eyes from you; even if you offer many prayers, I will not listen. Your hands are full of blood; wash and make yourselves clean. Take your evil deeds out of my sight! Stop doing wrong, learn to do right!... "Come now, let us reason together," says the LORD. "Though your sins are like scarlet, they shall be white as snow; though they are red as crimson, they shall be like wool. If you are willing and obedient, you will eat the best from the land; but if you resist and rebel, you will be devoured by the sword." For the mouth of the LORD has spoken.
>
> —ISAIAH 1:15–20, NIV

Abiding in Jesus and His Word, being in His heavenly family, having the authority of His name, seeking and knocking with faith, desiring His will, refraining from sin and greed—these are requirements for asking. And they assure results.

How can people be so expectant, yet so complacent in their spiritual lives? I believe it is partly because of the bounty entrusted to our nation. Many assume that their needs will always be met regardless of their commitment to God. In the midst of plenty they put Him in second place or give Him no place at all.

Sometimes my heart agonizes because of the spiritual blindness in our United States. Founded upon Christian principles, our nation has basked in the overflowing blessings of our heavenly Father. When we compare our abundance to the resources of pagan nations, there should be no doubt about the power of the Almighty to bless His own. But now, as we forsake the foundation of the Bible in our government, schools, and courtrooms, we tread on dangerous ground. Will He hide His eyes and cease to listen to our nation's pleas? It is a scary thing to defy the Word of God.

How can we justify requests for God to meet material needs without ever tasting the spiritual bread? How can we expect to "eat the best from the land" without ever wanting to dine with the Provider, the very One who taught us to pray, "Give us this day our daily bread"? How long can the Judge be patient?

Yes, let's ask for our daily bread, our daily natural needs. But let's eat first of the spiritual bread—Jesus, our staff of life, our bread from heaven.

> Our fathers did eat manna in the desert; as it is written, He gave them bread from heaven to eat. Then Jesus said unto them, Verily, verily, I say

unto you, Moses gave you not that bread from heaven; but my Father giveth you the true bread from heaven. For the bread of God is he which cometh down from heaven, and giveth life unto the world. . . . I am the bread of life: he that cometh to me shall never hunger.

—John 6:31–33, 35

We must turn from the ways of the Israelites who veered so far from the purpose set for them, who betrayed the One who blessed them as His handpicked nation. In the wilderness they screamed for food other than the manna He so graciously gave, "Oh, if we just had some of the delicious fish we used to eat and taste the cucumbers, melons, leeks, onions and garlic" (Num. 11:4–6, author's paraphrase).

Egypt is a picture of sin. Although the people of Israel had been freed from its bondage by the supernatural rod of God, they still longed for worldly pleasures more than relationship with Him.

Manna foreshadows Jesus, our living bread. He is the staff of life who takes away all hunger. What a miracle sent from heaven to Earth.

I am that bread of life. Your fathers did eat manna in the wilderness, and are dead. This is the bread which cometh down from heaven, that a man may eat thereof, and not die.

—John 6:48–50

Heavenly manna should be our mainstay of existence, our daily sustenance to satisfy our spiritual hunger, our daily nutrition that provides for life hereafter. Not food that we reserve only for Sunday, it is vital for us every day, giving life to our spirits, souls, and bodies. Every day, every hour, with every tick of the clock, Jesus is our food, our drink, our life, forever.

I am the living bread which came down from heaven: if any man eat of this bread, he shall live for ever: and the bread that I will give is my flesh, which I will give for the life of the world.

—John 6:51

To partake of their life-sustaining manna the Israelites had to pick it up. With the exception of the Sabbath day, it spoiled unless they gathered it daily. We too must gather our manna daily—constantly abiding in Christ, depending on His name, seeking, knocking, and turning from sin and dissatisfaction to live by His kingdom rules.

BUT WE HAVE not yet covered one vital requirement for asking and receiving—giving! Yes, giving activates the kingdom law of reciprocity, a spiritual law as sure as the natural law of gravity. To comprehend it fully, we must step inside Mark 4:3–20 to witness the parable of the sower.

Why? This ranks as the parable above all parables. It reveals mysteries of the kingdom—disclosing the purpose of sowing seed to prepare hearts for kingdom living and showing how sowing seed activates the wonders of kingdom economics.

What a parable! In it we discover the blueprint of kingdom administration on Earth both spiritually and materially. The ground is a symbol of man's heart, and the seed represents the gospel. We are challenged by the necessity of planting seed in all we do. And we see that the master key into all the kingdom is sowing, God's plan for receiving an abundant life of daily bread.

With a jolt and a heavy wheeze our train shuts down. Oh, the beauty of the countryside! We gaze across open farmland, where freshly plowed crops cover hill after hill, acre upon acre. Amid rows of budding seed we alight along with our Conductor.

"Behold!" He exclaims, "Listen with a learning ear! A farmer sowed these fields of grain..."

Handing seed to us He motions toward the black coal and cross-ties lining the railroad tracks. He wants us to toss the seed on the coals, but how will it ever come up?

It won't. As soon as the seed lands, blackbirds swoop down to devour it. We try to shoo them away, but it's no use. They just dive again.

Our Conductor says, "Just as some of the farmer's seed falls by the wayside and birds devour it, so does much of the good news of Christ you broadcast to the world. The seed descends on hostile hearts, and Satan immediately snatches it away."

What a perfect simile of his cunning ways! A stony heart is an open sports arena for Satan and his demons. They dive like an infectious team of germs gobbling up the good and casting their own evil in its place. We've all seen the devastation caused by their viruses of deadly words:

God? He's just a crutch.

You, created by a higher being? How absurd! Man evolved.

Hell? It's just a fantasy. Forget the Ten Commandments. Do your own thing!

With no desire for God, the hard heart shuns the seeds of the gospel with contempt, choosing instead to listen to the rhetoric of the devil. Our Conductor speaks to them:

By hearing ye shall hear, and shall not understand; and seeing ye shall see, and shall not perceive: for this people's heart is waxed gross, and their ears are dull of hearing, and their eyes they have closed.

—Matthew 13:14–15

It hurts to come face to face with reality. Sometimes attempts to sow the Word prove futile. Not only do many reject it, but they also relish poking fun of it. Harboring blind and rebellious infection from the deceiver, they choose to live in their disease.

We follow our Conductor along a bare stretch of dirt. With one foot He scrapes packed soil away, exposing solid rock. "Sometimes seeds land on stony ground with only shallow soil. They spring up, but when the sun scorches them, having no root, they wither away."

Nearby we spy fragile plants that have turned brown and brittle and cannot be revived.

He explains, "This portrays the hearts of those who hear the Word and receive it with joy. While at first seeds appear to flourish, they have no depth for roots to establish. As persecutions come, the tender shoots simply wilt and die."

We have all seen people who, overjoyed at first, absorb the seed of the Word in their hearts. But from their first utter of salvation the devil begins his work.

He sends a former buddy to the newborn Christian with a tongue of poison: "You have to clean up your life before you can be a Christian. And what makes you think you can ever be good enough for God? How can you expect God to forget all the horrible things you've done?"

About this time some legalistic do-gooder shows up to scorch any tender growth with religious rules: "You can't worship in those clothes. Your hairstyle is revolting, and just look at your tattoos! Don't you know you can't smoke and make it into heaven?"

If these ploys don't work, the devil throws in some problems. The car breaks down. The baby gets sick. The job doesn't work out.

Next he shoots fiery darts of negative thoughts.

Christians don't give one hoot about you! Where are they when you need help?

Life got worse since you started this church stuff. If God is real, why does He allow so much trouble?

Then comes the clincher. The old buddy shows up again sympathizing, offering a helping hand and knowing just the right words to sway this shallow soul back to the devil's ways: "Oh, how much all your old friends miss you..."

Soon the glorious budding withers, unable to withstand the pressure. Excitement about Jesus dwindles. Enthusiasm fades in the face of temptation. The deceiver wins.

Oh, where are compassionate believers to help cultivate shallow hearts? Ashamed, we hang our heads. We pray for God to not simply show us wilting souls but to also give us a burning desire to counteract all satanic traps that block growth in tender spirits.

In silence we walk along with our Conductor. He stops to point out a weedy patch. "See this? Some seeds fell among thorns. They grow together now, but before long the thorns will choke the good seed and they'll never produce."

Thorns represent more demonic weapons that work to stifle and suffocate the spiritual life of one who receives the truth and has every intention to live by it. Forces of darkness attack any progression toward maturity in the Word, any growing relationship with the Lord, any desire to thrive as a Christian. Three factors—the cares of this world, the deceitfulness of riches, and the lusts of other things—pierce the heart like thorns, causing a blossoming Christian to be unfruitful.

Worldly cares are the first thorn. The enemy appears in appealing garments of modernism, which can soon change from comfortable attire to costumes of exhausting mania. He turns wholesome things into obsessions, binding hearts to notions of earthly excellence and making them slaves to idealism.

Perhaps he will play on the desire for a dream home with a velvet lawn, an ultra landscape, a swimming pool, and a tennis court. Or he may create an obsession with automobiles, boats, and the latest styles of name-brand clothes. Some may be frantic to keep a youthful appearance and good looks with excessive weight-control sessions, bodybuilding equipment, flawless hair, and manicured nails. Such worldly cares choke time for God.

Schedules may become overcrowded as parents juggle the children between lessons in music, dance, gymnastics, swimming, and tennis and chauffeur them to Scout meetings, band practice, and ballgames. Time for church is choked. Stress becomes overwhelming, and money for giving is choked by the practice of living from payday to payday, stretching every penny, accumulating debt, and working more hours to make ends meet.

We wonder, what is OK for a Christian to do? It is not doing, but obsession, that causes the problem. Making a pleasant family life, rising above poverty, and appreciating the opportunity for betterment are blessings of God. But an endless burden grows when we are totally caught up in the cares of this world, trapped by secular society, and a slave to debt.

Does God want His children to enjoy natural things in life? Yes, yes, God says yes. The Bible tells us so.

> Here is what I have seen: It is good and fitting for one to eat and drink, and to enjoy the good of all his labor in which he toils under the sun all the days of his life which God gives him; for it is his heritage. As for every man to whom God has given riches and wealth, and given him power to eat of it, to receive his heritage and rejoice in his labor—this is the gift of God.
>
> —ECCLESIASTES 5:18–19, NKJV

God Himself is the ultimate Giver of all good. He wants to see His children happy. He is a God of blessings. Enjoyment of wholesome activities and possessions become wrong only when they replace fellowship with Him. Wealth becomes wrong only when it is used in wrong ways, when in self-esteem a heart boasts:

> My power and the might of mine hand hath gotten me this wealth.
>
> —DEUTERONOMY 8:17

The deceitfulness of riches—the second thorn—often stems from striving to keep up with the cares of this world. As we try to meet financial obligations, we may come to believe that money solves all our problems and buys love and happiness. The seduced heart lives not only to "keep up with the Joneses" but also to "bask on easy street," staking his soul on riches that often prove to be only temporary and can instantly vanish. An insatiable appetite for more evolves into a vicious cycle.

> He that loveth silver shall not be satisfied with silver; nor he that loveth abundance with increase.
>
> —ECCLESIASTES 5:10

Desire for money is never satisfied. Greediness supersedes desire for the Word, want replaces God, and chasing wealth captures top priority. Choke, choke, choke.

Obtaining prosperity God's way lifts the heart to wondrous heights, but without God the deceitfulness of riches snares the soul. It is not money itself, but the love of money that is the root of all evil (1 Tim. 6:10). A person without even one dime in his pocket can fall into the trap of loving money—ever longing for and seeking after it. But every dollar in existence can't buy one more breath when death closes in.

For what profit is it to a man if he gains the whole world, and loses his own soul? Or what will a man give in exchange for his soul?
—MATTHEW 16:26, NKJV

The lusts of other things—Satan's third thorn—dangles like the glitter of the world to bring about addiction.

Drugs. *Just try it once,* Satan reasons. *Everyone's doing it. Be part of the "in crowd." A little bit makes it easier to cope. Then if a little helps, just think what more of it will do. You'll never get hooked. And nobody ever needs to know.*

Alcohol. *Just be a social drinker so you can be accepted by your peers,* our enemy says. *It's fun, fashionable, relaxing. No need to worry. You're too intelligent to ever be an alcoholic.*

Pornography. *Nudity is so natural,* the deceptive thought suggests. *Skim over a few sexy magazines and take in an X-rated movie now and then. It's only entertainment. What can it hurt? Obsession? Na, who ever heard of such a thing!*

Immoral sex. *Why not sleep around before marriage and enjoy affairs during marriage?* the tempter asks. *Go ahead, try spouse-swapping parties. Enjoy an alternative lifestyle. Why bother getting married? Just live together. Bible teachings? Oh, they were written as ancient customs and are so out of touch with society today. Abstinence before marriage, a man and woman faithful to one another for life, gay marriage unacceptable—these biblical notions went out with the Dark Ages!*

Satan conceals any consequence that may arise because of drugs and alcohol. He never mentions recovery problems and treatment centers. Nor does he bring up the ultimate payment for extremes—spending every penny to support a habit, getting fired, serving time behind bars, sleeping on a park bench, living in a box, overdose, suicide.

He hides the fact that most rapists started by indulging in pornography and that a very high percentage of convicts on death row were first involved in this obscenity. With his lure of unbridled immorality he never mentions sexual disease, broken hearts, broken homes, or hurting children.

On and on the devil coaxes with excuses for all sorts of vices. Lust for violence, gluttony, gossip, manipulation of others, gambling, laziness.

To help secure success in the evil work of his thorns—the cares of this world, the deceitfulness of riches, and the lusts of other things—Satan has conveniently placed cheating, stealing, and murder in his briar patch. With endless lies he seeks to entrap the heart, squeezing, refusing to let go. He chokes until all the seeds of God's Word die in his patch of thorns.

Satan delights in being an enslaver, agitator, liar, and thief. And he is greatly pleased when the world and often churches present him as a mere storybook character like the big bad wolf or a man in a red suit. Satan is by no means fictional or a humorous subject.

Jesus refers to Satan as a murderer from the beginning, with no truth in him, "for he is a liar, and the father of it" (John 8:44). He also says:

> The thief cometh not, but for to steal, and to kill, and to destroy: I am come that they might have life, and that they might have it more abundantly.
>
> —JOHN 10:10

Chose abundant life! Let the seed of the Word grow and multiply in you. Until we reject Satan's gimmicks and face the fact that true and lasting happiness never grows from passing pleasures or perishable treasures, we will never know genuine joy, peace, and maturity in God's kingdom. Righteous living thrives with age, promising an everlasting harvest of joy. But lusts for temporal gratifications wane as either failing health or old age takes its toll, leaving a wasted life as its bonus and pain for all eternity.

Again we peer over the fields in sadness. We turn to our Conductor. Won't any of the seed reach full harvest?

His voice rings out, "Yes! Some seed falls on good ground. A crop springs up, increasing and producing. Some yield thirtyfold, some sixty, and some a hundredfold. These are hearts that hear the Word, truly receive it and bring forth a bountiful harvest of precious godly fruit."

Just like soil, hearts require cultivation. Before seeding, even the finest loam needs plowing. Likewise every heart must bow, broken and contrite, before the Giver of our daily bread:

> The LORD is near to the brokenhearted, and saves the crushed in spirit.
>
> —PSALM 34:18, RSV

How God delights in a heart that gladly bows before Him. How He honors and rewards a broken heart and a crushed spirit that calls to Him, "Here I am, send me. I'll do whatever You ask me to do, speak whatever You ask me to speak, give whatever You ask me to give. Wherever and whenever You send me, I'm willing to go."

To bear a successful crop soil requires ample water, fertilizer, and care. All hearts must drink of His truth and feed on His bread for successful growth in His kingdom. What we absorb determines how our hearts develop.

> A good man out of the good treasure of his heart bringeth forth that
> which is good; and an evil man out of the evil treasure of his heart
> bringeth forth that which is evil.
>
> —LUKE 6:45

Good soil doesn't happen naturally, but it is developed by constant effort. The heart sold out to God must be courageous enough to endure heat and drought, wise enough to detect a satanic thorn, and strong enough to pluck it out before it chokes the roots of a developing crop. It must be determined enough to be regularly cultivated, watered, and fed. And it must become mature enough to produce bountiful fruit, planting the seed of the Word, giving time and energy both spiritually and materially for the multiplication of His kingdom. And that's how His entire system works!

Sowing and reaping, seedtime and harvest. "So is the kingdom of God, as if a man should cast a seed into the ground" (Mark 4:26).

After Jesus told the parable of the sower, His disciples asked Him what it meant. He answered:

> To you is granted the secret of the kingdom of God, but to those who
> are outside everything comes in parables.... Do you not understand
> this parable? Then how will you understand any of the parables?
>
> —MARK 4:11, 13, NJB

YES, THIS PARABLE with its seedtime and harvest stands as the basis of all parables about the kingdom. Planting and harvesting is the way the kingdom works. It was established from the time of Creation.

> And the LORD God *planted* a garden eastward in Eden; and there he
> put man whom he had formed.
>
> —GENESIS 2:8, EMPHASIS ADDED

Then came sin with its curse upon the soil:

> Cursed is the ground for thy sake; in sorrow shalt thou eat of it all the
> days of thy life; thorns also and thistles shall it bring forth to thee; and
> thou shalt eat the herb of the field: in the sweat of thy face shalt thou
> eat bread.
>
> —GENESIS 3:17–19

After the Flood, God vowed:

> While the earth remaineth, seedtime and harvest, and cold and heat,
> and summer and winter, and day and night shall not cease.
>
> —GENESIS 8:22

In the spiritual realm seedtime and harvest govern the kingdom of God—sowing the Word, reaping souls. And sowing and reaping also endure without fail as the ruling agent in God's principles of giving and receiving.

When we pray, "Give us this day our daily bread," we are in effect pledging to plant seeds into good soil. If we expect to receive, we must first sow into His kingdom. Giving (planting) is the kingdom way of receiving (reaping). How much should we sow?

> But this I say: He who sows sparingly will also reap sparingly, and he
> who sows bountifully will also reap bountifully....Now may He who
> supplies seed to the sower, and bread for food, supply and multiply the
> seed you have sown and increase the fruits of your righteousness.
>
> —2 CORINTHIANS 9:6, 10, NKJV

Our God is the multiplier. By His very nature He returns more than we can ever give. Second Corinthians 9:10 in the Living Bible says:

> For God, who gives seed to the farmer to plant, and later on, good
> crops to harvest and eat, will give you more and more seed to plant and
> will make it grow so that you can give away more and more fruit from
> your harvest.

Should we give to get? Yes! To get to *give*, to get to *give*, to get to *give* more and more into the kingdom. And so His Word lives on, and His covenant is fulfilled.

> And you shall remember the LORD your God, for it is He who gives
> you power to get wealth, that He may establish His covenant.
>
> —DEUTERONOMY 8:18, NKJV

What should be the purpose of our wealth? This verse teaches that it is to establish His covenant, to spread His Word, to further His kingdom.

Our thoughts are interrupted by the summons of the train whistle as it calls for us to climb on board and head for a territory that is sometimes unpopular. Although some avoid this area, it holds vital secrets governing God's economic plan.

On our way we pass by more scenic farmland—green fields of corn, swaying wheat, and rows of cotton. *Good seed,* we smile, *so many crops growing to maturity.*

Sowing brings growing. We recall the words, "He who sows sparingly shall also reap sparingly, and he who sows bountifully shall also reap bountifully."

We notice a distant farmhouse shaded by waving oak trees and enclosed by a rambling white fence. Cattle graze in an adjoining pasture. Not far away a huge red barn, its loft stuffed with hay, rises against a sky of powder blue.

"Honor the LORD with your income and the firstfruit of every crop," exclaims our Conductor, "then your barns will be filled to capacity and your vats will spill over with the best of wine!" (Prov. 3:9–10, author's paraphrase).

Do your really want your daily bread? Then give of your *first* fruits! Genesis 4:2–5 tells that Cain, a tiller of the ground, made an offering of produce, which displeased the Lord. But Abel, a shepherd, brought the *firstlings* of his flock. The Lord was pleased with his offering.

Our train roars through the countryside, over hills and plains intertwined with crops and woodlands. We pass small farm villages and zip high above rushing streams and rivers.

Looking down at the water our Conductor delights in reciting Ecclesiastes 11:1, "Cast thy bread upon the waters: for thou shalt find it after many days."

This is another parable. What does it mean?

The answer rises from the knowledge we have gained about the sower. Just as sowing seed in good soil brings a bountiful harvest, giving our provisions for good causes results in their return to us. And what happens to bread dropped in water? It expands!

Our God—our bread of life—is the God of expansion. He is the multiplier, the One who increases. Our provider is Jehovah Jireh. More than enough, He is El Shaddai.

What abundance comes from Him to the giver. All we own actually belongs to God, yet as we give it back, He promises returns greater than the amount we give. Why are so many afraid to take Him at His Word?

If every Christian returned the first 10 percent of his income to God's kingdom, churches would be debt free. They would flourish and supply the needs of everyone. People would no longer be dependent on government subsidies but would turn to God through the generous body of Christ. Oh, how souls could be won to the kingdom of God.

This is the Lord's financial design. After all, Jesus instructed us to look to our Father—not the government—and pray, "Give us this day our daily bread."

OUR TRAIN SLOWS down. With searching eyes we peer out. Where are we? Oh, no! It's *tithing* territory! But isn't tithing Old Testament law?

No, the tithe existed long before. From the beginning God ordered that a portion be set aside specifically for Him:

> And the LORD God commanded the man, saying, Of every tree of the garden thou mayest freely eat: But of the tree of the knowledge of good and evil, thou shalt not eat of it.
>
> —GENESIS 2:16–17

This one tree belonged only to the Lord God. It was a test of obedience for mankind, a foreshadowing of the tithe.

Dashing on, we zoom into a mysterious setting, Genesis 14:17–20. Here we find ourselves in the presence of Melchizedek, king of Salem (the shortened title for Jerusalem).

Look! Abram *pays tithes* to him! Is it a tribute to his kingship?

No. Melchizedek also presides as a priest of the Most High God. What! How can he be a priest? This is long before the time of Moses when God designated Jewish priests to officiate in the tabernacle.

Abraham himself fathered the Jewish race. At this time Jews were nonexistent. This encounter with Melchizedek takes place before Abraham's son Isaac is even conceived. Isaac's son Jacob provided the twelve sons whose descendants become the twelve tribes. And it was from the tribe of Levi that all priests were appointed under the Law.

Who, then, is this priest, Melchizedek, who was worthy of receiving tithes from Abraham? As we've established, he is definitely not a Jew, definitely not appointed by the Law.

Melchizedek was appointed by the Most High God! He was priest to all—priest to the Gentiles and priest to the first Jew, Abraham!

What a picture of our High Priest in the heavenlies. Jesus is priest to all! Though He was a Jew, He was not in the lineage of Levi. Instead, He came from the kingly line of Judah:

> For it is evident that our Lord arose from Judah, of which tribe Moses spoke nothing concerning priesthood. And it is yet far more evident

if, in the likeness of Melchizedek, there arises another priest who has come, not according to the law of a fleshly commandment, but according to the power of an endless life. For He testifies: "You are a priest forever according to the order of Melchizedek."
—HEBREWS 7:14–17, NKJV

Jesus Christ. He is our Priest forever—not under the Law, not to the Jews only—but to all who believe. His priesthood is not after the order of Hebrew appointment but after the order of Melchizedek! Jesus is worthy of our tithe!

Melchizedek was not only a priest but also the king of Salem (Jerusalem). No Hebrew other than Jesus ever claimed both titles.

Jesus came from the lineage of King David of the tribe of Judah. He stands forever as the King of all kings and He bears the title of High Priest. After the order of Melchizedek, He is a Priest for all mankind!

What intrigue surrounds the identity of Melchizedek:

For this Melchizedec, king of Salem, priest of the most high God, who met Abraham returning from the slaughter of the kings, and blessed him, to whom also Abraham gave a tenth part of all, first being by interpretation King of righteousness, and after that also King of Salem, which is King of peace; without father, without mother, without descent, having neither beginning of days, nor end of life, but made like unto the Son of God; abideth a priest continually.
—HEBREWS 7:1–3

Who knows his true identity? Some believe he like the angel of the Lord, was a preincarnate appearance of the Messiah. Others say he was a symbolic type of Christ. No person can positively declare who he was, but we do know that the priestly order of Melchizedek remains forever through Jesus Christ.

Abraham, through whom all nations would be blessed, tithed not under the Law, but long before the Law, to a man who was priest to all—both Gentile and Jew. He tithed to Melchizedek, the one the very Son of God followed in priesthood

Before Abraham gave him a tithe, "Melchizedek king of Salem brought forth bread and wine" (Gen. 14:18). As we recognize this preview of Holy Communion, we ask how Melchizedek had such perception. It came from his relationship to the Most High God.

Why did Melchizedek share the bread and wine? J. Vernon McGee has this to say: "I know now why Melchizedek does this. It is because the

Scriptures say, 'For as often as ye eat this bread, and drink this cup, ye do shew the Lord's death till he come' (1 Cor. 11:26). Melchizedek is anticipating the death of Christ here!"[1]

How much of this did Abraham understand? Jesus once said:

> Your father Abraham rejoiced to see my day: and he saw it, and was glad.
> —John 8:56

Abraham knew both Holy Communion, an ordinance in remembrance of Christ, and tithing, an ordinance in obedience to Him. He paid tithes to Melchizedek and Melchizedek blessed him. When we tithe to our High Priest, He blesses us as we will discover in our travels deeper into tithing territory.

AS THE DAY draws to a close the Jubilee Express speeds under a sky of glowing pink. From our windows we notice birds beginning to roost. We watch a straight line of cows amble toward a dairy barn as evening calls them home. Just as twilight approaches we feel the train wheels begin to brake. Soon they stop rolling altogether.

"Come and follow me," our Conductor whispers.

As darkness falls we leave the train. With moonbeams and stars lighting our way, we pick our steps behind Him across slopes and valleys, delightfully breathing in the crisp night air. It smells like fresh-cut hay.

At the top of the next hill our hearts tingle with excitement as we step over into Genesis 28:10–22. In suspense we pause to listen. Sounds of a deep voice wail as if it is mourning. We hurry in its direction.

Beside a dying campfire a handsome young man kneels with his face turned toward the sky. His black hair shimmers in the amber glow, and under sweeping lashes his enormous eyes glisten with fresh tears. We notice the smoothness of his olive skin, and in an instant we recognize him as Jacob.

"Woe am I! Why did I disguise myself as my brother to trick my aging father? Oh, father Isaac! Oh, brother Esau! How I disgraced you! And instead of blessings on my own life, what misery my deceit has caused!"

We feel his frustration, loneliness, and exhaustion. We see fright in his trembling body as his fire gives up its light. He curls up in the dark with a stone pillow his only companion.

Restless with regret and remorse he recalls the quiet life he had once enjoyed. How he had loved staying at home near his tent, close by his mother

Rebekah. Squirming on the ground he tries to settle down, but what if a wild beast shows up? What if the temperature drops? What about the danger of wind and rain, scorpions or snakes, slave traders?

For hours he turns anxiously from side to side. Every vein in his body screams, *I want to go home!* Yet he knows that he can't. Somehow he must find strength to accept the consequences for his rashness. Sleep finally relieves his agony.

Suddenly a vision appears before our eyes. We find ourselves standing in the middle of Jacob's dream.

What beauty we behold. Reaching from Earth far into heaven's glory a majestic staircase glitters with millions of lights. In dazzling color they gleam in sharp contrast to the black sky. Angels with flowing robes and massive wings travel up and down the staircase with sweeping steps. At the very top we behold the Supreme Creator.

Yahweh Elohim—the Lord God Himself! His voice rumbles, "I am the Lord God of Abraham and of Isaac! The ground where you lie belongs to you and your descendants. Your offspring will multiply as the dust of the earth—spreading abroad everywhere, from the east and west, from the north to the south. In your seed shall all be blessed!"

Like lightning His words electrify the night. "I am with you, and wherever you go I will watch over you. Someday I will bring you back into this land, for I will not leave you until I have done all that I have promised you!"

The vision disappears. Jacob's dream is over. With a start he sits up. "Surely the Lord is in this place and I didn't even realize it!"

As the magnitude of his dream sinks in, his huge eyes fly open in shock from the sight of the sovereign, holy Being. "How awesome this place is! It has to be the actual house of God and the very gate to heaven!"

At dawn Jacob sets his stone pillow upright. Pouring oil over it, he dedicates it as a memorial pillar to the Lord and names the place Bethel, meaning the House of God. In his new awareness of such an almighty living Ruler, Jacob vows, "If He will be with me and will protect me as I go—providing food and clothing, bringing me back in peace to my father—then He will be my God. And this pillar will be as the house of God, a place of worship."

Then he prays, "Of all that You give me I will return a tenth of it to You."

From that day forward Jacob surely tithed, for God prospered him immensely. Later in his life Jacob—no longer a cheater and deceiver, as his name had so accurately announced—received a new name from the angel of the Lord. Israel! "For as a prince has thou power with God and with men, and thou hast prevailed" (Gen. 32:28). As Israel he would father the twelve tribes of God's chosen people.

IN THE DISTANCE we hear voices soaring in songs of praise from the Jubilee Express, beckoning us to return, eager to accompany us deeper into the land of tithing.

History shows that giving a tenth in tribute to emperors and monarchs was a recognized custom down through the ages. In antiquity it was practiced among heathen nations—Persia, Egypt, Babylon, and China. Perhaps nobody knows precisely how or when tithing began. However, it is recorded in the stories of Abraham and Jacob in the very first book of the Bible, and it is established as a time-honored financial order by the Creator Himself. As we consider this, tithing takes on a new meaning.

Why is tithing important to the Christian? It shows our faith in God. It opens a window of distribution for our Father who loves to give back to us. Certainly this test of our faithfulness provides the springboard for launching His power of multiplication into action.

Just what makes it work? To our human minds it is as much a mystery as the old adage, "No one but God knows how many apples are in one seed." What a miracle it is when one single seed springs up into a full-grown tree that produces bushel after bushel of fruit and more and more seed to sow, year after year.

How can one seed multiply beyond calculation? It's simply a natural kingdom law that we accept without question. This principle also works in the spiritual realm, multiplying the seed we sow into the God's kingdom, yet other than the One who designed its system of operation, who can truly understand how and why it works?

As we study the tithe we find that a person really hasn't given at all until he sows more than 10 percent with God. Ten percent isn't a gift but rather a return of what already belongs to Him.

> Will a man rob God? Yet ye have robbed me. But ye say, Wherein have we robbed thee? In tithes and offerings. Ye are cursed with a curse: for ye have robbed me, even this whole nation.
>
> —MALACHI 3:8–9

Jim and I robbed God! After thirteen years of knowing about tithing and doing it, we stopped point blank. In bewilderment we cried, *How could we as faithful tithers lose our business? Why has this happened to us?*

We didn't see this as a test of our faith or as God's means to steer us onto the path of His perfect will for us. Nor did we see it as a demonstration of His faithfulness to us despite our disobedience. Only time ushered in these revelations.

But our faith did blossom, and we found our destiny according to His will. Strength grew through our suffering, and understanding developed through our situation. Glory arose from our outcome and taught us to look at problems as a challenge of our faith.

What a time of progress it was. What a time of war we had with Satan. What a time of victory we experienced with our Savior. Yet how deep and rough the waters of calamity lashed against our lives before we found His answers. And how foolishly we first responded to our turbulence.

When we lost our business Satan whispered, "How can you even think of tithing? You owe so much money. Nothing you earn belongs to you. It belongs to your creditors. If you tithe, you'll be stealing their money!"

And we listened. Not only our store but also our common sense swirled down the drain and into a sewer of self-pity. It never crossed our minds that if nothing we earned belonged to us, we would also be stealing from our creditors when we made house payments, paid utilities, and bought food or clothes.

Though we continued in prayer and in our love for Jesus, we failed our test of faith and did not tithe regardless of our circumstances. How mixed up we became, paddling along and not going anywhere. We tried to accomplish God's will our own way, and that really isn't His will at all.

True, we didn't backslide into blasphemous sin or blatant rebellion. But in failing to tithe we placed our needs above obedience to His Word. Even while we were so blinded by our financial mess, we still claimed that God would bring us through. However, we never stopped to realize that not only had we robbed Him, but we had also shut the windows of abundant heavenly blessing.

> Bring ye all the tithes into the storehouse, that there may be meat in mine house, and prove me now herewith, saith the LORD of hosts, if I will not open you the windows of heaven, and pour you out a blessing, that there shall not be room enough to receive it. And I will rebuke the devourer for your sakes, and he shall not destroy the fruits of your ground; neither shall your vine cast her fruit before the time in the field, saith the LORD of hosts. And all nations shall call you blessed: for ye shall be a delightsome land, saith the LORD of hosts.
>
> —MALACHI 3:10–12

Oh, what a price we paid for our shallow faith. Like the Israelites in the desert, we existed with the bare necessities. With every ounce of strength I sought after a new job to bail us out, but we got no closer to being out of debt. The harder Jim and I worked, the further we slipped from shore. The prophet Haggai once spoke to the Jews who spent all their income on themselves instead of building God's house. Finally, his words became our reality:

> Now therefore thus saith the LORD of hosts; Consider your ways. You have sown much, and bring in little; ye eat, but ye have not enough; ye drink, but ye are not filled with drink; ye clothe you, but there is none warm; and he that earneth wages earneth wages to put it into a bag with holes. Thus saith the LORD of hosts; Consider your ways.
>
> —HAGGAI 1:5–7

But did I consider my ways?

No. And I ignored my conscience. Yet from a chamber deep within my mind a sermon from the past rumbled—if Satan can't get you into sin, he just gets you too busy!

Yes, I was too busy to listen to God's voice, too busy to spend intimate time with Him. I was preoccupied, disregarding the Most High's purpose for life, spending every penny on our own needs, no longer giving.

> Ye looked for much, and, lo, it came to little; and when ye brought it home, I did blow upon it. Why? saith the LORD of hosts. Because of mine house that is waste, and ye run every man unto his own house. Therefore the heaven over you is stayed from dew, and the earth is stayed from her fruit.
>
> —HAGGAI 1:9–10

It is a serious thing to put anything or ourselves before God. If we stop giving and disobey His command to tithe, this shows that we fear our creditors more than the Almighty, that we give honor to man more than to Him. But once we are on the treadmill of the world, how do we get off?

Four years would pass before we found the answer, four years without tithing. In the midst of our foolishness more calamity pounced on us without warning. Less than two years after we lost our store and stopped tithing, Jim found himself unemployed.

As I dressed for work that morning the phone rang. Calling from the headquarters in St. Louis, Jim's supervisor asked to speak to him. He'd never called our house before.

"Isn't he working at the local plant here?"

"Oh, he's not home yet? I'll call back later."

With that he hung up. *What in the world is going on?* my thoughts swirled as I tucked my blouse into my skirt. Hearing our car whip into our driveway I raced to the front door to greet my husband as he entered.

"Jim, why are you home?"

He shuffled inside, shaking his head and forcing a smile. "God's opening another new door in our lives." He said it lightly, but I read deep seriousness in his eyes.

As if struggling for the right words he paused, glancing at his watch. "One hour ago I was told that I no longer have a job. Early retirement, they called it."

"But why?"

"They're closing our department. In a few years it looks as if the entire company will be moved to Mexico. But no one in our division had any inkling before today."

If Jim chose immediate withdrawals, his retirement check would amount to $150 a month. What a cruel joke!

All of our savings as well as our portion of the inheritance received at my father's death had been sucked into the quagmire of our debt. In addition to our present money burdens, our son James planned to enter college in the fall. We wanted to say, "God, where are You?" But we knew that He had never left us.

God led us to read the praises of Habakkuk. As we related our needs to his burdens, we found comfort:

> Although the fig tree shall not blossom, neither shall fruit be in the vines; the labour of the olive shall fail, and the fields shall yield no meat; the flock shall be cut off from the fold, and there shall be no herd in the stalls: yet I will rejoice in the LORD, I will joy in the God of my salvation. The LORD God is my strength, and he will make my feet like hind's feet, and he will make me to walk upon mine high places.
> —HABAKKUK 3:17–19

What desolation this prophet faced, and yet he praised God. Leaning on his words we counted our blessings and found our joy in the LORD. In His never-ending goodness God honored our praise, kept us from bankruptcy once again and furnished our necessities in natural ways. Through the returns from my work and Jim's unemployment benefits He kept us afloat. At age fifty-seven Jim searched for new employment to no avail, but with unexpected grants and financial programs James entered college on schedule.

Still we didn't tithe. In our negligence we continued to pour all our earnings into a bag with holes. We were only able to pay the interest on our store notes and barely meet our personal needs.

Before our store collapsed we had proclaimed that our faith was deep and genuine. But if that was so, why did we panic at our first big trial? Why didn't we stand in obedience to His Word and continue to tithe? Why didn't we have the faith and courage believe Him when He said, "Prove Me (by bringing your tithes) ... if I will not open the windows of heaven, and pour you out a blessing, that there shall not be room enough to receive it"?

Looking back we acknowledge that our actions were more than foolish. We understood the kingdom principle of tithing. We knew that 10 percent belongs to God. We realized that God established the tithe, not because He depends on the wealth of man, but to open an avenue whereby He can supply our needs according to His riches in glory. Yes, we knew all this. Still we listened to the devil's lies. Whatever were we thinking?

We knew the words of Malachi 3:9–12 by heart. We were aware of God's promises to provide not just the bare essentials, but more than enough to those who trust Him and obey by giving. Our Father offers to open the windows of heaven and pour out blessing upon blessing, more than one can contain. It is His good will to rebuke the devourer until even outsiders take notice of His favor.

Tithing plus giving beyond the 10 percent furnish a natural way for God's people to substantiate their faith in His Word and their trust in Him. He encourages us to step out in His supernatural realm and try Him. We knew this, but we still failed.

We also realized that tithing is a holy ordinance ordained by God Himself:

> And all the tithe of the land, whether of the seed of the land, or of the fruit of the tree, is the LORD's: it is holy unto the LORD.
>
> —LEVITICUS 27:30

We knew so much. And still we failed to act in faith. Much like the Israelites, we had years to go before we crossed over into the promised land.

OUR TRAIN RUMBLES on. Where are we headed now? From our seats we scan the barren plains of a desert that stretches in every direction. The heat is stifling, but if we lower our windows, grit blows into the cabin.

In the distance we see what seems to be a huge settlement of buildings. We strain our eyes. No, it's tents that we see—miles and miles of them.

Can this be a mirage? No, as our train advances we discern a multitude of men and women clad in sun-faded robes with heads draped to protect them from the torrid rays. We squint through the blowing sand.

The people appear to be assembling for a meeting. In the desert? Is this a figment of our imagination? No, look! We catch sight of someone we know. It's Moses! We have come once again to the campsite of the Israelites. Now in the plains of Moab, they are gathering to hear the farewell address of Moses as recorded in the Book of Deuteronomy.

We feel the train wheels slowing. With eager hearts, almost before the train is completely stopped, we leap out to join the crowd.

Years of wilderness wandering have carved deep furrows across Moses' forehead, and the blazing sun has bleached his beard to snowy white. Yet, we recognize his age more by the distinguished maturity that marks his stature. With perfect agility he walks with his head erect and weaves through the multitude to scramble up on a raised platform near the tabernacle. His eyes, which provide perfect sight, gleam brightly. He stands with the stamina of youth and speaks with vibrant voice.

How different the Hebrews appear since the last time we visited them. We see a younger generation, their faces glowing with excitement and their hearts overflowing with hope and faith. The murmurs and whining of their deceased parents have vanished, and the strength of God fills their spirits. Forty years of wandering have passed. And very soon this new generation of Hebrews will enter the Promised Land.

What a wondrous time for us to join them once again!

A hush falls over the gathering. The sand settles, for not even one finger seems to move. All eyes are fixed on Moses. With remorse he recounts the time when their parents, weak in faith and afraid, rebelled against God's plan and refused to go in and possess the land of Canaan. What blessings they forfeited by rejecting this glorious place that awaited with rest for their souls. This fabulous country flowing with milk and honey was a vital part of the divine inheritance from their ancestor Abraham. It lay at their fingertips, just waiting for them to conquer.

"Even though I begged them to not be afraid of the enemies of the land and assured them that the Lord would go before us and fight for them as He did in Egypt, they would not listen." With sadness Moses lowers his glistening eyes.

He reminisces about their entire wilderness journey, the battles they won and hardships they endured. All around us heads nod in understanding.

A happy stirring breaks out as Moses assigns portions of the Promised Land to each Hebrew tribe. Eyes twinkle as families hug and others clap, all with eager smiles. All their lives they've yearned for freedom from this barren soil. At last the time has come.

"I am not permitted to enter this good land with you. I pleaded with the Lord, but because of His anger with me on your account, He refused. He told me, 'Let it satisfy you to go to the heights of Mount Pisgah where by peering into the distance you'll be able to see the Promised Land in every direction. But you cannot cross over the Jordan River to enter.'" Moses' voice breaks when he says, "As the Lord has ordered, I commission Joshua to take charge over you."

Silence resumes. Our hearts mourn as we watch tears spill over many cheeks. How deeply these people love their leader. All they have known is the guiding hand of Moses. They wait for him to speak again.

"Now listen intensely to these instructions and obey them if you wish to take possession of the land."

Reviewing the Law, he reminds them how necessary it is for them to be dedicated to Yahweh. Over and over he stresses the perils of idolatry. With great fervor he recalls the glorious experience of Mount Sinai and the making of the Ten Commandments.

We stare in total awe at the magnificence of this human being. At the burning bush so long ago, he was reluctant to address the people, and God appointed his brother Aaron to speak for him. But now, even at 120 years of age, this man needs no one to do his speaking. How marvelous Moses has become in his destiny with the Almighty.

Moses covers the rules of Passover and all the feasts God has established for them. Demanding undivided attention he reminds them of the ordinances of the Law. With complete confidence he assures the people that by their hands the Lord will defeat evil nations in their wake.

"But," he stresses, "Yahweh requires full obedience from you."

We listen to his instructions for them when they settle in the land and hear serious rules that apply to giving. With a growing awareness we realize that God does not take giving lightly, neither does He allow for inconsistency.

> When you arrive in the land and have conquered it and are living there, you must present to the Lord at his sanctuary the first sample from each annual harvest.
>
> —Deuteronomy 26:1–2, TLB

Moses details these gifts of the first fruits and gives instructions that after they present their produce to the priests, they must pray aloud, remembering their forefathers' plight of Egyptian bondage and acknowledging how God delivered them into their bountiful land. Next the priests will place their baskets of produce on the altar and a worship service will begin. Rejoicing in God's goodness, all will celebrate with joy these offerings from their harvest.

Moses also introduces a new requirement:

> Every third year is a year of special tithing. That year you are to give all your tithes to the Levites, migrants, orphans, and widows, so that they will be well fed.
>
> —DEUTERONOMY 26:12, TLB

In response to specific rules, the people are to declare their acts of tithing, and tell God that they are giving as He requires. And then they are instructed to go a step further and ask for a return of blessings for their giving:

> Look down from your holy home in heaven and bless your people and the land you have given us, as you promised our ancestors; make it a land "flowing with milk and honey"!
>
> —DEUTERONOMY 26:15, TLB

No wonder the Jews even today recognize their covenant of prosperity through Abraham. These divine instructions remind them, as well as God, of their inheritance and the rewards He promises through their giving.

Shouldn't we do the same and also declare His promises as we give today? If this pleased God in the days of old, surely it remains pleasing to Him now. After all, He is our covenant-fulfilling God, too!

Giving and receiving, sowing and reaping—what a glorious kingdom principle since the beginning of time. It is a sure foundation for His kingdom on Earth, an evidence of our faith, His channel of blessing. We are no longer under the Law as the Israelites were. However, we must recognize His commands for giving and receiving and abide by them to reap the fullness of His blessings and dwell in His land that flows with milk and honey. This land of perfect rest in Him is still a promise of His New Covenant and is available for obedient Christians.

> For who, having heard rebelled? Indeed, was it not all who came out of Egypt, led by Moses? Now with whom was He angry forty years? Was it not with those who sinned, whose corpses fell in the wilderness? And to whom did He swear that they would not enter His rest, but to those who did not obey? So we see that they could not enter in because of unbelief. Therefore, since a promise remains of entering His

rest, let us fear lest any of you seem to have come short of it.... Since therefore it remains that some must enter it, and those to whom it was first preached did not enter because of disobedience....Today, if you will hear His voice, Do not harden your hearts.

—HEBREWS 3:16–4:1, 6–7, NKJV

Yes, the land of rest can be ours today. We can possess it from now until the promised land of ultimate rest begins in eternity. What a joyous time when the kingdom of God will abide forever in power and glory and His will at last is done on all the earth as it is in heaven.

Until then, in His kingdom here today, God gives us ability to enter our promised land with Him. This land of rest is a place of assurance in Jesus, peace in Him, and hope and joy right now. The provision of His kingdom in our hearts is available at this moment for all who abide in faith and live in obedience.

We, like Israel, have battles to fight and evil to conquer in the land God has promised. He gives us seeds to plant, harvests to reap, and the fortitude to faithfully continue sowing seed. As we return to the Jubilee Express, we hear Moses speaking in Deuteronomy 28 and promising great blessings if the people obey all of God's commandments: "...blessed in the city, blessed in the field...blessed with children, bountiful crops, livestock...blessed with food, blessed coming in and blessed going out...blessed with divine protection and prosperity in everything..."

Just as we step aboard our train the voice of Moses shouts forth warnings of gruesome curses, the complete opposites of the blessings, if they choose to disobey.

God still demands obedience, and the repercussions of disobedience remain. Jim and I discovered this as we struggled in our cesspool of financial woes and did not tithe.

But Jesus is a faithful shepherd. He walks with us even when we stray. Over time we recognized our disobedience and corrected it. It was then that He, with His *rod,* gently lifted us from our despair. However, at this point we had miles to go.

Chapter 11

And Forgive Us Our Debts

H ow I THANK the Lord for the fountain of encouragement and
optimism that flows from Jim even in times of crisis. He was so
positive when his job suddenly ended. "God is opening a new
door in our lives," he declared.

It wasn't the first time I'd heard this. Seven years before, after we had spent
over seventeen years of marriage in the same small town—in fact, in the
same house—Jim's employment transferred us more than 250 miles away. As
we pulled up roots, selling our home and rental property and relocating our
prospering retail business—Jim affirmed that God was opening a new door.

Within five years our store collapsed. Now after a year and a half of struggling with debt, Jim no longer had a job. He had no salary, not even sever-
ance pay. How could a measly unemployment check ever suffice?

As his rosy attitude spread to me, I too knew that it would all work out.
God's presence overshadowed our hardships as we determined to be positive. As always His Word brought consolation:

> We are hard pressed on every side, but not crushed; perplexed, but not in
> despair; persecuted, but not abandoned; struck down, but not destroyed.
> —2 CORINTHIANS 4:8–9, NIV

We would not be destroyed. God had not abandoned us. With ongoing hope we continued to confess that He would see us through. Nevertheless, still blinded by Satan's lies and dumbfounded by financial burden, we neglected to tithe.

Jim sent résumés, followed word-of-mouth referrals, and worked with job-search companies. However, he was unable to find an industry that needed his skills, and after three long months of seeking and praying, we decided to go back to our hometown. Fifteen years before Jim had owned a cabinet shop there. Maybe he could build cabinets again. How hard it was to start over at fifty-seven.

As we loaded our possessions, my eyes brimmed with tears. We had never been frivolous spenders. Before we went into business we were practically debt-free. We had not been able to pay anything off since we lost our business, but at least we had managed to not sink deeper into debt. Now we had no choice but to finance this move on credit cards. How much our lives had changed. Before opening our store we didn't even have a credit card.

I sat down on our front steps and sobbed. The Word of God is so true when it declares that the debtor becomes servant to the lender. I recalled how we had once rejoiced in giving, not just our tithes, but also offerings and gifts. Someone once remarked to me, "You lost your store because you gave too much away." How selfishly the world thinks, and how repulsed I felt by that remark. It was such a joy to give as time and time again we furnished clothes for the needy. Proverbs 28:27 leaped into my mind, "He that giveth unto the poor shall not lack."

So why did we lose our business? Why did Jim lose his job? Why, why, why has all this happened to us?

I felt Jim's strong hand touch my shoulder. "Someday we'll look back and realize that the things we're going through were just stepping stones in our lives. God has never forsaken us—and now is no exception."

How right Jim would prove to be. And in time I would find answers to all my questions. I would understand the spiritual reason that our business went under.

Jim plopped down beside me. For a while we just leaned against each other in silence. Our Siamese cat, Sissy Blossom, purred and rubbed against our legs. Jim, in ragged jeans and a plaid flannel shirt, and I, in baggy sweatpants with half-combed hair and a red nose, must have been a sight for the neighbors. Realizing this we burst into laughter.

Yes, we agreed, we will not be destroyed! God will see us through! With our pickup truck loaded to the brim, our car bulging at the seams and pulling a heaped-up fishing boat, we started on our way back home looking like full-fledged hillbillies. Later we'd return and rent a moving van for furniture and big appliances. Despite our hardships, it felt good to at last begin moving through our "new door."

One step at a time our covenant-fulfilling heavenly Father showed us the depth of His commitment to His people. Jim, driving the car and pulling the boat while I followed in the truck, felt the presence of the Holy Spirit in the car with him. Though it was not an audible voice, Jim heard God prompting him to check with a company located seventy miles from the town where we had lived before his transfer. Three months earlier he had contacted this company at their headquarters in another state but received no reply.

With excitement in his voice Jim told me of his word from God as we ate dinner in a noisy truck stop restaurant. "I am confident a job is there for me. First thing tomorrow I'll contact them."

How hard he had tried to find employment. Would this pan out? Had he really heard from God? I prayed, *Don't let him be disappointed.*

At my mother's house the next day Jim drew a deep breath and dialed the company. I sat nearby on pins and needles while he spoke with the plant manager. As he listened, I watched amazement flood into his face. Only days before an employee had unexpectedly retired, leaving a position that required Jim's exact expertise. Following an interview that very day Jim was hired.

What a faithful God we serve!

Now Jim and I realize in full measure that each "new door" led us through a pilgrimage of maturity with God. However, at that moment we hardly noticed the seeds that were beginning to germinate in our hearts. Little by little God continued sowing His love and faithfulness into our lives, turning bad situations into blessings to reveal His perfect will for us. He led us into the awesome awareness of the necessity to completely trust His wisdom, walk daily in His kingdom ways, and seek His forgiveness for our errors.

AND FORGIVE US OUR DEBTS, AS WE FORGIVE OUR DEBTORS

The Conductor bids us to climb inside the glory train for the next destination on our treasure map. It's the place of God's forgiveness. Here we'll explore chambers of endless mercy and discover springs of undying grace. We'll learn our part in receiving pardon for our sins.

Come, the whistle blows. With extended nail-scarred hands our Conductor waits. The choir begins to sing, "Amazing grace! how sweet the sound, that saved a wretch like me! I once was lost, but now am found, Was blind but now I see."[1]

We rest in assurance as the Jubilee Express chugs along its scarlet rails. Gaining full speed, it travels through deep jungles, inside black tunnels, past dark shadows.

Oh, look! A beautiful sea, calm and sparkling red like rubies in bright sunshine. How comforting to see it streaming far into the distance as a token of the precious blood that flowed from Calvary. Oh, wonderful Sea of Forgetfulness!

> Who is a God like you, who pardons sin and forgives the transgression of the remnant of his inheritance? You do not stay angry forever but delight to show mercy. You will again have compassion on us; you will tread our sins underfoot and hurl all our iniquities into the depths of the sea.
>
> —Micah 7:18–19, NIV

At our sincere repentance God vows to not just forgive our sins, but to also forget them, never to be reminded of them again.

> As far as the east is from the west, so far hath he removed our transgressions from us.
>
> —Psalm 103:12

Oh, the magnitude of this verse!

Hold on! Our train leaps to a speed we didn't know was possible. Like a rocket ship it heads north. Before long it zooms by the North Pole. As we see it behind us, we wonder, are we still traveling north? No, south! In a matter of minutes we circle the globe. Oh, now we have just zipped past the South Pole! We're pointing north again.

Whoops! We switch course to travel east. Round and round we go along the equator. Regardless of the lands we sweep over, we can never travel west if we are going east. We'll always be eastbound. And if we turn around to travel west, we can never go east no matter how many hundreds of miles our train covers, no matter how fast it goes.

As far as the east is from the west—that's how far our sins, when forgiven, are removed from the mind of our heavenly Father. What unfathomable forgetfulness. What complete pardon. This is forgiveness so supreme that it washes even the deepest, darkest, bloodiest sin clean and spotless.

> Come now, and let us reason together, saith the LORD: though your
> sins be as scarlet, they shall be as white as snow.
> —ISAIAH 1:18

How do we reason together with God? How do we do our part to receive His grand acquittal? What is required for us to have our sins cast into the Sea of Forgetfulness?

The answer is so simple.

We must come to Him in repentance, our hearts broken with remorse, and lay our sinful filth before Him, determined never to pick it up again. At that moment He replaces our sin with the righteousness and purity of the spotless blood. He gives us a new heart as white as snow, a slate wiped clean, as innocent as a newborn baby.

In the ever-cleansing flow of His blood, His forgiveness endures forever and is endlessly available. Anytime we fall short, whenever we miss the mark, we need only to return to Him in sincere repentance.

Is there ever a time He won't forgive? Yes.

But when? When we ourselves fail to forgive. Just as He forgives us, so must we forgive others.

> For if ye forgive men their trespasses, your heavenly Father will also
> forgive you: But if ye forgive not men their trespasses, neither will your
> Father forgive your trespasses.
> —MATTHEW 6:14–15

Oh, how hard this is. What about the one who told lies about us, the thief who stole from us? What about the drunk driver who killed someone we loved, the adulterer who broke up our marriage? Why do we have to forgive?

As Christians we must be like Jesus. Not only did He bear our every sin and give His life so we may live, but He also cried out for man's forgiveness as He hung on the cross. In our own selves we could never earn such grace or deserve such mercy. But He did it anyway. Now by His strength in us we must follow His example and forgive others—whether or not they earn or deserve it.

This requires sacrificial love. Jesus says love your enemies and pray for those who do you wrong so that you may be the children of your Father in heaven. (See Matthew 5:44.) Paul backs up His words, telling us to let God deal with those who harm us.

> Bless them which persecute you: bless, and curse not.... Recompense
> to no man evil for evil.... Avenge not yourselves, but rather give place

unto wrath: for it is written, Vengeance is mine; I will repay, saith the Lord. Therefore if thine enemy hunger, feed him; if he thirst give him drink: for in so doing thou shalt heap coals of fire on his head. Be not overcome of evil, but overcome evil with good.

—ROMANS 12:14, 17, 19–21

This is impossible in the natural. But as we discipline our spirits to obey, blessings emerge. Proverbs 25:22 says, "For thou shall heap coals of fire upon his head, and the LORD shall reward thee."

Try it. It's fun. I remember our neighbor across the street. No one got along with her. She put up fences, disputed boundary lines, and dared anyone to touch her property.

Before he knew of her self-centeredness, Jim backed into her driveway to keep from getting stuck in newly fallen snow when he left for work one day. Although no damage was done to her property, she immediately called the police, who showed up at our door after Jim returned home that evening.

"Mr. Perrin," the officer said shaking his head, "this is so petty I hate to even bother you, but your neighbor across the street doesn't want you backing into her driveway anymore."

We waited until it snowed again. Then I called her. "Mrs. Cooper," I said, "I know with the weather so terrible it's hard for you to get out. Jim goes through town every day, and if there's anything you need—groceries, medicine, whatever—just let us know. He'll be glad to stop and pick it up for you."

From that point we remained neighbors without conflict. When we moved away we were the only neighbors who had relationship with her.

It was such a trivial thing—my husband backing into her driveway—but it could have swelled into a full-blown feud. Instead, what joy we received. And what a lesson we learned as we experienced the reward of forgiving others no matter what. What blessings we receive as we live by the motto—even if a person doesn't fit our mold or measure up to our expectations, even if they come against us without reason, we'll love them anyway.

A while back at a ladies' meeting one of my friends told about problems she was having with her in-laws. She stopped in the middle of a sentence, peered at me and laughed, "I know, you'll tell me to love them anyway!"

Yes, try it. It's fun. Heaping coals of goodness sows tenderness in a stony heart, reaps repentance instead of rebellion, and causes love to bloom. What bountiful rewards. And even more, when we forgive although the offender may not deserve it, our heavenly Father forgives us also, even though we don't deserve it.

But you say, what if someone murders my child? Can such a horrendous act be forgiven? Yes, it can. I once worked with a lady who forgave her daughter's cold-blooded killers. Before the girl's death they raped her. They stabbed her repeatedly. Still, this mother forgave. She made a trip to the prison, visited the convicted murderers, and prayed for their salvation.

How can this be? Only by the strength of Jesus. We can forgive this way only by placing our hatred upon His cross and never again picking it up. We must replace our natural human reactions with the God-kind of love described in 1 Corinthians 13. We must practice this love that never gives up and never fails, this love that sets us free.

No matter what the circumstances, we must forgive or we will die in bitterness. Unforgiveness yields only misery and torment. Unforgiveness literally eats us up with stress.

Oh, the joy that forgiving brings. It releases us for divine blessing, rewards us with peace, and leads us unencumbered to fulfill our destiny with God.

THE MOST ENDEARING biblical record of human forgiveness unfolds in the account of Joseph. How important his pardon was in the course of history.

Joseph, the son of Jacob (renamed Israel by God), was the great-grandson of Abraham, the man from whom the Hebrew nation originated. With unmerited mercy, Joseph forgave his brothers and became not only their savior but also the savior of the future Hebrew population. Jacob's sons were the heads of twelve tribes, and from their loins arose the entire Jewish nation of Israel. With his act of mercy Joseph saved the nation from death by famine.

For background, we start the story with Jacob, years before Joseph's birth. (See Genesis 29, 30:1–24.) How quickly Jacob falls head over heels in love with Rachel! She is the first relative he meets when, after fleeing from the wrath of his brother Esau, he arrives at Laban's ranch. Oh, Rachel, how beautiful she is!

After residing just one month with his Uncle Laban, Rachel's father, Jacob agrees to work seven years for her hand in marriage. In his desire to have Rachel as his own, the years fly by like a few days. Happiness beyond words surely swell like flooding rivers in his heart when at last he can say, "Uncle Laban, my time is now complete. Give me my wife."

But woe to Jacob! A sower of deception with his own father (Gen. 27:1–40), he now reaps the same from his uncle. What a letdown it is when, after so diligently fulfilling his part of the bargain for Rachel, he discovers that Laban has tricked him into marrying Rachel's older and not so attractive sister, Leah. Although he allows Jacob to marry Rachel only a week later, Laban demands another full seven years of work for her.

Will trouble never cease? Jacob must pine for children by the wife he dearly loves, but pregnancy evades Rachel. On the other hand, fruitful Leah gives birth to four fine sons. Likely from a sense of rejection for being the wife less loved, she proudly flaunts her role of motherhood.

Poor Rachel. Imagine her agony as she watches Leah nurture her babies and please their husband with her sons. Stewing in envy, she says, "Jacob, give me children or I'll die!"

In frustration he yells back, "Who do you think I am? God? Only He can take responsibility for your barrenness!"

"Well, then sleep with my servant Bilhah so her children can be mine!"

To appease her Jacob agrees. And Bilhah blesses him and Rachel with two sons.

"In rivalry with my sister, I have won!" Rachel rages.

Oh, the women Jacob married! Now Leah pouts. Since her child-bearing is at a standstill, she demands children from her servant Zilpah, who then births two sons by Jacob.

Leah gloats, "I'm so happy. All the women will see how blessed I am!"

Rachel's agony deepens even further when Leah has more babies—two additional sons and a daughter. Leah's goal to gain the greater part of Jacob's affection and Rachel's resentment of Leah's children keep their fires of jealousy ablaze.

Leah boasts, "I myself have given my husband six sons. Now he will honor me!"

Like needles this shoots into Rachel's heart. How inadequate she feels because of her infertility. With each passing day her torment intensifies. And so does Jacob's. Despite ten sons and one daughter he aches for offspring from Rachel, his beloved, the woman who holds his deepest devotion.

Then, finally, after all their years of barren marriage, God blesses Rachel. She conceives. Joseph is born!

Now from Genesis 37 and 39–47 the long story of this treasured son Joseph and the wonder of his forgiveness unfolds.

There he is! See him in the distance, roaming across green pastureland to locate his ten older brothers. Let's catch up with him. But hurry. At age seventeen Joseph leaps like a young deer, quick and nimble, almost dancing with each step.

Where are those brothers of mine? Are they hiding from me to make my work hard? He laughs at the thought and slows in his walk to scan the rolling fields.

What an exquisite garment he wears. Swinging from side to side it gleams like a bridal gown in the sunshine. Unlike the simple sleeveless tunic that hangs just below the knees—the kind worn by herdsmen—his vesture sports elegant sleeves full to his wrists and with it a hemline resting at the top of his sandals. Delicately woven of superb linen, white and shiny, it almost takes our breath.

We pause to consider this. White? So often we've heard about Joseph's coat of "many colors" from the King James Version of the Bible.

But the Hebrew word for *colors,* instead of referring to the dye of the garment, indicates a long and sleeved tunic.[2] The Revised Standard Version describes it as a long robe with sleeves. The New International Version says, "richly ornamented robe," while the Amplified Bible calls it a "[distinctive] long garment" (Gen. 37:23).

None of these sources mention its colors. Most likely Joseph's coat was sown from the finest linen of ancient times, the same fabric as that used in the gowns of King David's daughters. As it says of Tamar in 2 Samuel 13:18—"Now she was wearing a long robe with sleeves; for thus were the virgin daughters of the king clad of old" (RSV). *Tanakh: The Holy Scriptures* calls her attire and also the garment of Joseph, "ornamented tunics."

Joseph's robe most likely was very soft with the sheen of satin. In Matthew 11:8 Jesus makes reference to such fine fabric when He says, "Behold, those who wear soft clothing are in the houses of kings" (AMP).

With youthful vigor Joseph scours the hillsides, oblivious to the fact that his brothers harbor deadly envy against him because of the partiality their father Jacob showed by giving him his distinctive robe. Although he is the eleventh son, Joseph's coat distinguishes him with the blessings of the firstborn—a very prestigious position in the family. Its priestly design sets Joseph aside as the spiritual leader of Jacob's household. Its luxurious weave gives him the stature of a king.

At this very moment the jealous hatred of the older sons smolders like a sleeping volcano ready to erupt. Neither Joseph nor his father has an inkling of its magnitude.

It's no wonder that Jacob favors Joseph above all his older sons. His beloved Rachel died giving birth to her second child, Benjamin, the twelfth and last son of the family.

What grief Jacob bears. He so adored his Rachel. And she, who longed with all her heart to give birth, had no chance to rear her boys to manhood. Joseph probably has no recollection of her at all. He probably knows only Bilhah, his mother's servant and father's concubine, as his mother.

Joseph slows his pace. *Where can my brothers be today?* Actually, except to please his father he has no reason to want to rush to them. In fact, he dreads seeing them. One day after shepherding with them, he told their father of their indecent behavior in the field. Since then they've done nothing but ridicule him. And telling them his dreams made them even more hostile.

"Let me tell you what I dreamed," he had said. "We were all working in the field together binding sheaves. My sheaf stood up straight. Your sheaves gathered around mine and bowed down before it."

"Do you think you'll reign over us like a king?" they sneered.

Things got much worse after he told them his second dream. They had no kind words for him at all. But for some reason he felt compelled to tell them how the sun, moon, and eleven stars all bowed to him. When he told this dream to his father, even he rebuked him, saying, "Shall I and the entire family bow ourselves to you?"

Why did they get so upset? Joseph thinks as he reaches the top of a hill. *After all, these weren't my thoughts. I only told them what I dreamed.*

At that moment a man appears and interrupts his thoughts, "Are you looking for someone?"

"Yes, have you seen my brothers and their flock?"

"Yes, they left here saying they were going to Dothan."

In the next instant we find ourselves zooming ahead to Dothan where Joseph's ten older brothers watch their father's flock. Listen to what they say. How could they even think such things? We wish we could warn Joseph!

Under the shade of a large bush they recline on rocks they've piled together. Wearing sleeveless tunics of drab material they watch their younger brother approach in his special robe that glimmers in the sun. "Look, the dreamer! Just skipping along without a care in the world. We ought to murder that kid and be done with him."

The idea ignites. "Hey, we can dump his body in that old dry well we found."

"We'll tell Father that a wild animal ate him."

"Ha, ha! Then we'll see what becomes of his dreams!"

When Reuben, the oldest brother, realizes the seriousness of the others, he pipes in, "No, let's not kill him. Instead let's throw him alive into the well. Then he can die without us ever raising a hand to take his life." We sense Reuben's plans to rescue the boy later and send him home to Jacob.

By the time Joseph arrives, the brothers are primed to execute their evil deed. They grab him brutally, strip off his special coat, and wrestle him all the way to the well.

"Stop!" he yells. "What have I ever done to you? Let me go!" When he thuds on the dry bottom they jeer, "Go to sleep and have more dreams!" Leaning over the pit they stare down at him and laugh.

"Why are you doing this?" Joseph screams, "Get me out! Don't leave me to die in this hole!"

"Let's go eat," one brother says. Still laughing, they turn away and leave young Joseph crying.

"I'm not hungry," Reuben mumbles and walks away to think. How can they eat knowing what they've just done?

Swallowing a mouthful of bread, one brother leaps up. "Look, camels! A caravan of traders is coming!"

"Let's sell Joseph to them!" Judah exclaims. The others agree—all but Reuben, who hasn't come back yet.

When he does return, expecting to retrieve Joseph, he finds him gone. "Where is our little brother?"

"We're rid of him for good! Right now he's on his way to Egypt to be a slave. You missed the fun! You should have heard him squalling and bawling. Look at what those men gave us for our little spoiled brat," they roar with glee, holding out twenty pieces of silver.

Reuben weeps, "The child is gone, the child is gone. And I, oh, where shall I go?"

But the rest carry on as if Reuben has said nothing. Doubling over with exuberant laughter they slaughter a goat and dip Joseph's gorgeous robe in its bright red blood. They'll take it home for Jacob. On the way they pass the dripping garment around, waving it in the air, poking fun.

"Now what does this fine coat mean?"

"How beautiful it looks, fit for a king!"

"We'll see who Father favors now. Who will he pick to wear it next?"

Arriving home, with serious faces they approach Jacob. "Father, is this Joseph's coat?"

Jacob's eyes well with tears. Gasping he pulls the bloody garment to his chest and falls on his knees. "Oh, my son Joseph! He has surely been torn to pieces and eaten by wild animals!" For hours on end Jacob howls in sobs that tear his heart into a million pieces.

His precious Joseph, Rachel's firstborn, is gone from his life. Without Joseph, his joy of living, how can he ever know true happiness again? Day after day, week after week he grieves. No one can console him.

"I'll go to my death in mourning," he cries again and again, wailing louder with each cry.

Did his sons realize what this would do to Jacob? Were they prepared for all the grief they've caused their aging father? How they must suffer inwardly because they put him in such a state of agony. But it's done, and they can never take it back.

Quickly we skim over twenty-two years of Joseph's separation from his family. At first things in Egypt aren't completely horrible. Joseph serves as a slave to Potiphar, an officer of the pharaoh. God blesses the young lad and the prestigious home he tends, giving him complete run of the household and prospering his master's crops and livestock.

All goes well until Potiphar's wife, infatuated with Joseph's good manner and handsome appearance, tries in vain to seduce him. After his continued refusal she falsely accuses him of making a play for her. Potiphar throws innocent Joseph into the dungeon under the palace, where Pharaoh's prisoners reside in chains.

Still God blesses Joseph. He receives favor from the chief jailer and soon acquires full charge over the prisoners. When an angry Pharaoh jails both his chief butler and his chief baker, God gives Joseph the ability to interpret their dreams. Both dreams come to pass exactly as Joseph says, with Pharaoh putting the baker to death and reinstating the butler to his former duties.

When he told the butler the good meaning of his dream, Joseph had asked him for help. "Please show me kindness by making mention of me to Pharaoh to get me out of this place. As a young boy I was stolen out of my home and sold as a slave. Now even though I've done no wrong, I'm locked up."

But back at his old job the butler forgets all about Joseph's plea. How dim the future looks for this beloved son of Jacob. In every waking moment he surely recalls the privileges of home and yearns for the love his father showed him before his brothers sold him. His own brothers! How Joseph's heart must grieve as he remembers.

Two more dreary years drag by, making a total of thirteen since his fateful day in the dry well. Will he ever see the light of day again?

Yes! God has not forsaken Joseph.

Pharaoh has two dreams that stump all his wise men. Recalling the interpreter of his dream in jail, at last the butler tells Pharaoh about Joseph. Now the number one man in all of Egypt sends for the prisoner, and good things begin for Joseph.

In the first of Pharaoh's dreams seven fat healthy cows feed on reeds along the banks of the Nile and are joined by seven starving cows that eat them.

In the second dream seven ears of corn, filled out to perfection, grow on one stalk. Then seven blighted ears, withered and with little grain, devour the good ears.

Joseph has no problem explaining the dreams. "After seven prosperous years, seven years of famine will occur across the entire land. It will totally consume the people's minds, even to the point of causing them to forget the good years. Having two dreams with the same meaning indicates that this cannot be averted. It is fixed by God!"

Joseph suggests that Pharaoh appoint the wisest, most capable man he knows to oversee the project of gathering and stocking produce during the plentiful years so he can feed his country throughout the famine. Pharaoh not only listens, but he also chooses Joseph as overseer, appointing him to the position of second in authority in all his kingdom!

"Only in issues of the throne will I be greater than you," decrees Pharaoh, "I hereby place you in charge over all the land of Egypt." He removes his signet ring from his own finger and puts it on Joseph's. He dresses Joseph in a robe of fine linen and loops a gold chain around his neck.

What a switch—from prison to the right hand of the pharaoh. As the second in command passes people in his travels throughout Egypt, officials cry out and insist to bystanders, "Bow the knee!"

During the seven abundant years Joseph, now known by an Egyptian name and married to an Egyptian woman, governs the stockpiling of food until the land of Egypt bursts with overflowing surplus. Then just as he predicted, in the eighth year a devastating famine hits. It spreads far beyond the borders of Egypt, reaching even into Canaan, Joseph's homeland.

AND NOW OUR story of Joseph and his brothers resumes after twenty-two years. After suffering with a scarce supply of food for two years, Jacob, his one daughter, eleven remaining sons, and their families face starvation. As we enter Jacob's house, we find him slumped in his chair in a dim corner of the room. Years of grief have left their mark. Deep wrinkles line his hollow checks, and dark circles outline his sunken eyes.

Benjamin, a robust man in his early thirties, flanks his aged father. Since the tragic fate of Joseph, Jacob seldom lets this son, the second and only other child born of his cherished Rachel, escape his sight. Today his other ten sons, appearing very grim, also gather around him.

"Why do you just stand there staring at each other?" Jacob says. "I hear they have food in Egypt. Go there and buy some grain, or else we die!"

Though they must dread the journey, the ten older sons pack without grumbling. They know that Benjamin has to stay. If their younger brother met with ill fate, Jacob would surely lose any will to go on.

Meanwhile we look in on Joseph, the now famous governor of Egypt. Just a skinny teenager who was hardly old enough to shave when he was snatched from his homeland, he is now a handsome muscular man of thirty-nine. His thick hair and beard are such a shiny black that they catch highlights of his purple linen robe and gold necklaces. The only uncovered parts of his face are his broad cheek bones and his wide-set eyes.

In his royal position Joseph supervises the distribution of the reserves with a masterful mind as family after family, many from distant lands, approach him to buy food. He presides behind a heavy table, issuing orders for his personal stewards to fill each one.

Look! His brothers have arrived. Weary from traveling they stand in line hardly speaking to one another. At last their turn comes. Approaching the table each bows his face to the ground before the mighty ruler.

Oh, will they recognize this man as the little brother they sold twenty-two years ago? No, not one of them has any inkling whatsoever of his true identity. "We've come hoping to buy grain," one says in the Hebrew language.

Oh, will Joseph realize who they are? If so, what will he do to them? He must resent them with a passion for revenge after their uncaring brutality toward him and the years of suffering their betrayal put him through. Now he has power to sentence them to death!

We catch a painful twitch in Joseph's eye. He knows who they are! But he keeps his recognition of them a secret, not even speaking in his native tongue. Speaking through an interpreter, he exclaims in a stern voice, "Where have you come from?"

"All the way from the land of Canaan."

We detect unbearable memories clanging in Joseph's brain. How they ridiculed him, made fun of his dreams, and sold him without mercy. Drawing a deep breath, he glances toward the sky. Today those dreams have been fulfilled!

Joseph's dark eyes glare as his interpreter repeats his words to his unsuspecting siblings. "Aha! You can't fool me. You've come as spies to search out unprotected areas of food in our land!"

"No, no, our lord! We come only to purchase food! We're brothers, all sons of one man, twelve of us in all. One son is gone, and the youngest stayed at home with our aged father."

Joseph's heart leaps. His father and little brother still live! Yet with a stern face he continues, "What does it matter if you're brothers? What do I care about your family history? You claim you aren't spies? Well, prove your word! One of you return home, bring this little brother of your back here for me to see. Then I will know you speak truth."

With that Joseph orders all of them to be thrown in jail. Baffled at his accusations and horrified by his exercise of authority, they yield like lambs led to slaughter. What else can they do? Who besides Pharaoh himself has power to contradict this man?

Watching them as they are hustled away, Joseph's lips tighten. A faraway gaze consumes his eyes. Whatever is he thinking? Perhaps he wants these men, guilty of his boyhood cruelty, out of sight until he decides their fate. Oh, will he have them executed?

Three days pass before he calls for them. With trembling bodies they fall prostrate at his feet. Arising to face him, each eye looks at him with anxiety. Each heart beats with the silent pleading: give us grace, show us mercy, please let us go home in peace!

The moments drag by like hours while this ruler of all of Egypt, arrayed in his fine apparel, paces back and forth in front of them. Finally he speaks, again by an interpreter, "Because I am a God-fearing man I will give you an opportunity to live. I've decided to keep only one of you in jail while the rest return with grain for your families. Afterwards you must bring your younger brother to appear before me so your word can be verified."

The conversation of the brothers rings like sweet music in Joseph's ears. Unaware that he understands their Hebrew words, they discuss their guilt for selling their brother so long ago: "We saw his terror and heard his cries, yet we sold him anyway. Our horrible act has brought this judgment upon us."

A tear rolls down Reuben's cheek, "I told you not to do it."

Joseph leaves the room and weeps. How he desires to blurt out the words, "I am Joseph!" But he can't—not yet, maybe never. That will be determined by their hearts.

The men watch helplessly as their brother Simeon is chained and dragged back to prison, his face drained white with panic. His eyes cry, please hurry back with Benjamin!

Overwhelmed with sadness and despair, they load their donkeys to begin their trip home. At least they're going back with food. But how will their father react when Simeon isn't among them? And how will they tell him that Benjamin must return with them to Egypt? How well they remember his weeping over Joseph. Oh, what will he do now?

Little do they know what else lies in store, for this is only their first predicament. Trials by Joseph have just begun. What an ingenious plan he has devised, a test to show if their regret is truly heartfelt. Yes, he overheard them admit their guilt in sorrow, but he must know more. Were their words simply due to their dilemma at that moment, or have the years really changed them? Before he can tell them who he is, he must be sure of genuine remorse. Otherwise, revealing himself might simply open a vial of venom—resentment, hatred, vengeance, more heartbreak for his father. He can't take that chance.

Old injuries bleed afresh as if a flaming blade were thrust into his chest. Every cell within his body aches to see his father and Benjamin. But he must wait—and hope.

Standing on the palace balcony, he shades his eyes with one hand and stares after his brothers' donkey caravan until they fade from view. Watching them depart for his old home inflicts another gash to his now-reopened wounds.

Yet his idea to test their hearts brings consolation. As he returns to selling grain, we discern a slight smile on his lips. Despite his sorrow Joseph throbs with anticipation for the unfolding of his plot.

When his workers filled his brothers' orders, Joseph had slipped them money with the instructions, "Fill every sack to overflowing, then put the amount paid for each on top."

As we travel with the nine brothers on their way back to Canaan, gloom and dread steal their words. Dust swirls around the donkey's hoofs until one can hardly breathe, and a baking sun glares from a cloudless sky. But they don't even notice.

Changing from blazing yellow to a glowing ball of red the sun gives up her heat and sinks behind the horizon. At the brink of darkness our weary group trudges into a city and locates an inn where they can spend the night. As one brother opens a sack to feed the donkeys, he stares in disbelief.

"Oh, no! How can this be? The money I paid for grain is here in my sack!"

All the men shake with fright. They know that the governor who so unjustly accused them, threw them without reason into prison, and forced them to give up Simeon will surely believe that they stole from him. He will want them killed if they return. But if they don't, what will be the fate of Simeon? All along the way they attempt to understand the injustice that has fallen on them.

"Just look at what God is doing to us..."

"What repercussions for selling Joseph..."

When they finally pull up to their home site, they do their best to slip in quietly, hoping their father won't be around to notice that they are leading

Simeon's donkeys. But Jacob watches from the doorway.

In broken voices they blurt out their entire ordeal. With a sinking stomach Jacob listens.

"How could you let such things happen?" he cries.

One son exclaims, "But Father, just look at the amount of grain we brought home! The workers filled our sacks fuller than those of all the other buyers. See how this one bulges!"

He unties the bag, and there on top lies his money. All the others rip into theirs and find their money, too. Together they all freeze in horror.

Jacob rages, "You have ripped my heart apart anew. First Joseph is taken from me. Now Simeon. And you want to take Benjamin away? No, he can't leave me! He is my only remaining son from Rachel. I cannot bear losing him!"

How wise Joseph's test was. If the brothers return with Benjamin, willing to put their own lives in jeopardy for Simeon's freedom, if they confess that they returned home with all the money they paid for their food and bring it back to him in honesty—Joseph will know their hearts have changed. Yet how long this leader of Egypt must wait until they come again. Jacob cannot bear the thought of danger for his remaining sons, especially Benjamin.

Finally the famine gives them no choice. They have to return to Egypt for food, and Benjamin must go. Jacob cries, "May Almighty God give you favor before this ruler, that he in mercy will release Simeon and not harm Benjamin. But regardless, even if I must bear the pain of losing them, this trip has to be taken, or we all will starve."

At his orders the departing sons take double the money for the original grain, along with special gifts for the governor. Mile after mile they travel in silent fear.

Joseph awaits their return. Every day he scan the crowds. Maybe his plan has failed. His heart throbs with anxiety. Aren't they ever coming back?

At last the day arrives when he spies them. He blinks back tears. Benjamin stands with them! What a superb-looking man he has become, so tall and muscular with dark hair and creamy skin. Joseph yearns to rush to him and take him in his arms. But not yet, if ever. His test still has a way to go.

Without acknowledging them, Joseph excuses himself and heads for the palace. Pointing them out to his steward, he says, "Prepare a banquet at noon today. See those ten men huddled together? Bring them to dine with me."

When they hear Joseph's orders to join him at his home, the brothers panic.

"Oh, why are we ordered to the palace? Do you think it's because he thinks we stole the money that was in our sacks? Is he going to arrest us and make us slaves? Maybe put us in prison for life! Or sentence us to death!"

In a cold sweat they gather around the steward at the palace entrance and, jabbering all together, tell how they found the money in their sacks.

"We have no idea how it got there!"

"Here! We are bringing back double the amount!"

"Our father even sends extra gifts!"

The steward laughs, "Put it all away. You need not be afraid. Your God must have put money in your sacks, because I received your money." Turning to leave he adds, "Wait here. I have a surprise for you."

Moments later he comes back with Simeon. No physical harm has come to him, and he looks healthy. Reunited, the brothers rejoice together as they follow the palace official down the massive hallway to a room where they can freshen up. Servants bring water to wash their feet and tell them that their donkeys are being attended.

How baffling. On their first trip to Egypt they were accused as spies, and now they are treated like royal guests in the governor's palace. How can this be?

Before long the steward ushers them into an exquisite dining hall. "You'll be eating here today."

With amazement they scan the luxurious table settings. They gawk in disbelief. *We will be eating here?* Uneasiness ties their hearts in knots, and they dare not move or talk.

Governor Joseph enters with his interpreter. Quickly they bow at his feet, fumbling to present their gifts.

"And how is your aged father you spoke about? Is he alive and well?"

"Oh, yes, he is."

Joseph points to Benjamin. "Is this the youngest brother you mentioned before?"

"Yes, our lord."

At such close contact with his sibling Joseph's heart melts. Do they really love this brother as it appears, or do they belittle him when no one is looking? Hundreds of times he's wondered about Benjamin's welfare. What a joy to see him in his manhood, a picture of health.

"May God's blessing be on you, my son," Joseph says, then quickly turns his face away.

To the surprise of all he suddenly races from the dining room. When he reaches the privacy of his personal chambers, he weeps in heaving sobs until no more tears will come. Finally regaining his composure, he washes his face and returns to his guests.

"Let the meal begin," he orders.

How he wants to confront his brothers and cry, "I am Joseph, I am Joseph!" But the last part of his plan must unfold before he can, the test of the silver cup.

Excitement bubbles over as the brothers load their grain for the return trip home. All eleven are unharmed and returning safely. They have received royal treatment. What a glorious report they will have for Jacob this time.

How could they suspect Joseph's plot? Again he tells his steward to stuff their sacks full and then place every man's money at the mouth. "Put my silver cup in the sack of the youngest," he adds and then gives him extra instructions.

No sooner have the brothers departed than the steward and his men overtake them in a royal chariot. Blocking their procession the steward steps down, following Joseph's orders to the letter. "Why do you return evil for good by stealing my lord's silver cup from his palace?" he yells.

In shock, the brothers exchange glances, all shaking their heads in bewilderment. "What? How can you even say such a thing? Haven't we shown our honesty by bringing back all the money we found in our sacks? It isn't even conceivable that we would steal from your master!"

Positive that they do not have the cup one of them declares, "If you find it in anyone's possessions, let that person die, and the rest of us will be the governor's slaves."

"No," the steward says, "the one who has the cup will be a slave, but the rest may go free."

Convinced of their innocence they readily consent. But when the cup is uncovered in Benjamin's sack, their blood runs cold. Oh, no! In a fit of terror they realize what they have promised the steward. They stand petrified while he and his men shackle Benjamin and hoist him into the chariot. In a puff of dust their little brother is taken away.

Now they're free to go with no restraints. Nothing stops them from fleeing this madness. They can tell their father that just as their brother Joseph, Benjamin also met his death by some wild animal.

But years of guilt and seeing their father's grief have softened them. Such thoughts never enter their minds. In despair they rip their tunics, reload their donkeys, and head back to the palace.

Joseph stands on the balcony. What a relief to see his brothers coming like a stampede. They care! They really do care about their youngest brother! As they rush to the palace, Joseph meets them at the door. "Why have you stolen from my home? Don't you realize that a man of God such as I can discern these things?"

Through tear-blurred eyes Judah looks up. "Oh, my lord, how can we even defend ourselves, since it is God who has exposed our past iniquity? From now on all of us will be your slaves as well as the brother whose sack contained your silver cup."

Joseph frowns. "God forbid that I should consider such a thing. Why should all of you pay for his thievery? Only the guilty one will be my slave. As for the rest of you, get up! Go home in peace to your father."

Judah leaps to his feet. "Oh, my lord, please listen to me for a moment and do not strike me down in anger. Do you remember the first time we came for food, how you asked if we had a father or any other brothers?"

"Yes."

"In truth, we told you of our father who is very old and of our youngest brother—the child of his old age—at home. Since the only other son by our father's wife, Rachel, is dead—this lad means more to our father than I can tell. His entire life centers around him. His soul is knit as one with him. He will surely die without this son!"

Judah is the very brother who had insisted on selling Joseph to the slave traders. To conceal the pounding of his heart Joseph steps back. In the shadow of the doorway he clenches his fists and swallows hard. He doesn't speak. He can't.

"Oh, my lord, I come to you with the same respect as if I were pleading with the pharaoh himself. I beg of you to let me remain as your servant. But please, release my youngest brother. Let him return with the others to our father!"

Joseph can refrain himself no longer. He turns to his officers commanding, "Go away and leave me alone with these men."

As they walk away, the mighty governor of Egypt breaks down and sobs aloud, speaking to them for the first time without an interpreter. In the language of his brothers he exclaims, "I am Joseph! I am your brother Joseph whom you sold so long ago!"

Still within earshot the Egyptians hear him and hurry to tell Pharaoh the good news. The brothers cling to each other, gaping at the powerful figure who looms over them. This mighty ruler is the brother they sold so heartlessly! No words, only gasps of fear, escape their lips. There is nowhere to run, no place to hide. Now they must pay for their sin against the brother they betrayed. Surely they are doomed!

But forgiveness fills the heart of Joseph. Undeserved mercy flows and grace abounds. Holding out his arms Joseph utters, "Come close to me.

There is no need to be afraid. Don't even be ashamed any longer for what you did to me. God Himself sent me ahead of you to preserve your lives!"

He falls on Benjamin's neck, and they weep together. Then he kisses each brother as they tremble in his presence. Tears gush from their eyes as they release the guilt and pain they have bottled up for the twenty-two long years since they double-crossed their younger brother. Oh, what pleasure to touch him now in love, to have him back as one with them, to gain his pardon—even though they know they don't deserve it.

What a man, this Joseph. What a heart of forgiveness.

It is a joyous day when the eleven return for Jacob and he learns that Joseph lives. The precious firstborn son of Rachel is alive. It's as though he has risen from the dead!

Words cannot explain how Jacob rejoices to hold his long-lost son in his arms again when he arrives in Egypt. Here he will live out the rest of his days on the best land of the kingdom. It is a gift from Pharaoh to the family of Joseph, the savior of his nation.

When we can find it in our hearts to offer forgiveness as this man did, we will find ourselves yielded to the very nature of Christ Himself. Joseph, though he was deeply hurt, readily forgave and held no bitterness against his brothers. In many ways his life profiles that of our Redeemer.

Joseph was born of a woman highly favored by his father; Jesus was born of a woman highly favored by His Father (Luke 1:30).

Joseph wore a coat that distinguished him as priest and king in his family; Jesus, as seen by John in Revelation, wears the distinguishing garment of the heavenly High Priest (Rev. 1:13) and reigns with the words *King of kings and Lord of lords* written on His robe (Rev. 19:16).

Joseph's coat was dipped in blood. When Christ returns He will be wearing "a vesture dipped in blood" (Rev. 19:13).

Joseph, the special subject of his father's affection, received the firstborn blessing; Jesus, the special subject of His Father's affection, became the "firstborn among many brethren" (Rom. 8:29).

Joseph left the glories of home to become a savior in another land; Jesus left the glories of His heavenly home to become the Savior of Earth (John 3:13, 16).

Joseph was sold as a slave by his brothers at the insistence of Judah for twenty pieces of silver; Jesus was sold by His disciple Judas (spelled Judah in Hebrew) Iscariot for thirty pieces of silver (Matt. 26:15), the price of a slave in that day.

Joseph was honored like a king by people who shouted "Bow the knee!" as he road through the land; Jesus was honored like a king as he rode through the streets of Jerusalem (Matt. 21:8–9). Before Him every knee will bow and every tongue confess that He is Lord (Phil. 2:10–11).

Joseph and Jesus were both innocent but condemned. By the hand of God they arose to a position of royalty, Joseph, at the right hand of the pharaoh, and Jesus, at the right hand of the Majesty in heaven (Heb. 8:1).

Yes, over and over we see Jesus in the life of Joseph—rejected, jeered, hated by his brothers, and suffering at their unmerciful hands. But he pardoned their sins and forgave them at the moment of their true repentance. He exalted them to live in the kingdom of his rule, a land of plenty in the midst of famine, a place of peace and deliverance.

Yet in all these parallels the one that shines the brightest is the forgiveness Joseph so freely gave to his undeserving brothers. Similarly, how wonderful and merciful is the forgiveness our Savior gives. Even from the cross He cried:

> Father, forgive them; for they know not what they do.
>
> —LUKE 23:34

GOD'S FORGIVENESS STILL flourishes for the believer today, no matter how deep, malicious, or foolish the sin is. The Great I AM is now and has always been a forgiving God who loves unconditionally. To see His forgiveness in action we step into another story—the stormy struggles of King David, His beloved. Oh, what complicated messes are caused by sin!

Proverbs 6:16–19 lists seven things that God hates: a proud look. a lying tongue, hands that shed innocent blood, a heart that devises wicked imaginations, feet that are swift in running to mischief, a false witness that speaks lies, and he who sows discord among his brethren. Even if we commit all seven, God is willing to forgive and forget every single one if we cry to Him with a sincere heart.

He did for David. Let's look at these seven sinful acts in the life of this chosen king.

A proud look. It proceeds from one who is swollen with pride, arrogance, and excessive self-esteem. Does this apply to David?

Yes. Engulfed in pride an aging King David took a census of Israel against God's wishes. King David repented of his sin:

> Lo, I have sinned and I have done wickedly.
>
> —2 SAMUEL 24:17

But demons had a heyday, and seventy thousand lost their lives because of his egotism.

A lying tongue, hands shedding innocent blood, a heart devising wicked imaginations, feet running swiftly to mischief, a false witness, sowing discard among the people. Sad to say, David committed all these ugly deeds, too.

We all know the story. Not content with all his kingly riches, not satisfied with all his wives and concubines—he gazed with lustful eyes at a gorgeous lady named Bathsheba as she bathed on a nearby rooftop.

Even though she was the wife of Uriah, one of David's top soldiers and probably his own companion in past battles, David's heart raged with desire for this woman. Unconcerned for anyone or anything other than his lust, David stayed home from combat and summoned Bathsheba to his royal quarters for his sexual gratification.

And then Bathsheba got pregnant! Since her husband, Uriah, had been living on the battlefield for months, David hurriedly called him home. He must cover the adulterous act he and Bathsheba had committed by making sure that Uriah slept with his wife immediately. Then who would dare to doubt that the baby in Bathsheba's womb belonged to any other than her own husband?

How miserably David's devious plot failed.

A tired Uriah shuffles into the palace. In ragged battle clothes he has worn for days on end he faces his friend King David. A soiled cummerbund belted around his waist supports a dusty water flask made from furry animal skin. A dirty cloth banded around his sweaty head shades his sunken eyes and sun-baked cheeks. In meticulous detail he relays an update of the fighting.

Then David's scheme begins. Arrayed in a rich robe of the finest linen, his clean shiny hair resting like well-placed copper coils on his brawny shoulders, and his beard trimmed to perfection, he insists that his exhausted soldier go home and rest.

"Refresh yourself. Enjoy a nice bath. Spend time with your wife. Get a good night's sleep," David urges.

With parched lips Uriah speaks, not with disrespect for the king but out of commitment to his duties, concern for his fellow fighters, and reverence for the ark of the covenant. "The troops of Israel and Judah camp in tents in open fields with the ark in their midst. How can I even think of such pleasure as going home and sleeping with my wife?" In dismay he shakes his head, "As surely as I live, I cannot consider such a thing."

Even though King David stages a banquet and serves hard liquor until

Uriah staggers in a drunken stupor, the devoted soldier still refuses to go home. Instead he beds down in the servant's quarters of the palace.

In his dilemma David decides to cover his adulterous tracks by ordering that Uriah be placed in the front line of battle. There, he knows, his dedicated confidant and prized warrior will be killed.

What can King David be thinking? He can't conceal the facts. Surely all his kingdom can figure out that Uriah couldn't father Bathsheba's child from the battlefield. Even if people do not realize the disgrace of Bathsheba's pregnancy when their king takes her as his wife, they only need to count the months until the baby's birth.

David seems oblivious to his evil deeds until the prophet Nathan rebukes him. As his eyes are opened to the sickening disgust of his sin, David repents on the spot. Nevertheless the son conceived in sin still dies.

From this point on dishonor and rebellion run rampant in the royal family. David's son Amnon is overcome with desire for his half-sister Tamar and rapes her. Perhaps because David identifies with Amnon's uncontrollable lust, or maybe because of the guilt he suffers from his sin with Bathsheba, he fails to take action against his unscrupulous son.

Tamar, so innocent and untouched before the rape, now lives in disgrace. She no longer qualifies to wear the special garment designed only for virgin daughters of the king. What heartache she must suffer. This infuriates Tamar's full-brother Absalom. For two years resentment stews in Absalom until he murders his rapist brother Amnon.

While David grieves for Amnon, Absalom flees his wrath. After three years David says he wants reconciliation with his fugitive son. But does he really? Even though he has Absalom returned to Jerusalem, he disgraces him by denying him residence in the palace. He refuses to even see his son. Still harboring bitterness, David makes no genuine effort to mend any differences or show forgiveness.

Tension smolders and rebellion fumes in Absalom's heart. Eventually defiance flames unrestrained, and he revolts against his father's reign. With a passion to overthrow his father and gain rule of his kingdom, Absalom persuades many to take his side. What a shock when even Ahithophel, David's longtime counselor and trusted companion, joins ranks with Absalom.

Civil war erupts, and David flees. In total confusion he escapes to the Mount of Olives, his heart convulsing with grief. Barefoot and sobbing, his head covered with a mourning cloth, the king stumbles up the mountain. His faithful followers also throw off their sandals, drape their heads, and weep at his side.

How can Absalom do this to his father? David loves him so. But he loved his dead son Amnon, too. Total pardon for Amnon's murder proved to be more than David could give. Yet this whole agonizing predicament might well have been averted with a sincere attempt at reconciliation.

David is crushed because Ahithophel, his confidant who had served at his side throughout his kingship, is now was aligned with Absalom. He tears his robe and cries, "O Lord, I pray that you will make the advice of Ahithophel to my son be nothing but foolishness!"

With trembling voice he turns to another advisor, his dedicated friend Hushai, "I want you to return to Jerusalem to give instruction to my son. Hopefully your words will override the counsel of Ahithophel."

While it is natural for David to grieve just at the thought of Ahithophel's treason, his distress seems so deep. Why? Why did Ahithophel turn against David so readily after he had served him for so many years? Because Ahithophel is the grandfather of Bathsheba! (See 2 Samuel 23:34–35.) All these years vengeance for the dishonor placed on his lovely granddaughter must have silently seethed in his heart.

In addition, Ahithophel had undoubtedly loved Uriah very much and had considered it an honor to have such a recognized warrior in the family. Since Uriah had served on the battlefield with Ahithophel's son, Eliam, he had firsthand knowledge of Uriah's loyalty to his fellow soldiers and his dedication to the kingdom and the sacred ark.

It seems that Ahithophel, like a caged lion, has awaited his opportunity to get even. Now at last the door of vengeance is flung open. The moment of retribution has arrived!

Back in Jerusalem Ahithophel advises, "Absalom, gather your father's concubines and lie with them. Then all of Israel will see you've betrayed your father beyond any chance of reconciliation. Witnessing your strength over him, they'll claim you as their king."

A tent is pitched on the roof of the palace so everyone in the kingdom can behold Absalom as he commits sexual acts with King David's concubines. What disgrace! It is a true display of treason for Absalom and a triumphant day of revenge for Ahithophel.

We might wonder what Ahithophel would have dreamed up next, but we can never know for sure. In answer to David's prayer, when his trustworthy friend Hushai arrives on the scene, Absalom prizes his advice over Ahithophel's. But does Ahithophel care that much? Probably not. He's found his satisfaction in his long-awaited day of reprisal.

Full-fledged war breaks out, and David pleads with his men to spare Absalom's life in combat. Perhaps David plans to pardon the despicable acts of his son when the fighting ends and finally settle their differences with love and forgiveness. But if so, his desire to make things right comes too late. In spite of his appeal, Absalom perishes during the battle. His long thick hair gets caught in a tree, and one of David's men kills him while he hangs there. What a horrible and unnecessary death.

When King David, now back at the palace, receives the dreadful news of his son, he rushes to his chamber with bursting heart. Wailing through his tears he cries, "Oh, my son Absalom! My son, my son Absalom! I wish I had died instead of you! Oh, my son Absalom!"

Overcome by shame and grief, the men who betrayed King David for Absalom's reign creep quietly back into the city. Weeping engulfs the entire population. Tragedy prevails, outweighing any triumph. Oh, the price of sin.

> For they have sown the wind, and they shall reap the whirlwind.
>
> —HOSEA 8:7

David's personal life exploded into a total mess beginning with his fleshly appetite for Bathsheba. How differently the chronicles of history would read if David had exercised restraint and turned away from carnal pleasure. But instead we read of his treacherous act that bred a lifetime of diabolic hostility for himself, his family, and his right-hand man Ahithophel.

Sin ruined his model as a father. How could David, tarnished as he was, punish his son Amnon for the brutal rape of his virgin daughter Tamar? The tainted shadow of his uncontrolled lust for Bathsheba hung like a noose around his neck.

How could he denounce his son Absalom's blatant sexual conspiracy against his kingship, after his own betrayal of his friend and confidant Uriah? Even the passing of years could not erase the fact that he not only stole Uriah's wife but also took his life.

David couldn't even condemn the blasphemous disloyalty of his trusted and long-time advisor Ahithophel. Understanding of the reason for Ahithophel's rebellion must have surfaced in the recesses of his heart. As an employee of the king, Ahithophel had only been able to stand silently by while David disgraced his granddaughter and set her husband up for slaughter.

Oh, the payment for sin! Despite the gift of God's forgiveness, consequences still demand their toll. Though David readily fell on his knees before God each time he sinned, all his sorrow and regret could not erase the repercussions of his wrongdoings.

At the prophet's rebuke, David sought forgiveness for his sexual sin with Bathsheba and his murder of Uriah. In great remorse he composed this psalm:

> Have mercy upon me, O God, according to thy loving-kindness: according unto the multitude of thy tender mercies blot out my transgressions. Wash me thoroughly from mine iniquity, and cleanse me from my sin. For I acknowledge my transgressions: and my sin is ever before me.... Hide thy face from my sins, and blot out all mine iniquities. Create in me a clean heart, O God; and renew a right spirit within me.
>
> —PSALM 51:1–3, 9–10

Did God accept David's repentance? Did He forget his evil deeds?

Yes, we know He did. With everlasting blessings God honored him. God forgave David so completely that He called him a man after His own heart and gave him a throne from which the government of Christ extends forever.

> Of the increase of his [the Messiah's] government and peace there shall be no end, upon the throne of David, and upon his kingdom, to order it, and to establish it with judgment and with justice from henceforth even for ever. The zeal of the LORD of hosts will perform this.
>
> —ISAIAH 9:7

And He blessed his lineage. Although the son conceived out of wedlock died, the second son of David and Bathsheba followed his father as God's appointed king. Solomon, the man endowed with untold wisdom, was anointed to build the spectacular temple in Jerusalem. He was named by Matthew in the lineage of the Messiah. Yes, we can say with certainty that at David's repentance God forgave and forgot his sins.

The achievements of David's public life add up to definite success starting with his victory over Goliath, continuing through his flight from King Saul, and culminating in his reign as king. Despite his personal shortcomings he is looked upon as the greatest statesman in the history of Jewish monarchy.[3]

Few, if any, have ever outranked David's performance as a mighty warrior, a highly respected leader, and a master of diplomacy. In the hands of Yahweh he succeeded in establishing a strong government and forging a common bond of unity in Israel. He promoted a healthy sense of pride among the Jewish people and made Jerusalem a great capital city and a focal point for his people.

Even with all his faults, his spirit stayed attuned to the higher things of God. What a marvelous composer he was as he opened his heart in the beauty of his psalms. How musically talented he must have been to be invited as a youngster to play his harp in the courts of King Saul.

What respect he demonstrated for God's anointed when a jealous Saul turned against him, hunting him like a criminal, seeking to murder him. Yet David refused to take Saul's life even when opportunity arose. What dedication David displayed in friendship and endearing love for Jonathan, showing kindness to his crippled son Mephibosheth long after the death of his faithful friend. David, with his sins and successes, shows us the most human and loveable character of the Old Testament.

How exciting it is to realize that someday all who are in heaven will meet King David face-to-face. And how assuring it is to realize that the God of David still forgives today.

Although he was forgiven, David reaped the consequences of his sin. Perhaps things would have turned out better if he would have fully pardoned his son Absalom for the murder of his rapist son Amnon (just as God gave him full pardon for the death of Uriah, an innocent man). But he didn't. He suffered the repercussions of his ungodly choices until his dying day.

The Bible refers to him as "old and stricken in years" at his death (1 Kings 1:1). Yet David, who became king at age thirty and reigned for forty years, was only seventy when he died. Even when he was bedfast near the end of his life, havoc still persisted in his royal household. His son Adonijah schemed to overthrow Solomon, the son David had named as his successor. Physically broken, with a pathetic legacy as a father, David departed this life. Yet because of God's forgiveness he soared in death to heights beyond the realm of mortals, to a place where his reign is everlasting.

Oh, the wonders of God's perfect forgiveness. Oh, the glories of His faithfulness that pardons and forgets when we turn to Him in sorrow for our sins. Yes, we are fickle and foolish. However, He doesn't choose only perfect hearts, but accepts our broken and contrite hearts as we admit our sins, repent, and turn away from evil deeds.

What a compassionate, loving Lord we serve. A God of total forgiveness and supernatural forgetfulness, He says, "For I will forgive their iniquity, and I will remember their sin no more" (Jer. 31:34).

The majority of Christians never fall prey to willful acts of blatant wrongdoings like David. But if we do, what a consolation to know that we can renew our hearts to Him in repentance and receive the mercy and grace of His forgiveness and forgetfulness—just as David did.

WE ALL FALL short. "For all have sinned, and come short of the glory of God" (Rom. 3:23).

The apostle John uses a Greek word for sin that means to simply miss the mark with God. He tells us, "If we say that we have no sin, we deceive ourselves, and the truth is not in us" (1 John 1:8).

All of us miss the mark at times.

How well I know the results of falling short and the hopelessness in straying from His perfect will. Jim and I, floundering in our sea of debt and reluctance to tithe, lost sight of how to rest in God. How could we have been so blind to think that our own efforts could ever set us free?

Stretched between two jobs, I hardly saw Jim anymore. Even with our combined income, we barely made ends meet. While we managed to pay the interest on our loans, our debt remained the same. And we continued to put our money into a "bag with holes." Something had to give.

One day it did—but in a much different manner than I expected.

"Are you OK! Can you hear me?" A deep voice bellowed from outside my smashed car window.

"Yes, but my right arm is broken," I yelled upside down in the tangled wreckage. Reaching for the key with my left hand, I shut off the smoking engine. "If you'll cut my seat belt I can get out."

"You'll have to wait for help to come."

"No! If I can get this seat belt loose I will get out!"

Again using my left hand I managed to unlatch the lap belt, but the strap over my left shoulder remained taut. "Please help me!"

"No, I can't. You'll have to wait."

"How can I dangle upside down until help arrives?" I yanked at the belt with my uninjured fingers until at last I wriggled free. At that exact moment the stranger jerked the passenger door open. I scrambled out and crouched on the ground.

In dismay I stared at my arm. My crushed forearm, a zigzagging monstrosity, dangled from my mangled elbow. With my other arm, I cuddled it against my chest and waited for the ambulance.

Mist had tinted the sky gray as I set out for work that fateful day. With my never-ending schedule the hour's drive would have been a drudgery except that it had become my only time alone with God. I generally chose this route through winding countryside because it had less traffic and yielded better concentration for fellowship with Him.

As I drove that morning I prayed, *Heavenly Father, please deliver me from this rat race. Free me from this job. Lead me to Your purpose for me.* I began repeating over and over, *In Jesus' name ... in Jesus' name ...*

Rounding a curve I tapped my brakes as I met a car. My brakes locked up, and the damp pavement reacted like a road of ice. In the next instant my car skidded in a circle to the right, plowing head-on into a tree and flipping over.

Through it all my spirit kept whispering, *In Jesus' name... in Jesus' name.* And in the middle of confusion I felt calm.

It wasn't until later that fear tried to sneak in. Following surgery and several days in the hospital, I returned home with internal pins and plates holding my shattered bones together. An external fixture, which would stay in place for three months, protruded from my arm. During this time I would not be able to work. How could we make it?

My natural inclinations said, *Sink into depression; accept defeat.* After the loss of our store, Jim's job loss and our relocation life consisted of never-ending financial struggle. *Where are You, Lord?* my heart cried. Down deep I knew that He had never left me. And as I turned to Him instead of self-pity, He used my broken bones as a stepping stone back into His glory.

Nursing my arm alone at home, I found myself with hours of quiet fellowship with Him for the first time in several years. Depression left as I threw myself into His Word. His presence, soft and gentle, calmed my soul and assured me of His ever-abiding love. And He began to show me the error of my ways.

When I took on a second job, Jim and I had intended to start tithing again. And we had at times. But we had not become dedicated churchgoers since our move because I worked many Sundays.

Now we began attending church on a regular basis again, and we repented of our failure to tithe. Even with my inability to bring in income, we faithfully gave our 10 percent, knowing that God would meet out needs. And He did.

God never fails His children. When we do our part, He fulfills His promise in Malachi 3:10. He opens the windows of heaven and pours out blessings until they overflow. Within three years of my accident, our business debt was paid in full, and He furnished us with a debt-free car and truck as a bonus.

As soon as I could use my hand, I exercised it by writing lessons from His Word. This is what I used to do before my life filled up with busyness. *Why am I writing these?* I wondered. *I have nowhere to teach them.*

Then I heard His gentle voice, *Write them in a book.*

And that is how this book was born.

At last I knew the underlying reason for our business failure. I had not obeyed God.

Twelve years before in the spring of 1983, I had been in an undesirable job situation. I had asked God to show me His will for my life, and He had immediately led me to a verse in Ezekiel. As surely as if He had spoken in an audible voice it sprang to life within my heart:

> Then the spirit entered into me, and set me upon my feet, and spake with me, and said unto me, Go, shut thyself within thine house.
> —EZEKIEL 3:24

I knew, of course, that these words were given to Ezekiel thousands of centuries ago. Yet they also brought me to a personal encounter with the Lord. That's the wonder of His Word. It remains so alive that sometimes it just leaps into our hearts! Verse 27 says, "But when I speak with thee, I will open thy mouth, and thou shalt say unto them, Thus saith the Lord GOD..."

God gave me the same awareness of His presence as I had sensed when He put Psalm 27:13–14 in my heart and comforted me as I waited on Him in the dilemma of my son's addiction. (See chapter five.) At the moment I read God's Word in Ezekiel 3, I felt God calling me to stay at home and write for Him.

I had always loved writing, even as a child. In my early twenties I graduated from an extensive correspondence school in creative writing. After this I wrote articles and feature stories for local newspapers, more as a hobby than anything else.

But write full time? Did I have such courage and faith? I needed the income from my job. With Jim's support I quit work and disciplined myself. That summer I sat at the typewriter every day and wrote diligently.

But how short that lasted! In the fall my father approached Jim and me with the idea of an outlet clothing business. Without much thinking or serious prayer, we jumped in head first. Then came the merry-go-round, the roller coaster, the sinking ship.

What a long road we traveled to come back to God's will! God didn't cause our business to crash, but He wasn't included in our decision and it wasn't His purpose for me. God didn't break my arm. He didn't tell me to get two jobs and stretch myself beyond my limit. Everything that happened was the result of my own wrong decisions and my disobedience to His will.

Oh, what consequences we suffer when we miss the mark. But what joy we find in His forgiveness.

After three months, the external fixture on my crushed bone was removed. However, the bone collapsed, and I returned to surgery for a bone graft. (This was when I met God in His heavenly realm and witnessed His tunnel of vivid lights, as I told in chapter two.)

"You'll spend at least six months in physical therapy after this surgery," my family doctor told me.

A friend who had suffered a broken elbow said, "You'll never be able to straighten your arm completely again."

"You will always have pain, and without a doubt you'll develop arthritis," a nurse insisted.

"No," I said, "I will not have pain or arthritis."

"Yes, you will," she said. "I'm a nurse, and I know!"

Oh, the power of faith and the blessings of submission and obedience. My spirit kept claiming, *My God is bigger than that!* I spoke the Word, "By His stripes I am healed! He is the Lord my God who healeth me! I will not forget His benefits—that He forgives my iniquities, heals all my diseases, saves my life from destruction, crowns me with loving kindness and tender mercy! He is the Sun of Righteousness with healing in His wings!" I fed daily on Psalm 91.

Within three weeks following the bone graft the surgeon completely dismissed me. I did not have one physical therapy session, and my arm and elbow have been as good for past ten years now. Other than a few scars I have no reminder of my injury—no pain, no arthritis, no restraints.

I have one last word about our business debt. We found a church and started faithfully tithing and giving again. For the most part I stayed at home, selling life insurance and mutual funds part-time. Even with less income all our needs were met and our debt dwindled. By His goodness God provided money to pay two sizeable notes in full. But one large note still remained.

One day in 1998, as we heard a pastor preach on the Year of Jubilee, Jim and I both felt the Holy Spirit nudge us to forgive all the debts of those who owed us money. Although this amounted to a hefty sum, we told each of them, "You no longer owe us anything."

Three days later we received a phone call. Although the person on the line knew nothing about our decision to cancel the debts others owed us, the lender of our last remaining note spoke these words, "You no longer owe me anything. I'm canceling your note."

The last of our business debts was erased! What a supernatural God we serve. How great is His faithfulness. When we repent, He forgives all our disobedience and remembers it no more.

Are you missing the mark with God? Compromising His will for your life? Harboring bitterness for someone? Refusing to trust Him with your giving and tithing?

Ask God's forgiveness and start anew. Make things right with those you have wronged. Do good to those who have wronged you and completely forgive them. Commit your finances to kingdom principles. Choose to live in the center of His will.

You may face consequences for past actions, but His strength will pull you through. You will find that you can soar with Him into the heights above all worry and despair. Not only will He provide your daily bread, but He will also bless you in ways you never imagined.

God's faithfulness is real, and His forgiveness is certain.

Chapter 12

Deliver Us From Evil

TEENAGERS—WHAT EASY PREY for the tempter! He slips in unawares with his hordes of demonic forces disguised in garments of excitement, curiosity, and glamour. His evil design is more than simply having them stretch the truth to their parents, cheat on a history test, or steal a best friend's sweetheart. Satan sets out to lure these fun-seeking future leaders of society into his sticky web of intrigue that soon holds them so tightly they may never get loose.

What an enticing game he plays! He dangles alcohol, drugs, tobacco, permissive sex, and the mystical world of the occult like delicious bait within easy reach. Then he dares these young inquisitive minds to nibble. With an addictive hook embedded inside his seductions, he aims to puncture unsuspecting souls with deadly poison until they no longer fight for freedom. How subtle are his tactics.

It was a hot, boring day after school. Two of my classmates, Penny and Trish, listened to Elvis records with me in my bedroom. Friends since elementary school, we had hiked over all the surrounding farmland, hung from every tree limb possible and secretly swam in every muddy pond.

But in those days we had simply been mischievous little brats. Now we had grown too big for such baby stuff. Now we were seniors in high school—practically adults.

Sitting cross-legged in the center of my bed with a mirror propped on her lap, Penny dabbed her long lashes with mascara, dotted rouge on her high cheekbones, and painted her full lips pink. Smacking them together she jumped up and said, "Let's go somewhere!"

With her blonde ponytail bouncing, Trish nodded in agreement and leaped up, too. I shut off the record player.

"What can we do for fun?" I said hurriedly brushing through my poodle haircut and powering my nose to conceal embarrassing freckles. "Where can we go?"

"I know," Trish chimed in, her blue eyes shining. "We can go to a fortune-teller! I know where one lives."

"How far is it?" asked Penny, who had driven her parents' car to my house. "I can drive if it's not too far." She glanced at her watch. "We can't be gone long though."

With Penny behind the wheel we all piled in the front seat. "Turn here," Trish pointed and giggled as we wove down narrow streets in a remote section of town. "There's the house," she finally said.

I expected to spot a sign displaying "palm reader" or "fortune-teller." But this unpainted shack not only lacked identifying markings, it also appeared deserted. Stepping with Trish onto a rickety porch Penny and I questioned together, "Are you sure we're at the right place?

"Positive. I've been here before," Trish assured us as she banged on a torn screen door.

A tiny lady with black shriveled skin and white woolly hair appeared. Her shoulders were stooped, and she leaned on a cane as she walked on wobbly legs. Squinting her eyes, she peered at us over round wire-rimmed glasses, recognized Trish, and smiled. In a trembling voice she invited us inside. My heart went out to her, and I immediately began fishing in my purse for a donation to get my fortune told.

As we stepped into the front room, a combination bedroom and living area, its sultriness bombarded us. The air hung thick with funny smells like a mixture of mildew, stale smoke, and incense. With heavy drapes drawn over the windows, hazy shadows hovered all around.

She pointed and said, "You can sit on my bed."

With wrinkled noses we glanced at each other and grinned while she pulled up a wooden chair to face us. Then one by one she held each of our hands and studied our palms. No longer did I notice her frailness, the shaking of her voice, or our surroundings. *How can she know these things?* I wondered.

She told me that I had met a young man and fallen in love, but a problem had arisen. "You have a major decision to make. You must choose between the advice of people you highly admire and the call of love on your life. Always remember," she said, "love never gives a wrong answer. Love never fails."

Only a few months later, ignoring my parents' warning I made my mistake in marriage. Would I have done so without the fortune-teller's encouragement?

Maybe so. But once I swallowed this bait of psychic powers, my mind was deeply influenced by the mystical realm of the unnatural. A door into demonic darkness, cracked open earlier by foolish childhood games, now swung wide open.

My first actual taste of the occult occurred when as a youngster, a friend and I tinkered with a Ouija board. We also amused ourselves with an "eight ball" that answered questions when it was turned upside down. Even our parents viewed these games as harmless play, but without a doubt they set the stage for the uncanny predictions of the fortune-teller to sway me fully into the intrigue of supernatural phenomena.

Oh, I didn't forget Jesus. I didn't fail to go to church or say prayers. But I knew so little about the profound nature of God or His Word. Sure, I knew some things about sin—that murder, stealing, lying, and immoral sex headed a list of forbidden acts—but no one ever mentioned the occult. Never did I hear it taught that fortune-telling, divination, horoscopes, witchcraft, reincarnation, and even superstition, hypnotism, and handwriting analysis are abominations to a holy God—and straight from the pits of hell.

Observing my ignorance, a few years later the deceiver shrewdly threw out more enticement.

Shortly after the drowning incident with my daughter, as I was marveling at her miraculous resurrection, Satan pounced on another opportunity to allure me. *Reader's Digest* published a condensed book about the clairvoyant Jeanne Dixon.[1] Astonished by the reported accuracies of her supposed predictions, I bought her full-length book, and soon other articles about her found their way into my library.

How shrewdly the devil works. Mrs. Dixon claimed that her ability to see future events in a crystal ball was a talent from God. Described as a warm and friendly person whose days began with devotion at her church, she sounded so virtuous. A loving wife, she even prayed over the bushes she planted in her garden.

I swallowed it all—hook, line, and sinker. Why could I not decipher the obvious? Even common sense eluded me.

Her prophetic ability began as a child when a snake coiled itself around her body. In its eyes she beheld what she called the all-knowing wisdom of the ages. A snake! This alone should have alerted me that her power represented anything but godliness. Would God send a *snake* to bestow a prophetic gift from Him? No!

In the Garden of Eden the serpent promised all-knowing wisdom to Eve if she ate of the forbidden fruit, "...then your eyes shall be opened, and ye shall be as gods, knowing good and evil" (Gen. 3:5).

How could I not have seen the similarities? But I was so blind and ignorant. Snared by Satan's lures, wading in the dangers of demonic worship wrapped in colorful deceit, I sank deeper into a state of vulnerability and confusion.

WHAT EXCUSE CAN I give for not knowing the devil's trickery? None. I should have known. When a person seeks any source other than the Word of God for answers, he is turning to another god. Yes, I should have known.

Throughout the Bible God gives warnings about dabbling in such forbidden areas. Yahweh's voice speaks plainly about seeking advice, searching for answers, or placing trust in any but Himself. Four of the Ten Commandments, the only revelation to man that God wrote with His own finger, demand that He alone must be worshiped.

The first two commandments emphatically declare:

> Thou shalt have no other gods before me. Thou shalt not make unto thee any graven image, or any likeness of anything that is in heaven above, or that is in the earth beneath, or that is in the water under the earth. Thou shalt not bow down thyself to them, nor serve them: for I the LORD thy God am a jealous God.
>
> —EXODUS 20:3–5

His Word never varies in commanding us to totally worship Him, look only to Him, and wholly rely on His wisdom. By the prophet Jeremiah He exclaims:

> Don't act like the people who make horoscopes and try to read their fate and future in the stars!
>
> —JEREMIAH 10:2, TLB

Take heed also in His orders to the Hebrews before they entered the Promised Land:

No Israeli may practice black magic, or call on evil spirits for aid, or be a fortune teller, or be a serpent charmer, medium, or wizard, or call forth spirits of the dead. Anyone doing these things is an object of horror and disgust to the Lord, and it is because the nations do these things that the Lord your God will displace them.

—Deuteronomy 18:10–12, TLB

Could it be any plainer? God pronounced destruction upon all nations that indulge in occult worship! Today I cringe to think of the countless games, toys, books, movies, and even cartoons that have occult overtones. I fear for the many naive girls who conduct seances at slumber parties... the teens who experiment with mind-altering drugs, indulge in hard-rock music, and feed on horror movies . . . the millions who read their daily horoscopes "for fun."

Any believer who lacks instruction and insight into God's Word wanders through life as defenseless as a baby toddling toward an open pool of quicksand. "My people are destroyed for lack of knowledge," the Lord cautions in Hosea 4:6. So many go through life never knowing a true spiritual realm exists. But believe me when I tell you that a world beyond our human perception is alive and real!

My heart erupted like an atomic bomb inside my chest as I staggered from the lawyer's office in January 1969. I had just finished my first counseling session, which initiated divorce proceedings.

In a state of grief I drove to the outskirts of the city. With tears streaming down my face I whipped into a busy shopping center. Maybe I could gain composure in a crowd of strangers. Maybe focusing on after-Christmas bargains would take my mind off the days ahead. Maybe then I'd find the courage to go home and face my tomorrows—as a single mom. *Oh,* I cried, *what happened to the "love that never fails?"*

Perhaps these words I penned those many years ago can best express the emotions I felt. Even after all this time they still echo the agony of my soul that day.

Only yesterday you loved me,

Yesterday it's true,

You wanted me to be with you,
But that was yesterday,
I reached out, you turned away,
It seems so long ago,

A thousand years ago I'd say,
But it was only yesterday.
I must begin my life anew
Forget the yesterday I knew,
Where once we walked now I must tread
With so much left undone, unsaid.
Our future plans, our hopes, our dreams,
An eternity away it seems,
But as you turn to go I know
That they were only yesterday.
I cannot live in yesterday,
The memories must fade away,
And I must find myself again,
The yesterday I knew must end.
Tomorrow is all that I have now,
I must forget the past somehow...
But a son and daughter turn to me,
And yesterday is all I see.

With feeble steps I made my way across the parking lot to a variety store. A little something to take home to the kids would be nice. Deep breaths held my tears at bay while I shuffled through packaged toys dangling on a peg board.

"Why, hello," came a voice at my side. "How was your Christmas?"

I turned to face a slight acquaintance and fellow member of our community club. An immaculate woman with dark thick hair flowing to her shoulders, a creamy complexion, and a graceful walk, her charm always impressed me. Now dressed in a bright holiday sweater and accompanied by her husband who was pushing a cart brimming with sales items, her cheery smile was more than I could bear.

No words would emerge. Without explanation I turned away from her and fled the store.

Afterwards I ached with regret for my abrupt action and my surmise that she probably thought I had deliberately shunned her. I felt I owed her an apology, yet I wasn't even sure of her last name to find her phone number.

Since I was living in a sizable city, the odds of bumping into the same person again while I was shopping would be beyond reason. Yet only a week later it happened again—this time downtown, a considerable distance from the shopping center.

Immediately I began to explain my brusque departure, and without stopping I unloaded the dilemma of my marriage. Over a cup of coffee our friendship blossomed. We discovered that we both lived in the same suburb not far from each other. And she related how as a young person she, too, had gone through divorce.

"Why some things happen to us is hard to understand, but maybe I can help you," she said. "I'm an astrologer. Would you let me study your horoscope?"

She needed the exact places and times when my husband and I were born, and I obtained this information right away. A few days later I visited her house.

"How astonishing!" I exclaimed as I read the results of her stargazing profile. "Without ever meeting my husband you describe him to a tee. And these things about me, so accurate."

How I welcomed this new friendship. I no longer had family nearby. Three years earlier my husband and I relocated to this city after a separation in our marriage. Even though I placed high hopes in our recommitment to each other within two months after our move the same pattern of problems began all over. Before I sought divorce proceedings, I desperately sought marital direction from two pastors. Neither offered any biblical advice or guidance—but instead fled the scene of my agony like a deer from a hunter. I felt so deserted and alone, not knowing where to turn for help. In Beth, the astrologer, I found a listening ear, someone to understand my pain and help repair my heart.

With compassion she took me under her wing. I basked in her kindness and we became the best of companions. Treating my children and me like family members, she and her husband invited us on weekend trips to meet their relatives. Often they planned adventures that included my children along with their grandchildren—like a day at the zoo, excursions to car racing events that my son adored, educational outings to art galleries and special shows. After my divorce I moved back to my hometown to live near my parents, but for a time I remained in close touch with Beth, sometimes visiting on weekends.

Yes, believe me when I tell you there is a spiritual world beyond our human realm! The bizarre phenomenon I now share happened during one weekend stay at Beth's house...

My children slept together in one bedroom, and Beth and her husband in another. I lay awake alone in a bedroom across the hall. Sleep evaded me, and an unexplainable sensation fluttered in my chest. An uncanny stillness, a stony quietness, hovered around me like a dark, thick cloud.

And in a flash it happened!

Beth's poodle pierced the night's silence with shrill barking from another room. At that precise instant a gleaming circle of light appeared before my eyes.

How strange! Unlike the beam of a flashlight that follows the wall, this light floated in suspension. In its center I saw the head of a man whose beady eyes gazed down at me. An odd-looking page-boy hairstyle framed his round and aged face, and with a glimmer of admiration he smiled.

Then in a split second the brightness with its image disappeared. At that exact time the dog stopped barking. As though captivated by a mystical spell, I experienced no fright, not even the slightest tinge of anxiety. Instantly I fell asleep and slept soundly through the rest of the night.

Rising the next morning I burst with excitement to tell Beth about the incident. I found her at the kitchen table sipping coffee. "Did Rebel's barking wake you last night?" I asked.

"No. I'm sorry. Did he keep you awake?"

Without hestitating I blurted out the bizarre details. As I talked, Beth began to chuckle. "Oh, I just know that was my dad!" she said. "He always admired redheads, and he just wanted to meet you. Evidently he is waiting to be reincarnated."

She leaped from her chair. "I'll be right back."

As she hurried from the kitchen, her long velvet robe swished gracefully. In a few minutes she returned, thumbing through an old photo album as she walked over to my side. "Did he look like this?"

I gasped. Before my eyes she held a picture of the same face I had seen the night before. Although the hairstyle was different, the facial features were exactly the same. Without a doubt the apparition was the likeness of her dead father!

In time, Beth and I drifted apart. I met Jim and remarried. After her husband died, she remarried and moved away. While our beliefs may differ, at a time when I needed help, she reached out in love, and I appreciate her kindness deeply. I pray that wherever she is today she knows Jesus as God's Son.

When I told two people very close to me about this bizarre phenomenon, they responded with ridicule and unbelief. After that, I kept it bottled in my heart, not daring to reveal it to another soul for years. During that period the vision at Beth's home played silent havoc in my mind. Before it I doubted reincarnation. Afterwards I wasn't sure what to believe. *Where do the spirits of people go after death?* I questioned. *Do they float around waiting for another life? Do people really live one life after another until they reach a level of perfection? How else could this apparition of Beth's father be explained?*

As I indulged in psychic books the battle raged in me. If reincarnation is real, what about the other things they taught? I read that Jesus was not really the Son of God—He was only a great prophet like Buddha, Muhammad, or Edgar Cayce. Were they right? How could I know for sure?

Several years later, discovering the depth of God's Holy Word, I found the truth I needed. But until then I carried a heavy weight of uncertainty like an anchor in my heart.

TRAVEL WITH ME now into the sphere of spiritual warfare. Hopefully you'll emerge with belief in the existence of a spiritual world with active satanic forces and find insight to identify their source. Only then can you learn to fully stand against their might. Friends, with all my heart I stress that the powers of the devil remain alive, active, and dangerous in this unsuspecting secular world today.

But with God comes victory. Overcome demonic forces by letting the knowledge of His Word reign in you:

> You are of God, little children, and have overcome them, because He who is in you is greater than he who is in the world.
>
> —1 JOHN 4:4, NKJV

Knowing the reality of the spiritual realm, stand guard and never allow the devil's cunning bait to trap you in his web.

> For we wrestle not against flesh and blood, but against principalities, against powers, against the rulers of the darkness of this world, against spiritual wickedness in high places.
>
> —EPHESIANS 6:12

In the next venture on our treasure map, the Jubilee Express begins a chilling trip of many miles until we gain strength to win over temptations, win victory over the kingdom of darkness, and by new insight realize the importance of this prayer:

AND LEAD US NOT INTO TEMPTATION, BUT DELIVER US FROM EVIL

"What a dilapidated depot!" a member of our group exclaims.

With reservation we approach its entrance. The midnight air sends a chill up our spines, and bitter dread squeezes at our hearts as we step inside to wait. Black spiders dangle in every corner hoping for a victim. Bats flutter among the rafters. A rat scurries across the floor. Shivering we gather in a cluster and stare out a window, longing for our glory train to show up.

A light bursts through the darkness. "Here it comes!" someone shouts. "The Jubilee Express has arrived!"

As it screeches into the station, a bed of hibernating snakes awaken in its path and slither across the tracks into the night. Without warning jagged streaks of lightning split the inky sky. The heavens tremble in an aftermath of booms, and within seconds icy needles of rain plummet down on us as we make our way across the outside platform to the train.

We push inside the security of our train and seek our Conductor. As we grope for seats in the darkness we yell for Him in panic.

Instantly He comes to us. Our cabin floods with the light of His presence. Shamefaced we duck our heads. Didn't we realize that He never leaves us or forsakes us? But He isn't angry. How wonderful to feel His compassion and know His grace.

We sigh with blessed relief. Even when night hovers all around us, we need not fear. In His kingdom ways and with Him at our side evil never wins. And nothing or anyone has the power to come between us and His love.

> Who shall separate us from the love of Christ? shall tribulation, or distress, or persecution, or famine, or nakedness, or peril, or sword?...Nay, in all these things we are more than conquerors through him that loved us. For I am persuaded, that neither death, nor life, nor angels, nor principalities, nor powers, nor things present, nor things to come, nor height, nor depth, nor any other creature, shall be able to separate us from the love of God, which is in Christ Jesus our Lord.
> —ROMANS 8:35, 37–39

The wee hours of the night close in around our train. Except for the mighty pounding of the rain and the rumbling of the wheels on the track, all is silent now. Shielded by the comfort of our Conductor we no longer need to fear.

Glowing through the eerie darkness, our scarlet rails stretch ahead in reassuring splendor. From the deepest abyss of sin to the most wretched wickedness in high places, they will remain faithful to lead us out of harm's way as we travel on the Jubilee Express. Oh, but never be complacent. We must always stay alert!

Be careful—watch out for attacks from Satan, your great enemy. He prowls around like a hungry, roaring lion, looking for some victim to tear apart. Stand firm when he attacks. Trust the Lord.

—1 PETER 5:8–9, TLB

Satan is the tempter (Matt. 4:3; 1 Thess. 3:5), a murderer from the beginning and the father of lies (John 8:44). Aided by his hosts of fallen angels and demons (Eph. 6:12), he seeks to steal, kill, and destroy (John 10:10).

By all means, tuck these things into your memory bank. Bind them to your heart so that you never doubt the extent of Satan's maliciousness, and never fall victim to his seductive bait or fail to understand the eternal danger of his traps. Don't ignore his tactics, reason him away, or be ignorant of his vicious strategies of war against the kingdom of God. Always be on guard!

Deliver us from evil actually means "Deliver us from the evil one," and some versions of the Bible state it this way. Few characters are cited so broadly and explicitly in Scripture as this evil one who is described as the prince of demons (Matt. 12:24), the prince of the power of the air (Eph. 2:2), the prince of this world (John 14:30), the ruler of darkness (Eph. 6:12), the wicked one (Matt. 13:19), and the god of this world (2 Cor. 4:4).

His titles include Satan, the devil, Lucifer (Isa. 14:12), Beelzebub (Matt. 12:24), Belial (2 Cor. 6:15). Revelation 9:11 calls him Abaddon, Apollyon, and the angel of the bottomless pit. In Revelation 12:9 he is the great dragon and the old serpent who deceives the whole world. He was the serpent in the Garden of Eden (Gen. 3:4).

Yet what a most beautiful anointed cherub he was in the beginning—the highly esteemed Lucifer, who occupied an honored position.

> Thus says the Lord GOD: "You were the signet of perfection, full of wisdom and perfect in beauty. You were in Eden, the garden of God; every precious stone was your covering...and wrought in gold were your settings and your engravings....With an anointed guardian cherub I placed you; you were on the holy mountain of God; in the midst of the stones of fire you walked. You were blameless in your ways from the day you were created, till iniquity was found in you."
>
> —EZEKIEL 28:12–15, RSV

Filled with pride, Lucifer rebelled against the supreme authority of his almighty Creator.

> You said in your heart, "I will ascend to heaven; above the stars of God I will set my throne on high; I will sit on the mount of assembly

in the far north; I will ascend above the heights of the clouds, I will make myself like the Most High."

—ISAIAH 14:13–14, RSV

In his rebellion he enlisted one-third of the angels in heaven and rose up against the almighty power of the God of all the ages.

> And there was war in heaven: Michael and his angels fought against the dragon; and the dragon fought and his angels. And prevailed not; neither was their place found any more in heaven. And the great dragon was cast out, that old serpent called the Devil, and Satan, which deceiveth the whole world: he was cast out into the earth, and his angels were cast out with him.
>
> —REVELATION 12:7–9

From the time he was cast out of heaven, Satan turned wild, inflamed with an evil passion to control every inch of Earth and its surrounding heavens. He craves every nation and every soul. His bloodthirsty wrath searches out any corner of the heart that is not totally submitted to God. If there is a single spot of compromise, a tiny speck of unforgiveness, one particle of doubt, any area of ignorance, a secret site of lust, Satan sends his flood of temptation into that locality.

The Jubilee Express speeds full blast into the dangers of his wicked domain, hurling us head-on toward the seductiveness of his temptations. To give us a buffer against the tempter, our Conductor steps out and teaches from the book of James:

> Blessed is the man that endureth temptation: for when he is tried, he shall receive a crown of life, which the Lord hath promised to them that love him.
>
> —JAMES 1:12

For our survival we must realize that God does not lead anyone into sin. He does not tempt anyone with evil.

> Let no man say when he is tempted, I am tempted of God: for God cannot be tempted with evil, neither tempteth he any man.
>
> —JAMES 1:13

God is never bad! He only bestows excellence. "Every good gift and every perfect gift is from above" (James 1:17).

We must engrave this in our thoughts and receive it in our spirit. Success against the forces of evil depends on it. God is good. God is love. Let us repeat this day by day and absorb its truth. God desires that all would be saved and know His glory. He does not want any to be pulled away by temptation:

> ...not willing that any should perish, but that all should come to repentance.
>
> —2 PETER 3:9

We also need to face the fact that we either turn away from or cave in to temptation by our own choice. Just as surely as repentance must come from each of us, we cannot shift blame to someone else when we yield to wrongful acts. The choice is our very own:

> But every man is tempted, when he is drawn away by his own lust, and enticed.
>
> —JAMES 1:14

Temptation stems from the devil. Giving in to his seduction leads to misery and eventually death.

> Then when lust hath conceived, it bringeth forth sin: and sin, when it is finished, bringeth forth death.
>
> —JAMES 1:15

This trip will not be easy. To win over temptation and defeat evil requires steady combat and a committed soul. We must stand strong for righteousness, or we will succumb to the world. Unless we resist we will knuckle under. Only a heart of submission to God can send the devil running!

> Submit yourselves therefore to God. Resist the devil, and he will flee from you.
>
> —JAMES 4:7

FEELING SECURE INSIDE the Jubilee Express, we roll along reclining in our seats. The rain lets up. A glow of dawn glitters on the scarlet rails ahead, and soon warm sunshine streams through the windows, shooing away the last trace of night. What a lovely day for traveling.

We feel the train slowing. Soon it stops, and we raise our seats to peer out with eager eyes. Why, look at this depot! It is so opposite from the depot where we boarded the train last night. Its polished windows reflect diamond sunbeams, causing a rainbow of colors to dance along its loading dock. A round bearded man in gray pinstripe overalls with a red bandanna knotted at his neck whistles a tune while he sweeps the walkway. He smiles as a spotted puppy frolics by him and chases a rolling ball. Not far behind laughing children follow.

The man calls, "Welcome!" as we step down from the train to view a charming village nestled in a misty valley. Its lines of quaint little shops and cobblestone streets beckon us to come. We're going shopping!

In ecstasy we inhale the tantalizing aromas of spices, exotic coffee, roasting meats, and pastries from a small sidewalk café. Our mouths water, but we don't stop. We stick close to our Conductor and hurry on, knowing that He will lead us to the right food for our hungry souls.

We pass by people who nod with happy faces and kind greetings. Our hearts sing with delight. The dreadful night lies far behind, and all evil seems to have vanished with the darkness. Surely nothing bad can lurk in such a pleasant town as this.

At first we stay in step with our Conductor. After a while, however, the temptation to do more than simply follow behind Him gets the best of us, and we linger to window shop. Just as we lose sight of Him, a handsome stranger begins to stroll along beside us. Dressed to the utmost in an exquisitely tailored business suit accented by a satin white shirt and red silk tie, he shines with great finesse. With captivating charm his black eyes twinkle as he smiles. Oh, how he sparks our curiosity.

"Come with me," he urges. "There are fortunes to be made, and fun is just beyond this street. It can all belong to you. I'll be your friend, teach you the ropes, show you the way. Hurry, follow me."

Oh, the walk on which he leads us. How easily we glide upon its marbled surface. This is like a fairytale! Fresh puffs of cotton candy cascade from barrels made of gingerbread and streetlights with peppermint poles line the curb. We linger under a tree that dangles chocolate kisses. Feeling hungry after our night's ordeal we desire to nibble the enticing goodies that surround us.

"Taste everything," urges the stranger.

Should we? No, we decide, *we need to check first with our Conductor.* Then we realize that we have strayed away from His perfect path. *But do we have to turn back now? This way is so enchanting.*

No, we decide, *we'll catch up with Him later.*

With a flick of his wrist the handsome man motions, and a shimmering carriage of gold drawn by spirited white horses pulls up. A free ride!

Without a thought we climb aboard. A balmy breeze delights our faces as we ride along on velvet seats until the carriage halts at the entrance of a charming park.

"Welcome to the playground of fanciful ideas. So much fun awaits!" the stranger sings out to us as he leaps to the sidewalk.

Gazing into the park over a gate gleaming like rubies, we spy a jovial crowd drinking from sparkling fountains and feasting at overflowing banquet tables. Many dance to alluring music. Some play games with silver coins. Still another group delights in watching panoramic episodes inside a colossal crystal ball that foretells their future. We can see into game rooms where people play on huge screens. Theaters and casinos line a walkway that seems to stretch for miles.

Spellbound, we descend from our ride to stand outside and observe. Moments later we move closer to the gate. We touch its ruby surface. *Dare we go inside?*

"Oh yes," the handsome stranger coaxes as if he read our minds. "It doesn't cost anything to enter and enjoy the pleasures."

We move eagerly to step through the gate, but a sudden Voice shrieks, "Beware! Evil lurks inside the park!"

We look around but see no one. *Where did the Voice come from? Maybe we should turn and run!* Then we realize that the Voice sounded from within our hearts. *Yes, probably we should go, but....*

The handsome stranger scoffs at our misgivings, "Could something so lovely and intriguing as this delightful place be bad? No, that warning was only a delusion that likely stemmed from strict religious upbringing. Don't pay heed to such nonsense. Can't you see that this park offers marvelous opportunity and bustles with fun and new friends? It's a relaxing retreat from the daily routine and humdrum living, an open door to wealth and fame."

Then he flashes his diamond watch, gold cuff links and tie tack, and a wallet fat with hundred-dollar bills. "Look at me. Am I a picture of defeat? This park made me the man I am. Don't tarry any longer. Step inside with me now while opportunity remains."

Our minds tingle with the temptation. *This place is so inviting and aglow with light and cheer, just as the nice man said. It can't be bad. After all, wouldn't evil be draped in black and filled with horror like our experience last night? Bats, spiders, rats and snakes, lightning, thunder and violent storms, coldness and darkness—isn't that the way evil shows its face?*

Oh, Conductor, where are you? Certainly you can tell us.

Instantly He appears among us. How wonderful it is to know that He always stands nearby waiting for our call, ready to answer with the Word of God.

> And no marvel; for Satan himself is transformed into an angel of light. Therefore it is no great thing if his ministers also be transformed as the ministers of righteousness; whose end shall be according to their works.
>
> —2 CORINTHIANS 11:14–15

Hearing this, we realize the mysterious Voice warning us about the park was actually the Holy Spirit who abides in our hearts. With our spiritual eyes opened, we now discern entangled souls slinking in shadows behind the dazzling glare of the park's alluring entertainments. Victims of despair, they are cold, alone, sold out to addictions. Compulsive gamblers, alcoholics, the drug dependent, gluttonous eaters, pornographers, compulsive shoppers, Internet slaves, computer-game fanatics, witches, sorcerers—all are hooked and out of control. How sad! They entered the ruby gates intending to participate in playground activities just a tiny bit. How quickly the enemy seduced them and then wrapped them in his hidden web inside the playground. And this is the park where we stood with hands on the gate, ready to go in!

We recall the parable of the sower and the way tender hearts can become baked, trampled, and choked. Our spirits weep in prayer for those who are bound inside the ruby gate, stumbling in darkness behind the glitter of the park, unable to find their way out.

As we turn to our Conductor, He shines in such bright splendor that the radiance of the park loses its luster. How false it was! Immediately its phony glamour fades away, leaving the whole vicinity cold and dreary.

Where is the handsome stranger who, camouflaged as a minister of righteousness, sought to misguide us? As our eyes spot him, he transforms into a grotesque imp that reeks of demonic filth. Anger floods his now twisted face as he steals through the gate that has also lost its attraction. Scowling at our revelation of his playground's hidden ugliness and doom, he vanishes into utter darkness.

Our Conductor reassures us, "I am the light of the world. He that follows Me will not walk in darkness, but will have the light of life" (from John 8:12).

The light of life shines strongly to lead us away from evil. It beams brightly to reveal the tempter's traps. It enlightens us to darkness. As we walk with the light we also shine with His glory.

"Ye are the light of the world!" He exclaims, "Let your light so shine before others so they can see your good works, and glorify your Father which is in Heaven" (from Matt. 5:14, 16).

Much wiser now, we continue in our excursion with great desire to overcome and expose the devil's kingdom. No longer tempted to stray, we march in the authority of the light of life, shining in His brightness, wearing our new light like armor to stand against the ploys of Satan.

> The night is far spent, the day is at hand: let us cast off the works of darkness, and let us put on the armour of light. Let us walk honestly, as in the day; not in rioting and drunkenness, not in chambering and wantonness, not in strife and envying. But put ye on the Lord Jesus Christ, and make not provision for the flesh, to fulfill the lusts thereof.
>
> —ROMANS 13:12–14

By keeping on our armor of light we can breathe in freedom from the seduction of the park. Oh, how close we came to falling headlong into his clutches of fleshly evil!

"The works of the flesh," our Conductor names each one, "are adultery, fornication, uncleanness, lewdness, idolatry, sorcery, hatred, contentions, jealousies, outbursts of wrath, selfish ambitions, dissensions, heresies, envy, murders, drunkenness, revelries. Those who practice such things will not inherit the kingdom of God!" (See Galatians 5:19–21, NKJV.)

How thankful we are to have the light of life!

Now safely shining in His brightness, in step with our Conductor we tread through hideous winding streets where the park once stood. Buildings flash neon signs that advertise girly shows and liquor. While shutters fit tight against all the windows and keep disapproving eyes at bay, we hear loud music and detect addictive sin and chaos inside. Without a doubt all the works of the flesh abound.

With all our strength we shine our lights into the darkness. A few lost souls emerge to receive the light of life with us. Hallelujah! Saved from the deceiver, they will join us on the Jubilee Express to glory! With high hopes we continue shining, encouraging others to come.

Clinging to the heels of our Conductor, at last we turn back onto the friendly cobblestone streets. Golden steams stretch down through clouds above as if to welcome our return. Look! On the sidewalk a vendor is pushing an old-fashion wooden wagon that brims with produce. How hungry we are for proper nourishment. With the consent of our Conductor we stop to make a special purchase.

THE FRUIT OF THE SPIRIT

> But the fruit of the Spirit is love, joy, peace, longsuffering, kindness, goodness, faithfulness, gentleness, self-control.
> —GALATIANS 5:22–23, NKJV

Our Conductor smiles at the wisdom of our choices, for these nine delicacies display His very character. If we digest their sweetness, they'll mold our spirits into the image of His perfection and steer us from the wiles of Satan. One by one we savor each one.

Love. This is the special, flawless excellence that loves even the unloving. It is concern that sees the need of others as more vital than its own. A bond that holds regardless of extreme difficulties, it is unconditional loyalty without end.

Joy. That feeling unspeakable and full of glory, it is jubilation that never ceases. It supplies rock-solid strength even in times of mourning. Continual bliss locked into a sovereign God, it provides an inner reserve so strong that even the attacks of hell can't penetrate it.

Peace. A virtue beyond understanding, it is calmness that supersedes the havoc of the world and wraps the heart in tranquility. It is powerful serenity that is able to look beyond worldly turbulence and perceive the spiritual realm behind it, never doubting that good will win out. Faith in action, peace is trusting God in stillness.

Longsuffering. Patience without anger or disgust, it is the capability to endure the trials of life without buckling under their pressure. It is perseverance that waits untiringly and never gives up.

Kindness. This is a sincere word or deed that reaches out even to those who reek with rudeness. A hand of mercy that gives even to the undeserving, it is benevolence making considerate choices on the spot. Kindness is unexpected compassion, expecting nothing in return.

Goodness. A desire to bless, it shuns the very thought of evil tidings. Goodness is a life of righteous acts that keeps on caring after others turn their backs. It is the character to turn the other cheek and go the second mile.

Faithfulness. Staunch trust despite times of struggle, it is unfailing confidence even when God's Spirit seems far away. Faithfulness is steadfast devotion that causes the tempter to whimper in defeat and flee.

Gentleness. This is a tender response regardless of ill treatment or heated words from others. It is warmth and caring that, when harshness tries to bring contempt, chases it away like a calm summer's breeze.

Self-control. A monitoring system that keeps emotions in check, it is moderation that inhibits any indulgence. Self-control holds back even when all signals flash go. It is unwavering restraint even when all reason whispers that nobody is looking.

How blessed we feel with our hunger pangs now relieved. Our Conductor nods in approval as we buy extra to eat along the way.

"Walk in love, dear children," He begins to speak as we go along. "Don't be partakers of sexual sins, greed, impure thoughts, foolish talking, and dirty jokes. Those yielding to such things have no inheritance in the kingdom of Christ and God. Let no one entice or deceive you with empty promises and persuasive arguments, because this brings the wrath of God upon rebellious and defiant sons, so never even associate with them. Even though you were once darkness, now you are light in the Lord. Walk as children of light, for the fruit of the Spirit is in all goodness, righteousness, and truth. Have no fellowship with unfruitful works of darkness, but rather expose them" (Eph. 5:1–9, 11, author's paraphrase).

What a responsibility it is to always walk in the light. What devotion and determination it takes. Our minds spin uneasily as questions bombard our thoughts. *Even if we wear the armor of light, stay filled with spiritual fruit, and develop our characters in goodness, righteousness, and truth—how can we obtain enough wisdom and endurance to always overcome temptation? How can we always discern how and when to expose the unfruitful works of darkness?*

Our Conductor glances our way and smiles. *Does He always see our every thought?* Somehow we sense that wherever He is leading us will provide what we need to find our answers.

Before long we turn with Him to face a brightly lit building. Why, it looks like a white country church with beautiful rainbows streaming from its stained-glass windows. But no, it must be a store. Above the double doors a sign reads, "Warfare Shop."

A jolly gentleman behind the counter greets us with a hearty smile. He, like us, glows in the light of life. "I have the packages You ordered for Your passengers," he announces to our Conductor.

Our Conductor turns to us. "As you use the contents inside these boxes, you'll find solutions to relieve your uneasiness. You'll discover wisdom and endurance to always walk as children of light, exhibit the fruit of the Spirit, and expose all the unfruitful works of darkness. Yes, once you are fully clad in all the items your package contains, you'll be able to stand in the power of God's might."

Our minds relax as He hands a package to each of us, even those who just joined our group from dark corners of the sin. What a nice surprise for everyone.

Whatever can be inside? we wonder. But we have no time to check. Our train whistle sounds in the distance, and we know it's time to run. With our arms loaded, we scurry down the cobblestone streets. Spying the vendor who also glows with the light of life as he pushes his wagon of spiritual fruit, we nod good-bye for now. We know that someday we'll see him and the keeper of the warfare shop in realms of glory.

As we proceed we return smiles to all the friendly passersby and invite all who want the light of life to join us. We beam with excitement as we and our new friends step through the portals of the Jubilee Express to travel on in our adventure. Without delay we tear into our packages. At the top of each we discover a label reading, "spiritual attire for combat." We know beneath the label lie garments for our wisdom and endurance and tools for standing against the unfruitful works of darkness. We'll soon examine each one by one.

Hurray! The whole armor of God belongs to us!

> Finally, my brethren, be strong in the Lord and in the power of His might. Put on the whole armor of God, that you may be able to stand against the wiles of the devil. For we do not wrestle against flesh and blood, but against principalities, against powers, against the rulers of this age, against spiritual hosts of wickedness in the heavenly places. Therefore take up the whole armor of God, that you may be able to withstand in the evil day, and having done all, to stand.
> —EPHESIANS 6:10–13, NKJV

Get ready! Our battle against temptation and evil has only just begun.

Chapter 13

Spiritual Armor of Truth, Righteousness, and Peace

O LORD, I SOMETIMES prayed, *show me what to believe!*
After I saw the apparition of my friend Beth's dead father, my spirituality steeped in a brew of Christianity and psychic power. One fought to mix with the other, but like oil and water they just couldn't combine. Eventually one had to rise. I thank the Lord that by the light of His Word, truth arose to unscramble my jumbled thoughts.

Until then my mind continually clamored. *Is reincarnation possible? What really happens after death? Is Jesus the actual Son of God? Is He the only way to heaven or just one of many avenues?*

The answers came in such a simple way and at such an appropriate place—Sunday school. As I listened to the teacher, a valuable truth nestled inside one tiny Bible verse illuminated my fitful darkness:

> And as it is appointed unto men once to die, but after this the judgment.
>
> —HEBREWS 9:27

Once to die! A light bulb popped on in my head. At that second a divine witness within my spirit set the truth on fire. Man has only one earthly life and one earthly death; therefore, reincarnation ranks as no more than an absurd, boldfaced lie!

Once to die! This single phrase cleared the idea of reincarnation from my mind. How Satan had duped me! With this realization, all the mystical teachings I had ever encountered registered as preposterous. The instant I saw the truth, it set me free from all occult concerns.

If God is God—and He is!—then everything He says is true. Now without one qualm I embraced the actuality of Christ as His Son. In a heartbeat I saw Jesus alone as the only way to heaven, the only source of God's truth, the only door to eternal life. He is Christ, the anointed Messiah, the Son of the living God!

What dangerous ground I had tread by questioning the deity of Jesus. Without the sacrifice of spotless blood, without this only plan of redemption, the human soul faces eternal doom. All other plans are fabrications.

> Neither is there salvation in any other: for there is none other name under heaven given among men, whereby we must be saved.
>
> —ACTS 4:12

> Whosoever transgresseth, and abideth not in the doctrine of Christ, hath not God. He that abideth in the doctrine of Christ, he hath both the Father and the Son.
>
> —2 JOHN 9

Time and time again the Bible declares that no way other than Jesus leads us to the Father:

> Jesus saith unto him, I am the way, the truth, and the life: no man cometh unto the Father, but by me.
>
> —JOHN 14:6

> Who is a liar but he who denies that Jesus is the Christ? He is antichrist who denies the Father and the Son. Whoever denies the Son does not have the Father either; he who acknowledges the Son has the Father also.
>
> —1 JOHN 2:22–23, NKJV

From the promise of the Seed of the woman in Genesis 3:15 the Bible proclaims one Messiah. We must find our answers not just in part of the Scriptures, but from their entirety. We must shun misconstrued portions of Scripture that are pulled out of context by the occult and diabolical testimonies that don't line up with God's Word or come through any psychic means. To truly walk with the Almighty you and I and every person who lives to reach an age of accountability must believe in Jesus as God's Son. In doing so we must also trust His Word completely, honoring it alone as perfect truth.

Think about it. If any statement from God proves false, then God Himself becomes a liar and all His Word may as well be lies. If even one tiny part of His Word is untrue, what other parts can we believe? None!

When sects, both of the occult and the cults, claim the Bible has become distorted by evil men, poor copying, or wrong translation, they fail to give God the credit He deserves. Friends, we have a wonder-working Most High Master, who from age to age watches over His Word to keep it intact.

How can man profess to be so wise as to scoff at the capability of the One who inspired the writing of His Word for an everlasting covenant? The Creator of all matter, the Lord of hosts who controls the earth and all the heavens, who knows every star by name and the number of hairs on our head, can most certainly protect His truth from satanic perversion.

The Bible stands forever. Its truth can never be destroyed!

> Heaven and earth shall pass away, but my words shall not pass away.
> —MATTHEW 24:35

God Himself is Truth. Therefore He has to be all that His Word declares He is or He isn't God at all. He must be the all-knowing, ever-seeing, always-present Deity who consists of perfect purity and holiness, excellence and goodness. He is a supreme Being who can never lie (Titus 1:2).

How could the One of perfect and total light ever stand aside and allow darkness to infiltrate His Word?

> This is the message which we have heard from Him and declare to you, that God is light and in Him is no darkness at all.
> —1 JOHN 1:5, NKJV

If His Word were to become distorted, we couldn't walk wholly in His light. No one could completely determine right from wrong, and fellowship with God would be lost.

> If we say that we have fellowship with Him, and walk in darkness, we lie and do not practice the truth.
> —1 JOHN 1:6, NKJV

How true this is! I was so fortunate to already know Jesus as my Savior before I wavered into occultic teachings. Even under the influence of such falsehoods I could never quite relinquish the heartfelt knowledge I had in Jesus as the Son of God. Yet even though I did it in ignorance, I paid a price for dabbling in Satan's dark domain. Not only did it confuse my mind, but like a choking weed, it also blocked my growth and intimate fellowship with God. How wonderful it was when I recognized His truth.

Yes, His truth freed me from the snare of sorcery. For the first time I understood why Satan manifested the illusion at Beth's house. By it he launched an all-out attempt to fully win me over to his hypocrisies, corrupt my confidence in the gospel, and bind my heart in his web of lies.

Instead his plan backfired. By standing face-to-face with the reality of his supernatural power, I know firsthand the factual existence of the spiritual realm and the devil's unrelenting passion to capture the human soul. The very thing he meant for bad engulfs my heart with blazing zeal to alert the world of his deception and shout the truth of God!

> That we should no longer be children, tossed to and fro and carried about with every wind of doctrine, by the trickery of men, in the cunning craftiness of deceitful plotting, but, speaking the truth in love, may grow up in all things into Him who is the head—Christ.
> —EPHESIANS 4:14–15, NKJV

Oh, what a blessing it is to know the truth!

BACK ON THE Jubilee Express, zooming upon our scarlet rails, the moment arrives for us to unwrap the first piece of our spiritual armor.

> Wherefore take unto you the whole armour of God, that ye may be able to withstand in the evil day, and having done all, to stand. Stand therefore, having your loins girt about with truth...
> —EPHESIANS 6:13–14

THE BELT OF TRUTH

What is this? A wide belt?

In a broad sense, yes, it is. In olden Jewish dress they called it a girdle. Today it becomes our own spiritual belt of truth to protect us from the lies of Satan.

What a history it holds in the natural realm. The girdle was vital for carrying endeared possessions like money and wallets and priceless documents such as written contracts and records too valuable to leave unprotected.

Girdles aided in trips of extensive walking and gave men freedom to run when they tucked the hem of their robes under it. From this the phrase *girding up for the journey* became a saying that signified perseverance and courage to undertake any task and made the girdle a symbol of being ever-ready to serve.

Girdles gave identity. Townsmen sported belts of wool, linen, or silk wound with folds to act as pockets. In the field men shielded their midriff with broad belts of durable leather studded with metal. With an attached shoulder strap they secured personal items along with a dagger or sword. Both Elijah and John the Baptist wore leather girdles.

In the dress code of His day Jesus would have worn a girdle. Isaiah portrays Him also wearing a spiritual girdle, saying:

> Righteousness shall be the belt of His loins, and faithfulness the belt of His waist.
>
> —Isaiah 11:5, NKJV

The garments of a Jewish high priest included an elaborate girdle. Winding around his midsection from his chest to his waist, it had enough sash to flow all the way to the ground.

The soldier's girdle denoted strength and power. Usually constructed completely of metal, it kept him primed for battle, not just as a safe covering but also as a means for keeping his sword ever available by his side. The soldier's girdle was mandatory equipment. Without it no armor could be complete.

Oh, this belt that we have taken from our armor box! It is our belt of truth, the symbolic piece of our warfare attire that holds the priceless truth of His Word. It binds us with ever-readiness, perseverance, and courage to serve in every race we run for Him.

The belt of truth, the first source of defense God gives us against the wiles of Satan, keeps His covenant intact. Studded with the fear of the Lord, it keeps the sword of the Spirit always at our sides.

And the belt of truth carries the substance of His Word. It is mandatory equipment for Christian battle, brimming with righteousness and faithfulness at the very center of our beings. Its sash streams all the way to the ground where Jesus' blood flowed to make us free.

> If ye continue in my word, then are ye my disciples indeed; and ye shall know the truth, and the truth shall make you free.
>
> —John 8:31–32

And now we must explore this truth, a truth so powerful that it lifts man's heart into heavenly realms and unites a human spirit with the Holy Spirit of God.

> God is Spirit, and those who worship Him must worship in spirit and truth.
> —JOHN 4:24, NKJV

As surely as God is Spirit, He is also Truth. Truth, like a mirror of His character, reflects the very essence and expression of His total being. Jesus, "the express image" of God (Heb. 1:3), declares Himself to be the way, the *truth* and the life (John 14:6). He defines the Holy Spirit as the Spirit of *truth* (John 14:17). To the Father He says, "Thy word is *truth*" (John 17:17).

From Him stems all truth of all the ages—the awesome truth that creates an awareness of His deity, the saving truth that triumphs over the devil and his cohorts, the spiritual truth that makes worship come alive, all the provisions of His covenant, His message of eternal truth, His plan for man's redemption.

God gave His Son, the Seed of the woman, who born of a virgin mother, as a mortal lived without sinning, doing the perfect will of His Father; who became the unblemished sacrifice, crucified for the sin of humanity, dying on a cross for man's redemption; who by His spotless blood won the victory over Satan and obtained the keys of hell and of death.

Who in His resurrected body walked among men, then ascended into Heaven where He now sits at the right hand of the Father as Most High Priest, interceding for mankind; who did not leave man comfortless, but forty days after His ascension sent the Holy Spirit to guide, console, teach, edify and give power to believers during their earthly life; who promises to return to reward His faithful with everlasting life to claim them as His bride, to let them reign at His side as kings and priests on Earth for a thousand years; who afterwards in the glories of New Jerusalem will dwell among His people as their Bridegroom in a perfect union of love and peace under His banner of all truth and flawless light forevermore.

This is the vibrant truth our belts must hold! It is so simple and beautiful. Why has the world today complicated its simplicity and perverted its beauty? Why have so many lost all concept of the truth of God's Word? Four reasons come to mind.

First, the world possesses no fear of the Lord. All truth begins with the fear of the Lord.

The fear of the LORD is the beginning of knowledge.

—PROVERBS 1:7

The fear of the LORD is the beginning of wisdom.

—PSALM 111:10

This wisdom and knowledge give revelation of His truth. Without them no human mind recognizes the reality of the judgment of God or discerns good from evil. Without the fear of the Lord, ignorance of His Word abounds.

Ignorance is the second reason the world has no concept of truth. The saying ignorance is bliss is so foolish. How dangerous ignorance is!

My people are destroyed for lack of knowledge: Because thou hast rejected knowledge, I will also reject thee.

—HOSEA 4:6

Without the fear of the Lord, not only is ignorance of God's Word prevalent, but indifference is also rampant. This is the third reason the world has no concept of the truth. It has no desire to know.

Even in religious orders, indifference produces an insensitivity that has no conscience and expresses no feelings for the spiritual needs of others. It is such a deadly tool of Satan! Knowledge reveals the truth, ignorance conceals the truth, the fear of the Lord instills the truth, but indifference *kills* the truth.

How sad that many who profess Christianity sit in indifference, closing their eyes to sin around them, satisfied as long as their cubby hole remains unscathed. How easily they accept compromise to keep things running smoothly.

The forth reason is compromise—letting sin creep into society, even into our churches, because of "political correctness." With God's truth there can be no middle ground. If we totally believe His Word, we will proclaim the truth without fear or compromise.

A war for souls is raging. Christianity is not a game we play if we feel like it. Christianity calls for a dedicated lifestyle. It means that we combat all evil to spread the truth of righteousness and bring forth fruit. Christianity doesn't glide through life in a state of indifference or compromise. Christianity has boldness to stand up for the gospel. Christianity has a burden for souls.

Where is our fruit? Are we living the truth or just playing a game? We must step out for Jesus wearing our belt of truth. Let us fight the battle for Him. Truth working through us will win the lost.

Oh, yes, Satan defies our efforts, but so what if he sends a messenger to buffet us? Overall it will be worth it. Our life here lasts for such a brief time. Eternity lasts forever. As soldiers of God we must step out and change the world. If Christians don't, Satan will!

We must be unafraid of repercussions from the world! Christianity calls us to put concern of another's salvation above our own concerns. What has happened to courage to speak truth about areas of darkness that our mainstream culture portrays as OK?

To openly disagree with the media and political or educational views may be uncouth to secular society, but for the sake of eternity we have no choice. As Christians we must fear the Lord enough to declare the truth regardless of negative responses, to care about souls who need the truth, to lock horns with the apathy and sin-tolerance that is so prevalent today. Our Commander plainly makes His stand for righteousness. Unpopular or not, only His opinion will matter on Judgment Day.

At the risk of offending, yet with deep concern for those who are ignorant of God's truth and also those who know the truth but remain in Satan's clutches, we must sound an alarm to save a soul. His Word is plain. To deny its truth leads to doom.

ABORTION AND HOMOSEXUALITY are two sinful acts that the world presents as "choices." Uh-oh, I've opened a can of worms. It seems so much of today's society vibrates with support of these sins that those who speak against them place themselves in jeopardy. The truth has been reversed.

> Woe unto them that call evil good, and good evil; that put darkness for light, and light for darkness; that put bitter for sweet, and sweet for bitter!
>
> —Isaiah 5:20

How well we know, and often deeply love, people who are caught in these deceptions. Nevertheless God's truth remains. No one or anything can change its consequences. All who take part in, stand up for, or just agree with abortion, and any who indulge in any aspect of sexual perversion, put their approval on ungodliness and expose themselves to the judgment set forth in the unchangeable Word of God.

> For the wrath of God is revealed from heaven against all ungodliness and unrighteousness.
>
> —Romans 1:18, NKJV

Does God truly look at abortion and homosexuality as ungodly and unrighteousness? Yes. According to His Word, He clearly does.

It's a scary thing to toy with the wrath of God by turning a deaf ear to the teachings of the Bible. Whether we like it or not, despite popular opinion we have to look at sin as sin and accept it as sin.

Abortion. Somehow the world slipped in the impersonal word *fetus* to conceal the idea of a baby struggling for life in abortion clinics. Somehow the world influences politicians to fear the loss of votes more than the judgment of God. Somehow the world manages to sear consciences in the matter of determining who should live and who should die. But in the end only the truth will matter.

What is the truth? How does God really feel about abortion? Does He care about the lives of unborn babies? We search the Scriptures:

> Behold, children are a heritage from the LORD, the fruit of the womb is a reward.
>
> —PSALM 127:3, NKJV

> For You have formed my inward parts; You have covered me in my mother's womb.
>
> —PSALM 139:13, NKJV

> By You I have been upheld from my birth; You are He who took me out of my mother's womb.
>
> —PSALM 71:6, NKJV

Before the birth of Samson came the prophecy, "The child shall be a Nazirite unto God from the womb" (Judg. 13:5). The Lord told Jeremiah, "Before I formed thee in the belly I knew thee; and before thou camest forth out of the womb I sanctified thee" (Jer. 1:5). When Mary, the expectant mother of Jesus, visited Elisabeth—the expectant mother of John the Baptist—Elisabeth became filled with the Holy Ghost and cried, "The babe leaped in my womb for joy" (Luke 1:44).

I feel such alarm about the wrath of the Judge of Righteousness upon those who are sedated by the views of the world and have seared consciences and hearts of indifference. History records that Hitler murdered some six million innocent Jews during World War II, a horror that will never be forgotten and certainly shouldn't be. But without an ounce of shame we have taken the lives of nearly forty million innocent babies by intentional abortions between 1973 and the end of 1999 in the United

States alone. How can this be justified?

It can't. There can never be a point of justification for these killings. Our Maker values human life so supremely that He gives us provisions for eternity. What suffering Jesus endured to give us abundant life on Earth. How then can mankind be so uncaring and so foolish to destroy the lives of unborn children?

Satan must gloat as he sees the horrid deception of abortion wreak death across the world. How he undoubtedly swells with pride as each baby terminated becomes another blood sacrifice of the innocent to cover the sin of his parents. How he must delight as mothers and fathers legally present the fruit of the womb to the demon of sensual pleasure and the god of self-gratification. And how the holy Judge of Righteousness must agonize because of such indifference. In strong words He expresses His desire for mankind to turn from such sadistic acts:

> And they shall no more offer their sacrifices unto devils, after whom they have gone a whoring. This shall be a statute for ever unto them throughout their generations.
>
> —Leviticus 17:7

Yes, abortion easily fits into the category of blood sacrifice—to Satan. In no way can the murder of babies please the God of holiness who not only gives life but also hates hands that shed innocent blood (Prov. 6:17). What blood is more innocent than that of an unborn child?

And now we look at homosexuality. Homosexuals can be such caring, talented people. Yet, all the good qualities in the world cannot make sin right.

My heart goes out to all who are caught up in the web of homosexuality. Deluded by the terms *alternative lifestyle* and *gay,* they are told that they are born to this fate and can never overcome it. How they need the truth!

I've heard wonderful testimonies from overcomers, but they found deliverance only by super strength from God. An ironclad commitment to God and a supernatural move of His Spirit are required to break the bondage of this act of immorality that is so deeply rooted in the heart. But in a willing vessel it can be done. Jesus Himself says that with God all things are possible (Matt. 19:26).

What does God's Word say about homosexuality? The Old Testament speaks strictly against such matters:

> If a man also lie with mankind as he lieth with a woman, both of them have committed an abomination: they shall surely be put to death; their blood shall be upon them.
>
> —Leviticus 20:13

The New Testament sounds as though it was written for this very day:

> Although they knew God, they did not glorify Him as God, nor were thankful, but became futile in their thoughts, and their foolish hearts were darkened. Professing to be wise, they became fools, and changed the glory of the incorruptible God into an image made like corruptible man—and birds and four-footed animals and creeping things.
>
> Therefore God also gave them up to uncleanness, in the lusts of their hearts, to dishonor their bodies among themselves, who exchanged the truth of God for the lie, and worshiped and served the creature rather than the Creator, who is blessed forever. Amen.
>
> For this reason God gave them up to vile passions. For even their women exchanged the natural use for what is against nature. Likewise also the men, leaving the natural use of the woman, burned in their lust for one another, men with men committing what is shameful, and receiving in themselves the penalty of their error which was due.
>
> —ROMANS 1:21–27, NKJV

What is the penalty due them? This passage goes on to say that because they fail to accept it as worthwhile to acknowledge God, He gives them up to a reprobate (unapproved, rejected, cast away, abominable, to be abhorred by God and man.[1] A mind rejected by God and a conscience that is seared and turned off to conviction of the Holy Spirit—what a terrifying matter!

> Though they know God's degree that those who do such things deserve to die, they not only do them but approve those who practice them.
>
> —ROMANS 1:32, RSV

Jesus tells us to judge not. God is the Judge. Yet, here we see His ultimate judgment plain and pointblank not only for those who practice homosexuality but also for those who approve of them and their unrighteous acts. As Christians we do not judge the person, but we do judge sin by the Word of God—standing against it, never agreeing to exchange the truth of God for a lie, shunning evil, and never becoming involved with darkness or accepting it.

Most of us know talented, loving, and compassionate homosexuals. Many know caring women who, seemingly without a second thought, aborted their baby. We come in contact with people steeped in all types of ungodliness. Though we are not their judge, we should speak the truth with fear for their eternal souls.

Christ calls us to love our neighbor as ourselves, caring so deeply that we agonize for all who are in sin and work with fervor by prayer, example, word, and deed to lead them to God. We must never give up. This is our Christian duty.

> But you, beloved, remember the words which were spoken before by the apostles of our Lord Jesus Christ: how they told you that there would be mockers in the last time who would walk according to their own ungodly lusts. These are sensual persons, who cause divisions, not having the Spirit. But you, beloved, building yourselves up on your most holy faith, praying in the Holy Spirit, keep yourselves in the love of God, looking for the mercy of our Lord Jesus Christ unto eternal life. And on some have compassion, making a distinction; but others save with fear, pulling them out of the fire, hating even the garment defiled by the flesh.
>
> —JUDE 17–22, NKJV

More often than not people put up fronts to keep from admitting their sin. Or like cornered animals, they fight back viciously when they are confronted in their area of wrongful acts. They may go deeper into their sin and befriend those who agree with their unrighteousness deeds. These are the tactics of Satan's deception. But knowing that we hold the truth in our belt gives us the advantage over Satan. The Spirit of truth will lead us into battle.

Detesting one's sin never means that we hate the person. We wrestle not against flesh and blood, but against demonic forces. The enemy who drives a person to sin should be the target of our warfare, not the person.

We must never stop caring and turn away. How urgently these people need the truth. They are not too far for God to reach through our prayers and acts of love.

> And now abide faith, hope, love, these three; but the greatest of these is love.
>
> —1 CORINTHIANS 13:13, NKJV

> Love never fails...
>
> —1 CORINTHIANS 13:8, NKJV

The time has come for each of us to search ourselves.

> For all have sinned, and come short of the glory of God.
>
> —ROMANS 3:23

Yes, that includes you and me.

Does any darkness hide within your heart? Turn it over to your heavenly

Father who already knows about it. Nothing is hidden from Him, and nothing is too big for Him to conquer if you'll let Him.

Perhaps you yourself have participated in abortion or homosexuality, or maybe you harbor a secret lust. Is there a temptation stronger than you can bear alone? Has the ungodly power of the world pulled you astray? Have you wandered in ignorance, not knowing the teachings of God's Word? Has defeat conquered your soul? Has darkness seduced you, blinding your eyes, deafening your ears, and searing your conscience to the truth?

Wake up to the truth of God! You will discover not only the mighty Word of God, but also the mighty God of the Word. His grace will pardon your sin. Regardless of your past He stands by with compassion, always inviting and never rejecting or refusing. You may be broken and spent, your sin may be hideous, but He still wants you.

Whosoever will may come—homosexual, abortionist, drunkard, addict, glutton, gossiper, liar, cheater, thief, adulterer, rapist, child abuser, murderer. He will replace the filthiest of rags with garments of righteousness, pure and white. Let His forgiveness bind up your agony with mercy, and you can live abundantly in the light and freedom of His truth, now and for eternity.

Where would we be without His truth? Salvation comes by our acknowledgment of it. Accepting it cleanses, sanctifies, and delivers our souls to make us overcomers. By faith in God's truth, the sick are made whole, the weak made strong, the oppressed set free.

Treasure truth. Band your loins with it. Buckle it around your waist. Secure it over the very "gut-feeling" of your makeup, strapping it like a girdle of steel to guard your belly—from which rivers of living waters flow.

> He that believeth on me, as the scripture hath said, out of his belly shall flow rivers of living water.
>
> —John 7:38

No demon can even begin to tread such waters. Let us go forth in the wisdom and knowledge of the fear of the Lord, displaying our belt of truth and letting our rivers of living water proclaim the truth of all the ages to those in darkness.

Oh, the benefits of truth. How blessed to be protected in its knowledge and by its freedom as we travel on in the Jubilee Express. Now with our belts of truth in place, we open our packages again and pull out our second provision for spiritual warfare.

OH, WE GASP, such a fabulous piece of armor! We sense great honor in being chosen to wear it. But how can we be worthy to even put it on? Humbly we press it against our hearts with tender care.

> ...having on the breastplate of righteousness.
>
> —EPHESIANS 6:14

THE BREASTPLATE OF RIGHTEOUSNESS

In ourselves we can never measure up to standards required to wear this pristine vest of warfare. Only because of the perfect righteousness of our Savior do we have this privilege. With a sense of obligation to attain our best for Him we fasten it in place, hungering and thirsting to learn the wonders of its benefits.

What defense! While the belt of truth alerts us to Satan's schemes, the breastplate of righteousness annuls his filth and sends him running, because he knows he can never penetrate the righteousness of the Son of God.

The breastplate of the Roman soldier covered his entire chest. Its metal guarded vital organs—especially the heart—from arrows and swords. Troops could never charge into battle without their hearts protected and expect to stand for any time against the enemy.

The fight is on! Satan rages. Never can we stand without the righteousness of Christ. Never can we be good enough to battle on our own unless He is guarding our hearts.

The breastplate of righteousness is the sturdy shield that protects our innermost being. It covers our vital chamber where sensitivity dwells and intimacy blooms. Sheltering the secret place of the Most High where the Holy Spirit abides, it safeguards the holy of holies in His temple deep inside our beings.

As we consider the breastplate of righteousness, we must also look into the symbolism veiled in the spiritual breast ensemble worn by the high priest. Oh, what majesty it presented in Jewish worship!

The breast piece highly accentuated the elaborate garments worn for ceremonial occasions. How brilliant, how valuable it must have been, embellished as it was with twelve precious jewels. On each gem the name of a tribe of Israel was engraved. Covering the chest, the breastplate was fastened to the high priest's shoulders by golden chains. Blue ribbons connected it to his girdle.

As well as being beautiful in worship, it was significant to Jewish life because it provided guidance. Tucked inside a pocket behind the jewels were two mysterious and wonderful objects, the Urim and the Thummin. Perhaps they too were costly stones. Nobody can be positive of their composition or appearance. However, we do know their important function. The Urim and the Thummin revealed the will of a righteous holy God and gave surety of His care for His people.

Just as the ark of the covenant was a tangible evidence for the presence of the Almighty, the Urim and the Thummim served as a tangible expression of the Holy Spirit. As God worked through these two sources of guidance, the high priest received the direction that Israel needed.

Since the Holy Spirit did not yet abide in the hearts of men and lead through His internal voice, the Urim and the Thummim—carried just outside, yet against the heart—served as a touchable substitute. In crucial times the high priest interceded with Yahweh by the Urim and the Thummim to steer man from the slyness of the deceiver and reveal the way of righteousness. Having these objects gave counsel and comfort as well.

John saw Jesus in His priestly dress in his vision of the majesties of heaven; He wore "a girdle of gold about His breast" (Rev. 1:13, AMP).

A golden vest! This is the breastplate of righteousness worn by Christ, our High Priest!

Only because of His righteousness can we wear the breastplate of righteousness. Our own righteousness would never hold up against the evil one. Endued with the Holy Spirit who abides in our hearts, just behind our breastplates, we receive direction from a pure and holy God.

Envision yourself placing your breastplate of righteousness across your chest, securing it with chains of shining gold that extend over your shoulders and lacing it to your belt of truth with ribbons of blue, symbolic of heaven. What an honor to wear spiritual armor that covers our breasts in the purity and holiness of our Savior. How can we even begin to do it justice? We can seek His righteousness in all we do!

> Blessed are they which do hunger and thirst after righteousness: for they shall be filled.
>
> —Matthew 5:6

Desiring righteousness moves us to do our utmost to build a personal relationship with Jesus, to truly know the Father, Son, and Holy Spirit. It means that we long to be filled with righteousness by love, not by superficial acts. Yes, we seek righteousness, not religion.

Religion consists of doing outward acts of rituals and restraints to be approved and seen of men. It is reflected in legalism, traditions that proceed from the head, not the heart. This way of life is far removed from a righteous heart.

True worship is an act of righteousness. It is the expression of an inward relationship between an individual and God. This intimacy with Him marks a person whose spirit is yielded and sincere. God desires true worship. Righteousness itself comes only by the Righteous One who shed His blood for us. We receive this gift when we give our hearts to Him and share relationship with Him. In His righteousness we find true abiding power, the ability to give up the world and dwell in His holiness forever. We receive a supernatural strength that is not found in the religious acts of pleasing man and showing others.

Legalism never produces righteousness. Righteousness isn't gained by the way we dress or wear our hair, how frequently we go to church or how many Bible verses we memorize. Righteousness is not found in church work—organizing activities, planning meetings, serving on the board, singing in the choir. Righteousness is not achieved by lighting candles of by the use of "holy water" or prayer beads.

The Pharisees kept outward ordinances. They were sticklers for tradition, rigid in the Law, unyielding in their doctrine. John the Baptist called them a generation of vipers (Matt. 3:7).

Jesus called them hypocrites. "Why do you transgress the commandment of God by your tradition?" He asked them, "How correctly Isaiah prophesied of you when he said, 'These people honor me with their lips, but their heart is far from me. In vain they worship me, teaching for doctrines the commandments of men'" (Matt. 15:2, 7, 9, author's paraphrase).

With sadness I recall our neighbor. An upstanding young man of the community, he was on the ministerial staff of his church and a seemingly devoted husband and father. Dogmatic in his doctrine, he and his family followed the stiff regimen of his church to the letter. His wife never cut her hair or wore slacks, jewelry, or makeup. Even on the hottest summer days, he dressed in long sleeve shirts to, as he put it, "prevent women from lusting after me."

I respected his deep dedication to his beliefs. However, did it work to make him more righteous? No, tragically it didn't. This married man and the pastor's wife became involved in an affair.

Later my heart sobbed over their traumatic situation. I saw neighbor lose his family and leave the church for worldly living. The pastor and wife moved away.

Anyone who makes one wrong decision might find themselves overcome with temptation and yield to the pleasure of the moment. Though the consequences may seem unbearable, God forgives. When there is a repentant heart, God forgives.

But does legalism help make us righteous? I think not. If it takes strict rules and regulations, constant religious programs, or man-devised "holy" rituals to keep you personally right with God, then by all means do them. But legalism isn't God ordained. It is devised by man.

> The LORD seeth not as man seeth; for man looketh on the outward appearance, but the LORD looketh on the heart.
>
> —1 SAMUEL 16:7

Yes, we can be sure that righteousness doesn't manifest itself in outward appearances or in following certain traditions. Only a heart that is true before God puts us in right standing with Him and makes us right in His sight. This can never be achieved by rules, manipulations, or hype. It's a desire to truly know Him, not to merely know *about* Him through religious acts and laws.

The apostle Paul knew the Law frontward and backward, inside and out. Most certainly he believed in God. But he didn't *know* God until after his heart-changing conversion. Then and only then could he proclaim, "I know whom I have believed" (2 Tim. 1:12).

Seeking righteousness enlightens us with heart knowledge, not merely head knowledge, of our Savior. Then we recognize the Son of God for who He is—not simply Mary's baby in a manger or just as a prophet who walked the earth—but the righteous Redeemer of all mankind.

He is Christ the anointed Messiah, the One foreordained as the Lamb to be slain before the foundation of the world, the ageless Deity whom we find at the setting of creation: "In the beginning Elohim (God in plurality) created the heaven and earth" (Gen. 1:1), and at the end of the ages, "I am Alpha and Omega, the beginning and the ending, saith the Lord, which is, and which was, and which is to come, the Almighty" (Rev. 1:8).

CHRIST IS THE PROMISED ONE OF THE OLD TESTAMENT, THE FULFILLING ONE IN THE NEW

The One

> ...in whom we have redemption through His blood, the forgiveness of sins. He is the image of the invisible God, the firstborn over all creation. For by Him all things were created that are in heaven and that are on earth, visible and invisible, whether thrones or dominions or principalities or powers. All things were created

through Him and for Him. And He is before all things, and in Him all things consist. And He is the head of the body, the church, who is the beginning, the firstborn from the dead, that in all things He may have the preeminence. For it pleased the Father that in Him all the fullness should dwell.

—COLOSSIANS 1:14–19, NKJV

The One

...whom He [God the Father] has appointed heir of all things, through whom also He made the worlds; who being the brightness of His glory and the express image of His person, and upholding all things by the word of His power, when He had by Himself purged our sins, sat down at the right hand of the Majesty on high, having become so much better than the angels, as He has by inheritance obtained a more excellent name than they.

—HEBREWS 1:2–4, NKJV

The One

...like unto the Son of Man, clothed with a garment down to the feet and girded about the chest with a golden band. His head and hair were white like wool, as white as snow, and His eyes like a flame of fire; His feet were like fine brass, as if refined in a furnace, and His voice as the sound of many waters.

—REVELATION 1:13–15, NKJV

Yes, oh, yes! This is the Almighty Redeemer who shed His spotless blood for you and me so that we might walk in His righteousness. He is the Righteous Branch who opened the way for us to step without fear into the awesome presence of His Father's majesty. Immanuel, God with us, revealed the wonders of the Father's grace, the glories of His mercy. The Perfect Son of Man gave us the right to call His own Father our Abba Father—to know Him as our Daddy, crawling upon His lap, falling asleep in the comfort of His arms.

Starving for Christ's righteousness brings us to a place where we no longer care what the world thinks. Instead, we only desire closer union with Him no matter what. Regardless of our former conceptions or the things that others say or do, we want Him and all He has to offer. Above all else we long for more of His precious righteousness.

And this is where I found myself in 1978.

I had been delivered from the confusion of the occult. No longer bound by chains of guilt from my divorce, I was freed from the shame of failure and rejection. I realized that a God who still works miracles had raised my baby girl from a death of drowning, and I had experienced and observed His physical healing. God had given me His words of peace concerning my elder son. And now I was growing with hunger and thirst for His glorious Word.

What a marvelous God I had come to know. And I longed to know Him more.

"WON'T YOU AND Jim please come to our Thursday night sharing group?" my sister asked.

After several invitations to attend this home prayer meeting, Jim and I reluctantly decided to go. We loved the Lord and worked hard in church, but we weren't too enthused about frivolous socializing.

Wow, were we surprised! No idle talking here. With the accompaniment of a guitar these people sang with gusto, lifted their hands unashamedly in worship, and prayed out loud. For the first time we heard people speaking in tongues! And these were not so-called "Pentecostals," but just everyday people like us. How could this be?

The only person who ever told me about speaking in tongues was a class-mate who moved to town for a brief time during my freshman year in high school. Her father, the new pastor of a local Pentecostal denomination, refused to allow her to dress in stylish fashions, wear jewelry, apply any cos-metics, or cut her long bushy hair. But not only that, she couldn't shave her legs or underarms. This lifestyle served to make her holy, she explained.

What a difficult age to be classified as different. Though many students avoided or ignored her, I befriended her. I grew to like her a lot. And she told me about "speaking in unknown tongues."

I couldn't quite grasp why God would require a person to endure ridicule and look so hopeless in order to "bless" her with this unknown language. And despite her appearance of "holiness," my friend admitted that she had never spoken in tongues. She said some members in her church told her she couldn't go to heaven unless she received this blessing.

Now that's all I knew about speaking in tongues. But from the shar-ing-group meeting at my sister's house, I realized these tongue-talking people had something that I lacked in my spiritual life. And I so wanted more of God!

I begin asking people about speaking in tongues and studied everything I could get my hands on. Typed sermons of Jim's late father, a lay speaker for a strictly regimented denomination, stated point-blank that speaking in tongues today comes from the devil. A neighbor who attended my church gave me literature that said all the spiritual gifts listed in 1 Corinthians 12:8–10 (the word of wisdom, word of knowledge, faith, gifts of healing, working of miracles, prophecy, discerning of spirits, different types of tongues and interpretation of tongues) passed away with the early New Testament church.

The article indicated that a personal Father, a miracle-working and healing God is no longer for today. No! It couldn't be. From my own experiences I now knew that just wasn't so.

Conflicting thoughts bounced around in my head. If speaking in tongues is of the devil, why are these people who speak in tongues so on fire for the Lord? If it is the devil's language, why aren't criminals, idolaters, heathens, and atheists—those who serve him—all speaking in tongues? And if tongues passed away, why do people who are dedicated to God still receive it?

With an eagerness I had never known before I began to search the Bible on my own, starting with the chapters and verses the negative material used to support its opposition. Using their strongest argument I read and reread 1 Corinthians 13:8, "Charity never faileth: but whether there be prophecies, they shall fail; whether there be tongues, they shall cease; whether there be knowledge, it shall vanish away."

Prophecies failed and tongues ceased? Well, maybe . . . but knowledge—vanished away? In dismay I shook my head. Certainly knowledge has never vanished; instead it has escalated phenomenally, especially during the last century. With the speed of technology today, a person falls behind if he only blinks his eyes. Just look at television, computers, and space travel. In the medical realm laser surgery, transplants, and life-extending medicines boggle the average mind. Discovery of the x-ray, unknown to the world until 1895, ushered in a new level of perception in many fields.

Even spiritual awareness has advanced with an availability of Christian history, archaeology, concordances of Greek and Hebrew, and commentaries compiled through the ages. We could fill a book and still not exhaust the volume of new and astounding knowledge since the writing of this scripture.

As I continued in the following verses, I read:

> For we know in part, and we prophesy in part. But when that which is perfect is come, then that which is in part shall be done away.
> —1 CORINTHIANS 13:9–10

When did that which is perfect come? I wondered. *Isn't the Perfect One Jesus?*

Opposing doctrines claimed the phrase *that which is perfect* meant the New Testament at its completion. I may have considered this as a possibility if I hadn't read verse 12, "For now we see through a glass, darkly; but then face to face."

See the face of the Bible? my head questioned.

No, the face of my Savior! my spirit cried. All will be fulfilled when Jesus, the One who is perfect, comes for us and we see Him face-to-face! At the point of eternity we will no longer need prophecy. Being able to speak to our Redeemer face-to-face will nullify any need for tongues. And undoubtedly the "in-part" carnal knowledge we've acquired as mere mortals will be insignificant in the eternal realm.

The Revised Standard Version states verse 9–10, "For our knowledge is imperfect and our prophecy is imperfect; but when the perfect comes, the imperfect will pass away."

In our mortality tongues, prophecy, and knowledge are no more than the tools of a child:

> When I was a child, I spake as a child, I understood as a child, I thought as a child: but when I became a man, I put away childish things.
> —1 Corinthians 13:11

Our knowledge in the eternal state will be wholly mature, and it will likely include all the mysteries of the universe. Just listen to the next verse! "For now we see in a mirror dimly, but then face to face. Now I know in part; then I shall understand fully, even as I have been fully understood" (RSV). This will happen when we see Christ face-to-face. What a day that will be!

Other verses spoke to me. First Corinthians 12 begins, "Now concerning spiritual gifts, brethren, I would not have you ignorant." I reasoned, if the word of wisdom, word of knowledge, faith, gifts of healing, working of miracles, prophecy, discernment of spirits, various kinds of tongues, and interpretation of tongues no longer apply today, what difference would it make if we are ignorant of them? Also I wondered why God would bestow such wonderful gifts in manifestation of His Spirit, have Paul write so extensively about their operation, then jerk them away.

In 1 Corinthians 14 Paul tells the people not to speak in tongues in a church service "except he interpret, that the church may receive edifying" (v. 5). As an example he says that if he speaks to them in tongues, how would it profit them "except I speak to you either by revelation, or by knowledge, or by prophesying, or by doctrine?" (v. 6). In summary, Paul is explaining that without interpretation, all speaking in tongues should be done, not as a gift to the church, but in private.

When does Paul ever forbid anyone to speak in tongues in private, between only him and God? He doesn't. On the contrary, he says of himself, "I will pray with the spirit, and I will pray with the understanding also: I will sing with the spirit, and I will sing with the understanding also. . . . I thank my God, I speak with tongues more than ye all: Yet in church I had rather speak five words with my understanding, that by my voice I might teach others also, than ten thousand words in an unknown tongue" (vv. 15, 18–19).

Was he planning to continue speaking in tongues in prayer between him and God? Of course! In reading this chapter time and time again, I began to see that Paul was simply guarding against confusion and disruption that resulted in church services when many spoke aloud in tongues and no one interpreted. The last two verses of the chapter tie his teachings together and state his position, leaving no reason for question. "Wherefore, brethren, covet to prophesy, and forbid not to speak with tongues. Let all things be done decently and in order" (vv. 39–40). How could he make it any clearer?

Later I found other studies, this time positive, at a Christian bookstore. I also discovered two different television preachers who taught on the baptism of the Holy Spirit and the evidence of speaking in tongues. I devoured their every word.

In the meantime, Jim and I hungered for the Thursday night sharing group, and we counted the days between. We had never experienced such uplifting prayer and such true worship. Soon I realized that the baptism of the Holy Spirit is genuine. Not only did I desire it, but I also knew I needed it. Yet how could I receive it?

I tried everything I heard and read about the way others had received the baptism of the Holy Spirit. One television preacher said he received his Spirit baptism in the woods behind his house while he shouted hallelujah at the top of his lungs. Since we lived in town, I didn't think it would be appropriate to yell in the backyard. However, once Jim left for work and my two older children went to school, I would place James in front of *Captain Kangaroo*, shut myself in the bathroom, and cry hallelujah over and over. Did this work for me? No! And neither did anything else I tried.

Finally one day I said, "OK, Lord, I know that the baptism of the Holy Spirit with the evidence of speaking in tongues is real. But I don't know how to receive it. If You want me to have it, You'll just have to give it to me."

Alone in prayer that afternoon, I found myself in deep repentance for my past involvement in the occult. Although I had turned from all sorcery and burned every psychic book I owned, it had never crossed my mind to get on my knees and ask forgiveness. When I did, a heavy weight literally lifted from my shoulders. My body seemed so light I felt I could fly.

Before retiring that evening I read the second chapter of Acts, which tells of the Day of Pentecost when the 120 in the upper room were "filled with the Holy Ghost, and began to speak with other tongues, as the Spirit gave them utterance" (v. 4). Just reading about it caused my heart to flutter. I felt so alive in Him. But things got even better.

During the night I awoke from a deep sleep sitting up in bed, speaking a phrase of words that were unknown to me. *Oh, what a wonderful dream,* I thought as I nestled back under the cover.

Get up and go to the living room, something inside me whispered. I felt a gentle nudge as if an unseen hand had touched my shoulder. Being careful not to wake my husband, I tiptoed from the bedroom, and before I reached the living room I overflowed in jubilation. That same unrecognizable phrase kept bubbling over and over, rising from the depths of my chest and rolling from my lips. In the next few minutes a whole new vocabulary sprang out of me like a fountain of never-ending bliss.

I was speaking in tongues!

Dancing around the room I spoke to the light as I switched it on. I spoke to the sofa, the cuckoo clock, the piano, the curtains. Then with lifted hands I prayed to a wonderful supernatural God in a language just for Him. I prayed and prayed this way until almost dawn.

O Lord, I asked, *how shall I tell Jim about this?* While he knew I had been studying, he didn't know how deeply I had been seeking. And though he loved the sharing group as I did—how would he feel about my speaking in tongues? *O Father,* I added, *if You want me to tell him, please wake him.*

On other nights I had gotten up alone to pray and intercede for others, and Jim had never noticed. But this night, within moments of my prayer, he appeared tying the belt of his robe and frowning, "What are you doing? I felt for you, and your side of the bed was cold!"

As I began to talk my words shifted from the natural to my new spiritual language. Jim's eyes twinkled. His frown turned to laughter. Together we laughed and laughed until the light of dawn began coming through the window to remind us that Jim had to go to work and the children must get up for school.

What a night of glory!

Did it make me holier than before? No, holiness grows in our daily walk with God as He teaches us to love and establishes our hearts.

And may the Lord make you increase and abound in love to one another and to all...so that He may establish your hearts blameless in holiness before our God and Father at the coming of our Lord Jesus Christ with all His saints.

—I THESSALONIANS 3:12–13, NKJV

Did the baptism of the Holy Spirit make me better in God's sight than others who have not received such a wonderful encounter? Has it earned me more merits of righteousness than other believers? No, no, no! Such thinking would make it a prideful thing.

Since the Holy Spirit baptism didn't make me holier, more righteous, or better than others, what did it do for me? Oh, the beauty of it all! It broadened my spiritual sensitivity and awakened an eagerness to learn more and more of God. I hungered, I thirsted after righteousness.

With intense commitment I pledged to seek harder for the ways of Jesus to rule in my life. Consumed with a deeper awareness of a supernatural heavenly Father, my entire being throbbed with wonder and gratitude toward Him. To think that such an awesome almighty Being actually let His Spirit surge in such abundance in someone as insignificant as I.

I grew to have a richer understanding of His Word. And I craved it. Sometimes I would stay up until the wee hours of the morning and pore over my Bible. During the day I would find myself searching through Scripture, feeding on it, zealous for more of it, never satisfied. And in all the years since, this overwhelming passion for His Word, the prayer language He gave me, and my longing after His righteousness have never subsided. In fact, it is ever-increasing.

The baptism of His Holy Spirit set me ablaze with boldness. Never before had I dared to teach His Word to anyone other than small children in Sunday school or vacation Bible school. Immediately after the overflow of His Spirit, I burned with a passion to teach and spread the gospel to everyone. With every heartbeat, even today, that eagerness flames hotter and higher, and His Spirit continues to abound within me.

Soon after receiving this baptism I felt the need for immersion in water baptism. I had been "sprinkled" around age eleven. Although young I regarded this ceremony with heartfelt significance as a true commitment to Jesus, but now I wanted to show the world my full submersion in His love and full submission to His righteousness.

Two years after the night of my initial Holy Ghost encounter, Jim, my husband who had been so reared in legalist doctrine that forbade speaking in tongues, also received the baptism of His Spirit with an unknown language of his own. It also ignited his spirit. Nothing has ever quenched our fires.

Establishing a deeper perception of the wonders of His Being, this glorious and dynamic glimmer of His Spirit fills and refills our hearts with inexpressible joy. During the dark times of dealing with my older son it has reaffirmed God's promise of deliverance and supernatural peace. In our financial dilemma it gave us strength and sustaining trust. It continually blesses our days, turning ordeals into optimism. Oh, the beauty of it all!

> Until the Spirit is poured upon us from on high, and the wilderness becomes a fruitful field, and the fruitful field is counted as a forest.
> —Isaiah 32:15, NKJV

From the time of His first outpouring on me and then on Jim, we each experienced this prophecy of Isaiah, seeing His Spirit transform the wilderness in our spirits into a fruitful field. Despite any hardship that has surfaced, our fruitful field abounds, growing steadily every day, expanding more and more into a vast and flourishing forest.

Even with all its bliss, this experience doesn't make any person perfect. God knows that we failed to tithe even after we knew Him in this supernatural manner!

But it does instill an inextinguishable call to repent when we realize that we've fallen short. It does give a greater durability in serving Him when things go belly-up. And it plants an ever-present longing to fulfill His will and allow His gift of righteousness to reign in a greater dimension every passing day.

Some who have not sought the baptism of the Holy Spirit may say, "I already possess these expressions of God's work in my life." But oh, you just don't know the beauty of it all until you have personally experienced the fullness of the Spirit. I once heard a preacher explain it this way—you may know how to bat a ball because you've studied every aspect, watched famous players bat, even taught young children how. But until you've held the bat in your own hands and hit the ball, watching it soar into the air by your own swing—you actually cannot know the beauty of it all.

It is a spiritual experience unlike any other. Water baptism, which Jesus Himself commanded for a person who comes to Him in faith, is also a beautiful act. However, any person, sincere or not, can participate in this baptism that is performed by man; only God knows his heart. On the other hand, God Himself performs Holy Spirit baptism only to yielded hearts that are truly seeking His righteousness.

With His baptism the Holy Spirit lights a firestorm of desire to alert the world of the wonders of His might. He gives boldness and power to share the gospel as never before. How does the Bible put it?

> But ye shall receive power, after that the Holy Ghost is come upon you: and ye shall be witnesses unto me both in Jerusalem, and in all Judea, and in Samaria, and unto the uttermost part of the earth.
>
> —Acts 1:8

These are the last words Jesus spoke before His ascension. When the Holy Spirit came upon them ten days later, they "began to speak with other tongues, as the Spirit gave them utterance" (Acts 2:4).

What a miracle occurred! Jews who spoke many different languages and had gathered from many regions to celebrate Pentecost heard their own languages being spoken by the Spirit-filled people. What an initial outpouring! All through the Book of Acts the people who were baptized in the Holy Ghost spoke in unknown tongues. However, this phenomenon of others understanding their words is not reported again.

The personal language of unknown tongues is not always a sign for others. Paul teaches:

> For he that speaketh in an unknown tongue speaketh not unto men, but unto God: for no man understandeth him; howbeit in the spirit he speaketh mysteries.
>
> —1 Corinthians 14:2

This type of tongues works "internally, in a good sense, to build us up in the faith and cause us to advance in the divine light."[2]

> He who speaketh in an unknown tongue edifieth himself.
>
> —1 Corinthians 14:4

According to the Amplified Bible, one who prays in an unknown tongue "edifies and improves" himself. The Living Bible says, "A person 'speaking in tongues' helps himself grow spiritually."

How can enough ever be said about the ongoing nonpareil power, intimacy, boldness, and enlightenment that the Holy Spirit baptism imparts? Truly the initial infilling marks an unforgettable occasion, but repeated fillings bestow joy indescribable, renewing inner strength day by day and providing an unparalleled manner of prayer in words that are unique to you.

EVEN WITH ALL its benefits, the baptism of the Holy Spirit does not make a person more righteous than any other believer or more worthy than another to stand in His presence. Only the spotless blood shed for man's redemption makes us righteous. Righteousness does not come by spiritual experiences or by a person's own merit. Instead, it comes only by the righteousness of our Savior.

> For He made Him who knew no sin to be sin for us, that we might become the righteousness of God in Him.
> —2 CORINTHIANS 5:21, NKJV

Think about the richness of that verse. We are the righteousness of God when we are in Jesus!

> ...much more they which receive abundance of grace and of the gift of righteousness shall reign in life by one, Jesus Christ...by the righteousness of one the free gift came upon all men unto justification of life...so by the obedience of one shall many be made righteous....That as sin hath reigned unto death, even so might grace reign through righteousness unto eternal life by Jesus Christ our Lord.
> —ROMANS 5:17–19, 21

Yes, the baptism of His Holy Spirit is a magnificent blessing. But thank God for the Lamb! Nothing but the atonement and its work of reconciling sinful man to a holy God can impart righteousness to the defective human heart. Given to us by His obedience, only His righteousness makes it possible for us to come into the presence of the Father as though we never sinned. Only His perfect righteousness gives us imperfect mortal beings the ability to reign with Him.

He makes His gift of righteousness available to everyone. All it requires is a repentant heart and faith to believe in Jesus as the Son of God. How blessed your life will be!

> And the work of righteousness will be peace, and the effect of righteousness, quietness and assurance for ever.
> —ISAIAH 32:17, NKJV

The high priest's breastplate with its jewels and engravings was so decorative. As a reminder of the blessings and protection our breastplate bestows, let's decorate it with the righteous jewels of everlasting works and glorious effects from the scripture we just read.

We place assurance on our vest. W never need to doubt the righteousness of Jesus as our refuge, our place of safety from the enemy, and our sureness of entrance into the Father's holy presence.

Let us inscribe quietness across our breastplate for two reasons. First, it is to hear His still small voice inside our heart. Then it is for the quietness that replaces worldly havoc—the serenity of abiding in the righteous blood and the calmness of knowing the Father's mercy and grace.

And then we add peace. Oh, the wonders of His peace!

> And the fruit of righteousness is sown in peace of them that make peace.
> —James 3:18

Now we secure our breastplate across our chest and vow to never take it off. Then the work and effect of His righteousness with its quietness and assurance will be instilled like precious stones upon our heart. The fruit of our righteousness will spread to others, bursting forth in abundant peace, because righteousness walks hand in hand with peace. This is a peace that knows God's acceptance, grace, mercy, and love. It is an inner, enduring peace that is not obtainable through legalistic, religious activities. This peace comes only by dwelling in the security of our perfect Savior's righteousness and abiding by the spiritual principles of His kingdom.

> For the kingdom of God is not meat and drink; but righteousness, and peace, and joy in the Holy Ghost.
> —Romans 14:17

How blessed we are as citizens of God's kingdom to partake of Christ's righteousness and be accounted worthy by His perfection to stand holy before the Almighty. We experience the joy of His Holy Spirit and know His peace.

So proudly we must stand in our belts of truth and breastplates of righteousness. Now in the knowledge of His truth and having become the righteousness of God in Christ, you and I are called to take this good news to a lost and dying world. The Hebrew word for *work* of righteousness in Isaiah 32:17 is an action word. The word *effect* of righteousness in the same verse refers to laboring and ministering. And so our time has come to sow the good fruit of righteousness by learning His way of peace.

Are we prepared? Not yet. First we must discover how to wear our third piece of spiritual armor, having our—

> ...feet shod with the preparation of the gospel of peace.
> —Ephesians 6:15

The Gospel Boots of Peace

We now unpack gospel boots. Oh, look. This is heavy combat footwear to spread the good news of God's peace and to enlighten all who are unsaved. By announcing a peace of total wholeness, restoration, and deliverance everywhere we go, those who have burdens are set free.

> How beautiful upon the mountains are the feet of those who bring happy news of peace and salvation, the news that the God of Israel reigns.
> —Isaiah 52:7, TLB

Just like the girding of the loins in ancient times, having one's feet shod signaled readiness for any journey or assignment. Sturdy footwear was essential for a warrior to advance in battle without concern for rugged ground. Even sandals used for fighting were built of thick leather with spikes on the soles to protect the foot from any protruding objects.

Why should we preach peace? Oh, the marvel of this word in the Hebrew language. As you recall the name *Yahweh Shalom*, you will remember that the Hebrew word for *peace* is *shalom*. Yes, what a word! Its meaning speaks so much stronger than our simple English expression.

Shalom means entire wholeness, "safe, well, happy, friendly, health, welfare, prosperity, rest and safety."[3] Wow! Just pause and think about that!

Yet, the word takes on even greater meaning as we dig into the origin of its root. Do you recall our earlier discussion about the way a Hebrew word extends from the form of a verb and always retains its verbal meaning? Well, what insight that adds to *shalom!*

Its verbal root, *shalam,* extends the awesome nature of its definition to "be safe in mind body or estate, to be completed, reciprocate, make amends, repay, make restitution, restore, reward."[4] In addition to producing safety, wellness, happiness, friendliness, health, wealth, and rest, the peace of God by its root *shalam* also restores and repairs anything the enemy has ever stolen!

In biblical days and still today many Jews greet each other by asking, "Shalom?" meaning, "Is anything about your life wanting? Are you whole in every way?"

Shalom is the peace that leaves no room for worry or despair. Greater than earthly contentment, it is complete gladness and fulfillment from on high. More than the absence of fighting, more than family harmony and neighborly friendliness, more than a treaty signed by nations—this peace gives superabundant serenity, restoration, and satisfaction. It is nothing missing, nothing lacking, nothing damaged!

Yes, what marvels *shalom* bestows. No wonder Isaiah calls it perfect peace

(Isa. 26:3), and Paul from his Jewish background speaks of the peace of God that passes all understanding (Phil. 4:7). Jesus identifies it as His peace not of this world (John 14:27).

As we look further into these scriptures, we will become prepared to march forth bearing this gospel of *shalom* to all, proclaiming the covenant promises of God's perfect peace and all its benefits.

> For the mountains shall depart, and the hills be removed; but my kindness shall not depart from thee, neither shall the covenant of my peace be removed, saith the LORD that hath mercy on thee.
>
> —ISAIAH 54:10

We have a covenant of peace from Almighty God! In the midst of worldly chaos we can stand on His assurance of *shalom* and know that when we abide in Him, there should never be anything missing, lacking, or even damaged. Very few are conscious of the existence of this promise, and fewer still realize the magnitude of this, His pledge to all believers.

This wholeness of this covenant flows continually from Yahweh Shalom, the God of Peace who sent the Prince of Peace to fulfill His promises. Just hours before our redeeming Prince of Peace surrendered His human life for sacrifice, He gave His word that His ultimate *shalom* would remain intact.

> Peace I leave with you, My peace I give to you; not as the world gives do I give to you. Let not your heart be troubled, neither let it be afraid.
>
> —JOHN 14:27, NKJV

On the cross of Calvary our Savior's death sealed the covenant of God's peace. Jesus not only bore our sins, griefs, sorrows, and sickness, but He also endured horrendous physical abuse that we might have all benefits of *shalom*. "The chastisement for our peace was upon Him" (Isa. 53:5, NKJV).

The New International Version words it, "The punishment that brought us peace was upon him." In The Living Bible we read, "He was chastised that we might have peace." The Revised Standard Version says, "Upon him was the chastisement that made us whole." The Amplified Bible calls it "peace and well-being." In Hebrew it is *shalom*.

What a price He paid. How sad that so few really grasp the extent of His suffering to give to us safety, rest, happiness, friendliness, health, prosperity, and restoration. Oh, the importance of spreading this gospel of peace to help the lost and dying understand the total well-being that Jesus obtained for us by His spotless blood. But even now we aren't quite ready for such a task until we learn how to walk in this peace ourselves.

We must lace our gospel boots securely as we try them on for size. Let us walk carefully as step by step we discover how to live in His perfect peace. How vital this groundwork is.

This part of spiritual armor is the only gear that calls for preparation before we march into battle. It orders us to shod our feet "with the *preparation of* the gospel of peace" (emphasis added). So how do we prepare?

We keep our minds on Him!

> Thou wilt keep him in perfect peace [shalom] whose mind is stayed on thee: because he trusteth in thee.
>
> —Isaiah 26:3

How do we achieve such a mind-set and total trust? In Philippians 4 Paul gives us precise instructions. Yet what a challenge to follow them!

Do we truly desire God's covenant of peace to be real in our lives—to daily experience His perfect *shalom* with nothing missing, nothing lacking, nothing damaged?

Then we must step down from the glory train and brace ourselves for boot camp. Here we'll encounter very rigid exercises that earn us the peace of God in all situations and prepare us to carry the gospel of peace to a hurting world. Let us resolve to follow these directions no matter how tight our gospel boots may get. It is necessary to complete this training. Full obedience is mandatory for success.

Our first requirement is. Rejoice always! We are to rejoice even when times get tough, not just once, but time and time again. Always rejoice. Rejoice. Rejoice.

> Rejoice in the Lord alway: and again I say, Rejoice.
>
> —Philippians 4:4

The second requirement. Shine as an example to all men! We do this by self-control—practicing temperance, sobriety, and restraint in all unpleasant situations. Yes, it's hard. But those who are weak in faith and also unbelievers will witness the evidence of the Lord's ever-abiding presence with His children. What could offer a better example of peace to the world? "Let your moderation be known unto all men. The Lord is at hand" (v. 5).

A third and even harder requirement. Never worry about anything. Never? Never! "Be anxious for nothing" (v. 6, NKJV). What fortitude this demands. Yet giving up all anxiety is not an option; it's a must.

But can anyone really accomplish this? Yes! When we consider the horrendous pain and danger in the life of Paul, the very one who gave these orders, it should build our confidence. If Paul accomplished this—and he did!—surely we can, too. So let us discipline, discipline, discipline ourselves not to worry.

The fourth requirement comes a little easier. It consists of simply asking with a grateful heart for God to meet all our needs. We are called to share our every thought and desire with Him, presenting our every request to Him in prayer with thanksgiving. Yes, everything. Let us always being thankful that He hears, that He cares, that He answers.

"... in every thing by prayer and supplication with thanksgiving let your requests be made known unto God" (v. 6).

Once we master these four things, His covenant promises of peace arise inside our inner man to rule and reign beyond all expectation and explanation. Oh, what reward we receive when the wonders of His perfect *shalom* spring to life! The next verse says, "And the peace of God, which passeth all understanding, shall keep your hearts and minds through Christ Jesus" (v. 7).

How are your gospel boots fitting so far? Keep them laced tight as Paul presents the rest of his instructions.

What can be left? It's choosing positive thoughts! Experiencing the God of Peace in all His fullness demands that we abandon any negative thinking:

> For the rest, brethren, whatever is true, whatever is worthy of reverence and is honorable and seemly, whatever is just, whatever is pure, whatever is lovely and lovable, whatever is kind and winsome and gracious, if there is any virtue and excellence, if there is anything worthy of praise, think on and weigh and take account of these things [fix your minds on them].
>
> —PHILIPPIANS 4:8, AMP

As we practice positive thinking, peace will rise above hardship and grief. It is difficult to train the mind, but what powerful results are produced by wholesome thoughts. Everyone can do it. Paul did. And so can you and I. Let's discipline ourselves and do it!

How? Instead of conjuring thoughts of worry and imagining negative things that may happen, let us choose to remember good things that have already taken place, the times God has delivered us from past storms. We are to rejoice in worship and put on "the garment of praise for the spirit of heaviness" (Isa. 61:3).

Anxiety generates fear. Praise generates cheer. As we fill our thoughts with praise, our spirit will take us to God's perfect peace, above all troubles.

God's Word teaches us to let good thoughts rule our minds. Our thoughts control our actions, mold our behavior, and develop our personality. Mastering them is mighty defense in warfare.

> Casting down imaginations, and every high thing that exalteth itself against the knowledge of God, and bringing into captivity every thought to the obedience of Christ.
>
> —2 Corinthians 10:5

This holds the secret of Paul's contentment and how he knew the peace of God in any situation. He says:

> I have learned, in whatsoever state I am, therewith to be content.
>
> —Philippians 4:11

With our boots fitting snugly, our preparation to carry the gospel of peace would seem complete. But no, there's still more. One more painstaking assignment emerges as lastly Paul tells us to pattern our lifestyles after his.

> Practice what you have learned and received and heard and seen in me, and model your way of living on it, and the God of peace (of untroubled, undisturbed well-being) will be with you.
>
> —Philippians 4:9, AMP

What an added challenge! With zeal and dedication Paul adjures us to follow in the footsteps of his gospel boots, so that we, as he did, can walk daily in the supernatural contentment he found in his God of peace. Oh, how much this require of us!

Paul not only found contentment wherever God led him, but also his life consisted of so much more. With dynamic boldness he not only preached but also demonstrated a miracle-working gospel. Empowered by the Holy Spirit, he mightily practiced the gifts of the Spirit (1 Cor. 12:4–10). Accepting the great commission of Christ, he demonstrated his anointing to the world with the miraculous signs that follow believers (Mark 16:15–18).

Paul was a powerhouse for God!

> And God wrought special miracles by the hands of Paul: So that from his body were brought unto the sick handkerchiefs or aprons, and the diseases departed from them, and the evil spirits went out of them.
>
> —Acts 19:11–12

He poured his entire being into preaching the simple saving message of Jesus Christ and His power. Without looking back, Paul, once the killer of the Christians, dedicated his reborn life as clay in the Potter's hands.

> And I, brethren, when I came to you, did not come with excellence of speech or of wisdom declaring unto you the testimony of God. For I determined not to know anything among you except Jesus Christ and Him crucified.... And my speech and my preaching were not with persuasive words of human wisdom, but in demonstration of the Spirit and of power, that your faith should not be in the wisdom of men but in the power of God.
>
> —1 CORINTHIANS 2:1–2, 4–5, NKJV

Paul gave his life for the souls of others.

> But I will most gladly spend [myself] and be utterly spent for your souls.
>
> —2 CORINTHIANS 12:15, AMP

This speaks the essence of Paul, the man who qualifies to give specifications, precept upon precept, for receiving *shalom*—the complete peace of God. How difficult it is to follow after the example of this dedicated apostle.

Yes, it is difficult to always rejoice, be in control of our emotions, never worry but give thanks in everything with prayer, think only on good things. But with determined discipline we can do it all. Paul says:

> I can do all things through Christ which strengtheneth me.
>
> —PHILIPPIANS 4:13

As we make a wholehearted commitment to begin practicing Paul's concepts, we will find victory in personally knowing the God of Peace, Yahweh Shalom, and Jesus as the Prince of Peace. We can walk in His covenant of peace—anywhere we go, with every step taking the gospel of peace to all.

Wait! We have one more thing to learn before we travel on. As we grow by Paul's instructions, we must be on constant alert because our enemy, the thief and murderer, stands nearby in the shadows. He generally plays along with religious acts, ignorance, and ho-hum attitudes. But when we begin to discipline ourselves in the supernatural peace of God and mature in God's Word—he arrives with vengence to reclaim his strongholds.

I speak a warning from experience! Without total repentance and denouncement of my past occult involvement, I know I could never have received the baptism of the Holy Spirit. Even after my heartfelt cry for forgiveness Satan wasn't about to surrender without war.

Shortly after I was filled with the Holy Ghost, Jim and I begin attending a church where the spiritual gifts moved freely and in power. With the anointed Christ of the Bible and the Spirit's fire within us, we increased in fervor and relationship with a holy, awesome God.

Then one morning I awoke with a splitting headache. Far worse than any head pain I'd ever encountered, it proved to be a direct invasion from the demonic realm. Like a sledge hammer thudding inside my skull, violent curse words that used the Lord's name in vain bombarded my brain. Never in my life had I indulged in cursing, yet these words shrieked over and over with every throb. I could not control them!

I wanted to scream, not only in pain but also from the emotional stress. What was happening to my mind? Was I going crazy? Was I having a nervous breakdown?

Frantically I dialed the pastor of our new church. Satanic bombs ripped through my head. His profanity continued to explode hard and loud, and I almost hung up.

Don't call him, all reason shouted. *Remember how the preachers scattered when you needed marital help? He'll shun you, too. And not only that, he'll also think you're stark-raving mad.*

Just as I started to slam down the receiver I heard the pastor's voice. In agony I blurted out the situation.

What a liar Satan proved to be! There on the phone line, the pastor responded without hesitation against the forces of darkness. Offering a prayer in the name of Jesus, he spoke directly to my diabolic attack and took authority over the vile words that pulsated in my brain. Instantly they fled. My headache vanished. The peace of God flooded my being.

I have refused to relate this incident to anyone until this writing. I have never allowed myself to even think about it. *To recall it could encourage demons to storm my mind again,* I reasoned. *The devil loves attention.* I told myself, *To tell others might glorify him.*

Then I felt the Holy Spirit nudging me to tell about it in this book. I now realize that reluctance to reveal Satan's tactics translates as fear of him—to his delight! It also leaves others unaware of his vices.

Now free from fright, I have overcome the enemy by the power of the spotless blood and the authority in Jesus' name. I abide in His covenant of peace, and I walk with my feet shod in the gospel of peace. Daily I abide in God's *shalom* with nothing missing, nothing lacking, and nothing damaged. The evil liar may have plotted long and hard for my soul, but he lost!

> He who is in you is greater than he who is in the world.
>
> —1 JOHN 4:4, NKJV

Now together you and I can fight the enemy, protected in belts of truth and breastplates of righteousness, prepared in gospel boots for combat. Yet we still have miles to go and more armor to unpack.

The Jubilee Express presses onward. More dangers still lurk amid the gloom of Satan's unseen spirit world as we move deeper and deeper into the darkness to fight the enemy. But each piece of our armor makes us stronger. From our boxes we take out the next of God's provisions: the shield of faith.

> Above all, taking the shield of faith wherewith ye shall be able to quench all the fiery darts of the wicked.
>
> —EPHESIANS 6:16

Chapter 14

Shield of Faith, Helmet of Salvation

O UT OF THE corner of my eye I caught sight of it hurtling through the air like a spear. Its open jaws were aimed straight at me.

"Hurry, Norma!" I screamed, shoving her slow and stocky body into a run. With strength I didn't know I possessed, I threw us both upon the plank porch of her parents' white farmhouse. I turned my head just in time to see the vicious reptile land in the spot where only seconds ago I had followed along behind the nine-year-old girl.

"Are you OK?" I asked, wondering how much this student at my workplace, a school for the mentally disadvantaged, understood.

Norma nodded and pointed. "Nake!" she said laughing. What a delightful child. Baby-soft blonde curls framed her round pudgy cheeks and warm blue eyes, and she always wore a smile. As we sprawled there on the porch, she leaned in total trust against my leg.

Though I was still horrified, I breathed in relief as I watched a long black streak slither toward a nearby cotton field. By my split-second glimpse of the white interior of its mouth as it leaped toward me and now zeroing in on its diamond-shaped head I easily identified it as a poisonous water moccasin.

But why had it, of all snakes, ventured into this well-traveled lawn? It was so uncanny. I guess a snake could turn up anywhere, yet like most wild creatures, they generally steer clear of areas with frequent human activity. And since water moccasins, as their name implies, prefer being around still water, they normally stay in or near a pond or lake. How unusual that this one lay concealed in the brittle grass of a dry front yard with no body of water anywhere near. It was as if it was waiting for its victim.

"Did you see it jump up at me, Norma? It wanted to bite me! We both had to get out of its way; that's why I pushed you. Are you sure you're OK?"

Nodding she pointed to where the snake had been. "It gone..."

I gave her a quick hug, and she readily hugged me back. Knowing Norma didn't fully comprehend danger, a sense of gladness washed over me that her mother wasn't standing at the door as she generally did. Otherwise I wouldn't have hopped off the school bus to walk along with the child.

When I got back to the bus, the driver's eyes were like saucers, her usual rosy face drained of color. "I've never seen anything like that snake!" her voice quivered. "It leaped out of the grass coming for you so fast I didn't have time to warn you. I don't know how you managed to see it, much less get out of its way!" With a deep sigh she shifted gears and muttered, "I hope I can pull myself together enough to drive."

This turned out to be the first bizarre incident of the day. Were they all mere coincidences? You be the judge.

For months I had taught the church congregation on Wednesday nights. On this particular evening, I began relating my former occult involvement, even though it was not in my notes. *Why am I telling this?* my brain clicked as I described the apparition of my friend's dead father then eleven years passed. Soon I felt I knew the answer when after church dismissed, Lena, a lady in her early twenties, rushed to me.

"I have to talk to you!" she exclaimed with wide eyes.

Lena always looked so attractive and neat. That night a yellow chiffon blouse accented her shiny black hair and bronze complexion, and being so petite she resembled an innocent little girl. Although I didn't know her well, she had appeared calm, in control, never without a friendly smile anytime our paths had crossed. But not tonight.

Shuddering she collapsed on a pew. With tears forming she peered up at me, "Because I usually help in children's church, I've only heard you teach twice. Both times you talked about demonic powers."

During all my nights of teaching I had mentioned the occult only one other time. As I listened to Lena, I came to believe that God Himself had directed my comments on the kingdom of darkness for her benefit.

"After the first time I longed to come to you, but I didn't have the courage. I've never told a soul about my problem, but I want to tell you now because I believe if anyone can understand, you can. Until I heard you teach I thought I might be crazy."

I heard fear in her voice and felt the trembling of her thin body as I dropped down beside her. Concerned, yet apprehensive about what she might say next, I merely muttered, "I'll do my best to help you."

"Oh, I so hope you can!" Her naturally tan face turned pale and drawn as she began her story. "As a teenager my friends and I conducted séances and called on spirits of the dead. We looked on it as just a scary game. Then one night in a room illuminated only by a candle, we sat around a table and were chanting when suddenly it lifted off the floor and floated in midair between us. It scared us so much that we never did any séances again, yet some weird presence I can't explain always lingered around me after that. And there's so much more." She paused, eyeing me for reaction.

"Go on," I said with heartfelt voice.

"Years later when my husband and I first married we lived in a trailer park. I got to know the woman next door pretty well. One morning I noticed that she didn't leave for work as usual. When she didn't come out all day, I decided she might be sick and I went over to check on her." Lena closed her eyes and bit her lower lip.

"And was she sick?"

Lena sobbed, "No, oh no! She was dead! Overdosed on heroine, I found out later. From the door I saw her sprawled across the bed. I knocked. She didn't move. I knew where she kept an extra front door key, so I let myself in and rushed to her. Her head was drawn backwards, her mouth wide open. I knew she was dead and couldn't be revived, but I tried anyway. Oh, it was awful! Her body, so stiff, so cold! For a long time I rocked her in my arms and wept.

"And then," she continued, "a horrible thing happened to me while I held her. Something, maybe the lingering evil that followed me from the days of the séances or maybe a demonic spirit coming from my dead neighbor—I don't know what—but something zoomed into my mind, and even though now that I'm a Christian it has never left. In fact, the closer I draw to Jesus, the more I go to church, the worse it gets. I have terrible nightmares. I feel constantly tormented and afraid. I cry and cry for peace, but it doesn't come!"

Fighting tears myself, I swallowed the lump in my throat and fumbled for tissues in my purse. I handed one to Lena.

"And not only that, some kind of ghosts have moved into my house!

My husband works nights, so I'm all alone, and sometimes in the middle of the night lights come on for no reason. Even when he's home during the day, jar lids pop off and move across the kitchen cabinet. Water faucets turn on by themselves. Neither of us knows what to do. We're scared that it might get worse." Her gaze met mine, "I've never told him or anyone before now about the evil presence that keeps me bound. Oh, can I ever be free?"

In search of answers her pleading eyes cut to my heart. *Holy Spirit,* my spirit cried, *give me words of wisdom.*

"Lena, the demonic world is real and dangerous. When Jesus becomes alive in a person's life, it seems that the devil steps in with a vengeance to maintain his strongholds. You gave him the upper hand by keeping his control over you a secret, and that's exactly what he wanted. I'm so glad that you found courage to expose him tonight. You need believers to stand with you in combat."

My heart throbbed as I relived the satanic cursing that had stormed my mind two years before. Though my encounter had been on a smaller scale, it gave me an understanding of her torment. What if I hadn't reached out for help? How could I have overcome the powers of darkness alone?

"Would you allow my husband and me, and our pastor if he can, to come to your house tomorrow evening and unite in force with you against these unnatural occurrences?"

Taking a long breath she closed her eyes. I waited. She finally uttered, "Yes." With the tissue she wiped her cheeks and tried to smile, "As long as you don't think I'm nuts, hopefully they won't either."

"If we come about six, will you go with us to a meeting afterwards?"

"What kind of meeting?"

"We call it our sharing group, and we meet every Thursday night. A few weeks ago one of the leaders, Mr. Smith, told us about his confrontation with a demon. It was so strange that if I hadn't experienced an uncanny vision myself, I might have had a hard time believing him. Do you have time now for me to tell you what happened to him?"

With interest Lena nodded for me to go on.

"Mr. Smith said he was driving home from a business trip when he felt an overwhelming urge to turn into a subdivision and stop at a house where several cars were parked. Met by strangers at the door he blurted out, 'I don't know why, but the Holy Spirit led me here.'

"He said the people were overjoyed and whisked him inside, explaining they'd prayed for God to send someone to help their friend. 'He's emotionally distraught, haunted by nightmares,' they told him, 'crying for no apparent reason. Last week he suffered two seizures, yet his doctors can't find any reason for them.'

"Mr. Smith said they motioned to a corner of the room where a frail man in pajamas stared at him from a chair. As he approached, the man wept uncontrollably and pleaded for help. At first he prayed for the man's healing. Nothing changed. But then when he began speaking against the powers of Satan, Mr. Smith claims that he literally saw a snake crawl from the man's mouth and slither out the front door. Instantly the man was set free."

Taking the young lady by the hand I asked, "Would you consider telling your story to Mr. Smith and have him pray for you?"

"Yes, oh, yes," she gasped.

Lena left after we confirmed with the pastor that we would meet at her house the following night. *What a day!* I thought as I scooped up my Bible and lesson material. Little did I realize that its perils were not yet over.

Since Jim had needed to leave earlier, our six-year-old son James and I caught a ride home with a teenage girl. Anne had scattered books and gym clothes for school in the backseat of her car, so James and I crowded together in a front bucket seat. I sat against the door.

"My seat belt on your side isn't working," Anne apologized. "And slam your door real hard because sometimes it flies open."

"Since we only have a mile or so to go we should be OK, but you really need to get these things fixed before someone gets hurt."

She laughed, "You sound like my mother!"

Piling my Bible and notes on my lap, I closed the car door with all my might and checked it. It seemed secure. But as our youthful chauffeur whipped around a corner, the door swung open, just as she had forewarned. Like a human bullet I shot from the car. With a thud I hit the street and skidded on my left thigh across blacktop that had been sealed with chipped gravel and dug into my flesh like hundreds of tiny razor blades.

"Are you OK?" Anne screamed, screeching to a halt and jumping out. Like lightning she raced to my aid.

"Yes." I struggled up. My dress was ripped, my pantyhose were in shreds, and blood streamed down my leg. An area the size of a football resembled charred hamburger meat.

"I'm so sorry," she moaned, "and you are so right. I have to get my car fixed!"

James chased down whirling papers and retrieved my Bible, then scooted to the back seat on top of Anne's belongings while I managed to pull myself back into the car. "I'm OK, healed by Jesus' stripes," I insisted, carefully balancing on one side.

Oh, it burned! Jim helped me clean out stony grit and medicate and dress the oozing wound before I tumbled into bed. Yes, what a day it had been.

The next morning I could barely walk. My leg blazed like embers eating to the bone. But having no one to fill in on the spur of the moment, I forced myself to go to work. Hobbling onto the school bus, I related my mishap to the driver.

"First a snake strikes at you, then you fall out of a car? Sounds like something's out to do you in!" she joked.

While she spoke it in jest, her words erupted a torch in my soul. Were the dangers from the day before direct demonic assaults intended to block Lena's cry for help? Of course, one can only speculate, but unearthly events that followed certainly pointed to satanic workings.

All day long fire raged in my leg. By the time I got home tightness gripped it in a smoldering ache. *O God,* I cried, I *can't let Lena down. Please deaden the pain and give me strength. Jesus did not die in vain. With His stripes I am healed!*

After prayer I recalled how my mother always used zinc oxide ointment on my childhood cuts and scrapes "to take the soreness out." I found a tube, smeared it lavishly on my raw and throbbing abrasion, and rewrapped it. Within the hour the burning let up and the aching pressure subsided.

Early that evening Jim and I met the pastor at Lena's house, a gathering that took only moments. While he prayed, pleaded the blood of Jesus, and anointed every room with oil, Lena, Jim, and I stood in agreement. Afterwards he had another engagement. The three of us scurried off to the sharing group meeting.

On the way we picked up Joe, a big rugged man who wore western shirts and cowboy boots and always had a tall tale or joke to share. His wife worked on Sundays, so he had started going to church with Jim and me a few weeks before. At the last service Joe had rushed to the altar, prayed to receive Jesus, and was planning to be baptized the upcoming Sunday. While his move to receive salvation was a step to appease his Christian wife and mend their teetering marriage, it seemed genuine. In fact, still elated over his decision, he settled into the front passenger seat, announcing that he had been counting the hours until Sunday. Like Lena, this was Joe's first time to attend our Thursday night fellowship.

Songs of worship were already underway when we arrived, and we hurriedly found chairs. One man who was on fire with the Word of God led a devotion. Then Mr. Smith, a wiry middle-aged man with a vivacious personality, took over, inviting people to give praise reports or share prayer needs. The boldness of his testimony for Jesus always made everyone feel at ease about pouring out their feelings. After several spoke up, Lena needed no prompting.

"I need help..." her voice broke. A hush fell over the room as she related her dilemma.

At first Mr. Smith asked God for direction and prayed with Lena for deliverance and peace. Then he directly addressed the demonic forces tormenting her.

Without warning Lena sprang forward as if struck by a lightning bolt. Letting out an earsplitting shriek, she leaped into the air then collapsed on the floor. With her slender body writhing she squealed like a trapped wild animal. Undaunted Mr. Smith persisted. "In Jesus' name depart from this child of God, you demons!"

Just when her screaming and thrashing relented, Joe flopped to the floor as though he was having a seizure. He moaned in guttural tones. Flying to his side Mr. Smith prayed. Joe's moaning ceased. He lay still.

Lena jumped up. With arms outstretched she danced around the room weeping in utter joy, "I'm free! I'm free!" In delight we all rejoiced with her.

Joe raised up, sat cross-legged in the floor with his face cupped in his hands. In an attempt to minister further, Mr. Smith knelt beside him, but at that instant Joe raised his head and declared, "I'm free, too."

Immediately Joe hoisted his lanky frame back into his chair. Everyone again rejoiced, assuming that Joe had also experienced deliverance, as he claimed.

But after we left the meeting Jim and I sensed that things were amiss with Joe. He was usually talkative, but he seemed withdrawn and hardly spoke. Lena laughed and praised God all the way home.

At church on Sunday Lena flitted over to us like an uncaged bird. "I'm free," she sang, "and the demons have left my house!"

Even though it should have been the day of his baptism, Joe declined to come. Despite all the efforts to minister to him, he never again returned to church. Joe fell deeper into a sinful life than ever before. In a rage he stormed from his home, and for months neither his wife nor aging mother knew his whereabouts. Joe's marriage ended in divorce.

Lena's personality soared. What a privilege to watch her spirit blossom. After a few months she and her husband moved away. Five years passed before I saw her again.

"I'm still free," she beamed, "Whatever haunted me has never returned. Jesus is so real in my life. I pray all the time. I hunger to be in church and learn more of God. Sometimes I get to sing solos."

My heart overflows with gratitude. What an awesome God we serve.

Every demon on this earth must bow to the power in the name of Jesus, the One who won our freedom. I weep for Joe. What happened to him the night of Lena's deliverance?

Witnessing that manifestation of God's authority over the forces of darkness gave an inkling of what it was like in the region of the Gadarenes when two men violent with demons approached Jesus and His disciples.

> They began screaming at him, "What do you want with us, O Son of God? You have no right to torment us yet." A herd of pigs was feeding in the distance, so the demons begged, "If you cast us out, send us into that herd of pigs." "All right," Jesus told them. "Be gone." And they came out of the men and entered the pigs.
>
> —MATTHEW 8:29–32, TLB

These demons were banished from the men and entered into the pigs. However, can demons from one person possibly enter another human being? Is this what happened to Lena when she cradled her neighbor's lifeless body against her breast? Could this also be what happened to Joe at our sharing group?

With all my heart for Joe's sake, I hope not. Yet all indications point to this conclusion. Why else would he collapse on the floor and moan as Lena was set free? What made him immediately turn from his new commitment to the Lord, sever all Christian connections, and return to his former sinful ways even worse than before?

Jesus says:

> When an evil spirit comes out of a man, it goes through arid places seeking rest and does not find it. Then it says, "I will return to the house I left." When it arrives, it finds the house unoccupied, swept clean and put in order. Then it goes and takes with it seven other spirits more wicked than itself, and they go in and live there. And the final condition of that man is worse than the first.
>
> —MATTHEW 12:43–45, NIV

Did Joe truly desire to be a Christian, or was his decision a superficial act? No one knows another's heart, but certainly a sincere conviction generates a will to overcome. A heart filled with Jesus leaves no room for evil to enter. An empty heart is Satan's delight.

True Christians cannot be totally possessed by demons in their spirit, or they would have no desire for God. From my experience with Lena as well as the demonic invasion that attacked my mind with curse words against

God, I believe demons can hang on to areas and fight until believers stand in faith against such strongholds. Diabolical forces can assault a person's mind and possibly take over even to the point of causing what the world calls a "nervous breakdown." They can also attack the body, consuming it in sickness and disease.

And it doesn't always take exposure to the occult for demons to strike. Whether by thought or action, dabbling in any sin—lying, gossiping, taking drugs, drunkenness, sexual immorality, negative thinking, murmuring, unforgiveness, or just plain doubt and unbelief—can give evil spirits grounds for entrance into the mind or body.

However, the heart of man, the inner entity that fellowships with God, would have to knowingly and willingly give itself over to evil for the person to be what we term as "possessed." Demons may find a weakness in a mortal mind and body and enter through that avenue to afflict and torment. But I truly believe they can never take over the spirit without open permission from the owner himself.

As humans we may not entirely understand demonic behavior. Only by reading related scriptures can we catch a glimpse into their ways. But because the Bible says we wrestle against principalities and powers of darkness, we can be sure that they attack in every possible way. Yet with the shield of faith we can triumph over them and all their fiery darts.

THE SHIELD OF FAITH

And now we hold up from our box of spiritual armor the fourth vital piece by which we can withstand Satan and his armies.

> Above all, taking the shield of faith, wherewith ye shall be able to quench all the fiery darts of the wicked.
>
> —EPHESIANS 6:16

How magnificent this shield of faith is. It comes with the special promise that it will enable us to quench not just some, but all the fiery darts of the wicked.

In biblical times a shield served an essential part in military defense. When a soldier charged in battle, wearing protective armor with his shield in position, he became a human tank. There were many shapes and sizes of shields, and some were so large that when they were locked together, they formed an instant fort around the troops. The enemy sometimes shot flaming arrows in an effort to break up their united screen of protection.

More than any other battle equipment, shields made all opposing arrows of less effect. Our shield of faith makes *all* of no effect!

"Above all," this passage says, we must take up our shields of faith. Only by faith can we come to God. By grace we are saved through faith (Eph. 2:8). It is His grace, our faith. Without faith it is impossible to please God (Heb. 11:6). It is not merely improbable. It is impossible, totally unachievable.

Faith must be our daily walk, "for whatsoever is not of faith is sin" (Rom. 14:23). *Whatsoever* means anything and everything.

Faith reveals God's righteousness in us. "For therein is the righteousness of God revealed from faith to faith: as it is written, the just shall live by faith" (Rom. 1:17).

Who are the just? They are Christians, those who believe in Jesus as the Son of God and follow Christ the Anointed One.

Yes, take the shield of faith above all—in everything you do, in every word you speak, everywhere you go.

Faith says, **F**orsaking **A**ll **I T**rust **H**im. It is trust in an unfailing God, and it never gives up. Faith forges ahead with steadfastness, without apprehension. It means that we keep believing, putting our trust in God's ability. If an answer is delayed—we remain confident in word and deed. We never waver in unbelief but wait patiently, staying obedient to the ways of God.

> For ye have need of patience, that, after ye have done the will of God,
> ye might receive the promise.
>
> —HEBREWS 10:36

"Now faith," Hebrews 11:1 says, "is the assurance of things hoped for, the conviction of things not seen" (RSV). In plain talk this means that we have complete confidence in something happening *before* we see it come to pass.

The number one enemy of faith is fear—Faith's **E**liminator, **A**nnihilator, **R**evoker. Fear kills faith. No one who fears has faith, and without faith no one can triumph over Satan's fiery darts. Jesus says:

> Be not afraid, only believe.
>
> —MARK 5:36

Faith is believing without fear or worry despite the circumstances.

It is once again time for us to leave the comforts of the Jubilee Express. Renouncing fear, we emerge to walk the road of faith. To observe faith take action over fear, we go back two thousand years to visit Matthew 8:23–27 and peer into an ancient ship that is gliding calmly across still waters.

Night's darkness envelops the sea. Hazy reflections of a half moon cast eerie shadows upon a large sea vessel. On board twelve able-bodied men, some of them former professional fishermen who know how to handle a ship, talk softly so as not to awaken their Leader, Jesus.

Look out! Without warning a huge storm arises. Wind whips against the sails. Gigantic waves rage and surge over the sides of the boat. As water rushes in, the boat rocks from side to side despite the frantic efforts of the sailors to stabilize it. Help, they're about to sink!

"O Lord, wake up!" wail the twelve, weak with terror. "Save us before we die!"

Jesus awakes. Seeing the storm He seems amused at their alarm. He laughs, "Why are you fearful? Oh, you of little faith!" He simply rebukes the wind, and calmness returns. Chuckling to Himself, He wraps up in His fringed cloak, rolls over, and falls back to sleep.

In their never-ending amazement of their Leader, His disciples just shake their heads and also laugh, "What kind of man is this! Even the winds and the sea obey Him."

How quickly faith overcomes fear. Fear was about to drown them, but Jesus came through with faith. He never feared. He always trusted His Father.

And now we come to another enemy of faith. It is doubt—**D**istrust **O**bstructing **U**nfailing **B**ible **T**ruths. Not only did the wind and the sea obey this Man who had no fear, but a fig tree also obeyed this Man who had no doubt. We stop next in Matthew 21:17–22; Mark 11:12–14, 20, 22.

After staying overnight in Bethany, Jesus and His disciples hike along the road to Jerusalem. Gnawing hunger alerts them that it is time to eat, but where can they find food so early in the morning? Oh, how nice to spy a fig tree in the distance. Happily they rush to it.

"Oh, no," they sigh, examining its branches, "not one single fig!"

Jesus says, "Let this tree never bear fruit again."

What a surprise the disciples have when they pass by the very next day and find a dead tree, completely dried up from its roots. Just as they had that night on the rolling waters, they marvel at their Leader's capability. "How did it wither so soon?"

Just beyond them stands the Mount of Olives. Turning His eyes in its direction He answers, "Have faith in God. In all truth I tell you this, if you have faith instead of doubt, not only can you make a fig tree wither away, but you can also command this very mountain to be removed and fall into the sea, and it will be done. All things, anything you ask in prayer—believing—you'll receive."

Oh, the strength of faith! Without fear, without doubt, faith reverses natural situations. It brings calmness in the eye of the storm. It overpowers the force of the wind and stops the waves. It takes authority over dark clouds and gives courage to trust until the sun shines through. Faith sees the assurance of sunshine ahead and claims it as so. It "calleth things that be not as though they were" (Rom. 4:17).

Our words are the expression of faith. We've touched on this before. Now with the shield of faith in hand, we can go deeper into this domain. We will not emerge until we learn to speak His Word and His will despite the way things appear in the natural. We turn first to Abraham, our prime example, the father of our faith.

What made Abraham so special to produce the seed that spawned the entire Jewish nation? Why did God bring forth the Promised Seed by Abraham's offspring? Why would the whole world be blessed through this one man?

> We say that he [Abraham] received these blessings through his faith. Was it by faith alone? Or because he kept the Jewish rules? For the answer to that question, answer this one: When did God give this blessing to Abraham? It was before he became a Jew—before he went through the Jewish initiation ceremony of circumcision....It is clear, then, that God's promise to give the whole earth to Abraham and his descendants was not because Abraham obeyed God's laws but because he trusted God to keep his promise....So God's blessings are given to us by faith, as a free gift; we are certain to get them whether or not we follow Jewish customs if we have faith like Abraham's, for Abraham is the father of us all when it comes to these matters of faith. That is what the Scriptures mean when they say that God made Abraham the father of many nations. God will accept all people in every nation who trust God as Abraham did. And this promise is from God himself, who makes the dead live again and speaks of future events with as much certainty as though they were already past.
> —ROMANS 4:9–10, 13, 16–17, TLB

The King James Version words the last part of verse 17, "... even God, who quickened the dead, and calleth those things which be not as though they were." Like a lighthouse this scripture can direct our faith through all the storms of life. Some of the most inspiring insight I've seen on this subject comes from Mrs. C. Nuzum in her tiny book *The Life of Faith*:

> Perhaps there is nothing spoken of in the Bible which is quite so hard for most Christians to do as to call "those things which be not as

though they were." Many honest people think they would be lying if they did this, and so fear to do it. But consider a moment; the Bible tells us that God cannot lie, and God calls the things that be not as though they were.

God says that we were chosen in Christ from the foundation of the world, and we were not yet born. God said to Abraham, "I have made thee a father of many nations," before he even had one child. God's greatest desire for His children is that they be like Him in all things. He says that Abraham was made "like unto Him...whom he believed, even God who quickeneth the dead and calleth those things which be not as though they were" (Rom. 4:17).

Abraham was made like unto God in this thing, and we are told to follow in the footsteps of Abraham. Because God does this and tells us to do it, it is impossible to be wrong in the least degree. Sin is disobeying God, and holiness is simply obeying and pleasing God in all things, at all times. God is holy and His will is holy, and when Christ dwells within us, He works through us His own obedience and holiness. One part of God's will is that we shall call those things which be not as though they were. This attitude honors God because we are believing His Word without outward evidence and thus we please Him; it also puts us in an attitude of faith to receive great things from God.[1]

Many times Abraham spoke of things that had not yet taken place as if they had already come about. This happened when he called himself Abraham, meaning "father of multitudes," even before the conception of his promised son Isaac. Before climbing the mountain to sacrifice his son, he declared to his men:

> Stay here with the donkey while I and the boy go over there. We will worship and then we will come back to you.
>
> —GENESIS 22:5, NIV

When Isaac asked where the lamb for sacrifice was, he replied:

> God himself will provide the lamb for the burnt offering, my son.
>
> —GENESIS 22:8, NIV

Why did Abraham speak this way? Because of faith. This demonstrates the ultimate of faith, speaking of things that be not as though they were. This activates an "assurance of things hoped for and the conviction of things not seen."

How can we reach such potential?

So then faith cometh by hearing, and hearing by the word of God.

—ROMANS 10:17

Faith grows by God's Word. It manifests as we read, study, memorize, and meditate on His Word. Knowing His Word gives wisdom of how and what to speak in the time of need. Faith to speak His Word brings answers and solves problems.

After I fell from the car on the way home from church I spoke, "I am healed by the stripes of Jesus." In spite of the burning pain I continued to claim God's Word. To the amazement of all who saw the initial wound, it healed completely in three days, leaving only pink smooth skin. Within a week even that faded away.

We must speak words of faith! All our words are so important. The rhyme "Sticks and stones can break my bones, but words can never hurt me" is hogwash! Words cause much deeper wounds than broken bones! Who cries when they recall the pain of a bone that has healed? But years pass and hurtful words can still bring tears.

Words create the atmosphere of our surroundings, building or destroying character, determining who we are, forming attitudes. Words shape destinies by bringing blessings or curses, healing or pain. Words direct success or cause failure, develop faith or tear it down.

Thou art snared with the words of thy mouth, thou art taken with the words of thy mouth.

—PROVERBS 6:2

Death and life are in the power of the tongue: and they that love it shall eat the fruit thereof.

—PROVERBS 18:21

And the tongue is a fire, a world of iniquity: so is the tongue among our members, that it defileth the whole body, and setteth on fire the course of nature; and it is set on fire of hell.

—JAMES 3:6

It is vital that we keep our tongues in line with faith. Let us put away the negative, stand on the positive, and strongly believe in a good outcome. Faith victories demand it. Real feelings, whether faith or doubt and fear, surface by our words. Real feelings cannot be hidden:

A good man out of the good treasure of his heart bringeth forth that which is good; and an evil man out of the evil treasure of his heart bringeth forth that which is evil: for of the abundance of the heart his mouth speaketh.

—LUKE 6:45

People say what they believe. They may speak words of faith in one breath, but if they whine about their problems in the next, we can be sure that their faith is not genuine. They may say that they believe in divine healing and claim scripture to support it, but if they talk doubt—I just don't know why God doesn't heal me, I'm afraid I may die—then their faith has failed, cursed by doubt and fear.

Out of the same mouth proceedeth blessing and cursing. My brethren, these things ought not to be.

—JAMES 3:10

God is our Rewarder, not our condemner. He designed the Garden of Eden for mankind, and for six thousand years He's been working with man to bring him back to that place with Him. During this time He has promised to never leave us or forsake us (Heb. 13:5). Well, you say, I just don't feel His presence with me today. You've just canceled your faith and opened yourself up for the devil to move in with depression, loneliness, despair.

We are called to trust God's Word. Instead of speaking defeat, we are to speak Bible promises from the heart and believe nothing else.

Keep thy heart with all diligence; for out of it are the issues of life. Put away from thee a froward mouth, and perverse lips put far from thee.

—PROVERBS 4:23–24

Let us repent of past negative words, proclaim faith, and steer our speech according to His Word. As we weigh our words wisely, we will see prayers answered, problems solved, and victory abound. Just as Jesus spoke scripture to the devil in the desert, so can you and I in the middle of our temptation, in the eye of any storm. We can overcome Satan as He did. By faith we can believe until the solution comes, remaining stable and verbalizing the answer as if it has already taken place. This means that we never envision ourselves as overtaken by the problem. Instead, by faith we see ourselves as free and clear, looking only at the fullness of His glory. By faith we will have it.

The Bible contains solutions for every problem, answers for every need. As we find the promises that fit our situations, we must believe and stand by faith upon His Word. Instead of coming unglued if the going gets tough, we can persevere and praise the Lord. Let us, like Abraham, call things that be not as though they were.

At first our flesh may tremble when instead of talking about symptoms to our friends, we say, "I am healed by Jesus' stripes, my youth is renewed like the eagle's." But as we train our faith to take charge, we will find that trust and belief, fueled by hope, outweigh every doubt and fear. Then, constructed by faith-filled words, our shield of faith will come alive to quench *all fiery* darts of the enemy.

But wait! Words along are not enough. Each shield must be fortified with benevolence:

> What good is it, my brothers, if a man claims to have faith but has no deeds? Can such faith save him? Suppose a brother or sister is without clothes and daily food. If one of you says to him, "Go, I wish you well; keep warm and well fed," but does nothing about his physical needs, what good is it? In the same way, faith by itself, if it is not accompanied by action, is dead.
>
> —JAMES 2:14–17, NIV

Here we see that conversation alone cannot suffice, nor can belief without action to back it up. James goes on to say:

> You believe that there is one God. Good! Even the demons believe that—and shudder.
>
> —JAMES 2:19, NIV

Christians must show their faith. A life of faith is a life of love. Without love accompanying faith, the abilities of the most educated prophet, even if he has superior understanding that makes him able to solve great mysteries, amount to zero.

> And though I have all faith, so that I could remove mountains, but have not love, I am nothing.
>
> —1 CORINTHIANS 13:2, NKJV

God calls us to reach out with compassion for humanity and help those in need.

> Blessed is he that considereth the poor: the LORD will deliver him in time of trouble.
>
> —PSALM 41:1

Yes, we need to lend a helping hand. Then when times get hard for us—the car breaks down, the refrigerator quits, bills pile up—we can rely on His Word, knowing that we have done our part. Oh, what abundant blessings this psalm lists for the person "who considers the poor."

> The LORD will preserve him and keep him alive, and he will be blessed on the earth; You will not deliver him to the will of his enemies. The LORD will strengthen him on his bed of illness; You will sustain him on his sickbed.
>
> —PSALM 41:2–3, NKJV

By all means let us reach out to the less fortunate and stand on God's Word without fear and doubt. That's faith in action.

In addition to love for our fellow man, faith must show our obedience and love for God.

> Was not our ancestor Abraham considered righteous for what he did when he offered his son Isaac on the altar? You see that his faith and his actions were working together, and his faith was made complete by what he did.
>
> —JAMES 2:21–22, NIV

Hebrews 11 tells of many who exhibited their faith by their actions: Abel, Enoch, Noah, Abraham, Isaac, Jacob, Joseph, Moses, Rehab, Gideon, Barak, Samson, Jephthah, David, and Samuel. What feats they accomplished for God. Although their examples are hard to follow, great rewards await those who do.

> And these men of faith, though they trusted God and won his approval, none of them received all that God had promised them; for God wanted them to wait and share the even better rewards that were prepared for us.
>
> —HEBREWS 11:39–40, TLB

We can be like the patriarchs of old. When God calls we can move by faith! Years ago someone advised me to attempt something so big for God that unless He intervenes, it cannot succeed. This stuck in my heart. God places a calling on every life and sets a destiny for everyone. Let us trust Him and step forth by faith to fulfill His dreams and goals for us. He walks with us every step to guide and show the way.

Trust in the LORD with all thine heart; and lean not unto thine own understanding. In all thy ways acknowledge him, and he shall direct thy paths.

—PROVERBS 3:5–6

WITH OUR FAITH now at its optimum, we once again ride on the Jubilee Express and press forward toward the realms of glory. Proceeding in the belt of truth and the breastplate of righteousness, prepared in gospel boots—above all, we add the shield of faith. Reaching into our armor box we bring out a sturdy type of headgear, our fifth provision for spiritual warfare.

THE HELMET OF SALVATION

And take the helmet of salvation...

—EPHESIANS 6:17

How important our helmets are! Worn not only in olden days, this protection is so crucial that soldiers still wear them despite our modern weapons. Construction workers and sportsmen wear helmets, aware of the possible consequences of injury to an unprotected head.

The helmet of salvation is a vital part of God's armor. It divinely protects our mind and administers salvation in spiritual battle. Salvation is God's mighty provision of rescue, safety, deliverance, health, and preservation from danger and destruction! Now we see that it is a defensive covering, a complete spiritual safeguard for our heads.

The head—the home of our mind and our brain—is the grand central station, bus terminal, airport of our being. Entrance is gained through the eyes and ears, and it is the birthplace of every attraction, the incubator for every idea. The head is the classroom where notions graduate to become actions, the storage unit for man's personal computer. The information we allow to enter, take root, grow, and amass inside our mind is what comes out in crisis moments. This explains why protection is so critical!

The testimony of Norman Williams's most amazing and harrowing encounter demonstrates this fact. Return with me now to a Full Gospel Businessmen's Meeting in 1980 to hear his glowing account of victory over tragedy.[2]

In March 1977 he departed California with his business partner aboard a 747 Pan American jet, planning to enjoy a nice vacation. Instead, he wound up in a fiery furnace and witnessed the agonizing deaths of many unsuspecting, unprepared people. In a matter of moments, raging flames and exploding metal ushered 593 souls into eternity. Only 70 people survived, and 10 of those soon died from injuries and burns. Others endured skin grafts and suffered prolonged illnesses, both physical and emotional. One ended up insane. Yet, Norman Williams stood before us that night in flawless appearance.

It began as a normal flight. However, because of a terrorist threat, officials prohibited the jet that transported Norman, 417 other passengers, and its crew members from landing at its planned destination. Along with other huge aircraft, they found themselves detained at the tiny airport of Tenerife in the Canary Islands. Most travelers were vacationers, impatient to get on their way. While they sat for hours, a solid blanket of fog settled over the area.

Then came the fateful mistake. Although they were still enveloped in the blinding density of the atmosphere, the pilot of Norman's flight received approval for take-off. He taxied across the overcrowded runway to move into position even though he had no visual control from above and his physical sight was virtually zero. Literally no one could see the impending danger!

Just moments before a KLM 747 jet from Holland had also received orders for departure. By refueling at Tenerife it had taken on 21,000 gallons of liquid and now weighed about 144,000 pounds.

Now with the pilots of both jets unable to see each other, the Pan American entered the path of the oncoming Holland KLM. As the KLM jet roared with its added fuel weight at its full lift-off speed of approximately 200 miles per hour, the pilot was unable to stop or turn aside by the time he came near enough to discern the American plane.

In the next moment its landing gear plowed through the roof of the American plane, dumping jet fuel on top of the passengers and saturating everything. Fire exploded everywhere. Above, every single soul aboard the Holland flight died within a matter of seconds.

In the middle of the flames and explosions Norman leaped to his feet. He turned to help the two women in the seats next to him, but flames already engulfed them. Directly in front of him he saw that his business partner was also burning beyond the point of rescue. Norman Williams stood there overwhelmed in shock and confusion.

Then a wonderful thing took place in his mind. As if in a vision, the prayer time he and his mother had shared before he left on his trip turned into a living reality. He heard her prayer for his safe journey. He saw her tears. He saw their hands together on the open Bible.

Confusion fled, and clear, rational thoughts burst forth. In the thick of the turmoil a sense of calmness swept through him. Boldness to fight took over, and like a computer screen his mind displayed the Word of God.

"I will never leave you or forsake you. I am the same, yesterday, today, and forever." Scripture after scripture flashed through his head. The words of Isaiah 43, "When thou walkest through the fire, thou shalt not be burned; neither shall the flame kindle upon thee," came alive inside his being.

As loudly as he could he began yelling, "In the name of Jesus and through His shed blood I stand upon Your Word, I stand upon Your Word, I stand upon Your Word, I stand upon Your Word!" Over and over he cried these words as he battled his way to safety.

Debris flew all around. A huge object knocked him off his feet and caused him to look up and see a hole gleaming in the ceiling at least ten feet above him. How did he get up to it? He had no recollection, but only remembered that sharp metal shredded his hands as he pulled his body through.

Still shouting, "I stand upon Your Word," he now stood upright on one wing, its surface slick and cold from fuel. Protruding at least thirty feed above the ground, he saw an appalling sight! He stared as people leaped to their deaths. Some killed themselves and others who had already jumped because they landed on them.

Knowing that another explosion was inevitable because the drenched wings carried fuel inside, Norman also took the plunge. He landed in safety on some grass and suffered only a broken left foot. "Father, I praise You, I praise You, I praise You," he cried over and over as he hobbled away. Still shouting praise, his heavenly language took over.

What a miracle this godly man experienced. Of the 348 persons who died on the Pan American, 114 were burned beyond recognition. Among them were the two ladies who had been beside him, his business partner who had been seated in front of him, and also the passengers who had been directly behind him. None of the people who had been around him could be identified, and they were part of a final mass burial in California.

Norman Williams had no burns whatsoever, not even one singed hair. His only injuries were the deep cuts on his hands and the shattered bones in his foot, and he completely recovered from them. But it was such a tragedy that so many met such a terrifying death. How horrifying it was for him to witness such horrendous pain and hear the helpless cries of frantic voices wailing in agony and screaming for their loved ones. Some people just sat, evidently overcome with shock and unable to move.

Perhaps the most penetrating memory Norman had was the curses that escaped the lips of dying souls. He later learned that the last recorded words on the Holland jet's black box were violent swearing by the pilot. Oh, just to think, that the pilot was taking the Lord's name in vain as he entered eternity.

How contrary this was to Norman's nature. Reared in a Pentecostal home, he had accepted Jesus as his Savior at age seven. Aghast at the outburst of obscenities by people as they faced sudden death, he researched human behavior to discover the reason. His findings about the conduct of people at their point of no return carved a lasting impression in my heart, as much as the wonder of his deliverance from the fiery crash. In his taped testimony he said, "I found where they said that human beings respond in moments of disaster, in moments of crisis, as they have programmed themselves in life to respond. It's an automatic thing with them. If they have been blasphemers, for example, in their lifetime and they have programmed themselves to be blasphemers, this is the way they automatically respond in a moment like that."[3]

Norman Williams had programmed himself in God's ways! Oh, what a wonderful revelation to realize that you're automatically set to breathe the name of Jesus in a moment of disaster. Even in a fiery furnace Jesus abides with the person plugged into the Word. As I listened to Norman Williams, I realized that I had experienced the same saving power when my daughter drowned. As a young, unlearned mother I had possessed no theological knowledge to cry out in Jesus' name, but my heart knew the Son of God. And He was on my software!

Why, oh, why do so many gamble with eternity? Those who think that they will call out to God in a crisis moment are greatly fooled. They won't do it. Whatever exists in their "computer" will come out. We must put on the helmet of salvation and cover our thoughts with the power of deliverance! Let us fill our heads with a database for God and guard our eyes and ears from evil, daily renewing our mind.

> And be not conformed to this world: but be ye transformed by the renewing of your mind, that ye may prove what is that good, and acceptable, and perfect, will of God.
>
> —Romans 12:2

The time of our trip to glory passes quickly, and our miles on the Jubilee Express grow shorter. Soon we will face our Maker. Are we mature and ready for entrance into heaven? Can we stand before the scrutiny of His eyes and hear Him say, "Well done, My good and faithful servant?"

Are we transformed into God's goodness with minds renewed to "prove what is that good, and acceptable, and perfect will of God?" Or are we conformed to the world more than we realize? How can we be certain? Our train pulls into a depot, and as we get off we notice a building across the street. Over its entrance a sign reads, "Testing Center." *Oh, no,* our hearts flip-flop. *We don't want a test!*

For our own good we must find the courage to walk over to the building for an examination of our thinking. For eternity's sake we all need to take an honest inventory of the data in our minds. What captures our thoughts? Day by day, little by little, does the world win out? We say we love God, but how much of His Word have we actually stored inside our being? Let's take this comparison test and dare to face the truth.

1. Name twelve different kinds of cereal. Now name the twelve disciples of Jesus.

2. List ten current secular television programs and the times they are aired. Now recite the Ten Commandments in order.

3. What are the names of Santa's reindeer? The seven dwarfs of Snow White? The twelve tribes of Israel? The seven churches in Revelation?

4. Do you know your telephone number and address? Of course, you do. Your social security or driver's license number? If not, can you find them quickly? Sure you can. But do you know where the Lord's Prayer is located in the Bible? If not, how quickly can you find it?

5. Can you show someone how to read a road map and follow its directions? If you have an opportunity to lead a person to Jesus, can you quickly show them scriptures that reveal biblical teaching about salvation?

6. Can you recite "Mary Had a Little Lamb," "Twinkle, Twinkle Little Star," or "Humpty Dumpty"? How much of "The Night Before Christmas" can you quote? How long would it take you to say all the nursery rhymes and poems you know from memory? How many Bible verses do you know by heart? What about chapters? How long would it take you to quote all the scriptures you have memorized?

This could go on and on with questions about sports figures, newscasters, and movie stars we can name versus the judges, prophets, kings of Israel, and books of the Bible. But enough testing. We get the picture.

How did you score? What occupies your "computer files"? Consider this—if all the Bibles were destroyed, how much could your knowledge help reproduce it? How short most of us fall! I felt very conscience-stricken the first time I took this test. It revealed how little I knew of God's Word.

At a revival meeting in a small Methodist church the speaker asked if anyone could recite various selections from the Bible—simple and familiar things like the Ten Commandments, the beatitudes, the fruit and gifts of the Spirit, the whole armor of God. Not a single person could name them. I was ashamed and appalled. How can we who claim to be Christians sit in church week after week, live in houses overrun with Bibles, and yet know so little? That very night I made a commitment to begin studying and memorizing God's Word. It wasn't easy, but I stuck to it.

Jesus said, "You shall love the LORD your God with all your heart, with all your soul, with all your strength, and with all your mind" (Luke 10:27, NKJV). He is the Word (John 1:1, 14). How can we profess to know Him and yet not know what is written in His love letter—a message so important that He has preserved it for us throughout the centuries?

Do you remember what it was like to fall in love? Oh, how that special person's name echoed with your every heartbeat. Every thought centered on your cherished one. With every breath feelings of love swelled until it seemed that your lungs would burst. How you longed to be with, to talk to, and to know more about your sweetheart.

Jesus chose us to be His bride. He is our Bridegroom! Shouldn't every cell of our body, every reflection of our mind, every throb of our heart cry out for Him? Are we yearning to know Him better and ardent to be with Him? Are we prepared and ready, watching and hoping for His coming? Do we love Him with all our heart, soul, strength, and mind?

We must try harder! With heartfelt devotion let us vow to maintain and monitor our "computers" with daily diligence. As we learn His Word, we will recognize every satanic virus and close the window of invasive ideas that are intended to delete our relationship with the Almighty.

God calls us to put on the helmet of salvation and thereby guard every thought. As we march forth in the divine power of God's Word, we defeat every notion that pops into our head and attacks the ways of righteousness. When we put the Holy Word to use, it produces power so tremendous that it conquers every stronghold.

Oh, those strongholds! Besetting sins hold us from our destiny with God.

They first appear as tempting inclinations that zoom without warning into our intellect. Then as we let them linger, they move in and expand into binding vices and addictive habits that hold us captive and control our will and emotions.

How can we fight? Certainly not by mortal struggle against flesh and blood, but by spiritual combat against demonic forces. We must attack with the Word in the spiritual realm. It gives protection far more durable than that provided by any human resource.

> For though we live in the world we are not carrying on a worldly war, for the weapons of our warfare are not worldly but have divine power to destroy strongholds. We destroy arguments and every proud obstacle to the knowledge of God, and take every thought captive to obey Christ.
>
> —2 CORINTHIANS 10:3–5, RSV

It is vital that we know His Word and let it be the focus of our minds. No matter what our age or present agenda, we can begin today to program ourselves to memorize. Yes, what a task this proves to be. It demands diligence, discipline, and grueling exercise of the mind. But what an effective means of warfare!

> For the word of God is quick, and powerful, and sharper than any twoedged sword, piercing even to the dividing asunder of soul and spirit, and of the joints and marrow, and is a discerner of the thoughts and intents of the heart.
>
> —HEBREWS 4:12

After I was convicted at the revival meeting, I focused on storing His Word in my memory bank, word for word. While I still have far to go, I am greatly blessed by the scriptures that are now imprinted in the crevices of my mind. If sleep evades me, all I need to do is recall these verses, and my attention ceases to dwell on the cares of the world. His Word takes over and sleep soon comes. By training my thoughts, I automatically pray and then remember specific scriptures anytime I awaken during the night. Soon I fall asleep again.

Night or day I find myself in prayer speaking Bible promises that build faith or quoting psalms of praise to Him. When temptations arise, I follow Jesus' example. With the data I have stored I tell Satan, "It is written..."

How grateful I am for that preacher who cast such shame on me! His words lit a spark within my heart and moved me to program God's Word in my mind. How this man enriched my future. If you didn't do so well on the test a few moments ago, don't be offended or offer excuses. Instead, let it produce that same spark in you and discover how memorizing God's Word gives you a weapon to fight against the devil.

Stand on God's Word! Stand on God's Word! Stand on God's Word! Although Norman Williams couldn't recall how he rose over ten feet inside a blazing plane and reached the hole to freedom, his mother offered a simple solution. She suggested that perhaps he formed a new rung on his ladder to the top each time he cried, "I stand upon Your Word!" Oh, the almighty power of His Word. Nothing, absolutely nothing in the power of man or demons will ever overcome it.

Now back on the Jubilee Express, we find our seats and peer into our armor box. Carefully wrapped in a cloth trimmed in fringe we locate our sixth piece of spiritual armor. Even before we pick it up, we sense that it represents the very subject we've been discussing:

> . . . the sword of the Spirit, which is word of God.
>
> —EPHESIANS 6:17

Chapter 15

Sword of the Spirit, Mantle of Prayer

"I ATTEND A NEW Testament church," Wayne told me. "The Old Testament," he pursed his lips and shook his head, "is just a history book, that's all."

Although I didn't respond then, I confronted my co-worker the next day in the employees' lounge. "Wayne, I've been thinking about what you said yesterday, and I searched my Bible last night. I read where Isaiah says that the grass withers, the flower fades, but the Word of God stands forever. In Psalms it says that His Word is forever settled in Heaven. Second Timothy, in the New Testament, tells us that all scripture is given by the inspiration of God—but I never found any scripture that calls the Old Testament just a history book."

"I didn't say it was in the Bible," he retorted.

"Ohhh..." I replied thoughtfully, "then God didn't say it. Some *person* did."

How do people come up with notions that contradict the Word of God? I once heard a Sunday school teacher say that the story of Jonah never happened. "It's simply a parable," he told us. "Medical experts say no human could survive in the belly of a whale or fish."

Not long after he made this declaration, I read an account of a man who lived in the nineteenth century and survived after he was ingested by a whale. This report related that his skin had bleached white from the whale's digestive juices.[1]

Whose report do most believe? The Bible says that God prepared the fish that swallowed Jonah (Jon. 1:17).

How often we overlook the fact that the One who designed man has sovereign power to accomplish anything He pleases? The general public believes that if medical science declares it, if man says it, that's the way it is. The following verses describe the haughty attitude of people who exalt their ideas above the knowledge of God and His written Word. They "became vain in their imaginations, and their foolish heart was darkened. Professing themselves to be wise, they became fools...changed the truth of God into a lie" (Rom. 1:21–22, 25).

But how can we accept the Bible as the Word of God verbatim? Can we by any natural means prove it to be above reproach? Take your seats and buckle up! Prepare for another adventure on our train to glory. The wheels are poised, eager to spin on the scarlet rails again. The engine is in gear, ready to begin our trip. Our Conductor's twinkling eyes reveal His enthusiasm for discoveries that are just around the bend. As the train gains speed, in anticipation we hold up our next piece of spiritual armor.

Why, it's a Bible!

> ...the sword of the Spirit, which is the word of God.
>
> —Ephesians 6:17

The Bible, our sword, is the only aggressive weapon we need to battle with the enemy! However, for this Book to serve as our spiritual sword we must erase every doubt that it could be anything other than what it claims to be—the inexhaustible, inflexible, impeccable Word of God. We set out now to subject it to various tests that will verify its absolute authenticity.

Will it pass? Yes, yes, God says, yes! Its validity is declared throughout His Word.

> For ever, O Lord, thy word is settled in heaven.
>
> —Psalm 119:89

> Thy word is true from the beginning: and every one of thy righteous judgments endureth for ever.
>
> —Psalm 119:160

The grass withereth, the flower fadeth: but the word of our God shall stand for ever.

—ISAIAH 40:8

Heaven and earth shall pass away, but my words shall not pass away.

—MATTHEW 24:35

The Jubilee Express streaks through the darkened hillsides with blazing light that outshines the notions of all skeptics and brings us into the full awareness of the magnitude of His sword. We ride in tingling anticipation as we embark upon this exploration of invaluable insight to verify the Book of all books, to prove the phenomenon of this Holy Writ of God by the tangible, concrete discoveries of man.

Oh, the wonders of this Book! None other can compare in age, in circulation, in revelation. Yes, this solemn oath of God, sharper than any two-edged sword, overcomes all attacks by the intellectual elite. It survives any criticism from liberals. It rises above the challenges of science. Throughout the age of mankind it has always maintained its supreme place as the Book of all books. And it always will.

What a Book! It was compiled over at least 1,500 centuries from the writings of at least forty-four different authors from varied locations and numerous walks of life. Some were educated, but often they were not. Their number included kings, judges, public officials, teachers, farmers, fishermen, and shepherds. One writer was a physician, and another, a tax collector. Yet this Book flows with a harmony that is mathematically impossible for so many separate human intellects to have assembled in such a span of years—unless there was a supernatural Presence directing them.

Whether they wrote prose or poetry, each author had his own unique style. They addressed many subjects, from the dawn of creation until the end of time. Their writings included biographies of successes and failures and descriptions of culture, customs, and traditions. They taught about religion, covenants, love and hate, and good and evil. They gave us a library that included a Book of drama, a Book of prophecy, a Book of redemption, and yes, also a Book of history.

Though it was penned by many men, this superhuman Book of all books has only one Author. Its contents are inspired by the Holy Spirit of God Himself. Given by inspiration of the whole Being of Elohim, it is His Word and reveals His will, His work, and His plan for all mankind. He, and only He, is the real Writer.

FIRST WE PROBE its validity as a history book. Thumbing through its pages we read of the divine design of Creation, the Flood, the wanderings of Abraham, the exodus from Egypt, the fall of Jericho, and the frequent falterings of a chosen people. We view the birth and life of a Savior—finding accounts of His miracles and details of His crucifixion and resurrection. But are these writings true and accurate?

As our train stops, we grab our khaki shorts and wide-brim hats and descend with pick and shovel to dig into lost sites for hidden evidences that have been covered by the sands of time. As we delve into these long-lost treasures with experts in this field, we will seek to confirm God's Word as historically factual.

The most indisputable physical proof of God's undying truth undoubtedly lies in the astounding accuracy of biblical parchments known as the Dead Sea Scrolls. A native of the region of the Dead Sea accidentally stumbled across the first of these numerous discoveries in a remote cave in 1947. From then until 1962 searchers uncovered many more manuscripts with writings that date back to days long before Jesus' birth and continue until probably right before His death.

What a find! Except for the Book of Esther, every book of the Hebrew Bible was unearthed, each one when compared to today's Bible proved to be in precise text! Later we'll inspect them more thoroughly, but for now we turn our attention to other archeological treasures that have not been so widely reported. Findings that substantiate actual Bible events await as we leave our train to dig into Jerry M. Landay's book *Silent Cities, Sacred Stones.*[2]

We quickly revert to 1862 to join George Smith, a young gentleman who practically camps out at the British Museum in London. Why? He is engrossed in the huge collection of approximately twenty thousand clay tablets that have been preserved from ancient Nineveh. At this point no person of modern times has ever been able to read them.

Twenty thousand documents? How did so many happen to be kept together? An Assyrian king in the seventh century b.c. gathered and stored every writing he could for his own kingdom library. How important are they to biblical history? These tablets "represented the sum total of the written heritage of Mesopotamian civilization (the land of the Bible) which had been copied and recopied by scribes for hundreds of generations stretching back to the days of... the third millennium b.c."[3]

It's no wonder that Mr. Smith can hardly bear to be away from them. A museum official, impressed by his obsession with the clay inscriptions, hires him to organize and repair the very artifacts he loves so much! For ten years

Mr. Smith catalogs them. And in the process he discovers the mystery of deciphering this ancient cuneiform of Assyria!

"One day in 1872, Smith was studying a fragment, the now famous Tablet XI. Suddenly he sat bolt upright and caught his breath. He reread the passage."[4]

Oh, what evidence of biblical accuracy is revealed as he reads for the first time a long poem about the Flood of Noah's day. Here is just a portion— "...When the seventh day arrived I sent forth and set free a dove. The dove went forth, but came back; since no resting-place for it was visible, she turned round."[5]

Soon at a meeting of the Society of Biblical Archaeology Mr. Smith stuns the audience with his announcement—"On reviewing the evidence, it is apparent that the events of the Flood narrated in the Bible and the inscription are the same, and occur in the same order."[6]

Mr. Smith "...succeeded in piecing together a complete version of the Mesopotamian flood saga before his death. It leaves us in no doubt about the connection of early Hebrew tradition with Mesopotamia."[7]

According to *Silent Cities, Sacred Stones*, other finds that have been dated to the time of Abraham produce bona fide documentation of the cities mentioned in his day. Inscriptions even list the same names as Abraham's relatives. Whether they identify his actual kinsmen may be argued, but this discovery definitely proves that the origin of such names stems from ancient Mesopotamia.

Additional archeological discoveries that are documented in Landay's book relate and confirm the customs and cultures of societies and communities from times of antiquity to as recent as A.D. 135. But this time span presents far too many sights for us to visit on the Jubilee Express. We must move on to examine the evidence of others' findings.

Our digs into past eras would not be complete without searching out some of the amazing discoveries noted in *The Signature of God*. Its Christian author, Grant Jeffrey, tells about many documents that testify to the Bible's credibility. Inscriptions from ruins of the Tower of Babel authenticate the Genesis account.[8] A poetic writing supports the famine in Egypt during the time of Joseph.[9] Engravings on the rocks of Mount Sinai prove to be written in ancient Hebrew. They describe wilderness events that followed the Jewish exodus from Egypt and include a record of the crossing of the Red Sea, the murmurings against Moses, and the supernatural provision of water in the desert.

All these are amazing finds, but one discovery stands out to me. Immense burial grounds have been found in the Sinai Desert. The author says that all indications point to these graves as those of the children of Israel who died at the hand of judgment when they demanded meat instead of manna and God sent them multitudes of quail to eat (Num. 11:13).

Gravestones were engraved in legible writings and bore carved drawings of quail. Some pictures showed quail flying or just standing. Others illustrated what appeared to be birds propped up for cooking. The inscriptions of the artifacts have been translated to read:

> The apostates smitten with disease by God, by means of feathered fowls. Smitten by God with disease in the sandy plain, (when) exceeding the bounds of moderation.
> Sickening, smitten by God with disease; their marrow corrupted by God by means of the feathered fowls. The people, given over to destruction, cry aloud. God pours down deep sleep, messenger of death, upon the pilgrims. The tomb is the end of life to the sick, smitten with disease by God.[10]

How perfectly this lines up with the story in Numbers 11. It leaves no room to question the reason for this cemetery.

Another remarkable discovery described in *The Signature of God* surfaces in Professor John Garstang's excavations of Jericho in the 1930s. His findings revealed that the walls of Jericho actually fell outward, giving Joshua and his men easy entrance over the ruins into the city. The author states, "This fact is important because the evidence from all other archeological digs around ancient cities in the Middle East reveal that walls of cities always fall inwards as invading armies push their way into a city."[11]

What does the Bible say?

> The wall fell down flat, so that the people went up into the city, every man straight before him, and they took the city.
> —JOSHUA 6:20

Why don't the secular media publicize such archaeological discoveries? To do so would mean that they acknowledge God and admit His Word as truth. Although reporters give a small fanfare to the fantastic discovery of the Dead Sea Scrolls, it seems that they prefer to sensationalize unsolved mysteries. They present questions about the possibility of locating Noah's ark, the whereabouts of the ark of the covenant, or the authenticity of the shroud of Turin as Jesus' actual burial cloth.

As intriguing as these subjects may be, rehashing them over and over tends to make even definite Bible truths debatable. To a Christian, however, true intrigue comes from the joy of locating ancient sites and inscribed words and artifacts that bear proof of the historical accounts in God's Word.

Without a doubt, the Dead Sea Scrolls are the most outstanding positive natural evidence for the accuracy of the Bible. Many may wonder how their wording so long ago can compare so exactly to Scripture in Hebrew today.

When one considers the diligence of the Jewish scribes, the precision of these ancient scrolls is no surprise. Copying Scripture required strenuous training, flawless discipline, and grueling responsibility. Every jot and tittle had to be printed by hand, error-free and to perfection. Each letter in every single line was counted to be sure that it was an exact match of the manuscript being copied. If *one* *w*ord was misspelled or *any letter* was left out or formed incorrectly, the *entire* document was quickly destroyed and often buried.

The Dead Sea Scrolls, dating back as far as the second century B.C., contain all the books of the Old Testament with the exception of the Book of Esther. They also yield marvelous evidence of Jesus, referring to Him as Messiah and telling of His crucifixion. Until the discovery of these scrolls, the writings of Flavius Josephus were the main reliable source of history during the times of Jesus. From around A.D. 37 to A.D. 95 Josephus wrote extensively, detailing culture and events. In his account of Pontius Pilate, he inserts this confirmation of Jesus:

> Now there was about this time Jesus, a wise man, if it be lawful to call him a man; for he was a doer of wonderful works, a teacher of such men as receive the truth with pleasure. He drew over to him both many of the Jews and many of the Gentiles. He was [the] Christ. And when Pilate, at the suggestion of the principal men amongst us, had condemned him to the cross, those that loved him at first did not forsake him; for he appeared to them alive again the third day; as the divine prophets had foretold these and ten thousand other wonderful things concerning him. And the tribe of Christians, so named for him, are not extinct to this day.[12]

Many sites in Israel also verify the existence of Jesus. Writing in the *Prophecy Study Bible*, John C. Hagee says:

> New Testament archaeology has enjoyed spectacular finds since World War II. The Dead Sea Scrolls give glimpses into the life of the Essenes, a sect of Judaism that influenced the culture of Jesus' time. References have been found in inscriptions to Herod, Pilate, Sergius, Paulus, Erastus, and Gallio among the political figures of the Gospels and Acts.

The synagogue of Capernaum and Peter's nearby house have been excavated. Recent tunneling along the foundation of the temple in Jerusalem has uncovered evidence of the Roman destruction from A.D. 70 as well as the kinds of stalls set up there by merchants and money changers. The Bible is rooted in reality; archaeology keeps digging up more of those roots.[13]

No matter how much we probe in natural discoveries, the greatest proof for the accuracy of biblical teaching about Jesus exists in plain old common sense. Think about it—the New Testament was written by eyewitnesses and completed less than fifty years after Christ's death and resurrection. Can you imagine what an uproar it would have caused among the people of the day if the written accounts had not been true?

Grant Jeffrey says it this way:

> To put this in proper perspective, imagine that some writer wanted to create a false story in the 1990s about President Kennedy performing miracles and being raised from the dead for forty days after his tragic assassination in November 1963. To succeed with his plan the writer would have to accomplish two impossible things: (1) He would have to simultaneously acquire every one of the millions of books and newspaper reports about the president and insert his counterfeit passages in this material without being detected by a single reader. (2) He would have to simultaneously convince millions of people around the world to accept his forgery as true, despite the fact that these people who were alive when Kennedy lived have independent recollections that contradict his invented story.[14]

Someone once gave me a book that said Jesus plotted His own crucifixion. It also claimed that His resurrection was a hoax. Even as the author explained how this was accomplished, I wondered who could believe such a story. Perhaps the body of Jesus could have somehow been stolen from the tomb if the huge stone blocking its entrance was rolled away even while the Roman soldiers were standing guard, but...

Why would anyone endure such torture just to have some imposter pose as his resurrected self? How could all His family, friends, and disciples not recognize a phony? Even if they were in on the scheme, wouldn't there have been at least one person to cry fraud? After seeing Christ in His risen state, ten of the disciples willingly died violent deaths for proclaiming the gospel of Christ. Why would anyone willingly give his life for something he knew or suspected to be nothing but a ridiculous chain of lies?

These are the questions I asked as I looked at the accusations of this book from a natural standpoint. If only I had known the Bible to be the book of prophecy that it is. Setting all other literature aside, one can be convinced of the Bible's authenticity by merely considering this:

How could any mere mortal plot his death and its aftermath so well that every single prediction of the Scriptures was carried out to the letter? At least three hundred prophecies of the Old Testament speak of the birth, ministry, and death of the Messiah. All were precisely fulfilled in the earthly life of Jesus Christ. The Scriptures foretold that He would descend as the seed of the woman (Gen. 3:15), from the tribe of Judah (Gen. 49:10), through the lineage of David (2 Sam. 7:12–16). Isaiah 7:14 declares His virgin birth, and Micah 5:2 places it in Bethlehem. Psalm 41:9 speaks of His betrayal by Judas, and other passages such as Isaiah 53:3–7 and Psalm 22 give details of His suffering and death. We could go on and on.

YES, THE WORD of God stands solid as a history of the past, and it also endures as so much more. Even more than the discovered documentations of the past, prophecy proves the divine inspiration of the Word of God. Not conceived by the minds of men but given instead by the Holy Spirit, Bible prophecy withstands the test of exactness without one failure.

> And we have the prophetic word [made] firmer still. You will do well to pay close attention to it as to a lamp shining in a dismal (squalid and dark) place, until the day breaks through [the gloom] and the Morning Star rises (comes into being) in your hearts. [Yet] first [you must] understand this, that no prophecy of Scripture is [a matter] of any personal or private or special interpretation (loosening, solving). For no prophecy ever originated because some man willed it [to do so—it never came by human impulse], but men spoke from God who were borne along (moved and impelled) by the Holy Spirit.
>
> —2 PETER 1:19–21, AMP

At its writing some 25 percent of the Bible was prophecy waiting to be fulfilled. Can any other religion dare to risk its reputation by foretelling hundreds of events before they happen? No!

But in this respect the Word of God stands 100 percent perfect. Approximately half of its prophecies have come to pass, without flaw, exactly as proclaimed. Who besides a sovereign omniscient Being could know these things, sometimes thousands of years in advance, without one shred of inaccuracy?

Of all the Old Testament books, none gives such graphic prophetic detail as Daniel. Daniel's prophecy was an accurate preview of significant events that would happen in the history of Israel starting with the time of Nehemiah in 444 B.C. While some of Daniel's prophecies came to pass in his lifetime, others, such as his prediction of Alexander the Great, took place long after his death. Liberal scholars who seek to explain away such impeccable proclamations once claimed that the words of Daniel were forged, written much later by some unknown author. However, when the Book of Daniel was found intact among the Dead Sea manuscripts, their accusations proved groundless.

What are the prophecies of Daniel? They range from describing the outcome of the empires of Babylon, Medo-Persia, Greece, and Rome, which have been fulfilled, to End-Time events, some of which we see unfolding before our very eyes today.

He says that at the time of the end, "Many shall run to and fro, and knowledge shall be increased" (Dan. 12:4). Civilization rode into the twentieth century on horses and in wagons, not much different than transportation in Daniel's day. In a span of only one hundred years it zoomed into the twenty-first century in rocket ships. Medical, scientific, technological, and spiritual knowledge have exploded. Doesn't Daniel's insight into the future fit our times to a tee? Who other than a supreme, all-knowing Deity could reveal such things to a mortal man so long ago?

Daniel details events of the End Times and describes the Antichrist. Since all of Daniel's prophecies that have happened proved to be true, isn't it safe to say his prophecies yet to be fulfilled will also happen exactly as he declared?

Without a doubt all Bible prophecies continue in perfection. Perhaps the most outstanding fulfillment in recent times is that Israel after all her years of wandering without a homeland became recognized as a nation in 1948. Who could have predicted such a thing? Yet, over and over God's Word insisted it would happen.

> And I will bring again the captivity of my people of Israel, and they shall build the waste cities, and inhabit them; and they shall plant vineyards, and drink the wine thereof; they shall also make gardens, and eat the fruit of them. And I will plant them upon their land, and they shall no more be pulled up out of their land which I have given them, saith the LORD thy God.
>
> —AMOS 9:14–15

> I will bring you out from the people, and will gather you out of the countries wherein ye are scattered.
>
> —EZEKIEL 20:34

Ezekiel 37 with its vision of the dry bones presents an allegory of the Jews reuniting as a nation and coming alive again in the last days. Has it happened? Yes! And they have rebuilt waste cities and now import produce from land that lay desolate for hundreds of years.

BESIDES THE SUPERNATURAL fulfillment of prophecy, what other proof should God need to display to reveal His Word as authentic? None!

He has now unsealed the Bible code, a mysterious series of letters embedded in the original Hebrew language of the Old Testament. If any one factor proves that God Himself directed absolute control over the composition of the Word, it is these thousands of messages hidden within the initial text of His Holy Script. Code experts explain that it is mathematically impossible for these implanted messages to occur by random chance.

Even though I did not learn of it until 1997, it has been known for quite sometime that rabbis had detected words encoded in original Hebrew text many years ago. Why wasn't this phenomenon widely publicized then? Because the messages were so few. Human brains alone were simply not equipped to find their letter sequence in great number. It took our age of high-speed computers.

Have you heard of the code? My knowledge of it stems simply from devouring books by a variety of authors,[15] reading other reports, and hearing various speakers on the subject. From my studies I offer this brief explanation of its workings.

By skipping letters in equal sequences—such as every fifth, seventh, even fiftieth letter—words and sometimes sentences are spelled out within passages of Scripture and pertain to the related subject. For instance, I read that *Yeshua,* the Hebrew name for Jesus, surfaces one letter at a time at equal sequences of letters where a prophetic scripture speaks about the Messiah. Also inserted in these verses in close sequence are the names of all the disciples, "Mary," and other related Bible names.

This in itself is overwhelming. Even more amazing is the fact that many modern historical events also emerge by skipping letters at equal distances. Examples are *Hitler, Nazi,* and *Holocaust* being found together with phrases such as *in Germany.* Still more mind-boggling, names associated with world-shattering assassinations surface—Mahatma Gandhi, Anwar Sadat, Yitzhak Rabin. Appearing with *A. Lincoln* is the name *Booth.* In words dealing with the assassination of John Kennedy, *Dallas, Oswald,* and *Ruby* are interlaced as is also the name of his brother R. F. Kennedy. And this provides only a minute sampling of the numerous discoveries of hidden past, recent, and current events communicated in the Bible code.

Can this code be found in other books? No! Many other Hebrew writings, ancient or otherwise, have been tested, but such intricate patterns of words cannot be detected in them. Although trained skeptics of science and theology have tried to refute the existence of the code in the Bible text, none have been able to do so. Its discovery is so extraordinary and its legitimacy is so undeniable that both *Time* and *Newsweek* magazines, as well as other magazines, journals, and books, have written of its incredible significance.

Who other than an all-seeing, all-knowing, almighty God could know of events that would take place thousand of years later and encode them in a book? How unique that He would allow them to be uncovered in our day and time. Is this a fulfillment of prophecy? Could this be what God spoke about so many hundreds of generations ago?

> But you, Daniel, shut up the words, and seal the book until the time of the end; many shall run to and fro, and knowledge shall increase. . . . Go your way, Daniel, for the words are closed up and sealed till the time of the end.
>
> —Daniel 12:4, 9, NKJV

Are you skeptical about the Bible code? Those who are untrained in the Hebrew language can purchase computer software programs that will enable them to examine it. Check out the wonders of His Word for yourself! Accurate history, perfect prophecy, a unique code within its pages—these affirm the authenticity of the Bible as God's Word. What a Book!

THE ABOVE ANSWERS may not completely satisfy our questions about the validity of the Bible. The reason for this is that God wants us to come to Him by faith, not by scientific findings or theological studies. We are called to faith in a wonder-working supernatural Being who designed all of creation and rules over it—in eternity past, in the beginning, in bygone eras, now, today, in eternity future. We must come to Him by faith. Only by faith can we discover the true wonders of His Word.

The Bible is alive! It is our strength against principalities, powers, and rulers of all wickedness in Satan's demonic realm. It gives us wisdom of discernment between good and evil. It is our triumphant weapon.

For the word of God is living and powerful, and sharper than any two-edged sword, piercing even to the division of soul and spirit, and of joints and marrow, and is a discerner of the thoughts and intents of the heart.

—HEBREWS 4:12, NKJV

His Word is our guide through dark times.

Thy word is a lamp unto my feet, and a light unto my path.

—PSALM 119:105

His Word is wisdom, completeness, and provision for His work.

…and that from childhood you have known the Holy Scriptures, which are able to make you wise for salvation through faith which is in Christ Jesus. All Scripture is given by the inspiration of God, and is profitable for doctrine, for reproof, for correction, for instruction in righteousness, that the man of God may be complete, thoroughly equipped for every good work.

—2 TIMOTHY 3:15–17, NKJV

His Word is the way into salvation.

Receive with meekness the implanted word, which is able to save your souls.

—JAMES 1:21, NKJV

His Word is truth.

Thy word is truth.

—JOHN 17:17

His Word is life.

My son attend to my words; incline thine ear unto my sayings. Let them not depart from thine eyes; keep them in the midst of thine heart. For they are life unto those that find them and health to all their flesh.

—PROVERBS 4:20–22

His Word is the Son of God Himself!

In the beginning was the Word, and the Word was with God, and the Word was God. He was in the beginning with God….And the Word became flesh and dwelt among us, and we beheld His glory, the glory as of the only begotten of the Father, full of grace and truth.

—JOHN 1:1–2, 14, NKJV

His Word is Jesus—the Lamb of God, our Savior! His Word is His Name!

He was clothed with a robe dipped in blood, and His name is called The Word of God.

—REVELATION 19:13, NKJV

When we pray to the Father in the name of Jesus, our prayers are backed by the entire glorious, miraculous, wondrous Word of God! What power we hold in our hands—the sword of the Spirit, the Word of God, the name of Jesus. Yes, we have the power of Jesus Himself!

THE PRAYER SHAWL

Physically exhausted but spiritually exhilarated, we once again take our places aboard the Jubilee Express with new and overflowing appreciation for the Word of God. At each seat our packages from the village now sit empty.

Well, that is except for one last article. We still have not examined the cloth that covered our sword. What is it? It appears to be merely a piece of woven fabric trimmed in fringe. A large scarf or cape perhaps? It certainly doesn't look like part of any military gear. Yet we know that someone intentionally placed it at the bottom of every box.

For what purpose? What more can we need for battle? We are decked out in uniform—our belt of truth, breastplate of righteousness, gospel boots, shield of faith, helmet of salvation—and armed with the mighty sword of the Spirit. Aren't these six pieces of armor adequate for our need to stand against the evil one and all his army?

Eyeing our Conductor, we see His approval as we gather the cloths to our laps. They feel soft and warm like virgin wool. As we unfold them, we find that they are large and rectangular with stripes running lengthwise, accented by a fringe sewn along its bottom edge and elaborate knotted tassels on all four corners. So intricate in design, it seems that it might be some type of sacred clothing fashioned under divine direction. Is it a special garment to accompany our armor?

Yes, our Conductor nods. It's a prayer shawl. He shows us how to position it over our shoulders. This, our seventh provision for spiritual warfare, is an excellent finishing touch to make our armor whole.

Praying always with all prayer and supplication in the Spirit, and watching thereunto with all perseverance and supplication for all saints.

—EPHESIANS 6:18

Seven is God's number for complete perfection and fullness. Prayer is a special mantle that adds an extra touch of splendor to our uniforms. With pride we place it over our shoulders, thinking of the prayer shawl that is worn in Jewish synagogues today. We recall that God's chosen have worn it in moments of peril and grief, in joy and celebration, for hundreds and hundreds of years. It is no wonder that it is a significant part of their religious practice.

But our Conductor attests that it is much more than an article of religious attire. While the train hums along on the scarlet rails, He urges us to rely on the light of our swords to search out the mystique of this time-honored cloak. He calls us to not only explore the external pathways of its past, but to also to embark upon its internal workings in the present. What insights lie ahead as we delve into the symbolism of the ancient Jewish mantle to discover its spiritual meaning for the Christian.

In the natural, it was a holy vesture of woven cloth fashioned in the days of Moses under the Old Covenant. Designed by the omniscient mind of almighty Yahweh Himself and created in simple man-made material for His Hebrew tribes to wear, it set them apart as His chosen in the eyes of the world.

In the spiritual, it is a part of His grace, a holy vesture, not of a touchable cloth but an invisible covering that reaches into the inward parts of a righteous heart. It is a dynamic warhead of holy apparel displayed, not upon the body, but in character and actions. It is available, not to a certain few He chooses, but to everyone who chooses Jesus.

Our train speeds now into a new adventure to uncover hidden parallels and shadows that reveal these concepts. Such delight will flood our souls as new perception of the mantle unfolds in wonder and magnificence before our eyes.

We begin our adventure in Numbers 15 with the Lord's instruction to Moses. "Speak unto the children of Israel, and bid them that they make them fringes in the borders of their garments throughout their generations" (v. 38).

The size of this garment was larger than the rectangular shawl of today, and it was fashioned as a tunic to wear over their robes. Called the *tallith* in Hebrew, in English the Bible refers to it as a cloak or mantle. With its added decoration it served as a holy raiment to constantly remind them of the Law and of God's greatness.

> And it shall be unto you for a fringe, that ye may look upon it, and remember all the commandments of the LORD, and do them; and that ye seek not after your own heart and your own eyes, after which ye use to go a-whoring: That ye may remember, and do all my commandments, and be holy unto your God. I am the LORD your God, which brought you out of the land of Egypt, to be your God: I am the LORD your God.
>
> —NUMBERS 15:39–41

How well this divine vesture instilled loyalty to God. Now the outer garment of His people displayed an obvious sign of commitment to Him, identified them as the seed of Abraham, and presented a visible means of separation from the pagan world. Its symbolic trim created a sense of dignity, building the esteem of Jewish heritage. Each thread of fringe at the hemline stood for one of the 613 statutes of the Law. Longer corner tassels gave representation to the Holy Name, *Yahweh*.

No Hebrew could ever overlook the supreme importance of this tunic. How could he? Swaying with his every step, its border continually relayed the precepts that governed every part of his life and reminded him that the sovereign One was his God. What a symbolic connection it established between its Designer and its wearer. Even the covering it provided for his body typified God's ever-abiding presence.

Draping the mantle over his head, the Jew transformed it into a tent of prayer. It became a protective canopy that provided warmth in times of cold and relief from the heat of a scorching sun. Because of all its benefits, the Jew valued it as a steadfast guide and welcomed comforter.

Remember Elijah's remarkable mantle? Under its anointing his accomplishments far surpassed the realm of mere human capability. Seven miracles are attributed to this prophet. His prayer stopped rain for three and one-half years (1 Kings 17:1; James 5:17). He made a widow's depleted supply of oil and meal last until the drought was over (1 Kings 17:12–16). He restored life to this woman's dead son (1 Kings 17:17–23).

Before the eyes of the prophets of Baal, he summoned fire from heaven. The fire consumed his sacrifice to Jehovah despite the fact that it had been drenched in water (1 Kings 18:36–38). His prayer brought a deluge of rain and ended the drought (1 Kings 18:41, 45). Twice he called down fire on companies of men the king had sent to arrest him (2 Kings 1:9–12). With his mantle he divided the waters of the Jordan River (2 Kings 2:8).

Elijah's faith may have lacked perfection when he fled in fear from the vengeance of Jezebel and hid out on Mount Horeb, but God never forsook him. Imagine him alone, huddled under his mantle, a weary prophet waiting for his Lord to speak. From One so powerful he expects a thundering voice. Yet a personal God descends with a quiet voice, so still and small. Can't you picture him humbly burying his face into his mantle while, like a close Friend, a Most High God softly gives direction to His servant?

Shortly after leaving Mount Horeb, with his courage restored, Elijah finds Elisha plowing in a field. He must detect a special quality in this farmer, because he casts his sacred cloak upon him, thereby calling Elisha to accompany him as his disciple. What an impression it makes on Elisha. Never again will he be the same. Bidding good-bye to his parents and farm life, he slaughters his oxen for food and gives it away. Without one qualm he strikes out after this miracle-working preacher, never to look back.

NOW THE JUBILEE Express slows down and stops. With our Conductor in the lead we hop off in 2 Kings 2:1–13 to join these two men in the land of the Bible, 850 B.C.

There they are! We spot them wending their way along the dry plains of Israel with dust stirring at their feet and tinting their sandals a dingy white. At the hems of their tunics tassels bounce as side by side they step with haste. While we scurry to get within earshot our spirits alert us, *Today the Lord will whisk Elijah into heaven!*

Both men, also by divine revelation, realize that the time for Elijah's departure is near. Their minds wrestle with this bombshell. Yes, they know that glory awaits, but facing the unknown weighs like lead upon their souls. Although Elijah yearns to watch and wait for His Maker's glorious arrival alone, young Elisha burns with determination to share his leader's every remaining moment. As they march along methodically we can just imagine Elisha's thoughts. *What will I do without my mentor? I am so inept alone. For months I've served the Lord under Elijah's protection, secure in his wisdom and maturity. Without his anointing, how can I even think of carrying on?*

In the shade of a big rock Elijah stops to catch his breath. Of course Elisha waits with him, not daring to let him out of his sight in this desert place. He knows that the Lord could appear any moment. Stroking his beard Elijah sighs, "Elisha, stay behind while I go to Bethel."

Elisha's eyes blur. How could he as Elijah's friend even consider letting him face this time alone? Taking an affectionate step toward the older prophet, he grips him by his shoulders and says with quivering voice, "As truly as the Lord and you both live, I'll not leave you!"

Elijah heaves and trudges onward with Elisha at his side. In silence they push ahead until they arrive at Bethel, where Elijah manages to step aside for a moment.

Seeing Elisha by himself a group of excited prophets rush up to him. "O Elisha, do you realize that the Lord will take your master away this very day?"

"Yes, I know." With a mourning heart he adds, "But please don't speak · of it again."

Ready to continue, Elijah returns to Elisha. Again he appeals, "Wait here. The Lord is sending me to Jericho."

Without hesitation Elisha repeats even more firmly than before, "As truly as the Lord and you both live, I will not leave you!"

On the road to Jericho time drags by like it does for a bride the morning before her wedding. Onward they push toward Elijah's destination with their hearts pounding wildly. Oh, how much longer now?

A dry breeze swirls the sand from time to time. In the distance we hear a donkey bray. They pass a few people, but both men seem unaware of anything other than their own deep feelings as they continue side by side hardly speaking. When they finally reach the city, several prophets pull Elisha aside and whisper, "Are you aware that the Lord will take your master away today?"

"Yes, I know. Please say no more about it."

Before long Elijah pleads a third time, "Stay here, Elisha. The Lord is sending me to Jordan."

Elisha cries, "I will not leave your side!"

Once more in pace together, Elijah and Elisha resume their journey, yet not entirely alone. Fifty prophets file behind keeping their distance. As they look on, the two men come to the river Jordan. How will they ever cross?

Elisha halts. He stares with wonder as Elijah, barely breaking his stride, whips his mantle off and twists it together. The younger prophet's eyes now sparkle in delight as he watches Elijah strike the flowing water with his garment. Behold! The river splits and Elijah steps on a supernatural path between two liquid walls. Laying aside all misgivings, a chuckling Elisha turns to wave farewell to the gaping prophets. He skips behind Elijah, grinning from ear to ear in admiration of his undaunted leader.

As Elijah reaches the far bank hearing the prancing behind him, he glances back and catches a glimpse of Elisha's beaming face. Despite himself a smile flickers across his lips. Yielding to Elisha's persistence he shakes his head and pauses for him to catch up. "Before I'm taken away tell me what what I can do for you."

Elisha's face lights up even more brightly, "I want a double portion of your spirit to be upon me!"

How honored and touched Elijah seems. His heart melts. Maybe instead of being so engrossed by his own anticipation of his departure he should have been more sensitive to Elisha's uneasiness. With moist eyes he extends an arm around his faithful follower's broad shoulders. As they continue together step by step, their spirits bond as one.

"You ask a difficult thing," Elijah says, "but if you see me taken away, your request will be granted." They proceed in deep conversation. Though we long to listen in, the words they share now are very personal and quiet, and we can no longer hear them. It seems that we trail behind for miles.

Without the slightest warning the heavens blare like thundering trumpets, nearly knocking us off our feet. The blue sky gives way to a blinding burst of red flames as a dazzling chariot pulled by blazing horses dives between the two prophets. In the twinkling of an eye Elijah is caught up into the chariot, raptured from Earth by a gigantic whirlwind into the untold heights of almighty God!

"I saw it! Yes, I saw him taken away!" Elisha cries. Ripping his own tunic from his body he reaches up to receive the mantle of Elijah as it floats down into his outstretched arms.

The Scriptures do not record that Elisha performed any miracles until after he received Elijah's cloak. But now what a mighty man of God is born! Under the anointing of Elijah's mantle, his ministry explodes with impelling force. Fourteen incredible feats—exactly double those of his predecessor—are listed to his credit.

The first happens almost immediately. On his way back he uses the phenomenal mantle and splits the Jordan River as Elijah had (2 Kings 2:14). Later, he purifies putrid water in Jericho (vv. 20–21). When he curses forty-two disrespectful youth in the name of the Lord, bears charge from the woods and maul them (v. 24). He miraculously supplies water for Israel's King Jehoshaphat (2 Kings 3:16–20). He multiplies a widow's oil supply (2 Kings 4:1–7), raises the Shunammite's child from the dead (vv. 19–37), and makes toxic pottage harmless (vv. 38–41).

With twenty loaves he feeds a hundred people (vv. 42–44). By his instructions Naaman receives healing (2 Kings 5:10–14), and then, because his servant, Gehazi, chases after Naaman for payment, Elisha pronounces the leprosy of Naaman upon him (vv. 20–27). He makes an axe-head float (2 Kings 6:5–7). By supernatural knowledge He reveals Ben-Hadad's secret battle plans (vv. 8–12) and defeats the Syrians by praying for them to become blind (vv. 14–23). The last wonder of Elisha occurs after his own death when a dead body touched his bones and came to life (2 Kings 13:21).

What a mantle!

WE STROKE OUR shawls with deep appreciation. Yes, it is a magnificent covering over our armor. Yet we've only scratched the surface of its significance. Much more enlightenment awaits. As we return to the train and our trip resumes, it suddenly dawns on us that Jesus Christ Himself is the predecessor of our mantle!

At Jesus' baptism by John the Baptist, the Spirit of God descended upon Him like a dove, enduing Him with power from on high, covering and enabling Him as a mighty spiritual cloak. Before this He had accomplished no miracles. From that day forward He ministered with fortitude, boldness, and wonders beyond the realm of mortal man. He withstood all the temptations of the devil in the wilderness, spoke to multitudes with astonishing wisdom and authority, overruled sickness and death, and overpowered demons. No circumstance could hold back His anointing. No influence could thwart His purpose.

Under this new dynamic mantle His ministry erupted like wildfire. People flocked to His side. Human eyes had never before witnessed the manifestation of such supernatural power. But mystery surrounded Him. He bore no outstanding physical features. People saw Him as a typical rabbi, who like all Jewish men wore His mantle with fringe and special knotted cords along the hemline.

We travel to the scene of the encounter between Christ and the woman with the issue of blood. With determination she fought the crowd to reach this Man of miracles—just to lay hands on the fringe of His mantle.

> And, behold, a woman which was diseased with an issue of blood twelve years, came behind him, and touched the hem of his garment: For she said within herself, If I may but touch his garment, I shall be whole.
>
> —MATTHEW 9:20–21

Without a doubt His tasseled cloak accompanied Him not only while He healed the sick, but also when He turned water into wine, multiplied tiny bits of food to feed thousands, cast out demons, and raised the dead. Even though the cloak customarily accompanied the Jew in burial, Roman soldiers gambled for Jesus' garment at the foot of the cross. This gives us a spiritual picture of His mantle spreading even to the Gentiles.

Once again we see our Lord at His last supper before the arrest leading to His crucifixion. We notice that He and His disciples all possess a fringed tunic of their own. Tomorrow Jesus will die upon the cross. Intently we listen as He speaks to His disciples. "Though I will no longer be with you, after I depart—the Comforter, who is the Spirit of Truth, will be with you as your Counselor and Guide." (See John 14:16–17; 16:7, 13.)

Foreheads wrinkle, and puzzled looks cross every face. How can they accept the idea that their faithful Master, this Man of wonders, will no longer be physically among them?

No! They must never let this happen. In denial they shake their heads. Until this point they have been able to approach their Friend in person with needs, questions, and requests. How can this Comforter take His place? How can the Spirit of Truth counsel and guide them as He has? Whatever can Jesus mean? While He continues, every eye stays glued on Him.

> In that day ye shall ask me nothing. Verily, verily, I say unto you, What-
> soever ye shall the Father in my name, he will give it you.
> —JOHN 16:23

Earlier Jesus had identified the Comforter as the Holy Spirit, who won't just abide with them, but will dwell in them. (See John 14:17, 26.) Now Jesus tells them that when this happens, they can come directly (without a priest) to the great and mighty Yahweh simply by praying in the name of Jesus. How can this be?

What new concepts these are. Though it is beyond their comprehension at this point, Christ is moving them from the natural realm into a spiritual realm. Things will change from this night forward. Yet for now, how can they grasp the magnitude of the moment? How can they even begin to perceive that this Man, their miracle-working Leader who has lived among them and guided them as a mortal Friend is now to be their Savior by His death? "Until now you've asked for nothing in My name, but from now on, ask and you will receive, that your joy may be full," Jesus reassures them. (See John 16:24.)

What a legacy He leaves His disciples as He gives them this infallible means of prayer by the authority of His name. And what a Comforter He promises in this One who will accompany their every step when His physical form departs from them. Not an earthly mantle like Elijah gave Elisha, this is a divine mantle, the Holy Spirit.

But what about us? Can we receive this mantle, too?

Before Jesus leaves the Passover meal for the Garden of Gethsemane on the night of His arrest, He pours His heart out in prayer, "Father, the hour has come. Glorify Your Son, that Your Son may also glorify You."

From this Man so torn apart inside we hear His prayer of John 17. Agonizing yet wonderful words escaping from the perfect heart of a Man so devoted to His Father's will, determined to complete His mission of redemption—regardless of the pain. Even in the gnawing dread of His awaiting torture, He calls out in behalf of others.

How heavy His petition for His disciples weighs upon His soul, as He knows He must leave them. "I don't pray that You take them out of the world, but that You will keep them from evil." Our hearts ignite in gratitude as His next plea echoes. A request that is not bound by time, it releases words that travel like healing balm to all future ages. Yes, oh, yes, with these words of hope for every generation, He intercedes for us!

"I don't pray for My disciples alone, but I also pray for them who shall believe on Me through their word." Undying love and saving power for everyone issued from His precious prayer that night. All souls come to the knowledge of the Son through the message of His disciples. Yes! This prayer was for all who have received the gospel during the last two thousand years, and it's for all who now are and those yet to come. Yes, His mantle includes you and me!

Oh, what a wondrous prayer. And what a glorious time of events that are about to unfold—the cross, Christ's death and resurrection, His ascension into heaven, and the coming of the Holy Spirit to all men. In a span of fifty days it all takes place.

Now we visualize the resurrected Jesus surrounded by many followers. Soon He will ascend to the Father's throne. He will transcend the boundary of Earth to prepare a wedding chamber for His bride and to serve as intercessor for believers and mediator for sinful man. A High Priest reigning in splendor at the Father's right hand, He will forever be a conqueror.

His loved ones who have witnessed His death in sadness are jubilant as they see Him alive again. And now they sense that they must give Him up a second time. Yet this parting is mixed with joy. By His resurrection they know without a doubt that His promises never fail. The Comforter will surely come in His place.

> And, [Jesus] being assembled together with them, commanded them that they should not depart from Jerusalem, but wait for the promise of the Father, which, saith he, ye have heard of me. For John truly

> baptized with water; but ye shall be baptized with the Holy Ghost not
> many days hence....But ye shall receive power, after that the Holy
> Ghost is come upon you: and ye shall be witnesses unto me both in
> Jerusalem, and in all Judea, and in Samaria, and unto the uttermost
> part of the earth.
>
> —ACTS 1:4–5, 8

An instant after this declaration we behold Jesus, their faithful Friend, the precious Son of Mary, lifted from their midst. As they stand below and stare upward, this Jesus, the glorified Savior of the world, the magnificent Son of God, disappears in a flash beyond the glory of the clouds.

Reach up! Reach up to catch His mantle! It is not a mantle that we can physically see and touch. No, it is a mantle we acquire only by His Spirit. Yes, keep reaching up until it comes to you.

In our mind's eye we follow the crowd now to the upper room to wait for the "promise of the Father," when His mantle will descend in glorious power. We recall Christ's words at His last supper.

> And I will pray the Father, and he shall give you another Comforter,
> that he may abide with you for ever; Even the Spirit of truth; whom the
> world cannot receive, because it seeth him not, neither knoweth him:
> but you know him; for he dwelleth with you, and shall be in you.
>
> —JOHN 14:16–17

For ten days of continuous prayer, believers abide in harmony until the Day of Pentecost. Oh, what excitement and anticipation stir among them. And what a group—Peter, James, John, Andrew, Philip, Thomas, Bartholomew, Matthew, James (the son of Alpheus), Simon Zelotes, Judas (brother of James), Mary (mother of Jesus), Jesus' brothers, along with many others. Altogether 120 are waiting. Then at last the appointed moment arrives for the Comforter, the promised Spirit of Truth, to appear in fullness.

> And when the day of Pentecost was fully come, they were all with one
> accord in one place. And suddenly there came a sound from heaven as
> of a rushing mighty wind, and it filled all the house where they were
> sitting. And there appeared unto them cloven tongues like as of fire,
> and it sat upon each of them. And they were all filled with the Holy
> Ghost, and began to speak with other tongues, as the Spirit gave them
> utterance.
>
> —ACTS 2:1–4

What a joyous day. The prophecy of John the Baptist has come to pass!

> I indeed baptize you with water unto repentance: but he that cometh
> after me is mightier than I, whose shoes I am not worthy to bear: he
> shall baptize you with the Holy Ghost, and with fire.
>
> —MATTHEW 3:11

It is the celebration of Pentecost, and hundreds of Jews who speak many different dialects have assembled in Jerusalem from many nations. They are amazed as they hear these Galilean followers of Jesus speaking words in languages native to their homelands. Peter explains:

> But this is that which was spoken by the prophet Joel; And it shall come
> to pass in the last days, saith God, I will pour out of my Spirit upon
> all flesh: and your sons and your daughters shall prophesy, and your
> young men shall see visions, and your old men shall dream dreams: and
> on my servants and on my handmaidens I will pour out in those days
> of my Spirit; and they shall prophesy.
>
> —ACTS 2:16–18

Look at Peter. What a transformation we see in this man who has been changed from coward to courageous! Can this be the same weakling who hid in the shadows and denied Jesus three times after His arrest? Yes! Now baptized in the Spirit of God, he speaks out in super boldness without fear, proclaiming before all that Jesus Christ is the Messiah.

Deeply moved by his dynamic message, the people cry, "What can we do?"

Peter answers, "Repent, and be baptized every one of you in the name of Jesus Christ for the remission of sins, and ye shall receive the gift of the Holy Ghost." And oh, just listen to his next words! "For the promise is unto you, and to all your children, and to all that are afar off, even as many as the Lord our God shall call" (Acts 2:38–39).

Hallelujah! The promise is for all who are afar off, as many as the Lord shall call! This also includes us! Yes, reach up and receive His promise!

After being baptized in this Spirit of Truth—the Holy Ghost, the Comforter, the Counselor, the Promise of the Father—the disciples, now immersed in His power, revolutionize the world. Over and over the Book of Acts reports how thousands upon thousands are converted to Christianity and receive this gift of power.

> And when they had prayed, the place was shaken where they were
> assembled together; and they were all filled with the Holy Ghost,

and they spake the word of God with boldness.

—ACTS 4:31

Now when the apostles who were at Jerusalem heard that Samaria had received the word of God, they sent Peter and John to them, who, when they had come down, prayed for them that they might receive the Holy Spirit. For as yet He had fallen upon none of them. They had only been baptized in the name of the Lord Jesus. Then they laid hands on them, and they received the Holy Spirit.

—ACTS 8:14–17, NKJV

And those of the circumcision who believed were astonished, as many as came with Peter, because the gift of the Holy Spirit had been poured out on the Gentiles also. For they heard them speak with tongues and magnify God.

—ACTS 10:45–46, NKJV

In Ephesus Paul asked the believers, "Did you receive the Holy Spirit when you believed?"

They answered, "We haven't so much as heard whether there is a Holy Spirit."

"Unto what then were you baptized?"

"Into John's baptism."

"John indeed baptized with a baptism of repentance, saying to the people that they should believe on Him who would come after him, that is, on Christ Jesus," Paul told them. Upon hearing this they were baptized in the name of the Lord Jesus, and when Paul laid hands on them, the Holy Spirit fell upon them. And they spoke with tongues and prophesied. (See Acts 19:1–6, NKJV.)

"You shall receive power after the Holy Ghost has come upon you," Jesus promised. This word *power* comes from the Greek word *dunamis*, the source for the word *dynamite*. Friends, that's power! It is power to stand by God's sufficient grace, power to proclaim the gospel with boldness, power to be a living testimony for Him in all situations. Superseding any human ability, this is a super power that no man, principality, or demonic spirit can hold back.

From the time the Holy Spirit fell, believers were transformed into explosive witnesses unable to keep silent.

For we cannot but speak the things which we have seen and heard.

—ACTS 4:20

Bold hearts burned with eagerness and devotion and spread the news of Jesus Christ as the Messiah regardless of any consequences. Why? What made them become so alive in God? It was the supernatural mantle of Christ in the form of the Holy Spirit. This glorious spiritual covering reaches the depths of a soul with an inward explosion so dynamic and divine that words cannot explain it.

Though a person may be dedicated to God's purposes, his submission to receive this power and boldness of the Holy Spirit deepens and broadens his prayer life in a way nothing else can. Unlike any other experience, it consummates a beautiful relationship between God and man.

WITHOUT A DOUBT the New Testament church consisted of Spirit-filled, tongue-talking assemblies. The last verse of our warfare scripture says, "Praying always with all prayer and supplication in the Spirit." Tongues give undisputable evidence that one is praying in the Spirit. A person may pray in the Spirit without speaking in tongues. However, this manifestation of the Holy Spirit's ministry transforms the mantle of Christ into a most glorious tent of prayer where the grandeur of God comes down in an awesome way that no other means of communication can produce. This prayer connection with the Father was normal and expected of all believers in the early church.

A few years ago I watched a news-magazine show on a major network. One of its topics that night revolved around Christians who speak in tongues. The investigative reporter admitted that skeptics expected to find people from the same congregations speaking in a similar manner. But guess what? They found that people, even though from the same church, all spoke quite differently.[16] That's the way our God works!

Though some try to explain it away and refuse its benefits, speaking in tongues is truly Spirit inspired. It is God activated, not a learned or practiced response, not initiated by human motivation. A prayer shawl designed and bestowed by the Master Himself, it allows us to pray at a higher level in an individual language meant only for Him.

> For he that speaketh in an unknown tongue speaketh not unto men, but unto God.
>
> —1 Corinthians 14:2

Because the Spirit always knows what is best, tongues give a means of praying about situations we otherwise do not know how to approach.

> So too the [Holy] Spirit comes to our aid and bears us up in our weakness; for we do not know what prayer to offer nor how to offer it worthily as we ought, but the Spirit Himself goes to meet our supplication and pleads in our behalf with unspeakable yearnings and groanings too deep for utterance.
>
> —ROMANS 8:26, AMP

When the Holy Spirit prays through us in tongues, we can be assured that we pray the perfect will of our Father since His very Spirit directs the words.

> And He Who searches the hearts of men knows what is in the mind of the [Holy] Spirit [what His intent is], because the Spirit intercedes and pleads [before God] in behalf of the saints according to and in harmony with God's will.
>
> —ROMANS 8:27, AMP

Praying in tongues uplifts.

> He that speaketh in an unknown tongue edifieth himself.
>
> —1 CORINTHIANS 14:4

> ...building up yourselves on your most holy faith, praying in the Holy Ghost.
>
> —JUDE 20

What an honor to be able to pray in tongues, knowing that the Holy Spirit of almighty God entrusts us with our own individual communication reserved only for Him. This precious overflowing is inconceivable until we experience it. It is simple once we receive it, yet so unimaginable and sometimes confusing to a person who has not received it.

Once again I declare, the personal language of tongues received at Holy Spirit baptism is for every believer! In fact, I believe with all my heart that God intends for every believer to receive his own.

What makes it so hard for some to be convinced? Doubters sometimes quote this scripture:

> Are all apostles? are all prophets? are all teachers? are all workers of miracles? Have all the gifts of healing? do all speak with tongues? do all interpret?
>
> —1 CORINTHIANS 12:29–30

However, once the Holy Spirit baptizes a person and tongues overflow from within him, he sees this scripture in a new light. No longer does he question if his newly received manner of prayer belongs to every believer. He knows it does.

He understands that Paul is referring to the "gift of tongues" that is given in an assembly and requires interpretation, as we discussed in chapter twelve. It is different from the personal utterance of tongues that is first evidenced at the moment of Holy Spirit baptism and continues day to day in private prayer.

This unique "gift," though it is certainly a wonderful inspirational experience for both the giver of the message and the hearers, is not private. It manifests only by a special anointing of the Spirit on a specific person and imparts words fresh from the heart of God to a congregation. Yes, it always requires an interpreter. Not every Christian experiences this "gift," just as not all are apostles, prophets, teachers, workers of miracles or possess special gifts of healing or receive interpretation of tongues.

God places various duties, callings, and responsibilities on individuals. But He favors no person above another. Just as He offers salvation through His Son to every human being, He also makes an unknown spiritual prayer language available for anyone who desires it.

In Acts 10:34–48 (NKJV) Peter preached, "In truth I perceive that God shows no partiality. But in every nation whoever fears Him and works righteousness is accepted by Him....He is Lord of all." He explained how at Jesus' baptism by John the Baptist God anointed Him with the Holy Spirit and power, and afterwards He did many good things such as healing those oppressed by the devil "for God was with Him."

As Peter continued, telling of Christ's death and resurrection, "the Holy Spirit fell upon all those who heard the word. And those of the circumcision [Jews] who believed were astonished...because the gift of the Holy Spirit had been poured out on the Gentiles also. For they heard them speak with tongues and magnify God." After this Peter commanded that the new believers be baptized in water.

Yes, the same baptism of the Holy Spirit with the confirmation of tongues as reported throughout the Book of Acts remains available today for all who will seek and accept it. How does one receive it? With a true heart's desire for God and all He has to offer. That's all it takes!

In his article "How to Take the Power of God Into Your Life to Meet Your Circumstances!" evangelist Dr. Morris Cerullo shares this story:

A man who came to me during a crusade and said, "Brother Cerullo, I want to get the baptism of the Holy Spirit so bad, I can taste it." I said, "Well, what's your problem?" He said, "Every time I get in the prayer room, somebody speaks in tongues and shouts in my ear, one says hold on, another says turn loose! My parents were Methodists, I was born a Methodist, and I'm going to die a Methodist!" He came back 3 or 4 days later, shouting and praising God. I said, "Hey, it looks like something happened to you!" He said, "It did, Brother Cerullo!" He explained how he told God in the prayer room, "God, I don't care if they spit on me, or shake me up and down, just give me the Holy Ghost!" And he got it! Many of us have been Christians for so long that we've become set in our ways. We want everything to be done a certain way. You must get to the end of your rope—to the end of yourself—let God take over and make of you what He wants![17]

Yes, that's all it takes!

Be completely in line with His Spirit and yielded to Him. Open yourself up to receive, and you will. This experience is not a prerequisite to "being saved." God's Spirit dwells with every believer, for "no man can say that Jesus is the Lord, but by the Holy Ghost" (1 Cor. 12:3).

When the believer is willing to lay aside all pride and surrender his will for the enrichment of an unknown language, the Holy Spirit dwells within him in a remarkable, indescribable dimension that is beyond human reasoning. Once he receives the manifestation of tongues, he never doubts whether the God of supernatural power abides with man today.

Many who have reservations about speaking in tongues or are unwilling to submit to Him in such deepness often ask, "Can't a person receive baptism of the Holy Ghost without speaking in tongues?" Perhaps. But to me it would seem like riding a bicycle with no handlebars. Why would anyone want to peddle without something to control direction?

It baffles me why some refuse to believe or just simply prefer to not receive. What makes a person who loves Jesus reject an overflowing communication that is supernaturally directed and inspired just for them? It seems to me that all Christians should desire all God has for them. But they don't.

After I received my initial outpouring, a friend said, "I'm happy for you, but I'll never want to speak in tongues!"

"No need for worry," I told her. "As long as you feel that way, you never will."

The Holy Ghost, a gentle Spirit, never imposes Himself on anyone. But oh, how He surely must grieve over those who deny Him because of tradition, unbelief, pride, or simply a lack of commitment. In reviewing the last verse of instruction about our spiritual armor we read again, "Praying always with all prayer and supplication in the Spirit..."

As I said earlier in this chapter, a person may pray in the Spirit without speaking in tongues. I believe that prayer in the Spirit takes place by simply connecting one's spirit to His in wholehearted sincerity and responsiveness to His voice. Before I received the prayer support of tongues I often shared this heart-to-heart closeness with the Father.

To pray in the Spirit is to place your soul in His presence. It may involve praying in tongues, or it may not. However, one thing is certain—it requires that your spirit be in harmony and fellowship with His. It is not just words from you to God. It is a two-way conversation in which you speak from your heart and wait quietly to hear from Him.

The deepest level of spiritual expression, praying in the Spirit is sometimes just being still in His presence, so filled with devotion for Him that your heart throbs in adoration. It is seeking the direction of the Counselor and placing all anxiety upon Him.

Prayer begins with the act of repentance, offering ourselves on the altar before a holy God and having our hearts cleansed of wickedness. We accept Jesus as Savior, the Lamb of God, the perfect sacrifice for our sin, and overflow with thankfulness for our salvation.

From this, prayer moves into its second phase, that of learning to know Abba Father and building relationship with Him. We recognize that He is worthy of all praise and admiration, and we serve Him, looking to His provision for our daily needs. Knowing that Jesus is the light of the world and we are part of that light, we desire to shine it everywhere.

From this we progress to prayer in the Spirit. Humbling ourselves in the presence an awesome God, we shut out the world and worship in the wonders of His glory. Perhaps nothing shows this progression like walking through the Old Testament tabernacle. In its design God provides a beautiful blueprint for our prayer life as well as types and shadows of the Christian faith. Now, to truly display this mantle that completes our spiritual armor, we must step behind the curtains of this sacred structure.

BEFORE THE COMING of the Holy Spirit, the only sanctuary of worship for the people of the living God existed in the tabernacle. Patterned after His heavenly throne, it provided a dwelling place for God to be among His people.

Though we assemble in a church building to fellowship and worship with other believers, God now dwells in the temple of a believer's heart through the Holy Spirit. Prayer is the only means for any man to reach God. Whether it be in songs of worship, speaking aloud, or quiet whispers from within our spirits, prayer gives us entrance into the meeting place inside the heart where His presence always dwells.

The tabernacle of Moses was a mobile structure. Later it progressed to the stationary temple of Solomon, a place of lavish beauty. This gives us a shadow or picture of good things to come. Today in the mobile temple in our hearts we converse with God. Someday in heaven we will meet Him in His stationary throne room of lavish beauty.

Like the Godhead, His tabernacle presents a trinity—the outer court, an open yard surrounded by curtains; the inner holy court, enclosed in a large tent; and the innermost holy of holies, a secluded room that was also enclosed within the tent.

As we advance through all three sections of the tabernacle we'll see a symbolic progression of our prayer life. First, in the outer court we come to God in repentance and give thanksgiving for His forgiveness. In the inner holy court we develop fellowship with God through praise and adoration. The innermost holy of holies brings us into solitude with Him, praying in the Spirit for ourselves and interceding for others. Shall we enter now?

A person may enter the outer court, the first area of the tabernacle, through only one entrance. Jesus provides our only entrance into the kingdom of God: "I am the door: by me if any man enter in, he shall be saved" (John 10:9). And He is the only access to the Father: "No man cometh unto the Father, but by me" (John 14:6). We also enter into prayer by one way— the authority of Jesus' name, "that whatsoever ye shall ask of the Father in my name he may give it you" (John 15:16).

The outer court permitted admittance for any sincere, unblemished person. Its large rectangular space, open overhead, surrounded the two secluded holy chambers. In the outer court a daily bustle of activity took place around its only two furnishings, an altar and a water basin positioned near the entrance.

The outer court had two functions. First, it was a place of daily sacrifice. Under the Law, people presented sacrifices upon the altar as acts of repentance to atone for their sin. The priest sprinkled the blood of these spotless offerings over them for their pardon. What atones for our sin under grace? The spotless blood of a perfect sacrifice. How? By our prayer of repentance and our offering of submission.

In the outer court we bow before the altar of Calvary and crucify our own flesh with His.

> I am crucified with Christ: nevertheless I live; yet not I, but Christ liveth in me: and the life which I now live in the flesh I live by the faith of the Son of God, who loved me, and gave himself for me.
>
> —GALATIANS 2:20

Offerings presented in the outer court were always perfect, always daily. Likewise, any prayer of repentance always requires a pure heart that is without one spot of insincerity and daily places shortcomings and wrongful deeds upon the altar. It is not a one-time act but an ongoing necessity. The apostle Paul said, "I die daily" (1 Cor. 15:31). In submission to Him we must be willing to "present [our] bodies a living sacrifice, holy, acceptable unto God" (Rom. 12:1).

Second, the courtyard was a place of cleansing. After the rituals of sacrifice in a purification ceremony, the priests washed themselves in the basin of water.

In this we see three correlations for the Christian. One, with repentance all former sin is washed away. Two, water baptism should always follow the initial prayer of repentance that brings one into the Christian walk. Three, afterwards one must stay cleansed by continual renewal of the mind and purification by the Word of God. Christ gave Himself for the church "that he might sanctify and cleanse it with the washing of water by the word" (Eph. 5:26).

The acts of sacrifice and cleansing concluded with joyous dedication. When the purifying rites were completed, the priests approached the inner holy place with thanksgiving. After truly repentant prayer, we spill over with joy and gratitude for the forgiveness we receive by His grace and mercy and the gift of salvation purchased by His spotless blood. Just like the Jewish priests, we can progress to the next area of the tabernacle only after we complete the duties of the outer court.

The inner holy place was an enclosed room where three objects resided. One was an altar not for sacrifice, but for burning incense. A second was a table holding twelve loaves of bread. This was the table of shewbread, also called the Bread of the Presence. A third was a seven-branched candelabra, a menorah that flamed constantly near the heavily veiled holy of holies.

Priests burned incense upon the special altar, and the incense rose with a pleasing aroma toward heaven. This represented prayer, as David's words show:

> Let my prayer be set forth before thee as incense.
>
> —PSALM 141:2

As prayer expands from repentance and thanksgiving to servitude, fellowship, praise, and adoration in our own inner holy place, it rises as a sweet-smelling savor before the Lord. Do you remember how we saw this when we visited heaven with John?

> And the smoke of the incense, which came with the prayers of the saints, ascended up before God out of the angel's hand.
> —REVELATION 8:4

In the inner holy place priests arranged fresh bread on the table every Sabbath day. This was not to feed their God as the pagans did, but it was a praise offering to remind them that their nation had been dependent upon His provision of manna. It was also an act of adoration for His continued supply.

As we praise our Savior for His provisions, we recognize Him as our bread of life: "I am the living bread which came down from heaven: if any man eat of this bread, he shall live for ever" (John 6:51). Jesus knows our needs and tells us to pray, "Give us this day our daily bread" (Matt. 6:11).

Priestly duty demanded that they keep the candlesticks of the inner holy place blazing continuously. Their flames produced the only light in the room, and their burning oil beautified the thickly veiled entrance into the innermost court, the holy of holies.

Our prayer of praise recognizes Christ as the true light, "which lighteth every man that cometh into the world" (John 1:9). It esteems Him as our light of life: "I am the light of the world: he that followeth me shall not walk in darkness, but shall have the light of life" (John 8:12). As His light continuously blazes in us, it provides the only light that can kindle hope for lost souls and beautify Him in a world that is veiled in darkness. "Let your light so shine before men, that they may see your good works, and glorify your Father which is in heaven" (Matt. 5:16). We must never let it go out.

Now we progress to the hidden court, the innermost holy of holies where only the high priest could go on the Day of Atonement. It housed only one object, the precious ark of the covenant. Completely shut off from the other two areas, no man-made light made its way into its chamber. In His *Shekinah* glory God consumed the room in His brilliance. On the Day of Atonement one mortal man met here with the Almighty in all His splendor.

At this point you and I must separate company. We must each go alone into our own innermost holy of holies. Only in solitude with Him can we behold His glory deep within the secret portals of our hearts. Only you and only I can enter this chamber within our individual spirit, the secret room where we meet individually with God. Unlike the high priest, we are no longer bound by a specific day. Our entrance into the innermost holy of holies and the prayer of total worship is always accessible.

In the light of His grace you and I bow alone before the mercy seat. We sense His splendor and behold His awesomeness. Enveloped in communication with the God of all the ages we lose ourselves in the splendor of His Spirit, engrossed in the wonder of His Being. In His infinite radiance we move from the realm of this world into an awareness of His eternal kingdom of power and glory.

Let us visit the tabernacle daily. As we travel through the prayer of repentance and thanksgiving, we will enter into a prayer of praise and petition and then find ourselves engulfed in the prayer of total worship. How blessed our souls will be!

Just as the tabernacle moved from place to place in the desert, we are mobile temples where His presence always abides. Everywhere we go our spirits can abide with Him, open to His voice, ready to receive. Perhaps this will help us understand what 1 Thessalonians 5:17 means when it tells us to "pray without ceasing."

How can a person pray all the time and still go about his daily duties? How can anyone constantly think thoughts of prayer? Even with the help of a heavenly prayer language, who can speak to God continuously? Nobody can.

However, if we keep an open prayer line with God, He will lead us by His Spirit. As we spend time communicating with Him from our hearts, we will begin to know His prompting. We will learn to differentiate between our inner voice and His. Our whole being—mind, will, and emotions—will tune in to His internal witness. We will become His willing vessels, His temples on the move, walking in the Spirit. And prayer will become a constant way of living.

As this takes place we will realize not only the miracle of prayer but also the wonderful privilege it is. It will develop a supernatural connection with a holy God and produce a living communion with the very One who created us. It will keep an ongoing relationship with Him burning at the deepest core of our beings.

In this setting, God will whisper instructions that we must obey, even if it seems foolish in the natural. If we allow Him, God will work even in simple everyday occurrences.

At a restaurant the other day a nice and accommodating young man took my order. Out of the blue I felt the Holy Spirit prompting me to tell him, "Jesus loves you." It seemed a childish thing to say. No personal words had been exchanged between us, so I felt somewhat embarrassed to relay the message. Then, although he had no idea that I could hear, I overheard his manager criticize him for not pushing the special of the day.

When he came back with my order I said, "The Holy Spirit told me to tell you that Jesus loves you."

"What?" he said.

I repeated it. A smile flashed across his face. His eyes sparkled. God knew that he needed His reassurance.

OUR LAST VERSE on spiritual warfare concludes, "Watching thereunto with all perseverance and supplication for all saints" (Eph. 6:18).

This prayer—the prayer of intercession—is not for ourselves but for others. This was also foreshadowed by the high priest in the holy of holies. He prayed not only for himself, but also for his family and the nation of Israel.

How vital it is for us to pray with heartfelt concern for others—family, friends, and the government. Praying for our leaders should assume utmost importance. In his letter to Timothy Paul stresses:

> I exhort therefore, that, first of all, supplications, prayers, intercessions, and giving of thanks, be made for all men; for kings, and for all in authority; that we may lead a quiet and peaceable life in all godliness and honesty.
>
> —1 TIMOTHY 2:1–2

Only eternity will reveal how many disasters have been averted, how many diseases have been cured, how many blessings have come about by the power of intercessory prayer. Many have asked where God was when the terrorists attacked our country, when we stared in horror as the twin towers of the World Trade Center tumbled to the ground in billowing clouds of dust and the Pentagon went up in flames. What happened to the protective hand that has always kept our nation safe?

It is often said that if God doesn't judge our nation, He will have to apologize to Sodom and Gomorrah. Some say that judgment has begun. If so, whose fault is it? The sinners of our society? The unbelievers?

No! The *believers*!

Oh, the power of unity in prayer. As individuals we are temples. Collectively we make an army. Believers who band together as prayer warriors have the ability to change a nation.

> If my people, which are called by my name, shall humble themselves, and pray, and seek my face, and turn from their wicked ways;

then will I hear from heaven, and I will forgive their sin, and will heal their land.

—2 Chronicles 7:14

All the prayer vigils, the singing of hymns and patriotic songs, the waving of flags, and our generosity are in vain unless the people of God seek His face in humble prayer and turn from their wicked ways. Only then can our land find healing. Only then can we be sure of His protective hand.

We must pray earnestly for God's forgiveness and direction, for our government and its leaders, for the unsaved, and for each other. We may never totally agree on every doctrinal point. Yet even if you don't fit my mold, I must lift you up in prayer. If you believe in Jesus as the Son of God we are on the same side, soldiers together for the kingdom of God. We must abide in harmony for His purposes, with understanding, tolerance, compassion, and love, being watchful and concerned.

Let us pray in humility—for America, the world, and the peace of Jerusalem, where terrorism is a constant threat. Let us pray that our government will always stand by Israel. Their miraculous existence alone should confirm that the God of their beginning is still working with them today. His covenants and promises remain forever.

Pray for the peace of Jerusalem: they shall prosper that love thee.

—Psalm 122:6

What is the best formula for praying? There is none.

Prayer is simply pouring out one's heart. It reflects our individuality, as we speak in our own words. It does not require the use of *thees* and *thous* or the repetition of memorized words. It is not a virtue to be displayed by the use of fancy speech, flowery phrases, or a certain tone of voice.

Prayer must come from the heart of one whose mind is attuned to God. Often the Bible links prayer with fasting and giving. James speaks of the prayer of faith that saves the sick (James 5:15) and the effectual fervent (heartfelt and continuing) prayer of a righteous person (v. 16). Faith requires expectancy. Effectual, fervent requests originate from one who asks in God's will from a pure heart and a humble and forgiving spirit. These seeds produce prayer that brings results.

In His sermon on the mount Jesus instructs us to not pray as the hypocrites who "love to pray standing in the synagogues and in the corners of the streets, that they may be seen of men" but to "enter into thy closet, and when thou hast shut thy door, pray to thy Father which is in secret...use not vain repetitions, as the heathen do: for they think that they shall be heard for their much speaking" (Matt. 6:5–7).

Our "closet" may not be a literal area. If it is, it should not be the only place we feel we must go to meet with Him alone. Prayer should not be some regimented hour that we set aside each day at a specific location. Though this may work for some and can certainly have value, many who have attempted such a strict routine only fail and wind up with a sense of guilt. Instead of striving for a programmed prayer time, we must commit ourselves to a lifestyle of continuous prayer. Which is better: to spend a whole hour in constant prayer, or to never go a whole hour without praying and sharing our words and thoughts with Him?

Oh, the wonder of prayer, our means of contact with the Creator. It is His divine provision for us to meet, abide, and settle down with Him under the mantle of His Sprit. In prayer words have no bounds. They can travel around the world in a single utterance and achieve the will of God. Words cannot explain the power of prayer or adequately express how it works. Only as we enter into prayer by faith can we conceive the wonder of its benefits. What an honor to have such an avenue to the eternal living Father.

Let us put on our mantle of prayer and run with it! As a covering over our armor it is priceless. Until we reach the heights of glory, the counsel of the prayer shawl will lead us from temptation. As it enshrouds us like a protective canopy, it will keep us from evil. When perilous times arise and war surrounds us, we can turn to it and be reassured that our Savior never leaves us or forsakes us. As we make it part of our daily apparel we will abide in its power from on high. It will keep our thoughts on Him in steadfast consecration to His will and purpose for our lives.

Yes, what a garment it is!

Now back on the Jubilee Express we lean back in our seats. The journey through the land of evil hasn't been easy, but with a deeper knowledge of the deceiver and his devices and dressed in the whole armor of the Almighty we move forward prepared to conquer.

Pulling our prayer shawl over our heads, our spirits travel back through the tabernacle. Offering a prayer of repentance and humbling ourselves, we enter into a place of solitude with our Father, the glorious awe-inspiring Master, who governs us. Gently He calls us into His secret place, where we are heart to heart with His Spirit. Here we encounter His protective hand. Here lies healing for our nation.

Our mantle cascades around us as a precious overlay of our military attire. Dressed in our whole armor, equipped with the sword of the Spirit and wrapped in our prayer shawls, the words "Deliver us from evil" take on a whole new meaning. Clearly now we see the way to victory as we ride unafraid into His prophetic Word to reach the glorious realms of heaven.

God's *Shekinah* glory lights our way. We hear the choir singing softly aboard the Jubilee Express as we glide into the end of our journey to behold His soon coming kingdom of spectacular power and fabulous glory. "Onward, Christian soldiers, marching as to war, with the cross of Jesus, going on before..."[18]

Chapter 16

For Thine Is the Kingdom

"COMING!"

Wrapping my wet hair in a towel I rushed to the knock on my apartment door and opened it to greet two women with friendly smiles. Both were neatly dressed in straight skirts and crisp white blouses and appeared to be in their early forties—about the same age as my mother. I was nineteen.

"We'd like to give you some free literature," said one as she pulled a magazine from a black satchel strapped over her shoulder. While I glanced at it the other lady said, "We're also offering these for twenty-five cents." She showed me an orange hardcover book that was filled with pictures and bore the title *Paradise Regained*.

I knew nothing about this religious sect that called themselves Jehovah's Witnesses, but the book appeared interesting and I love to read. Besides, for only a quarter I was willing to help any church.

"Wait here; I'll be right back." Hurriedly I counted out change from a jar of nickels and dimes and returned. Delight showed in their eyes. With enthusiasm one of them said, "As you read these write down any questions you may have. We'll come back next week to answer them from the Bible."

I desired to know more about God. And being shut in with a three-month-old baby, a husband who worked long hours and no car—I reasoned that it would be nice to have a Bible study in my home. "OK," I agreed, allowing them to set a day and time. As soon as they left I started poring over their material.

That afternoon my next door neighbor Mary dropped in. She and I had become good friends. Three years older than me, she also had married at age eighteen but she had no children. Very frail because of a heart defect, Mary did not work outside the home. She wore her long dark hair in a neat ponytail, and her clothes always looked freshly starched and ironed. What an encouragement she was amid my diaper pails and bottle formula. With a passion for babies she enjoyed helping me, and I looked forward to her daily visits.

Over a glass of iced tea I told her about my morning visitors and plopped their publications on the kitchen table. "They sure have some different views," I said.

Scanning the pages she muttered, "I know."

Since Mary's husband was studying to be a pastor and served as youth minister at their church, I realized that she might be able to answer some questions I already had about their beliefs. "Mary, what do you know about Jehovah's Witnesses?"

"They're a cult," she said sipping her tea, thumbing through the book.

"What's a cult?"

"First and foremost I'd identify a cult as a religious organization started by one person who claims new insight from God. Though they declare the Bible as their source, their teachings—each with their own unique dogma—stray from vital Christian beliefs. For instance, they reject Jesus as deity and the actual Son of God."

"Who do they say He is?"

"Oh, each cult gives their own portrayal—a created angel, even Michael the archangel, a unique or superhuman being, a spiritual brother, a highly enlightened prophet—but not God incarnate. Another mark of a cult is that they support their own ideas by pushing their printed material more than the Bible. They maintain that the Bible is inaccurately translated or insufficient by itself. All the while they declare that their private interpretation and special understanding stands without error and is the only way to God."

Now that sparked my interest. In school some of my classmates had attended a denominational church that also claimed their teachings presented the only right way. No one, they said, other than people baptized in their way and following their distinctive doctrine could make it to heaven. Their beliefs made me wonder, not if they alone knew the only true way to God, but if anyone actually possessed real answers.

"They believe in eternal existence for themselves," Mary continued, "earned by performing the required duties of their doctrine and adhering to all its teachings. These works establish their way to one of two perfect places—paradise on earth or realms of heaven. Both places are reserved solely for their followers."

Looking across the table at me Mary patted the literature. "Going house to house and distributing this stuff is part of the Jehovah's Witnesses' work requirements." She picked up the orange book. "I'd like for my husband to see this. Is it OK if I take it home for a day or two?"

By the next week I was loaded with inquiries. As I watched through the front window and waited for my religious visitors to arrive I held a whole page of questions Mary's husband sent over. I had jotted down a few myself.

The two ladies in their neat skirts and blouses were exactly on time. Armed with new reading material, they were accompanied by an older gray-haired man who looked like a preacher in his dark suit and tie. He answered all my questions without hesitation and amazed me by his ability to flip through pages of the Bible to support his explanations. After six weeks of their in-home teaching, I learned the crux of Jehovah Witnesses' doctrine.

I must admit that two positive things developed from my time of study. First, I began to realize that no select group has obtained exclusive insight from God. This happened as discrepancies in their teachings became apparent from outside research I did with the aid of Mary and her husband, and also from scriptures they showed me.

> Knowing this first, that no prophecy of the scripture is of any private interpretation.
>
> —2 Peter 1:20

No freshly acquired enlightenment or unique revelation is without flaw. The light of the New Covenant beams not just for one special sect that God chooses but for *whoever* seeks Him.

> For there is no respect of persons with God.
>
> —Romans 2:11

> For whosoever shall call upon the name of the Lord shall be saved.
>
> —Romans 10:13

> Then Peter opened his mouth, and said, Of a truth I perceive that God
> is no respecter of persons: But in every nation he that feareth him, and
> worketh righteousness, is accepted with him.
>
> —Acts 10:34–35

Salvation does not come by any remote teaching or new awakening. We do not receive it by the works we do or by our perfection. I stumbled for years before complete understanding dawned on my dark and misled self-searching. How simple His truth is! It is God's gift to all who have faith in His Son.

> For by grace are ye saved through faith; and that not of yourselves: it is
> the gift of God: Not of works, lest any man should boast.
>
> —Ephesians 2:8–9

The only road to salvation is the spotless blood of Jesus Christ. Over and over the Word declares it.

> That if thou shalt confess with thy mouth the Lord Jesus, and shalt
> believe in thine heart that God has raised him from the dead, thou
> shalt be shalt be saved.
>
> —Romans 10:9

> ...whosoever believeth in him should not perish, but have everlast-
> ing life.
>
> —John 3:16

Why do men make it so complicated by adding their own devised ideas?

Second, and this is a good thing, these Jehovah's Witnesses awakened my young mind to prophecy. The church I attended never taught about Christ's Second Coming. These people presented it in a pronounced way. As they showed me verses in Matthew 24, the End-Time scene leaped to life.

How wrong they were to set dates. They declared that the actual end of the world began in 1914 with World War I, "Before the generation of 1914 ceases to be," they said, "even before your baby reaches the age of accountability, Jesus will return."

Today my son is over forty years old! This experience taught me one thing—never, never put a date on any prophecy of God until it actually takes place. Yes, we can know the season, but we must leave the date-setting to the omniscient One. He alone knows the time!

Only recently as I watched a television program about the history of the Jehovah Witnesses I learned that all their past predictions failed. Their original prophecy of 1914 claimed it as the year to end the gospel age and bring the time of the Gentiles to a close with the battle of Armageddon. Later they announced 1925 as the beginning of paradise on Earth with the soon return of Abraham, Isaac, and Jacob from the dead.

As World War II brewed and then broke out, they said that it was ushering in Armageddon. Still later came the declaration that 1975 would bring an end to six thousand years of man's history.[1] Despite their "new light," their teachings have demanded alteration because of these false claims and other inaccuracies in their doctrine.

Their organization doesn't stand alone by any means. Many others have predicted exact dates and set precise times that passed without any unusual event. I recall much excitement over a publication that detailed why Jesus would return in 1988. At times misguided groups have shut themselves in houses and waited for a specific day they had set for Christ to return. To their disappointment those dates came and went. Y2K date-setters predicted Christ would rapture His church at the turn of the twenty-first century.

No mortal mind can pinpoint the day of Christ's return, nor can any man grasp the precise way prophecy will unfold. Even the best students of the Bible fail to agree wholly on the time frame, sequence, or particulars of events. Let's face the facts—although God reveals future happenings in His Word, nobody knows the exact details before they occur. This knowledge belongs to the Father.

The time has come for our travels to take us into the end of the age. As we imagine ourselves in the center of End-Time situations, we must never forget that while the Bible gives insight, God alone sets the how, when, and where of their fulfillment.

One thing stands certain and unchangeable. Every single proclamation in God's Holy Word will happen, not according to your or my assumption, but exactly as He plans. Someday every human being who has ever lived will behold Him in all His power and glory. Some will enter into eternal life with Him, and some will face eternal separation from Him—but all will meet Him face-to-face at their appointed times. And all will hail His greatness.

WITH THIS KNOWLEDGE we travel to the last location on our treasure map. The Jubilee Express will take us on this daring trip into End-Time prophecy to probe our final destination.

"For thine is the kingdom, and the power, and the glory, for ever. Amen."

A whirlwind of questions swirls across the track of the Jubilee Express as we race together toward our journey's end. Why does God tarry so long for His Day of Judgment? Is He putting it off? What will become of our world when that ultimate Day arrives?

Many proclaim that the time of Christ's return as very soon. Can this be true? Are we actually living at the end of the "last days?" Without pinpointing precise dates, can we predict that these times are upon us?

Do we want to seek answers, or be as the many who prefer to glide aimlessly along, simply brushing aside any prophetic issue that arises? It is so tempting for us to ignore all storm warnings about future events as prophesied in the Bible and bring our journey to a close. But it would be so sad if we failed to finish the mission of our treasure map.

The train whistle musters our attention. Its clanging bell rings into the future. Its brilliant light glitters upon the scarlet rails rushing ahead into God's prophetic Word, shining on a place of mystery and wonder, exposing secrets of things to come, revealing the marvels of His timetable. With our Conductor near, we know that we have no need for apprehension.

We begin our search for answers by pausing for a brief encounter with Peter. As we present our questions to him, we gain introductory insights on the end of this age.

Why does God tarry so long for His Day of Judgment? Is He putting it off?

> The Lord is not slack concerning his promise, as some men count slackness; but is longsuffering to usward, not willing that any should perish, but that all should come to repentance.
>
> —2 PETER 3:9

What will become of our world when that ultimate Day arrives?

> But the day of the Lord will come as a thief in the night; in which the heavens shall pass away with a great noise, and the elements shall melt with fervent heat, the earth also and the works that are therein shall be burned up.
>
> —2 PETER 3:10

Are we at the end of the "last days?" Can we predict that the End Times are upon us? In the two verses preceding these, Peter gives us a metaphor that reveals a hidden composite picture of God's timetable.

> But the heavens and the earth, which are now, by the same word are kept in store, reserved unto fire against the day of judgment and perdition of ungodly men. But, beloved, be not ignorant of this one thing, that *one day is with the Lord as a thousand years, and a thousand years as one day.*
>
> —2 PETER 3:7–8, EMPHASIS ADDED

A thousand years equals the span of one day with God. What does this mean, and why does Peter mention this in his discourse on the coming Day of Judgment? What significance does it have? Our train jolts to a stop, and we are thrust into the exploration of the "sixth-day" time theory and its relationship to the coming of the Lord. Oh, what intrigue we are about to encounter!

From the Garden of Eden until today the history of man covers six thousand years. Approximately two thousand years elapsed first from Adam to Abraham, then from Abraham to Jesus, and finally from Jesus until now. Altogether, that is six thousand years. Since a thousand years are as one day to God, this would be six days for Him. So what comes on His seventh day?

Consider the Creation. For six days God worked planting, forming, creating, and establishing man's system of rule on this planet. On the seventh day with Creation completed in fullness and perfection, He rested from His work to celebrate His accomplishment.

For six thousand years—"six days"—God has worked and guided man's rule of the Earth. It is nearly time for the "seventh day." Could this indicate that the millennium, His coming thousand-year reign of peace on Earth, is about to usher in His perfect rest?

What a parallel, what a pattern God hides in His Word! Just as the number *seven* stands for complete fullness and perfection, the number *six* represents mankind. Are the last sands of this age sifting into the lower compartment of His hourglass of time? Is the world system as we know it almost at an end?

By accepting the seven days of Genesis chapters 1–2 as a prophetic pattern, we can see that a thousand-year Sabbath day is about to embark when Christ returns to reign on the Earth. The millennium will bring fulfillment to God's plan of redemption that was promised at the initial fall of man and established before the foundation of the world. Satan will be locked up for a thousand years and will never again reign as the god of this world. For one thousand years the tranquility of the Garden of Eden will be restored. True and perfect rest will return to the Creator and His creation on the seventh day. The writer of Hebrews verifies it:

> For we which have believed do enter into rest, as he said, As I have sworn in my wrath, if they shall enter into my rest: although the works were finished from the foundation of the world. For he spake in a certain place of the *seventh* day on this wise, And God did rest the *seventh* day from all his works. And in this place again, If they shall enter into my rest.
>
> —Hebrews 4:3–5, emphasis added

Are there other hidden nuggets foreshadowing the number of "days" until Christ's return? Yes, oh yes, God says yes!

What treasures I discovered when I first looked into scriptures that casually mentioned a number of days as possible hidden references to the ultimate Timekeeper's thousand-year day. Amazed I scanned verse after verse. In the following two examples, the complexity of God's Book astounds my heart anew.

The prophet Hosea says:

> After *two days* He will revive us; on the *third day* He will raise us up, that we may live in His sight.
>
> —Hosea 6:2, nkjv, emphasis added

Oh, see how this verse alludes to God's thousand-year day! In our generation, two thousand years (*two days*) since the victory of the cross, the nation of Israel has been miraculously revived. Could the *third day* allude to the rapture when those who have accepted the Messiah, both Jew and Gentile, will be "raised up" and "live in His sight?"

This next example creates even more excitement.

> For the Son of man shall come in the glory of his Father with his angels; and then he shall reward every man according to his works. Verily I say unto you, There be some standing here, which shall not taste of death, till they see the Son of man coming in his kingdom.
>
> And *after six days* Jesus taketh Peter, James, and John his brother, and bringeth them up into a high mountain apart, and was transfigured before them: and his face did shine as the sun, and his raiment was white as the light. And, behold, there appeared unto them Moses and Elias talking with him.
>
> —Matthew 16:27–17:3, emphasis added

Oh, what a glorious secrets this scripture reveals! First, Jesus sets the stage by telling of His coming when He will "reward every man according to his works." This describes the judgment of the righteous following the rapture.

The very next words at the beginning of Matthew 17 read, "And *after six days*...." That is six thousand years by man's calendar!

Many scholars deem the transfiguration as a foreshadowing of the rapture. Moses symbolized the resurrected dead, and Elijah symbolized those who are caught up alive. This thinking stems partially from the fact that Elijah was caught up alive and also from the mysterious circumstances of Moses' death and burial.

Before the children of Israel crossed over into the Promised Land, God instructed Moses to go alone up the mountain of Nebo (the same area from which Elijah would ascend). There Moses died and the Lord Himself buried his faithful servant. "No man knoweth of his sepulchre unto this day" (Deut. 34:6).

But did Moses' body stay in the grave? Evidently not. In Jude 9 we find, "Yet Michael the archangel, when contending with the devil he disputed about the body of Moses..."

Friends, we stand at the brink of God's seventh day. Will it close six thousand years of history on Earth with first the rapture, then the Great Tribulation, and finally the return of the Messiah to reign on the earth for a thousand years?

You may think that although this thousand-year-day scenario is a nice concept, it still stands as only a theory. And yes, I must agree. If this presented the only evidence of the soon appearing of Christ, the case would be shallow at best.

BUT AS ALWAYS the Bible is one step ahead of us. Every unfulfilled prediction in Scripture stands poised like a battalion ready to fire. At no other time in history has the possible completion of every End-Time prophecy existed. Today it does.

Take, for instance, the "mark of the beast" and its mandatory issue during the tribulation.

> And he caused all, both small and great, rich and poor, free and bond, to receive a mark in their right hand, or in their foreheads: And that no man might buy or sell, save he that had the mark, or the name of the beast, or the number of his name.
>
> —REVELATION 13:16–17

Until a few decades ago people wondered what this "mark" might be. Every idea had its flaws. A stamp, maybe? Any stamp would eventually wash off. What about a tattoo? Although it is a permanent marking, it is time-consuming to imprint and easy to misread. Perhaps a mark branded into the skin. This would never work, considering distortions from possible infection or differences in scarring. And counterfeits could be easily produced for all these methods.

How things have changed. Today, scanners can instantly read computer chips, and nobody questions the possibility of a unique and positive personal identification "mark." Many animals have had chips embedded beneath their skin to identify and keep track of them. Not long ago I watched a television interview with a person who wears an embedded chip that reveals information about his health conditions in case of a medical emergency. There is now talk about using these tiny devices in masses of people, perhaps starting with soldiers at war. Today, the question is not about the nature of the End-Time mark. It's when!

Jesus tells us that no one can know the day and the hour of His return to Earth:

> But of that day and hour knoweth no man, no, not the angels of heaven, but my Father only.
>
> —MATTHEW 24:36

> And he [Jesus] said unto them, It is not for you to know the times or the seasons, which the Father hath put in his own power.
>
> —ACTS 1:7

Yet the signs Jesus gives in Matthew 24, as well as many other Bible prophecies, alert us that His coming may be right around the corner.

> So likewise ye, when ye shall see all these things, know that it is near, even at the doors.
>
> —MATTHEW 24:33

One of the most obvious fulfillments of prophecy in our day is Daniel's prediction of the state of this world in the End Times: "Many shall run to and fro, and knowledge shall be increased" (Dan. 12:4).

Even though we have discussed this in chapter 14, let's consider it once again. Have you looked at the highways or been to the airport lately? The amount of running to and fro astounds the mind. Who would have pictured such travel just fifty years ago?

And what about knowledge? Can you believe the expansion of technology in our lifetime? Recently it was reported that knowledge now doubles every two and one-half years. Explosions in scientific and electronic capabilities bring us everything from microwaves, cell phones, and personal computers to satellites and spaceships. Medical ability astonishes us with test-tube babies, laser surgery, and artificial hearts, not to mention cloning.

Another prophecy surfaces in the signs that are appearing on the face of God's last-days timepiece—Israel, the fig tree.

> I found Israel like grapes in the wilderness; I saw your fathers as the firstripe in the fig tree.
>
> —HOSEA 9:10

In verses nestled throughout God's Word the nation of Israel is illustrated by the fig tree and the olive tree. Why both? The fig tree denotes the governmental aspect of Israel. On the other hand, the olive tree reveals its spiritual side. Gentile believers in Christ are not of the fig tree, but they are part of the olive tree.

> For if God was willing to take you who were so far away from him—being part of a wild olive tree—and graft you into his own good tree—a very unusual thing to do—don't you see that he will be far more ready to put the Jews back again, who were there in the first place?
>
> —ROMANS 11:24, TLB

God has never forgotten His everlasting covenant with Israel. He never will. This is a glorious concept to pursue, but at this time our travels lead us a different direction. We will look at prophecies of political Israel budding as the fig tree as we begin our tour of Matthew 24.

"Now learn a parable of the fig tree," Jesus explains in His discourse on End-Time events. "When his branch is yet tender, and putteth forth leaves, ye know that summer is nigh. So likewise ye, when ye shall see all these things, know that it is near, even at the doors. Verily I say unto you, This generation shall not pass, till all these things be fulfilled" (vv. 32–34).

In 1948 Israel reestablished their nation after nearly two thousand years of wandering the globe. Then, "In the Arab-Israeli War of 1967, Israeli forces took the Old City. The Israeli government then formally annexed the Old City and placed all of Jerusalem under a unified administration."[2]

So has the fig tree budded? Yes! Are we living within the generation that has witnessed it? Yes, oh yes! The psalmist says:

> When the LORD shall build up Zion [Jerusalem], he shall appear in his glory.
>
> —PSALM 102:16

What is the "parable of the fig tree?" Jews know this parable from the Song of Solomon. All Christians should know this book for its lovely allegory of our Bridegroom and realize the wonders of its parable of the fig tree.

> The fig tree putteth forth her green figs, and the vines with the tender grape give a good smell. Arise, my love, my fair one, and come away.
>
> —SONG OF SOLOMON 2:13

This is "the parable of the fig tree!" Has it put "forth her green figs"? Yes! Following the miraculous victory in 1967 with Israel establishing Jerusalem as their capital city and unifying their governmental system, this parable unfolded before our very eyes. Oh friends, can the rapture of the saints, when believers "arise" and "come away" with Him be very far off? Jesus said the generation that sees the budding of the fig tree will behold the Son of man coming in His glory (Matt. 24:29–30).

We have seen its budding!

How long is a generation? The Bible does not give a definite length of time. But thirty-eight years have passed from 1967 until 2005. Oh, how much longer until all "these things" Jesus identifies in Matthew 24 are fulfilled?

In this prophetic chapter the subject of End Times arises when His disciples ask, "What shall be the sign of Your coming and of the end of the world?" (v. 3). Jesus' begins His answer by listing five things that will happen during a period He calls "the beginning of sorrows" (v. 8) and explains, "The end is not yet" (v. 6).

Today we see all these things—the deception of false christs, wars and constant talk of war, famine, pestilences, earthquakes. Let's examine each of them one by one.

First, Jesus says, "Many shall come in my name, saying I am Christ; and shall deceive many" (v. 5).

People who claim to be Christ have surfaced in record numbers in our day. Daymond R. Duck discusses this in his book *On the Brink*.

> In recent years, the Church has seen "Sweet Daddy Grace," "Father Divine," Jim Jones, Charles Manson and others who claimed to be the Christ. In the late '80s and early '90s, a Korean Messiah, Rev. Sun

Myung Moon, appeared. At the same time, a British Messiah, Lord Maitreya, showed up in London. In 1990 a black Messiah, Hulon Mitchell, Jr., otherwise known as "Yahweh ben Yahweh," turned up in Florida and an Arab Messiah, Saddam Hussein appeared in Iraq. In 1992, the followers of Rabbi Menachem Schneerson of Brooklyn, N.Y. claimed he is the Jewish Messiah and newspapers dubbed Marcos Antonio Bonilla of Nicaragua "Jesus of the poor." In 1993 David Koresh, leader of the Branch Davidians in Waco, Texas, called himself the Lamb of God. We could go on. But altogether, there have been at least fifty men and two women in the United States alone who have claimed to be the Christ. This is the beginning of sorrows and they have deceived many.[3]

Jesus continues, "You will hear of wars and rumors of wars, but don't be troubled, because all these things must come to pass, but the end isn't yet. For nation shall rise against nation, and kingdom against kingdom" (vv. 6–7).

In modern times nation has risen against nation and kingdom against kingdom in ways mankind has never before conceived. Until the twentieth century we had never seen world wars that encompassed the whole globe.

Now Jesus adds, "There shall be famines and pestilences" (v. 7).

Even with all our knowledge of agriculture and nutrition, people die of starvation in untold numbers, and all our efforts do little to abate it. Disease runs rampant. With the discovery of antibiotics in 1948 many authorities claimed that disease would be eradicated. Today antibiotics have lost their effect as immune systems no longer respond to them and stronger strains of bacteria emerge. The dangers of the Ebola virus demand new handling and cooking of foods.

A possible forty million cases of AIDS exist in the world, with no cure in sight; other sexual diseases are increasing at a frightful rate. New outbreaks of tuberculosis continue to surface. Cancer, heart disease, diabetes, arthritis, and multiple sclerosis abound in record numbers. With the anthrax scare released on society and the threat of smallpox baring its teeth, one has to wonder what more our planet can endure before the "beginning of sorrows" ends and the tribulation takes over.

Finally Jesus says, "And earthquakes in divers (various and many) places" (v. 7).

In modern times earthquakes have greatly increased. Accurate records of ancient eras may not exist, but modern records show far more eruptions in the twentieth century than in the nineteenth. And hundreds more occurred in its last quarter than in its first seventy-five years.

"All these are the beginning of sorrows," Jesus concludes in verse 8. The deception of Jesus impostors, wars, famine, disease and earthquakes all happen during this time period.

So what happens next, after the time of "beginning of sorrows?" "Then," Jesus says in verse 9, "shall they deliver you up to be afflicted, and kill you: and ye shall be hated of all nations for my sake."

After much reflection on the entire discourse of Matthew 24, I have concluded that the use of the word *then* in this verse ushers in an era much worse than simply "the *beginning* of sorrows!" It implies an act following something that took place immediately before. For instance, one may say, "I took a shower this morning, then I ate breakfast." Of course, eating breakfast followed taking a shower. That's only common sense.

The eighth verse ends "the beginning of sorrows" era. I believe that at the last happening Jesus mentions, the "earthquakes in divers places," the rapture of the saints occurs and the time of the tribulation begins. *Then* a time of greater sorrow shows its face in the ninth verse—"they shall deliver you up to be afflicted, and shall kill you." During the Great Tribulation the full-fledged fury of the Antichrist escalates against the Jews and any new Christians to a point of horror never before witnessed by mankind.

Before I understood this sequence I struggled in my attempts to decipher Matthew 24. However, as I placed the events listed after verse 8 in the time of the tribulation, it became completely logical.

Verse 15 speaks of the Antichrist standing in the Jewish temple and declaring himself to be God. At that moment the Jews in Judea will flee into the mountains. The following verses therefore apply to their flight, not the rapture as some have taught:

> Let him which is on the housetop not come down to take any thing out of his house....But pray ye that your flight be not in winter, neither on the sabbath day.
>
> —Matthew 24:17, 20

With the rapture occurring "in the twinkling of an eye," who will have time to even think of grabbing anything out of his house? No one. What difference will it make if the rapture takes place in winter or on the Sabbath? None. But it will make a great difference if a Jew has to flee from the Antichrist and his fury in winter or on the Sabbath.

The last half of the Great Tribulation will dawn with the events of Matthew 24:15–20. The next verse tells us, "For then shall be great tribulation, such as was not since the beginning of the world to this time, no, nor ever shall be" (v. 21). At the end of these extreme perils and troubles "the tribes of the earth shall mourn, and they shall see the Son of man coming in the clouds of heaven with power and great glory" (v. 30).

The coming of the Son of man refers to the arrival of Christ as King of kings and Lord of lords upon the earth at the end of the tribulation. It does not identify His appearing in the clouds to catch His bride away at the rapture.

Understanding this clears up the passage, "But as the days of Noah were, so shall also the coming of the Son of man be. For as in the days that were before the flood they were eating and drinking, marrying and giving in marriage, until the day that Noe entered into the ark, and knew not until the flood came, and took them all away; so shall the coming of the Son of man be. Then shall two be in the field; the one shall be taken, the other left. Two women shall be grinding at the mill; the one shall be taken, and the other left" (vv. 37–41).

It becomes apparent that this is the time of Christ's return to Earth to reign, as we study the word *taken* in the phrase "the one shall be taken." *The Complete Word Study Dictionary* of New Testament words states:

> In these verses, those taken are not to be misconstrued as those whom the Lord favors...who will be raptured....It is used to refer to those in the days of Noah who were taken away, not being favored but being punished, while Noah and his family were left intact. Therefore this passage...must not be equated to the believers who are to be raptured at the coming of the Lord for His saints. It refers rather to those who, as in the days of Noah, are taken to destruction. The others are left alone for the purpose of entering into the blessings of Christ's kingdom (identified by some as the Millennium) and the righteous rule of Christ upon earth.[4]

What a time awaits! What a time of horror. Yet also, what a time of glory.

HOW LONG IS "the beginning of sorrows?" No one can say for certain, but without any question we live in the time when the five things Jesus prophesied are happening. Are you ready for the Bridegroom's trumpet? Are you prepared to stand before the Judgment Seat of Christ?

For we must all appear before the judgment seat of Christ; that every one may receive the things done in his body, according to that he hath done, whether it be good or bad.

—2 CORINTHIANS 5:10

For we shall all stand before the judgment seat of Christ. For it is written, As I live, saith the Lord, every knee shall bow to me, and every tongue shall confess to God. So then every one of us shall give account of himself to God.

—ROMANS 14:10–12

The Jubilee Express lifts like a jumbo jet at takeoff to scale an incline reaching into the heavens. Lights dim inside our coach, and instantly a panoramic screen blazes in the sky outside our windows. The Judgment Seat appears! There He is! The Son of man in all His glory!

Angels sing. Multitudes of newly raptured saints stand, clad in gleaming white. Ecstasy radiates from every face. Amid heaven's glory all bow in devotion before the Lamb of God. Translated out a world of sin and sorrow, temptation and disappointment into a utopia of unity with Elohim forever, their hearts erupt in total worship. With loving eyes and outstretched arms the Lamb, now arrayed in splendor and endowed with power, accepts His position as their Judge.

"Come unto Me," we hear Him say.

One by one, He selects individuals to step forward. In an instant of time every person's life flashes like a vivid drama as their works are tried. There is nothing secret, nothing hidden.

For God shall bring every work into judgment, with every secret thing, whether it be good, or whether it be evil.

—ECCLESIASTES 12:14

Only deeds that flowed from a faithful heart can endure the test.

For no one can lay any foundation other than the one already laid, which is Jesus Christ. If any man builds on this foundation using gold, silver, costly stones, wood, hay or straw, his works will be shown for what it is, because the Day will bring it to light. It will be revealed with fire, and the fire will test the quality of each man's work. If what he has built survives, he will receive his reward. If it is burned up, he will suffer loss; he himself will be saved, but only as one escaping through the flames.

—1 CORINTHIANS 3:11–15, NIV

No one who is raptured is condemned to die. Not one risks being turned away from eternal glory. Since some deceived even themselves in their shortcomings, they expect more deeds to survive as gold, silver and precious gems—yet now they see themselves as they really are. All deceit and pride is burned away, and only truth remains as each life plays like a movie.

We recognize Deacon Dominate approaching the Seat of Judgment. With his leadership talent His service for Christ included feats that leaped from the fire as gold and silver forever to be sown into his garment. Yet some of his works burn to ashes. There were the times he had chosen to glorify himself instead of God. When the Holy Spirit had nudged him to step aside and let others lead, he had sometimes insisted on taking control for the sake of his self-esteem. All these works dissolve forever in the flames.

In the presence of the Judge, Deacon Dominate bows his head. When he lifts his eyes, a totally new expression spreads over his face. Does he appear sad or discouraged? No! Free at last from a controlling spirit that had plagued his earthly mission, he beams with joy.

Sister Blab takes the stand. We know her! Though she was a wonderful intercessor, at times she gave in to gossip and blurted out things people had told her in confidence "so others could pray about the problem." Sometimes though vowing to pray for someone, she got busy with other things and failed to do so. Engulfed by flames these acts perish before her eyes. Is she sad? No, she accepts her failures and views all deeds in truth and honesty. She beams to see all her intercession that had been done in sincerity turn to gold threads across her robe and gleam across her chest. With her sinful nature conquered, she lifts her voice in praise.

Brother Flaunt. Remember him? He bragged so much about the good things he did that most of his deeds are consumed in the fire. Only a select few come out as precious metal. Is he distressed? No, he sees the judgment of the Lamb as just and pure. With his weight of egotism burned to ashes, he steps aside, giving thanks with a perfect heart.

In astonishment we recognize Rev. National Evangelist who blessed millions with his gospel message. Responsible for the salvation of multitudes, many deeds emerge in sparkling gold. Yet with nothing hidden now, even this one who has works that burn—faults in his personal life, an occasional moment when he gloated in his fame, the few times he shunned the needs of others to seek a larger congregation. Though flames devour these like wood and straw, he walks away rejoicing, free from earthly pressures, secure in the perfect holiness of God.

People from all the historical ages of mankind must have a turn at judgment. We see a man who accepted Jesus only moments before his death. Although he has no deeds to survive the fire, he glows in gratitude for an eternity of happiness. Some approach shyly, having barely made it in the rapture. Yet the Bridegroom loves all the same.

What works make it through the fire? Works of faith, standing in the name of Jesus, finding peace in God during trying situations, enduring by looking to Him, preaching and teaching the gospel with a pure heart, demonstrations of the power of the Spirit, loving and helping the less fortunate, reaching out in compassion, offering encouragement to the hurting, being a sacrificial giver, obeying His call, studying His Word, praying, worshiping.

Only heartfelt acts that honor God survive. All achievements for self-glorification dissolve in flames. We watch with wonder as flimsy acts of religion go up in smoke—church programs, special baptisms, prayer activities, symbols and traditions, superficial acts of worship. All efforts that were rooted in the world are reduced to ashes. The holy blaze of justice extinguished all vices—every stronghold, false sentiment, secret fantasy, hidden feeling. Purity and freedom flood into their place.

By the power of the spotless blood every raptured saint reigns in victory over human weakness. Any sense of guilt for neglected deeds, overlooked needs, thoughtless acts, insincerity or insensitivity is consoled in the anticipation of the eternal opportunity to accomplish true services of excellence. A mortal life of loss transforms into an eternal life of holiness. Gratefulness replaces shame. With the weight of sin destroyed forever, all are free in the magnitude of God's love, compassion, and understanding. All know that they have eternal life only by His mercy and grace.

Sin that was confessed on Earth has been long washed away and forgotten. Yet every soul who stands before Him at some time fell short. Only a few approach having confessed all their faults while they were mortals. Even these could do better, if they could go back to Earth knowing themselves as they do now. Yet if they were given a choice, nobody here would elect to return. Not one, not ever.

The accomplishments offered for Christ in mortal life are sealed now for eternity. As a reminder gleaming gold, silver, and gems remain with the ones who earned them. No person begrudges the result of judgment. Flawless love and harmony overflow from everyone as praises ring throughout the kingdom. Only the recognition of God's perfection could accomplish such excellence of heart.

> Therefore judge nothing before the time, until the Lord come, who both will bring to light the hidden things of darkness, and will make manifest the counsels of the hearts: and then shall every man have praise of God.
>
> —1 CORINTHIANS 4:5

With every soul basking in God's forgiveness, grace, and mercy, His righteousness shines brighter than the sun upon their countenance. No contention can ever flare up within the bride of Christ. Regret, jealousy, envy, and fear have forever lost their power. Free at last, free at last. All tears are wiped away for all eternity.

With judgment complete the glorious moment of rewards unfolds. What beauty we behold. Mountains of glittering crowns wait for all who deserve them. With hands lifted, the assembled saints sway in harmony like miles of golden wheat in the autumn breezes. The Lamb of God—the Righteous Judge steps forth.

We gaze as the One who died for sin now in untold glory presents the special crowns of life to all who overcame temptation. These are the ones who in their devotion for Him stood in His strength and by His power against the lure of Satan.

> Blessed is the man that endureth temptation: for when he is tried, he shall receive the crown of life, which the Lord hath promised to them that love him.
>
> —JAMES 1:12

Oh, what joy we have as we witness billions of faithful saints streaming forward to accept their crowns! Yet many still wait to be presented.

Next, Judge Jesus awards crowns of righteous. Who is the first man in line? How familiar he looks. With his robe so radiant we have to squint to make him out. The apostle Paul! We recognize him from our visit to prison where just days before his beheading we heard him speak these words:

> Henceforth there is laid up for me a crown of righteousness, which the Lord, the righteous judge, shall give me at that day: and not to me only, but unto all them that love his appearing.
>
> —2 TIMOTHY 4:8

He steps from the crowd, no longer emaciated but robust and tall. How complete and perfected he appears in his immortal body. In a glistening robe embossed with gold and silver and arrayed in sparkling stones, he bows before the Master he served on Earth. Paul ran his earthly race with honor, keeping his faith to the finish, never wavering despite all hardships.

Still another crown is given to all who ran the race of mortal life with persistence to attain the eternal heavenly goal. The Perfect Winner entrusts a victorious crown, incorruptible and everlasting, to every man and woman who threw aside any weight that would have slowed them down or held them back. He honors them for keeping their eyes focused on God's will and refusing anything that would weaken their ability to win the prize of glory.

> Everyone who competes in the games goes into strict training. They do it to get a crown that will not last; but we do it to get a crown that will last forever.
>
> —1 CORINTHIANS 9:25, NIV

Now as the Chief Shepherd, Jesus reaches out to all who obeyed His call to pastor, teach, nurture, and feed His flock. We recall His words to Peter, three times saying, "Do you love me? Feed my sheep." Look! Now Peter steps up for his crown of glory. Others also follow to receive crowns that will gleam brightly for all eternity.

> Be shepherds of God's flock that is under your care, serving as over-seers—not because you must, but because you are willing, as God wants you to be; not greedy for money, but eager to serve; not lording it over those entrusted to you, but being examples to the flock. And when the Chief Shepherd appears, you will receive the crown of glory that will never fade away.
>
> —1 PETER 5:2–4, NIV

> For what is our hope, our joy, or the crown in which we will glory in the presence of our Lord Jesus when he comes? Is it not you? Indeed, you are our glory and joy.
>
> —1 THESSALONIANS 2:19–20, NIV

Many soulwinners dance in jubilation to accept this crown of rejoicing. Each disciple receives one. Along with Peter, Andrew, James, John, and Matthew are leading the parade. Faithful patrons of the early church, other forefathers from ages of old, believers of our time pass by. Doctors, nurses, fishermen, farmers, storekeepers, teachers, students, secretaries, housewives—every single person who planted seeds, who watered and cultivated another's heart with the gospel, twirl like dazzling stars in worship. Oh, the joy of this Judgment Seat!

> And many of them that sleep in the dust of the earth shall awake. . . . And
> they that be wise shall shine as the brightness of the firmament; and
> they that turn many to righteousness as the stars for ever and ever.
>
> —DANIEL 12:2–3

Many prizes remain to be presented. All of them are awesome beyond words with some of them so mysterious our mortal minds are unable to understand their meaning.

We see privileges given to partake of the Tree of Life in the midst of the Paradise of God, to dine on the hidden manna, to receive a white stone containing a new and special name. There are the honors of gaining power over nations, possessing the Morning Star, wearing garments of purest white. Heaven's glories include the joy of hearing Jesus confess each name written in the Book of Life before the Father and His angels and having the name of the Bridegroom and New Jerusalem written on all redeemed by Christ Himself. There is also the award for all overcomers to become a pillar in the temple of God and to sit with Christ in His throne. (See Revelation 2:7, 17, 26; 3:5, 12, 21.)

All these rewards last for eternity. None will ever pass away, and nobody at this judgment will face the White Throne Judgment of the wicked. This is the greatest reward—just to obtain life everlasting with the precious Lamb of God, to reign with the King of kings and Lord of lords, to dwell with the Alpha and Omega, to abide forever as His bride and to be assured that as overcomers none will ever face the second death:

> He that hath an ear, let him hear what the Spirit saith unto the churches;
> He that overcometh shall not be hurt of the second death.
>
> —REVELATION 2:11

What is the second death?

> But the fearful, and unbelieving, and the abominable, and murderers, and whoremongers, and sorcerers, and idolaters, and all liars, shall have their part in the lake which burneth with fire and brimstone: which is the second death.
>
> —REVELATION 21:8

Now the Lamb takes His place as the Bridegroom. With tenderness He beams at the gathering of His bride. He died for her. During centuries of anticipation He prepared wedding chambers. At last the day is here! The union planned before the world's foundation culminates in joyous fulfillment.

How can we with human minds understand the depth of our glimpse into glory? We can't. Even as children of God, we can't yet grasp it all.

> Beloved, now are we the sons of God, and it doth not yet appear what we shall be: but we know that, when he shall appear, we shall be like him; for we shall see him as he is.
>
> —1 John 3:2

We strain to scan the multitudes in the presence of the Savior. Can we find ourselves? Have we made it to the believer's Judgment Seat? Have our works survived the fire? Have we received a crown? Oh, how can we be sure of eternal life?

> He that hath the Son hath life; and he that hath not the Son of God hath not life. These things have I written unto you that believe on the name of the Son of God; that ye may know that ye have eternal life, and that ye may believe on the name of the Son of God.
>
> —1 John 5:12–13

How can we be overcomers?

> Who is he that overcometh the world, but he that believeth that Jesus is the Son of God?
>
> —1 John 5:5

> And they have overcome (conquered) him by means of the blood of the Lamb and by the utterance of their testimony, for they did not love and cling to life even when faced with death [holding their lives cheap till they had to die for their witnessing].
>
> —Revelation 12:11, AMP

We must be willing to give Him our all:

> If any man will come after me, let him deny himself, and take up his cross, and follow me. For whosoever will save his life shall lose it: and whosoever will lose his life for my sake shall find it. For what is a man profited, if he shall gain the whole world, and lose his own soul? or what shall a man give in exchange for his soul? For the Son of man shall come in the glory of his Father with his angels; and then he shall reward every man according to his works.
>
> —Matthew 16:24–27

Then what joy to hear Him say:

> Well done, good and faithful servant: thou has been faithful over a few
> things, I will make thee ruler over many things: enter thou into the joy
> of thy lord.
>
> —MATTHEW 25:23

Oh, what wonders are prepared for the raptured saints! What joy will
ring in heaven! Yet what perils await for those who are left to face the wrath
on Planet Earth. How hard it is for us to leave such bliss to witness them.

Chapter 17

The Power and the Glory Forever

A FRIEND OF MINE had a dream about the rapture. She was standing on the ground with a loved one when she suddenly rose into the sky. As she reached out beside her for the one she loved, he wasn't there. For a split-second she caught a glimpse of him still on Earth, and she realized that he had been left behind. With a saddened heart my friend awoke.

We must reach out *now* before it is too late! Why? To understand the reason more fully we continue on the Jubilee Express for our last ride, our final adventure.

As we gaze at the cinema of glory displayed across the sky, the screen blackens and disappears. For a second we sit without moving in total darkness. What's happening?

Hold on! A nasty jolt thrusts the Jubilee Express into a nosedive. Racing downward it pierces the air like a lightning bolt. A sense of anguish penetrates our cabin with an icy chill as our faithful train seems to be zooming out of control! Oh, have we lost our direction to glory?

With a thud we hit the ground. Oh, look at the horror! Complete turmoil engulfs Planet Earth. We see fire, smoke, dust, debris. The wreckage is unmanageable, the panic unrestrainable.

What caused such total chaos? Some gigantic earthquake? Yes!

But why? The answer stuns us like a shock wave. The rapture caused it. What? The rapture?

Three New Testament accounts tell of dead bodies being resurrected to eternal life. All the resurrections took place with earthquakes. One happens during the tribulation when two witnesses who come down from heaven to Earth lay dead, yet unburied, in the streets of Jerusalem:

> And after three days and an half the spirit of life from God entered into them, and they stood upon their feet; and great fear fell upon them which saw them. And they heard a great voice from heaven saying unto them, Come up hither. And they ascended up to heaven in a cloud....And the same hour was there a great earthquake, and the tenth part of the city fell, and in the earthquake were slain of men seven thousand.
>
> —REVELATION 11:11–13

Matthew records the other occurrences. First he told about the righteous dead who awakened at the triumph of the cross.

> And, behold, the veil of the temple was rent in twain from the top to the bottom; and the earth did quake, and the rocks rent. And the graves were opened; and many bodies of the saints which slept arose, and came out of the graves...
>
> —MATTHEW 27:51–53

His second narrative, of course, was the resurrection of the Triumphant One Himself:

> And, behold, there was a great earthquake: for the angel of the Lord descended from heaven, and came and rolled the stone from the door, and sat upon it.
>
> —MATTHEW 28:2

In both of Matthew's accounts earthquakes not only occurred, but graves also literally opened to free earthly bodies. Not one mortal zipped through solid matter. I've heard it taught that the stone blocking the tomb of Jesus was rolled away for man's benefit so they could see that the body was gone. No! Jesus possessed a human body that had to be resurrected. Only later, after He walked on Earth in immortality, did He supernaturally emerge through walls or transcend from place to place.

Just when did Jesus' body change from mortal to immortal? In truth, this actual moment is unclear. Some teach that when Mary met Jesus at the tomb shortly after He came back to life, He was still in his mortal body because He told her, "Touch me not; for I am not yet ascended to my Father."

Those who stand by this teaching say that He returned to earth in immortality only after He ascended to the Father, where in the heavenly holy of holies He performed the ritual of the high priest who, according to Jewish law, sprinkled the blood of animals on the mercy seat of the ark of the covenant in the earthly holy of holies for the sins of all of the Israelites. Fulfilling this function of the Law Jesus entered this most sacred place with His own blood for us:

> He came as High Priest of this better system which we now have. He went into that greater, perfect tabernacle in heaven, not made by men nor part of this world, and once for all took blood into that inner room, the Holy of Holies, and sprinkled it on the mercy seat; but it was not the blood of goats and calves. No, he took his own blood, and with it he, by himself, made sure of our eternal salvation.
> —HEBREWS 9:11–12, TLB

This portrays a beautiful scene. This teaching tells a lovely story. But who actually knows that it is completely accurate in placing the time of Jesus' change from bodily mortality into an everlasting body?

Others believe that Jesus' body changed immediately at the tomb, believing no ascension (or rapture) was necessary. I would say to this, if rapture is required for us to receive our incorruptible bodies, why not for Jesus' human body also? Yet, who can say for certain? However, we do know from Scripture that the stone was rolled away, His earthly remains no longer there!

Just think about this. The burial site of every righteous person from eons past until the moment of the rapture will pop open one day. What immense upheaval it will cause. How can anyone even calculate its extent?

It won't simply be modern-day cemeteries that erupt, but thousands upon thousands of graves from bygone eras. Burial sites that have been lost or long forgotten—perhaps under buildings and highways, in mountains and jungles, in the depths of the sea—will all explode at the same microsecond. A force far beyond human capability and inconceivable by any imagination will transport resurrected bodies high into the sky to join Jesus and His angels.

Who knows how many Christians have been buried in unknown, unmarked graves? Uncountable numbers were martyred down through the centuries for their Christian beliefs. Thousands upon thousands of deaths, "tragical sufferings...too numerous to detail" are recorded in the Christian classic *Fox's Book of Martyrs*.[1] Just think! All will shoot forth when the trumpet sounds. Who would dare to estimate the number waiting to arise?

Oh, what an event! But it's not over. Make way for millions of believers who are still living. Those "which are alive and remain" will be "caught up together with them in the clouds, to meet the Lord" (1 Thess. 4:17).

These will also have to break through earthly bounds like houses, cars, and even airplanes as they zip with bullet speed into the air! How quickly they'll rise in their mortal state—"in a moment, in the twinkling of an eye!" (1 Cor. 15:52)—to receive their immortal bodies when they meet Jesus in the air. Most likely no human eye will be able to detect their faster-than-lightning-speed departure.

I say again, what an event! Its magnitude transcends our understanding.

Now picture the havoc that is left on our globe. It is inadequate to imagine that people who are left will only witness a few car and airplane accidents and find piles of clothing where someone stood when they were caught away. Instead, thousands will be buried in rubble with thousands of others injured. In the midst of such deep misery, will the world as a whole even realize that all true Christians have departed?

Concluding His detailing of "the beginning of sorrows," Jesus declares that there will be eruptions of "earthquakes in divers places" (Matt. 24:7).

Are these the result of the rapture? The Amplified Bible states the above phrase as "earthquakes in place after place." With all its increased tremors in recent years, might our planet be moaning and groaning like a woman in labor, getting ready to release the buried saints with a super eruption "in place after place" all over this world?

Describing what the King James Version calls "the beginning of sorrows," the Amplified Bible says, "All this is but the beginning [the early pains] of the birth pangs [of the intolerable anguish]" (Matt. 24:8). The Greek word for *sorrows* here means, "a pang or throe, esp. of childbirth."[2]

First Thessalonians 5:2–3 speaks of "the day of the Lord" coming "as a thief in the night" with "sudden destruction...as travail upon a woman with child." The day of the Lord is one of many titles for the tribulation period. Others include the day of wrath, the day of judgment, the time of indignation, and the time of Jacob's (Israel's) trouble.

Countries that have borne missionaries, preached the gospel, supported the church, and followed Jesus will be the most distressed by the rapture. Oh, what will it do to the United States? At the dawning of our nation, the pilgrims risked their lives to come here and find freedom to worship Christ. Our pioneers established Bible-believing churches everywhere. There was no thought of the "separation of church and state." Our Founding Fathers based the constitution on Christian principles.

Think of all our American ancestors who will rise to meet Jesus. Add to this number the living who stand ready, watching, and waiting for the trumpet of the Lord to sound even at this moment. An enormous cataclysm of unbelievable magnitude will no doubt cripple the strength of the United States.

How can one even think about our great society falling? It seems unpatriotic to even hint at such an idea. Yet we must be realistic. For End-Times prophecy to be fulfilled, the United States cannot continue as the superpower of the world. Who can know if her downfall will come by terrorism, war, natural disaster, or the after-effect of the rapture? But one thing is certain. During the tribulation, power shifts to Europe with the Antichrist controlling the world.

Unless she was at a state of absolute collapse, how would the United States ever submit to the rule of any foreign dictator? Chances are she wouldn't. In that day she, like all other nations, buckles under the control of a new world regime—that is, if she exists at all. Many have searched diligently to locate even one Bible verse that gives ironclad testimony to the place of the United States in End-Time prophecy. Their efforts have been to no avail. There is none.

Our hearts break with sorrow as the Jubilee Express chugs amid the rubble of the earth. How can we bear to travel through the hideous time of horror and deception that lies ahead? Can we endure watching the world as it is torn apart in tragedy? Yes, although the darkest time in human history descends upon us, our train chugs on.

Terror rules. A frantic, dying public moans for basic needs and comfort—shelter, drinking water, clothing, electric generators, gasoline. Food, oh food—where can it be found? Famine now blankets every continent. Starvation, disease, death, and stench are rampant. And in the midst of all this there is a search for lost loved ones.

Money has no value. Neighbors bicker over simple necessities. Utter selfishness takes over, and looting, stealing, hoarding, rioting, and racial clashes are epidemic. Governments search for solutions to alleviate fear and poverty, but they find none. Hysteria spins out of control. Rationality cringes in hopelessness as panic rules. Brotherhood is dead.

Despite such calamity, only a few people turn to Jesus for an answer. We long to shout, "Cry out to God!" Yet even if we could, who would listen? The true church is gone.

Above the shock, fright, pain, and bedlam, a desperate groan rises from the bowels of society and pleads to frenzied leaders, "Where can we find someone with the insight to end our horrid existence? We need a wise man who understands the interdependence of all nations and can put a stop to our fighting against each other. We need someone who can unite the world in politics, economy, and religion."

Has any religion survived? Will, as many believe, an apostate Catholic church rule from Rome? Or can it be that Islam will reign by terrorism, demanding that people honor their doctrine by the worship of Allah or face death by *beheading*? Their Quran reads, "And who is more wicked than the man who pays no heed to the revelations of the Lord when he is reminded of them? We will surely take vengeance on the guilty."[3]

By midtribulation a bloodthirsty holocaust barrels over the globe to eradicate both Judaism and Christianity. Jews and any who have turned to Christ will in no way accept a one-world religion or look up to any pagan ruler. And Satan desires death for all who worship the true and living Jehovah.

Secluded in the safety of the Jubilee Express, our tears run down the aisle like a river. Appalled by the hardness of man's heart, we wonder how can any who missed the rapture escape?

WITH THIS QUESTION, our train backs up to a time just before the rapture. As we reenter the Book of Revelation, our minds replay the symbolic picture of the rapture, the scene where John heard the voice calling, "Come up hither..." and was lifted into the heavens.

In an instant we find ourselves once again standing in the vision Jesus gives John. Is it possible that we are in the same era as "the beginning of sorrows" that Jesus described in Matthew 24:4–8? Can it be that He now gives John actual sight of this period? Certainly the portrayal of the six seals in Revelation match the events in the "beginning of sorrow."

The first sign Jesus gives in Matthew is *false christs*. In the first seal in Revelation 6:2 we see "a white horse: and he that sat on him had a bow; and a crown was given unto him: and he went forth conquering, and to conquer." Here we see a counterfeit of Christ. In Revelation 19:11–13 Christ, wearing many crowns, descends on a white horse from the portals of heaven to Earth.

First John 2:18–20 speaks of the spirit of antichrist that was prevalent even in John's day. Today this spirit saturates the world and is out to conquer Christianity. It defies the Bible and portrays darkness as light, evil as good, and truth as a lie. It uses many avenues—New Age ideas, Eastern mysticism, cults, witchcraft, "political correctness," and the secular media, as well as people who claim to be the true Messiah in flesh.

The other "horseman" that will follow each symbolize a *spirit*, not a person, so it stands to reason that this horseman is also a spirit, not the actual Antichrist. This rider carries a bow but no arrows. As he goes about conquering and to conquer, it is evidently not by vicious means as the Antichrist will do—but by deception.

The second sign given in Matthew 24:6–7 is *"wars and rumors of wars*... nation shall rise against nation, and kingdom against kingdom"* The second seal shown in Revelation 6:4 is also *wars*. It reads, "And there went out another horse that was red: and power was given to him that sat thereon to take peace from the earth, and that they should kill one another: and there was given unto him a great sword."

The third and fourth signs in Matthew 24:7 were *famines and pestilences*. The third seal in Revelation 6:5 presents a rider on a black horse with highly inflated prices: "A quart of wheat for a day's wages, three quarts of barley for a day's wages" (v. 6, NIV). *Famines*! With sky-high prices in many countries, even in the United States, families go hungry.

The fourth seal in Revelation 6:8 is *famines and pestilences*—"And I looked, and behold a pale horse: and his name that sat on him was Death, and Hell.... And power was given unto them over a fourth part of the earth, to kill with sword, and with hunger, and with death, and the beasts of the earth." Famine, death, animals. We see pestilences cropping up from mosquitoes, ticks, and even cows. Mounting evidence shows the plague of AIDS (HIV-1) likely originated with apes.[4]

While it is commonly taught that these seals are opened during the Great Tribulation period, by their parallels to Matthew 24 the first six fall into place as the birth pangs just prior to the tribulation. Yes, they are "the beginning of sorrows!"

The fifth sign in Matthew 24:7 is *earthquakes in many* and *various places*. In the fifth seal of Revelation 6:9–11 we see souls crying out to God from "under the altar." It seems as though they are crying for the tribulation to begin as they ask, "How long, O Lord, holy and true, dost thou not judge and avenge our blood on them that dwell on earth?" Then with the sixth seal an *earthquake to top all earthquakes erupts*! Oh, woe unto the earth and all of its inhabitants! The heavens convulse with rage as our planet writhes in violent shock waves.

> And, lo, there was a great earthquake; and the sun became black as sackcloth of hair, and the moon became as blood; and the stars of

heaven fell unto the earth, even as the fig tree casteh her untimely figs, when she is shaken of a mighty wind. And the heaven departed as a scroll when it is rolled together; and every mountain and island were moved out of their places. And the kings of the earth, and the great men, and the rich men, and the chief captains, and the mighty men, and every bondman, and every free man, hid themselves in the dens and in the rocks of the mountains; and said to the mountains and rocks, Fall on us, and hide us from the face of him that sitteth on the throne, and from the wrath of the Lamb: For the great day of his wrath is come; and who shall be able to stand?

—REVELATION 6:12–17

The rapture has happened! *Now* the tribulation begins! Even if it is traditionally taught that the tribulation period begins before the seals are broken, *no scripture* says it starts until Revelation 6:17 states pointblank, "The great day of God's wrath is come."

Now with all hindrance to the Antichrist removed from Planet Earth, Satan launches his long-awaited plot. How he laughs and pounds his chest while his demons squeal in ecstasy. From the moment of his victory in the Garden of Eden he schemed for this very day. The stage stands ready for his Antichrist to leap out. At last, at last, evil rules over all the world!

Without restraint from the Christian church Satan's venom spews freely to poison every vein of man. Consciences diminish. At every corner shamelessness, corruption, and antagonism toward God abound unbridled. As Satan speeds full-throttle and Earth reels under the fury of the Holy Judge of Righteousness, the terrible time of the Great Tribulation bursts forth in fullness.

Where, oh, where can man turn? Has God withdrawn His presence from all those who were left behind? No! Our Lord can never change. He remains always omnipresent and in control. And He still longs for man to turn to Him. In spite of Satan's heyday, the greatest revival ever known to humanity flames like wildfire across the world, fueled by the Holy Spirit.

Yes, lift up your hearts! Although the church has departed, hope still lives!

Who will carry the message of truth? Jews! One hundred forty-four thousand anointed preachers, twelve thousand from each tribe of Israel with divine protection by God's seal upon their foreheads, shout the revelation that Jesus indeed is the real Messiah (Rev. 7:1–8).

Two supernatural witnesses arrive from the ranks of heaven and join in the quest to spread the message and rebuild the Jewish temple (Rev. 11:1–6). The truth will be preached! In the last half of the Great Tribulation, angels fly from the midst of heaven broadcasting the everlasting gospel to all who dwell below (Rev. 14:6–7).

The power of the Holy Word never ceases. Despite Satan's madness, God's good news of redemption thrives as multitudes, many being Jews, come to know the Son of God. Yes, Jews. Even as His judgment falls, the God of all the ages has not forgotten them.

> And these are the words that the LORD spake concerning Israel and concerning Judah. For thus saith the LORD; We have heard a voice of trembling, of fear, and not of peace. Ask ye now, and see whether a man doth travail with child? wherefore do I see every man with his hands on his loins, as a woman in travail, and all faces turned into paleness? Alas! for that day is great, so that none is like it: it is even the time of Jacob's trouble; but he shall be saved out of it.
>
> —JEREMIAH 30:4–7

The covenant spoken by the Lord God to Abraham for His chosen people can never be renounced. His political fig tree may be shaken by His wind of wrath, but she shall never be cut down to her death. His vow to restore His original spiritual olive tree still stands. In the tribulation judgment God turns His heart toward His treasured Israel—His wondrous race who bore His Seed but rejected His salvation.

> He came unto his own, and his own received him not.
>
> —JOHN 1:11

Amid the anguish of the time of Jacob's trouble His people come to know His saving truth. Why does God still care so about the Jews? Because He is God, His Word stands true. His heart never changes. At this point let's take a pause from our study of tribulation times to search God's Word to understand the seriousness of His unending covenant with His chosen people.

THE APOSTLE PAUL says:

> Dear brothers, the longing of my heart and my prayer is that the Jewish people might be saved. I know what enthusiasm they have for the honor of God, but it is misdirected zeal. For they don't understand that Christ has died to make them right with God. Instead they are trying to make themselves good enough to gain God's favor by keeping the Jewish laws and customs, but that is not God's way of salvation. They

don't understand that Christ gives to those who trust in him everything they are trying to get by keeping his laws.

—ROMANS 10:1–4, TLB

Paul, educated to the highest degree in these very laws and customs, goes on to tell about God's intention for the unbelieving Jew:

But what about the Jews? Have they heard God's Word? Yes, for it has gone wherever they are; the Good News has been told to the ends of the earth. And did they understand [that God would give his salvation to others if they refused to take it]? Yes, for even back in the time of Moses, God had said that he would make his people jealous and try to wake them up by giving his salvation to the foolish heathen nations.

—ROMANS 10:18–19, TLB

But did God throw away His covenant with them because they rejected Jesus? No. Paul continues, "In the meantime, he keeps on reaching out his hands to the Jews, but they keep arguing and refusing to come. I ask then, has God rejected and deserted his people the Jews? Oh, no, not at all. . . . No, God has not discarded his own people whom he chose from the very beginning" (Rom. 10:21–11:2 , TLB).

Even though God left His chosen ones to their own doing for the last two thousand years, His supernatural abiding has never departed, His preservation has never ceased—even in all their persecutions and wanderings. Will His bond with them always be unending? Yes, yes, God says, yes!

He hath remembered his covenant for ever, the word which he commanded to a thousand generations. Which covenant he made with Abraham, and his oath unto Isaac; and confirmed the same unto Jacob for a law, and to Israel for an everlasting covenant.

—PSALM 105:8–10

God renewed His promise through David.

My covenant will I not break, nor alter the thing that is gone out of my lips. Once have I sworn by my holiness that I will not lie unto David. His seed shall endure for ever, and his throne as the sun before me. It shall be established for ever as the moon, and as a faithful witness in heaven. Selah.

—PSALM 89:34–37

Some claim that God washed His hands of Israel because the Jews rejected His Son. They say that Christians replaced the Jews and identify themselves as "spiritual Israel." When they are asked where the Bible states this, they usually give an answer like, "It's just understood."

This is such a misconception. Indeed, Christians can be called spiritual Jews in some respects. By accepting Jesus, we are adopted into the seed of Abraham and become members of the family of God. (See Galatians 3; 4:1–6.) And yes, by faith in His Son, God grafts Gentile believers into His olive tree—but only as branches—not to replace those of natural Hebraic roots. It was never His intention that anyone should replace His chosen, Israel.

Jews will always be the natural seed of Abraham. Our Savior Christ Himself is a Jew. So are Isaac, Jacob, and all Jacob's children, Moses, King David, Daniel, Elijah and Elisha, Mary and Joseph, John the Baptist, every one of Christ's disciples. Even the apostle Paul, the special one God called to take the gospel message to the Gentiles, is a Jew.

Let's face it. The Jew is the root of the Christian's heritage. The writings we call our Old Testament are none other than the Jewish Tanakh. Have you ever stopped to realize that *Jews* inspired by the Holy Spirit wrote *all* of the Old and New Testaments?

Because of Israel's rejection of Jesus as Messiah and by God's merciful grace we Gentiles are given a place in His spiritual olive tree. Paul explains:

> And since Abraham and the prophets are God's people, their children will be too. For if the roots of the tree are holy, the branches will be too. But some of these branches from Abraham's tree, some of the Jews, have been broken off. And you Gentiles who were branches from, we might say, a wild olive tree, were grafted in. So now you, too, receive the blessings God has promised Abraham and his children, sharing in God's rich nourishment of his own special olive tree.
>
> —Romans 11:16–17, TLB

Christians should beware of placing themselves above the position God has so graciously has given them. Paul warns of such a haughty attitude,

> But you must be careful not to brag about being put in to replace the branches that were broken off. Remember that you are important only because you are now a part of God's tree; you are just a branch, not a root.... For if God was willing to take you who were so far away from him—being part of a wild olive tree—and graft you into his own good tree—a very unusual thing to do—don't you see that

he will be far more ready to put the Jews back again, who were there in the first place?

—ROMANS 11:18, 24, TLB

The Jews as a whole may have turned their back on God's plan of redemption by refusing to affirm Jesus as Messiah. But Paul states:

Yet the Jews are still beloved of God because of his promises to Abraham, Isaac, and Jacob. For God's gifts and his call can never be withdrawn; he will never go back on his promises.

—ROMANS 11:28–29, TLB

How much clearer can it be? God will "never go back on His promises!"

SINCE 586 B.C. Jewish people—trampled by an unbelieving, misguided world—have suffered uncountable persecutions. During the Great Tribulation it gets even worse. With no true church of God left on Earth or any new believers with governmental authority, the degree of abuse toward Jews accelerates into a raging fury of uninhibited hatred and diabolical mania as never seen before.

And they shall fall by the edge of the sword, and shall be led away captive into all nations: and Jerusalem shall be trodden down by the Gentiles, until the times of the Gentiles be fulfilled.

—LUKE 21:24

How could Jews trust those who do not believe in Jehovah? All history bears record that they shouldn't. Yet during the first half of the seven years of judgment, they evidently swallow the Antichrist's bogus pledges—hook, line, and sinker.

Like the rest of the world they put their safekeeping in the extraordinary insight of Satan's man. When he steps out to sign a treaty that ends friction in the Holy Land, all seems well. However, it is only for a season. As peace settles upon the Jews and their land is no longer under threat, they foolishly dismantle all walls of defense. They have no need for worry. Peace abides. Or so they think.

But unseen trouble lurks! According to the End-Time prophecies of Ezekiel 38 and 39, three malicious nations situated directly north of Israel plot a surprise ambush with an untold number of soldiers. Scripture dubs the players in this scheme "Magog, Meshech and Tubal," calling their human leader, "Gog." Theologians identify Russia as Magog, the ringleader nation, because of its northern location above Israel and its ancient historical name. Oh, no! After the rapture the nation Israel has no Christian allies. Once she signs the peace treaty her military becomes inactive. What will she do!

Relax. There is no need for alarm. The Almighty is always in control. This crisis sparkles as His spectacular production, a diamond of divine design that radiates His eternal awesomeness to the world just as He had planned. How astounding it is when the same Yahweh who delivered His chosen Hebrews from Egyptian slavery thirty-five hundred years before shines forth as their Defender.

In His Word He vows:

> I stand against you, Gog, leader of Meshech and Tubal. I will turn you and drive you toward the mountains of Israel, bringing you from the distant north. And I will destroy 85 percent of your army in the mountains. I will knock your weapons from your hands and leave you helpless. You and all your vast armies will die upon the mountains. I will give you to the vultures and wild animals to devour you. You will never reach the cities—you will fall upon the open fields; for I have spoken, the Lord God says. And I will rain down fire on Magog and all your allies who live safely on the coasts, and they shall know I am the Lord. Thus I will make known my holy name among my people Israel; I will not let it be mocked any more. And the nations too shall know I am the Lord, the Holy One of Israel. That day of judgment will come; everything will happen just as I have declared it.
> —Ezekiel 39:1–8, TLB

What an awesome victory! These would-be invaders could obliterate the state of Israel in one assault by natural means. However, by the majestic force of Jehovah the Jews triumph in a single day—letting all nations behold firsthand how the wondrous God of Abraham, Isaac, and Jacob keeps watch over His people now as in the days of old.

The number of the dead is appalling. There are so many the Jews bury bodies for seven months. The debris is so large that they burn demolished weapons for fuel for seven years.

Will this prophecy of Ezekiel happen before or during the tribulation? I believe it takes place shortly after its onset, but God's Word states no precise time. John F. Walvoord discusses its possible effect on the world. "As the battle described here is a disaster for the invading countries, it may change the political power structure to such an extent that it will be possible for the Roman leader of the ten nations to become a world dictator."[5]

This conflict may actually be the stepping stone needed for the Antichrist to rise to full power!

Some time before the seven years of wrath or shortly thereafter, the Jews rebuild their temple. I believe it will be built during the first three and one-half years of the tribulation while the supernatural power and protection of the 144,000 Jews and the two witnesses prevail.

What will happen to the Moslem mosque that at this moment sits on the sacred temple site? At this point one can only speculate. Could it be that the earthquake of the rapture destroys it? If so, with the two witnesses on the scene, no one would have the power to rebuild it!

Who can say for sure? The Word of God is silent on when and how the temple will be built. It declares only that it will.

Imagine the anger of Satan. He attempts to rule through his total possession of the Antichrist, but the presence of an active Jewish temple gnaws at his ego. It displays a constant witness of the faithful One who oversees Israel. It is a daily reminder of His covenantal people and fuels insane jealousy.

After God allows the two witnesses to die and they no longer stand in Satan's way, he explodes, pushing the Antichrist into a hysterical rage. Manipulated by Satan, this man storms into the newly built site of Jewish worship. He probably unveils the holy of holies and stands there—maybe even sits on the sacred mercy seat of the newly constructed (or relocated) ark of the covenant, shouting, "*I* am the world's messiah! I am God!"

What an awakening for Jews who worship according to Old Testament teaching. When the Antichrist defiles their sacred temple, defies their Eternal Yahweh, makes a mockery of their worship before the world—they realize his demonic power. Never again will they look to him for guidance or swallow his lies.

How the man of Satan hates rebellion! At their rejection of his deity he strikes back like a mad monster at breakneck speed to exterminate them all.

> When ye therefore shall see the abomination of desolation, spoken of by Daniel the prophet, stand in the holy place, (whoso readeth let him understand:) Then let them which be in Judea flee into the mountains.... For then shall be great tribulation such as was not since the beginning of the world to this time, no, nor ever shall be.
>
> —MATTHEW 24:15–16, 21

Does God's faithfulness still abide with Israel? Can He bring good from this? Yes! Fleeing into the mountains, many Jews escape to a place of safety prepared by God Himself (Rev. 12:6).

There He protects and cares for them as He did in the desert in the time of Moses. Under His divine security they wait in anticipation of the arrival of the Messiah. Oh, what a majestic sight it will be when He breaks into Earth's atmosphere enshrouded with glory and surrounded by all His raptured saints and heavenly hosts. Yet, what a day of great remorse it will be as they lay eyes on the Messiah they have rejected so long.

> Then I will pour out the spirit of grace and prayer on all people of Jerusalem, and they will look on him they pierced, and mourn for him as an only son, and grieve bitterly for him as for an oldest child who died.
>
> —ZECHARIAH 12:10, TLB

At the revolt of the Jews the Gentile world becomes restless and uneasy. Evidently scores of people all over the globe reject the Antichrist's claims to deity. After all, everyone has witnessed the splendor of Israel's God in their victory over Gog. The world has also been appalled when the two witnesses, after lying dead in the streets of Jerusalem for three and a half days, suddenly revived, stood on their feet, and rose from Earth by a supernatural force (Rev. 11:9–12).

It is no wonder that so many have questions about this man who proclaims that he is God.

Ferocious battles break out in bold opposition to the authority of the self-acclaimed deity who now sits on the Jewish throne in Israel. Their defiance spurs ravenous greed plus a lust for power themselves. Nations soon march in force to seek the treasures of the Promised Land and the valuable minerals of the Dead Sea, which has abundant produce that is needed by a starving world, plus a possible vast supply of oil hidden beneath its surface.

Can even the strongest army of men triumph over the superhuman strength of Satan without the hand of God to back them? No! So will he wipe them out completely? Not at all. Satan doesn't wish to destroy Earth's population. Instead, in his hatred of Yahweh he craves complete loyalty and subjection from human beings. How he dreams of all creatures created in the image of God worshiping him! What an excellent way to ridicule the Creator! What a perfect display of defiance!

As a first step he must end the world's rebellion by proving that the man he possesses is God. True to his character, the master of deception comes up with a plot so cunning that it fools even the most elite. He allows the Antichrist to be killed!

Speaking of the Antichrist's battles and shocking death, Daniel says:

> News from the east and north will alarm him and he will return in
> great anger to destroy as he goes. He will halt between Jerusalem and
> the sea, and there pitch his royal tents, but while he is there his time
> will suddenly run out and there will be no one to help him.
>
> —DANIEL 11:44–45, TLB

Surely the devil gloats at the feebleness of humankind as mortal devotees
of the Antichrist try in vain to save him. After the world grasps the news
of his demise, Satan—called "Dragon" here in Revelation—resurrects his
fallen ruler. Behold, the Antichrist—identified as the "Creature" and the
one empowered with Satan's "own power and throne and great authority"
(Rev. 13:2, TLB)—lives again!

> I saw that one of his heads seemed wounded beyond recovery—but
> the fatal wound was healed! All the world marveled at this miracle and
> followed the Creature in awe They worshiped the Dragon for giving
> him such power, and they worshiped the strange Creature. "Where is
> anyone as great as he?" they exclaimed. "Who is able to fight against
> him?" Then the Dragon encouraged the Creature to speak great blas-
> phemies against the Lord; and gave him authority to control the earth
> for forty-two months.
>
> —REVELATION 13:3–5, TLB

The Dragon wins the battle! A deceived world worships the Creature, the
antichrist, and takes his mark. And without question they also believe the
Dragon's false prophet, who is appointed to stand by his Creature's side and
has satanic power to perform miracles.

Does everyone worship the Antichrist? No, those who have their names
written in God's Book of Life are wise to his deception. Why? Because
they belong to the "Lamb that was slain from the foundation of the world"
(Rev. 13:8).

Others still undecided in their loyalty buckle under when, unless they
bear his mark on their forehead or right hand, they can no longer buy or sell.
Those who do not bear the mark and refuse to follow after the Antichrist live
in constant danger, and many are beheaded. How the man of Satan throbs
with passion to annihilate all believers of the true and living God. He won
the battle, yet to win the war of all the ages he must usurp the power of the
Almighty Himself!

Satan's strategy centers on the extinction of the Jews. His scheme fell short
with Hitler, but how can he lose this time with the church of God removed
and Gentiles across the world joining full rank with him? Coldhearted, savage,

horrifying—these words are too mild to describe the Dragon's maneuvers against the chosen of God.

God is not surprised. He and He alone stands as the Master Planner.

> Behold, I will make Jerusalem a cup of trembling unto all the people round about, when they shall be in the siege both against Judah and against Jerusalem. And in that day will I make Jerusalem a burdensome stone for all people: all that burden themselves with it shall be cut in pieces, though all the people of the earth be gathered together against it.
>
> —ZECHARIAH 12:2–3

Oh, why don't the heathens accept the truth? How do they expect to defeat the descendants of Abraham whose God wiped out Magog, Meshech, and Tubal with one fatal sweep of His might? How can they dare to come against the Power who raised the two witnesses from the dead before their very eyes?

They can't see. By taking the mark of the beast as a pledge of allegiance to him, they have closed their spirits to God. Their eyes are blinded to the truth, and no place of redemption abides for them. Their decision cannot be recanted. There is no turning back.

As they follow the lies of the Antichrist's cohort, the false prophet, and the demands of the Antichrist himself, their minds have lost all reason and their hearts all moral judgment. Like puppets of the Dragon, all the armies of the world gather in the valley of Megiddo to strike out against all remaining children of God. The Battle of Armageddon dawns!

IS GOD EVER surprised? No, never. Even though the world is in slavery to Satan, the Holy Creator will never lose His sovereignty. He designed this very day:

> For I will gather all nations against Jerusalem to battle.
>
> —ZECHARIAH 14:2

His glorious moment of reckoning arrives!

> Then the Lord will go out fully armed for war, to fight against those nations. That day his feet will stand upon the Mount of Olives, to the east of Jerusalem, and the Mount of Olives will split apart.
>
> —ZECHARIAH 14:3–4, TLB

How foolish the Antichrist and his followers are! How helpless they stand against the sword of Christ. The entire heavens burst open at His coming. The Mount of Olives splits apart. What a picture of glory! What a display of power! In the nick of time the Conqueror shows up!

> I saw heaven standing open and there before me was a white horse, whose rider is called Faithful and True. With justice he judges and makes war. His eyes are like blazing fire, and on his head are many crowns. He has a name written on him that no one but he himself knows. He is dressed in a robe dipped in blood, and his name is the Word of God. The armies of heaven were following him, riding on white horses and dressed in fine linen, white and clean. Out of his mouth comes a sharp sword with which to strike down the nations. He will rule them with an iron scepter. He treads the winepress of the fury of the wrath of God Almighty. On his robe and on his thigh he has this name written: KING OF KINGS AND LORD OF LORDS.
> —REVELATION 19:11–16, NIV

Surely this stops the Dragon in his tracks and his armies retreat. But no, his hatred for almighty God and His eternal Savior erupts like a volcano inside the Antichrist and his false prophet. Like robots the armies of the world march to the Antichrist's command, pleased to carry out his morbid lust for power, thrilled to collide with the Word of God and all His saints.

> Then I saw the Evil Creature gathering the governments of the earth and their armies to fight against the one sitting on the horse and his army.
> —REVELATION 19:19, TLB

How can man be so ignorant? What a grip Satan has on the souls of those who reject the truth of Christ.

> And the Evil Creature was captured, and with him the False Prophet.... Both of them—the Evil Creature and his False Prophet—were thrown alive into the Lake of Fire that burns with sulfur. And their entire army was killed with the sharp sword in the mouth of the one riding the white horse.
> —REVELATION 19:20–21, TLB

The King wins! The rule of the Antichrist is ended by the unconquerable strength of the Almighty. The Antichrist and his false prophet are thrown into the lake of fire. The Gentile armies fall dead on the spot. Now for the climax!

> Then I saw an angel come down from heaven with the key to the bot-
> tomless pit and a heavy chain in his hand. He seized the Dragon—that
> old Serpent, the devil, Satan—and bound him in chains for 1,000
> years, and threw him into the bottomless pit, which he then shut and
> locked, so that he could not fool the nations any more until the thou-
> sand years were finished. Afterwards he would be released again for a
> little while.
>
> —REVELATION 20:1–3, TLB

Oh, what a day of wonder on Planet Earth. This is true victory at last as good triumphs over wickedness. Divine majesty and glory shine throughout the world. Paradise is restored! This story would earn rave reviews as a novel. But this is not a novel. This is real.

AND NOW COMES the judgment for those who have survived the Great Tribulation. Yes, those who are still alive assemble to receive justice for their acts during these seven years. They face the King of kings, who is flanked by countless martyrs slaughtered during the horror of Satan's rampage and now deemed worthy to join Him in His judgment.

> Then I saw thrones, and sitting on them were those who had been
> given the right to judge. And I saw the souls of those who had been
> beheaded for their testimony about Jesus, for proclaiming the Word
> of God, and who had not worshiped the Creature or his statue, nor
> accepted his mark on their foreheads or their hands. They had come
> to life again.
>
> —REVELATION 20:4, TLB

In the presence of the King all mankind confesses Him as Lord and every knee bows at His feet. Will all who call upon Him at this late date be saved? Or is it too late for some?

All people will not be saved. Yes, many come too late. While none at this judgment have been resurrected from the dead, the dispensation of unearned grace no longer abides. Only those who have earned His grace by their kindness to God's people can live. Matthew 25:31–46 tells the story:

> When the Son of Man comes in his glory, and all the angels with him,
> he will sit on his throne in heavenly glory. All the nations will be gath-
> ered before him, and he will separate the people one from another as a

shepherd separates the sheep from the goats. He will put the sheep on his right and the goats on his left.

—MATTHEW 25:31–33, NIV

Oh, what a glorious day for those who are on His right. "Come," says the King, "you who are blessed by my Father. Accept your inheritance—the kingdom prepared for you since the creation of the world. For I was hungry and you fed me. I was thirsty and you gave me something to drink. I was a stranger, yet you took me in. I needed clothes, and you clothed me. I was sick, and you cared for me. I was in prison, and you visited me."

Grateful eyes behold Him. Humble hearts question how they can be so deserving. "Whenever did we do such things?"

The King points to the martyred saints at His side—saints from Heaven, "who had been given the right to judge," "who had been beheaded for their testimony about Jesus."

The "sheep" scan the faces of those who were once slain and are now alive. Recognition dawns. When the Antichrist in his rampage hunted down these brothers of Christ, they risked their own safety to help them. Then the King says, "Whatever you did for the least of these, My brothers, you also did for Me."

Yes! Let us peer into the faces of His brothers. We distinguish His Jewish siblings, for Jesus is a Jew. We also spot some Gentiles, unbelievers at the rapture, who turned to Him during the Tribulation. As they accepted the Son of God as their Redeemer, they were grafted into the olive tree. And just as many of the natural seed of Abraham, they too are brothers of the King.

What rewards the mortals on His right receive. Because of their goodness to His brothers, these who stand before the King inherit the kingdom of paradise on Earth with Satan locked away for a thousand years.

How hard it is to watch the King turn to His left. "Away with you! Depart into the eternal fire prepared for the devil and his angels. When I hungered and thirsted you gave me nothing. As a stranger you shunned me. You left me naked, and cared not that I was in prison!"

A moment ago they seemed repentant, but Jesus knew their true character. After He pronounced judgement, they sneer at Him. They gave inhumane treatment to His brothers in the tribulation, and even now they haven't changed. We cannot tell if any or all of them bear the mark of the beast, but they all stagger from the throne of righteous judgment into everlasting punishment, banished from the love of God forever.

Those who were judged righteous reclaim at last man's rightful place of rule over Planet Earth with the Eternal Creator as their leader. The One who came to fellowship in the Garden of Eden with Adam and Eve now dwells among His humankind again as Redeemer of the world, King of kings, Lord of lords, and high priest to all. He is assisted by all His raptured bride, the tribulation saints, and all His angels. Oh, what a supreme existence for a span of a thousand years.

Is the Lord pleased? Yes, yes, God says yes!

> "Be glad and rejoice forever in what I will create, for I will create Jerusalem to be a delight and its people a joy. I will rejoice over Jerusalem and take delight in my people; the sound of weeping and of crying will be heard in it no more. Never again will there be in it an infant that lives but a few days, or an old man who does not live out his years; he who dies at a hundred will be thought a mere youth; he who fails to reach a hundred will be considered accursed. They will build houses and dwell in them; they will plant vineyards and eat their fruit. No longer will they build houses and others live in them, or plant and others eat. For as the days of a tree, so will be the days of my people; my chosen ones will long enjoy the works of their hands. They will not toil in vain or bear children doomed to misfortune; for they will be a people blessed by the LORD, they and their descendants with them. Before they call I will answer; while they are still speaking I will hear. The wolf and the lamb will feed together, and the lion will eat straw like the ox, but dust will be the serpent's food. They will neither harm nor destroy in all my holy mountain," says the LORD.
>
> —ISAIAH 65:18–25, NIV

A GLORIOUS TEMPLE graces the city of Jerusalem during the millennial kingdom. Ezekiel beholds its magnificence in a vision and describes it as so majestic in size and lavish in decoration that it far outshines the wonders of Solomon's temple. The glory of God overflows from its quarters. This temple furnishes a dwelling for King Jesus and His saints, who came with Him from heaven in their incorruptible bodies and reign as kings and priests at His side. It gives all mortal people the assurance that He is constantly abiding in their midst.

What a marvelous period of time. This is the long-awaited joy and peace on Earth, the fabulous thousand-year sabbath day of God!

But wait! What about the Dragon? After a thousand years God allows him to ravage the Earth again. Why, oh, why does He release this wicked menace?

God in fairness must allow evil to try the hearts of those who were born during the millennium. They have never experienced temptation, so how can they choose between the nature of Elohim, who breathed life into man at the dawning of creation, and the Adamic nature that Satan corrupted with sin in the Garden? Both natures remain within their souls.

We have beheld Satan as that serpent in our travels. We have encountered him as a roaring lion throughout the ages and have looked at the devastation he did as the mighty dragon in the tribulation. Knowing all his lying, murdering tricks—can we now attempt to imagine his last assault on humanity?

The final war of wills begins! Free at last after a thousand years of being locked away, the Serpent dupes the hearts of many with his cunning lies and con-artist disguise one last time. While he was in captivity, he no doubt plotted his final masterpiece of delusion, and in this closing act he still dreams of victory.

Now, foaming at the mouth like a rabid werewolf, he wildly infects the earthly paradise again. Yet he appears so beautiful and brilliant, like a glorious angel of light, bursting forth with promises of wealth and power behind a facade of innocence. Sticky with poisoned sweetness, he paints fanatical pictures and offers overpowering propositions in a dynamic combination of all his tricks throughout history.

Perhaps he will say, "God keeps you bound by subjection to Him. He suppresses your capabilities to keep you from becoming omnipotent as He is. He kept me from you for a thousand years because He knows I possess superhuman knowledge that will give you the eternal wisdom of all the ages and powers far beyond any mortal realm. But His so-called majesty and authority couldn't hold me back! I fought my way to freedom, and look—I won! Freedom can be yours, too, when together we gain control over all creation. All its riches, all its beauty shall be ours from the soil beneath your feet to the vanishing point of outer space."

"Follow me," he might say, "and you'll become almighty and all-knowing like the King upon the throne in Jerusalem. No longer will you need to bow to Him; you'll be worshiped as a god yourself. Angels will be at your command. Only the tyranny of the Godhead stands in your way. With me at your side we can defeat Him!"

Perhaps he'll promise to give them rule over kingdoms, the kind of supernatural abilities he gave the Antichrist and false prophet and fleshly pleasures never before encountered or even imagined by mortal beings. No human mind can compute the magnitude of deception that Satan dares to use, but we see the awful results. Millions yield to his wooing. In wholehearted allegiance they prepare to battle against the kingdom of

God, eagerly submitting as soldiers in Satan's grand finale.

How foolish can these humans be? Unlike Eve in her innocence, they have surely heard the story of Eden and the agony sin brought into the world. They must know by heart the details of Armageddon that have been handed down year after year by witnesses who are still living. Don't they understand how God's redemptive plan delivered man from the destruction of evil? Or how the world was transformed into a utopia of goodness when Satan was locked away? Don't they know what a curse the world endured when wickedness had its way?

Who could be so naive as to believe the devil's nonsense? How can anyone believe that his plan to overtake God's throne might succeed this time? None of us can comprehend such reasoning. But as Satan lines up his followers for battle, "their number is like the sand of the sea" (Rev. 20:8, RSV).

Sheltered aboard the Jubilee Express, we are in utter shock as we hear ear-shattering shouts of obscenities and see stampedes of countless infantries and roaring artillery outside our windows. We stare, unaware of just how horrible the massacre will be. Armed and ready millions march by, insane with bloodthirsty passion, trusting the devil's fraudulent promises. They storm from every corner of the world to surround the camp of the saints in Jerusalem and overtake the beloved city of the King where the glorious temple stands.

Then suddenly the Holy Avenger declares, "Enough!" Lightning blazes across the skies of Jerusalem. In deafening thunder the wrath of the Almighty sweeps the battle zone around the city with torrid winds. Ferocious clouds roll back with whirling fury to reveal the heavens as a sheet of fire. Stretching for miles across the land, the troops are petrified with fear, and blood-curdling screams escape their lips. In an instant, white-hot flames devour every soldier in his tracks!

Amid the inferno countless explosions eject huge fireballs into the air. Military tanks and weapons that are not blown to bits melt like small wax toys. The earth's surface shrivels like tissue paper. Anything caught in the fiery breath of wrath—houses, buildings, trees—disintegrates on the spot. Churning high above the land of Israel black smoke billows carrying the stench of roasting flesh.

How sick the devil must feel! His final war to top all wars ends before one shot is fired. And he has lost forever. Our hearts are in anguish as we look upon the far-reaching devastation. How unbearable it is to witness so many die and watch so much of the Earth dissolve in flames. We bow our heads and weep. Yet, despite our overwhelming sorrow, we feel safe inside our quarters.

Then, without warning, a deafening boom jars us from our seats. An enormous gaping hole ruptures the crust of the entire battleground to reveal a roaring lake of fire and sulfur. With gigantic heaves hungry lava leaps out to lap up any victim within its reach. Like a seething underground ocean it ripples spasmodically beneath the Jubilee Express. Smoldering mire mounds up around our wheels. A whirlwind of charred debris turns the air to inky black. With vicious force, it threatens to swirl our train into the flaming pit and end our trip to glory.

But our Conductor is greater than all this, and He shines beside us with everlasting light. Nothing can destroy the scarlet rails before us. In the blackness ahead we detect the glittering tracks as they stretch into the heavens. Our ever-faithful Engineer revs the engine to a high velocity, and with supersonic speed we lift up, up, up into the sky far above the pandemonium and angry fire below.

THE WHOLE EARTH trembles. Its core bubbles with molten slush, and its surface pulsates like a time bomb ready to explode. How can it survive?

All at once a glaring brilliance streaks from the portals of infinity and pours out another roaring flood of fire. Transfixed in our seats we watch in horror as it illuminates the entire atmosphere of Earth. The sky becomes ablaze with holy thrones that flame with fires of judgment.

The Eternal Godhead appears, towering over them all in glorious blinding white. As the Ancient of Days, He abides in solemn sovereignty.

> As I looked, thrones were set in place, and the Ancient of Days took his seat. His clothing was as white as snow; the hair of his head was white like wool. His throne was flaming with fire, and its wheels were all ablaze. A river of fire was flowing, coming out from before him. Thousands upon thousands attended him ten thousand times ten thousand stood before him. The court was seated, and the books were opened.
> —Daniel 7:9–10, NIV

Bleakness engulfs the moment. No rainbow streams from this throne. No angels sing, and no palm branches wave. We see no crowns, no rewards. Except for His splendor, all beauty has departed. Before our eyes "ten thousand times ten thousand" stand before Him to be judged.

What a sight as the sea and all hell convulse to release the bodies of the damned. Some souls have resided in Hades thousands of years until this appointed day. No white robes cover their nakedness as they tremble with-out hope, knowing their everlasting doom. Speechless they gaze into the blazing eyes of the One they rejected.

> And I saw a great white throne and the one who sat upon it, from whose face the earth and sky fled away, but they found no place to hide. I saw the dead, great and small, standing before God; and The Books were opened, including the Book of Life. And the dead were judged according to the things written in The Books, each according to the deeds he had done.
>
> —REVELATION 20:11–12, TLB

Enthroned in sheer perfection and flawless justice the Righteous Judge thunders:

> But cowards who turn back from following me, and those who are unfaithful to me, the corrupt, and murderers, and the immoral, and those conversing with demons, and idol worshipers and all liars— their doom is in the Lake that burns with fire and sulphur. This is the Second Death.
>
> —REVELATION 21:8, TLB

One by one their deeds are read from The Books, and our hearts throb with remorse for the billions upon billions who lived so foolishly. We see unrighteous souls from the beginning of time—people from the tower of Babel and Sodom and Gomorrah, the Egyptians and those who died in the wilderness in Moses' day, the persecutors of Christians from the days of Jesus through the Middle Ages until now. Anyone who rejected God, all unbelievers, now weep before the throne. Though they are in a crowd too huge to number, they pass by utterly alone and stark naked.

On and on they file, each to face their sentence of eternal doom. We recognize presidents, kings, and celebrities from the annals of history. No amount of prestige or wealth could save their souls. Most who move by are unknown to us, but...

"Oh, no!" wails a passenger aboard our train, "There's my Uncle Ed. He was a good man. I thought he was saved. I never even talked to him about Jesus! Oh, how could I have been so blind?"

Another cries, "I see my neighbor. She belonged to a New Age group. I tried to tell her about the saving blood of Jesus once. When she didn't listen, I just turned away. Why, oh, why wasn't I more persistent?" Sobs flood our coach as over and over we recognize someone we know—friends, relatives, brief acquaintances, bosses, co-workers. Some even see their lost spouses, children, and parents.

What a dreadful time of weeping and remorse! As we scan the crowd, we see people we told about Jesus or lifted up in prayer. We also see those whom we failed to offer a word of hope. Oh, why don't we work harder to reach the lost? Begging, wailing, gnashing of teeth breaks out among the condemned as they are thrown into the lake of fire.

Guilt, regret, total agony grips our souls. Aloud we moan, "Lord, forgive us for failing the unsaved. Ignite in our hearts a blazing torch for the lost from this point on! Let us not be timid, ashamed, or afraid of ridicule. Anoint us with wisdom and power to win people to You and keep them from an everlasting hell!"

How our hearts break as we ponder the punishment of those who will someday stand before this Judgment Throne with all hope gone.

> And if anyone's name was not found recorded in the Book of Life, he was thrown into the Lake of Fire.
>
> —REVELATION 20:15, TLB

The unsaved go to their eternal doom. Our hearts still mourn, but we know that each person chose their fate. Even in our sadness we rejoice to know that righteousness prevails and we will live forever in its graces.

What about the devil? Has he received his just dues? "I kept looking until the beast was slain and its body destroyed and thrown into the blazing fire" (Dan. 7:11, NIV).

What an ending for Satan. Though he is such a maniac for evil, he once stood as a star of loveliness in eons past, the most magnificent of all the holy angels, "the signet of perfection, full of wisdom, perfect in beauty" (Ezek. 28:12, RSV).

Created in the highest form of excellence, he could have been a glorious being who walked hand in hand with God forever. But no, he relinquished his position for the sake of pride. Seeking self-esteem, he chose the way of iniquity and sealed his fate.

> And the devil, who had deceived them, was thrown into the lake of burning sulfur, where the beast and the false prophet had been thrown. They will be tormented day and night for ever and ever.
>
> —REVELATION 20:10, NIV

Satan gave up his glorious standing with his Creator for this tragic end. Now he will never rule again or rise to power. Oh, Satan—you father of lies, you deceiver of the nations, once god of this world, prince and power of the air—forever face your doom.

> "So, you too are now as weak as we are! You, too, have become like us. Your pride has been flung down to Sheol with the music of your lyres; under you a mattress of maggots, over you a blanket of worms. How did you come to fall from the heavens, Daystar, son of Dawn? How did you come to be thrown to the ground, conqueror of nations? You who used to think to yourself: I shall scale the heavens; higher than the stars of God I shall set my throne. I shall sit on the Mount of Assembly far away to the north. I shall rival the Most High." Now you have been flung down to Sheol, into the depths of the abyss!"
>
> —ISAIAH 14:10–15, TNJB

The dragon, the old serpent, the devil—yes, Satan meets his ruin. Never again will the earth entertain his ploys. Only holiness reigns. There is no more threat of sin, wickedness, rebellion. The tempter can never raise his ugly head again. And along with him the Adamic nature of man has perished in the lake of fire. The final judgment ends, and death will be no more!

WHAT A CELEBRATION we now see. Around a breathtaking throne that is ablaze with holy flames of white, multitudes of the heavenly hosts rejoice and worship the Ancient of Days. Suddenly all creation stands at attention as the Son of Man arrives in glory to take His honored place beside the Ancient of Days.

> Next I saw the arrival of a Man—or so he seemed to be—brought there on clouds from heaven; he approached the Ancient of Days and was presented to him. He was given the ruling power and glory over all the nations of the world, so that all people of every language must obey him. His power is eternal—it will never end; his government shall never fail.
>
> —DANIEL 7:13–14, TLB

All that remains—every living soul and all of creation—belongs totally to Jesus. The One who came as a babe in a manger so many years ago at last completes the promise in Isaiah to the fullest degree.

> For unto us a Child is born, unto us a Son is given; and the government will be upon His shoulder, and His name will be called Wonderful, Counselor, Mighty God, Everlasting Father, Prince of Peace. Of the

increase of His government and peace there will be no end, upon the throne of David and over His kingdom, to order it and establish it with judgment and justice from that time forward, even forever.

—ISAIAH 9:6–7, NKJV

What a day of glory. What a time of praise. There is endless praise, endless joy, endless peace. We abide forever in the presence of the One who lived as man and died for man's redemption.

He has so many glorious names: The Word of Elohim. The Seed of the woman. Bethlehem's baby. The prophet's Messiah. Holy Redeemer. The Righteous Branch. The Son of God. The Son of man. The Lamb without blemish. The Lion of the tribe of Judah. The Root of David. Faithful and True. Wonderful. Counselor. The Mighty God. The Prince of Peace. The true and eternal Daystar. The Bridegroom of the raptured. The Ruler of all nations. High Priest forever. The King of kings and Lord of lords. The Alpha and Omega. The Beginning and End. The First and the Last. Our Beloved forever and ever and ever. The everlasting Father of all inhabitants of Earth.

But what about Earth? How can it ever be populated by man again? It writhes with horror within its core. Engulfed in spreading flames its outer crust quivers and its waters boil. Glowing clouds of embers envelop all the sky around it and spew white-hot sparks beyond its sphere far into the universe.

Should we be alarmed? No, we heed the words of Peter:

> You should look forward to that day and hurry it along—the day when God will set the heavens on fire, and the heavenly bodies will melt and disappear in flames. But we are looking forward to God's promise of new heavens and a new earth afterwards, where there will be only goodness.
>
> —2 PETER 3:12, TLB

The seventh day of God draws to a close. *Seven*, used throughout God's Word to "represent God's complete provision both in Christ and in His dealings with man," is the number of perfect completion and fulfillment.[6] The day of renewal—the eighth day—begins. With God, the number *eight* means "something new." A new beginning has arrived!

> And I saw a new heaven and a new earth, for the first heaven and the first earth had passed away. Also there was no more sea.
>
> —REVELATION 21:1, NKJV

Before our panoramic view of all these End-Time events completely fades away we catch a glimpse of the New Jerusalem coming down. What a glorious Holy City. What a majestic sight. As the scene across the sky disappears, we recall our tour of heaven at the onset of our travels together in chapter two. Oh, the wonders of that city.

The city soars higher and stretches farther than mortal eyes can see. Ablaze with the reflection of God's *Shekinah* glory, it has gates of pearl, walls of gems, streets of gold, a crystal river, the fountain of the water of life, and the tree of life to bring healing for the nations. We certainly understand the necessity of healing for the nations.

Overflowing with happiness, we call to mind our Redeemer's mighty words at the beginning of this eternal Sabbath:

> I am the Alpha and the Omega, the beginning and the end. I will give unto him that is athirst of the fountain of the water of life freely. He that overcometh shall inherit all things; and I will be his God, and he shall be my son.
>
> —REVELATION 21:6–7

Resting in peacefulness we settle back against our seats as the Jubilee Express glides along. We've experienced many things on our journey together, but perhaps the most important is knowing beyond any doubt that all our God has said will come to pass. We never need to worry if He will keep His Word. His promises are true.

> For all the promises of God in Him are Yes, and in Him Amen...
> —2 CORINTHIANS 1:20, NKJV

Yes, yes, our hearts hear Him say. From the portals of our train the hallelujah choir once more rings with song. "And, Lord, haste the day when the faith shall be sight, the clouds be rolled back as a scroll, the trump shall resound and the Lord shall descend, even so—it is well with my soul."[7]

Like sparkling ribbons the scarlet rails still stretch before us reaching toward eternity and the land of glory. Somewhere far above at the right hand of His Father's throne a Son waits, anticipating His orders. *O Abba Father, is it time?* we hear Him say.

Yes, yes, God says. *Yes! Time is now fulfilled. Go and claim Your bride!*

From far beyond a trumpet blows. Shouts of angels vibrate in the sky. The clouds open to reveal His glory. Oh, what a sight!

The voice of my beloved! Behold, he comes, leaping upon the mountains, bounding over the hills. My beloved is like a gazelle, or a young stag. Behold, there he stands behind our wall, gazing in at the windows, looking through the lattice. My beloved speaks and says to me: *"Arise, my love, my fair one, and come away."*
—SONG OF SOLOMON 2:8–10, RSV, EMPHASIS ADDED

At this majestic moment a tugging in our spirits tells us to leave our glory train, to soar on wings of grace and mercy to the side of our Beloved. Oh, what a wonder! Have we really been accepted as His bride?

YES! YES! GOD SAYS, *YES!*

In the twinkling of an eye we arise and come away as His eternal helpmate. And so our journey ends with a new beginning at the final and eternal stop on our treasure map— "... the kingdom, and the power and the glory for ever. Amen."

The kingdom of eternity. Here we will dwell in joy, in bliss, in the splendor of His power and glory forever and ever and ever and ever and ever and ever...

Yes, yes, and amen!

Notes

Chapter 1
OUR FATHER

1. Merrill C. Tenney, gen. ed., *Zondervan Pictorial Bible Dictionary*, (Grand Rapids, MI: Zondervan Publishing House, 1978), 883.

2. *Indiana Jones, Raiders of the Lost Ark,* Paramount Pictures, produced by Frank Marshall, directed by Steven Spielburg, 1981.

3. Adapted from the video teachings of Dick Reuben, "The Pattern for Revival Fire." Dick Reuben Evangelist Association, Boonville, IN, 1993.

4. Biblesoft's *New Exhaustive Strong's Numbers and Concordance With Expanded Greek-Hebrew Dictionary*, s.v. 6754, "*tselem*." Copyright © 1994 Biblesoft and International Bible Translators, Inc. All rights reserved.

5. *Vine's Expository Dictionary of Biblical Words* (Nashville, TN: Thomas Nelson, 1985), s.v. 120, "*adam*."

6. Biblesoft's *New Exhaustive Strong's Numbers and Concordance With Expanded Greek-Hebrew Dictionary*, s.v. 6635, "*tsaba'*."

7. Ibid., s.v. 1288, "*barak*."

8. Ibid., s.v. 6942, "*qadash*."

9. Ibid., s.v. 7673, "*shabath*."

10. Ibid.

11. R. B. Thieme Jr., *Levitical Offerings* (Houston, TX: R. B. Thieme Bible Ministries, 1973), 72.

Chapter 2
HEAVEN

1. Original source unknown.

2. Biblesoft's *New Exhaustive Strong's Numbers and Concordance With Expanded Greek-Hebrew Dictionary*, s.v. "*paradeisos*."

3. *Vine's Expository Dictionary of Biblical Words*, s.v. "*paradeisos*."

4. Spiros Zodhiates, ThD, *The Complete Word Study Dictionary, New Testament*, 2nd printing (Chattanooga, TN: AMG Publishers, 1993), 1102.

5. Biblesoft's *New Exhaustive Strong's Numbers and Concordance With Expanded Greek-Hebrew Dictionary*, s.v. 7393, "*rekeb*."

6. Original source unknown.

7. Biblesoft's *New Exhaustive Strong's Numbers and Concordance With Expanded Greek-Hebrew Dictionary*, s.v. 3709, "*orge.*"

8. Ibid., s.v. 4991, "*soteria.*"

9. "The Global War on Christians," *Reader's Digest*, August 1997, 51.

10. Lawrence O. Richards, *The Bible Reader's Companion* (Colorado Springs, CO: Victor Books, 1992), 912.

11. William Barclay, *The Revelation of John*, Daily Study Bible Series, volume two, revised edition (Philadelphia, PA: Westminster Press, 1976), 209.

Chapter 3
HALLOWED BE THY NAME—YAHWEH

1. Matthew Henry, *Matthew Henry's Commentary on the Holy Bible* (Nashville, TN: Thomas Nelson, Inc., n.d.), 20.

2. The definition of *Enoch* is taken from several Bible dictionaries, including *Nelson's Illustrated Bible Dictionary*, Herbert Lockyer, senior editor (Nashville, TN: Thomas Nelson Publishers, 1986); *Hitchcock's Dictionary of Bible Names, Easton's Bible Dictionary* (both public domain), and others.

3. *Nelson's Illustrated Bible Dictionary*, s.v. "Abram."

4. Ibid., s.v. "Abraham."

5. Dr. William Smith, *Smith's Bible Dictionary*, 1901, s.v. "Sarai," "Sarah," http://www.biblestudytools.net/Dictionaries/SmithsBibleDictionary/smt.cgi?number=T3743 (accessed October 23, 2005).

6. *Nelson's Illustrated Bible Dictionary*, s.v. "Isaac."

7. J. I. Packer, Merrill C. Tenney, and William White Jr., *Nelson's Illustrated Encyclopedia of Bible Facts* (Nashville, TN: Thomas Nelson Publishers, 1980, 1995), 636.

8. Biblesoft's *New Exhaustive Strong's Numbers and Concordance With Expanded Greek-Hebrew Dictionary*, s.v. 3068, "*Yehovah.*"

9. Adapted from Philip S. Berstein, *What the Jews Believe* (New York: Funk & Wagnalls, 1950), 11–12.

10. Herbert Lockyer, DD, *All the Divine Names and Titles in the Bible* (Grand Rapids, MI: Zondervan, 1975), 17.

11. Biblesoft's *New Exhaustive Strong's Numbers and Concordance With Expanded Greek-Hebrew Dictionary*, s.v. 117, "*addiyr.*"

12. Andrew Jukes, *The Names of God* (Grand Rapids, MI: Kregel Publications, 1967), 53–54.

13. Zodhiates, *The Complete Word Study Dictionary*, 874.

14. Ibid., 273.

15. Ibid.

16. *Vine's Expository Dictionary of Biblical Words*, s.v. "*astheneia*."

17. Ibid.

18. Scripture used of Paul in prison is from 2 Timothy, some portions paraphrased.

Chapter 4

EL SHADDAI, EL ELYON, ELOHIM, AND ADONAI

1. Lockyer, *All the Divine Names and Titles in the Bible*, 34.

2. Jukes, *The Names of God*, 67.

3. Ibid., 68.

4. Original source unknown.

5. "Holy, Holy, Holy" by Reginald Heber. Public domain.

6. Walter C. Kaiser Jr., et al., *Hard Sayings of the Bible* (Downers Grove, IL: InterVarsity Press, 1996), 491.

7. Paul D. Gardner, ed., *The Complete Who's Who in the Bible* (Grand Rapids, MI: Zondervan Publishing House, 1995), 217.

Chapter 5

SHALOM, SABAOTH, AND SHAMMAH

1. *Nelson's Illustrated Bible Dictionary*, s.v. "Angel of the Lord."

2. Finis J. Dake, ed., Dake's Annotated Reference Bible (Lawrenceville, GA: Bible Sales, Inc., 1978), 88, col.1, OT.

3. *Zondervan Pictorial Bible Dictionary*, 40.

4. Wyn Craig Wade, *The Titanic—End of a Dream* (New York: Penguin Group, 1979, 1986), 75.

Chapter 6

TSIDKENU AND M'KADDESH

1. Norman Vincent Peale, *The Power of Positive Thinking* (New York: Prentice-Hall, 1952).

2. Abridgment of Andrew Murray, *The Holiest of All* (Grand Rapids, MI: Baker Book House, 1894), retypeset edition published by Kenneth Copeland Ministries, Fort Worth, TX, 1993, pages 506 and 363.

3. Henry Harrison with Cliff Dudley, *Second Fiddle* (Los Angeles: New Leaf Press, 1977), 90–91.

Chapter 7
ROPHE

1. Biblesoft's *New Exhaustive Strong's Numbers and Concordance With Expanded Greek-Hebrew Dictionary*, s.v. 3679, "*oneidizo.*" Also, Zodhiates, *The Complete Word Study Dictionary*, 1047.

2. Biblesoft's *New Exhaustive Strong's Numbers and Concordance With Expanded Greek-Hebrew Dictionary*, s.v. 1383, "*dokimion.*"

3. Biblesoft's *New Exhaustive Strong's Numbers and Concordance With Expanded Greek-Hebrew Dictionary*, s.v. 4991, "*soteria.*" Also, Zodhiates, *The Complete Word Study Dictionary*, s.v. "*soteria.*"

4. Biblesoft's *New Exhaustive Strong's Numbers and Concordance With Expanded Greek-Hebrew Dictionary*, s.v. 5849, "*awtar.*"

5. Ibid., s.v. 2896, "*tobe.*"

6. Adapted from sermons of Joyce Meyer of Life in the Word Ministries, Fenton, MO, and Rod Parsley, pastor of World Harvest Church, Breakthrough Ministries, Columbus, OH.

7. Zodhiates, *The Complete Word Study Dictionary*, s.v. "*anaxios.*"

8. Perry Stone Jr., *The Meal That Heals* (Cleveland, TN: Voice of Evangelism, Inc., Pressworks, n.d.), 54.

9. Biblesoft's *New Exhaustive Strong's Numbers and Concordance With Expanded Greek-Hebrew Dictionary*, s.v. 1897, "*hagah.*"

10. Ibid., s.v., 1643, "*tsalach.*"

11. Adapted from Oral Roberts, *Get off the Briar…and Get on the Wing* (Tulsa, OK: Guide to Seed Faith Living).

12. Grant R. Jeffrey, *The Signature of God* (Toronto, Ontario: Frontier Research Publications, 1996), 134–137.

13. Original source unknown.

Chapter 8
HALLOWED BE THY NAME

1. Kay Arthur, *To Know Him by Name* (New York: Random House, 1933).

2. "Along the Road" by Robert Browning Hamilton, in *The Best Loved Poems of the American People*, selected by Hazel Felleman (New York: Doubleday and Company, 1936).

3. Biblesoft's *New Exhaustive Strong's Numbers and Concordance With Expanded Greek-Hebrew Dictionary*, s.v. 4982, "*sozo.*"

Chapter 9

THY KINGDOM COME

1. "This Train," public domain.

2. "Just As I Am" by Charlotte Elliott. Public domain.

3. "Where He Leads Me" by E. W. Blandy. Public domain.

4. *Passover Haggadah*, distributed by The Maxwell House Family of Coffees Inc., 1999, 11.

5. Ibid., 18.

6. Ibid., 25.

7. Ibid., 26.

8. Ibid., 47.

9. Stanley Howard Frodsham, *Smith Wigglesworth: Apostle of Faith* (Springfield, MO: Gospel Publishing House, 1948, 1990).

10. Reuben, "The Pattern for Revival Fire."

Chapter 10

GIVE US THIS DAY OUR DAILY BREAD

1. J. Vernon McGee, *Through the Bible with J. Vernon McGee*, vol. 1 (Nashville, TN: Thomas Nelson Publishers, 1981), 65.

Chapter 11

AND FORGIVE US OUR DEBTS

1. "Amazing Grace" by John Newton. Public domain.

2. Biblesoft's *New Exhaustive Strong's Numbers and Concordance With Expanded Greek-Hebrew Dictionary*, s.v. 6446, "*pac*."

3. Abram Leon Sachar, *A History of the Jews* (N.p.: Alfred A. Knopf, 1965), 37.

Chapter 12

DELIVER US FROM EVIL

1. *Reader's Digest Condensed Books*, July 1965.

Chapter 13

BELT OF TRUTH, BREASTPLATE OF RIGHTEOUSNESS

1. Biblesoft's *New Exhaustive Strong's Numbers and Concordance With*

Expanded Greek-Hebrew Dictionary, s.v. 96, "*adkimos.*" Also, Zodhiates, *The Complete Word Study Dictionary*, s.v. "*adkimos.*"

2. Zodhiates, *The Complete Word Study Dictionary*, s.v. "*oikodomeo.*"

3. Biblesoft's *New Exhaustive Strong's Numbers and Concordance With Expanded Greek-Hebrew Dictionary*, s.v. 7965, "*shalom.*"

4. Ibid., s.v. 7999, "*shalam.*"

Chapter 14
SHIELD OF FAITH, HELMET OF SALVATION

1. Mrs. C. Nuzum, *The Life of Faith*, revised edition, 15th printing (Springfield, MO: Gospel Publishing House, 1928, 1996), 80–81.

2. From a testimonial account cassette tape of Normal Williams, Full Gospel Businessmen Association meeting, Union City, TN, July 1980.

3. Ibid.

Chapter 15
SWORD OF THE SPIRIT, MANTLE OF PRAYER

1. "Swallowed by a Whale," *True Tales of Terror on the High Seas*, http://www.ycaol.com/swallowed.htm (accessed October 30, 2005).

2. Jerry M. Landay, *Silent Cities, Sacred Stones* (New York: McCall Publishing Company, 1971), 80–81.

3. Ibid.

4. Ibid.

5. Ibid.

6. Ibid.

7. Ibid.

8. Jeffrey, *The Signature of God*, 40–47.

9. Ibid., 42–43.

10. Ibid., 62–64.

11. Ibid., 74–75.

12. *The Life and Works of Flavius Josephus*, translated by Willian Whiston, A.M. (Philadelphia, PA: John C. Winston Company, n.d.), 535, "The Antiquities of the Jews," chapter XVII.

13. *Prophecy Study Bible* (NKJV), with commentary and teachings of John C. Hagee, general editor (Nashville, TN: Thomas Nelson Publishers, 1997), 1239.

14. Jeffrey, *The Signature of God*, 89.

15. Michael Drosnin, *The Bible Code* (New York: Simon and Schuster,

1997. Grant R. Jeffrey, *The Mysterious Bible Code* (Nashville, TN: Word Publishing, 1998). Yacov Rambsel, *The Genesis Factor* (Beverly Hills, CA: Lion's Head Publishing, 2000).

16. *ABC Primetime Live*, October 19, 2000.

17. *Blessed*, vol. 1, issue 2, October 2001, 5.

18. "Onward, Christian Soldiers" by Sabine Baring-Gould. Public domain.

Chapter 16
FOR THINE IS THE KINGDOM

1. *Jehovah's Witnesses: A Non-Prophet Organization*, video by Witness, Inc., MacGregor Ministries, Metaline Falls, Washington.

2. The Columbia Electronic Encyclopedia, 6th ed. Copyright © 2005, Columbia University Press.

3. David Duck, *On the Brink* (Lancaster, PA: Starburst Publishers, 1995), 150–151.

4. Zodhiates, *The Complete Word Study Dictionary*, 1108.

Chapter 17
THE POWER AND THE GLORY FOREVER

1. John Fox, *Fox's Book of Martyrs* (Grand Rapids, MI: Zondervan Publishing House, 1973), 52.

2. Biblesoft's *New Exhaustive Strong's Numbers and Concordance With Expanded Greek-Hebrew Dictionary*, s.v. 5604, "*odin*."

3. Surah 32:21, translated with notes by N. J. Dawood (New York: Penquin Group, 1999).

4. Dale Peterson, *Eating Apes* (Los Angeles: University of California Press, 2001), 80–105, 246.

5. John F. Walvoord, *Every Prophecy of the Bible* (Colorado Springs, CO: Chariot Victor Publishing, 1999), 189.

6. Walter L. Wilson, *A Dictionary of Bible Types* (Peabody, MA: Hendrickson Publishers, 1999), 135.

7. "It Is Well With My Soul" by H. G. Spafford. Public domain.

Selected Bibliography

Alexander, David and Pat Alexander, editors, *Eerdman's Handbook to the Bible*, Grand Rapids, MI: William B. Eerdmans Publishing Company, 1992.

Arthur, Kay, *To Know Him by Name*, Sisters, OR: Multnomah Books, 1995.

Barclay, William: *The Daily Study Bible Series*, revised edition, Philadelphia PA: The Westminster Press, 1976.

Bernstein, Rabbi Philip S., *What the Jews Believe*, New York, NY: Funk & Wagnalls, 1950.

Brim, Billye, *The Blood and the Glory*, Tulsa, OK: Harrison House Inc., 1995.

Cornwall, Judson, *Heaven*, Van Nuys, CA: Bible Voice, Inc., 1978.

Dake, Finis Jennings, *Dake's Annotated Reference Bible*, Lawrenceville, GA: Dake Bible Sales, Inc., 1978.

Duck, Daymond R., *On the Brink*, Lancaster, PA: Starburst Publishers, 1994.

Freedman, David Noel, editor, *Eerdman's Dictionary of the Bible*, Grand Rapids, MI: William B. Eerdmans Publishing Company, 2000.

Gardner, Paul D., editor, *The Complete Who's Who in the Bible*, Grand Rapids MI: Zondervan Publishing House, n.d.

Hagin, Kenneth E., *The Name of Jesus*, Tulsa, OK: Faith Library Publications, 1979.

Hickey, Marilyn, *The Names of God*, Denver, CO: Marilyn Hickey Ministries, 1990.

Jeffrey, Grant R., *The Signature of God*, Toronto, Ontario: Frontier Research Publications, Inc, 1996.

Jukes, Andrew, *The Names of God*, Grand Rapids, MI: Kregel Publications, a division of Kregel, Inc., 1967.

LaHaye, Tim, *Revelation Unveiled*, Grand Rapids, MI: Zondervan Publishing House, 1999.

Levitt, Zola, *A Christian Love Story*, Dallas, TX: Zola Levitt, 1978.

Levitt, Zola, *The Seven Feasts of Israel*, Dallas, TX: Zola Levitt, 1979.

Liberman Paul, *The Fig Tree Blossoms*, San Diego, CA: Tree of Life, 1987.

Lockyer, Herbert, D.D., *All the Divine Names and Titles in the Bible*, Grand Rapids, MI: Zondervan Publishing House, 1975.

Richards, Lawrence O., *Complete Bible Handbook*, Dallas, TX: Word Publishing, 1987.

Richards, Lawrence O., *The Bible Reader's Companion*, USA, Canada, England: Victor Books, a division of Scripture Press Publications, Inc., 1991.

Sachar, Abram Leon, Ph.D., *A History of the Jews*, n.p.: Alfred A. Knopf, Inc., 1965.

Mike Shreve, *Our Glorious Inheritance*, Revelations of the Titles of the Children of God Series, volumes 1–3, Winter Park, FL: Deeper Revelation Books, 1988.

Tenney, Merrill C., editor, *The Zondervan Pictorial Bible Dictionary*, Grand Rapids, MI: Zondervan, 1978.

Thieme, R. B. Jr., *Levitical Offerings*, Houston, TX: R.L.B. Thieme Jr. Bible Ministries, 1973.

Thieme, R. B. Jr., *The Blood of Christ*, Houston, TX: R.L.B. Thieme Jr. Bible Ministries, 1989.

Thieme, R. B. Jr., *The Origin of Human Life*, Houston, TX: R.L.B. Thieme Jr. Bible Ministries, 1992.

Selected Videos and Cassette Tapes

American Portrait Films Inc., *Countdown to Eternity*, Cleveland, OH, 1997.

Brim, Billye, *The Overcoming Power of the Blood* six tape series, the teaching ministry of Billye Brim.

Copeland, Gloria with Brim, Billye, *Our Covenant of Peace* three tape series, Kenneth Copeland Ministries, Fort Worth TX, 1999.

Day of Discovery, *The Holidays of God*, volumes 1 & 2, 1997.

Hagee, John, *Israel: The Apple of God's Eye, Prophecy and the Seven Feasts, Abraham to Armageddon*, John Hagee Ministries, San Antonio, TX.

Hagee, John, *The Blood Covenant, The Marriage Covenant*, John Hagee Ministries, San Antonio, TX.

Levitt, Zola, *The Miracle of Passover*, produced and directed by Berg Productions, Dallas, Texas, 1995.

Nelson, Ed, *Jesus in the Torah*, Bellwether International, Lexington, SC.

Parsley, Ron, *A Walk Through the Tabernacle*, Breakthrough Ministries, Columbus, OH, 1996.

Parsley, Ron, *Behold His Glory* three tape series, Breakthrough Ministries, Columbus, OH, 1996.

Reuben, Dick, *The Pattern for Revival Fire*, Dick Reuben Evangelistic Association, Booneville, IN, 1993